Step by Step

Microsoft® Office XP

Perspection, Inc.,
Online Training Solutions, Inc.,
Curtis Frye, and Kristen Crupi

I Microsoft Word

II Microsoft Excel

III Microsoft Access

IV Microsoft PowerPoint

V Microsoft FrontPage

VI Microsoft Publisher

VII Microsoft Outlook

PUBLISHED BY
Microsoft Press
A Division of Microsoft Corporation
One Microsoft Way
Redmond, Washington 98052-6399

Library of Congress Cataloging-in-Publication Data
Microsoft Office XP Step by Step / Perspection, Inc., Online Training Solutions, Inc., Kristen Crupi, Curtis Frye.
    p. cm.
  Includes index.
  ISBN 0-7356-1294-3
  1. Microsoft Office. 2. Business--Computer programs. I. Crupi, Kristen. II. Frye, Curtis, 1968-
III. Perspection, Inc. IV. Online Training Solutions (Firm) V. Microsoft Corporation.

HF5548.4.M525 M5393   2001
005.369--dc21

                                              2001030873

Printed and bound in the United States of America.

8 9   QWT   6 5 4

Distributed in Canada by H.B. Fenn and Company Ltd.

A CIP catalogue record for this book is available from the British Library.

Microsoft Press books are available through booksellers and distributors worldwide. For further information about international editions, contact your local Microsoft Corporation office or contact Microsoft Press International directly at fax (425) 936-7329. Visit our Web site at www.microsoft.com/mspress. Send comments to *mspinput@microsoft.com*.

Acquisitions Editor: Kong Cheung
Project Editors: Judith Bloch, Wendy Zucker
Technical Editor: Jim Fuchs

Body Part No. X08-04484

Contents

Microsoft Word   1

Contents

Microsoft Excel   93

Contents

V Microsoft FrontPage 375

Contents

Chapter 25: Managing E-Mail Messages   576

Chapter 26: Customizing and Organizing E-Mail Messages   600

Chapter 27: Managing Your Calendar   630

Chapter 28: Scheduling and Managing Meetings   658

Quick Reference   677

Contents

What's New in Microsoft Office XP

You'll notice some changes as soon as you start Microsoft Office XP. The toolbars and menu bar have a new look, and there's a new task pane on the right side of your screen. But the features that are new or greatly improved in this version of Office go beyond just changes in appearance. Some changes won't be apparent to you until you start using the program.

To help you quickly identify features that are new or greatly enhanced with Office XP, this book uses the icon in the margin whenever those features are discussed or shown. If you want to learn about only the new features of the program, you can skim through the book, completing only those topics that show this icon.

Many of the enhancements to the Office suite are included in each of the applications but aren't necessarily discussed in each section of this book. For example, the Ask A Question Box is common to each of the applications in Office XP but is mentioned only in chapters about Word, Excel, and FrontPage.

The following table lists the new features that you might be interested in, as well as the chapters in which those features are discussed.

To Learn How To	Using This New Feature	See
Get help from the main Word window	Ask A Question Box	Chapter 1, page 6
Perform common tasks with a single click in Word	Task Pane	Chapter 1, page 5
Move and copy text in Word	Office Clipboard Task Pane	Chapter 1, page 18
Select blocks of text that are not adjacent to one another in Word	Select Nonadjacent Text	Chapter 1, page 17
Display formatting information of selected text in Word	Reveal Formatting	Chapter 2, page 28
Resize a table quickly in Word	Selection Handle	Chapter 3, page 60
Perform common tasks with a single click in Excel	Task Pane	Chapter 5, page 97
Get help from the main Excel window	Ask A Question Box	Chapter 5, page 97
Set the properties of pasted data in Excel	Paste options	Chapter 5, page 101

(continued)

To Learn How To	Using This New Feature	See
Set the properties of Auto Fill and Fill Series data in Excel	Auto Fill options	Chapter 5, page 108
Locate data with a specific format in Excel	Find Format	Chapter 5, page 113
Set the properties of inserted columns, rows, or cells in Excel	Insert options	Chapter 6, page 121
Draw borders with new tools in Excel	Borders	Chapter 6, page 132
Get information about an error in Excel	Error options	Chapter 7, page 163
Perform common tasks with a single click in Access	Task Pane	Chapter 9, page 191
Alternate between viewing slides in outline format and as thumbnails in PowerPoint	Outline/Slides Pane	Chapter 13, page 297
Perform common tasks with a single click in Access	Task Pane	Chapter 13, page 297
Control whether text is automatically corrected in PowerPoint	AutoCorrect options	Chapter 15, page 347
Control whether text is automatically resized in PowerPoint	AutoFit options	Chapter 15, page 347
Print a presentation in one of eleven size formats in PowerPoint	Page Setup	Chapter 16, page 362
Perform common tasks with a single click in FrontPage	Task Pane	Chapter 17, page 379
View a Web site in six different formats in FrontPage	Page Tabs	Chapter 17, page 389
Get help from the main FrontPage window	Ask A Question Box	Chapter 17, page 395
Move and copy text in FrontPage	Office Clipboard Task Pane	Chapter 18, page 416
Paste content in FrontPage	Paste options	Chapter 18, page 417
Format a table in FrontPage	Table-Formatting options	Chapter 19, page 445
Access and organize media files in FrontPage	Clip Organizer	Chapter 20, page 454
Use enhanced drawing tools in FrontPage	Office Drawings	Chapter 20, page 466

To Learn How To	Using This New Feature	See
Add photos to your Web site in FrontPage	Photo Gallery	Chapter 20, page 474
Publish a single page to the Web in FrontPage, rather than an entire site or file	Single-Page Publishing	Chapter 21, page 499
Create a new publication in Publisher	New Publication Task Pane	Chapter 22, page 506
Check the design, layout, and content of a Publisher file before printing	Print Preview	Chapter 23, page 532
Use an HTTP-based e-mail account, such as Hotmail, in Outlook	HTTP support	Chapter 24, page 549
View the full content of a message in Outlook	Enhanced Preview Pane	Chapter 24, page 553
Use Word as the e-mail editor in Outlook	Word As Default Editor	Chapter 24, page 557
Automatically complete e-mail addresses in Outlook	Automatic Address Completion	Chapter 24, page 558
Use friendly names in e-mail addresses in Outlook	Display As box	Chapter 24, page 562
Add multiple e-mail accounts to your profile in Outlook	E-Mail Accounts	Chapter 24, page 572
Find messages in Outlook	Find and Advanced Find	Chapter 25, page 589
AutoArchive all folders in the same way in Outlook	Global AutoArchive Settings	Chapter 25, page 593
Color-code appointments in an Outlook Calendar	Calendar Coloring	Chapter 27, page 642
Respond to an Outlook meeting invitation by proposing a different time	Propose New Time	Chapter 28, page 668

For more information about Microsoft Office XP, see *http://www.microsoft.com/office/xp.*

Getting Help

Every effort has been made to ensure the accuracy of this book and the contents of its CD-ROM. If you do run into problems, please contact the appropriate source for help and assistance:

Getting Help with This Book and Its CD-ROM

If your question or issue concerns the content of this book or its companion CD-ROM, please first search the online Microsoft Knowledge Base, which provides support information for known errors in or corrections to this book, at the following Web site:

http://mspress.microsoft.com/support/search.htm

If you do not find your answer at the online Knowledge Base, send your comments or questions to Microsoft Press Technical Support at:

mspinput@microsoft.com

Getting Help with Microsoft Office XP

If your question is about a Microsoft software product, including Office XP, and not about the content of this Microsoft Press book, please search the Microsoft Knowledge Base at:

http://support.microsoft.com/directory

In the United States, Microsoft software product support issues not covered by the Microsoft Knowledge Base are addressed by Microsoft Product Support Services. The Microsoft software support options available from Microsoft Product Support Services are listed at:

http://support.microsoft.com/directory

Outside the United States, for support information specific to your location, please refer to the Worldwide Support menu on the Microsoft Product Support Services Web site for the site specific to your country:

http://support.microsoft.com/directory

Using the Book's CD-ROM

The CD-ROM inside the back cover of this book contains all the practice files you'll use as you work through the exercises in the book. By using practice files, you won't waste time creating samples and typing spreadsheet data—instead, you can jump right in and concentrate on learning how to use Microsoft Office XP.

Important

The CD-ROM for this book does not contain the Office XP software. You should purchase and install that program before using this book.

Minimum System Requirements

To use this book's practice files, your computer should meet the following requirements:

■ **Computer/Processor**

Computer with a Pentium 133-megahertz (MHz) or higher processor

■ **Memory**

RAM requirements depend on the operating system used:

■ **Microsoft Windows 98 or Windows 98 Second Edition**

24 MB of RAM plus an additional 8 MB of RAM for each Office program (such as Microsoft Word) running simultaneously

■ **Microsoft Windows Millennium Edition (Windows Me) or Microsoft Windows NT**

32 MB of RAM plus an additional 8 MB of RAM for each Office program (such as Microsoft Word) running simultaneously

■ **Microsoft Windows 2000 Professional**

64 MB of RAM plus an additional 8 MB of RAM for each Office program (such as Microsoft Word) running simultaneously

■ **Hard Disk**

Hard disk space requirements will vary depending on configuration; custom installation choices may require more or less hard disk space.

■ 245 MB of available hard disk space with 115 MB on the hard disk where the operating system is installed. (Users without Windows 2000, Windows Me, or Office 2000 Service Release 1 require an extra 50 MB of hard disk space for System Files Update.)

■ An additional 136 MB of hard disk space is required for installing the practice files.

■ **Operating System**

Windows 98, Windows 98 Second Edition, Windows Me, Windows NT 4.0 with Service Pack 6 or later, or Windows 2000 or later. (On systems running Windows NT 4.0 with Service Pack 6, the version of Microsoft Internet Explorer must be upgraded to at least version 4.01 with Service Pack 1.)

Important

The exercises in the book were created on a computer running Windows 98. Other operating systems might display different results than those shown in this book.

■ **Drive**

CD-ROM drive

■ **Display**

Super VGA (800 × 600) or higher–resolution monitor with at least 256 colors

■ **Peripherals**

Microsoft Mouse, Microsoft IntelliMouse, or compatible pointing device

■ **Applications**

Microsoft Office XP

Installing the Practice Files

You need to install the practice files on your hard disk before you use them in the chapters' exercises. Follow these steps to prepare the CD files for your use:

1 Insert the CD-ROM into the CD-ROM drive of your computer.

A menu screen appears.

Important

If the menu screen does not appear, start Windows Explorer. In the left pane, locate the icon for your CD-ROM and click this icon. In the right pane, double-click the file named *StartCd*.

2 Click **Install Practice Files**.

3 Click **OK** in the initial message box.

4 If you want to install the practice files to a location other than the default folder (C:\Office XP SBS), click the **Change Folder** button, select the new drive and path, and then click **OK**.

5 Click the **Continue** button to install the selected practice files.

6 After the practice files have been installed, click **OK**.

Within the installation folder are subfolders for each chapter in the book.

7 Remove the CD-ROM from the CD-ROM drive, and return it to its envelope.

Important

If you install the practice files to a location other than the default folder, the file location listed in some of the book's exercises will be incorrect.

Using the Practice Files

Each chapter's introduction lists the files that are needed for that chapter and explains any file preparation that you need to take care of before you start working through the chapter.

Each topic in the chapter explains how and when to use any practice files. The file or files that you'll need are indicated in the margin at the beginning of the procedure above the CD icon:

GoalSeek

Throughout the Microsoft Outlook section of the book, you will be working with e-mail messages, calendar appointments, and contact information. To follow along with the exercises in this section, you need to copy the installed practice files from your hard disk to the correct Outlook folders. Here are the steps for doing this:

1 Start Outlook by double-clicking its icon on the desktop.

2 On the **Start** menu, point to **Programs** and then click **Windows Explorer** to open Windows Explorer.

3 If the Explorer window obscures the bar on the left side of the Outlook window, drag the **Explorer** window to the right side of the screen so that the **Inbox** icon on the Outlook bar is visible.

4 In the left pane of the Explorer window, browse to the Practice Files subfolder of the Office XP SBS\Outlook folders, which contain all the practice files for the Outlook section of this book.

The contents of the folders are displayed in the right pane.

5   Click the **Type** header in the right pane to sort the practice files by type.

6   Drag the .msg files **Kickoff**, **Status**, **TeamMeeting**, **NextShow**, **OrderStatus**, **ReNextShow**, **Schedule**, and **NewSupplier**, which are identified by the **message** icon, to the **Inbox** icon on the Outlook bar.

The items are added to your Inbox.

7   Drag all the .cal files (**DayCareVisit**, **TeamMeeting**, **HomeShow**), which are identified by the **Calendar** icon, to the **Calendar** icon on the Outlook bar.

The items are added to your Calendar.

8   Drag the .msg files **CatherineT** and **KimY**, which are identified by the **address card** icon, to the **Contact** icon on the Outlook bar.

The items are added to your Contacts folder.

9   Close Windows Explorer by clicking its **Close** button.

Important

If you have upgraded to Outlook 2002 from an earlier version of the program, the practice files will now be mixed with your real messages, appointments, contacts, and tasks.

The following table lists each chapter's practice files.

Chapter	Folder	Files
1	\Word\Chap01	ExistDoc, EditDoc, OpenDoc, and ReplaceText
2	\Word\Chap02	FormatText, FormatPara, CreateList, FormatPage, and FormatStyle
3	\Word\Chap03	CreateTable, FormatTable, DataTable, InsertTable, and CreateColumn
4	\Word\Chap04	SpellCheck and PreviewPrint
5	\Excel\Chap05	FileOpen, ZeroIn, DataEntry, and Replace
6	\Excel\Chap06	Easier, DataRead, Formats, CreateNew, EasyRead, and Conditional
7	\Excel\Chap07	NameRange, Formula, and FindErrors
8	\Excel\Chap08	Filter, Calculations, and Validate
9	\Access\Chap09	Open\GardenCo, Tables\GardenCo, Queries\GardenCo, Forms\GardenCo, and Reports\GardenCo
10	\Access\Chap10	CheckingDB\Contacts, Refining\GardenCo, and Manipulate\GardenCo

Chapter	Folder	Files
11	\Access\Chap11	FormByWiz\GardenCo, Properties\GardenCo, Properties\tgc_bkgrnd, Layout\GardenCo, Controls\GardenCo, Controls\tgc_logo2, Events\GardenCo, Events\AftUpdate, AutoForm\GardenCo, and Subform\GardenCo
12	\Access\Chap12	Sort\GardenCo, FilterDS\GardenCo, FilterForm\GardenCo, AdvFilter\GardenCo, QueryDes\GardenCo, QueryWiz\GardenCo, and Aggregate\GardenCo
13	\PowerPoint\Chap13	BrowsePres, EditText, and ViewPres
14	\PowerPoint\Chap14	EnterText, NewSlide, InsertSlide, SlideInsert, OrderSlides, EnterNotes, and StorePres
15	\PowerPoint\Chap15	AddText, AlignText, ReplaceText, CorrectText, and SpellCheck
16	\PowerPoint\Chap16	FilePrint, HeaderFooter, PrintSetting, PrintPreview, and PrintFile
17	\FrontPage\Chap17	GardenCo
18	\FrontPage\Chap18	TasksList\GardenCo, InsertText\GardenCo, InsertExist\GardenCo, InsertExist\Classes, InsertExist\PR2, FormatText\GardenCo, InsertHype\GardenCo, InsertHype\PR1, and PreviewPage\GardenCo
19	\FrontPage\Chap19	CreateList\GardenCo, CreateTable\GardenCo, Start\GardenCo, TableText\GardenCo, TableText\ClassList, TableStruct\GardenCo, FormatTable\GardenCo, TableInTable\GardenCo, Carniv, Organic, and Spring
20	\FrontPage\Chap20	AddPicture\Garden4, Start\GardenCo, Thumbnail\PH01245J[1], Thumbnail\pictures, WordArt\GardenCo, and PhotoGallery\GardenCo (and various pictures)
21	\FrontPage\Chap21	GardenCo
22	\Publisher\Chap22	BusinessCard, Garden_4color, and Gardenc_4color
23	\Publisher\Chap23	PrintDoc1, PrintDoc2, SpotColor, SpotColor2, and ProcessColor
24	\Outlook\Chap24	NewSupplier, NextShow, and Attachment
25	\Outlook\Chap25	NextShow, OrderStatus, ReNextShow, and Schedule

(continued)

Chapter	Folder	Files
26	\Outlook\Chap26	GardenCo, NextShow, OrderStatus, ReNextShow, and Schedule
27	\Outlook\Chap27	DayCareVisit and TeamMeeting
28	\Outlook\Chap28	Journal\CatherineT, Journal\KimY, Journal\OfferLetter, HomeShow, Kickoff, Status, and TeamMeeting

Uninstalling the Practice Files

After you finish working through this book, you should uninstall the practice files to free up hard disk space.

1 On the Windows taskbar, click the **Start** button, point to **Settings**, and then click **Control Panel**.

2 Double-click the **Add/Remove Programs** icon.

3 Click **Microsoft Office XP SBS Files**, and click **Add/Remove**. (If you're using Windows 2000 Professional, click the **Remove** or **Change/Remove** button.)

4 Click **Yes** when the confirmation dialog box appears.

If you've worked through the Outlook exercises, you've probably created some additional files (files with .msg, .cal, and .pst extensions, for example) that will not be deleted by the uninstall procedure shown above. To help you find and delete these files, you can follow these additional, optional steps:

1 In Outlook, on the **Tools** menu, click **Advanced Find**.

2 In the **Look for** list, click **Any type of Outlook item**, and when presented with a message indicating that this will clear your search, click **OK**.

3 Click the **More Choices** tab, and click the **Categories** button.

4 In the **Available categories** list, select the **Practice Files** check box, and click **OK**.

5 Click **Find Now**.

Outlook searches all your Outlook folders for items assigned to the Practice Files category.

6 When the search is complete, select all the found items, and on the **Edit** menu, click **Delete**.

7 If prompted to send any meeting responses, click the **Delete without sending a response** option, and click **OK**.

The items remain in the list but are placed in the Deleted Items folder.

8 Delete the remaining items you created during the lessons using the following table:

Location	Files
Inbox	Catherine Turner
	Kim Yoshida
	This is a message of high importance
	This is a message of low importance
	Any undeliverable messages or messages sent to yourself
Drafts	This is a message of low importance
Calendar	Budget Meeting, the day and week after you completed the exercise and 6/18/02
	Collaborate on Sales Report, the business day after you completed the exercise
	Day Care Visit, 6/18/02
	Plan for Home Show Exhibition, 6/18/02
	Out for Holidays, 12/23/02
	Team Meeting, 6/18/02
Contacts	Catherine T
	Catherine Turner
	Garden Co
	KimY
	Kim Yoshida
	Mike Galos

9 To empty your Deleted Items folder (optional), on the **Outlook Bar**, right-click the **Deleted Items** icon, and click **Empty "Deleted Items" Folder**. When prompted to confirm that you want to permanently delete the items, click **Yes**.

Important

If you need additional help installing or uninstalling the practice files, please see the section "Getting Help" earlier in this book. Microsoft's product support does not provide support for this book or its CD-ROM.

Conventions and Features

You can save time when you use this book by understanding how the Step by Step series shows special instructions, keys to press, buttons to click, and so on.

Convention	Meaning
1 2	Numbered steps guide you through hands-on exercises in each topic.
●	A round bullet indicates an exercise that has only one step.
(CD icon)	This icon at the beginning of a chapter appears next to the paragraph that lists the files that the lesson will use and explains any file preparation that needs to take place before starting the lesson.
FileName (CD icon)	Practice files that you'll need to use in a topic's procedure are shown above the CD icon.
new for **Office**XP	This icon indicates a new or greatly improved feature in this version of Microsoft Office.
Tip	This section provides a helpful hint or shortcut that makes working through a task easier.
Important	This section points out information that you need to know to complete the procedure.
Troubleshooting	This section shows you how to fix a common problem.
Save 🖫	When a button is referenced in a topic, a picture of the button with a label appears in the margin area.
Alt + Tab	A plus sign (+) between two key names means that you must press those keys at the same time. For example, "Press Alt + Tab " means that you hold down the Alt key while you press Tab .
Black boldface type	Program features that you click or press are shown in black boldface type.
Blue boldface type	Terms that are explained in the glossary at the end of the book are shown in blue boldface type within the chapter.
Red boldface type	Text that you are supposed to type appears in red boldface type in the procedures.
Italic type	Folder paths, URLs, and emphasized words appear in italic type.

Microsoft Word

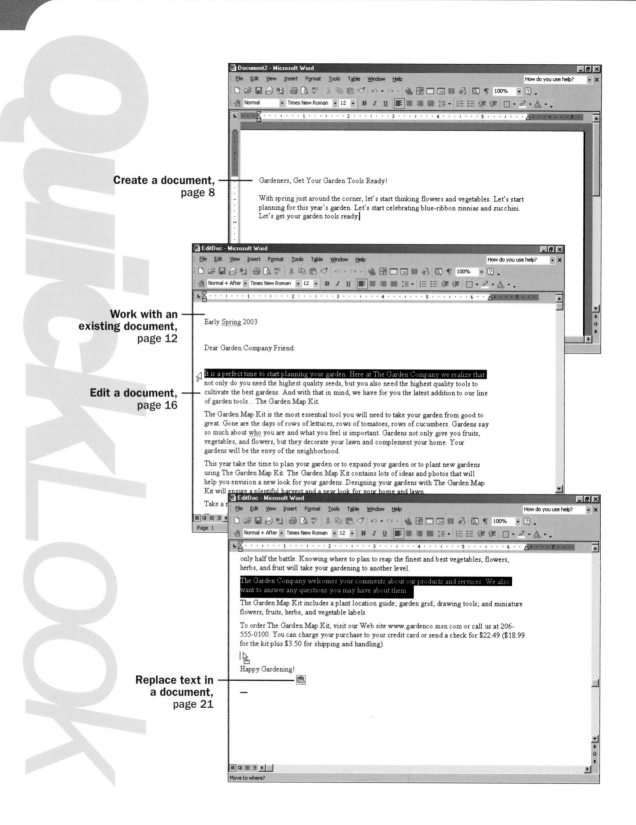

Gardeners, Get Your Garden Tools Ready!

With spring just around the corner, let's start thinking flowers and vegetables. Let's start planning for this year's garden. Let's start celebrating blue-ribbon zinnias and zucchini. Let's get your garden tools ready.

Early Spring 2003

Dear Garden Company Friend:

It is a perfect time to start planning your garden. Here at The Garden Company we realize that not only do you need the highest quality seeds, but you also need the highest quality tools to cultivate the best gardens. And with that in mind, we have for you the latest addition to our line of garden tools... The Garden Map Kit.

The Garden Map Kit is the most essential tool you will need to take your garden from good to great. Gone are the days of rows of lettuces, rows of tomatoes, rows of cucumbers. Gardens say so much about who you are and what you feel is important. Gardens not only give you fruits, vegetables, and flowers, but they decorate your lawn and complement your home. Your gardens will be the envy of the neighborhood.

This year take the time to plan your garden or to expand your garden or to plant new gardens using The Garden Map Kit. The Garden Map Kit contains lots of ideas and photos that will help you envision a new look for your gardens. Designing your gardens with The Garden Map Kit will ensure a plentiful harvest and a new look for your home and lawn.

Take a...

only half the battle. Knowing where to plan to reap the finest and best vegetables, flowers, herbs, and fruit will take your gardening to another level.

The Garden Company welcomes your comments about our products and services. We also want to answer any questions you may have about them.

The Garden Map Kit includes a plant location guide; garden grid; drawing tools; and miniature flowers, fruits, herbs, and vegetable labels.

To order The Garden Map Kit, visit our Web site www.gardenco.msn.com or call us at 206-555-0100. You can charge your purchase to your credit card or send a check for $22.49 ($18.99 for the kit plus $3.50 for shipping and handling).

Happy Gardening!

Chapter 1
Creating a Document

After completing this chapter, you will be able to:
- ✔ **Get started with Word.**
- ✔ **Create a document.**
- ✔ **Work with an existing document.**
- ✔ **Edit a document.**
- ✔ **Replace text in a document.**

Word processing is using a computer program to create, edit, and produce text documents. Word-processing programs help you create professional-quality documents because they let you type and format text, correct errors, and preview your work before you print or distribute a document.

Microsoft Word is a word-processing program that you can use to compose and update a wide range of business and personal documents. In addition, Word offers many **desktop-publishing** features that let you enhance the appearance of documents so that they are appealing and easy to read. Whether you need to create a letter, memo, fax, annual report, newsletter, or book, Word has the power and flexibility to produce professional documents quickly and easily.

In this chapter, you'll create and edit documents for The Garden Company, a business that provides supplies to gardeners. You'll start by entering text to create a document, and then you'll save the document as a file. You'll open other documents to navigate and switch between them. As you save a document with a new file name, you'll also create a folder for the file. Finally, you'll edit a document by inserting and deleting text, moving and copying text, and finding and replacing text.

This chapter uses the practice files ExistDoc, EditDoc, OpenDoc, and ReplaceText that are stored in the Office XP SBS\Word\Chap01 subfolder that you installed from this book's CD-ROM. For details about installing the practice files, see "Using the Book's CD-ROM" at the beginning of this book.

Important

If you haven't done so yet, you should install the book's practice files so that you can work through the exercises in this chapter. You can find instructions for installing the practice files in the "Using the Book's CD-ROM" section at the beginning of this book.

Getting Started with Word

When you start Word, the Word program window opens. This window contains many of the same menus, tools, and other features that every Microsoft Office XP program has and some that are unique to Word. You enter and edit text in the Word document window, which is part of the Word program window. The insertion point, the blinking vertical line that appears in the document window, indicates where the text will appear when you type.

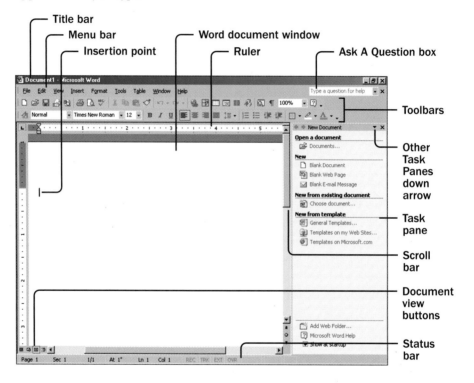

Title bar
Menu bar
Insertion point
Word document window
Ruler
Ask A Question box
Toolbars
Other Task Panes down arrow
Task pane
Scroll bar
Document view buttons
Status bar

Tip

Word uses personalized menus and toolbars to reduce the number of menu commands and toolbar buttons that you see on the screen and to display the ones that you use most often. When you click a menu name, a short menu appears, containing the commands that you use most often. To make the complete long menu appear, you can leave the pointer over the menu name for several seconds, double-click the menu name, or click the menu name and then click the small double arrow at the bottom of the short menu. When the long menu is open, the commands that did not appear on the short menu are light gray.

Important

When the Standard and Formatting toolbars share one row, which is the default set-ting, you can't see all the available buttons, but you can access other buttons by clicking the **Toolbar Options** down arrow at the end of the toolbar. If a button men-tioned in this book doesn't appear on a toolbar, click the **Toolbar Options** down arrow on that toolbar to display the rest of its buttons. To make it easier for you to find but-tons, the Standard and Formatting toolbars in this book appear on two rows. To change your settings to match the screens in this book, click **Customize** on the Tools menu, select the **Show Standard and Formatting toolbars on two rows** check box on the **Options** tab, and then click **Close**.

At the bottom of the document window are view buttons that allow you to look at a document in different ways. **Normal view** is the default editing view, which you use to write and edit your documents. **Web Layout view** shows your document as it appears as a Web page. This view is useful for viewing and editing text and graphics designed for use in a Web browser. **Print Layout view** shows your document as it appears on the printed page. This view is useful for changing page and column boundaries, editing headers and footers, and working with drawing objects. **Outline view** shows the structure of the document, which consists of headings and body text. This view is useful for viewing, moving, copying, and reorganizing text.

Task pane
new for
OfficeXP

Word organizes commands for common tasks in the **Task pane**, a small window next to your document that opens when you need it. For example, when you start Word, you see the New Document Task pane, which includes commands for opening and creating documents. Use the New Document Task pane to open a saved or blank document, to create a document based on an existing one, or to create a document from a **template**, a file containing structure and style settings that help you create a specific type of document, such as a memo or resume. You also can show or hide any Task pane when you like. If you want to use a Task pane and the one that you want does not appear, you can manually show the Task pane and then select the spe-cific Task pane that you want from the **Other Task panes** menu on the Task pane. If you no longer need the Task pane, you can hide it to free up valuable screen space in the program window. On the **View** menu, click Task pane; clicking the command hides the Task pane if it is currently displayed or shows it if it is currently hidden.

Tip

The Task pane opens each time you start Word and closes when you open a docu-ment. If you do not want the Task pane to appear each time you start Word, clear the **Show at Startup** check box in the Task pane.

When you have a question about using Word, you can save time by using the Ask A Question box rather than searching the table of contents or index in online Help. After you type a question or keyword and press the [Enter] key, Word lists Help topics so that you can choose the one that answers your question. Another way to get help is to use the **Office Assistant**. As you work, the Office Assistant appears, offering tips for completing your task, such as creating and formatting a letter. For complete access to Help topics, you can open the Help window and use its table of contents, index, and Answer Wizard, or you can visit the Microsoft Web site to find Help information.

In this exercise, you start Word, close the New Document Task pane, and ask a question about online Help.

1 On the taskbar, click **Start**, point to **Programs**, and then click **Microsoft Word**.

The Word window opens with a blank document and the New Document Task pane in the document window.

Tip

Another way to start Word and create a new document is to click the **New Office Document** command at the top of the **Start** menu. When the **New Office Document** dialog box appears, double-click the **Blank Document** icon.

2 In the title bar of the New Document Task pane, click the **Other Task panes** down arrow.

The **Other Task panes** menu opens.

3 Press the [Esc] key, or click an empty place in the document.

Word closes the **Other Task panes** menu.

Close

4 Click the **Close** button in the New Document Task pane.

The New Document Task pane closes.

5 On the **View** menu, click **Task pane**.

The New Document Task pane opens.

6 On the right side of the menu bar, click in the **Ask A Question** box.

7 Type **How do I use help?**, and then press [Enter].

A menu appears with help topics that relate to the question that you typed.

8 Click **About getting help while you work**.

The Microsoft Word Help window opens.

9 Click the **Ask A Question box**.

The Microsoft Word Help window displays more information about the Ask A Question box.

Close

10 Click the **Close** button in the Microsoft Word Help window.

The Microsoft Word Help window closes.

11 On the Help menu, click **Show the Office Assistant**.

The animated paper clip Office Assistant appears.

12 Click the **Office Assistant**.

A yellow help box appears, as shown in the following illustration. You can type a question in the box, and then click **Search** or a help topic provided.

13 Right-click the **Office Assistant**, and then click **Hide** on the shortcut menu to hide the Office Assistant.

Tip

You can open the Microsoft Word Help window instead of using the Ask A Question box or the Office Assistant. Right-click the **Office Assistant**, click **Options**, clear the **Use the Office Assistant** check box, and then click **OK**. On the **Help** menu, click **Microsoft Word Help**. To turn on the Office Assistant again, click **Show the Office Assistant** on the **Help** menu.

Creating a Document

Creating a Word document is as simple as typing text. The insertion point indicates where the text will appear in the document. As with most word-processing programs, in Word you don't have to press the [Enter] key after you type a full line of text. Instead of continuing the text past the right margin, Word "wraps" the text to the next line. **Word wrap** is a feature of word processing and desktop publishing that moves text to the next line when the insertion point reaches the right margin. You press [Enter] to start a new paragraph, not a new line.

The text that you type appears in the document window and is stored temporarily in your computer's memory. If you want to keep the text for future use, you must save the document to a **file**. You specify a name and location for the file. You can then retrieve the file later to continue working on the document.

Create New
Folder

To save a new document in Word, you click the **Save** button on the Standard toolbar. The first time that you save a document, you use the **Save As** dialog box to enter a file name and indicate where you want to save the file. To keep your documents organized and easily accessible, you can store them in folders that you create. You can store related documents in a single folder. To create a new folder, you click, the **Create New Folder** button in the **Save As** dialog box.

After you save a document once using the **Save As** dialog box, you can save changes that you make by clicking the **Save** button on the Standard toolbar. In other words, the newer version overwrites the original version. If you want to keep both the original file and the version with your recent changes, you click the **Save As** command on the **File** menu to save the new version with a new name. You can save the document with the new name in the same folder as the original or in a new folder, but you cannot store two documents in the same folder if the documents have the same name.

Tip

To help you locate the drive where you want to store a new folder and file, you can click the **Up One Level** button to move up a level in the hierarchy of folders, or you can use the Places Bar to move to another location on your computer. The Places Bar on the left side of the **Save As** and **Open** dialog boxes provides quick access to commonly used locations for storing and opening files.

The Garden Company is preparing a new garden supply catalog. The inside cover of the catalog will need some text that describes the new catalog's theme, which is planning a garden.

In this exercise, you enter text in a document and then save your new document.

New Blank
Document

1   On the Standard toolbar, click the **New Blank Document** button.

A new document window opens.

2   With the insertion point at the top of the new document, type Gardeners, Get Your Garden Tools Ready!, and then press ⏎ twice.

The text appears in the new document.

3   Press ⏎ again to insert a blank line below the heading.

4   Type With spring just around the corner, let's start thinking flowers and vegetables. Let's start planning for this year's garden. Let's start celebrating blue-ribbon zinnias and zucchini. Let's get your garden tools ready.

Notice that you did not need to press ⏎ when the insertion point reached the right margin because the text wrapped to the left margin.

Important

If a wavy red or green line appears under a word or phrase, Word is flagging text that it does not recognize as a possible spelling or grammar error. If a purple dotted line appears under a word or phrase, Word is displaying a Smart Tag, which recognizes certain types of text as data that you can use with other programs. For example, Word tags a person's name as data that you can add to an electronic address book. For now, ignore any errors and Smart Tags.

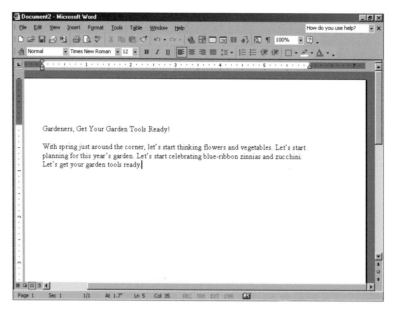

Save

5 On the Standard toolbar, click the **Save** button.

The **Save As** dialog box appears and displays the My Documents folder as the open folder.

Important

Use the Places Bar in the **Save As** dialog box to move to a location listed on the bar. For instance, to save a file to a floppy disk, you click the **Desktop** icon on the Places Bar, double-click the **My Computer** icon, and then double-click **3½ Floppy (A:)** drive.

6 Click the **Save in** down arrow, and then click your hard disk, typically drive C.

7 In the list of file and folder names, double-click the **Office XP SBS** folder, and then double-click the **Word** folder.

The contents of the Word folder appear in the **Save As** dialog box.

8 Double-click the **Chap01** folder.

The contents of the Chap01 folder appear in the **Save As** dialog box. You can see that the word *Gardeners*, the first word in the document, appears in the File Name box.

Tip

Word uses the first few characters (or words) in the document to suggest a file name. You can accept this suggested name or type a new one.

9   Click the **Create New Folder** button.

The **New Folder** dialog box appears. The folder that you are creating is a sub-folder within the CreatingDoc folder.

10   Type NewFolder, and then click **OK**.

NewFolder becomes the current folder.

11   In the File Name box, double-click **Gardeners**, type FirstSave, and then click the **Save** button.

The **Save As** dialog box closes, and the file name *FirstSave* appears in the title bar.

Close Window

12   Click the **Close** button in the document window.

The FirstSave document closes.

Saving a File for Use in Another Program

Word allows you to save a document in a **file format** other than the Word document format. A file format is the way that a program stores a file so that the program can open up the file later. Saving a document in another format is important if you share documents with others who use programs or previous versions of Word that have a different file format, such as Word 6.0/95 or WordPerfect. For example, if you use Word 6.0 on the computer that you have at home, you can create a document in Word 2002, save it in the Word 6.0 format, and then open and edit the document on your home computer.

To save a file in another file format:

1   On the **File** menu, click **Save As**.

   The **Save As** dialog box appears.

2   In the File Name box, type a new name for the document.

3   Click the **Save as type** down arrow, and then select the file format that you want to use.

4   Click **Save**.

Working with an Existing Document

Once you save a document to a file, you can open that document again. To open an existing document, you use the **Open** button on the Standard toolbar or an option on the New Document Task pane. Using the New Document Task pane, you can create a document based on an existing one. This is useful when you want to start a new document with existing text without changing the original document.

To enter or revise text, you start by positioning the insertion point. You can click to place the insertion point at a particular location, or you can press keys on the keyboard to move the insertion point in a document. When you use a **key combination,** you press two keys at the same time to perform an action. For example, pressing the [End] key moves the insertion point to the end of a line of text, whereas pressing the [Ctrl] and [End] keys at the same time moves the insertion point to the beginning of the document. To use a key combination, you hold down the first key (for example, [Ctrl]) and then press the second key. Once the action takes place, you release both keys.

The following table shows the keys and key combinations that you can use to move the insertion point quickly.

Pressing This Key...	Moves the Insertion Point
←	Left one character at a time (A character can be a letter, number, punctuation mark, or symbol.)
→	Right one character at a time
↓	Down one line at a time
↑	Up one line at a time
Ctrl + ←	Left one word at a time
Ctrl + →	Right one word at a time
Home	To the beginning of the current line of text
End	To the end of the current line of text
Ctrl + Home	To the beginning of the document
Ctrl + End	To the end of the document
Page Up	Up one full screen
Page Down	Down one full screen
Ctrl + Page Up	To the beginning of the previous page
Ctrl + Page Down	To the beginning of the next page

You can also use the vertical and horizontal scroll bars to move around in a document. However, using the scroll bars does not move the insertion point—it changes only your view of the document in the window. For example, if you drag the vertical scroll box down to the bottom of the scroll bar, the end of the document comes into view, but the insertion point does not move. The status bar shows the location of the insertion point (by page, section, inch, line, and column). Click the up or down scroll arrow on the vertical scroll bar to move the document window up or down one line of text. Click the left or right scroll arrow on the horizontal scroll bar to move the document window to the left or right several characters at a time.

Select Browse
Object

As you create longer documents, you can use the **Select Browse Object** menu at the bottom of the vertical scroll bars to move quickly through a document. When you click the **Select Browse Object** button, a menu appears with browsing options, such as Browse By Page, Browse By Comment, and Browse By Graphic.

When you open a document, a program button with the Word program icon and document name appears on the taskbar. You can have many documents open at the same time, but only one is the current or active document. The program button of the current document appears pressed in. To move between open documents, click the program button on the taskbar, or use the **Window** menu, which lists all open documents. The check mark to the left of the document name in the Window menu indicates the current document.

The Garden Company sends marketing letters to its customers during the spring to promote new products. Before the letter is updated, the copy editor wants to review last year's letter to see what needs to be changed.

ExistDoc,
OpenDoc

In this exercise, you move around a document and then switch between open documents. First, you open the document called ExistDoc, and then you move around the document to review the text.

Open

1   On the Standard toolbar, click the **Open** button.

The **Open** dialog box appears.

Tip

You can also click **Open** on the **File** menu or click **Documents** on the New Document Task pane to open an existing document.

2   Navigate to the Office XP SBS folder on your hard disk, double-click the **Word** folder, and then double-click the **Chap01** folder.

3   Double-click the **ExistDoc** file to open the document in the Word window.

The ExistDoc document opens.

4   In the greeting, click after the colon (:) to position the insertion point.

5   Press the [Home] key to move the insertion point to the beginning of the line.

6   Press the [→] key five times to move the insertion point to the beginning of the word *Garden* in the greeting.

7   Press the [↓] key two times to move the insertion point to the first paragraph.

8   Press the [End] key to move the insertion point to the end of the first line of text.

9   Press [Ctrl]+[End] to move the insertion point to the end of the document.

10   Press [Ctrl]+[Home] to move the insertion point to the beginning of the document.

11   Drag the vertical scroll box to the bottom of the vertical scroll bar.

The insertion point is still at the beginning of the document, but the end of the document now comes into view.

12   In the vertical scroll bar, click the Scroll Up arrow five times.

The document changes to show five more lines of text.

13 Click above the vertical scroll box to change the view of the document by one screen.

14 In the horizontal scroll bar, click the right scroll arrow twice so that the right side of the document comes into view by a few characters.

15 Drag the horizontal scroll box all the way to the left.

The document is repositioned. Note that the location of the insertion point has not changed—just the view of the document.

16 Press Ctrl+Home to move the insertion point to the beginning of the document.

Select Browse
Object

17 Click the **Select Browse Object** button on the right side of the window.

When you click the button, a palette of objects appears.

18 Move the pointer over the palette of objects.

The name of each object in the palette appears as you point to an object.

Browse by
Page

19 Click the **Browse by Page** button.

The insertion point moves from page 1 to the beginning of page 2.

Open

20 On the Standard toolbar, click the **Open** button.

The **Open** dialog box appears.

21 Navigate to the SBS folder on your hard disk, double-click the **Word** folder, double-click the **CreatingDoc** folder, and then double-click the **OpenDoc** file.

The OpenDoc document opens.

22 On the taskbar, click the **ExistDoc program** button to make it the current document.

The ExistDoc document opens. The taskbar now shows two program buttons, each with the name of an open document. The button that is pressed in indicates the active document, which is currently the ExistDoc document.

23 On the menu bar, click **Window**.

The two open files are listed at the bottom of the **Window** menu.

24 On the **Window** menu, click **Arrange All**.

The two document windows are resized and stacked one on top of the other.

Close

25 Click the **Close** button in the ExistDoc document window, and then click the **Close** button in the OpenDoc document window.

Maximize

26 Click the **Maximize** button in the Word window to return it to its original size.

Editing a Document

When you edit a document, you revise its text. Editing encompasses many tasks, such as inserting and deleting words and phrases, correcting errors, and moving and copying text to different places in the document. Editing also includes searching for words, phrases, or even formatting, and replacing that text with different text.

Inserting text is as easy as positioning the insertion point and typing. When you insert text, existing text moves to the right to accommodate the text that you are inserting, and the text that reaches the right margin wraps to the next line, if necessary.

Before you can edit or work with text, you first need to select it. Selected text appears highlighted on the screen. To deselect text, you click anywhere outside of the selected text. To select a block of text quickly, you can use the selection area. The **selection area** is any blank area to the left of the left margin in the document. When the pointer is in the selection area, the pointer changes from an I-beam to a right-pointing arrow.

Selection area

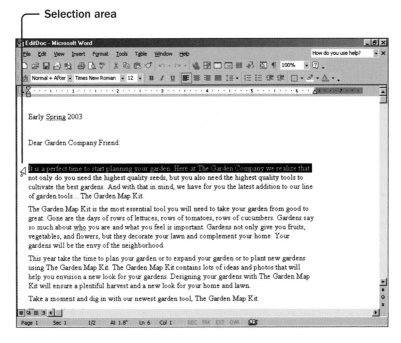

The following table describes methods that you can use to select text in a document.

Selection	Action
A word	Double-click the word.
A line	Click the selection area to the left of the line.
A sentence	Hold down the `Ctrl` key, and then click anywhere in the sentence. The first character in the sentence through the space following the ending punctuation mark is selected.
A paragraph	Double-click the selection area to the left of any line in the paragraph, or triple-click anywhere in the paragraph.
An entire document	Hold down the `Ctrl` key, and then click anywhere in the selection area, or triple-click anywhere in the selection area.

Select nonadjacent text

new for OfficeXP

To select blocks of text that are not adjacent in a document, you select the first block of text, hold down `Ctrl`, and then select the next block of text. You can also use the `Shift` key and the arrow keys to select adjacent words, lines, or paragraphs. You position the insertion point in the text that you want to select, hold down the `Shift` key, and then press an arrow key or click at the end of the text that you want to select.

Deleting text in a document is also an easy task. To delete a few characters, you can use the ⌫Backspace⌫ or ⌫Del⌫ key. Pressing ⌫Backspace⌫ deletes the character to the left of the insertion point. Pressing ⌫Del⌫ deletes the character to the right of the insertion point. Using these keys is a quick way to correct small errors. However, if you need to delete an entire sentence or a large block of text, first select the text, and then press ⌫Backspace⌫ or ⌫Del⌫.

Undo

As you edit a document, Word keeps track of the changes that you make so that you can easily remove a change and restore your original text. This is useful when you make a mistake, as when you inadvertently delete a word. To undo the last action that you performed, click the **Undo** button on the Standard toolbar. To display the last five or six actions that you have performed, click the down arrow on the **Undo** button. Click the action in the list that you want to undo, and that action and all subsequent actions in the list are undone.

Redo

If you undo an action, you can restore, or redo, the action by clicking the **Redo** button. You can click the down arrow on the **Redo** button to restore multiple undone actions.

Office
Clipboard
Task pane
new for
OfficeXP

You can move selected text by cutting it and then pasting it in another place in the document. Text that you move, or cut, no longer appears in the document but is temporarily stored in an area of the computer memory called the **Office Clipboard**. Copying text is similar to moving text. However, when you copy selected text, the selected text remains in its original location, and you paste a copy of the selected text in another location. When you paste the selection, the text appears at the location of the insertion point.

Office Clipboard

You can use the Office Clipboard to store multiple items of information from several different sources in one storage area shared by all Office programs. The Office Clipboard appears as a Task pane and shows all the items that you stored there. You can paste these items of information into any Office program, either individually or all at once.

The Office Clipboard appears when you copy multiple items, unless the Office Clipboard option is turned off. To manually open the Office Clipboard, you click **Office Clipboard** on the **Edit** menu or double-click the **Clipboard** icon in the status area of the taskbar. The Clipboard icon appears on the taskbar when the Office Clipboard contains items. The Office Clipboard is useful for moving and copying information between pages and documents. If you need to move or copy text within a paragraph or line, you can drag the text instead of using the Office Clipboard. To move text, you select the text and drag it to another place. To copy or select text, you hold down ⌫Ctrl⌫ and drag it to another place.

Now that the marketing letter from last year has been reviewed, an assistant at The Garden Company can use it to create a new letter for this year's marketing campaign. The most efficient way to create the new letter is to edit last year's letter.

In this exercise, you edit text in the existing document. You insert and delete text, undo the deletion, copy and paste a phrase, and move a paragraph.

EditDoc

Open

1 On the Standard toolbar, click the **Open** button.

The **Open** dialog box appears.

2 Navigate to the Office XP SBS folder on your hard disk, double-click the **Word** folder, double-click the **Chap01** folder, and then double-click the **EditDoc** file.

The EditDoc document opens.

3 Double-click the word *Early* at the top of the document to select it, and then press Enter to delete the word and create a paragraph.

4 Press End to move the insertion point to the end of the line, press Space , and then type **Has Arrived!**

The text appears at the end of the line.

5 Press ↓ four times, hold down Ctrl, and then click anywhere in the first sentence to select it.

6 Press Del to delete the sentence.

Undo

7 On the Standard toolbar, click the **Undo** button to restore the deleted text.

8 Click the down scroll arrow until the phrase *Happy Gardening!* appears, position the pointer in the selection area to the left of the text *Happy Gardening!*, and then click to select the entire line of text.

Copy

9 On the Standard toolbar, click the **Copy** button to copy the text to the Clipboard.

10 On the **Edit** menu, click **Office Clipboard**.

The Clipboard Task pane appears, displaying the current items in the Office Clipboard.

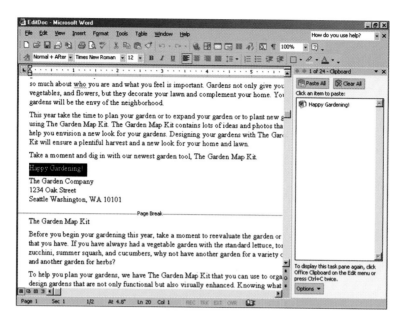

Troubleshooting

You can turn on and off Office Clipboard options in the Task pane. You can choose either to display the Office Clipboard when you are copying items or to copy items to the Office Clipboard without displaying the Office Clipboard. You can also choose to display the Clipboard icon on the taskbar when the Office Clipboard is turned on. To access these options, click **Options** at the bottom of the Clipboard Task pane.

11 Press [Ctrl]+[End] to move to the end of the document, and then press [Enter] to insert a blank line.

12 In the Clipboard Task pane, click the **Happy Gardening!** box to place the text from the Clipboard into the document.

Troubleshooting

If a **Paste Options** button appears next to the selection that you pasted, you can ignore it for now. The **Paste Options** button provides a list of options that allows you to determine how the information is pasted into your document.

Close

13 In the Clipboard Task pane, click the **Close** button to close the Task pane.

14 If necessary, scroll up to the paragraph that begins *The Garden Company welcomes your comments*, and then triple-click in the paragraph to select the paragraph.

15 Drag the paragraph text down to above the text *Happy Gardening!*.

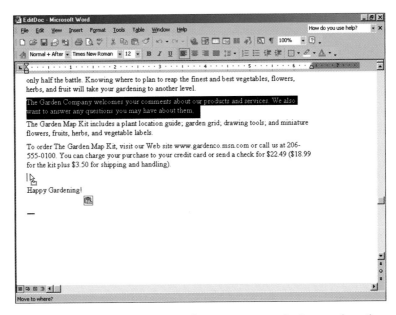

When you release the mouse, the text appears in its new location.

16 On the Standard toolbar, click the **Save** button to save the document.

Close

17 Click the **Close** button in the document window.

The EditDoc document closes.

Replacing Text in a Document

Word corrects commonly misspelled words as you type so that you don't have to correct them yourself. For example, if you type **teh**, Word changes it to *the* as soon as you press [Space]. Changing the text like this is called **AutoCorrect**. Besides correcting misspelled words, AutoCorrect can also insert a long phrase when you type an abbreviation. For example, if you type the abbreviation *gc* to represent the company name, you can have AutoCorrect insert the full phrase *The Garden Company*. To add your own AutoCorrect entry, you enter the abbreviation and the full phrase in the **AutoCorrect** dialog box and then add the entry to the list of corrections.

AutoCorrect
Options

If you don't want Word to automatically change text, you can undo the change or turn off AutoCorrect options by clicking the **AutoCorrect Options** button that appears after the change. The **AutoCorrect Options** button first appears as a small blue box near the changed text and then changes to a button icon. If you are uncertain about AutoCorrect options or if you want to change or modify an AutoCorrect setting, you can open the **AutoCorrect** dialog box. You also use this dialog box to add your own AutoCorrect entry.

Besides replacing misspellings and abbreviations, you can also find and replace other text. If you know that you want to substitute one word or phrase for another, you can use the **Find and Replace** dialog box to find each occurrence of the word that you want to change and replace it with another. On the Replace tab of the **Find and Replace** dialog box, use the **Find Next** button to locate the next occurrence of the text that you enter in the **Find what** box, and then use the **Replace** button to replace the text that you found with the text in the **Replace with** box. You can use the **Replace** button to continue to replace each occurrence individually, the **Replace All** button to replace all of the occurrences, or the **Find Next** button to locate the next occurrence. If you want to only find text and not replace it, you can use the Find tab in the **Find and Replace** dialog box and use the **Find Next** button. You can access the **Find and Replace** commands on the **Edit** menu.

An assistant at The Garden Company is fine-tuning a marketing letter and wants to send it to customers.

ReplaceText

In this exercise, you change an AutoCorrect setting, add an AutoCorrect entry, and change text as you type. You also find a phrase and replace it with another one throughout the entire document.

Open

1 On the Standard toolbar, click the **Open** button.

The **Open** dialog box appears.

2 Navigate to the Office XP SBS folder on your hard disk, double-click the **Word** folder, double-click the **Chap01** folder, and then double-click the **Replace-Text** file.

The ReplaceText document opens.

3 On the **Tools** menu, click **AutoCorrect Options**.

The **AutoCorrect Options** dialog box appears, displaying the **AutoCorrect** tab.

4 Clear the **Capitalize first letter of sentences** check box so that Word will not capitalize a letter or word that follows a period.

5 Click in the Replace box, and then type **gc**.

6 Press the ⎘ key to move the insertion point in the With box.

7 Type **The Garden Company**.

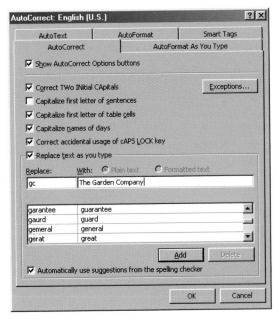

8   Click **Add** to add the entry to the correction list.

The text for the new AutoCorrect entry will display each time you type its abbreviation and press ⌴Space.

9   Click **OK** to close the **AutoCorrect** dialog box.

10 Press Ctrl+End to place the insertion point at the end of the document.

11 Type gc, and then press ⌴Space.

The text *gc* changes to *The Garden Company*.

12 Press Ctrl+Home to move to the beginning of the document.

13 On the **Edit** menu, click **Replace** to open the **Find and Replace** dialog box.

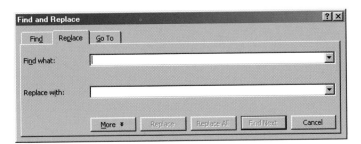

14   In the **Find what** box, type Garden Map Kit, and then press ⟨Tab⟩ to move the insertion point in the **Replace with** box.

15   In the **Replace with** box, type Interactive Garden, and then click **Find Next**.

Word finds and selects the first mention of *Garden Map Kit*.

16   Click **Replace**.

The selection is replaced with the text *Interactive Garden*, and the next occurrence is selected.

17   Click **Replace All**.

The Word message box that appears indicates that nine replacements were made.

18   Click **OK**, and then click **Close** to close the **Find and Replace** dialog box.

Save

19   On the Standard toolbar, click the **Save** button to save the document.

Close

20   Click the **Close** button in the document window.

The ReplaceText document closes.

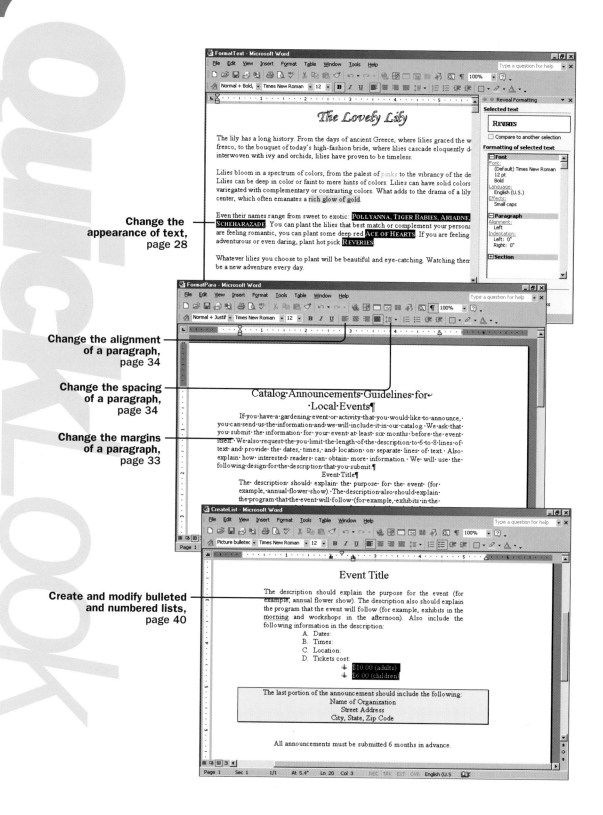

Change the appearance of text, page 28

Change the alignment of a paragraph, page 34

Change the spacing of a paragraph, page 34

Change the margins of a paragraph, page 33

Create and modify bulleted and numbered lists, page 40

Chapter 2
Changing the Look of Your Document

After completing this chapter, you will be able to:

✔ Change the appearance of text.

✔ Change the appearance of a paragraph.

✔ Create and modify a list.

✔ Change the way each page appears in a document.

✔ Change the look of a document with styles.

You want your documents to look professional—well designed and polished. The appearance of your text should reflect the content of your message. The format of your paragraphs and pages influences the appeal of your documents and helps draw the reader's attention to important information. To enhance the appearance of your documents, you can format the text to make your words stand out and arrange paragraphs to make them easy to read.

Word comes with formatting tools, such as styles, that you can use to enhance the appearance of your documents. You can change the characteristics, or attributes, of the text by applying bold or italics to words and phrases or by changing the color of the text that you type. You can also apply these visually enhancing attributes to paragraphs. To ensure a consistent and polished look for your document, you can apply those same attributes throughout your document.

In this chapter, you'll improve the appearance of the text in a document by changing text characteristics, or **attributes**. You'll change the appearance of the paragraphs in a document by indenting and changing the alignment and by setting tab stops for lines within paragraphs. You'll insert page and section breaks in a multiple-page document and make sure that the page breaks do not leave single words or phrases at the top or bottom of a page. You'll create and modify bulleted and numbered lists. Finally, you'll apply, modify, and delete a formatting style using the Styles and Formatting Task pane.

This chapter uses the practice files FormatText, FormatPara, CreateList, FormatPage, and FormatStyle that are stored in the Office XP SBS\Word\Chap02 subfolder that you installed from this book's CD-ROM. For details about installing the practice files, see "Using the Book's CD-ROM" at the beginning of this book.

Changing the Appearance of Text

The text that you type in a document appears in a font typeface. A **font typeface**, or simply **font**, is a complete set of characters that uses the same design. Depending on your printer, the fonts available on your computer may vary. Some fonts are more common than others, such as Times New Roman, Courier, and Arial. In addition to the design, the size of each character is also part of the font. The **font size** of text is measured in **points**. A point is equal to about 1/72 of an inch.

You can emphasize text using special **font effects**, such as bold type, italics, all capital letters, or shadows. For example, to make a heading stand out, you could make it bold. To draw attention to a warning, you could make it italic. You can also add emphasis by changing the color of the text in your document. For example, you could use white text on a black or gray background. If you plan to print your documents on a color printer or send them electronically, you can apply other colors to the text and its background.

Reveal
Formatting
new for
OfficeXP

When you are formatting a document, you can open the Reveal Formatting Task pane to display the format of selected text, such as its font and font effects. The Reveal Formatting Task pane allows you to display, change, or clear the formatting for the selected text. You also can use the Reveal Formatting Task pane to select text based on formatting so that you can compare the formatting used in the selected text with formatting used in other parts of the document.

The Garden Company catalog will include an article on lilies in its upcoming spring catalog. The text in the document will be formatted to visually communicate the beauty of this type of flower.

FormatText

In this exercise, you change the font typeface, font size, and font color to format text in a document.

1   Start Word, if necessary.

Open

2   On the Standard toolbar, click the **Open** button.

The **Open** dialog box appears.

3   Navigate to the Office XP SBS folder on your hard disk, double-click the **Word** folder, double-click the **Chap02** folder and then double-click the **FormatText** file.

The FormatText document opens.

4 Select the title *The Lovely Lily* at the top of the document.

5 On the Formatting toolbar, click the **Font** down arrow, scroll down in the list of available fonts, and then click **Monotype Corsiva**.

Tip

If Monotype Corsiva is not available, select a different font, such as Brush Script MT.

The title at the top of the document now appears in a new font.

Font Size

6 On the Formatting toolbar, click the **Font Size** down arrow, and then click **26** in the list.

The size of the title text is increased to 26 points.

7 On the Format menu, click **Reveal Formatting**.

The Reveal Formatting Task pane appears, displaying the formatting of the selected text.

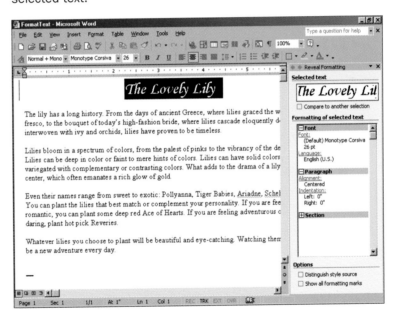

8 In the Reveal Formatting Task pane, click the **Font** link in the **Font** section.

The **Font** dialog box appears.

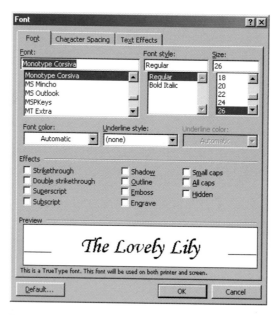

9 In the **Effects** area, select the **Outline** check box, and then click **OK**.

The selected text appears with an outline effect, and that effect is now listed in the Reveal Formatting Task pane in the **Font** section.

10 In the Reveal Formatting Task pane, point to the **Selected text** box at the top of the Task pane.

A down arrow appears on the right side of the **Selected text** box.

11 In the **Selected text** box, click the down arrow, and then click **Clear Formatting**.

The formatting for the selected text is removed.

Undo

12 On the Standard toolbar, click the **Undo** button.

The formatting for the selected text is restored.

13 Select the word *pinks* in the first sentence of the second paragraph.

Font Color

14 On the Formatting toolbar, click the **Font Color** down arrow, and then click the **Pink** color box (first column, fourth row) on the color palette.

The color of the selected word is now pink, and the formatting is listed in the **Font** section of the Reveal Formatting Task pane.

Tip

To apply the most recently selected color to other text, select the word or phrase, and then click the **Font Color** button (not the down arrow). The color that appears on the **Font Color** button is applied to the selected text.

Highlight

15 Select the phrase *rich glow of gold* at the end of the second paragraph, click the **Highlight** down arrow on the Formatting toolbar, and then click the **Yellow** color box (first column, first row).

The highlighted phrase now stands out from the rest of the text.

Tip

You do not have to select the text first before choosing a highlighting color. You can select a highlighting color from the color palette and then use the highlighting pointer to highlight the text.

16 Scroll to the right and then select the text *Pollyanna, Tiger Babies, Ariadne, Scheharazade* in the third paragraph.

Troubleshooting

If the Reveal Formatting Task pane overlays some of the text in the document, you can resize the Task pane. Position the pointer over the left edge of the Task pane, and when the pointer changes to the double arrow pointer, drag the edge to the right so that the text of the document is visible.

17 On the **Format** menu, click **Font** to open the **Font** dialog box, select the **Small caps** check box, and then click **OK**.

The lowercase letters in the names of the lilies now appear in small caps, making those names easier to find in the text.

18 In the same paragraph, select the text *Ace of Hearts*, and then hold down the ⌘ key and double-click the text *Reveries* in the last line of the paragraph to select the nonadjacent text.

19 Press the F4 key.

The other lily names appear in small caps. When you press F4, the change that you just made is applied to the selected text.

20 In the Reveal Formatting Task pane, point to the Selected Text box, click the **Selected text** down arrow, and then click **Select All Text With Similar Formatting**.

All the flower names that have been formatted in small caps are selected in the document.

Bold

B

21 On the Formatting toolbar, click the **Bold** button.

The flower names are now bold.

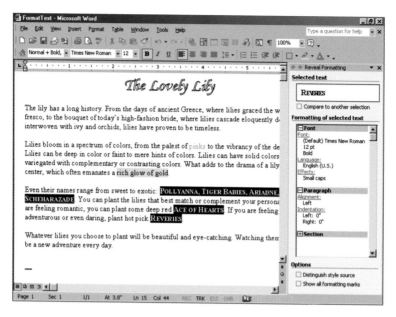

Close

22 In the Reveal Formatting Task pane, click the **Close** button.

The Reveal Formatting Task pane closes.

23 On the Standard toolbar, click the **Save** button to save the document.

24 Click the **Close** button in the document window.

The FormatText document closes.

Adding Animation to Text

If someone using a computer will be reading your document, you can add effects that will make the text in your document vibrant and visually alive. You can apply sparkling and flashing lights or a marquee that will draw your reader's attention to specific words and phrases in the document. To add these special effects, you can apply an animation to selected text in your document.

To add animation to selected text:

1 Select the text that you want to animate.

2 On the **Format** menu, click **Font**.

The **Font** dialog box appears.

3 Click the **Text Effects** tab.

4 In the Animations box, select the animation effect that you want to add to the selected text.

5 Click **OK**.

Changing the Appearance of a Paragraph

You can enhance the appearance of a paragraph by changing the way text is aligned, modifying the spacing between paragraphs, and adding borders and shading around text. In Word, a **paragraph** is any amount of text that ends when you press the `Enter` key. A paragraph can include several sentences or a single line of text consisting of one or more words.

You control the length of a line by setting the left and right margins and the length of a page by setting the top and bottom margins. The width of a margin controls the amount of white space that surrounds your text. You can use the options in the **Page Setup** dialog box to control the margins in the document.

After you've set up a document's margins, you can control the positioning of the text within the margins. In Word, you can align lines of text in different locations along the horizontal ruler using tab stops. You can also indent paragraphs. When you indent a paragraph, you control where the first line of text begins, where the second and subsequent lines begin, and where paragraph text wraps at the right margin.

You use the horizontal ruler, which you can display at the top of the Word document window, to set **tab stops**. Tab stops are locations along the ruler that you use to align text. By default, the tab stops in Word are set at every half-inch mark on the ruler. To set a tab using the ruler, you click the tab indicator, which is a button with a symbol on it, located on the leftmost end of the ruler. Each time that you click the tab indicator, a different type of tab stop indicator appears. When the type of tab stop that you want to set appears, you click the ruler where you want to set the tab. To remove a tab stop, you drag it down and away from the ruler.

After you set a tab stop, you position the insertion point to the left of the text you want to align and then press the `Tab` key. The text is aligned along the next tab stop. For example, if you set a center tab, when you press `Tab`, the text moves to the right and aligns itself using the center tab stop as the middle point. A decimal tab aligns numbers on their decimal points.

Tip

In Word, you can display formatting marks to help you align and space the text in a document correctly. Formatting marks do no print with your document. They display in the document just as an aide. To turn on formatting marks, you click the **Show/Hide ¶** button on the Standard toolbar. Examples for formatting marks include the paragraph mark, ¶, which marks the end of a paragraph of text, and the tab stop, which marks the location of a tab stop. To turn off formatting, click the **Show/Hide ¶** button again.

In addition to tab stops, the horizontal ruler also includes special markers that you can use to control how text wraps on the left or right side of a document. You use these markers if you want to **indent** the text toward the right or left. To indent text, you can use one of the indent markers located on the horizontal ruler. The following table describes each indent marker:

Marker on Ruler	Icon	Description
First Line Indent	▽	Sets where the first line of text in a paragraph begins.
Hanging Indent	⊔	Sets where the second and all subsequent lines of text wrap after reaching the right margin.
Left Indent	▢	Sets where the text indents when you press `Tab`.
Right Indent	△	Sets where the text wraps as it reaches the right margin. By default, the right indent marker is set at the right margin, but you can change that setting.

When you use the ruler to format paragraphs, you can use Print Layout view to see the page margins in relation to the borders of the page. Print Layout view also shows two rulers: the horizontal ruler at the top and the vertical ruler along the left side of the document window. The vertical ruler helps you judge the amount of spacing between the paragraphs in the document.

You can also position text within the document's margin using the alignment buttons on the Formatting toolbar. Click the **Align Left** button to align text along the left margin, click the **Align Right** button to align the text along the right margin, click the **Center** button to align a paragraph between the left and right margins, and click the **Justify** button to align between the margins, creating a flush-right edge for the text.

To add space between paragraphs, you can press `Enter` to insert a blank line. For more precise control, you can adjust the spacing before and after paragraphs. For example, instead of indicating a new paragraph by indenting the first line, you could create a more professional appearance by adding twelve points of blank space before a new paragraph. You use the **Paragraph** dialog box to adjust the paragraph spacing.

Tip

To format a paragraph, you can click in the paragraph or select any part of it and then apply the formats that you want.

To set off a paragraph from the rest of the document, you can add borders and shading. For example, if you are sending a long letter to a client, you can place a border around the paragraph that you want the client to pay the most attention to. You can also shade the background of a paragraph to create a subtler effect.

After you indent, align, space, border, or shade one paragraph, you can press ⌈Enter⌉ to apply these same effects to the next paragraph that you type. To apply the effects to an existing paragraph, you can use the Format Painter to quickly copy the format of one paragraph to another.

The Garden Company catalog includes an announcement, which needs to be formatted to fit the layout of the catalog and match its new color design.

FormatPara

In this exercise, you modify text alignment, insert and modify tab stops, modify line spacing, and add borders and shading around text to change the appearance of the paragraphs in the document.

Open

1 On the Standard toolbar, click the **Open** button.

The **Open** dialog box appears.

2 Navigate to the Office XP SBS folder on your hard disk, double-click the **Word** folder, double-click the **Chap02** folder, and then double-click the **FormatPara** file.

The FormatPara document opens.

Print Layout View

3 Click the **Print Layout View** button.

The document view changes. You can see how the work area is aligned between the left and right margins. In addition to the horizontal ruler at the top of the document window, a vertical ruler also appears on the left side of the document window.

Tip

In Print Layout view, you can show or hide the white space between the pages. Position the pointer between the pages until the Show White pointer or Hide White pointer appears, and then click the page.

4 On the Standard toolbar, click the **Show/Hide ¶** button to display the formatting marks.

5 Click immediately to the right of the word *for* in the title, hold down the ⌈Shift⌉ key, and then press ⌈Enter⌉.

Part of the title wraps to the second line of text.

Space character   Manual line break character

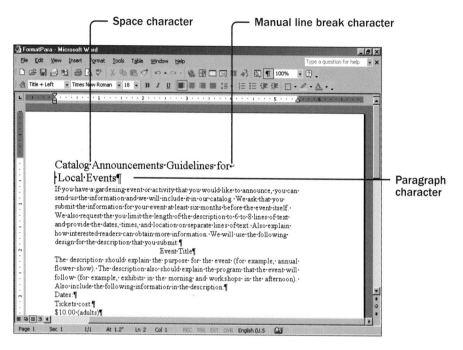

Paragraph
character

Center

6 On the Formatting toolbar, click the **Center** button to center the title to make it appear more balanced.

Justify

7 Click anywhere in the first paragraph, and then click the **Justify** button on the Formatting toolbar.

The paragraph is now formatted with the text flush against both left and right margins.

First Line
Indent

8 Drag the First Line Indent marker to the 0.5-inch mark on the horizontal ruler.

The first line of text in the paragraph is indented a half inch from the left margin.

Left Indent

9 Click anywhere in the paragraph that starts with the text *The description should explain*, and then drag the Left Indent marker to the 0.5-inch mark on the horizontal ruler.

The paragraph is indented on the left side.

Right Indent

10 Drag the Right Indent marker to the 5-inch mark on the ruler.

The paragraph now appears indented on the right side as well.

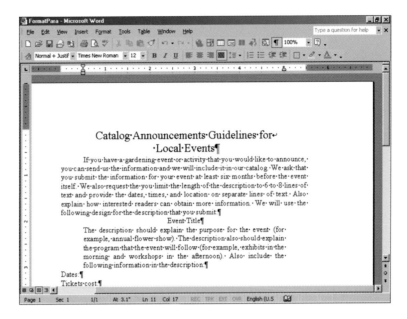

Left Tab icon

11 Scroll down the page, select the two lines that include the text *Dates: and Tickets cost:*, make sure that the **Tab Indicator** button shows the Left Tab icon, and then click the ruler at the 1.0-inch mark to set a left tab.

12 Click to the left of the word *Dates* to deselect all the text, and then press [Tab] to align the text at the new tab stop.

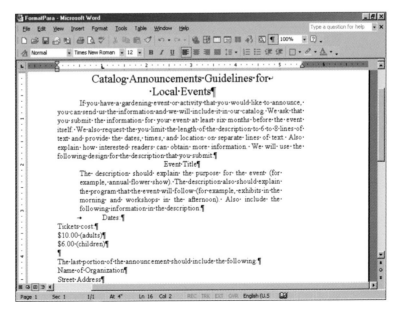

13 Press `End` to move the insertion point to the end of the line, and then press `Enter` to create a new line. Press `Tab`, and then type **Times:**.

14 Press `Enter` to create a new line, press `Tab`, type **Location:**, press the `→` key to move the insertion point to the beginning of the next line, and then press `Tab`.

Decimal Tab icon

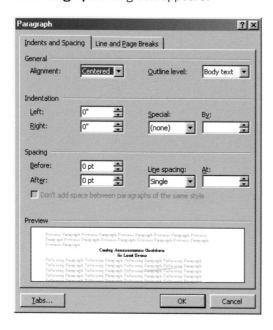

15 Select the two lines that start with text *$10.00* and *$6.00*, click the Tab Indicator three times to see a Decimal Tab icon, and then click the ruler at the 2.5-inch mark to set a decimal tab.

16 Click to the left of the text *$10.00* to deselect the text, press `Tab`, click to the left of the text *$6.00*, and then press `Tab`.

The dollar amounts are aligned along their decimal points.

17 Select the two lines of text with the dollar amounts again, drag the decimal tab from the 2.5-inch mark to the 2.0-inch mark to adjust the tab stop.

18 Press `Ctrl`+`Home` to move the insertion point to the top of the document, and then on the **Format** menu, click **Paragraph**.

The **Paragraph** dialog box appears.

Tip

You can also use the **Paragraph** dialog box to control the left and right indentation instead of using the ruler.

19 In the Spacing area, click the **After** up arrow two times to display 12 pt, and then click **OK**.

The paragraphs below the title move down. The added space helps to set the title off from the rest of the document.

Format Painter

20 On the Standard toolbar, click the **Format Painter** button, move the insertion point to the paragraph that begins *Event Title*, and then click the text to copy the formatting from the title paragraph.

Additional spacing appears between the *Event Title* text and the following paragraph.

21 On the **Format** menu, click **Paragraph** to open the **Paragraph** dialog box. In the **Spacing** area, click the **Before** up arrow to display 12 pt, and then click **OK**.

There is more spacing between the *Event Title* text and the paragraph before it.

Center

22 Scroll down the page, select the last four lines of text in the document, which start with the line *The last portion of*, and then on the Formatting toolbar, click the **Center** button to center these lines of text.

23 On the **Format** menu, click **Borders and Shading**.

The **Borders and Shading** dialog box appears, displaying the **Borders** tab.

24 In the **Setting** area, click the **Shadow** icon to select that border style.

25 Click the **Shading** tab, click the **Light Yellow** color box on the color palette (third column, last row), and then click **OK**.

A border with a shadow surrounds the text, and the background color is light yellow.

26 Click a blank area two lines below the yellow shaded box, and then move the pointer to the center of the line until it changes shape.

Align Center
Pointer

The pointer shape changes to the Click and Type's Align Center pointer to indicate that when you click and type, the text will be centered.

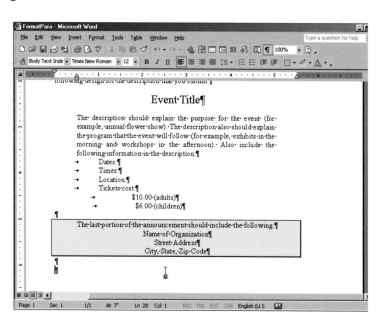

27 When the pointer changes shape, double-click to position the insertion point, and then type **All announcements must be submitted 6 months in advance.**

The newly inserted text appears centered in the document

Show/Hide ¶

28 On the Formatting toolbar, click the **Show/Hide ¶** button to hide the formatting marks.

29 On the Standard toolbar, click the **Save** button to save the document.

Close

30 Click the **Close** button in the document window.

The FormatPara document closes.

Creating and Modifying a List

To organize lists in your document, such as lists of events, names, numbers, or procedures, you can format the information in a bulleted or numbered list. A **bullet** is a small graphic, such as a large dot, that sets off an item in a list. Use numbers instead of bullets when you want to emphasize sequence, as in a series of steps. If you move, insert, or delete items in a numbered list, Word renumbers the list for you. If the items in a list are out of order, alphabetically or numerically, you can sort the items in ascending or descending order using the **Sort** command on the **Table** menu.

For emphasis, you can change any bullet or number style to one of Word's pre-defined formats. For example, you can switch round bullets to check boxes, or Roman numerals to lowercase letters. You can also customize the list style or insert a picture as a bullet. Use the **Bullets and Numbering** dialog box to modify, format, and customize your list.

Word makes it easy to start a bulleted or numbered list. For a bulleted list, you simply click at the beginning of a line, type * (an asterisk), and then press ⎣Tab⎦; for a numbered list, you type **1.**, press ⎣Space⎦, type the first item in the list, and then press ⎣Enter⎦. The next bullet or number in the list appears, and Word changes the formatting to a list. You can type the next item in the list or press ⎣Enter⎦ or ⎣Backspace⎦ to end the list.

You can change a bulleted or numbered list into an outline or create one of your own. Outlines are useful for organizing information, such as topics in an essay. An outline typically consists of main headings and subheadings. To start an outline, you click at the beginning of a line, type **I.**, press ⎣Tab⎦, type a main heading, and then press ⎣Enter⎦. You can type another main heading or press ⎣Tab⎦ to add a subheadings under the main heading.

The Garden Company needs to complete the announcement that will be used on the back pages of the catalog.

CreateList

In this exercise, you create a bulleted and numbered list, modify it by adjusting its indents, and then apply outline numbering.

Open

1   On the Standard toolbar, click the **Open** button.

The **Open** dialog box appears.

2   Navigate to the Office XP SBS folder on your hard disk, double-click the **Word** folder, double-click the **Chap02** folder, and then double-click the **CreateList** file.

The CreateList document opens.

3   Select the four lines that start with the word *Dates*.

Numbering

4   On the Formatting toolbar, click the **Numbering** button.

The selected text appears as a numbered list.

5   On the **Format** menu, click **Bullets and Numbering**.

The **Bullets and Numbering** dialog box appears, displaying the **Numbered** tab.

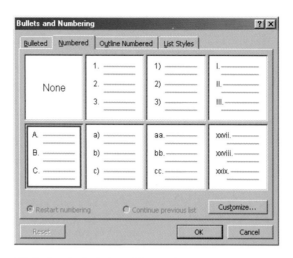

6 Click the A, B, C box (first column, second row), and then click **OK**.

The numbered list changes from numbers to letters.

7 Select the two lines that start with the text *$10.00* and *$6.00*.

Bullets

8 On the Formatting toolbar, click the **Bullets** button.

The selected text appears as a bulleted list.

Decrease Indent

9 On the Formatting toolbar, click the **Decrease Indent** button.

The bulleted list is indented to the left and becomes part of the alphabetical list.

Increase Indent

10 On the Formatting toolbar, click the **Increase Indent** button.

The bulleted list is indented to the right and becomes a bulleted list again under the text *Tickets cost*.

11 On the **Format** menu, click **Bullets and Numbering**.

The **Bullets and Numbering** dialog box appears.

12 Click the **Bulleted** tab, if necessary, click the colored bullet box (first column, second row), and then click **OK**.

The bullet character changes from circles to colored bullets.

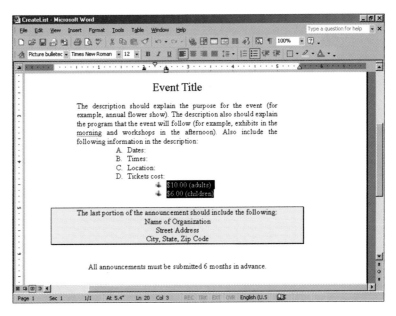

13 Select the six lines that start with the word *Dates*.

14 On the **Format** menu, click **Bullets and Numbering**.

The **Bullets and Numbering** dialog box appears.

15 Click the **Outline Numbered** tab, if necessary, click the **A Heading** box (third column, second row), and then click **OK**.

The lettered list changes from letters to numbers and the bulleted list changes to letters.

16 On the Standard toolbar, click the **Save** button to save the document.

Close

17 Click the **Close** button in the document window.

The CreateList document closes.

Changing the Way Each Page Appears in a Document

Using a template is a great way to begin your document. Many of the documents that you create (with or without a template) will be more than a page or two. When you create a document that contains more than one page, Word paginates your document for you. To paginate a document means to insert page breaks—the page breaks that Word inserts are called **soft page breaks**. A soft page break appears as a dotted line across the page. If you don't like where Word inserts a page break, you can insert one yourself. A page break that you insert is called a **manual page break**. A manual page break appears as a dotted line across the page with the words *Page Break* in the middle. You insert a manual page break when you want to begin a new page.

Tip

Word repaginates a document as you make changes to it. In other words, as you insert, delete, and move text, Word changes where it inserts soft page breaks. Word does not change the location of manual page breaks; you must do that yourself.

Regardless of whether you keep Word's soft page breaks or insert your own manual page breaks, you should make sure that the page breaks do not leave widows and orphans. A **widow** is the last line of a paragraph printed by itself at the top of a page. An **orphan** is the first line of a paragraph printed by itself at the bottom of a page. Leaving a word or short phrase at the top or bottom of a page can interrupt the flow of long documents. To eliminate widows and orphans and to further control where Word inserts page breaks, you can use the options in the **Paragraph** dialog box. The following table explains the options in the **Paragraph** dialog box that you can use to specify how Word should treat situations that might cause paragraphs to break at undesirable places.

Line and Page Break Options	
Widow/Orphan control	Prevents Word from printing the last line of a paragraph by itself at the top of a page (widow) or the first line of a paragraph by itself at the bottom of a page (orphan).
Keep lines together	Prevents a page break within a paragraph.
Keep with next	Prevents a page break between the selected paragraph and the following paragraph.
Page break before	Inserts a page break before the selected paragraph.

Important

You have to apply the options in the dialog box on a paragraph-by-paragraph basis.

You can also insert a section break in your document. A **section break** identifies a portion of the document that you can format with unique page settings, such as different margins. A section break appears as a double-dotted line across the page with the words *Section Break* and the type of section break in the middle. There are several types of section breaks that you can insert. For example, if you want a section to begin on a new page, you insert a New Page section break. You can also insert a Continuous section break or Even Page or Odd Page section breaks. Dividing a document into sections is especially helpful when you are creating long documents that cover a wide range of topics.

Tip

As you make changes to your document, you might want to preview the way that it looks. Previewing your document helps you determine if and where you might need a manual page break or where you might want to insert a section break. To preview your document, click the **Print Preview** button on the Standard toolbar. Not only can you review the layout of your document in the Print Preview window, but you can also make changes to the layout from within the Print Preview window.

The way in which a page is laid out in a printed document is called the **page orientation**. The default page orientation in Word is portrait. When the page orientation is **portrait**, the page is taller than it is wide. **Landscape** orientation, on the other hand, creates a page that is wider than it is tall. A document has only one page orientation unless you divide your document into sections. Then each section can have its own page orientation.

If you have a multiple-page document, you might want to insert page numbers so that you can keep track of where you are in the document. You can insert page numbers using the Page Numbers command on the **Insert** menu. When you insert page numbers, they appear in the lower-right corner of each page by default, but you can change their position and alignment by using the **Position** and **Alignment** options in the **Page Numbers** dialog box. You can change the position of the page numbers to the top and align them on the left or center them.

You can also add information, such as the name of your company or the author of the document, that is printed on every page of your document. The **header** is text that is printed at the top of each page. The **footer** is text that is printed at the bottom of each page. To enter text for a header or footer, you select the Header and Footer command on the **View** menu. When you select the command, the document view changes to Print Layout view, the Header section appears at the top of the page, and the Footer section appears at the bottom of the page. The Header and Footer toolbar appears as well. You can use the Header and Footer toolbar to enter document-related text, such as the name of the file or the date the document was last printed. You can also use the toolbar to insert page numbers and the current date and time. If your document contains section breaks, you can have different headers and footers for each section.

Tip

To display different headers and footers on different pages, click the **Page Setup** button on the Headers and Footers toolbar. In the **Page Setup** dialog box with the **Layout** tab open, select the **Different odd and even** check box, select the **Different first page** check box, or select both.

The Garden Company often sends articles to its customers to respond to many of the most commonly asked questions. One of the most frequently asked questions is about composting. An article written on composting needs to be paginated, and the last page about the do's and don'ts of composting needs to be formatted differently from the rest of the article. The company name should appear at the top of each page, except on the last page. Each page, except the last page, should have a page number.

FormatPage

In this exercise, you insert page and section breaks, make sure that page breaks do not leave widows and orphans, change the page orientation, and add a header and a footer in the document.

Open

1 On the Standard toolbar, click the **Open** button.

The **Open** dialog box appears.

2 Navigate to the Office XP SBS folder on your hard disk, double-click the **Word** folder, double-click the **Chap02** folder, and then double-click the **FormatPage** file.

The FormatPage document opens.

Print Preview

3 On the Standard toolbar, click the **Print Preview** button.

The Print Preview window appears.

Multiple Pages

4 Click the **Multiple Pages** button on the Print Preview toolbar, and then click and drag the pointer to select four pages (2 x 2 Pages).

The Print Preview window shows the four pages of the document with a widow at the top of the second page.

5 On the **File** menu, click **Page Setup**.

The **Page Setup** dialog box appears, displaying the **Margins** tab.

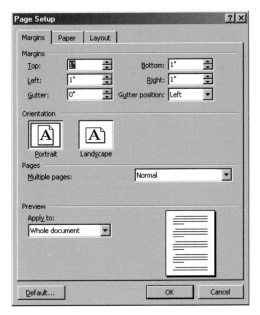

6   In the **Margins** area, select the value in the Top box and type **1.25"**, select the value in the Bottom box and type **1.25"**, and then click **OK**.

The amount of blank space at the top and bottom of each page increases from 1 inch to 1.25 inches. The changes in the margins eliminated the widow at the top of page 2.

Tip

The standard size of a page is 8.5 inches by 11 inches. With margins of 1.5 inches on each side, you are left with a work area that is 5.5 inches wide.

Close Preview

Close

7   On the Print Preview toolbar, click the **Close Preview** button to close the Print Preview window.

8   Press the ⌨Page Down⌨ key four times, and then click in the first line of text in the paragraph that begins with the text *If you take the time*. (You might need to press the ⌨Page Down⌨ key fewer times if your monitor is set to a resolution higher than 800 by 600.)

The first two lines of the paragraph appear at the bottom of page 2. You can keep these lines of text with the rest of the paragraph.

9 On the **Format** menu, click **Paragraph** to display the **Paragraph** dialog box, and then click the **Line and Page Breaks** tab, if necessary.

10 If necessary, select the **Widow/Orphan control** check box, select the **Keep lines together** check box, and then click **OK**.

The page break moves up so that all the lines of text in the paragraph appear on the same page.

11 Press ⌨ twice, and then click to the left of the text *Hot or Cold?*

12 On the **Insert** menu, click **Break** to display the **Break** dialog box.

13 In the **Break types** area, verify that the **Page break** option is selected, and then click **OK**.

A dotted line with the words *Page Break* appears, indicating that you inserted a manual page break.

14 Scroll down to the last paragraph, and then position the insertion point to the left of the title *COMPOSTING DO's AND DON'Ts*.

15 On the **Insert** menu, click **Break** to open the **Break** dialog box, click the **Next page** option in the **Section break types** areas, and then click **OK**.

A double dotted line with the text *Section Break (Next Page)* appears.

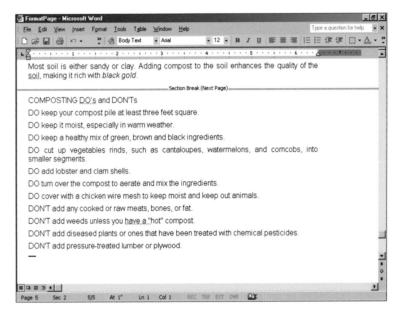

16 Press ⌷Ctrl⌷+⌷Home⌷ to move the insertion point to the beginning of the document, and then on the **View** menu, click **Header and Footer**.

The document is now in Print Layout view. At the top of the document window, there is an empty box in which you can enter the text for the header for section 1 of the document. The Header and Footer toolbar appears just below the box.

Insert page number

Insert number of pages

Format page number

Enter text for the header here

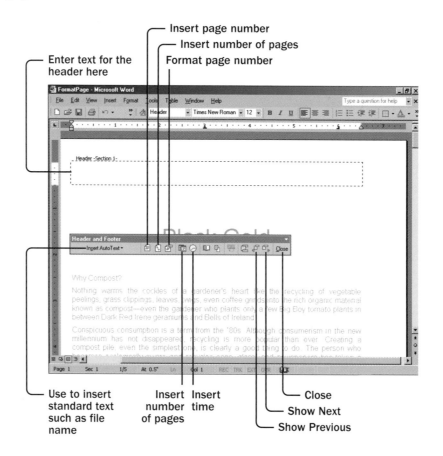

Use to insert standard text such as file name

Insert number of pages

Insert time

Close

Show Next

Show Previous

Show Next

17 Type **The Garden Company**, and then click the **Show Next** button on the Header and Footer toolbar.

The insertion point is now in the Header - Section 2 text box.

Same as Previous

18 On the Header and Footer toolbar, click the **Same as Previous** button, click the **Yes** button in the message box (if necessary), select the text *The Garden Company*, and then press [Del].

The company is deleted from the header so that it doesn't appear as the previous header.

Switch Between Header and Footer

19 Click the **Switch Between Header and Footer** button to switch to the footer text box. You do not want the same footer for section 2 as you have for section 1.

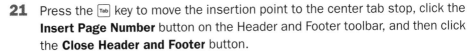

Same as Previous

20 On the Header and Footer toolbar, click the **Same as Previous** button, and then click the **Show Previous** button on the Header and Footer toolbar.

The insertion point is now in the Footer - Section 1 text box.

Insert Page Number

21 Press the Tab key to move the insertion point to the center tab stop, click the **Insert Page Number** button on the Header and Footer toolbar, and then click the **Close Header and Footer** button.

The first four pages in the first section of the document are numbered.

Print Preview

22 On the Standard toolbar, click the **Print Preview** button to display the print preview window.

Multiple Pages

23 On the Print Preview toolbar, click the **Multiple Pages** button, click and drag the pointer to select six pages (3 x 3 Pages) so that all five pages in the document display, click the **Magnifier** button on the **Print Preview** button, and then click the last page in the document to enlarge the view of the page.

24 On the **File** menu, click **Page Setup** to open the **Page Setup** dialog box, click the **Margins** tab, click the **Landscape** icon, make sure that the **This section** option in the **Apply to** section is selected, and then click **OK**.

25 On the Print Preview toolbar, click the **Multiple Pages** button, click and drag the pointer to select six pages (3 x 3 Pages) so that all five pages redisplay in the Print Preview window.

Note that the company name appears at the top of the first four pages of the document and that there are page numbers on the bottom of the first four pages. Note also that the last page is wider than it is tall and does not have header or footer text.

Close Preview

26 On the Print Preview toolbar, click the **Close Preview** button to close the Print Preview window.

27 On the Standard toolbar, click the **Save** button to save the document.

Close

28 Click the **Close** button in the document window.

The FormatPage document closes.

Changing the Look of a Document with Styles

As you change the appearance of the text in your documents, you might find that you have created a look, or style, of your own. You may want to take advantage of the styles that Word provides. A **style** is a collection of text and paragraph formatting that you can apply to text throughout your document.

You can apply a set of formatting changes to your documents at the same time using styles. **Character styles** format selected words and lines of text within a paragraph, whereas **paragraph styles** format entire paragraphs, including their indents, alignment, and tabs. For example, a character style might be 18-point, bold, underlined, and centered text, whereas a paragraph style might include a border and hanging indent. Instead of applying each of these formatting effects or attributes individually, you can apply all of the attributes using a style.

Unless you choose a template from the **Templates** dialog box, the documents that you create use the same default template, the Normal template. In the Normal template (as in all templates), there are styles that make up the formatting attributes of the template. For example, the Normal style includes the default font style, font size, and alignment. The default Normal style is 12-point Times New Roman text that is aligned on the left margin. (The Normal style is used in many of the available templates, not just in the Normal template.) The text that you type in your document uses the Normal style until you apply another style. For example, you might apply the Heading 1 style to text that you want to use as the title of your document.

To apply another style to the text in your document, you can use the Style down arrow on the Formatting toolbar. You can also create a new style. You can modify an existing style or create a new style based on text that you have formatted. When you modify a style, the text in your document associated with that style is updated to reflect the changes.

Displaying the Style Area

To help you apply styles consistently throughout a document, you can change your document window to include a style area along the left side that displays the style names. The style area lists the styles that are used in the document paragraph by paragraph. The document must be in Normal or Outline view to display the style area. Note that the style area is not printed with your document; the style area is part of the document window and a tool you can use to format your document.

To display the style area:

1   Click the Tools menu, and then click **Options**.

    The **Options** dialog box appears.

2   Click the **View** tab, if necessary.

3   In the **Outline and Normal options** area, click the **Style** area width up arrow to increase the style area in the document window, and then click **OK**.

    The style area will appear along the left side of the document window in Normal view. A thin vertical line appears between the style area and document text.

4   To close the style area, you can open the **Options** dialog box and decrease the width of the style area, or you can drag the vertical line to the left to close the style area.

To enhance the appearance of the article on composting, The Garden Company wants to format the main headings by using styles.

FormatStyle

In this exercise, you apply, modify, and delete a style using the Styles And Formatting Task pane.

Open

1   On the Standard toolbar, click the **Open** button.

The **Open** dialog box appears.

2   Navigate to the Office XP SBS folder on your hard disk, double-click the **Word** folder, double-click the **Chap02** folder, and then double-click the **FormatStyle** file.

The FormatStyle document opens.

3   Select the line of text *Why Compost?*

4   On the **Format** menu, click **Styles and Formatting**.

The Styles And Formatting Task pane appears.

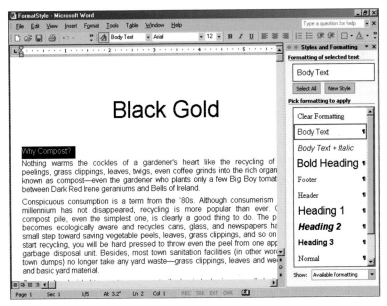

5   In the Styles And Formatting Task pane, point to the preview box in the **Formatting of selected text** section.

A ScreenTip appears, displaying the style and attributes of the selected text. In this case, the style is Body Text and the attributes are Normal style plus the default font Arial with the text justified and the spacing before and after the paragraph at 6 points.

6 In the Styles And Formatting Task pane, scroll down the list, and then click the Heading 2 style in the **Pick formatting to apply** section.

The selected text changes to the Heading 2 style.

7 Click in the document, scroll down the document, hold down the ⌃key, select the line of text *What Is a Compost Pile?*, scroll down the document, select the line of text *How Do You Make a Compost Pile?*, scroll down the document, select the line of text *Hot or Cold?*, and then select the line of text *Compost and Soil*.

8 In the Styles And Formatting Task pane, click the Heading 2 style to apply the style to the selected text.

9 Scroll to the top of the document, click in the line of text *Why Compost?*, and then click **Select All** in the Styles And Formatting Task pane.

Word selects all the text in the document with the style of the selected text, which is Heading 2.

10 In the Styles And Formatting Task pane, click **New Style**.

The **New Style** dialog box appears.

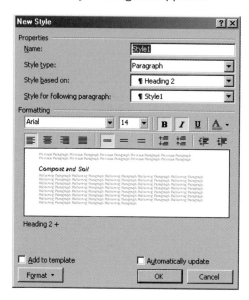

11 In the Name box, type **Heading 2 Plus** to create a new name for the style.

12 In the **Formatting** area, click the **Font Size** down arrow, click **16**, click the **Font Color** down arrow, click the **Blue** color box (sixth column, second row), and then click **OK**.

The Heading 2 Plus style appears in the Styles And Formatting Task pane.

Troubleshooting

If the name of the new style is not displayed completely in the Styles And Format Task pane, resize the Task pane. First, position the pointer over the left edge of the Task pane. When the pointer changes shape, click and drag the edge to increase the width of the Task pane.

13 In the Styles And Formatting Task pane, click the Heading 2 Plus style in the Pick formatting to apply section.

The new style is applied to the selected text.

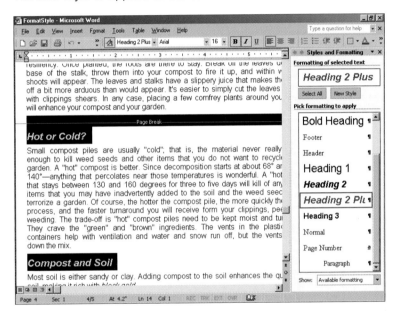

14 In the Styles And Formatting Task pane, point to the Heading 2 Plus style, click the Heading 2 Plus down arrow on the right, and then click **Modify**.

The **Modify Style** dialog box appears.

Italic

I

15 In the **Formatting** area, click the **Italic** button to deselect the attribute, and then click **OK**.

The Heading 2 Plus style is updated along with all text with the style.

16 In the Styles And Formatting Task pane, click **Heading 2**.

The selected text is formatted with the selected style.

17 In the Styles And Formatting Task pane, point to the Heading 2 Plus style, click the down arrow to the right, and then click **Delete**.

An **Alert** dialog box appears, asking whether you want to delete the style.

18 Click **Yes**.

The Heading 2 Plus style is deleted from the Styles And Formatting Task pane.

19 In the Styles And Formatting Task pane, click the **Show** down arrow, and then click **Formatting in use**.

The styles used in the document appear in the Styles And Formatting Task pane.

Tip

You can use the **Find and Replace** dialog box to search for a specific style and replace it with a different style. On the **Edit** menu, click **Replace**, click **More**, click **Format**, and then click **Style**. In the **Find Style** dialog box, click the style that you want to find, and then click **OK**. Click in the **Replace With** box, click **Format**, click **Style**, click the style that you want to use, and then click **OK**. Click **Find Next** to search for the next occurrence of the style, and then click **Replace**.

Close

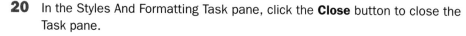

20 In the Styles And Formatting Task pane, click the **Close** button to close the Task pane.

Save

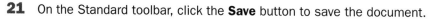

21 On the Standard toolbar, click the **Save** button to save the document.

22 Click the **Close** button in the document window.

The FormatStyle document closes.

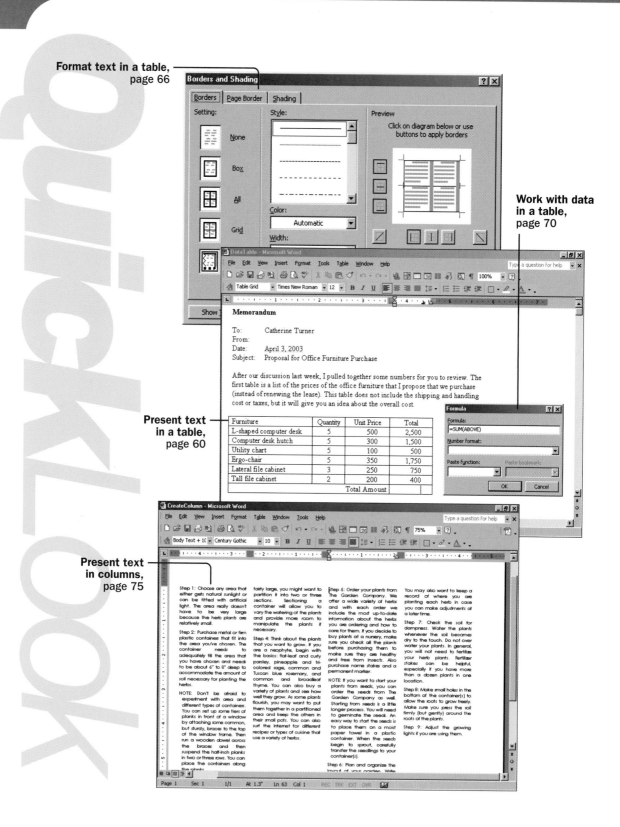

Format text in a table,
page 66

Work with data in a table,
page 70

Present text in a table,
page 60

Present text in columns,
page 75

Borders and Shading

Borders | Page Border | Shading

Setting:
None
Box
All
Grid

Style:

Color:
Automatic

Width:

Preview
Click on diagram below or use buttons to apply borders

Memorandum

To: Catherine Turner
From:
Date: April 3, 2003
Subject: Proposal for Office Furniture Purchase

After our discussion last week, I pulled together some numbers for you to review. The first table is a list of the prices of the office furniture that I propose that we purchase (instead of renewing the lease). This table does not include the shipping and handling cost or taxes, but it will give you an idea about the overall cost.

Furniture	Quantity	Unit Price	Total
L-shaped computer desk	5	500	2,500
Computer desk hutch	5	300	1,500
Utility chart	5	100	500
Ergo-chair	5	350	1,750
Lateral file cabinet	3	250	750
Tall file cabinet	2	200	400
		Total Amount	

Formula

Formula:
=SUM(ABOVE)

Number format:

Paste function: Paste bookmark:

OK   Cancel

Chapter 3
Presenting Information in Tables and Columns

After completing this chapter, you will be able to:

✔ **Present text in a table.**

✔ **Format text in a table.**

✔ **Work with data in a table.**

✔ **Present text in columns.**

You can use a table to group and organize the information in your document in a concise, consistent, and easy-to-read format. A table organizes information neatly into rows and columns. The intersection of a row and column is called a cell. You can create a uniform table with standard-sized cells or draw a custom table with various-sized cells, or you can create a table from existing text. Once you create your table, you can enter text, numbers, and even graphics into cells. To help readers interpret the information in your table, you can arrange, or **sort**, the information in a logical order.

Once you have created a table, you can change the size of the table or of individual columns and rows. You can also insert and delete columns and rows as needed. To make the table visually appealing, you can format table text and add borders and shading to part or all of the table.

Tables often present numerical data. To perform standard mathematical calculations on numbers in a table, you can use the **Formula** command on the **Table** menu to add a column or row of numbers, for example, or to find the average of the numbers. For more complex calculations, you can insert a Microsoft Excel worksheet into your document. Excel is a Microsoft Office program that you use to perform complex calculations or statistical analysis.

Columns of text are another way that you can group and organize information in a document. Dividing text into columns might be useful when you are creating a newsletter or brochure. In Word, you can define the number of columns that you want on a page. You can then choose to allow the text to flow from the bottom of one column to the top of the next column, as you see in newspapers. Or you can choose to end the column of text in a specific location, moving the subsequent text to the next column.

This chapter uses the practice files CreateTable, FormatTable, DataTable, InsertTable, and CreateColumn that are stored in the Office XP SBS\Word\Chap03 subfolder that you installed from this book's CD-ROM. For details about installing the practice files, see "Using the Book's CD-ROM" at the beginning of this book.

Presenting Text in a Table

To add a simple table to a document, you can use the **Insert Table** button on the Standard toolbar and then select the number of rows and columns you want from the menu that appears. If you want to set the size of the table along with other options, such as table formatting, you use the **Insert** command on the **Table** menu to open the **Insert Table** dialog box. You can also add a table by converting existing plain text to a table.

Once you create a table, you enter text or numbers into cells just as you would in a paragraph, except pressing the Tab key in a table moves the insertion point from cell to cell instead of indenting a paragraph. In addition to Tab, you can also use the arrow keys or the mouse pointer to move from cell to cell. The leftmost cell in a row is considered the first cell in the row. The first row in the table is usually used for column headings, whereas the leftmost column is used for row labels.

After you have created a table, you can modify its structure by inserting or deleting columns and rows. If the insertion point is positioned in the rightmost cell in the last row of the table, you can press Tab to quickly add another row to the bottom of the table. You can also use the **Table** menu to insert, delete, and select rows and columns. To insert a row or column, you click to place the insertion point in the row or column where you want to insert one, point to **Insert** on the **Table** menu, and then click **Rows Above**, **Rows Below**, **Columns to the Right**, or **Columns to the Left**. If you select more than one row or column and use one of the **Insert** commands, Word adds that number of rows or columns to the table.

Selection handle
new for
OfficeXP

You can resize an entire table or each column or row individually to accommodate the text that you are presenting. To resize a table quickly, you can click and then drag the selection handle that appears in the lower-right corner of the table.

You can also merge cells to create cells of varying sizes. For example, if you want the title to be in the first row of your table, you can merge the cells in that row to create one cell that spans the table's width. If you need to divide a cell into smaller cells, you can split a cell into additional columns or rows. You can use the **Merge Cells** and **Split Cells** commands on the **Table** menu to combine or separate cells.

To change a table, you might need to select the entire table or specific rows or columns. The following table explains how to select part or all of a table.

To Select	Action
A table	Click the **Select Table** button in the upper-left of the first cell in the table. Or on the **Table** menu, point to **Select**, and then click **Table**.
A column or a row	Point to the first row in a column or the first column in a row, and when the pointer changes to an arrow, click to select the column or row.
A cell	Double-click the cell.
Multiple cells	Click the first cell, hold down the Shift key, and then press the ↓ or → key to select cells in a column or row, respectively.

Tip

The document must be in Print Layout view before you can use the **Select Table** button and the selection handle.

To move a table in a document, you can click the **Select Table** button and drag the table to another location in the document. You can also use the **Cut** and **Paste** buttons on the Standard toolbar to move a table.

You will often create a table to accommodate multiple columns or lists of information. After you enter the text, you can sort the information in ascending or descending order, and you can sort the information by column or row by using the **Sort** command on the **Table** menu. For example, if you have a table with column headings for name, address, and phone number, you can sort the table in alphabetical order by name to make it easier to find a person in the table.

The Garden Company needs to design an insert for its catalog, *The Company Garden Herbs*. The owner of The Garden Company wants the insert to include three tables: an order form, a table of shipping and handling fees, and a table of optional delivery services.

CreateTable

In this exercise, you create three tables. In the first table, you merge cells, enter text, and add rows. To create the second table, you convert existing plain text to a table. Finally, you sort information in a third table.

1 Start Word, if necessary.

Open

2 On the Standard toolbar, click the **Open** button.

The **Open** dialog box appears.

3 Navigate to the **Office XP SBS** folder on your hard disk, double-click the **Word** folder, double-click the **Chap03** folder, and then double-click the **CreateTable** file.

The CreateTable document opens.

4 Press ↓ to position the insertion point in the blank line below the *Please complete this form* sentence.

5 On the **Table** menu, point to **Insert**, and then click **Table**.

The **Insert Table** dialog box appears.

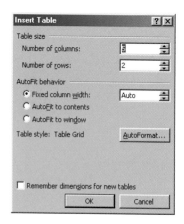

6 Make sure that the **Number of columns** box displays 5, click the **Number of rows** up arrow to display 5, and then click **OK**.

A blank table with five columns and five rows appears. The insertion point appears in the first cell.

7 Position the pointer in the selection area to the left of the first row, and then click to select the row.

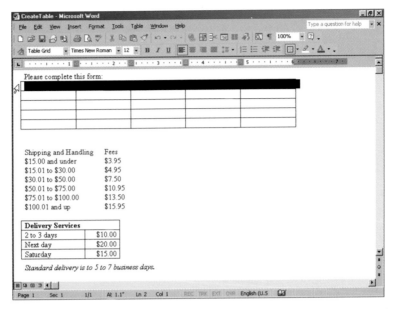

8   On the **Table** menu, click **Merge Cells** to combine the cells in the first row into one cell.

9   Type **The Garden Company Herb Plant Order Form**.

The text appears in the first row.

10   Click in the first cell in the second row, and then type **Page No**.

11   Press ⟦Tab⟧ and type **Description**, press ⟦Tab⟧ and type **Quantity**, press ⟦Tab⟧ and type **Unit Price**, press ⟦Tab⟧ and type **Total**, and then press ⟦Tab⟧ to move the insertion point to the first cell in the next row.

12   Type **25**, press ⟦Tab⟧ and type **Lemon Basil**, press ⟦Tab⟧ and type **3**, press ⟦Tab⟧ and type **2.29**, and then press ⟦Tab⟧ and type **6.78**.

The text appears in the second row.

13   Position the pointer in the selection area to the left of the fourth row, and then drag to select the last two rows.

14   On the **Table** menu, point to **Insert**, and then click **Rows Below** to add two more rows to the table.

Two rows appear below the two selected rows.

15   In the last row, click in the first cell, hold down ⟦Shift⟧, and then press ⟦→⟧ four times to select the first four cells in the row.

16   On the **Table** menu, click **Merge Cells** to combine the cells in the first row into one cell.

17   Type **Total Order Amount**, and then press ⟦Tab⟧ twice.

A new row is added to the bottom of the table. Note that the new row uses the structure of the preceding row.

63

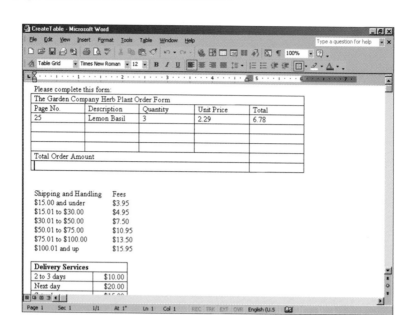

18 Type **Add Shipping and Handling Fee**, and then press [Tab] twice to add a new row.

19 Type **Add Delivery Service Fee, if necessary**, and then press [Tab] twice to add a new row.

20 Type **Total Amount Due**.

21 In the paragraphs below the table, select the block of text that begins *Shipping and Handling* and ends with *$15.95*.

22 On the **Table** menu, point to **Convert**, and then click **Text to Table**.

The **Convert Text to Table** dialog box appears.

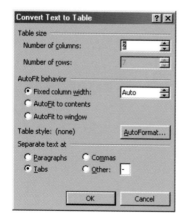

23 Make sure that the **Number of columns** box displays *2*, and then click **OK**.

The seven lines of selected text now appear in a table format with two columns and seven rows.

Double-headed
arrow pointer

↔

24 Click in the table to deselect the cells, point to the right edge of the table until the pointer changes to a thick double-headed arrow, and then double-click to resize the table to the width of the text in the cell.

25 Scroll down, and then click anywhere in the **Delivery Services** table to place the insertion point.

26 On the **Table** menu, click **Sort**.

The **Sort** dialog box appears.

27 Click the **Sort by** down arrow, and then click **(Column2)**. If necessary, click the **Descending** option, make sure the **Header row** option in the **My list has** area is selected, and then click **OK**.

Print Layout

▣

28 Click the **Print Layout View** button, and then scroll down the document window to bring the **Delivery Services** table, the **Shipping and Handling Fees** table, and the bottom of the **Order Form** table into view.

Select Table

⊞

29 Hold down the **Select Table** button in the upper-left corner of the **Delivery Services** table to select the table.

30 Drag the outline of the table up and to the right of the **Shipping and Handling Fees** table, aligning the top of the **Delivery Services** table with the top of the **Shipping and Handling** table and the right side of the **Delivery Services** table with the right side of the **Order Form** table.

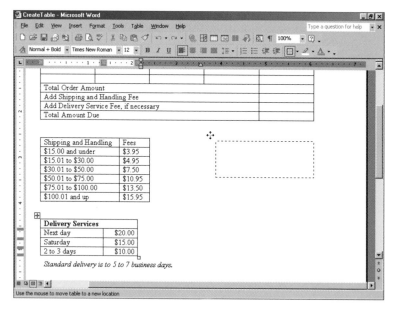

31 When the **Delivery Services** table is positioned correctly, release the mouse button.

32 Point to the **Delivery Services** table, and then drag the selection handle in the lower-right corner down, releasing the mouse button when the lower-edge of the **Delivery Services** table is aligned with the lower-edge of the **Shipping and Handling Fees** table.

33 On the Standard toolbar, click the **Save** button to save the document.

Close

34 Click the **Close** button in the document window.

The CreateTable document closes.

Formatting Text in a Table

To enhance the appearance of the text in a table, you can format it using the buttons on the Formatting toolbar, just as you would when formatting any text in a Word document. You can also format the structure of the table by adding borders and shading.

You can use the buttons on the Formatting toolbar to change the appearance and the alignment of the text in a cell. To modify the table or cell borders, you use the **Borders and Shading** command on the **Format** menu, which opens the **Borders and Shading** dialog box. You can also add shading to the table or cells using the options on the **Shading** tab in the **Borders and Shading** dialog box.

To format a table and its text quickly, you can apply a **Table AutoFormat** using the **Table AutoFormat** command on the **Table** menu. The **Table AutoFormat** dialog box provides 18 predesigned table formats that include a variety of borders, colors, and attributes, such as italics, that will give your table a professional look. This is useful for quickly formatting a table.

To make sure that the tables in The Garden Company's catalog are easily distinguishable from one another, but also complementary, the owner will format the tables.

FormatTable

In this exercise, you format the text in a table and add shading to a cell. You also add a border to the entire table and to selected rows. Finally, you apply an AutoFormat to a table.

1 On the Standard toolbar, click the **Open** button.

The **Open** dialog box appears.

2 Navigate to the **Office XP SBS** folder on your hard disk, double-click the **Word** folder, double-click the **Chap03** folder, and then double-click the **FormatTable** file.

The FormatTable document opens.

Troubleshooting

The document should open in the Print Layout view. If the document is in Normal view, click the **Print Layout View** button.

3 Position the pointer in the selection area to the left of the first row in the Order Form table, and then click to select the first row.

4 On the Formatting toolbar, click the **Font** down arrow, and then click **Arial**. Click the **Font Size** down arrow, and then click **16**.

The font style changes to Arial, and the size changes to 16 points.

Center

5 On the Formatting toolbar, click the **Bold** button, and then click the **Center** button.

The text appears in the center of the cell with the bold formatting style.

6 With the first row in the table still selected, on the **Format** menu, click **Borders and Shading**.

The **Borders and Shading** dialog box appears.

7 Click the **Shading** tab.

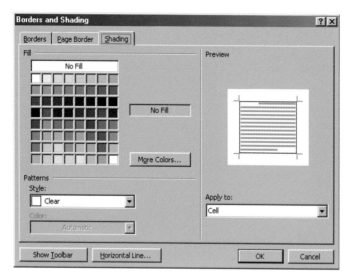

8   Click the **Light Yellow** color box in the color palette (last row, third column), and then click **OK**.

Word adds light yellow shading to the background of the first row of the table.

9   Select the third row in the table.

Italic

10   On the Formatting toolbar, click the **Italic** button to change the selected text to italic.

Font Color

11   On the Formatting toolbar, click the **Font Color** down arrow, and then click the **Red** color box in the color palette (third row, first column) to change the selected text to red.

12   Select the last four rows in the Order Form table.

Align Right

13   On the Formatting toolbar, click the **Align Right** button.

Word aligns the text in the last four rows of the table along the right margin.

14   Click anywhere in the Shipping and Handling table to place the insertion point.

15   On the **Table** menu, click **Table AutoFormat**.

The **Table AutoFormat** dialog box appears.

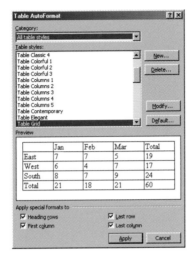

16 Scroll down the **Table Styles** list, click **Table List 8**, and then click **Apply**.

The Shipping and Handling Fees table is formatted in contrasting colors with a thick dark border.

17 Click anywhere in the Delivery Services table to place the insertion point.

18 On the **Format** menu, click **Borders and Shading**, and then click the **Borders** tab.

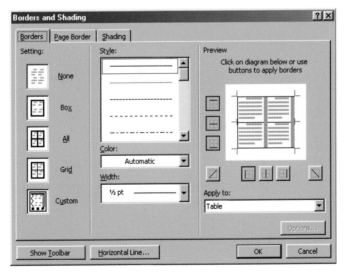

19 In the **Setting** area, click the **All** icon, if necessary, to select it.

20 In the **Style** list, click the scroll down arrow twice, and then click the double line border style.

21   Click the **Color** down arrow, click the **Red** color box in the color palette (third row, first column), and then click **OK**.

Word adds a red double border to the entire table.

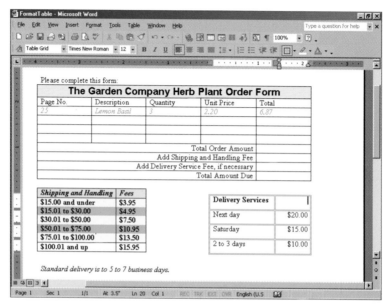

22   On the Standard toolbar, click the **Save** button to save the document.

Close

23   Click the **Close** button in the document window.

The FormatTable document closes.

Working with Data in a Table

You can perform certain calculations on the numbers in a Word table using one of Word's built-in formulas. A **formula** is a mathematical expression that performs calculations, such as adding or averaging values. To insert a formula, you use the **Formula** command on the **Table** menu to display the **Formula** dialog box. A formula starts with an equal sign. After the equal sign you insert a function, such as (SUM), which performs a calculation.

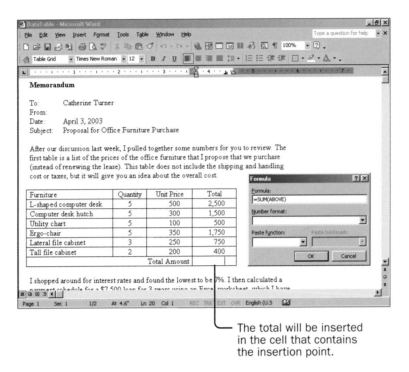

The total will be inserted in the cell that contains the insertion point.

Word anticipates what you want to calculate. In the previous illustration, the formula in the **Formula** dialog box will add (SUM) the values in the cell that appear to the left of the current cell (the cell that contains the insertion point).

To insert other functions into the **Formula** box in the **Formula** dialog box, click the **Paste function** down arrow, and then click a function. You can use other built-in functions to count (COUNT) the number of values or find the maximum (MAX) or minimum (MIN) value in a series of cells. Many Word formulas refer to the cells in the table; you can also specify cell references or values that are used as constants. To reference a cell in a formula, you type the cell location in parentheses in the formula. For example, the formula =SUM(b2, b3) uses cell references to cell b2 and b3. The formula adds the numbers in the two cells.

Tip

Click the **AutoSum** button on the **Tables and Borders** toolbar to add a column or row of numbers quickly and easily.

Although you can perform many standard calculations in a Word table, the available formulas might not address all your needs. For complex calculations or analyses, such as determining a payment schedule for a loan, you can include a Microsoft Excel worksheet in a Word document. Excel is an electronic spreadsheet program that provides extensive mathematical and financial capabilities.

Important

In a Word table, you must recalculate formulas manually if you change a value in the Word table. In an Excel worksheet, the formulas are automatically recalculated when you change a value in the worksheet.

To include an Excel worksheet in a Word document, you need to understand how Microsoft Office programs integrate data.

Object Linking and Embedding

To insert information from one Office program into another, you can use Microsoft's **object linking and embedding (OLE)** technology. OLE allows you to insert a file created in one program into a document that was created in another program. For example, you can insert an Excel file into a Word document. The object that you are inserting is called the **source file**, which is created in the **source program**. The file into which you are inserting the information is called the **destination file**.

The difference between linking and embedding is the type of connection that is maintained between the source and the destination. A **linked object** is an object that maintains a direct connection (or link) to the source file. The linked data is stored in the source file, not in the destination file; the destination file displays only a representation of the linked data. An **embedded object** is an object that becomes part of the destination file and is no longer a part of the source file.

When you link an object, the linked object is updated only when you update the source file. The update occurs when you open the destination file that includes the linked object. When you embed an object, you can make changes to the embedded object using the source program, but the source file is not updated. Determining whether to link or embed an object depends on whether the information in the destination file must be synchronized with the information in the source file. If more than one person needs to update a file, you can place the file in a central location and then link to the file so that both people will always get the latest information in the file.

If you do not need to maintain a connection between the source file and the destination file, you can copy and paste information between programs using the **Copy** and **Paste** buttons on the Standard toolbar. If you use this method, the source files and the destination files are not connected. The pasted information becomes part of the destination file, and you can use the tools in the destination file to edit the pasted information.

You can insert data from an Excel worksheet into a Word document in a few ways. Copy and paste the data if you do not need to maintain a connection between the source file and the destination file. You can use the **Object** command on the **Insert** menu to link or embed objects, such as graphics, slide presentations files, charts, graphs, and spreadsheets. You can also use the **Paste Special** command on the **Edit** menu to embed or link the object. Paste Special allows you to copy information from one location and paste it in another location using a different format, such as a Microsoft Excel Object, Picture, or Web format.

To update a linked or embedded object, you double-click the object. If the object is linked, the source file opens in the source program. When you save any changes that you've made, the linked object is updated. If the object is embedded, the source program opens, but the source file does not. You can use the source program commands to update the embedded object, saving the changes in the destination file.

The office manager at The Garden Company has written a memo outlining a proposal to purchase office furniture. The memo includes a table listing furniture and prices. The office manager has also created an Excel worksheet that provides the payment schedule for a loan needed to purchase the furniture. She wants to embed the worksheet because this is a preliminary proposal. She also wants to see how the payment schedule changes if the loan amount changes.

DataTable
InsertTable

In this exercise, you calculate data in a table. You embed an Excel worksheet in a Word document and then change the worksheet data.

1   On the Standard toolbar, click the **Open** button.

The **Open** dialog box appears.

2   Navigate to the **Office XP SBS** folder on your hard disk, double-click the **Word** folder, double-click the **Chap03** folder, and then double-click the **DataTable** file.

The DataTable document opens.

3   Click in the lower-right cell of the furniture table (after *Total Amount*).

4   On the **Table** menu, click **Formula** to open the **Formula** dialog box.

The **Formula** dialog box shows the formula *=SUM(ABOVE)*, meaning that the formula will add the numbers in the cells above the current cell.

5   Click **OK** to display the total amount for the furniture in the cell.

6   Press Ctrl+End to move the insertion point to the end of the document.

7   On the **Insert** menu, click **Object** to open the **Object** dialog box, and then click the **Create from File** tab.

8   Click **Browse**, navigate to the **Office XP SBS** folder on your hard disk, double-click the **Word** folder, double-click the **Chap03** folder, and then double-click the **InsertTable** file.

The InsertTable file appears in the **File Name** box.

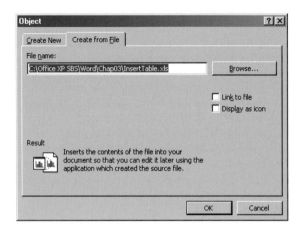

9   Click **OK**.

The Excel worksheet appears in the document.

10   Press the ⌈Page Up⌉ key to see the beginning of the inserted Excel worksheet.

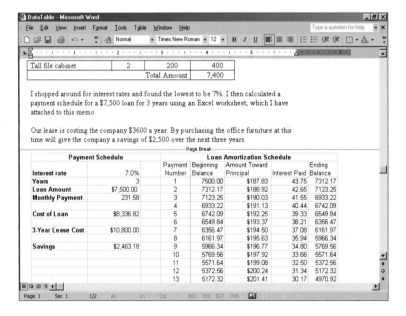

11 Double-click anywhere in the **Excel worksheet table**, click cell **B4**, type **10000**, and then press the `Enter` key.

Excel recalculates the data in the table to show how the payment schedule would change if the loan were for $10,000.

12 Scroll up, and then click just above the Excel worksheet table.

The worksheet table is updated with the costs for a loan of $10,000.

13 On the Standard toolbar, click the **Save** button to save the document.

Close

14 Click the **Close** button in the document window.

The DataTable document closes.

Presenting Text in Columns

When you want to create a document, such as a newsletter, columns are a useful way to present information. In Word, a column is a block of text that has its own margins. You can divide a document into two, three, or more columns of text. (If you decide that you don't want to divide your document into multiple columns, you can format the document as one column—which is the default setting for any Word document.) When you divide a document into columns, the text flows, or snakes, from the top of one column to the top of the next. If you want the columns to be equal in length, you can insert a column break to force the text to move to the top of the next column.

After you break text into columns, you can change the width of a column. You can also format column text as you would any other text. For example, you can change the indentation or the alignment of text in a column using the horizontal ruler or the alignment buttons on the Formatting toolbar.

The owner of The Garden Company has written a nine-step procedure for cultivating an herb garden. The document must be set up in four columns to match other marketing materials.

CreateColumn

In this exercise, you format text into four columns. You reduce the amount of space between the columns and indent column text. Finally, you break the columns at specific locations rather than allowing the text to flow naturally from one column to the next.

1 On the Standard toolbar, click the **Open** button.

The **Open** dialog box appears.

2 Navigate to the **Office XP SBS** folder on your hard disk, double-click the **Word** folder, double-click the **Chap03** folder, and then double-click the **CreateColumn** file.

The CreateColumn document opens.

3 On the **Format** menu, click **Columns**.

The **Columns** dialog box appears.

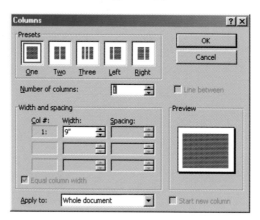

4 Click the **Number of columns** up arrow until **4** is displayed, and then click **OK**.

The document view changes to Print Layout view, and the document is divided into four columns.

5 On the **Edit** menu, click **Select All** to select all the text in the document.

Justify

6 On the Formatting toolbar, click the **Justify** button to align the text in the columns equally to the left and right margins, and then click in the document to deselect the text.

Zoom

100% ▾

7 On the Standard toolbar, click the **Zoom** down arrow, and then click **75%** so that more of the document is displayed in the document window.

8 Point to the **Right Indent** indicator for the second column on the horizontal ruler. The pointer changes shape.

Hanging Indent marker — Right Margin indicator

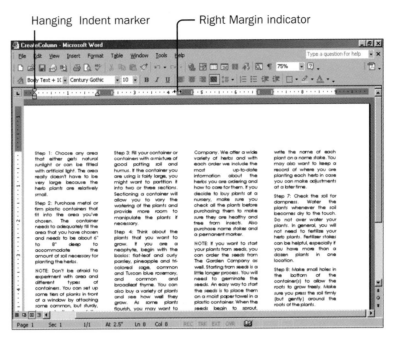

9 Click and drag the pointer 1/6-inch (one tick mark) to the right, and then release the mouse button to resize the columns.

By dragging the pointer to the right, you decrease the spacing between the columns, which decreases the amount of white space on the page, visually enhancing the overall appearance of the layout of the document.

10 Click in the *NOTE* paragraph that appears after the *Step 2* paragraph.

11 Drag the **Hanging Indent** marker on the ruler 1/6-inch (one tick mark) to the right.

All lines except the first line of text in the *NOTE* paragraph are indented, which offsets this text from the step text.

12 Click in the *NOTE* paragraph that appears after the *Step 5* paragraph, and then press the F4 key to apply the same formatting to this paragraph.

13 Click to the left of the text *Step 5* to place the insertion point.

14 On the **Insert** menu, click **Break** to open the **Break** dialog box, click the **Column break** option, and then click **OK**.

The text that appears after the column break moves to the top of the next column.

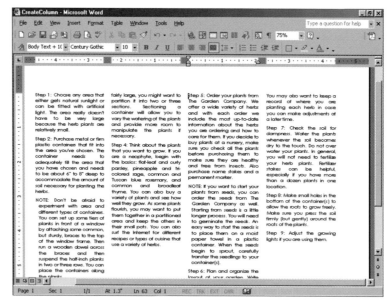

15 Click to the left of the text *Step 6*, and then press [F4].

The Step 6 paragraph moves to the top of the fourth column. The columns are now more evenly divided across the page.

Print Preview

16 On the Standard toolbar, click the **Print Preview** button to view the document formatted in columns.

Close Preview

17 On the Print Preview toolbar, click the **Close Preview** button to close the Print Preview window.

18 On the Standard toolbar, click the **Save** button to save the document.

Close

19 Click the **Close** button in the document window.

The CreateColumn document closes.

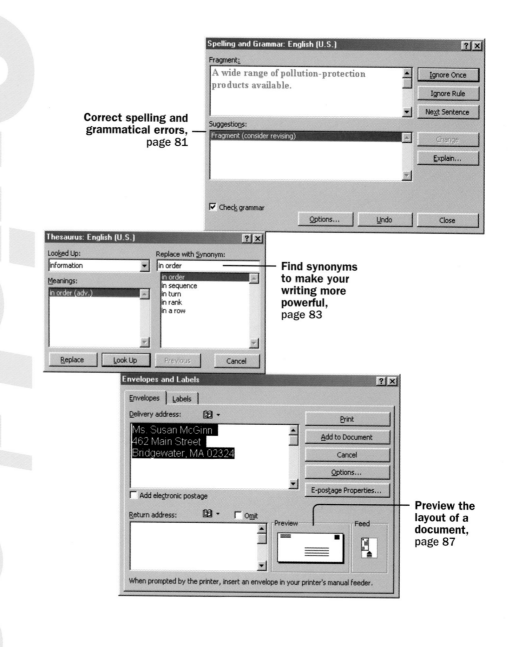

Correct spelling and grammatical errors, page 81

Find synonyms to make your writing more powerful, page 83

Preview the layout of a document, page 87

Chapter 4
Proofreading and Printing a Document

After completing this chapter, you will be able to:

✔ Check the spelling and grammar in a document.

✔ Preview and print a document.

Before you share your documents with others, you should take a few steps to ensure that the documents are ready for distribution. One of the most important steps to take is to check the document's grammar and spelling to ensure that the words are spelled correctly and that the text is grammatically correct. You can use Word's Spelling and Grammar Checker and Thesaurus to correct spelling and grammar errors, add new words to Word's online dictionary, and replace words with synonyms that improve readability and match the reading level of your audience. Because the online dictionary might not include specialized terms, proper names, or foreign words, you can use Word's AutoText feature to store and quickly insert these types of text. When you finish proofreading your document, you can preview the document to view and adjust the layout before you print it. Then you're ready to print the document and any related materials, such as an envelope.

In this chapter, you'll proofread and print a letter for the assistant buyer at The Garden Company. You'll check the spelling and grammar in the Word document and then preview the document before you print it. You'll also create and insert an AutoText entry and print an envelope.

This chapter uses the practice files SpellCheck and PreviewPrint that that are stored in the Office XP SBS\Word\Chap04 subfolder that you installed from this book's CD-ROM. For details about installing the practice files, see "Using the Book's CD-ROM" at the beginning of this book.

Checking the Spelling and Grammar in a Document

Proofreading a document involves checking the spelling of words, correcting grammatical errors, and choosing language that best conveys your message to your audience. You should always proofread a document *before* you print and share it with others. Sending a document that is filled with spelling and grammatical errors creates a poor impression on your reader. You can use Word's **Spelling and Grammar** features to correct errors and maintain professional writing standards.

As you type the text of your document, by default Word underlines spelling and grammar errors with red or green wavy lines. A red wavy line indicates that Word does not recognize the spelling of the word; that is, the word is not included in Word's online dictionary. A green line indicates a possible grammar error. To quickly fix individual spelling and grammar errors, you can right-click a word underlined with a red or green wavy line to display a list of corrections from which you can choose.

In addition to correcting individual errors, you can check the entire document for spelling and grammar errors by clicking the **Spelling and Grammar** button on the Standard toolbar. When you start checking spelling and grammar, Word compares each word in the document with the words in its dictionary. Word stops at each red and green wavy line and displays the possible reason for the error. For example, if a word is misspelled, the **Spelling and Grammar** dialog box identifies the misspelled word and provides a list of possible replacements. If Word finds a potential grammar error, the **Spelling and Grammar** dialog box identifies the problem and provides suggestions for correcting the error.

The options that are displayed in the **Spelling and Grammar** dialog box depend on the type of error that Word encounters. The following table describes the options in the **Spelling and Grammar** dialog box:

Button or Option	Function
Ignore Once	Leaves the highlighted error unchanged and finds the next spelling or grammar error. If you click in the document to edit it, this button changes to the **Resume** button. After you finish editing, click the **Resume** button to continue checking the spelling and grammar.
Ignore All or **Ignore Rule**	Leaves all occurrences of the highlighted spelling or grammar error unchanged throughout the document and continues to check the rest of the document. Word ignores the spelling or grammar of this word in this document and in all documents whose spelling was checked during the current Word session.
Next Sentence	Accepts manual changes in a document and continues to check the document.
Add to Dictionary	Adds the selected word in the **Not in dictionary** box to the custom dictionary. A custom dictionary contains your own words.
Change	Changes the highlighted error to the word that you select in the **Suggestions** box.

Button or Option	Function
Change All	Changes all occurrences of the highlighted error to the word that you select in the **Suggestions** box and then continues to check the rest of the document.
Explain	Provides more information about the grammar error.
AutoCorrect	Adds the spelling error and its correction to the **AutoCorrect** list so that Word corrects it automatically as you type.
Undo	Undoes the last spelling or grammar action that you performed.
Options	Opens the **Spelling and Grammar Options** dialog box. Use this dialog box to open a different custom dictionary or to change the rules that Word uses to check spelling and grammar.

Tip

Word's **AutoCorrect** feature corrects commonly misspelled and mistyped words as you enter text in a document. For example, if you type *adn* for *and*, AutoCorrect corrects the spelling as soon as you press the [Space]. You can add to the AutoCorrect list the words that you often misspell or mistype.

To make sure that you are using the correct words in your documents, you can use Word's **thesaurus**. For example, the language that you use in a letter to a friend is different from the language that you use in business correspondence. You can use the thesaurus to look up alternative words or synonyms for a selected word. To use the thesaurus, you select the word that you want to look up, point to **Language** on the **Tools** menu, and then click **Thesaurus**. The **Thesaurus** dialog box appears, displaying a list of synonyms.

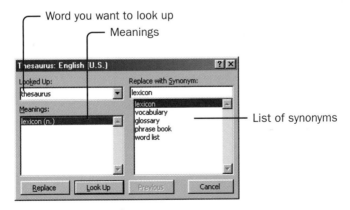

Word you want to look up

Meanings

List of synonyms

SpellCheck

In this exercise, you check the spelling in the document, and add common terms that are not already in the online dictionary. You find, review, and correct a grammar error, and use the thesaurus to replace one word with another.

1 Start Word, if necessary.

Open

2 On the Standard toolbar, click the **Open** button.

The **Open** dialog box appears.

3 Navigate to the Office XP SBS folder on your hard disk, double-click the **Word** folder, double-click the **Chap04** folder, and then double-click the **SpellCheck** file.

The SpellCheck document opens, displaying red and green wavy lines.

Spelling and Grammar

4 On the Standard toolbar, click the **Spelling and Grammar** button.

The **Spelling and Grammar** dialog box appears, highlighting the first word that Word does not recognize. The online dictionary contains many common first and last names, but it does not recognize unusual or foreign names.

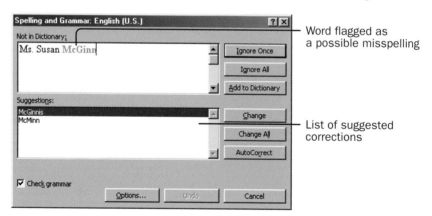

Word flagged as a possible misspelling

List of suggested corrections

Troubleshooting

If the Spelling and Grammar checker doesn't find the errors in this document, you need to reset the spelling and grammar checker. On the **Tools** menu, click **Options**, click the tab, click **Recheck Document**, and then click **Yes** to recheck words and grammar that were previously checked or that you chose to ignore.

5 Click **Ignore Once** to skip the name.

Word stops at the next word that it does not recognize—*bot*.

6 In the **Suggestions** box, click **both**, and then click **Change**.

Word corrects the misspelling. The next flagged word is *envrionmentally*.

7 In the **Suggestions** box, click **environmentally**, click **AutoCorrect**, and then click **Yes** to redefine the AutoCorrect entry.

Word adds the correction to the AutoCorrect list. The next time that you type *envrionmentally* by mistake, Word will correct the spelling for you as you type.

Word flags *harty* as a possible misspelling.

8 With the word *hearty* selected in the **Suggestions** box, click **Change All** to change this and subsequent occurrences of *harty* to *hearty*.

Word corrects both misspellings and then flags *crassula* as a word that it doesn't recognize.

9 Click **Ignore All**.

Because this is the correct spelling of *crassula*, a type of plant, you can skip any other instances of *crassula* in the letter.

Word stops at the next word that it does not recognize—this time a Latin word. (If your version of Word doesn't stop at the Latin word skip to step 11.)

10 Click **Add to Dictionary** three times to add to the custom dictionary the next three Latin words that Word does not recognize.

The three Latin words in italics are spelled correctly. By adding them to the custom dictionary, you prevent Word from flagging them later.

Word flags a possible grammar error in green and indicates that this text could be a sentence fragment. The sentence is missing a verb.

Grammar error highlighted in green

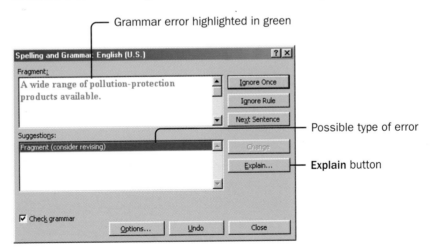

Possible type of error

Explain button

11 In the **Spelling and Grammar** dialog box, click before the word *available* in the highlighted text, type **are**, press ⌷Space⌷, and then click **Change**.

An alert message appears, indicating that Word has finished checking the spelling and grammar in the document.

12 Click **OK** to close the alert message.

13 Press ⌷Ctrl⌷+⌷Home⌷ to move the insertion point to the top of the document.

14 Double-click *important* near the end of the first paragraph to select the word.

15 On the **Tools** menu, point to **Language**, and then click **Thesaurus**.

The **Thesaurus** dialog box appears, displaying a list of meanings associated with the word and suggested synonyms for *important*.

16 With *significant* selected in the **Replace with Synonym** box, click the **Replace** button.

Word replaces *important* with *significant*.

17 On the Standard toolbar, click the **Save** button to save the document.

Close

☒

18 Click the **Close** button in the document window.

The SpellCheck document closes.

Translating Text in Another Language

Word provides a basic multi-language dictionary and translation feature so that you can look up text in the dictionary of a different language, translate simple, short phrases, and insert the translated text into your document directly from the Translate Task pane. You can often use these translations to determine the main ideas in a document written in a foreign language. If you need to translate longer sections of text, you can connect to translation services on the World Wide Web directly from the Translate Task pane. For important or sensitive documents, you might want to have a trained person do the translation, since computer translation might not preserve the text's full meaning, detail, or tone. You can also look up words or phrases in the dictionary of a different language, provided that the language dictionary is installed on your computer and enabled through Microsoft Office XP Language Settings. To enable a language, click the **Start** button on the taskbar, point to **Programs**, point to **Microsoft Office Tools**, click **Microsoft Office XP Language Settings**, click the **Enabled Languages** tab, select a language, and then click **Add**.

To translate text in another language:

1 Select the text in your document that you want to translate.

2 On the **Tools** menu, point to **Language**, and then click **Translate**.

The Translate Task pane appears.

3 In the Translate Task pane, click the **Current selection** option in the **Translate what?** section.

4 In the **Dictionary** box, select the languages that you want to translate from and to.

5 Click **Go**.

The translated text appears in the **Results** box.

6 In the **Results** box, select the translated text, and then click **Replace**.

The selected text in your document is replaced with the translated text.

Previewing and Printing a Document

Before printing a document, you should verify that its pages look the way that you want. You save time, money, and paper by avoiding duplicate printing. Print Preview shows you exactly how your text will be placed on each page. This is especially helpful when you have a multi-page document. The Print Preview toolbar provides the tools that you need to check the presentation of each page. If you have headers and footers in your document, they also appear in Print Preview. You can change the layout of your document in Print Preview, and you can even change the text.

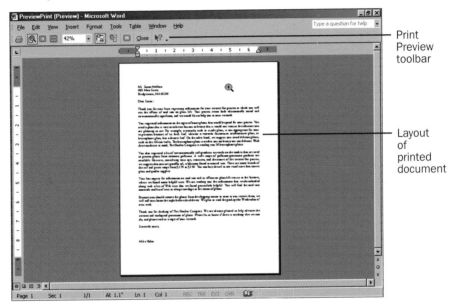

Print Preview toolbar

Layout of printed document

You can print your document by clicking the **Print** button on the Standard toolbar or the Print Preview toolbar. When you do, Word uses the current settings specified in the **Print** dialog box and prints to the default printer, which is the printer set as the one that you use most often. To open the **Print** dialog box to view or change print settings, on the **File** menu, click **Print**. In the **Print** dialog box, you can choose to print the current page or select certain pages that you want to print. You can also choose to print more than one copy of a document or print other document components, such as the list of comments or styles associated with the document.

You can print envelopes and labels using addresses that you have entered in a document. To do this, you select the lines of the address (or the text that you want for the label), point to **Letters and Mailings** on the **Tools** menu, and then click **Envelopes and Labels** to open the **Envelopes and Labels** dialog box. You then choose the type of envelope or label that you need. You can also choose to print the envelope and label text in the font and font size that match those used in the document, and you can include a return address on the envelope.

Tip

To provide a return address, Word uses the personalized information that you entered when you installed Word. You can change that information on the **User Information** tab in the **Options** dialog box, which you open by clicking **Options** on the **Tools** menu.

An assistant at The Garden Company wants to preview a letter before printing it and adjust the layout of the letter, if necessary. He wants to print the letter on a printer other than the one he normally uses and needs to print an envelope for the letter.

PreviewPrint

In this exercise, you preview a document, adjust the top margin in the print preview window, and select a new printer before sending the letter to be printed. After printing the document, you select the inside address and use it to print an envelope and label.

Tip

To complete this exercise, you need a printer connected to your computer and the printer software installed.

Open

1 On the Standard toolbar, click the **Open** button.

The **Open** dialog box appears.

2 Navigate to the Office XP SBS folder on your hard disk, double-click the **Word** folder, double-click the **Chap04** folder, and then double-click the **Preview-Print** file.

The PreviewPrint document opens.

Troubleshooting

If an information icon appears in the document window, you can ignore it for now. Words and phrases underlined with dotted lines have a Smart Tag. Smart Tags provide options for using text as data in other programs. For example, you might want to add Susan McGinn's name and address to your Contacts list in your Outlook program. To do so, click the **Smart Tag**, and then select **Add to Contacts** from the list of **Smart Tag** options.

Print Preview

3 On the Standard toolbar, click the **Print Preview** button.

The letter appears in the print preview window, showing the entire page as it would appear on the printed page.

4   Position the pointer (which changes to the two-headed arrow) over the Top Margin indicator on the vertical ruler, and then drag the pointer down about a half inch, making sure that the last line of text is not forced to another page, as shown in the following illustration:

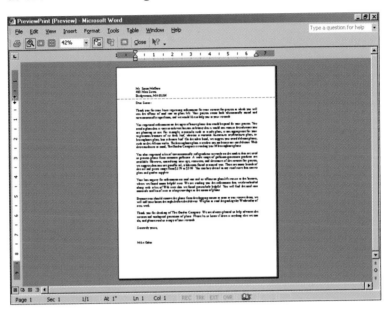

Magnifying Glass (+)

5   Position the Magnifying Glass (+) pointer over the document, and then click near the top of the document.

The document view zoom percentage changes to 100%, the actual size of the page.

Magnifying Glass (-)

6   Position the Magnifying Glass (-) pointer over the document, and then click near the top of the document.

The zoom percentage is reduced.

Close Preview

Close

7   On the Print Preview toolbar, click the **Close Preview** button.

The print preview window closes, and the Word document window appears in Normal view.

8   On the **File** menu, click **Print**.

The **Print** dialog box appears.

Your printer settings will differ.

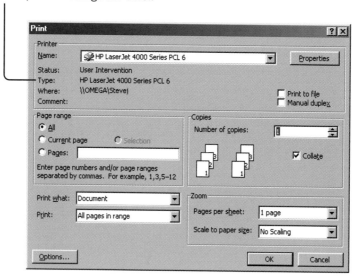

9 Click the **Name** down arrow, select a printer, if necessary, and then click **OK** to send the document to the printer.

Tip

If you are satisfied with the current **Print** dialog box settings, you can click the **Print** button on the Standard toolbar to print directly without first viewing the settings.

10 Select the three lines of the inside address at the top of the document. (Do not select the blank line below the inside address.)

11 On the **Tools** menu, point to **Letters and Mailing**, and then click **Envelopes and Labels**.

The **Envelopes and Labels** dialog box appears with the inside address selected in the **Delivery Address** box.

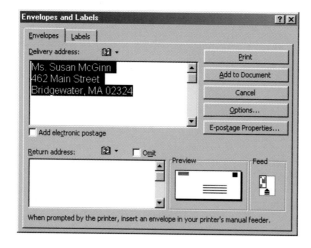

12 Select the **Omit** check box, and then click **Options**.

This option doesn't include the return address when you print envelopes.

The **Envelope Options** dialog box appears, displaying envelope types and styles that your printer accepts. The default size is 10, which is acceptable.

13 Click **OK**, insert an envelope in the printer according to your printer manufacturer's directions (optional), and then click **Print**.

The envelope is printed.

14 On the **Tools** menu, point to **Letters and Mailing**, click **Envelopes and Labels** to display the **Envelopes and Labels** dialog box, and then click the **Labels** tab.

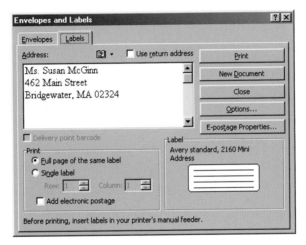

15 Click the **Single label** option.

Row 1 and Column 1 appear under the **Single label** option.

16 Click **Print**.

The label is printed.

17 On the Standard toolbar, click the **Save** button to save the document.

Close

18 Click the **Close** button in the document window.

The PreviewPrint document closes.

Microsoft Excel

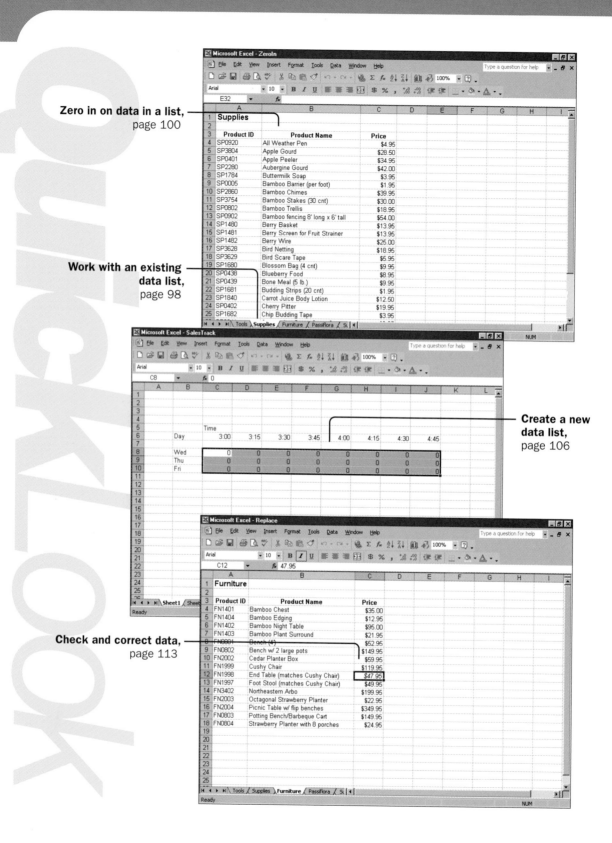

Chapter 5
Getting to Know Excel

After completing this chapter, you will be able to:

✔ **Work with an existing data list.**

✔ **Zero in on data in a list.**

✔ **Create a data list.**

✔ **Check and correct data.**

One thing all businesses have in common is the need to keep accurate records. As the range of products, services, and customers expands, businesses require a computer-based system to keep up with an avalanche of financial and other data.

Microsoft Excel is a spreadsheet program, one that lets you organize your data into lists and then summarize, compare, and present your data graphically. For example, you can have Excel find the sum, average, or maximum value for sales on a given day; create a graph showing what percentage of sales were in a particular range; and show how the total sales compared with the total sales of other days in the same week. In short, Excel saves you from having to create these summaries by hand.

The exercises in this section are based on data for The Garden Company, the fictional business used in the Step by Step series. In addition to taking care of the plants and gardening supplies offered by the company, the owner, Catherine Turner, and her employees need to maintain the data lists that let Catherine and The Garden Company's head buyer make informed decisions about the products the company carries.

In this chapter, you'll learn how to work with an existing data list and specific data within a data list, create a data list, and check and correct data.

This chapter uses the practice files FileOpen, ZeroIn, DataEntry, and Replace that you installed from this book's CD-ROM. For details about installing the practice files, see "Using the Book's CD-ROM" at the beginning of this book.

Important

Depending on the screen resolution you have set on your computer and which toolbar buttons you use most often, it's possible that not every button on every toolbar will appear on your Excel toolbars. If a button mentioned in this book doesn't appear on a toolbar, click the **Toolbar Options** down arrow on that toolbar to display the rest of the buttons available on that toolbar.

Introducing Excel

When you start Excel, a blank document appears. From this point, you can add data, change how the data looks, have Excel summarize data, or find information in Excel's Help files. The following graphic points out the most important parts of Excel, the last two of which are new in the current version: the Workbook window, the Main Menu bar, the Formula bar, the Standard and Formatting toolbars, the Status bar, and (new in this version), the **Ask A Question** box and the Task pane.

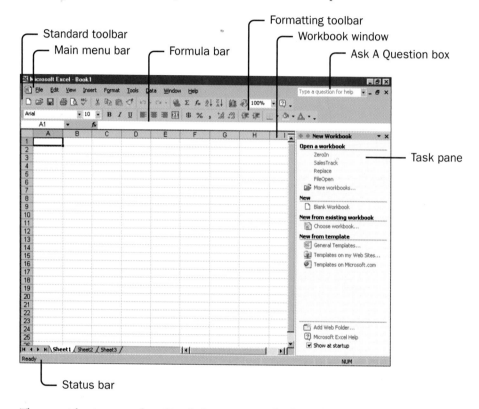

The most basic part of an Excel document is the box that holds an element of data—in Excel, that box is called a **cell**. Each cell is at the intersection of a **row** (a sequence of cells along a horizontal line) and a **column** (a sequence of cells along a vertical line); rows are identified by a number and columns by a letter. The row number and column letter that designate a specific cell are called a **cell reference**. For example, the cell in the upper left corner of the workbook window has the cell reference A1. A single set of columns and rows makes up a **worksheet**, which appears as a page in an Excel document. A **workbook**, in turn, is a collection of one or more worksheets.

Tip

When you create an Excel document, you create a workbook with three worksheets.

The workbook that owner Catherine Turner has developed for The Garden Company has three worksheets, with each worksheet holding data about products available at the company's retail location. She has named the workbook *Products*, and she records data about furniture items on one worksheet, gardening supplies on another worksheet, and tools on a third worksheet. On each worksheet, she uses three columns to record each product's identification code, description, and price. This collection of related information is called a **data list**.

You can include more than three categories in a workbook for a given subject by simply creating additional worksheets; if you want to store data about an entirely different subject, however, you must create a new workbook. For example, if Catherine wanted to record more data about different categories of products sold by The Garden Company, such as varieties of plants, she could create a new worksheet in the Products workbook and add the data to the worksheet. However, if she wanted to store data on a different subject, perhaps her customers and their contact information, she would need to create a new workbook.

Tip

Each workbook should contain information about a unique subject, such as Products, Customers, or Sales, while each worksheet should hold information about a subset of items in that category, meaning different types of products, preferred customers vs. nonpreferred customers, or sales information for a given month.

Ask A Question
new for
OfficeXP

The **Ask A Question** box is new in this version of Excel. Rather than get help through the **Help** menu, you can now type a question in the **Ask A Question** box and have Excel display the help topics that match your request. The benefit of placing the **Ask A Question** box in the main Excel window is that you can quickly and easily get help while your question is fresh in your mind, without adding any steps that might distract you from your question.

Task pane
new for
OfficeXP

The Task pane, also new in this version of Excel, lets you open files, paste data from the Clipboard, create blank workbooks, and create Excel workbooks based on existing files. A great advantage of the Task pane is that it groups many common actions, such as opening or creating new files, in one place and lets you perform them with a single mouse click. The only drawback of the Task pane is that it takes up valuable screen space. Fortunately, you can show or hide the Task pane easily. On the **View** menu, click **Task Pane**; Excel hides the Task pane if it is currently displayed or shows it if it is currently hidden.

Important

If you haven't done so yet, you should install the book's practice files so you can work through the exercises in this chapter. You can find instructions for installing the practice files in the "Using the CD-ROM" section at the front of this book.

Working with an Existing Data List

When you start Excel, the program displays a blank worksheet and has the Task pane open on the right side of the screen. You can begin to enter data in the worksheet's cells or open an existing workbook. In the exercises that follow, you'll be working with some of the workbooks that have already been created for The Garden Company. After you've made any desired changes to a workbook, you should save the workbook.

When you save a file, you overwrite the previous copy of the file. If you have made changes that you want to save but you want to keep a copy of the file as it was previously, you can use the **Save As** command to specify a name for the new file.

Tip

Readers frequently ask, "How often should I save my files?" It's good practice to save your changes every half hour, or even every five minutes, but the best time to save a file is whenever you have made a change you would hate to have to make again.

You can also use the controls in the **Save As** dialog box to specify a different format for the new file. For example, Catherine Turner, the owner of The Garden Company, might want to save an Excel file in a different format if she needs to share the file with the company's accountant, who happens to use another spreadsheet program.

FileOpen

In this exercise, you start Excel from the **Start** menu and then use the **Open** dialog box to open an existing workbook. Once you have opened the workbook, you update the price of an item and save the workbook twice: once as an Excel workbook and again as a Lotus file.

1 On the task bar, click the **Start** button, point to **Programs**, and then click **Microsoft Excel**.

The main Excel program window appears.

Open

2 On the Standard toolbar, click the **Open** button.

The **Open** dialog box appears.

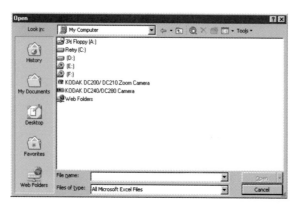

Tip

When the Task pane is displayed, you can also open a file by looking under the **Open a Workbook** heading and either clicking the name of the workbook you want to open or clicking **More Workbooks** to display the **Open** dialog box.

3 Click the **Look In** down arrow, and select the hard disk where you installed the Office XP SBS practice files.

The files and folders on your hard disk appear.

4 Locate the Office XP SBS folder, and then double-click the **Excel** folder to display its contents.

The files and folders in the Excel folder appear.

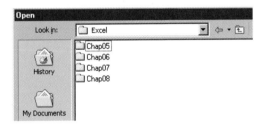

5 Double-click the **Chap05** folder.

The files and folders in the Chap05 folder appear.

6 Double-click the **FileOpen.xls** file.

The FileOpen.xls file opens.

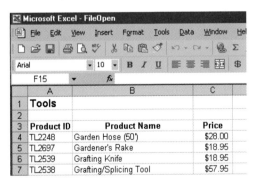

7 Click **cell C16**, and type **15.95**.

The data in cell C16 changes to $15.95.

Save

8 On the Standard toolbar, click the **Save** button.

Excel saves your changes.

9 On the **File** menu, click **Save As**.

The **Save As** dialog box appears.

10 Click in the **File name** box, delete the existing file name, and type SaveAs.

11 Click the **Save as type** down arrow to expand the list, and click **WK4 (1-2-3) (*.wk4).**

12 Click the **Save** button.

A dialog box appears, indicating that some features might be lost. Click **Yes** to have Excel save a new copy of your data in a Lotus file named SaveAs.wk4.

Zeroing In on Data in a List

Once you have opened a workbook, you can examine and modify its contents. To change specific data, such as the price of a pair of shears, you can move to that cell directly and then make your changes. Once in that cell, you can move to another cell in the same worksheet or move to another worksheet in the workbook. Moving to another worksheet is accomplished by clicking its **sheet tab**, located at the bottom left edge of the workbook window.

You can move to a specific cell in lots of ways, but the most direct method is to click the cell to which you want to move. The cell you click will be outlined in black, and its contents, if any, will appear in the formula bar. When a cell is outlined, it is the **active cell**, meaning you can modify its contents. You use a similar method to select multiple cells (referred to as a **cell range**)—just click the first cell in the range, and drag the mouse pointer over the remaining cells you want to select. Once you have selected the cell or cells you want to work with, you can cut, copy, delete, or change the format of the cells' contents. For instance, Catherine Turner, the owner of The

Garden Company, might want to copy the prices of her five most popular garden furniture pieces to a new page that summarizes the best-selling items in each product category that the company offers.

Important

If you select a group of cells, the first cell you click is designated the active cell.

You're not limited to selecting cells individually or as part of a range. For example, you might need to move a column of price data one column to the right to make room for a column of headings that indicate to which product category (Furniture, Tools, Supplies, and so forth) items belong. To move an entire column (or entire columns) of data at a time, you click the column's header, located at the top of the worksheet. Clicking a column header highlights every cell in that column and lets you copy or cut the column and paste it elsewhere in the workbook.

Paste Options
new for
OfficeXP

A new feature in this version of Excel is the **Paste Options** button that appears next to data you copy from a cell and paste into another cell.

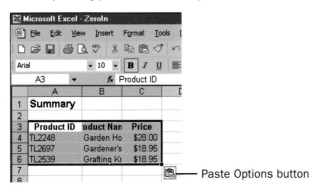

Paste Options button

Clicking the **Paste Options** button displays a list of actions Excel can take regarding the pasted cells. The options in the list are summarized in the following table.

Option	Action
Keep Source Formatting	Paste the contents of the Clipboard (which holds the last information selected via Cut or Copy) into the target cells, and format the data as it was formatted in the original cells.
Match Destination Formatting	Paste the contents of the Clipboard into the target cells, and format the data using the existing format in the target cells.
Values and Number Formatting	Paste the contents of the Clipboard into the target cells, keeping any numeric formats.

(continued)

continued

Option	Action
Keep Source Column Widths	Paste the contents of the Clipboard into the target cells, and resize the columns of the target cells to match the widths of the columns of the source cells.
Formatting Only	Apply the format of the source cells to the target cells, but do not copy the contents of the source cells.
Link Cells	Display the contents of the source cells in the target cells, updating the target cells whenever the content of the source cells changes.
Values Only	Paste the values from a column into the target column; use the existing format of the target column.
Values and Source Formatting	Paste a column of cells into the target column; apply the format of the copied column to the new column.

Troubleshooting

If the **Paste Options** button doesn't appear, you can turn the feature on by clicking **Options** on the **Tools** menu. In the dialog box that appears, click the **Edit** tab and then select the **Show Paste Options buttons** check box.

ZeroIn

In this exercise, you move from one worksheet to another to examine data about products The Garden Company sells, and then you select a range of cells whose contents you want to copy to the Summary sheet in your workbook. After you have copied and pasted that information, you select the first three columns of your Summary worksheet, copy them to the Clipboard, and move the columns (and their contents) over one column to make the first column available for text indicating which worksheet specific sets of data came from.

1 Navigate to the Chap05 practice folder, and open the file ZeroIn.xls.

2 In the lower left corner of the Excel window, click the **Furniture** sheet tab.

The Furniture worksheet appears.

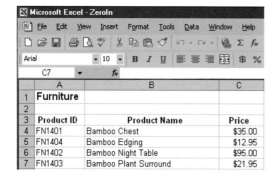

3   On the tab bar, right-click the arrow buttons and then, from the shortcut menu that appears, click **Passiflora**.

The Passiflora worksheet appears.

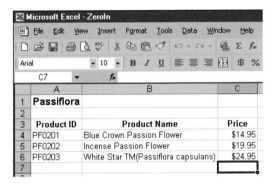

4   Click the **Tools** sheet tab to make the Tools sheet the active worksheet in the workbook.

5   Click **cell A3**.

Cell A3 becomes the active cell in the worksheet. The value in cell A3, *Product ID*, appears in the formula bar, and the cell identifier appears in the Name box.

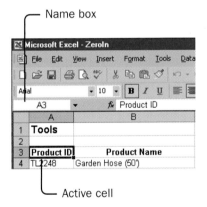

6   Drag from cell A3 to cell C6.

The selected cells are highlighted.

Copy

7   On the Standard toolbar, click the **Copy** button.

The contents of the selected cells are copied to the Clipboard. The selected cells retain their contents and are surrounded by a marquee outline (an outline that seems to move around the edge of the cells).

8   Click the **Summary** sheet tab.

Paste

9   The Summary sheet appears. Click **cell A3**, and then, on the Standard toolbar, click the **Paste** button.

      The values in the cells you copied appear in cells A3 to C6 of the Summary sheet.

Tip

In previous versions of Excel, you had to select the cells that were the destination for the values you copied. If the destination area wasn't the same size as the copied area, Excel wouldn't let the paste proceed. In this version of Excel, all you need to do is click the cell in the upper left corner of the group of cells that you want to hold the data and then paste the data into the sheet. The exception, which you will encounter later in this chapter, occurs when you cut and paste entire columns or rows.

10   Click the **Tools** sheet tab.

      The Tools worksheet appears.

11   Click the **Name box**.

      The value in the Name box is highlighted.

12   In the Name box, type **B9** and press Enter.

      Cell B9 is highlighted with the value *Long-handled Loppers*.

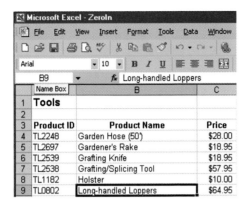

13 Click the **Name box**, type **B14**, and press Enter.

Cell B14 is highlighted with the value *Pruning Saw*.

14 Click the **Summary** sheet tab.

The Summary worksheet appears.

15 Click the column heading for column A.

Every cell in column A, including the column heading, is highlighted.

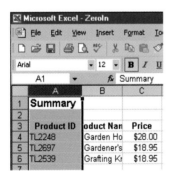

16 Drag to the column heading for column C.

Every cell in columns A through C, including the column headings, is high-lighted.

Cut

17 On the Standard toolbar, click the **Cut** button.

18 Click the column heading for column B, and drag to the column heading for column D.

Every cell in columns B through D, including the column headings, is highlighted.

19 On the **Edit** menu, click **Paste**.

The contents of the Clipboard appear in columns B through D.

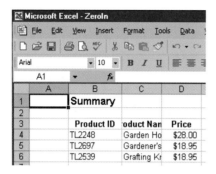

20 On the Standard toolbar, click the **Save** button to save your changes.

Close

21 Click the **Close** button to close ZeroIn.xls.

Tip

To select cell A1 in the active worksheet (that is, to return to the top of a worksheet immediately), press Ctrl + Home.

Creating a Workbook

Every time you want to gather and store data that isn't closely related to any of your existing data, you should create a new workbook. The default new workbook in the current version of Excel has three worksheets, although you can add more worksheets or delete existing worksheets if you want. Creating a new workbook is a straightforward process—you just click the appropriate button on the toolbar.

Once you have created a workbook, you can begin entering data. The simplest way to enter data is to click a cell and type a value, a method that works very well when you're entering a few pieces of data but that is less than ideal when you're entering long sequences or series of values. For example, Catherine Turner, the owner of The Garden Company, might want to create a worksheet listing hourly sales figures for the company from 1:00 p.m. to 7:00 p.m. for weekdays. To record those numbers, she would need to create a worksheet with the following layout.

Typing the sequence *Monday, Tuesday, Wednesday, Thursday, Friday* repeatedly can be avoided by copying and pasting the first occurrence of the sequence, but there's an easier way to do it using **AutoFill**. With AutoFill, you enter the first element in a recognized series, grab the **fill handle** at the lower right corner of the cell, and drag the fill handle until the series extends far enough to accommodate your data. A similar tool, **FillSeries**, lets you enter two values in a series and use the fill handle to extend the series in your worksheet. For example, if you want to create a series starting at 2 and increasing by 2, you would put *2* in the first cell and *4* in the second cell, select both cells, and then use the fill handle to extend the series to your desired end value.

Other data entry techniques you'll use in this section are **AutoComplete**, which detects when a value you're entering is similar to previously entered values; **Pick from List**, which lets you choose a value from existing values in a column; and Ctrl+Enter, which lets you enter a value in multiple cells simultaneously.

The following table summarizes these data entry techniques.

Method	Action
AutoFill	Enter the first value in a recognized series, and use the fill handle to extend the series.
FillSeries	Enter the first two values in a series, and use the fill handle to extend the series.
AutoComplete	Type the first few letters in a cell, and if a similar value exists in the same column, Excel will suggest the existing value.
Pick from List	Right-click a cell, and from the pop-up menu that appears, choose **Pick from List**. A list of existing values in the cell's column will appear.
Ctrl+Enter	Select a range of cells to contain the same data, type the data in the active cell, and press Ctrl+Enter.

Fill Options
new for
OfficeXP

A new feature in the current version of Excel is the **Auto Fill Options** button that appears next to data you add to a worksheet using either AutoFill or FillSeries.

Clicking the **Auto Fill Options** button displays a list of actions Excel can take regarding the cells affected by your Fill operation. The options in the list are summarized in the following table.

Option	Action
Copy Cells	Copy the contents of the selected cells to the cells indicated by the Fill operation.
Fill Series	Fill the cells indicated by the Fill operation with the next items in the series.
Fill Formatting Only	Copy the format of the selected cell to the cells indicated by the Fill operation, but do not place any values in the target cells.
Fill Without Formatting	Fill the cells indicated by the Fill operation with the next items in the series, but ignore any formatting applied to the source cells.
Fill <sequence>	This option changes according to the series Excel detects and seems to have the same effect as the Fill Series option. If you do not use a recognized sequence, the option does not appear.

Troubleshooting

If the **Auto Fill Options** button doesn't appear, you can turn the feature on by clicking **Options** on the **Tools** menu. In the dialog box that appears, click the **Edit** tab and then select the **Show Paste Options buttons** check box.

In this exercise, you create a workbook to track the number of customers of The Garden Company making purchases during a two-hour period for three days. The workbook will eventually have sheets recording the total number of customers making purchases (by quarter hour), items sold, and number of items in a given transaction. You use the data entry methods described earlier in this section, such as AutoFill, FillSeries, and $\boxed{\text{Ctrl}}+\boxed{\text{Enter}}$, to fill in the worksheets.

New

1 On the Standard toolbar, click the **New** button.

A blank workbook appears.

Save

2 On the Standard toolbar, click the **Save** button.

The **Save** dialog box appears.

3 If necessary, navigate to the Office XP SBS\Excel\Chap05 folder on your hard disk.

4 In the **File name** box, type **SalesTrack**.

Excel adds the .xls extension to your file.

5 Click **Save**.

Excel saves your file as SalesTrack.xls.

6 Click **cell B6**, and type **Day**.

7 Click **cell C5**, and type **Time**.

8 Click **cell B8**, and type **Wed**.

A black box appears around cell B8.

9 Move the mouse pointer over the lower right corner of cell B8.

The mouse pointer changes to a black plus sign, as shown on the next page.

10 Click the black plus sign at the lower right corner of cell B8, and drag it to cell B10.

Excel fills cell B9 with the value *Thu* and cell B10 with *Fri*. As you drag over cells B9 and B10, Excel displays a ScreenTip indicating which value will appear in each cell.

11 Click **cell C6**, and type **3:00**; then click cell D6, and type **3:15**.

Tip

You give Excel two values when you use FillSeries: the first value sets the starting point for the series, and the second sets the increment. In this example, 3:15 is 15 minutes greater than the starting value of 3:00, so Excel adds 15 minutes to the current cell to generate the value for the next cell in the series.

12 Click **cell C6**, and drag to cell D6.

A black box appears around cells C6 and D6.

13 Move the mouse pointer over the lower right corner of cell D6.

When the mouse pointer is over the lower right corner of the cell, it changes to a black plus sign.

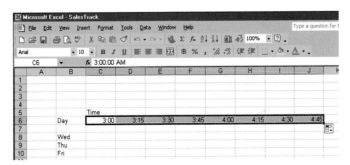

14 Click the black plus sign at the lower right corner of cell D6, and drag it to cell J6.

Excel fills the six cells from E6 through J6 with the next values in the series, namely 3:30 to 4:45, in 15-minute increments.

15 On the Standard toolbar, click the **Save** button to save your changes.

Close

16 Click the **Close** button to close SalesTrack.xls.

DataEntry

17 On the Standard toolbar, click the **Open** button.

The **Open** dialog box appears.

18 Click **DataEntry**, and then click **Open**.

DataEntry.xls appears.

19 Click the **Sheet2** sheet tab.

Sheet2 appears.

20 Click **cell C8** and type **Bamboo S**, but do not press ⌷Enter⌷.

Just after you type the S, Excel searches the existing items in the column and, finding a match, adds the highlighted text *takes (30 cnt)* to the contents of the cell, as shown on the next page.

21 To accept the suggested value, *Bamboo Stakes (30 cnt)*, for the cell, press the [Enter] key.

Excel completes the cell entry.

Important

Pressing [Del] before pressing [Enter] (or [Tab]) will delete the highlighted text and keep *Bamboo S* as the value of the cell you were editing.

22 Click **cell C9** and type **Bamboo T**, but do not press [Enter].

Just after you type the *T*, Excel adds the highlighted text *rellis*.

23 Press [Tab] to accept the suggested value, *Bamboo Trellis*.

Bamboo Trellis appears in cell C9.

24 Right-click **cell C10**, and on the shortcut menu that appears, click **Pick from List**.

A list of existing values in the column appears.

25 Click **Bird Netting**.

Bird Netting appears in cell C10.

26 Click the **Sheet1** sheet tab.

Sheet1 appears.

27 Drag from cell C8 to cell J10.

Excel highlights the cells in the rectangle defined at the upper left by cell C8 and at the lower right by cell J10. Note that cell C8 is still the active cell.

28 Type **0**, and press Ctrl + Enter.

The value *0* appears in every selected cell.

29 On the Standard toolbar, click the **Save** button to save your changes.

30 Click the **Close** button.

31 DataEntry.xls closes.

Checking and Correcting Data

Once you've entered your data, you should take the time to check and correct it. You do need to verify visually that each piece of numeric data is correct, but you can make sure that the text is spelled correctly by using the Excel Spell Checker. When the Spell Checker encounters a word it doesn't recognize, it will highlight the word and offer suggestions representing its best guess as to the correct word. You can then edit the word directly, pick the proper word from the list of suggestions, or have the Spell Checker ignore the misspelling. You can also use the Spell Checker to add any words that aren't in the standard dictionary so that Excel will recognize them later, saving you time by not requiring you to identify the words as correct every time they occur in your worksheets. Once you've made a change, you can remove the change so long as you haven't closed the workbook where you made the change. To undo a change, you click the appropriate toolbar button or open the **Edit** menu and choose the Undo command. If you decide you want to keep a change, you can use the **Redo** command to restore it.

Find by Format
new for
OfficeXP

You can use a distinct text format to identify data you may need to change later. As an example, a sales rep for one of The Garden Company's suppliers might give The Garden Company's owner, Catherine Turner, a list of prices for upcoming products, with a note that those prices could change at any time. Catherine could format the changeable prices differently from the rest of the prices in the worksheet and call the rep to update her worksheet just before the products became available. After she got the new prices, she could use **Find Format** in the **Find and Replace** dialog box to locate the old prices and then change them by hand.

Replace

In this exercise, you have just found out that the manufacturer of the Comfy Chair has changed the name of the product to Cushy Chair. You use **Find** to determine whether there are any occurrences of the word *Comfy*, and if there are, you use **Replace** to change them to *Cushy*. After you have made that change, you use **Find Format** to locate specially formatted data and change it. Finally, you use the Spell Checker to ensure that your text data has been entered correctly.

Open

1 On the Standard toolbar, click the **Open** button.

The **Open** dialog box appears.

2 Click **Replace.xls**, and then click **Open**.

Replace.xls appears.

3 If necessary, click the **Furniture** sheet tab to display the Furniture worksheet.

4 On the **Edit** menu, click **Find**.

The **Find and Replace** dialog box appears and opens to the **Find** tab.

Tip

You can also open the **Find and Replace** dialog box by pressing Ctrl+F.

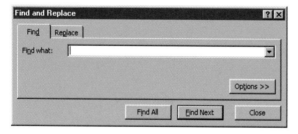

5 In the **Find what** box, type **Comfy**, and then click **Find Next**.

The first cell containing *Comfy* is highlighted.

6 In the **Find and Replace** dialog box, click **Find Next** again.

The second cell containing *Comfy* is highlighted.

Tip

Clicking **Find All** would generate a list of matching cells and their contents below the dialog box. Clicking one of the matches moves you to that instance of the matching word or phrase.

7   Click the **Replace** tab.

The **Find what** box still shows the word *Comfy*.

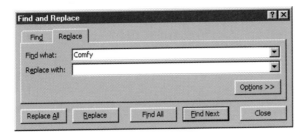

8   In the **Replace with** box, type **Cushy**.

9   Click **Replace All**.

A dialog box appears, indicating that Excel has completed the operation and that three replacements were made.

10   Click **OK**.

The three occurrences of the word *Comfy* have been switched to *Cushy*.

Important

You can change the occurrences of the word *Comfy* one at a time by clicking the **Replace** button instead of the **Replace All** button. You might do so to ensure that there are no instances in which you don't want to replace the original word.

11   In the **Find and Replace** dialog box, click the **Find** tab.

The **Find** tab page appears.

12   Clear the **Find what** box.

13   Click the **Options** button to expand the options on the **Find** tab page.

The **Find** tab page options appear.

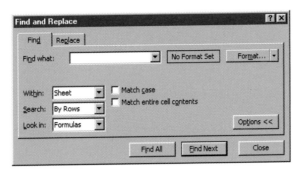

14   Click the **Format** button.

The **Find Format** dialog box appears.

15   If necessary, click the **Font** tab.

The **Font** tab page appears.

16   In the **Font style** list, click the word *Italic*, and then click **OK**.

The **Find Format** dialog box disappears.

17   In the **Find and Replace** dialog box, click **Find Next**.

Excel highlights the first cell containing italicized text.

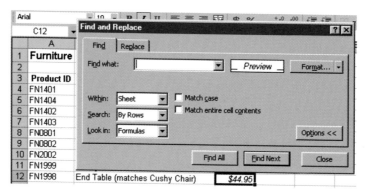

18   Click **cell C12**.

Italic

I

19   On the Formatting toolbar, click the **Italic** button.

Excel removes italics from the text in the selected cell.

10	FN2002	Cedar Planter Box	$59.95
11	FN1999	Cushy Chair	$119.95
12	FN1998	End Table (matches Cushy Chair)	$44.95
13	FN1997	Foot Stool (matches Cushy Chair)	$49.95
14	FN3402	Northeastern Arbo	$199.95

20 Type **47.95** and press ⌜Enter⌝.

Excel replaces the previous value in the cell with the value you just entered. You will now undo the change you just made.

Undo

21 On the Standard toolbar, click the **Undo** button.

The contents of cell C12 revert to 44.95.

22 Click the **Undo** button.

The contents of cell C12 are once again italicized.

Redo

23 Click the **Redo** button.

The contents of cell C12 are no longer italicized.

24 On the **Tools** menu, click **Spelling**.

The **Spelling** dialog box appears. The first misspelled word Excel detects appears in the **Not in Dictionary** box, while the list of suggested replacements appears in the **Suggestions** list.

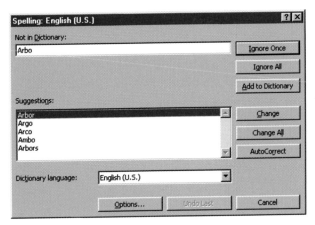

25 If necessary, in the **Suggestions** list, click *Arbor* and then click **Change**.

Excel changes *Arbo* to *Arbor* and displays a dialog box indicating that it found no more misspellings.

26 Click **OK**.

The dialog box disappears.

Tip

If you click **Change**, Excel inserts the suggested word. If you wanted Excel to ignore this occurrence of *Arbo*, you could have clicked **Ignore Once**; clicking **Ignore All** would cause Excel to skip over any occurrence of *Arbo* in the worksheet. Clicking **Add to Dictionary** means Excel would forever recognize *Arbo* as a word that did not need to be corrected.

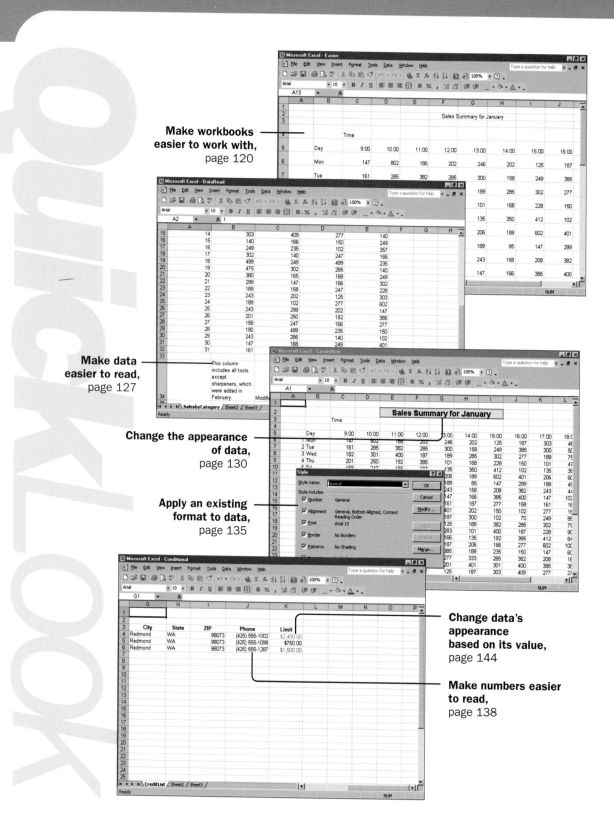

Make workbooks easier to work with, page 120

Make data easier to read, page 127

Change the appearance of data, page 130

Apply an existing format to data, page 135

Change data's appearance based on its value, page 144

Make numbers easier to read, page 138

Chapter 6
Making Changes to Your Workbook

After completing this chapter, you will be able to:

✔ Make workbooks easier to work with.

✔ Make data easier to read.

✔ Change the appearance of data.

✔ Apply an existing format to data.

✔ Make numbers easier to read.

✔ Change data's appearance based on its value.

One of the real strengths of Excel is that the program helps you manage large quantities of data with ease and ensures that the data is easy to read. Part of the reason managing large data collections is so easy with Excel is that you can change how Excel displays your data within a worksheet. If you want more space between the rows or columns of a worksheet, want to temporarily limit which data is shown on the screen, or even just want to add descriptions that make it easier for you and your colleagues to understand the data that's stored on a worksheet, you can do so quickly. Excel also gives you a wide variety of ways to make your data easier to understand; for example, you can change the font, letter size, or color used to present a cell's contents. You can also change how those descriptions appear in a cell, setting them apart from the data in the worksheet.

You might also want to specially format a cell's contents to reflect the value in that cell. For instance, Catherine Turner, the owner of The Garden Company, might grant some of The Garden Company's better customers credit, use Excel to track each customer's purchases, and use that information to determine which customers are close to their credit limit. A quick way to distinguish when a customer is close to their credit limit is to change how their outstanding balance is presented in its cell. Catherine might, for example, change the color of the font from the standard black to blue when a customer is within 10 percent of their limit.

In this chapter, you'll learn how to change the appearance of data and make it easier to read, apply existing formats to data, make numbers easier to read, and change data's appearance based on its value.

This chapter uses the practice files Easier, DataRead, Formats, CreateNew, EasyRead, and Conditional that you installed from this book's CD-ROM. For details about installing the practice files, see "Using the Book's CD-ROM" at the beginning of this book.

Making Workbooks Easier to Work With

An important component of making workbooks easy to work with is to give users an idea where to find the data they're looking for. Excel gives you several ways to set up signposts directing users toward the data they want. The first method is to give each workbook a descriptive name. Once users have opened the proper workbook, you can guide them to a specific worksheet by giving each worksheet a name; the names are displayed on the sheet tabs in the lower left corner of the workbook window. To change a worksheet's name, you right-click the sheet tab of the worksheet you want and, from the shortcut menu that appears, choose **Rename**. Choosing **Rename** opens the worksheet name for editing. You can also change the order of worksheets in a workbook by dragging the sheet tab of a worksheet to the desired position on the navigation bar, bringing the most popular worksheets to the front of the list.

After you have put up the signposts that make your data easy to find, you can take other steps to make the data in your workbooks easier to work with. For instance, you can change the width of a column or the height of a row in a worksheet by dragging the column or row's border to the desired position. Increasing a column's width or a row's height increases the space between cell contents, making it easier to select a cell's data without inadvertently selecting data from other cells as well.

Tip

You can apply the same change to more than one row or column by selecting the rows or columns you want to change and then dragging the border of one of the selected rows or columns to the desired location. When you release the mouse button, all of the selected rows or columns will change to the new height or width.

Changing column width and row height can make a workbook's contents easier to work with, but you can also insert a row or column between the edge of a worksheet and the cells containing the data. Adding space between the edge of a worksheet and cells, or perhaps between a label and the data to which it refers, makes the workbook's contents less crowded and easier to work with. You insert rows by clicking a cell and then, on the main menu bar, clicking **Insert** and then clicking **Rows**. Excel inserts a row above the active cell. You insert a column in much the same way, but you click **Insert** and then click **Columns**. When you do, Excel inserts a column to the left of the active cell.

Merge and
Center

Sometimes changing a row's height or a column's width isn't the best way to improve your workbook's usability. For instance, even though a worksheet's label might not fit within a single cell, increasing that cell's width (or every cell's width) might throw off the worksheet's design. While you can type individual words in cells so that the label fits in the worksheet, another alternative is to **merge** two or more cells. Merging cells tells Excel to treat a group of cells as a single cell as far as content and formatting go. To merge cells into a single cell, you click the **Merge and Center** toolbar button. As the name of the button implies, Excel centers the contents of the merged cell.

Tip

Clicking a merged cell and then clicking the **Merge and Center** toolbar button removes the merge.

If you want to delete a row or column, you right-click the row or column head and then, from the shortcut menu that appears, click **Delete**. You can temporarily hide a number of rows or columns by selecting those rows or columns and then, on the **Format** menu, pointing to **Row** or **Column** and then clicking **Hide**. The rows or columns you selected disappear, but they aren't gone for good, as they would be if you'd used **Delete**. Instead, they have just been removed from the display until you call them back; to return the hidden rows to the display, on the **Format** menu, point to **Row** or **Column** and then click **Unhide**.

Insert Options
new for
OfficeXP

When you insert a row or column in a worksheet with existing formatting, the **Insert Options** button appears. As with the **Paste Options** button and the **Auto Fill Options** button, clicking the **Insert Options** button displays a list of choices you can make about how the inserted row or column should be formatted. The options are summarized in the following table.

Option	Action
Format Same as Above	Apply the format of the row above the inserted row to the new row.
Format Same as Below	Apply the format of the row below the inserted row to the new row.
Format Same as Left	Apply the format of the column to the left of the inserted column to the new column.
Format Same as Right	Apply the format of the column to the right of the inserted column to the new column.
Clear Formatting	Apply the default format to the new row or column.

121

Easier

In this exercise, you make the worksheet containing last January's sales data easier to read. First, you name the worksheet and bring it to the front of the list of worksheets in its workbook. Next, you increase the column width and row height of the cells holding the sales data. In addition, you merge and center the worksheet's title and then add a row between the title and the row that holds the times for which The Garden Company recorded sales. Finally, you add a column to the left of the first column of data and then hide rows containing data for all but the first week of the month.

Open

1   On the Standard toolbar, click the **Open** button.

The **Open** dialog box appears.

2   If necessary, navigate to the Office XP SBS folder, and then double-click the **Excel** folder to display its contents.

The files and folders in the Excel folder appear.

3   Double-click the **Chap06** folder.

The files in the Chap06 folder appear.

4   Double-click the **Easier.xls** file.

The Easier.xls file opens.

5   In the lower left corner of the workbook window, right-click the **Sheet2** sheet tab.

6   From the shortcut menu that appears, click **Rename.**

Sheet2 is highlighted.

7   Type **January**, and press ⁣`Enter`⁣.

The name of the worksheet changes from Sheet2 to January.

20	Tue	202	102	277
21	Wed	300	401	150
22	Thu	189	299	102
23	Fri	101	166	401
24	Sat	135	235	299
25	Sun	206	140	382

Sheet1 \ **January** / Sheet3 /

Ready

8   Click the **January** sheet tab, and drag it to the left of the **Sheet1** sheet tab.

The **January** sheet tab moves to the left of the **Sheet1** sheet tab. As the sheet tab moves, an inverted black triangle marks the sheet's location in the workbook.

21	Wed	300	401	150
22	Thu	189	299	102
23	Fri	101	166	401
24	Sat	135	235	299
25	Sun	206	140	382

January / Sheet1 / Sheet3 /

Ready

9   Click the column head for column A, and drag to column M.

Columns A through M are highlighted.

10 Position the mouse pointer over the right edge of column A, and drag the edge to the right until the ScreenTip says *Width: 10.00 (75 pixels)*.

The width of the selected columns changes.

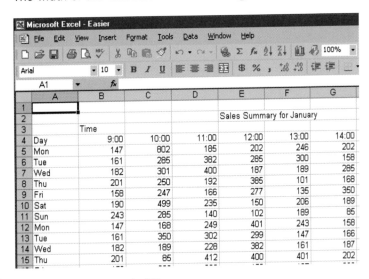

11 Select rows 3 through 35.

Rows 3 through 35 are highlighted.

12 Position the mouse pointer over the bottom edge of row 3, and drag the edge down until the ScreenTip says *Height: 25.50 (34 pixels)*.

The height of the selected rows changes.

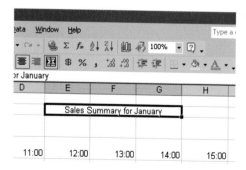

	A	B	C	D	E	F	G
1							
2					Sales Summary for January		
3		Time					
4	Day	9:00	10:00	11:00	12:00	13:00	14:00
5	Mon	147	802	185	202	246	202
6	Tue	161	285	382	285	300	158
7	Wed	182	301	400	187	189	285
8	Thu	201	250	192	385	101	168

13 Click **cell E2**, and drag to cell G2.

14 On the Formatting toolbar, click the **Merge and Center** toolbar button.

Cells E2, F2, and G2 are merged into a single cell, and the new cell's contents are centered.

Important

Depending on the screen resolution you have set on your computer and which toolbar buttons you use most often, it's possible that not every button on every toolbar will appear on your Excel toolbars. If a button mentioned in this book doesn't appear on a toolbar, click the **Toolbar Options** down arrow on that toolbar to display the rest of the buttons available on that toolbar.

	D	E	F	G	H
		Sales Summary for January			
	11:00	12:00	13:00	14:00	15:00

15 Click **cell A3**.

16 On the main menu bar, click **Insert** and then click **Rows**.

A new row, labeled row 3, appears above the row previously labeled row 3.

17 On the main menu bar, click **Insert** and then click **Columns**.

A new column, labeled column A, appears to the left of the column previously labeled column A.

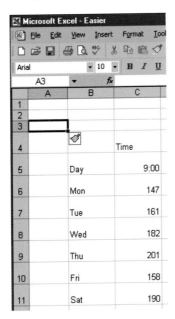

18 Select rows 13 through 36.

Rows 13 through 36 are highlighted.

19 On the main menu bar, click **Format**, then click **Row**, and then click **Hide**.

Rows 13 through 36 disappear from the worksheet.

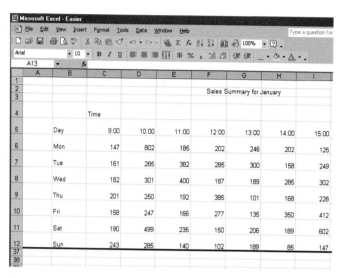

20 On the main menu bar, click **Format**, then click **Row**, and then click **Unhide**.

The hidden rows reappear in the worksheet.

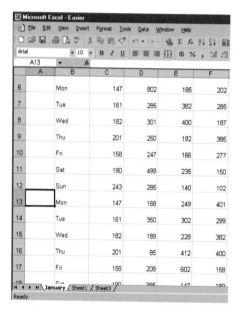

Save

21 On the Standard toolbar, click the **Save** button.

Excel saves the document.

Close

22 Click the **Close** button.

The file Easier.xls closes.

Making Data Easier to Read

After you have modified your worksheet so it is easier to work with, you can make the data easier to read by modifying how data is presented within the worksheet's cells. One case in which you might want to change how data is presented occurs if the data doesn't fit in a cell's boundaries and you don't want to merge the cells the data overlaps with. For instance, you could choose not to merge the cells because you might want to add data or comments to the neighboring cells later.

The following graphic shows what happens if there is a spillover in two adjacent cells.

161	350	302
This column include	Modified to remove overlap with Tools.	

If the right-hand cell were empty, the text in the left-hand cell would simply spill over into the right-hand cell. When there is data in the right-hand cell, however, Excel brings it to the front, hiding any data that spills over from the adjoining cell. To avoid hiding the text in the first cell behind the text in the second cell, you can have the text wrap within the first cell, as seen in the following graphic.

	This column includes all tools except sharpeners, which were added in	
34	February.	Modified to remove overlap with Tools.

Tip

It may be tempting to just change a column's width to accommodate your data, but remember that widening a single column will make that column stand out in the worksheet, possibly making data in other columns harder to read.

Another way you can make your data easier to read is to distinguish any data labels by changing how the data appears in a cell. One way to separate data labels from the data that follows them is to change the **alignment** of the labels in their cells. For example, you can center the data labels in their cells, setting the labels apart from the right-aligned data farther down in the column.

You can also make your worksheet data easier to read by ensuring that the data labels at the top of a column **freeze**, or remain on the screen regardless of how far down in the document you scroll. For instance, Catherine Turner, the owner of The Garden Company, might not remember which data is kept in which column on a worksheet. Freezing the data labels at the top of the column would let her scroll to the last row of the worksheet and still have the labels available as a reference. Excel marks the division between frozen and unfrozen cells with a **split bar**.

Split bar

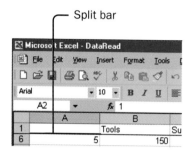

Troubleshooting

When you tell Excel to freeze rows in your worksheet, Excel freezes the rows above the active cell. So if you want to freeze the top three rows of your worksheet, click a cell in the fourth row and then turn on the freeze.

DataRead

In this exercise, you prevent the text in a cell from spilling over into adjoining cells, allowing you to enter comments in those adjoining cells without obscuring the contents of the first cell. You then change the alignment of the cells containing the data labels for the columns in your worksheet and then freeze those data labels so that they remain at the top of the page as you scroll down through the worksheet.

Open

1   On the Standard toolbar, click the **Open** button.

The **Open** dialog box appears.

2   Double-click the **DataRead.xls** file.

DataRead.xls opens.

3   If necessary, click the **SalesbyCategory** sheet tab.

4   Click **cell B34**.

5 On the **Format** menu, click **Cells**.

The **Format Cells** dialog box appears.

6 If necessary, click the **Alignment** tab.

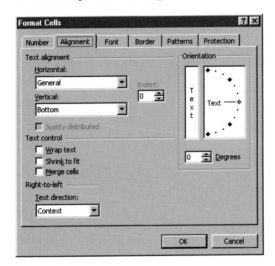

7 Select the **Wrap Text** check box, and click **OK**.

The text in cell B34 wraps to fit within the original borders of the cell.

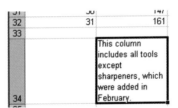

8 Click **cell B1** and drag to cell E1.

Center

9 On the Formatting toolbar, click the **Center** button.

The contents of the selected cells are centered within those cells.

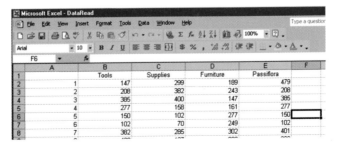

10 Click **cell A2**.

11 On the **Window** menu, click **Freeze Panes**.

A split bar appears between row 1 and row 2.

12 On the vertical scroll bar, click the down arrow.

Row 1 stays in place while the remaining rows scroll normally.

	A	B Tools	C Supplies	D Furniture	E Passiflora	F
15	14	303	409	277	140	
16	15	140	166	150	249	
17	16	249	235	102	357	
18	17	302	140	247	166	
19	18	499	249	499	235	
20	19	475	302	285	140	
21	20	380	165	168	249	
22	21	299	147	166	302	
23	22	189	158	247	228	
24	23	243	202	125	303	
25	24	189	102	277	602	
26	25	243	299	202	147	
27	26	201	250	192	385	
28	27	158	247	166	277	
29	28	190	499	235	150	
30	29	243	285	140	102	
31	30	147	168	249	401	
32	31	161	350	302	299	

13 On the **Window** menu, click **Unfreeze Panes**.

The split bar disappears, and all rows scroll normally.

Save

14 On the Standard toolbar, click the **Save** button.

Excel saves your changes.

Close

15 Click the **Close** button.

The file DataRead.xls closes.

Changing the Appearance of Data

Excel spreadsheets can hold and process lots of data, but when you manage numerous spreadsheets it can be hard to remember by a worksheet's title exactly what data is kept on that worksheet. Data labels give you and your colleagues information about data in a worksheet, but it's important to format the labels so they stand out visually. To make your data labels or any other data stand out, you can change the format of the cells in which the data is stored.

		Time	
Day		9:00 AM	10:00 AM
1 Mon		$ 147.00	$ 802.00
2 Tue		$ 161.00	$ 285.00
3 Wed		$ 182.00	$ 301.00
4 Thu		$ 201.00	$ 250.00

Most of the tools you need to change a cell's format can be found on the Formatting toolbar.

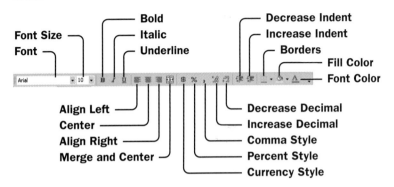

Depending on the screen resolution you have set on your computer and which tool-bar buttons you use most often, it's possible that not every button on every toolbar will appear on your Excel toolbars. If a button mentioned in this book doesn't appear on a toolbar, click the **Toolbar Options** down arrow on that toolbar to display the rest of its buttons.

Bold

B

You can apply the formatting represented by a toolbar button by selecting the cells to which you want to apply the style and then clicking the appropriate button. If you want to set your data labels apart by making them appear in boldface, click the **Bold** button. If you have already made a cell's contents bold, selecting the cell and clicking the **Bold** button will remove the formatting.

Tip

Deleting a cell's contents doesn't delete the cell's formatting. To delete a cell's for-matting, select the cell and then, on the **Edit** menu, point to **Clear**, and click **Formats**.

Items on the Formatting toolbar that give you choices, such as the **Font Size** control, have a down arrow at the right edge of the control. Clicking the down arrow displays a list of options available for that control, such as the fonts available on your system or the colors you can assign to a cell.

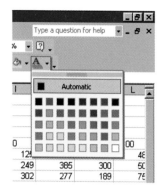

Borders

Another way you can make a cell stand apart from its neighbors is to add a border around the cell. In previous versions of Excel, you could select the cell or cells to which you wanted to add the border and use the options available under the Formatting toolbar's **Borders** button to assign a border to the cells. For example, you could select a group of cells and then choose the border type you wanted. That method of adding borders is still available in Excel, but it has some limitations. The most important limitation is that, while creating a simple border around a group of cells is easy, creating complex borders makes you select different groups of cells and apply different types of borders to them. The current version of Excel makes creating complex borders easy by letting you draw borders directly on the worksheet.

To use the new border-drawing capabilities, you display the Borders toolbar.

To draw a border around a group of cells, click the mouse pointer at one corner of the group and drag it to the diagonal corner. You will see your border expand as you move the mouse pointer. If you want to add a border in a vertical or horizontal line, drag the mouse pointer along the target grid line—Excel will add the line without expanding it to include the surrounding cells. You can also change the characteristics of the border you draw through the options on the Borders toolbar.

Another way you can make a group of cells stand apart from its neighbors is to change their shading, or the color that fills the cell. On a worksheet with monthly sales data for The Garden Company, for example, owner Catherine Turner could change the fill color of the cells holding her data labels to make the labels stand out even more than by changing the formatting of the text used to display the labels.

Formats

In this exercise, you change the format of cell data, add a border to a cell, and then change a cell's fill color.

Open

1   On the Standard toolbar, click the **Open** button.

The **Open** dialog box appears.

2   Navigate to the Office XP SBS\Excel\Chap06 folder, and double-click the **Formats.xls** file.

Formats.xls opens.

3   If necessary, click the **January** sheet tab.

4   Click **cell G2**.

Cell G2 is highlighted.

5   On the Formatting toolbar, click the **Font Size** down arrow and, from the list that appears, click **14**.

The text in cell G2 changes to 14-point type, and row 2 expands vertically to accommodate the text.

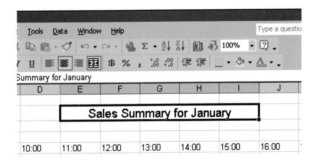

6   On the Formatting toolbar, click the **Bold** button.

The text in cell G2 appears in boldface.

7   Click the row head for row 5.

Row 5 is highlighted.

Center

8   On the Formatting toolbar, click the **Center** button.

The contents of the cells in row 5 are centered.

133

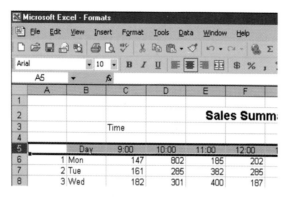

9 Click **cell G2**.

Cell G2 is highlighted.

Borders

10 On the Formatting toolbar, click the down arrow at the right of the **Borders** button and then, from the list that appears, click **Draw Borders**.

The Borders toolbar appears, and the mouse pointer changes to a pencil.

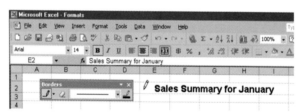

11 Click the left edge of **cell G2** and drag to the right edge.

A border appears around cell G2.

Close

12 On the Borders toolbar, click the **Close** button.

The Borders toolbar disappears.

FillColor

13 On the Formatting toolbar, click the **Fill Color** button.

The **Fill Color** color palette appears.

14 In the **Fill Color** color palette, click the yellow square.

Cell G2 fills with a yellow background.

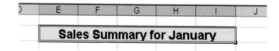

Save

15 On the Standard toolbar, click the **Save** button.

Excel saves your changes.

16 Click the **Close** button.

Formats.xls closes.

Applying an Existing Format to Data

As you work with Excel, you will probably develop preferred formats for data labels, titles, and other worksheet elements. Rather than add the format's characteristics one element at a time to the target cells, you can have Excel store the format and recall it as needed. You can find the predefined formats available to you in the **Style** dialog box.

You can apply an existing style to a cell from within the **Style** dialog box. If none of the existing styles are what you want, you can create your own by typing the name of your new style in the **Style name** box and then clicking **Modify**. The **Format Cells** dialog box appears.

Once you've set the characteristics of your new style, you click **OK** to make your style available permanently.

Format Painter

The **Style** dialog box is quite versatile, but it's overkill if all you want to do is apply formatting changes you made to a cell to the contents of another cell. To do so, you can use the Standard toolbar's **Format Painter** button; just click the cell with the format you want to copy, click the **Format Painter** button, and select the target cells.

CreateNew

In this exercise, you create a style, apply the new style to a data label, and then use the Format Painter to apply the style to the contents of another cell.

Open

1   On the Standard toolbar, click the **Open** button.

The **Open** dialog box appears.

2   Double-click the **CreateNew.xls** file.

CreateNew.xls opens.

3   If necessary, click the **January** sheet tab.

4   Click **cell C3**.

5   On the **Format** menu, click **Style**.

The **Style** dialog box appears, with *Normal* in the **Style name** box.

6   In the **Style name** box, delete the existing value and then type **Emphasis**.

The **Add** button is activated.

7   Click **Modify**.

The **Format Cells** dialog box appears.

8   If necessary, click the **Font** tab.

The **Font** tab page appears.

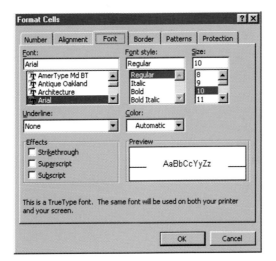

9 In the **Font style** box, click **Bold Italic**.

The text in the Preview pane, in the lower right corner of the dialog box, changes to reflect your choice.

10 Click the **Alignment** tab.

The **Alignment** tab page appears.

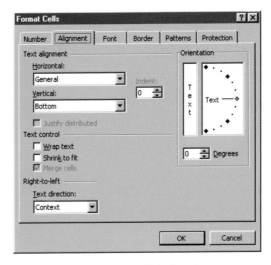

11 In the **Horizontal** box, click the down arrow and, from the list that appears, click **Center**.

12 Click **OK**.

The **Format Cells** dialog box disappears.

13 Click **OK**.

The **Style** dialog box disappears, and the text in cell C3 takes on the chosen style.

14 On the Standard toolbar, click the **Format Painter** button.

The mouse pointer changes to a white cross with a paintbrush icon next to it.

15 Click **cell B5**.

Cell B5 takes on the format of cell C3.

Save

16 On the Standard toolbar, click the **Save** button.

Excel saves your changes.

Close

17 Click the **Close** button.

CreateNew.xls closes.

Making Numbers Easier to Read

Changing the format of the cells in your worksheet can make your data much easier to read, both by setting data labels apart from the actual data and by adding borders to define the boundaries between labels and data even more clearly. Of course, using formatting options to change the font and appearance of a cell's contents doesn't help with idiosyncratic data types such as dates, phone numbers, or currency.

For example, consider U.S. phone numbers. These numbers are ten digits long and have a three-digit area code, a three-digit exchange, and a four-digit line number written in the form *(###) ###-####*. While it's certainly possible to type a phone number with the expected formatting in a cell, it's much simpler to type a sequence of ten digits and have Excel change the data's appearance.

You can tell Excel to expect a phone number in a cell by opening the **Format Cells** dialog box to the **Number** tab and displaying the formats available under the **Special** category.

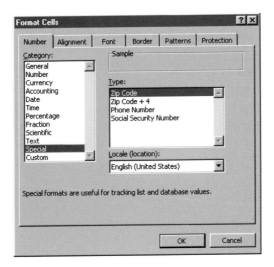

Clicking **Phone Number** from the **Type** list tells Excel to format ten-digit numbers in the standard phone number format. As you can see by comparing the contents of the active cell and the contents of the formula bar in the next graphic, the underlying data isn't changed, just its appearance in the cell.

Troubleshooting

If you type a nine-digit number in a field that expects a phone number, you won't see an error message; instead, you'll see a two-digit area code. For example, the number 425555012 would be displayed as (42) 555-5012. Eleven-digit numbers are displayed with a four-digit area code.

Just as you can have Excel expect a phone number in a cell, you can also have it expect a date or a currency amount. You can make those changes from the **Format Cells** dialog box by choosing either the **Date** category or the **Currency** category. The **Date** category lets you pick the format for the date (and determine whether the date's appearance changes due to the Locale setting of the operating system on the computer viewing the workbook). In a similar vein, selecting the **Currency** category displays controls to set the number of places after the decimal point, the currency symbol to use, and the way in which Excel should display negative numbers.

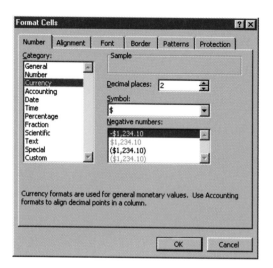

You can also create a custom numeric format to add a word or phrase to a number in a cell. For example, you can add the phrase *per month* to a cell with a formula that calculates average monthly sales for a year to ensure that you and your colleagues will recognize the figure as a monthly average. To create a custom number format, open the **Format** menu and click **Cells** to open the **Format Cells** dialog box. Then, if necessary, click the **Number** tab to display the **Number** tab page.

In the Category pane, click the **Custom** item to display the available custom number formats in the Type pane. You can then click the base format you want and modify it in the **Type** box. For example, clicking the *0.00* format has Excel format any number in a cell as a number with two digits to the right of the decimal point.

Tip

The zeros in the format mean that that place in the format can accept any number as a valid value.

To customize the format, click in the **Type** box and add to the format any symbols or text you want. For example, typing a dollar sign to the left of the existing format and then typing *"per month"* to the right of the existing format causes the number 1500 to be displayed as *$ 1500.00 per month*.

Important

You need to enclose any text in quotes so that Excel recognizes the text as a string to be displayed in the cell.

EasyRead

In this exercise, you assign date, phone number, and currency formats to ranges of cells in your worksheet. After you assign the formats, you test them by entering customer data.

Open

1 On the Standard toolbar, click the **Open** button.

The **Open** dialog box appears.

2 Double-click the **EasyRead.xls** file.

EasyRead.xls opens.

3 Click **cell B4**.

4 On the **Format** menu, click **Cells**.

The **Format Cells** dialog box appears.

5 If necessary, click the **Number** tab.

6 In the Category pane, click **Date**.

The Type pane appears with a list of date formats.

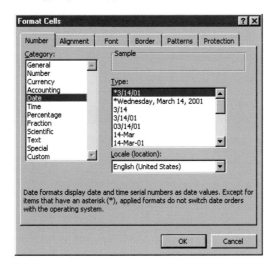

7 In the Type pane, click ***3/14/01**.

8 Click **OK**.

Excel assigns the chosen format to the cell.

Format Painter

9 On the Standard toolbar, click the **Format Painter** button.

Cell B4 is highlighted with a marquee outline.

10   Select **cell B5** and drag to cell B23.

Excel assigns the format from cell B4 to cells B5:B23.

11   Click **cell J4**.

12   On the **Format** menu, click **Cells**.

The **Format Cells** dialog box appears.

13   In the Category pane, click **Special**.

The Type pane appears with a list of Special formats.

14   In the Type pane, click **Phone Number** and then click **OK**.

The **Format Cells** dialog box disappears.

15   On the Standard toolbar, click the **Format Painter** button.

Cell J4 is highlighted with a marquee outline.

16   Select **cell J5** and drag to cell J23.

Excel assigns the format from cell J4 to cells J5:J23.

17   Click **cell K4**.

18   On the **Format** menu, click **Cells**.

The **Format Cells** dialog box appears.

19   In the Category pane, click **Custom**.

The contents of the **Type** box are updated to reflect your choice.

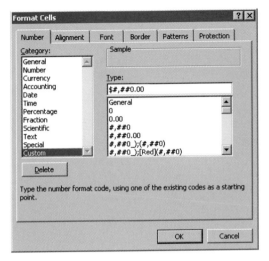

20 In the **Type** box, click the **#,##0.00** item.

#,##0.00 appears in the **Type** box.

21 In the **Type** box, click to the left of the existing format and type **$**, and then click to the right of the format and type **"total"**.

22 Click **OK**.

The **Format Cells** dialog box disappears.

23 On the **Standard** toolbar, click the **Format Painter** button.

Cell K4 is highlighted with a marquee outline.

24 Select **cell K5** and drag to cell K23.

Excel assigns the format from cell K4 to cells K5:K23.

25 In cell B4, type **January 25, 2001**, and press ⌨Enter.

The contents of cell B4 change to 1/25/01, matching the format you set earlier.

26 In cell C4, type **C100001**.

27 In cell D4, type **Steven**.

28 In cell E4, type **Levy**.

29 In cell F4, type **6789 Elm Street**.

30 In cell G4, type **Redmond**.

31 In cell H4, type **WA**.

32 In cell I4, type **98073**.

33 In cell J4, type **4255550102**.

The contents of the cell change to (425) 555-0102, matching the format you chose earlier.

34 In cell K4, type **2400**.

The contents of the cell change to *$2,400 total*, matching the format you created earlier.

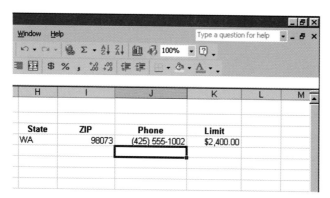

35 On the Standard toolbar, click **Save** to save your changes.

Close

36 Click the **Close** button to close EasyRead.xls.

Changing Data's Appearance Based on Its Value

Recording sales, credit limits, and other business data in a worksheet lets you make important decisions about your operations. And as you saw earlier in this chapter, you can change the appearance of data labels and the worksheet itself to make interpreting your data easier.

Another way you can make your data easier to interpret is to have Excel change the appearance of your data based on its value. These formats are called **conditional formats** because the data must meet certain conditions to have a format applied to it. For instance, if owner Catherine Turner wanted to highlight any Saturdays on which daily sales at The Garden Company were over $4,000, she could define a conditional format that tests the value in the cell recording total sales and that will change the format of the cell's contents when the condition is met.

To create a conditional format, you click the cells to which you want to apply the format and open the **Conditional Formatting** dialog box. The default configuration of the **Conditional Formatting** dialog box appears in the following graphic.

The first list box lets you choose whether you want the condition that follows to look at the cell's contents or the formula in the cell. In almost every circumstance, you will use the contents of the cell as the test value for the condition.

Tip

The only time you would want to set a formula as the basis for the condition would be to format a certain result, such as a grand total, the same way every time it appeared in a worksheet.

The second list box in the **Conditional Formatting** dialog box lets you select the comparison to be made. Depending on the comparison you choose, the dialog box will have either one or two boxes in which you enter values to be used in the comparison. The default comparison, *between*, requires two values, whereas comparisons such as *less than* require one.

After you have created a condition, you need to define the format to be applied to data that meets that condition. You do that in the **Format Cells** dialog box. From within this dialog box, you can set the characteristics of the text used to print the value in the cell. When you're done, a preview of the format you defined appears in the **Conditional Formatting** dialog box.

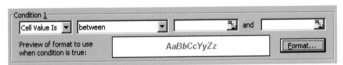

You're not limited to creating one condition per cell. If you like, you can create additional conditions by clicking the **Add** button in the **Conditional Formatting** dialog box. When you click the **Add** button, a second condition section appears.

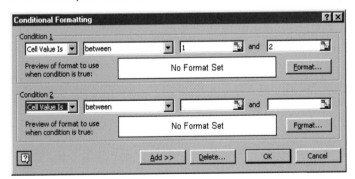

Important

Excel doesn't check to make sure your conditions are logically consistent, so you need to be sure you enter your conditions correctly.

Excel evaluates the conditions in the order you entered them in the **Conditional Formatting** dialog box and, upon finding a condition the data meets, stops its comparisons. For example, suppose Catherine wanted to visually separate the credit limits of The Garden Company's customers into two different categories: those with limits under $1,500 and those with limits from $1,500 to $2,500. She could display her customers' credit limits with a conditional format using the conditions in the following graphic.

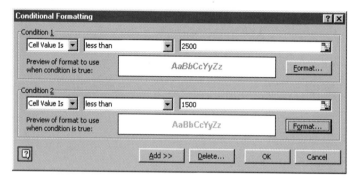

In this case, Excel would compare the value *1250* with the first condition, *<2500*, and assign that formatting to the cell containing the value. The fact that the second condition, *<1500*, is "closer" is irrelevant—once Excel finds a condition the data meets, it stops comparing.

Tip

You should always enter the most restrictive condition first. In the example presented above, setting the first condition to *<1500* and the second to *<2500* would result in the proper format being applied.

Conditional

Open

In this exercise, you create a series of conditional formats to change the appearance of data in worksheet cells listing the credit limit of The Garden Company's customers.

1 On the Standard toolbar, click the **Open** button.

The **Open** dialog box appears.

2 Double-click the **Conditional.xls** file.

Conditional.xls opens.

3 If necessary, click **cell K4**.

4 On the **Format** menu, click **Conditional Formatting**.

The **Conditional Formatting** dialog box appears.

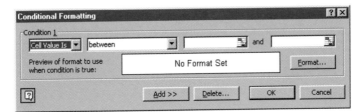

5 In the second list box, click the down arrow and then, from the list that appears, click *between*.

The word *between* appears in the second list box.

6 In the first argument box, type **1000**.

7 In the second argument box, type **2000**.

8 Click the **Format** button.

The **Format Cells** dialog box appears.

9 If necessary, click the **Font** tab.

The **Font** tab page appears.

10 In the **Color** box, click the down arrow and then, from the color palette that appears, click the blue square.

The color palette disappears, and the text in the Preview pane changes to blue.

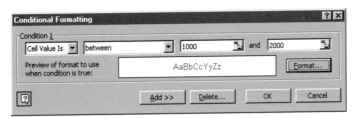

11 Click **OK**.

The **Format Cells** dialog box disappears.

12 Click the **Add** button.

The **Condition 2** section of the dialog box appears.

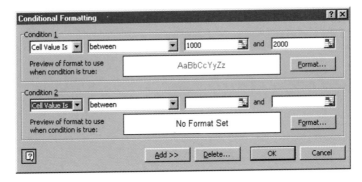

13 In the second list box, click the down arrow and then, from the list that appears, click *between*.

The word *between* appears in the second list box.

14 In the first argument box, type **2000**.

15 In the second argument box, type **2500**.

16 Click the **Format** button.

The **Format Cells** dialog box appears.

17 In the **Color** box, click the down arrow and then, from the color palette that appears, click the green square.

The color palette disappears, and the text in the Preview pane changes to green.

18 Click **OK**.

The **Format Cells** dialog box disappears.

19 Click **OK**.

The **Conditional Formatting** dialog box disappears.

20 In cell K4, click the **Fill Handle**, and drag it to cell K6.

FillOptions

The contents of cells K5 and K6 change to $2,400.00, and the **Auto Fill Options** button appears.

21 Click the **Auto Fill Options** button, and from the list that appears, click **Fill Formatting Only**.

The contents of cells K5 and K6 revert to their previous values, and Excel applies the conditional formats to the selected cells.

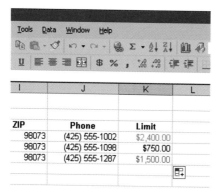

22 On the Standard toolbar, click the **Save** toolbar button to save your changes.

Close

23 Click the **Close** button to close Conditional.xls.

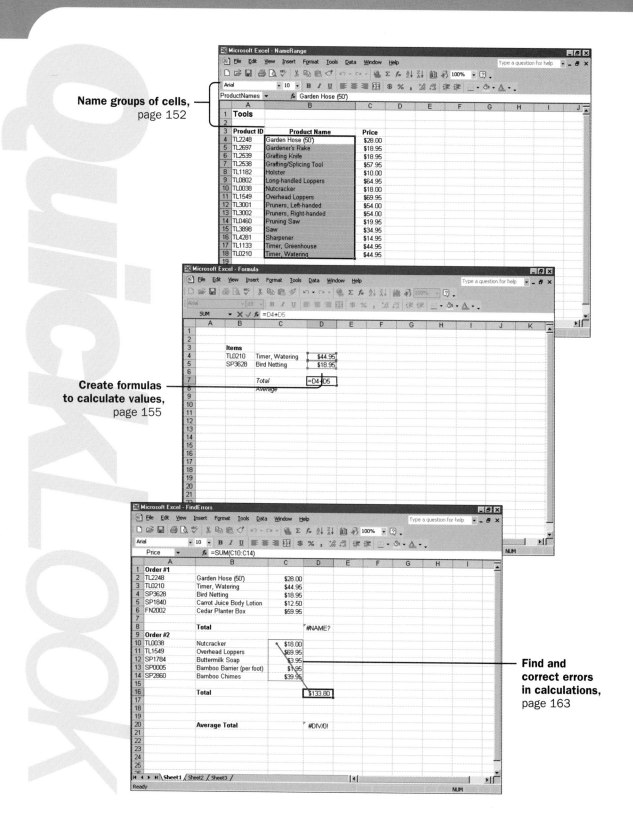

Name groups of cells, page 152

Create formulas to calculate values, page 155

Find and correct errors in calculations, page 163

Chapter 7
Performing Calculations on Data

After completing this chapter, you will be able to:

✔ Name groups of cells.
✔ Create formulas to calculate values.
✔ Find and correct errors in calculations.

Excel workbooks give you a handy place to store and organize your data, but you can do a lot more with your data in Excel. One important task you can perform in Excel is to calculate totals for the values in a series of related cells. You can also have Excel find out other things about the data you select, such as the maximum or minimum value in a group of cells. Finding the maximum or minimum value in a group can let you identify your best salesperson, product categories you might need to pay more attention to, or suppliers that consistently give you the best deal. Regardless of your bookkeeping needs, Excel gives you the ability to find the information you want. And if you should make an error, you can find the cause and correct it quickly.

Many times you can't access the information you want without referencing more than one cell, and it's also often true that you'll use the data in the same group of cells for more than one calculation. Excel makes it easy to reference a number of cells at once, letting you define your calculations quickly.

In this chapter, you'll learn how to streamline references to groups of data on your worksheets and to create and correct formulas that summarize the sales and product data from The Garden Company.

 This chapter uses the practice files NameRange, Formula, and FindErrors that you installed from this book's CD-ROM. For details about installing the practice files, see "Using the Book's CD-ROM" at the beginning of this book.

Naming Groups of Data

When you work with large amounts of data, it's easier to identify groups of cells that contain related data. In the following graphic, for example, cells C2 through C6 hold the prices of items from a customer's order.

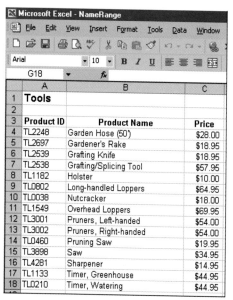

Rather than specify the cells individually every time you want to use the data they contain, you can define those cells as a **range** (also called a **named range**). For instance, you could group the items from the previous graphic into a range named *OrderItems1*. Whenever you wanted to use the contents of that range in a calculation, you could just use the name of the range instead of specifying each cell individually.

There are a number of ways to create a named range, two of which you can access through the **Insert** menu. The first method works well if you have a column of data with a label at the head of the column, as in the following graphic.

In this case, you access the **Create Name** dialog box by pointing to **Name** on the **Insert** menu and clicking **Create**. In the **Create Name** dialog box, you can define a named range by having Excel use the label in the top cell as the range's name. You can also create and delete named ranges through the **Define Name** dialog box, which you access by pointing to **Name** on the **Insert** menu and clicking **Define**.

A final way to create a named range is to select the cells you want in the range, click in the **Name** box next to the Formula bar, and then type the name for the range. You can display the ranges available in a workbook by clicking the **Name** box's down arrow.

Important

Every range in a workbook must have a unique name. Assigning the name of an existing range to a new range removes the original reference, likely affecting how your worksheet behaves.

NameRange

In this exercise, you will create named ranges to streamline references to groups of cells.

Open

1   On the Standard toolbar, click the **Open** button.

The **Open** dialog box appears.

2   Navigate to the Office XP SBS\Excel\Chap07 folder, and double-click the **NameRange.xls** file.

NameRange.xls opens.

3   If necessary, click the **Tools** sheet tab.

4   Click **cell C3** and drag to cell C18.

The selected cells are highlighted.

5   On the **Insert** menu, point to **Name**, and then click **Create**.

The **Create Names** dialog box appears.

6   If necessary, select the **Top row** check box.

7   Click **OK**.

Excel assigns the name *Price* to the cell range.

8   In the lower left corner of the workbook window, click the **Supplies** sheet tab.

The Supplies worksheet appears.

9   Click **cell C4** and drag to cell C29.

10 On the **Insert** menu, point to **Name**, and then click **Define**.

The **Define Name** dialog box appears.

11 In the **Names in workbook** box, type **SuppliesPrice** and then click **OK**.

Excel assigns the name *SuppliesPrice* to the cell range, and the **Define Name** dialog box disappears.

12 In the lower left corner of the workbook window, click the **Furniture** sheet tab.

The Furniture worksheet appears.

13 Click **cell C4** and drag to cell C18.

14 Click in the **Name** box.

The contents of the **Name** box are highlighted.

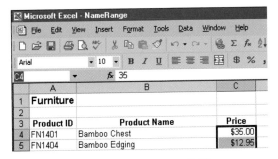

15 Type **FurniturePrice**, and press Enter.

Excel assigns the name *FurniturePrice* to the cell range.

16 On the **Insert** menu, point to **Name**, and then click **Define**.

The **Define Name** dialog box appears.

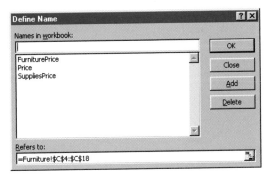

17 In the lower pane of the **Define Name** dialog box, click **Price**.

18 Price appears in the **Names in workbook** box.

19 In the **Names in workbook** box, delete *Price*, type **ToolsPrice**, and then click **OK**.

The **Define Name** dialog box disappears.

20 On the Standard toolbar, click the **Save** button.

Close

21 Click the **Close** button.

NameRange.xls closes.

Creating Formulas to Calculate Values

Once you've added your data to a worksheet and defined ranges to simplify data references, you can create a **formula**, or an expression that performs calculations on your data. For example, you can calculate the total cost of a customer's order, figure the average sales for all Wednesdays in the month of January, or find the highest and lowest daily sales for a week, month, or year.

To write an Excel formula, you begin the cell's contents with an equal sign—when Excel sees it, it knows that the expression following it should be interpreted as a calculation and not text. After the equal sign, you type the formula. For instance, you can find the sum of the numbers in cells C2 and C3 with the formula *=C2+C3*. After you have entered a formula into a cell, you can revise it by clicking the cell and then editing the formula on the formula bar. For example, you can change the preceding formula to *=C3-C2*, which calculates the difference of the contents of cells C2 and C3.

Troubleshooting

If Excel treats your formula as text, make sure you haven't accidentally put a space before the equal sign. Remember, the equal sign must be the first character!

Typing the cell references for fifteen or twenty cells in a calculation would be tedious, but Excel makes it easy to handle complex calculations. To create a new calculation, you click **Function** on the **Insert** menu. The **Insert Function** dialog box appears, with a list of **functions**, or predefined formulas, from which you can choose.

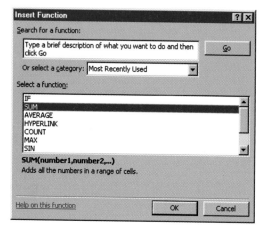

The most useful functions in the list are described in the following table.

Item	Description
SUM	Returns the sum of the numbers in the specified cells
AVERAGE	Finds the average of the numbers in the specified cells
COUNT	Finds the number of entries in the specified cells
MAX	Finds the largest value in the specified cells
MIN	Finds the smallest value in the specified cells

Two other functions you might use are the NOW() and PMT() functions. The NOW() function returns the time the workbook was last opened, so the value will change every time the workbook is opened. The proper form for this function is =NOW(); to update the value to the current date and time, just save your work, close the workbook, and then reopen it. The PMT() function is a bit more complex. It calculates payments due on a loan, assuming a constant interest rate and constant payments. To perform its calculations, the PMT() function requires an interest rate, the number of months of payments, and the starting balance. The elements to be entered into the function are called **arguments** and must be entered in a certain order. That order is written *PMT(rate, nper, pv, fv, type)*. The following table summarizes the arguments in the PMT() function.

Argument	Description
Rate	The interest rate, to be divided by 12 for a loan with monthly payments
Nper	The total number of payments for the loan
Pv	The amount loaned (pv is short for present value, or principal)
Fv	The amount to be left over at the end of the payment cycle (usually left blank, which indicates 0)
Type	0 or 1, indicating whether payments are made at the beginning or at the end of the month (usually left blank, which indicates 0, or the end of the month)

If you wanted to borrow $20,000 at an 8 percent interest rate and pay the loan back over 24 months, you could use the PMT() function to figure out the monthly payments. In this case, the function would be written *=PMT(8%/12, 24, 20000)*, which calculates a monthly payment of $904.55.

You can also add the names of any ranges you've defined to a formula. For example, if the named range *Order1* refers to cells C2 through C6, you can calculate the average of cells C2 through C6 with the formula *=AVERAGE(Order1)*. If you want to include a series of contiguous cells in a formula but you haven't defined the cells as a named range, you can click the first cell in the range and drag to the last cell. If the cells aren't contiguous, hold down the ⌷ key and click the cells to be included. In both cases, when you release the mouse button, the references of the cells you selected appear in the formula.

Another use for formulas is to print out messages when certain conditions are met. For instance, Catherine Turner, the owner of The Garden Company, might provide a free copy of a gardening magazine to customers making purchases worth more than $150. This kind of formula is called a **conditional formula** and uses the IF function.

To create a conditional formula, you click the cell to hold the formula and open the **Insert Function** dialog box. From within the dialog box, you select IF from the list of available functions and then click **OK**. The **Function Arguments** dialog box appears.

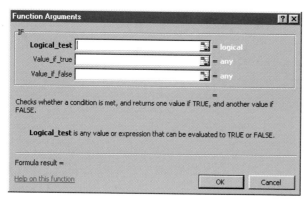

When you work with an IF function, the **Function Arguments** dialog box will have three boxes: **Logical_test**, **Value_if_true**, and **Value_if_false**. The **Logical_test** box holds the condition you want to check. To check whether the total for an order is greater than $150, the expression would be *SUM(Order1)>150*.

Now you need to have Excel print messages indicating whether the customer should receive a free magazine. To have Excel print a message from an IF function, you enclose the message in quotes in the **Value_if_true** or **Value_if_false** box. In this case, you would type **"Qualifies for a free magazine!"** in the **Value_if_true** box and **"Thanks for your order!"** in the **Value_if_false** box.

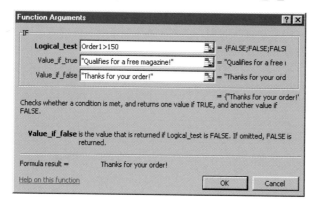

Once you've created a formula, you can copy it and paste it into another cell. When you do, Excel will try to change the formula so it works in the new cells. For instance, in the following graphic, cell D8 contains the formula *=SUM(C2:C6)*.

Clicking cell D8, copying the cell's contents, and then pasting the result into cell D16 writes *=SUM(C10:C14)* into cell D16. Excel has reinterpreted the formula so that it fits the surrounding cells! Excel knows it can reinterpret the cells used in the formula because the formula uses a **relative reference**, or a reference that can change if the formula is copied to another cell. Relative references are written with just the cell row and column (for example, *C14*). If you want a cell reference to remain constant when the formula using it is copied to another cell, you can use an **absolute reference**. To write a cell reference as an absolute reference, you type *$* before the row name and the column number. If you wanted the formula in cell D16 to show the sum of values in cells C10 through C14 regardless of the cell into which it is pasted, you would write the formula as *=SUM($C$10:$C$14)*.

As an example of how absolute references prevent misinterpretations, copy the formula *=SUM(C10:C14)* from cell D16 and paste it into cell D17.

As shown in the preceding graphic, Excel reinterprets the formula so that it doesn't include one of the cells with data that should be included. In this case, the proper way to write the formula so that the sum of the values in cells C10 through C14 appears in cell D17 is to use absolute references, as in the formula =SUM($C$10:$C$14).

Tip

If you copy a formula from the formula bar, use absolute references, or use only named ranges in your formula, Excel won't change the cell references when you copy your formula to another cell.

Formula

In this exercise, you create a formula to find the total cost of an order, copy that formula to another cell, and then create a formula to find the average cost of items in the order. The cells with the cost of products in this order are stored in the named range *OrderItems*.

Open

1 On the Standard toolbar, click the **Open** button.

The **Open** dialog box appears.

2 Double-click **Formula.xls**.

Formula.xls opens.

3 Click **cell D7**.

D7 becomes the active cell.

4 On the formula bar, type **=D4+D5** and press ⌈Enter⌋.

The value $63.90 appears in cell D7.

	A	B	C	D
1				
2				
3		Items		
4		TL0210	Timer, Watering	$44.95
5		SP3628	Bird Netting	$18.95
6				
7			Total	$63.90
8			Average	

Copy

5 Click **cell D7**, and then, on the Standard toolbar, click the **Copy** button.

Excel copies the formula in cell D7 to the Clipboard.

Paste

6 Click **cell D8**, and then, on the Standard toolbar, click the **Paste** button.

The value *$18.95* appears in cell D8, and *=D5+D6* appears in the formula bar.

7 Press ⌜Del⌟.

The formula in cell D8 disappears.

8 On the **Insert** menu, click **Function**.

The **Insert Function** dialog box appears.

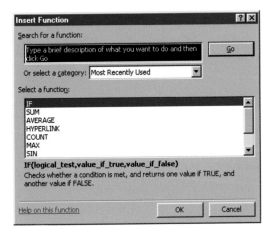

9 Click **AVERAGE**, and then click **OK**.

The **Function Arguments** dialog box appears, with the contents of the Number 1 box highlighted.

10 Type OrderItems, and then click **OK**.

The **Function Arguments** dialog box disappears, and *$31.95* appears in cell D8.

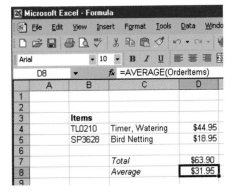

11 Click **cell C10**.

12 On the **Insert** menu, click **Function**.

The **Insert Function** dialog box appears.

13 In the Select A Function pane, click **IF** and then click **OK**.

The **Function Arguments** dialog box appears.

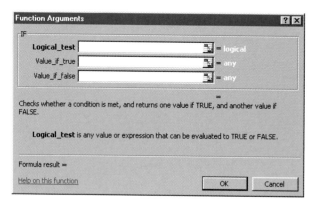

14 In the **Logical_test** box, type **D7>50**.

15 In the **Value_if_true** box, type **"5% discount"**.

16 In the **Value_if_false** box, type **"No discount"** and then click **OK**.

The **Function Arguments** dialog box disappears, and 5% discount appears in cell C10.

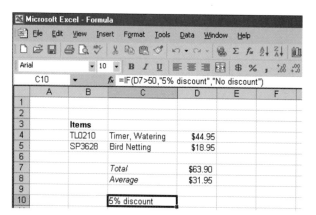

Save

17 On the **Standard** toolbar, click the **Save** button.

Excel saves your changes.

Close

18 Click the **Close** button.

Formula.xls closes.

Finding and Correcting Errors in Calculations

Including calculations in a worksheet gives you valuable answers to questions about your data. As is always true, however, it is possible for errors to creep into your formulas. Excel makes it easy to find the source of errors in your formulas by identifying the cells used in a given calculation and describing any errors that have occurred. The process of examining a worksheet for errors in formulas is referred to as **auditing**.

Excel identifies errors in several ways. The first way is to fill the cell holding the formula generating the error with an **error code**. In the following graphic, cell D8 has the error code *#NAME?*.

	A	B	C	D
1	Order #1			
2	TL2248	Garden Hose (50')	$28.00	
3	TL0210	Timer, Watering	$44.95	
4	SP3628	Bird Netting	$18.95	
5	SP1840	Carrot Juice Body Lotion	$12.50	
6	FN2002	Cedar Planter Box	$59.95	
7				
8		Total		#NAME?
9	Order #2			

Error

When a cell with an erroneous formula is the active cell, an **Error** button appears next to it. You can click the button's down arrow to display a menu with options that provide information about the error and offer to help you fix it. The following table lists the most common error codes and what they mean.

Error button
new for
OfficeXP

Error Code	Description
#####	The column isn't wide enough to display the value.
#VALUE!	The formula has the wrong type of argument (such as text where a TRUE or FALSE value is required).
#NAME?	The formula contains text that Excel doesn't recognize (such as an unknown named range).
#REF!	The formula refers to a cell that doesn't exist (which can happen whenever cells are deleted).
#DIV/0!	The formula attempts to divide by zero.

Another technique you can use to find the source of formula errors is to ensure that the appropriate cells are providing values for the formula. For example, you might want to calculate the total sales for a product category but accidentally create a formula referring to the products' names, not their prices. You can identify that kind of error by having Excel trace a cell's **precedents**, which are the cells with values used in the active cell's formula. Excel identifies a cell's precedents by drawing a blue tracer arrow from the precedent to the active cell.

You can also audit your worksheet by identifying cells with formulas that use a value from a given cell. For example, you might have the total cost of a single order used in a formula that calculates the average cost of all orders placed on a given day. Cells that use another cell's value in their calculations are known as **dependents**, meaning that they depend on the value in the other cell to derive their own value. As with tracing precedents, you can open the **Tools** menu, point to **Formula Auditing**, and click **Trace Dependents** to have Excel draw blue arrows from the active cell to those cells that have calculations based on that value.

If the cells identified by the tracer arrows aren't the correct cells, you can hide the arrows and correct the formula. To hide the tracer arrows on a worksheet, you point to **Formula Auditing** on the **Tools** menu and click **Remove All Arrows**.

FindErrors

In this exercise, you use the formula auditing capabilities in Excel to identify and correct errors in a formula.

Open

1   On the Standard toolbar, click the **Open** button.

The **Open** dialog box appears.

2   Double-click the **FindErrors.xls** file.

FindErrors.xls opens.

3   Click **cell D8**.

=SUM(C2:C6) appears in the formula bar.

4   On the **Tools** menu, point to **Formula Auditing**, and then click **Trace Precedents**.

A blue arrow appears between cell D8 and the group of cells from C2 to C6, indicating that cells in the C2:C6 range are precedents of the value in cell D8.

5   On the **Tools** menu, point to **Formula Auditing**, and then click **Remove All Arrows**.

The arrow disappears.

6   Click **cell D20**.

=AVERAGE(D7,D15) appears on the formula bar.

7   On the **Tools** menu, point to **Formula Auditing**, and then click **Trace Error**.

Blue arrows appear, pointing to cell D20 from cells D7 and D15. These arrows indicate that using the values (or lack of values, in this case) in the indicated cells is generating the error in cell D20.

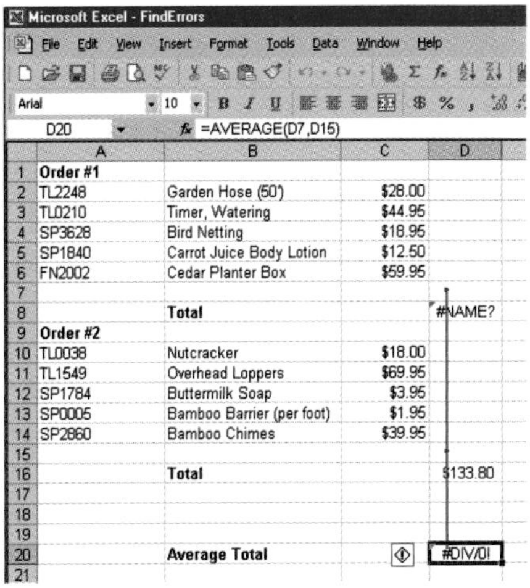

8   On the **Tools** menu, point to **Formula Auditing**, and then click **Remove All Arrows**.

The arrows disappear.

9   In the formula bar, delete the existing formula, type **=AVERAGE(D8,D16)**, and press Enter .

The value *$149.08* appears in cell D20.

Save

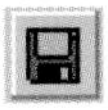

10 On the Standard toolbar, click the **Save** button.

Excel saves your changes.

Close

11 Click the **Close** button.

FindErrors.xls closes.

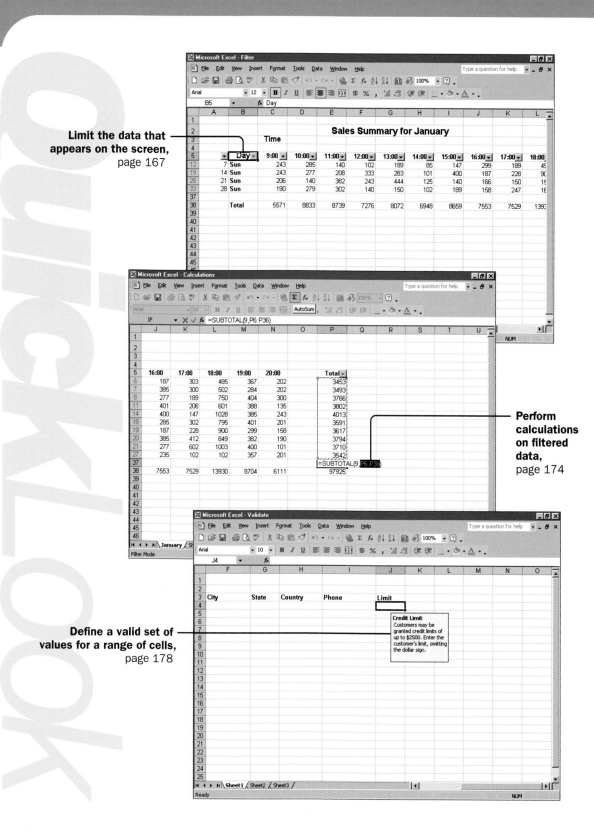

Limit the data that appears on the screen, page 167

Perform calculations on filtered data, page 174

Define a valid set of values for a range of cells, page 178

Chapter 8
Focusing on Specific Data Using Filters

After completing this chapter, you will be able to:

✔ Limit the data that appears on the screen.

✔ Perform calculations on filtered data.

✔ Define a valid set of values for a range of cells.

An important aspect of working with large amounts of data is the ability to zero in on the most important data in a worksheet, whether that data represents the best ten days of sales in a month or slow-selling product lines that you may need to reevaluate. In Excel, you have a number of powerful, flexible tools with which you can limit the data displayed in your worksheet. Once your worksheet displays the subset of your data that you need to make a decision, you can perform calculations on that data. You can discover what percentage of monthly sales were made up by the ten best days in the month, find your total sales for particular days of the week, or locate the slowest business day of the month.

Just as you can limit the data displayed by your worksheets, you can limit the data entered into them as well. Setting rules for data entered into cells lets you catch many of the most common data entry errors, such as entering values that are too small or too large, or attempting to enter a word in a cell that requires a number.

In this chapter, you'll learn how to limit the data that appears in your worksheets, perform calculations on the remaining data, and limit the data that can be entered into specific cells.

 This chapter uses the practice files Filter, Calculations, and Validate that you installed from this book's CD-ROM. For details about installing the practice files, see "Using the Book's CD-ROM" at the beginning of this book.

Limiting the Data That Appears on the Screen

Excel spreadsheets can hold as much data as you need them to, but you may not want to work with all of the data in a worksheet at the same time. For example, you might want to see the sales figures for your company during the first third, second third, and final third of a month. You can limit the data shown on a worksheet by creating a **filter**, which is a rule that selects rows to be shown in a worksheet.

To create a filter, you click the cell in the group you want to filter and use the **Data** menu to turn on **AutoFilter**. When you turn on AutoFilter, which is a built-in set of filtering capabilities, a down arrow button appears in the cell that Excel recognizes as the column's label.

Important

When you turn on filtering, Excel treats the cells in the active cell's column as a range. To ensure that the filtering works properly, you should always add a label to the column you want to filter.

Clicking the down arrow displays a list of values and options. The first few items in the list are filtering options, such as whether you want to display the top ten values in the column, create a custom filter, or display all values in the column (that is, remove the filter). The rest of the items on the list are the unique values in the column—clicking one of those values displays the row or rows containing that value.

Choosing the **Top 10** option from the list doesn't just limit the display to the top ten values. Instead, it opens the **Top 10 AutoFilter** dialog box.

From within this dialog box, you can choose whether to show values from the top or bottom of the list, define the number of items you want to see, and choose whether the number in the middle box indicates the number of items or the percentage of items to be shown when the filter is applied. Using the **Top 10 AutoFilter** dialog box, you can find your top ten salespeople or identify the top five percent of your customers.

When you choose **Custom** from the **AutoFilter** list, you can define a rule that Excel uses to decide which rows to show after the filter is applied. For instance, you can create a rule that only days with total sales of less than $2,500 should be shown in your worksheet. With those results in front of you, you might be able to determine whether the weather or another factor resulted in slower business on those days.

Two related things you can do in Excel are choose rows at random from a list and display the unique values in a column in the worksheet (not in the down arrow's list, which you can't normally work with). Generating a list of unique values in a column can give you important information, such as from which states you have customers or which categories of products sold in an hour.

Selecting rows randomly is useful for selecting customers to receive a special offer, deciding which days of the month to audit, or picking prize winners at an employee party. To choose rows, you can use the RAND function, which generates a random value and compares it with a test value included in the statement. A statement that returns a TRUE value 30 percent of the time would be *RAND()<=30%*; you could use this statement to select each row in a list with a probability of 30 percent.

Filter

In this exercise, you create a filter to show the top five sales days in January, show sales figures for Mondays during the same month, display the days with sales of at least $3,000, pick random days from the month to audit, and then generate a list of unique values in one of the worksheet's columns.

Open

1   On the Standard toolbar, click the **Open** button.

The **Open** dialog box appears.

2   Navigate to the Office XP SBS\Excel\Chap08 folder, and double-click the **Filter.xls** file.

Filter.xls opens.

3   If necessary, click the **January** sheet tab.

4   Click cell P5.

5   On the **Data** menu, point to **Filter**, and then click **AutoFilter**.

A down arrow appears in cell P5.

6   In cell P5, click the down arrow and, from the list that appears, click **(Top 10...)**.

The **Top 10 AutoFilter** dialog box appears.

7   Click in the middle box, delete *10*, type **5**, and click **OK**.

Only the rows containing the five largest values in column P are shown.

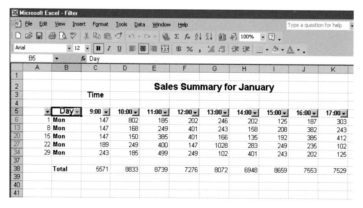

8   On the **Data** menu, point to **Filter**, and then click **AutoFilter**.

The filtered rows reappear.

9   Click **cell B5**.

10   On the **Data** menu, point to **Filter**, and then click **AutoFilter**.

A down arrow appears in cell B5.

11   In cell B5, click the down arrow and, from the list of unique column values that appears, click **Mon**.

Only rows with *Mon* in column B are shown in the worksheet.

12   On the **Data** menu, point to **Filter**, and then click **AutoFilter**.

The filtered rows reappear.

13   Click **cell P5**, and then, on the **Data** menu, point to **Filter**, and then click **AutoFilter**.

A down arrow appears in cell P5.

14 In cell P5, click the down arrow and then, from the list that appears, click **(Custom...)**.

The **Custom AutoFilter** dialog box appears.

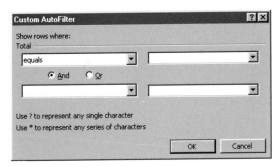

15 In the upper left box, click the down arrow and, from the list that appears, click **is greater than or equal to**.

16 In the upper right box, type **3000** and then click **OK**.

Only rows with totals of at least 3000 are shown in the worksheet.

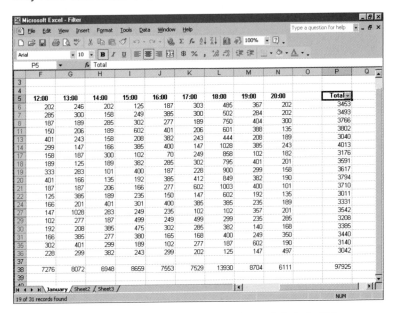

	F	G	H	I	J	K	L	M	N	O	P	Q
		12:00	13:00	14:00	15:00	16:00	17:00	18:00	19:00	20:00	Total	
6	202	246	202	125	187	303	485	367	202		3453	
7	285	300	158	249	385	300	502	284	202		3493	
8	187	189	285	302	277	189	750	404	300		3766	
11	150	206	189	602	401	206	601	388	135		3802	
13	401	243	158	382	243	444	208	189			3040	
14	299	147	166	385	400	147	1028	385	243		4013	
17	158	187	300	102	70	249	858	102	182		3176	
18	189	125	189	382	285	302	795	401	201		3591	
19	333	283	101	400	187	228	900	299	158		3617	
20	401	166	135	192	385	412	849	382	190		3794	
21	187	187	206	166	277	602	1003	400	101		3710	
22	125	385	189	235	150	147	602	192	135		3011	
24	166	201	401	301	400	385	385	235	189		3331	
27	147	1028	283	249	235	102	102	357	201		3542	
29	102	277	187	499	249	499	299	235	285		3208	
30	192	208	385	475	302	285	382	140	168		3385	
31	166	385	277	380	165	168	400	249	350		3440	
35	302	401	299	189	102	277	187	602	190		3140	
36	228	299	382	243	299	202	125	147	497		3042	
38	7276	8072	6948	8659	7553	7529	13930	8704	6111		97925	

17 On the **Data** menu, point to **Filter**, and then click **AutoFilter**.

The filtered rows reappear.

18 On the **Data** menu, point to **Filter**, and then click **AutoFilter**.

A down arrow appears in cell P5.

19 In cell P5, click the down arrow and then, from the list of unique column values that appears, click **2236**.

All rows except the row containing *2236* in column P disappear.

20 On the **Data** menu, point to **Filter**, and then click **AutoFilter**.

The filtered rows reappear.

21 In cell Q5, type **Audit**.

22 In cell Q6, type **=RAND()<17%**.

If the result of the RAND function is less than *17%*, cell Q6 will display *TRUE*; otherwise, cell Q6 will display *FALSE*.

23 Drag the **AutoFill handle** from cell Q6 to cell Q36.

TRUE and *FALSE* values appear in the cells from Q6 to Q36 with a frequency of 16 percent and 84 percent, respectively.

24 Click **cell B5** and drag to cell B36.

Cells B5 through B36 are highlighted.

25 On the **Data** menu, point to **Filter**, and then click **Advanced Filter**.

The **Advanced Filter** dialog box appears.

26 Select the **Unique records only** check box, and then click **OK**.

Rows with the first occurrence of a value are displayed in the worksheet.

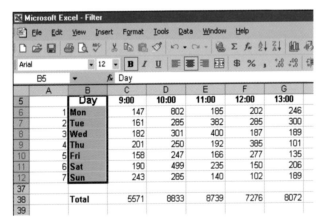

27 On the **Data** menu, point to **Filter**, and then click **Show All**.

The filtered rows reappear.

28 On the Standard toolbar, click the **Save** button.

Excel saves your changes.

29 Click the **Close** button.

Filter.xls closes.

Performing Calculations on Filtered Data

When you filter your worksheet, you limit the data that appears. The ability to focus on the data that's most important to your current needs is important, but there are a few limitations. One limitation is that any formulas you have created don't change their calculations, even if some of the rows used in the formula are hidden by the filter. The following graphic shows a filtered worksheet in which the total at the bottom of the filtered column hasn't changed.

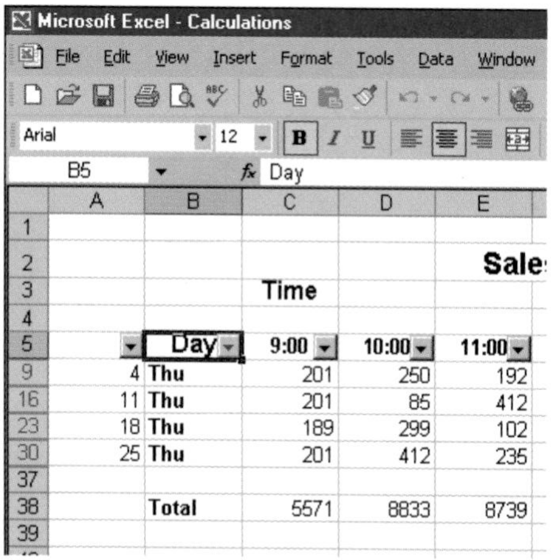

There are two ways you can find the total of a group of filtered cells. The first method is to use AutoCalculate. To use AutoCalculate, you select the cells you want to find the total for. When you do, the total for the cells appears on the status bar, at the lower edge of the Excel window.

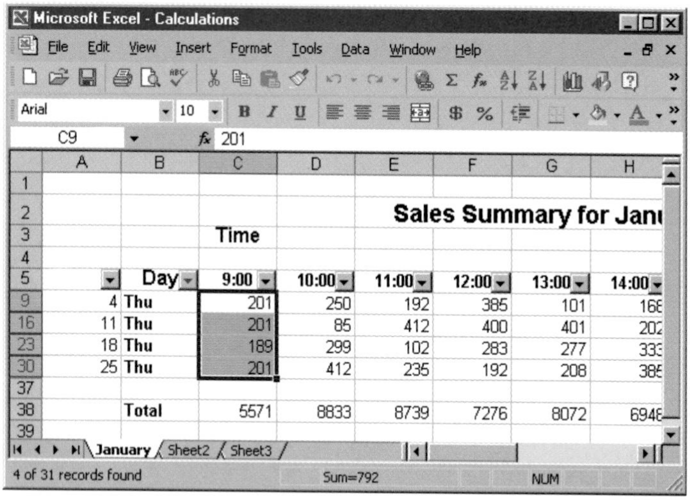

When you use AutoCalculate, you aren't limited to finding the sum of the selected cells. To display the other functions you can use, you right-click the AutoCalculate pane and select the function you want from the shortcut menu that appears.

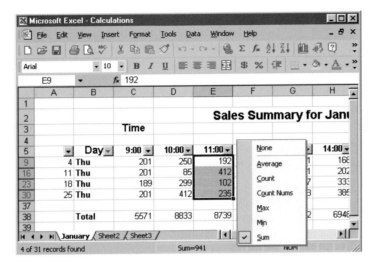

AutoCalculate is great for finding a quick total or average for filtered cells, but it doesn't make the result available in the worksheet. To make the value available in your worksheet, you can create a SUBTOTAL function. As with AutoCalculate, you can choose the type of calculation the function performs.

Calculations

In this exercise, you use AutoCalculate to find the total of a group of cells in a filtered worksheet, create a SUBTOTAL function to make the same value available in the worksheet, and then edit the SUBTOTAL function so that it calculates an average instead of a sum.

Open

1   On the Standard toolbar, click the **Open** button.

The **Open** dialog box appears.

2   Double-click the **Calculations.xls** file.

Calculations.xls opens.

3   If necessary, click the **January** sheet tab.

4   Click **cell P5**.

5   On the **Data** menu, point to **Filter**, and then click **AutoFilter**.

A down arrow button appears in cell P5.

6   In cell P5, click the down arrow button and then, from the list that appears, click **(Top 10...)**.

The **Top 10 AutoFilter** dialog box appears.

7 Click **OK**.

Tip

Clicking **OK** here accepts the default setting of the **Top 10 AutoFilter** dialog box, which is to show the top ten values in the selected cells.

The **Top 10 AutoFilter** dialog box disappears, and the rows with the ten highest values in column P are displayed.

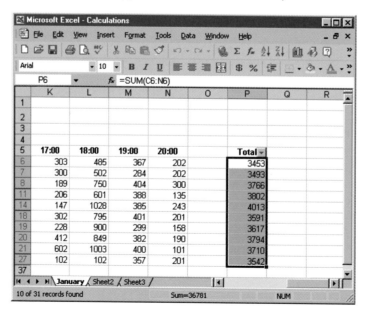

8 Click **cell P6** and drag to cell P27.

The cells are selected, and on the status bar, in the middle of the Excel window, *SUM=36781* appears in the AutoCalculate pane.

AutoSum

Σ

9 Click **cell P37**, and then, on the Standard toolbar, click the **AutoSum** button.

The formula =SUBTOTAL(9,P6:P36) appears on the formula bar.

10 Press [Enter].

The value 36781 appears in cell P37. The value in cell P38 also changes to *134706*, but that calculation includes the subtotal of the filtered cells in the column.

11 Click **cell P37**, and then, on the formula bar, edit the formula so that it reads =SUBTOTAL(1,P6:P36) and then press [Enter].

By changing the 9 to a 1 in the SUBTOTAL function, the function now calculates an average instead of a sum. The average of the top ten values in cells P6 through P36, *3678.1*, appears in cell P37. The value in cell P38 also changes to *101603.1*, but that calculation includes the average of the filtered cells in the column.

12 If necessary, click **cell P37** and then press [Del].

Excel deletes the SUBTOTAL formula from cell P37, and the total in cell P38 changes to *97925*.

Save

13 On the Standard toolbar, click the **Save** button.

Excel saves your changes.

Close

14 Click the **Close** button.

Calculations.xls closes.

Defining a Valid Set of Values for a Range of Cells

Part of creating efficient and easy-to-use worksheets is to do what you can to ensure that the data entered into your worksheets is as accurate as possible. While it isn't possible to catch every typographical or transcription error, you can set up a **validation rule** to make sure the data entered into a cell meets certain standards.

To create a validation rule, you open the **Data Validation** dialog box.

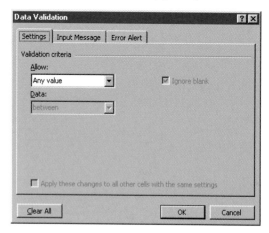

You can use the **Data Validation** dialog box to define the type of data that Excel should allow in the cell and then, depending on the data type you choose, to set the conditions data must meet to be accepted in the cell. In the following graphic, Excel knows to look for a whole number value between 1000 and 2000.

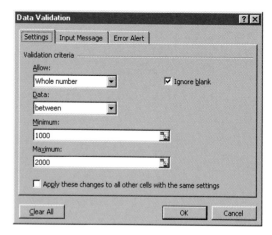

Setting accurate validation rules can help you and your colleagues avoid entering a customer's name in the cell designated to hold their phone number or setting a credit limit above a certain level. To require a user to enter a numeric value in a cell, display the Settings page of the **Data Validation** dialog box, in the Allow box, click the down arrow, and depending on your needs, choose either **Whole Number** or **Decimal** from the list that appears.

Of course, it's frustrating if you want to enter data into a cell and, when a message box appears telling you the data you tried to enter isn't acceptable, you aren't given the rules you need to follow. Excel lets you create messages that tell the user what values are expected before the data is entered and then, if the conditions aren't met, reiterate the conditions in a custom error message.

You can turn off data validation in a cell by displaying the Settings page of the **Data Validation** dialog box and clicking the **Clear All** button in the lower left corner of the dialog box.

Validate

In this exercise, you create a data validation rule limiting the credit line of The Garden Company customers to $2,500, add an input message mentioning the limitation, and then create an error message should someone enter a value greater than $2,500. After you've created your rule and messages, you test them.

Open

1   On the Standard toolbar, click the **Open** button.

The **Open** dialog box appears.

2   Double-click the **Validate.xls** file.

Validate.xls opens.

3   Click **cell J4**.

4   On the **Data** menu, click **Validation**.

The **Data Validation** dialog box appears with the **Settings** tab page in front.

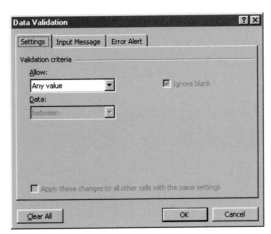

5   In the **Allow** box, click the down arrow and, from the list that appears, click **Decimal**.

Boxes labeled **Minimum** and **Maximum** appear below the **Data** box.

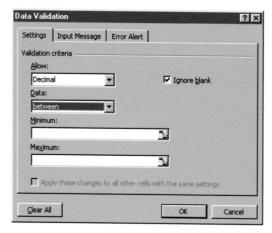

6 In the **Data** box, click the down arrow and, from the list that appears, click **less than or equal to**.

The **Minimum** box disappears.

7 In the **Maximum** box, type 2500.

8 Clear the **Ignore blank** check box.

9 Click the **Input Message** tab.

The **Input Message** tab page appears.

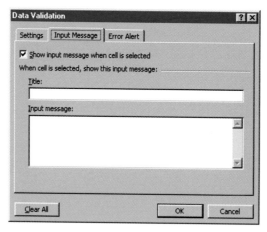

10 In the **Title** box, type Enter Limit.

11 In the **Input Message** box, type Please enter the customer's credit limit, omitting the dollar sign.

12 Click the **Error Alert** tab.

The **Error Alert** tab page appears.

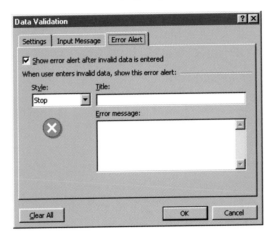

13 In the **Style** box, click the down arrow and, from the list that appears, choose **Warning**.

The icon that will appear on your message box changes to the **Warning** icon.

14 In the **Title** box, type Error.

15 Click **OK**.

Tip

Leaving the **Error Message** box blank causes Excel to use its default message: *The value you entered is not valid. A user has restricted values that can be entered into this cell.*

A ScreenTip with the title *Enter Limit* and the text *Please enter the customer's credit limit, omitting the dollar sign* appears near cell J4.

16 Type 2501, and press Enter.

A **warning box** with the title **Error** and default text appears.

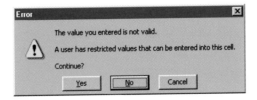

17 Click **Yes**.

The warning box disappears.

Important

Clicking **No** lets you edit the bad value, while clicking **Cancel** deletes the entry.

18 Click **cell J4**.

Cell J4 becomes the active cell, and the ScreenTip reappears.

19 Type **2500**, and press ⌷Enter⌷.

Excel accepts your input.

20 Click **cell J4**.

21 On the **Data** menu, click **Validation**.

The **Data Validation** dialog box appears.

22 Click the **Settings** tab.

The **Settings** tab page appears.

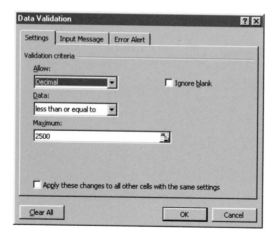

23 In the **Allow** box, click the down arrow and, from the list that appears, click **Whole number**.

24 Click **OK**.

25 In cell J4, type **2499.95** and press ⌷Enter⌷.

A warning box with the title *Error* and default text appears.

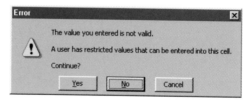

26 Click **No**.

The warning box disappears, cell J4 becomes the active cell, and the ScreenTip reappears.

27 Type **2500**, and press Enter.

28 Excel accepts your input.

29 On the Standard toolbar, click the **Save** button.

Close

![X]

30 Click the **Close** button.

Validate.xls closes.

Microsoft Access

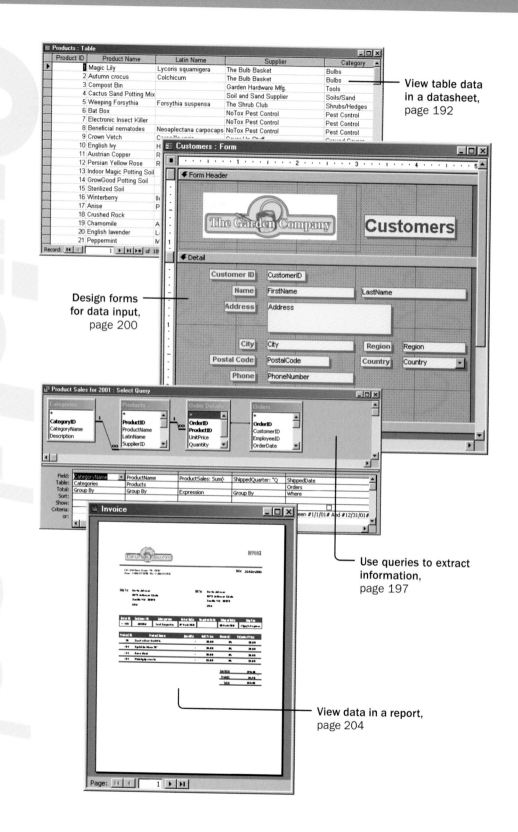

View table data
in a datasheet,
page 192

Design forms
for data input,
page 200

Use queries to extract
information,
page 197

View data in a report,
page 204

Chapter 9
Getting to Know Access

After completing this chapter, you will be able to:

✔   **Open an existing database.**

✔   **Open tables in different views.**

✔   **Open and run queries.**

✔   **Open a form in different views.**

✔   **Open a report in different views.**

This section of the book gives you straightforward instructions for using Microsoft Access 2002 to create databases. It takes you from knowing nothing about Access—or, for that matter, about databases—to a level of expertise that will enable you to develop database applications for use by one person or by many.

This chapter introduces the concept of a database, explains a little about Access, and then takes you on a tour. The database you will use for the tour belongs to The Garden Company, a fictional garden supply and plant store. (You will be working with this database throughout the book.) Although looking at someone else's work might not be as exciting as jumping in and creating your own database, this tour will give you a firm foundation from which to begin working with Access to create your own databases.

In this chapter, you will open the GardenCo database, explore its structure, and look at some of the objects used to store and manipulate the data it contains. You will be working with the GardenCo database files that are stored in the following sub-folders of the Office XP SBS\Access\Chap09 folder: Open, Tables, Queries, Forms, and Reports.

Tip

To follow along with the exercises in this book, you need to install the practice files from the companion CD. (You cannot just copy the files.) You'll find instructions for installing the files in the "Using the Book's CD-ROM" section at the beginning of the book.

What Is a Database?

In its most basic form, a database is the computer equivalent of an organized list of information. Typically, this information has a common subject or purpose, such as the list of employees shown here:

ID	Last Name	First Name	Title	Hire Date
1	Dale	Martha	Sales Rep	May 1, 1992
2	Fuller	Joanna	V.P., Sales	Aug 14, 1992
3	Lee	Mark	Sales Rep	Apr 1, 1992
4	Penn	Daniel	Sales Rep	May 3, 1993

This list is arranged in a **table** of columns and rows, called **fields** and **records** in database terms. Each column (field) stores a particular type of information about an employee: first name, last name, date of hire, and so on. Each row (record) contains information about a different employee.

If a database did nothing more than store information in a table, it would be as useful as a paper list. But because the database stores information in electronic format, you can manipulate the information in powerful ways to extend its utility.

For example, a phone book for your city is probably sitting on a shelf within a few feet of you. If you want to locate a person or a business in your city, you can do so, because the information in the telephone book is organized in an understandable manner. If you want to get in touch with someone a little further away, you can go to the public library and use its collection of phone books, which probably includes one for each major city in the country. However, if you want to find the phone numbers of all the people in the country with your last name, or if you want the phone number of your grandmother's neighbor, these phone books won't do you much good because they aren't organized in a way that makes that information easy to find.

When the information published in a phone book is stored in a database, it takes up far less space, it costs less to reproduce and distribute, and, if the database is designed correctly, the information can be retrieved in many ways. The real power of a database isn't in its ability to store information; it is in your ability to quickly retrieve exactly the information your want from the database.

What's Special About Access?

Simple **database programs**, such as the Database component of Microsoft Works, can store information in only one table, which is often referred to as a flat file. These simple databases are often called **flat databases**. More complex database programs, such as Microsoft Access, can store information in multiple related tables, thereby creating what are often referred to as **relational databases**. If the information in a relational database is organized correctly, you can treat these multiple tables as a single storage area and pull information electronically from different tables in whatever order meets your needs.

A table is just one of the types of **objects** that you can work with in Access. The following figure shows all the Access object types:

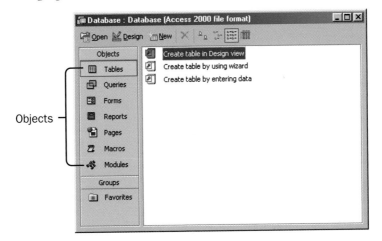

Tip

For maximum compatibility with existing databases, the default format for new databases created with Access 2002 is Access 2000.

Of all these object types, only one—tables—is used to store information. The rest are used to manage, manipulate, analyze, retrieve, display, or publish the table information—in other words, to make the information as accessible and therefore as useful as possible.

Over the years, Microsoft has put a lot of effort into making Access not only one of the most powerful consumer database programs available, but also one of the easiest to learn and use. Because Access is part of the Microsoft Office suite of programs, you can use many of the techniques you know from using other Office programs, such as Microsoft Word and Microsoft Excel, when using Access. For example, you can use familiar commands, buttons, and keyboard shortcuts to open and edit the information in Access tables. And because Access is integrated with other members of the suite, you can easily share information between Access and Word, Excel, or other programs.

Opening an Existing Database

The database for The Garden Company, which is called *GardenCo*, contains information about its employees, products, suppliers, and customers that is stored in a series of tables. As you complete the exercises in this book, you will work with these tables and develop an assortment of queries, forms, reports, data access pages, macros, and modules that can be used to enter, edit, and manipulate the information in the tables in many ways.

GardenCo

In this exercise, you will open the GardenCo database, explore some of its objects, and then close the database. You won't find a lot of detailed explanation here, because this is just an overview. The working folder for this exercise is Office XP SBS\Access\Chap09\Open. Follow these steps:

1 At the left end of the taskbar at the bottom of your screen, click the **Start** button, point to **Programs**, and then click **Microsoft Access**.

When Access first opens, your screen looks like this:

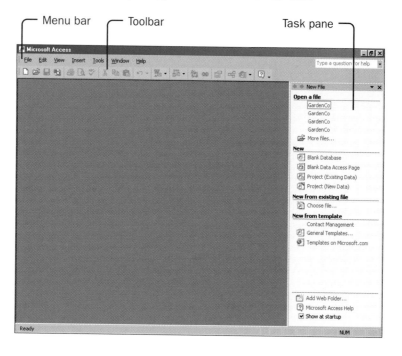

Important

What you see on your screen might not match the graphics in this book exactly. The screens in this book were captured on a monitor set to 800 x 600 resolution with 24-bit color and the Windows Standard color scheme. The book starts with the Access default settings, and the screens reflect any changes to those settings that are called for by the steps in the exercises.

Task pane
new for
OfficeXP

As with other Microsoft Office applications, Access has a menu bar and one or more toolbars across the top of the window. New to programs in Office XP is the **task pane** shown at the right side of this window. In Access, a different version of the task pane appears when you click either **New** or **Search** on the **File** menu, or click **Office Clipboard** on the **Edit** menu.

Open

2 Click the **Open** button on the toolbar, browse to the Office XP SBS\Access\Chap09\Open folder, and double-click **GardenCo**.

The Garden Company introductory screen, called a **splash screen**, appears.

Tip

You will normally open a database by double-clicking its file name in Windows Explorer. (Access databases have a filename extension of *.mdb*.) Or you can start Access and click **New** on the **File** menu to display the **New File** task pane, which offers a variety of options for opening new or existing databases.

3 Select the **Don't show this screen again** check box, and then click **OK**.

You see this **switchboard**, which is used to easily access the database objects needed to perform common tasks:

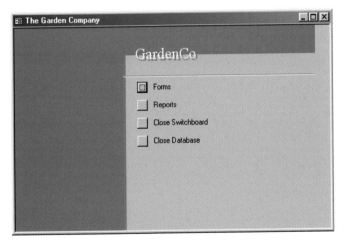

4 Click **Close Switchboard** to close the switchboard.

Restore

5 The database window is minimized as a small title bar in the lower left corner of your screen. Click the **Restore** button in this title bar to expand the database window.

The GardenCo **database window** looks like the one shown on the next page.

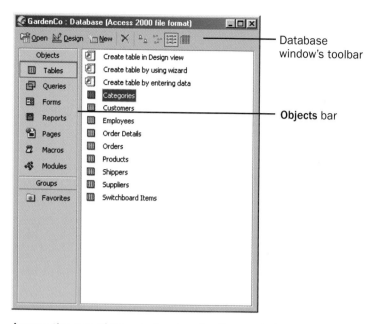

Database
window's toolbar

Objects bar

Across the top of the window is a toolbar and along the left edge is the **Objects** bar, which lists the Access database objects. Because **Tables** is selected, the right pane of the window lists the tables contained in the database.

6 Close the **GardenCo** database by clicking **Close** on the **File** menu.

Exploring Tables

Tables are the core database objects. Their purpose is to store information. The purpose of every other database object is to interact in some manner with one or more tables. An Access database can contain thousands of tables, and the number of records each table can contain is limited more by the space available on your hard disk than anything else.

Tip

For detailed information about Access specifications, such as the maximum size of a database or the maximum number of records in a table, click the Ask A Question box at the right end of the menu bar, type **Access specifications**, and press [Enter].

Every Access object has two or more **views**. For tables, the two most common views are **Datasheet view**, where you can see and modify the table's data, and **Design view**, where you can see and modify the table's structure. Clicking the **View** button toggles the view of the open table between Datasheet and Design views. You can also click the arrow to the right of the button and select a view from the drop-down list.

When you view a table in Datasheet view, you see the table's data in columns (fields) and rows (records) as shown here:

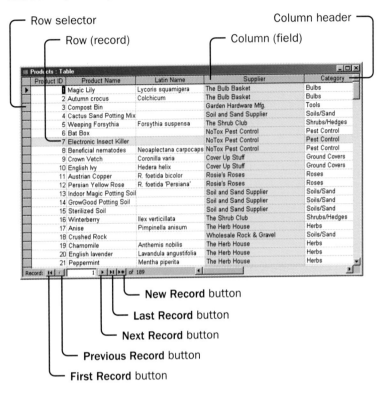

If two tables have one or more fields in common, you can embed the datasheet for one table in another. The embedded datasheet, which is called a **subdatasheet**, allows you to see the information in more than one table at the same time. For example, you might want to embed an Orders datasheet in a Customers table so that you can see the orders each customer has placed.

GardenCo

In this exercise, you will open tables in the GardenCo database and explore their structure in different views. The working folder for this exercise is Office XP SBS\Access\Chap09\Tables. Follow these steps:

1 Open the **GardenCo** database located in the working folder.

2 Click **Tables** on the **Objects** bar.

Details

Because the **Details** button has been clicked on the toolbar at the top of the database window, a description of each of the objects listed in the window is displayed to the right of its name.

193

Tip

You can resize the columns in the database window by dragging the vertical bar that separates columns in the header. You can set the width of a column to the width of its widest entry by double-clicking the vertical bar.

Maximize

3   Click the **Maximize** button in the upper right corner of the database window.

The database window expands to fill the Access window, and you can now read the table descriptions. Note that the first three items in the Name list are not tables; they are shortcuts to commands you can use to create a new table.

Tip

If you don't want these shortcuts at the top of each list of objects, click **Options** on the **Tools** menu, click the **View** tab in the **Options** dialog box, clear the **New object shortcuts** check box, and click **OK**.

4   Click the **Restore** button to shrink the database window again.

Open

5   Click the **Categories** table, and then click the **Open** button at the top of the database window.

The table opens in Datasheet view, as shown here:

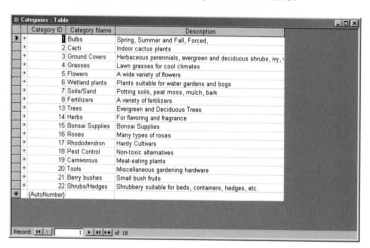

This datasheet contains a list of the categories of products sold by The Garden Company. As you can see, there are fields for Category ID, Category Name, and Description.

6   Click the plus sign to the left of the record for the Bulbs category.

Clicking the plus sign expands an embedded subdatasheet. You are now looking at category records from the Categories table and product records from the Products table simultaneously, as shown on the next page.

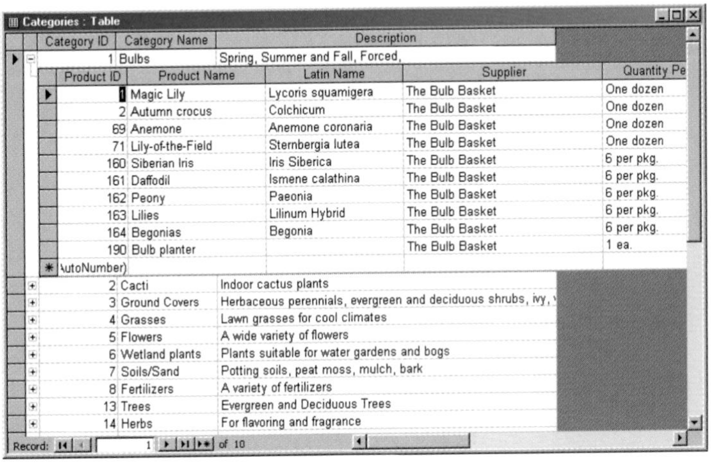

Notice that the plus sign has changed to a minus sign.

7 Click the minus sign to the left of the Bulbs record to collapse the sub-datasheet.

8 Close the **Categories** table by clicking **Close** on the **File** menu. If you are prompted to save changes to the table layout, click **Yes**.

Tip

You can also close a window by clicking the **Close** button in the window's upper right corner. When an object window is maximized, this button is called the **Close Window** button to avoid confusion with the **Close** button at the right end of the Access window's title bar. Be careful to click the right button, or else you will exit Access.

9 On the **Objects** bar, double-click the **Orders** table to open it in Datasheet view, like this:

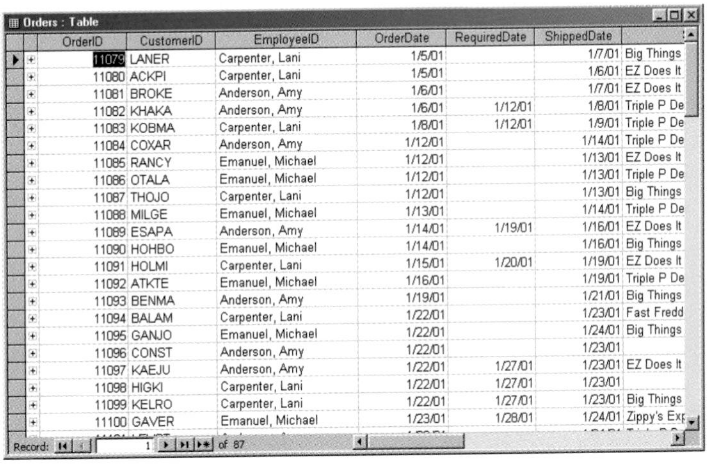

195

The navigation area at the bottom of the window indicates that this table contains 87 records and that the active record is number 1.

Next Record

10 Move the selection one record at a time by clicking the **Next Record** button several times.

The selection moves down the OrderID field, because that field contains the insertion point.

Tip

You can move the selection one record at a time by pressing the ⬆ or ⬇ keys, one screen at a time by pressing the [Page Up] or [Page Down] keys, and to the first or last field in the table by pressing [Ctrl]+[Home] or [Ctrl]+[End].

11 Move directly to record 40 by selecting the current record number, typing **40**, and pressing [Enter].

12 Close the **Orders** table, clicking **No** if you are prompted to save changes to the table's layout.

13 Double-click **Products** in the list of tables to open it in Datasheet view.

Notice that this table contains 189 records.

View

14 Click the **View** button on the toolbar to switch the view of the Products table to Design view.

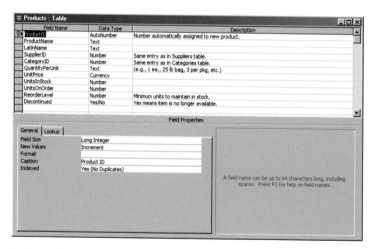

In Datasheet view, you see the data stored in the table, whereas in Design view, you see the underlying table structure.

Close

15 Close the **Products** table by clicking its **Close** button. If prompted to save changes to the table layout, click **No**.

16 Close the **GardenCo** database by clicking its **Close** button.

Exploring Queries

One of the ways you can locate information in an Access database is to create **queries**. You use queries to locate information so that you can view, change, or analyze it in various ways. You can also use the results of queries as the basis for forms, reports, and data access pages.

A query is essentially a question. For example, you might ask, "Which records in the Customer table have the value 98052 in the Postal Code field?" When you **run a query** (the equivalent of *asking a question*), Access looks at all the records in the table or tables you have specified, finds those that match the criteria you have defined, and displays them in a datasheet.

In order for Access to be able to answer your questions, you have to structure queries in a very specific way. Each type of question has a corresponding type of query. The primary query types are select, crosstab, and parameter. Less common types are action, AutoLookup, and SQL (Structured Query Language). Access includes wizards that quickly guide you through the creation of the more common queries; the less common ones have to be created by hand in a **design grid** in Design view. Here's what a typical query looks like:

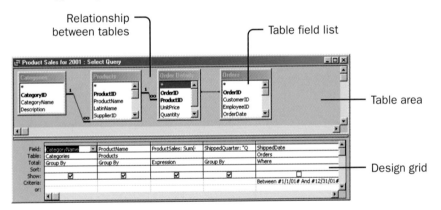

At the top of the query window are four small windows, listing the fields in the four tables that will be included in this query. The lines connecting the tables indicate that they are related by virtue of common fields. The first row of the grid contains the names of the fields to be included in the query, and the second row shows which table each field belongs to. The third row (labeled *Total*) enables you to perform calculations on the field values, and the fourth indicates whether the query results will be sorted on this field. A check mark in the check box in the fifth row (labeled *Show*) means that the field will be displayed in the results datasheet. (If the check box is not selected, the field can be used in determining the query results, but it will not be displayed.) The sixth row (labeled *Criteria*) contains criteria that determine which records will be displayed, and the seventh row (labeled *or*) sets up alternate criteria.

197

Don't worry if this all sounds a bit complicated at the moment. When you approach queries logically, they soon begin to make perfect sense. And don't worry if they sound like a lot of work. The **Query Wizard** is available to help you structure the query, and if you create a query that you are likely to run more than once, you can save it. It then becomes part of the database and is displayed in the database window when you click **Queries** on the **Objects** bar.

GardenCo

In this exercise, you will explore a few of the queries that have already been defined and saved in the GardenCo database. The working folder for this exercise is Office XP SBS\Access\Chap09\Queries. Follow these steps:

1 Open the **GardenCo** database located in the working folder.

2 Click **Queries** on the **Objects** bar.

The database window displays all the queries that have been saved as part of the GardenCo database.

3 Double-click the title bar of the database window to maximize the window.

Your screen looks like this:

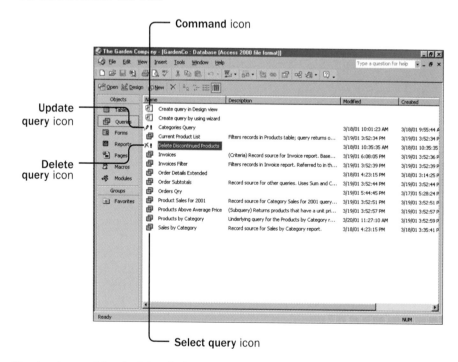

The top two entries in this window are commands you can use to create queries. The remaining entries are queries that have already been created. The description of each query explains its purpose. The icon in the Name field is an indication of the query's type, as is the information in the Type field, which you can see by scrolling the window to the right.

4 Restore the database window by clicking its **Restore** button.

Open

5 Open the **Products by Category** query in Datasheet view by selecting it and clicking the **Open** button at the top of the database window.

When you open the query, Access processes, or *runs*, it and produces a datasheet that displays these results:

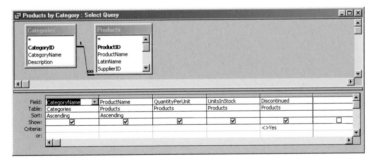

The navigation bar tells you that 171 records are displayed. The Products table contains 189 records. To find out why 18 of the records are missing, you need to look at this query in Design view.

6 Click the **View** button on the toolbar to view the query in Design view, like this:

In the top part of the query window, two boxes list the fields of the tables this query is designed to work with. The bottom part is the design grid, where the query is formed. Each column of the grid can refer to one field from one of the tables above. Notice that **<>Yes** (*not equal to Yes*) has been entered in the **Criteria** row for the Discontinued field. This query therefore finds all the records that don't have a value of *Yes* in that field (in other words, that have not been discontinued).

199

Run

7 As an experiment, select **<>Yes** in the **Criteria** row for **Discontinued**, type **=Yes**, and then click the **Run** button on the toolbar.

Tip

You can also run a query by switching to Datasheet view.

You changed the query so that it finds all the records that have a value of Yes in the Discontinued field (in other words, that have been discontinued). Here are the results:

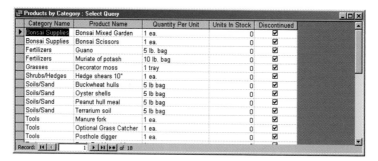

The 18 discontinued products account for the difference in the number of records in the Products table and the number of records displayed by the original query.

8 Close the query window, clicking **No** when prompted to save the design changes.

9 Close the **GardenCo** database.

Exploring Forms

Access tables are dense lists of raw information. If you create a database that only you will use, you will probably be very comfortable working directly with tables. But if you create a database that will be viewed and edited by people who don't know much about it—and don't necessarily want to know about it—working with your tables might be overwhelming. To solve this problem, you can design **forms** to guide users through your database, making it easier for them to enter, retrieve, display, and print information.

A form is essentially a window in which you can place **controls** that either give users information or enable them to enter information. Access provides a toolbox that includes many standard Windows controls, such as labels, text boxes, option buttons, and check boxes. With a little ingenuity, you can use these controls to create forms that look and work much like the dialog boxes in all Microsoft Windows applications.

You use forms to edit the records of the underlying tables or enter new records. As with tables and queries, you can display forms in several views. The three most common views are **Form view**, where you enter data; Datasheet view, which looks essentially like a table; and Design view, where you work with the elements of the form to refine the way it looks and works. Here's what a form looks like in Design view:

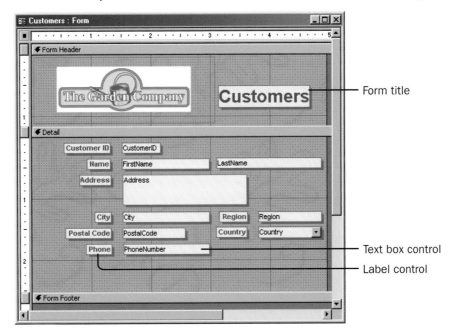

This form consists of a **main form** that is linked to just one table. But a form can also include **subforms** that are linked to other tables. Arranged on the form are **label controls** containing text that appears on the form in Form view, and **text box controls** that will contain data from the table. Although you can create a form from scratch in Design view, you will probably use this view most often to refine the forms you create with a wizard.

GardenCo

In this exercise, you will take a look at a few of the forms that have been designed to make viewing and editing the information in the tables of the GardenCo database easier and less error prone. The working folder for this exercise is Office XP SBS\Access\Chap09\Forms. Follow these steps:

1 Open the **GardenCo** database located in the working folder.

2 Click **Forms** on the **Objects** bar, and then double-click **Switchboard**, to open the main switchboard.

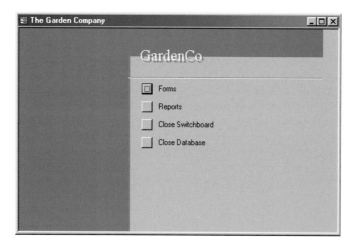

The Switchboard form has a title bar at the top, a title for The Garden Company, and four command buttons. The first two buttons open switchboards—other forms—that have the same name as the button.

3 Click the **Forms** button on the switchboard to display the Forms switchboard.

4 Click **Edit/Enter Orders** to display this Orders form:

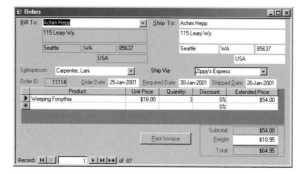

This form consists of a main form and a subform.

New Record

5 Click the **Next Record** button on the navigation bar to display that record's information, and then click the **New Record** button (the right-facing triangle with an asterisk) to display a blank form where you could enter a new order.

6 Close the **Orders** form, and click **Return** in the **Forms** switchboard to redisplay the main switchboard.

7 Click the **Close switchboard** button.

8 In the database window, double-click **Products** in the **Forms** list to open this form:

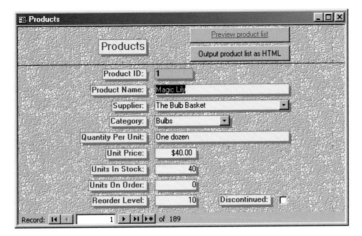

You use this form to edit the records of current products or enter new ones. You are currently looking at the form in Form view.

9 Click the **View** button's arrow, and click **Datasheet View**.

Now the form looks essentially like the Products table in Datasheet view but without gridlines, as shown here:

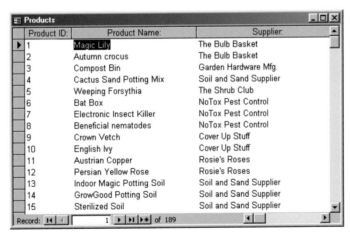

10 Click the **View** button again to switch to Design view, and maximize the form window.

Toolbox

11 If the toolbox is not displayed, click the **Toolbox** button on the toolbar.

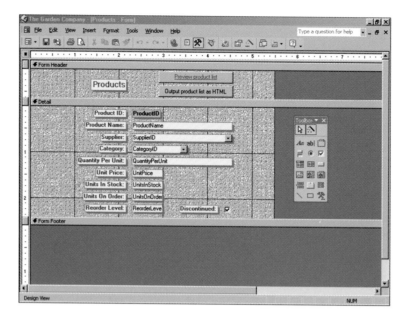

Tip

If the toolbox is in the way, drag it by its title bar to the side of the form as shown above.

12 Point to each of the icons in the toolbox until the name of the tool is displayed.

These are the tools you use to build custom forms for your database.

13 Close the **Products** form, and then close the database.

Exploring Reports

You use **reports** to display the information from your tables in nicely formatted, easily accessible ways, either on your computer screen or on paper. A report can include items of information selected from multiple tables and queries, values calculated from information in the database, and formatting elements such as headers, footers, titles, and headings.

You can look at reports in three views: Design view, where you can manipulate the design of a report in the same way that you manipulate a form; **Print Preview**, where you see your report exactly as it will look when printed; and **Layout Preview**, which shows you how each element will look but without all the detail of Print Preview. Here's how a report looks in Design view:

Function to insert current date

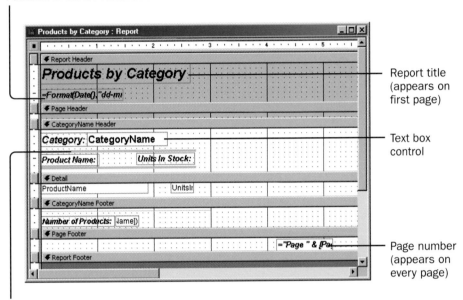

Report title (appears on first page)

Text box control

Page number (appears on every page)

Label control

GardenCo

In this exercise you will take a look at a report that has been saved as part of the GardenCo database, just to get an idea of what is possible. The working folder for this exercise is Office XP SBS\Access\Chap09\Reports. Follow these steps:

1   Open the **GardenCo** database located in the working folder.

2   Click **Reports** on the **Objects** bar.

     The top two entries in this window are commands you can use to create reports. The remaining entries are reports that have already been created.

Preview

3   Click **Customer Labels**, and then click the **Preview** button at the top of the database window to display the report.

     This report prints customer names and addresses in a mailing label format. You are looking at it in a view that is much like Print Preview in other Microsoft Windows programs.

Tip

Access provides a wizard that creates a mailing label report. You can also use the Customer table in this database with Word's mail merge feature to create these labels.

4   Click in the form to change the zoom level.

Tip

If the report is too small to read in Preview view, you can also select a zoom level in the **Zoom** box on the toolbar.

5   Close the **Customer Labels** report.

6   In the database window, click the **Invoice** report, and click the **Preview** button to see the invoice shown here:

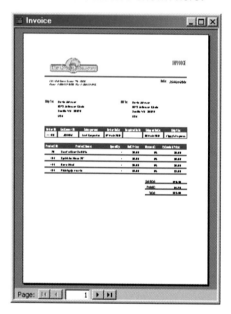

7   Check out each page by clicking the navigation buttons at the bottom of the window.

View

8   Click the **View** button on the toolbar to display the report in Design view, and then maximize the report window so that your screen looks like this:

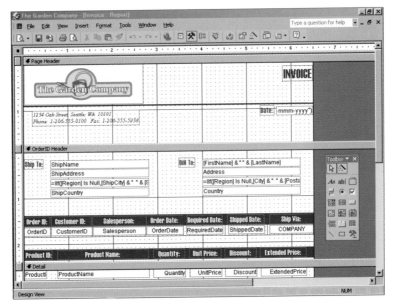

In this view, the report looks similar to a form, and the techniques you use to create forms can also be used to create reports.

9   Close the **Invoice** report, and then close the **GardenCo** database.

10   If you are not continuing on to the next chapter, exit Access.

Exploring Other Access Objects

Tables, queries, forms, and reports are the objects you will use most frequently in Access. You can use them to create powerful and useful databases. However, if you need to create a sophisticated database, you can use data access pages, macros, and modules to substantially extend the capabilities of Access. To round out this introduction to Access databases, this section provides a brief overview of these objects.

Pages

To enable people to view and manipulate your database information via an intranet or the Internet, you can create **pages**, also known as *data access pages*. Working with a data access page on the Web is very much like working directly with a table or form in Access—users can work with the data in tables, run queries, and enter information in forms.

Although publishing database information on the Web seems like a fairly difficult task, Access provides a wizard that does most of the tedious work of creating data access pages for you. You can use wizard-generated pages as-is, or you can add your own personal touch in Design view.

Macros

You use **macros** to have Access respond to an event, such as the click of a button, the opening of a form, or the updating of a record. Macros can be particularly handy when you expect that other people who are less experienced with Access than you will work in your database. For example, you can make routine database actions, such as opening and closing forms or printing reports, available as command buttons on switchboards. And by grouping together an assortment of menu commands and having users carry them out via a macro with the click of a button, you can ensure that everyone does things the same way.

Modules

More powerful than macros, **modules** are Microsoft Visual Basic for Applications (VBA) programs. VBA is a high-level programming language developed by Microsoft for the purpose of creating Windows applications. A common set of VBA instructions can be used with all Microsoft Office programs, plus each program has its own set. Whereas macros can automate four to five dozen actions, VBA includes hundreds of commands and can be extended indefinitely with third-party add-ins. You could use VBA to carry out tasks that are too complex to be handled with macros, such as opening an Excel spreadsheet and retrieving some information.

Tip

The Microsoft Office XP installation CD-ROM includes several sample databases that illustrate many of the principles of creating and using a database. One of these, the Northwind Traders database, is used as an example in many topics in Access online Help, so it is a particularly good database for you to explore. You'll find a link to this database on the Access **Help** menu, under **Sample Databases**.

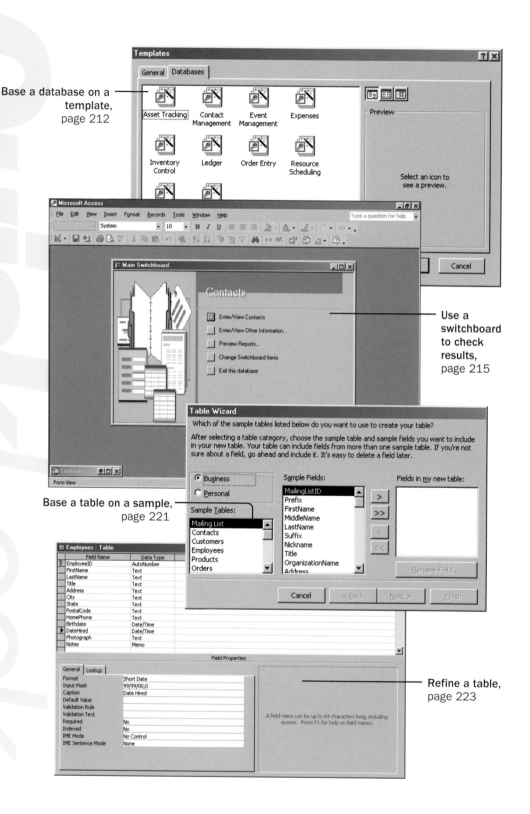

Base a database on a template, page 212

Use a switchboard to check results, page 215

Base a table on a sample, page 221

Refine a table, page 223

Chapter 10
Creating a New Database

After completing this chapter, you will be able to:

✔ Create a new database structure using a wizard.

✔ Check the work of the wizard.

✔ Create an empty database, and add tables using a wizard.

✔ Refine the way your data is displayed.

✔ Manipulate columns and rows in tables.

Creating the structure for a database is easy. But an empty database is no more useful than an empty Microsoft Word document or an empty Microsoft Excel worksheet. It is only when you fill, or **populate**, a database with data in tables that it starts to serve a purpose. As you add queries, forms, and reports, it becomes easier to use. If you customize it with a switchboard and your tools, it moves into the realm of a **database application**.

Not every database has to be refined to the point that it can be classified as an application. Databases that only you or a few experienced database users will work with can remain fairly rough-hewn. But if you expect an administrative assistant to enter data or your company's executives to generate their own reports, then spending a little extra time in the beginning to create a solid database application will save a lot of work later. Otherwise, you'll find yourself continually repairing damaged files or walking people through seemingly easy tasks.

Microsoft Access takes a lot of the difficult and mundane work out of creating and customizing a database by providing **wizards** that you can use to create entire databases or individual tables, forms, queries, and other objects. It is generally easier to use a wizard to create something that is similar to what you need and then modify it than it is to create the same thing by hand.

In this chapter you will first use a wizard to rapidly create the structure for a sophisticated contact management database, complete with tables, queries, forms, and reports. After exploring this database and entering a few records to get an idea of what a wizard can provide in the way of a starting point, you will discard this database and start working on a simpler contacts database for The Garden Company. By the end of this chapter, you will have a GardenCo database containing three tables that will serve as the foundation for many of the exercises in this book.

In this chapter, the working folder is Office XP SBS\Access\Chap10. You'll be creating a couple of databases from scratch in the CreatingDB subfolder. You will also use the Contacts and GardenCo database files that are stored in the following subfolders of the working folder: CheckingDB, Refining, and Manipulating.

Creating a Database Structure the Simple Way

In the distant past (a few years ago in computer time), creating a database structure from scratch involved first analyzing your needs and then laying out the database design on paper. You would decide what information you needed to track and how to store it in the database. Creating the database structure could be a lot of work, and after you had created it and entered data, making changes could be difficult. Wizards have changed this process. Committing yourself to a particular database structure is no longer the big decision it once was. Using the **Database Wizard**, you can create a dozen database applications in less time than it used to take to sketch the design of one on paper.

In this exercise, you will use the **Database Wizard** to create a new database structure. Access wizards may not create exactly the database application you want, but they can quickly create something very close. In this case, the new database will contain the structure for a contact management database. The working folder for this exercise is Office XP SBS\Access\Chap10\CreatingDB. Follow these steps:

1 Start Access.

New

2 If the Task pane is not displayed, open it by clicking the **New** button on the Standard toolbar.

3 In the **New from template** section of the Task pane, click **General Templates**, and then click the **Databases** tab to display these options:

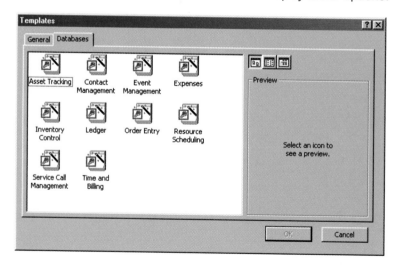

Tip

The **Database Wizard** uses predefined **templates** to create fairly sophisticated database applications. In addition to the templates provided with Access, if you are connected to the Internet, you will find additional templates and other resources by following the link to **Templates on Microsoft.com** that is in the **New from template** section of the Task pane.

4 Double-click **Contact Management**.

A **File New Database** dialog box similar to this one appears so that you can provide a name for your new database and specify where to store it:

Tip

The default folder for storing Access database files is *My Documents*. You can change this default to any other folder by clicking **Options** on the **Tools** menu when a database file is open, entering a new path in the **Default database folder** box on the **General** tab, and clicking **OK**.

5 Navigate to Office XP SBS\Access\Chap10\CreatingDB (the working folder for this exercise), type **Contacts** as the file name, and click **Create**.

Tip

Naming conventions for an Access database file follow those for Microsoft Windows files. A file name can contain up to 215 characters including spaces, but creating a file name that long is not recommended. File names cannot contain the following characters: \ / : * ? " < > |. The extension for an Access database file is *.mdb*.

First the database window is displayed, and then you see the first page of the **Database Wizard**, which tells you the type of information that will be stored in this database.

6 This page requires no input from you, so click **Next** to move to this second page of the **Database Wizard**:

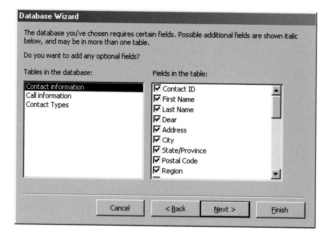

This page lists the three tables that will be included in the Contacts database. The box on the right lists the fields you might want to include in the table selected in the box on the left. Required fields have a check mark in their check boxes. Optional fields are italic. You can click the check box of an optional field to include it in the selected table.

7 Click each table name, and browse through its list of fields, just to see what is available. Then indicate that you want to include all the selected fields in the three tables by clicking **Next** to move to the next page of the wizard.

On this page, you can select from a list of predefined styles that determine what the elements of the database will look like.

Tip

Whenever the wizard's **Back** button is active (not gray), you can click it to move back through previous pages and change your selections. If the **Finish** button is active, you can click it at any time to tell a wizard to do its job with no further input from you. Most of the options set by a wizard can be modified later, so clicking **Finish** does not mean that whatever the wizard creates is cast in stone.

8 Click each of the styles to see what they look like. Then click **Blends**, and click **Next**.

9 Take a look at each of the report styles. Then click **Bold**, and click **Next**.

10 Change the proposed database name to Contacts, leave the **Yes, I'd like to include a picture** check box clear, and click **Next**.

The **Next** button is unavailable on this page, indicating that this is the wizard's last page. By default, the **Yes, start the database** check box is selected, and the **Display Help on using a database** check box is clear.

11 Leave the default settings as they are, and click **Finish**.

The process of creating a database can take from several seconds to a minute or more. While the wizard creates the database, an alert box tells you what is happening and how far along the process is. When the wizard finishes, it opens the newly created Contacts database with this switchboard displayed:

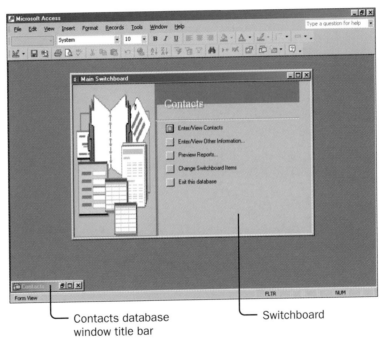

Contacts database window title bar

Switchboard

12 Click the Main Switchboard window's **Close** button.

13 When the switchboard opened, the Contacts database window was minimized. (You can see its title bar in the lower left corner of the Access window.) Click the database's **Close** button to close the database.

Checking the Work of a Wizard

Using a wizard to create a database is quick and painless, but just what do you end up with? The **Database Wizard** creates a database application, complete with a switchboard, several tables, and some combination of other objects. In many cases, all you have to do to have a working database application is add the data. If the wizard's work doesn't quite suit your needs, you can modify any of the database objects, or use another type of wizard to add more objects.

For example, if you tell the **Database Wizard** to create a contact management database, it creates three tables. It doesn't create any queries for this type of database, but it does for some of the other types. It creates forms that you can use to enter or view data, and two reports that you can use to list contacts or summarize the calls made or received during the week. Finally, it creates a switchboard so that users can quickly access the parts of the database needed to perform specific tasks.

Contacts

In this exercise, you will use the switchboard to take a quick tour of a Contacts database that the **Database Wizard** has created. You can't check out some of the objects unless the database contains some data, so along the way, you will enter information in several of the tables. The working folder for this exercise is Office XP SBS\Access\Chap10\CheckingDB. Follow these steps:

1 Open the **Contacts** database located in the working folder.

2 In the switchboard, click the **Enter/View Other Information** button to display the Forms Switchboard window.

This switchboard has two buttons: the first opens a form you can use to enter or view contact types, and the second returns you to the Main Switchboard window.

3 Click **Enter/View Contact Types** to display this Contact Types form:

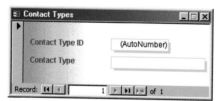

If the underlying Contact Types table contained any records, you could use this form to view them. The only action you can take now is to add a new record.

4 Type **Supplier** in the **Contact Type** box, and press ⌷Enter⌷.

As you typed, Access supplied the entry for the **Contact Type ID** field. Access keeps track of this number and enters the next available number in this field whenever you add a new record.

5 Repeat the previous step to enter records for **Customer** and **Shipper**.

6 Now that the underlying Contact Types table contains a few records, use the **navigation buttons** at the bottom of the form to scroll through them. Then click the **Close** button to close the Contact Types form.

Important

With most computer applications, **saving** your work often is important, to avoid losing it if your computer crashes or the dog chews through the power cord. With Access, it is not only *not* important to save your data, it is *not possible* to manually save it. When you move the insertion point out of a record after entering or editing information, Access saves that record. This mixed blessing means that you don't have to worry about losing your changes, but you do have to remember that any data entry changes you make are permanent and can be undone only by editing the record again.

7 Click **Return to Main Switchboard**.

8 Click **Enter/View Contacts** to display this Contacts form:

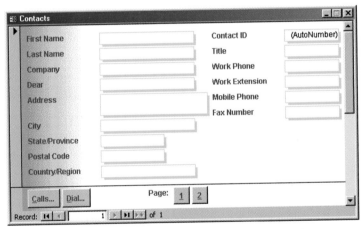

You use this two-page form to enter records in the underlying Contacts table or to view records that are already there. The form has buttons at the bottom to switch between pages and to open other forms from which you can place calls (**Dial**) or where you can record information about communications you've had with the contact (**Calls**).

9 Enter some information on this form—your own first and last name will do—and notice that when you enter your name, Access provides a Contact ID.

10 Click the **2** button at the bottom of the form to move to page 2, and then open the list of contact types.

The list contains the three types you just entered in the Contact Types table through the Contact Types form.

11 Select one of the contact types.

12 Return to the first page, click in the **Work Phone** box to place the insertion point there, type **555-0100**, and press Enter.

13 Click in the **Work Phone** box again, and click the **Dial** button.

The **AutoDialer** dialog box appears, with the contents of the **Work Phone** box that is currently selected on the form displayed as a potential number to dial.

Tip

This dialog box is not part of Access; it is a Windows utility. When you click the **Dial** button, VBA code attached to the button calls the utility. If you were to click **Setup** in the **AutoDialer** dialog box, the **Windows Phone And Modem Options** dialog box would be displayed. (If you don't have a modem installed, the **Install New Modem** dialog box appears instead.)

14 Click **Cancel** to close the **AutoDialer** dialog box, and then click the **Calls** button to display this Calls form:

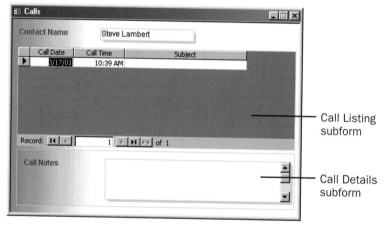

Call Listing
subform

Call Details
subform

This form includes the Call Listing subform, which lists any previous calls you have recorded, and the Call Details subform, which displays details of the selected call. You can record information about communications (phone calls, email exchanges, and so on) that you've had with this contact.

15 Click in the **Subject** field of the new record, and enter **Order information** as the subject.

Access adds a **New Record** line, where the **Call Date** and **Call Time** fields default to the current date and time, as shown here:

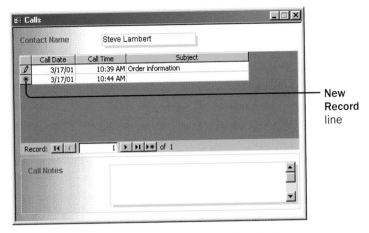

New
Record
line

16 Click in the **Call Notes** box, and type a short note.

17 Click the **Close** button to close the Calls form, and then click **Close** again to close the Contacts form.

18 Click **Preview Reports** to display the Reports Switchboard window.

19 Preview the two short reports by clicking the button for each one, reading the report, and then closing it.

When you preview the Weekly Call Summary report, the Report Date Range form is displayed to allow you to enter a range of dates for the report. If you accept the default range of the current week, the summary of the call you just added is included in the report.

20 Click **Return to Main Switchboard**, and then click the **Close** button to close the Main Switchboard window without closing the database.

21 Double-click the database window's title bar to restore the window, which looks like this:

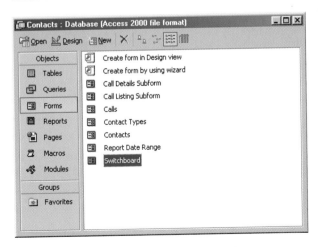

22 Explore all the tables, forms, and reports in the database by clicking each object type on the **Objects** bar and then opening the individual objects.

You won't be able to open the Report Date Range form directly, because it is designed to be opened by VBA code that supplies the information that the form needs.

23 Close the **Contacts** database.

Creating Tables the Simple Way

When you use the **Database Wizard** to create a contact management database, the database has all the **components** needed to store basic information about people. But suppose The Garden Company needs to store different types of information for different types of contacts. For example, they might want to maintain different types of information about employees, customers, and suppliers. In addition to the standard information—such as names, addresses, and phone numbers—the company might want to track these other kinds of information:

- Employee Social Security number, date of hire, marital status, deductions, and pay rate
- Customer order and account status
- Supplier contact, current order status, and discounts

They could add a lot of extra fields to the Contacts table and then fill in just the ones they need for each contact type, but cramming all this information into one table would soon get pretty messy. Instead, they should create a database with one table for each contact type: employee, customer, and supplier.

The **Database Wizard** doesn't offer exactly this combination of tables, so in this exercise, you will create a GardenCo database with an empty structure. You will then add several tables to the database using the **Table Wizard**. The working folder for this exercise is Office XP SBS\Access\Chap10\CreatingDB. Follow these steps:

New

1 Click the **New** button on the toolbar to display the Task pane.

2 In the **New** section of the Task pane, click **Blank Database**.

3 Navigate to the working folder for this exercise, type **GardenCo** as the name of the new database, and click **Create**.

Access displays a database window that contains no tables, queries, forms, or other database objects. (You can confirm that the database is empty by clicking each of the object types on the **Objects** bar.)

4 Click the **New** button on the database window's toolbar to display the **New Table** dialog box.

Tip

Instead of clicking the **New** button, you can click the **New Object** button's arrow on the Standard toolbar and then click **Table**; or you can click **Tables** on the **Objects** bar and then double-click **Create table by using wizard**; or you can click **Table** on the **Insert** menu.

5   Double-click **Table Wizard** to display the wizard's first page, shown here:

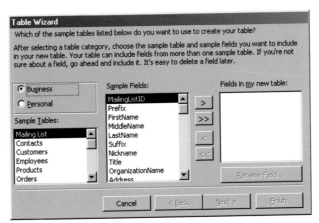

You can display a list of either business tables or personal tables. Although these categories are generally oriented toward business or personal use, depending on the nature of your business or personality, you might find the sample table you want in either list.

6   Take a few minutes to browse through first the business list and then the personal one.

Each category contains a list of sample tables. When you click an item in the **Sample Tables** list, the **Sample Fields** list to the right displays all the fields available for that table. (You can add more fields after creating the table if you need them.) Selecting an item in the **Sample Fields** list and then clicking the **>** button moves the selected field to the **Fields in my new table** list. Clicking the **>>** button moves *all* sample fields to the **Fields in my new table** list. The **<** and **<<** buttons remove one or all fields from your new table list.

7   With the **Business** category selected, select **Customers** in the **Sample Tables** list.

8   Click the **>>** button to copy all the fields to the **Fields in my new table** list, and then click **Next** to move to the next page of the wizard.

On this page you can provide a name for your new table and specify whether the wizard should set a **primary key** for the table. A primary key consists of one or more fields that differentiate one record from another.

9   Leave **Customers** as the table name, click **No, I'll set the primary key**, and then click **Next**.

The wizard suggests **CustomerID** as the field that will uniquely identify records, and asks what type of data the field will contain.

10   Click **Numbers and/or letters I enter when I add new records**, and then click **Next** to move to the last page of the wizard.

You can select one of the three option buttons on this page to determine whether the table should open in Design view or in Datasheet view, or whether a wizard-generated form should open so that you can enter data.

11   Accept the default selection, **Enter data directly into the table**, and click **Finish** to create and open the Customers table.

12   Scroll horizontally through the table to view all the fields created by the wizard based on your selections on its first page. Then close the table.

The Customer table now appears on the **Tables** pane of the database window.

13   Start the **Table Wizard** again, this time by double-clicking **Create table by using wizard** in the database window.

14   Select **Employees** in the **Sample Tables** list, and move only the following fields to the **Fields in my new table** list, by selecting each field in the **Sample Fields** list and clicking the **>** button.

EmployeeID	**PostalCode**
FirstName	**HomePhone**
LastName	**Birthdate**
Title	**DateHired**
Address	**Photograph**
City	**Notes**
StateOrProvince	

15   In the **Fields in my new table** list, select **StateOrProvince**, click **Rename Field**, change the name of the field to State, and click **OK**.

16   Click the **Next** button twice to move two pages forward, naming the table **Employees** and allowing Access to create a primary key.

Because one table already exists in the database, the wizard attempts to establish a relationship between the tables and displays a new page.

17   You will be able to establish relationships later, so skip over this page by clicking **Next**.

18 Click **Finish**, and then close the **Employees** table.

19 Use the **Table Wizard** to create a **Suppliers** table that includes all the fields provided. Click **Finish** to accept all the suggestions and defaults.

20 Close the **Suppliers** table.

Three tables are now listed in the **Tables** pane of the database window.

21 Close the database.

Refining How Data Is Displayed

When you use the **Table Wizard** to create tables and populate them with the fields you specify, it sets a variety of **properties** for each field. These properties determine what data can be entered in a field and how the data will look on the screen.

The field properties set by Access are a good starting place, and most of them are probably fine as they are. However, suppose some of the properties don't meet your needs. You can change some of them without affecting the data stored in the table; others might affect the data, so it pays to be cautious about making drastic changes until you have some experience working with Access.

GardenCo

In this exercise, you will review and edit a few of the property settings for one of the tables in the GardenCo database located in the working folder for this exercise, Office XP SBS\Access\Chap10\Refining. Follow these steps:

1 Open the **GardenCo** database located in the working folder.

2 In the database window, double-click **Employees** in the **Tables** pane to open the table in Datasheet view, like this:

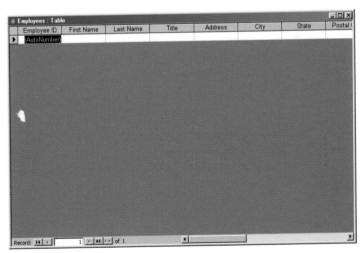

Your table window might be a different size than this one. Notice that any field name that is composed of two words has a space between the words, whereas the name you specified in the wizard had no space. Remember this when you are looking at the table in Design view later.

Tip

As with other Microsoft Office XP applications, you can change the size of the window by moving the pointer to a window border and, when the pointer becomes a double-headed arrow, dragging to expand or reduce the size of the window.

View

3 Click the **View** button on the toolbar to display the table in Design view, like this:

Primary key ———

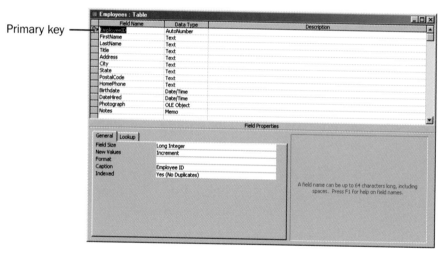

In Design view, the top portion of the window contains a list of the table's fields. The **Field Name** column contains the names you specified when creating the table. Notice that there are no spaces in the names. The **Data Type** column specifies the type of data that the field can contain. The **Description** column can contain a description of the field.

Primary Key

Notice the **Primary Key** icon to the left of the EmployeeID field. The value in the primary key field is used to uniquely identify each record; that is, no two records can have the same value in this field. You can take responsibility for entering this value, or you can let Access help you with this chore. When the data type of a field is set to **AutoNumber**, Access fills this field in every new record with the next available number.

Tip

If you no longer want the table to have a primary key, select the field designated as the primary key in the top portion of the window, and click **Primary Key** on the **Edit** menu. If you want to assign a different field as the primary key, select that field, and click **Primary Key** on the **Edit** menu.

4   Click in the **Data Type** cell for the **EmployeeID** field—the one with **Auto-Number** in it—and then click the down arrow that appears.

Important

If you delete a record that has an **AutoNumber** value, that value will never be reused in the same table. For example, if you add records for ten employees to a table, their ID numbers will be 1 through 10. If you then delete the last three records and add a new one, the new ID number will be 11. Numbers 8, 9, and 10 will never again be available for use in this table.

The cell expands to show a list of all possible **data types**. Each data type cell contains this list, allowing you to set the appropriate data type for each field. The data type setting restricts data entry to that specific type. If you try to enter data that is incompatible with that type, Access rejects it.

Tip

For a description of all the data types, search on *data type* in Access online Help.

5   Press the ⎋ key to close the list without changing the data type.

6   Click in each box in the **Field Properties** section at the bottom of the window.

The number of properties in the **Field Properties** section varies with each data type. For example, the **AutoNumber** data type has five properties, four of which have drop-down lists from which you can select settings. As you click each property, a description of that property appears in the area on the right, as shown on the next page.

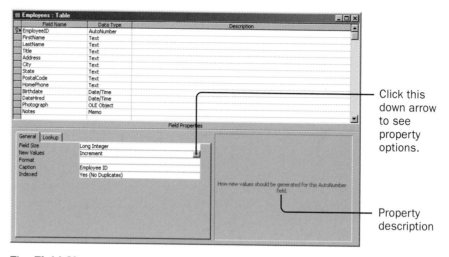

Click this
down arrow
to see
property
options.

Property
description

The **Field Size** property determines the size and type of value that can be entered in the field. For example, if this property is set to **Long Integer** the field will accept entries from –2,147,483,648 to 2,147,483,647. If the data type is **AutoNumber**, entries in this field will start with 1, so you could conceivably have over two billion employees before you outgrew this table.

The **Increment** setting for the **New Values** property specifies that Access should use the next available sequential number. The alternative (which you can see by expanding the list for this cell) is **Random**.

The **Format** property determines how data from the field is displayed on the screen and in print; it does not control how it is stored. Some data types have predefined formats, and you can also create custom formats.

Remember that when you displayed the table in Datasheet view, some of the field names had spaces in them? The way the field names are displayed in Datasheet view is controlled by the **Caption** property. If there is an entry for this property, it is used in place of the actual field name.

The **Yes (No Duplicates)** setting for the **Indexed** property indicates that the information in this field will be indexed for faster searching, and that duplicate values are not allowed. For the primary key field, this property is automatically set to **Yes (No Duplicates)**, but a field can also be indexed without being a primary key.

Tip

For more information about a particular property, click in its box, and press F1 to see the pertinent Access online Help topic.

7 With the **EmployeeID** field still selected (as indicated by the right arrowhead in the **row selector**), click in the **Format** box, and enter three zeros (**000**).

The ID number generated by Access will now be displayed as three digits. If the number isn't three digits long, it will be padded on the left with zeros.

8 Click the **Photograph** field, and change its data type from **OLE Object** to **Text**.

The **Table Wizard** included the **Photograph** field in this table. Notice that its data type is set to **OLE Object** so that you can store a graphic in the field. But you will be storing the file name of a graphic, not the graphic itself, so **Text** is a more appropriate data type. Select Text from the drop-down list.

9 Click in the **HomePhone** field to display these properties:

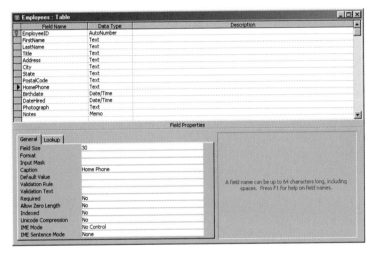

The data type for **HomePhone** is **Text**, even though the data will be a string of numbers. Because this entry can also contain parentheses, dashes, and spaces and is not the type of number that you would use in a calculation, **Text** is the appropriate data type.

Looking at the **Field Properties** section for this field, you can see that fields with this data type have more properties than fields with the **AutoNumber** data type.

The **Field Size** property for a field with the **Text** data type determines the number of characters that can be entered in the field. If you attempt to enter too many characters, Access displays a warning message, and you can't leave the field until you reduce the number of characters to this many or fewer.

The **Caption** property is set to **Home Phone**. This name is used at the top of the field's column in Datasheet view. The wizard supplies these more readable names, but you can change them.

10 Click in the **DateHired** field to display the properties shown here:

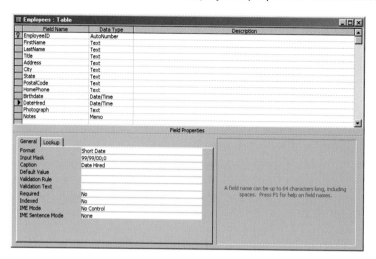

The **Format** property for this field is set to **Short Date**, which looks like this: 4/21/01. If a valid date is entered in just about any standard format, such as 21 April 01, this property displays the date as 4/21/01.

Important

Exercises in this book that use the short date format assume that the year display is set to two digits (M/d/yy) in the **Regional Settings Properties** dialog box in Windows 98 or the **Regional Options** dialog box in Windows 2000. You can check this on your computer by opening Control Panel (click **Start**, move the pointer over **Settings**, then click **Control Panel**) and then double-clicking **Regional Settings** or **Regional Options**, as appropriate. In either case, the setting is found on the **Date** tab.

This field also has its **Input Mask** property set to **99/99/00;0**. An **input mask** controls how data looks when you enter it and the format in which it is stored. Each 9 represents an optional numeral, and each 0 represents a required one. When you move to this field to enter a date in Datasheet view, you will see a mask that looks like this: __/__/__. The mask indicates that the date must be entered in the 4/21/01 format, but as soon as you press Enter to move to the next field, the date will change to whatever format is specified by the **Format** property.

Another interesting property is **Validation Rule**. None of the wizard-generated tables use **validation rules**, because the rules are too specific to the data being entered to anticipate, but let's take a quick look at how they work.

11 Click in the Validation Rule box, and type <Now(). Then click in the **Validation Text** box, and type Date entered must be today or earlier.

This rule states that the date entered must be before (less than) the current date, as determined by the system clock of the computer where the database is stored. If you enter a date in the future, Access will not accept it and will display the validation text in an alert box.

Important

The **Format**, **Input Mask**, and **Validation Rule** properties seem like great ways to be sure that only valid information is entered in your tables. But if you aren't careful, you can make data entry difficult and frustrating. Test your properties carefully before releasing your database for others to use.

View

12   Click the **View** button to return to Datasheet view, clicking **Yes** when prompted to save the table.

Tip

When you try to switch from Design view to Datasheet view after making changes (and sometimes even if you haven't made any changes), you are presented with an alert box stating that you must save the table. If you click **No**, you remain in Design view. If you click **Yes**, Access saves your changes and switches to Datasheet view. If you want to switch views without saving changes that you have made inadvertently, click **No**, and then click the table's **Close** button. When Access displays another alert box, click **No** to close the table without saving any changes.

13   Enter a future date in both the **Birthdate** and **DateHired** fields.

The **Birthdate** field, which has no validation rule, accepts any date, but the **DateHired** field won't accept a date beyond the current date set on your computer.

14   If necessary, click OK to close the alert box, change the DateHired value to a date in the past, and click the **Close** button to close the Employees table.

Design

15   In the database window, select **Suppliers**, and click the **Design** button to open the table in Design view.

16   Double-click the **StateOrProvince** field name to select it, and change it to State. The **Caption** doesn't change, so change it to State, too.

17   Delete the **Country/Region**, **PaymentTerms**, **EmailAddress**, and **Notes** fields by clicking in the row selector and pressing the Del key.

Tip

Access alerts you that deleting the **EmailAddress** field requires deleting the field and all its indexes. Click **Yes**. (You will see this alert again in step 19; click **Yes** each time to delete the fields.)

18 Click the **Close** button to close the Supplier table, clicking **Yes** to save your changes.

19 Open the **Customers** table in Design view, and delete the following fields: **CompanyName**, **CompanyOrDepartment**, **ContactTitle**, **Extension**, **Fax-Number**, **EmailAddress**, and **Notes**.

20 Click in the **CustomerID** field, and change the **Field Size** property to **5**.

21 Change the following fields and their captions: *ContactFirstName* to **First-Name** and **First Name**, *ContactLastName* to **LastName** and **Last Name**, *BillingAddress* to **Address**, *StateOrProvince* to **Region**, and *Country/Region* to **Country**.

22 Click the **Close** button to close the Customers table, clicking **Yes** to save it.

23 Close the **GardenCo** database.

Manipulating Table Columns and Rows

When you refine a table's structure by adding fields and changing field properties in Design view, you are affecting the data that is stored in the table. But sometimes you will want to adjust the table itself to get a better view of the data. For example, if you want to look up a phone number but the names and phone numbers are several columns apart, you will have to scroll the table window to get the information you need. You might want to rearrange columns or hide a few columns to be able to see the fields you are interested in at the same time.

You can manipulate the columns and rows of an Access table without in any way affecting the underlying data. You can size both rows and columns, and you can also hide, move, and freeze columns. You can save your table formatting so that the table will look the same the next time you open it, or you can discard your table adjustments without saving them.

GardenCo

In this exercise, you will open a table and manipulate its columns and rows. To make the value of table formatting more apparent, you will work with a version of the GardenCo database that has several tables containing many records. The working folder for this exercise is Office XP SBS\Access\Chap10\Manipulate. Follow these steps:

1 Open the **GardenCo** database located in the working folder.

2 Click **Tables** on the **Objects** bar.

3 Double-click the **Customers** table to open it in Datasheet view.

4 Drag the vertical bar at the right edge of the **Address** column header to the left until the column is about a half inch wide.

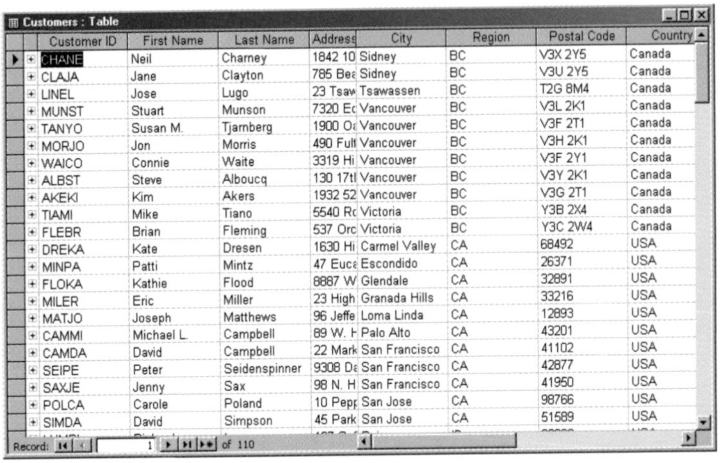

The column is now too narrow to display the entire address.

5 Point to the vertical bar between the **Address** and **City** column headers, and double-click.

The column to the left of the vertical bar is now the minimum width that will display all the text in that field in all records. This technique is particularly useful in a large table where you can't easily determine the length of a field's longest entry.

6 On the left side of the datasheet, drag the horizontal bar between any two record selectors downward.

As you can see here, this increases the height of all rows in the table:

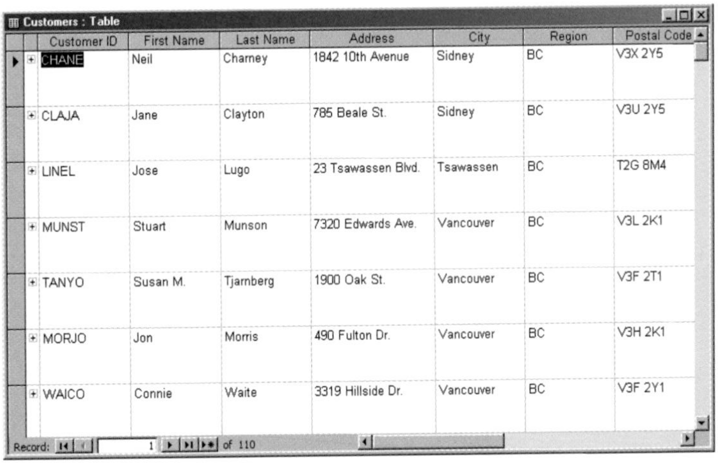

231

7   On the **Format** menu, click **Row Height** to display the **Row Height** dialog box.

8   Click the **Standard Height** check box, and then click **OK**.

The height of all rows is returned to the default setting. (You can also set the rows to any other height in this dialog box.)

9   Click in the **First Name** column, and then click Hide Columns on the Format menu.

The First Name column disappears, and the columns to its right shift to the left. If you select several columns before clicking Hide Columns, they all disappear.

Tip

You can select adjacent columns by clicking in the header of one, holding down the [Shift] key, and then clicking in the header of another. The two columns and any in between are selected.

10   To restore the hidden field, click **Unhide Columns** on the **Format** menu to display this dialog box:

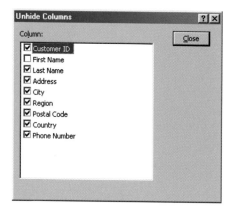

11   Select the **First Name** check box, and then click **Close**.

Access redisplays the First Name column.

12   Drag the right side of the database window to the left to reduce its size so that you are cannot see all fields in the table.

13   Point to the **Customer ID** column header, hold down the mouse button, and drag through the **First Name** and **Last Name** column headers. Then with the three columns selected, click **Freeze Columns** on the **Format** menu.

Now as you scroll the window horizontally to view columns that are off-screen to the right, the first three columns will remain in view.

14 On the **Format** menu, click **Unfreeze All Columns** to restore the columns to their normal condition.

15 Close the table, without saving your changes, and then close the **GardenCo** database.

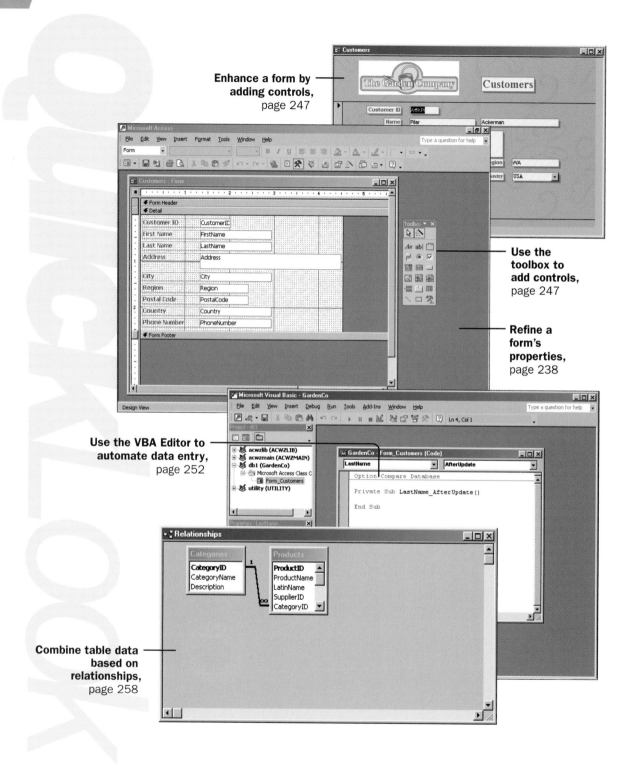

Enhance a form by adding controls, page 247

Use the toolbox to add controls, page 247

Refine a form's properties, page 238

Use the VBA Editor to automate data entry, page 252

Combine table data based on relationships, page 258

Chapter 11
Simplifying Data Entry with Forms

After completing this chapter, you will be able to:

✔ **Create a form using a wizard.**

✔ **Refine the properties and layout of a form.**

✔ **Add controls and VBA code that help enter data.**

✔ **Create a form using AutoForm.**

✔ **Create a form based on more than one table.**

A database that contains the day-to-day records of an active company is useful only if it can be kept up to date and if particular items of information can be found quickly. Although Microsoft Access is fairly easy to use, entering, editing, and retrieving information in Datasheet view is not a task you would want to assign to anybody not familiar with Access. Not only would these tasks be tedious and inefficient, but working in Datasheet view leaves far too much room for error, especially if details of complex transactions have to be entered into several related tables. The solution to this problem, and the first step in the conversion of this database to a database application, is to create and use forms.

A form is an organized and formatted view of some or all of the fields from one or more tables or queries. Forms work interactively with the tables in a database. You use **controls** on the form to enter new information, to edit or remove existing information, or to locate information. Like printed forms, Access forms can include **label controls** that tell users what type of information they are expected to enter, as well as **text box controls** in which they can enter the information. Unlike printed forms, Access forms can also include a variety of other controls, such as **option buttons** and **command buttons**, which transform Access forms into something very much like a Microsoft Windows dialog box or one page of a wizard.

Tip

Some forms are used to navigate among the features and functions of a database application and have little or no connection with its actual data. A **switchboard** is an example of this type of form.

As with other Access objects, you can create forms by hand or with the help of a wizard. Navigational and housekeeping forms, such as switchboards, are best created by hand in Design view. Forms that are based on tables, on the other hand, should always be created with a wizard and then refined by hand—not because it is difficult to drag the necessary text box controls onto a form, but because there is simply no point in doing it by hand.

In this chapter, you will create some forms to hide the complexity of the GardenCo database from the people who will be entering and working with its information. First you will discover how easy it is to let the **Form Wizard** create forms that you can then modify to suit your needs. You'll learn about the controls you can place on a form, and the properties that control its function and appearance. After you have created a form containing controls, you will learn how to tell Access what to do when a user performs some action in a control, such as clicking or entering text. You will also take a quick look at subforms (forms within a form). You will be working with the GardenCo database files and other sample files that are stored in the following sub-folders of the Office XP SBS\Access\Chap11 folder: FormByWiz, Properties, Layout, Controls, Events, AutoForm, and Subform.

Creating a Form Using a Wizard

Before you begin creating a form, you need to know what table it will be based on and have an idea of how the form will be used. Having made these decisions, you can use the Form Wizard to help create the basic form. Remember though, that like almost any other object in Access, after the form is created you can always go into Design view to customize the form if it does not quite meet your needs.

GardenCo

In this exercise, you'll create a form that will be used to add new customer records to the Customers table of The Garden Company's database. The working folder for this exercise is Office XP SBS\Access\Chap11\FormByWiz. Follow these steps:

1   Open the **GardenCo** database located in the working folder.

2   On the **Objects** bar, click **Forms**.

3 Double-click **Create form by using wizard** to start the **Form Wizard,** whose first page looks like this:

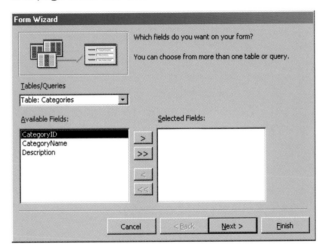

4 In the **Tables/Queries** list, click **Table: Customers** to display the fields from that table in the **Available Fields** list.

5 Click the **>>** button to move all the fields from the Customers table to the **Selected Fields** list, and then click **Next**.

You use the second page of the **Form Wizard** to select the layout of the fields on the new form. When you click an option on the right side of the page, the preview area on the left side shows what the form layout will look like with that option applied.

6 Click **Columnar**, and then click **Next**.

In this page, you can click a style option to see how the selected style will look when applied to the form.

7 Click the **Sumi Painting** style from the list, and click **Next**.

8 Because this form is based on the Customers table, Access suggests *Customers* as the form's title. Accept this suggestion, leave the **Open the form to view or enter information** option selected, and click **Finish**.

The new Customers form opens, displaying the first customer record in the Customers table, like the one on the next page.

Customers			_ □ ×
▶	Customer ID	ACKPI	
	First Name	Pilar	
	Last Name	Ackerman	
	Address	8808 Backbay St.	
	City	Bellevue	
	Region	WA	
	Postal Code	88337	
	Country	USA	
	Phone Number	(206) 555-0194	

Record: ◄◄ ◄ [1] ► ►I ►* of 110

9 Use the navigation controls at the bottom of the form to scroll through a few of the records.

10 Close the form and the database.

Refining Form Properties

As with tables, you can work with forms in multiple views. The two most common views are Form view, which you use to view or enter data, and Design view, which you use to add controls to the form or change the form's properties or layout.

When you use the **Form Wizard** to create a form in a column format, every field you select from the underlying table is represented by a text box control and its associated label control. A form like this one, which is used to enter or view the information stored in a specific table, is linked, or **bound**, to that table. Each text box—the box where data is entered or viewed—is bound to a specific field in the table. The table is the **record source**, and the field is the **control source**. Each control has a number of properties, such as font, font size, alignment, fill color, and border. The wizard assigns default values for these properties, but you can change them to improve the form's appearance.

In this exercise, you will edit the properties of the Customers form so that it suits the needs of the people who will be using it on a daily basis. The working folder for this exercise is Office XP SBS\Access\Chap11\Properties. Follow these steps:

1 Open the **GardenCo** database located in the working folder.

Design

2 With **Forms** selected on the **Objects** bar, select **Customers** in the list of forms, and click the **Design** button.

This form opens in Design view, like this (the toolbox has been moved):

Text box control — Toolbox

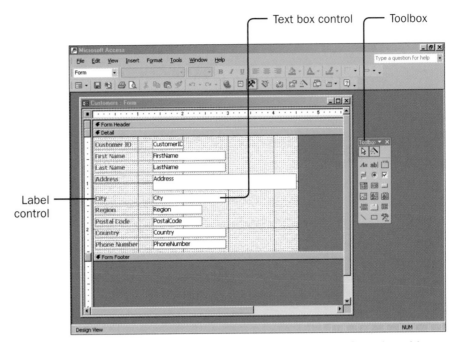

Label control

When a form is created, some of its properties are inherited from the table on which it is based. In this case, the names assigned to the text boxes (*First-Name*, *LastName*, and so on) are the field names from the Customers table, and the labels to the left of each text box reflect the **Caption** property of each field. The size of each text box is determined by the **Field Size** property.

Tip

After a form has been created, its properties are not bound to their source. Changing the table's field properties has no impact on the corresponding form property, and vice versa.

3 Change the font of the **Customer ID** label by clicking the label and clicking **Microsoft Sans Serif** in the **Font** list on the Formatting toolbar. (If you don't see **Microsoft Sans Serif**, click **MS Sans Serif**.)

4 With the label still selected, click **8** in the **Font Size** list to make the font slightly smaller.

5 Right-click the **CustomerID** text box, and click **Properties** on the shortcut menu to display this **Properties** dialog box for the **CustomerID** text box.

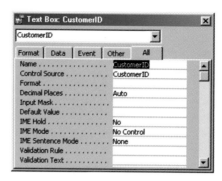

All the settings available on the toolbar are also available (with other settings) in a **Properties** dialog box that is associated with each control. You can use this dialog box to display the properties of any object on the form, including the form itself: simply select the object from the drop-down list at the top of the dialog box.

You can display related types of properties by clicking the appropriate tab: **Format**, **Data**, **Event**, and **Other**. Or you can display all the properties by clicking the **All** tab.

6   Click the **Format** tab, scroll to the **Font Name** property, and change it to **Microsoft Sans Serif** (or **MS Sans Serif**). Then set **Font Size** to **8**, and set **Font Weight** to **Bold**.

On the form behind the dialog box, you can see how these changes affect the *CustomerID* text in the text box.

Tip

When you are working in Design view with the **Properties** dialog box open, you can drag the dialog box by its title bar to the side of the screen so that you can see the changes you're making to the form.

7   Click **FirstName_Label** in the drop-down list at the top of the **Properties** dialog box, to select the label to the left of the **FirstName** text box.

8   Change the font settings for this control, as you did for the previous one.

These different ways of selecting a control and changing its properties provide some flexibility and convenience, but you can see that it would be a bit tedious to apply any of them to a few dozen controls on a form. The next two steps provide a faster method.

9   Click in the form and press ⌃+Ⓐ to select all the controls in the **Detail** section of the form.

Tip

Small black handles appear around all the controls to indicate that they are selected. The title bar of the Properties dialog box now displays *Multiple selection*, and the **Objects** list is blank. Only the **Format** settings that have the same settings for all the selected controls are displayed. Because the changes you made in the previous steps are not shared by all the selected controls, the **Font Name**, **Font Size**, and **Font Weight** settings are now blank.

10 To apply the settings to all the selected controls, set the **Font Name**, **Font Size**, and **Font Weight** as you did in step 6.

11 With all controls still selected, click **Back Style** on the **Format** tab, and set it to **Normal**. The background of the labels will no longer be transparent.

12 Click **Back Color**, and then click the **...** button to display this **Color** dialog box:

13 Click pale yellow, and click **OK**.

Tip

The background of all the controls changes to a pale yellow.

14 Set **Special Effect** to **Shadowed**, and set **Border Color** to a shade of green (such as 32768).

15 Click the **Detail** section of the form to deselect all the controls. Your form should now look something like this:

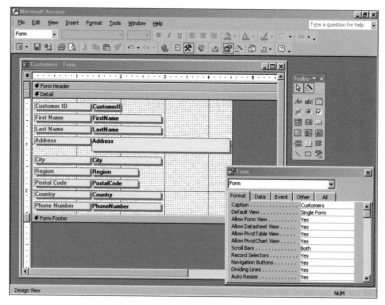

16 Click the label to the left of **FirstName**, and in the **Properties** dialog box, change the caption to **Name**.

17 Repeat the above step to change *Phone Number* to **Phone**.

Tip

You can edit the **Caption** property of a label or the **Control Source** property of a text box by selecting it, clicking its text, and then editing the text as you would in any other Windows application. However, take care when editing the **Control Source** property, which defines where the content of the text box comes from.

18 Remove the label to the left of **LastName** by clicking it and pressing the ⌫ key.

19 Select all the labels, but not their corresponding text boxes, by holding down the Shift key as you click each of them. Then in the **Properties** dialog box, set the **Text Align** property to **Left**.

20 On the **Format** tab, point to **Size**, and then click **ToFit**, to size the labels to fit their contents, as shown here:

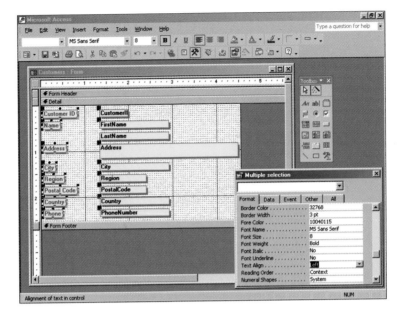

Tip

The order in which you make formatting changes, such as the ones above, can have an impact on the results. If you don't see the expected results, click the **Undo** button or press Ctrl+Z to step back through your changes, and then try again.

21 Now select all the text boxes, but not their corresponding labels, and in the **Properties** dialog box, change the **Left** setting to **1.5"** to insert a little more space between the labels and the text boxes.

22 Change **Font Weight** to **Normal**, and then click anywhere outside the controls to deselect them.

23 To change the background to one that better represents The Garden Company, select **Form** from the drop-down list of objects at the top of the **Properties** dialog box, click the **Picture** property—which shows *(bitmap)*—and then click the **...** button to open the **Insert Picture** dialog box.

24 Navigate to Office XP SBS\Access\Chap11\Properties the folder, change the **Files of type** setting to **Graphics Interchange Format**, and double-click **tgc_bkgrnd**.

The form's background changes, and the path to the graphic used for the new background is displayed in the **Picture** property.

25 Close the **Properties** dialog box to view your form, which should now look similar to the one on the next page.

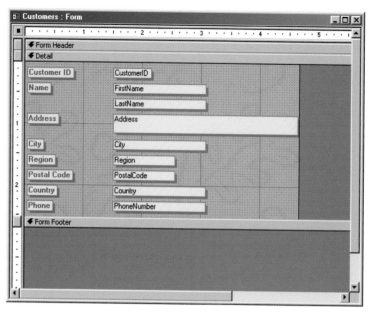

Save

26 Click the **Save** button to save the design of your Customers form.

27 Close the form and the database.

Refining Form Layout

The forms created by a wizard are functional, not fancy. However, it's fairly easy to customize the layout to suit your needs. You can add and delete labels, move both labels and text controls around the form, add logos and other graphics, and otherwise improve the layout of the form to make it attractive and easy to use.

As you work with a form's layout, it is important to pay attention to the shape of the pointer, which changes to indicate the manner in which you can change the selected item. Because a text box and its label sometimes act as a unit, you have to be careful to notice the pointer's shape before making any change. This table explains what action each shape indicates.

	Shape	Action
🖐	Hand	Drag to move both controls together, as one.
👆	Pointing finger	Drag to move just the control.
↕	Vertical arrows	Drag the top or bottom border to change the height.
↔	Horizontal arrows	Drag the right or left border to change the width.
↘	Diagonal arrows	Drag the corner to change both the height and width.

GardenCo

In this exercise, you will rearrange the label and text box controls on the Customers form to make them more closely fit the way people will work with them. The working folder for this exercise is Office XP SBS\Access\Chap11\Layout. Follow these steps:

1   Open the **GardenCo** database located in the working folder.

2   Open the **Customers** form in Design view.

3   If necessary, drag the lower right corner of the Form window down and to the right until you can see the **Form Footer** at the bottom of the form and have an inch or so of blank area to the right of the background, like this:

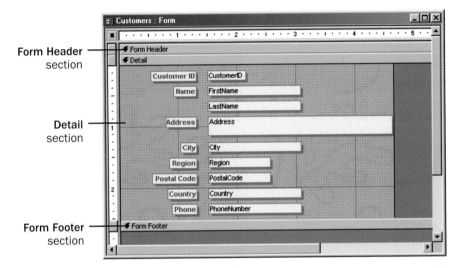

The form is divided into three sections: **Form Header**, **Detail**, and **Form Footer**. Only the **Detail** section currently has anything in it.

4   Point to the right edge of the **Detail** background, and when the pointer changes to a two-way arrow, drag the edge of the background to the right until you can see about five full grid sections.

5   Click the **LastName** text box, and then slowly move the pointer around its border, from black handle to black handle, noticing how it changes shape.

6   Move the pointer over the **LastName** text box and when it changes to a hand, drag it up to the right of the **FirstName** text box.

7   One by one, select each control, resize it and move it to the location shown in the figure on the next page.

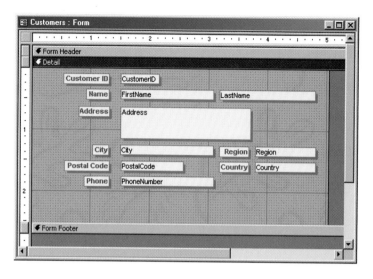

Tip

To fine-tune the size or position of a control, click it, move the pointer over the control until it becomes the shape for the change you want, and then press the appropriate Arrow key to move the control, in small increments, in a specific direction.

8   Now create and save a style based on this form so that you can apply it to any new form you create in the future, instead of having to make all of these manual adjustments each time. On the **Format** menu, click **AutoFormat** to display this **AutoFormat** dialog box:

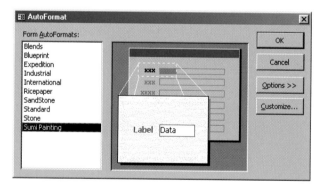

9   Click the **Customize** button to display the **Customize AutoFormat** dialog box.

10   Click **Create a new AutoFormat based on the Form 'Customers'**, and then click **OK**.

11   In the **New Style Name** dialog box, type The Garden Company as the name of the new style, and then click **OK**.

Back in the **AutoFormat** dialog box, the new style appears in the **Form Auto-Formats** list. From now on, this style will be available in any database you open on this computer.

12 Click **OK** to close the **AutoFormat** dialog box.

13 Click the **Save** button.

14 Close the form and the database.

Adding Controls to a Form

Every form has three basic sections: **Form Header**, **Detail**, and **Form Footer**. When you use a wizard to create a form, the wizard adds a set of controls for each field that you select from the underlying table to the **Detail** section and leaves the **Form Header** and **Form Footer** sections blank. Because these sections are empty, Access collapses them, but you can size all the sections by dragging their **selectors**. Although labels and text box controls are perhaps the most common controls found on forms, you can also enhance your forms with many other types of controls. For example, you can add groups of option buttons, check boxes, and list boxes to present people with choices instead of making them type entries in text boxes.

More Controls

The most popular controls are stored in the toolbox. Clicking the **More Controls** button displays a list of all the other controls that Access has discovered on your computer. The controls displayed when you click the **More Controls** button are not necessarily associated with Access or even with another Microsoft Office application. The list includes every control that any application has installed and registered on your computer.

Important

Some controls, such as the Calendar Control, can be very useful. Others might do nothing when you add them to a form, or might do something unexpected and not entirely pleasant. If you feel like experimenting, don't do so in a database that is important to you.

In this exercise, you will use the Customers form from the GardenCo database to add a graphic and a caption to the **Form Header** section. You will also replace the **Country** text box control in the **Detail** section with a combo box control. The working folder for this exercise is Office XP SBS\Access\Chap11\Controls. Follow these steps:

1 Open the **GardenCo** database located in the working folder.

2 Open the **Customers** form in Design view.

Toolbox

3   To get an idea of what controls are available, move the pointer over the buttons on the toolbox, pausing long enough to display each button's Screen-
Tip. (If the toolbox isn't displayed, click the **Toolbox** button.)

4   Point to the horizontal line between the **Form Header** section selector and
the **Detail** section selector and, when the pointer changes to a double arrow,
drag the **Detail** section selector down about 1 inch.

The form now looks like this:

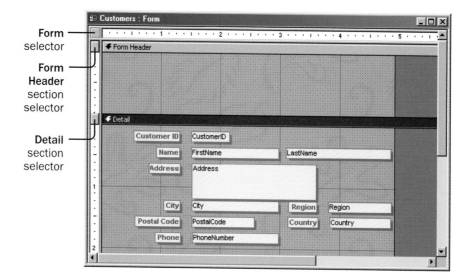

Image

5   Click the **Image** control on the toolbox, and then drag a rectangle about 1
inch high and 3 inches wide at the left end of the **Form Header** section.

When you release the mouse button, Access displays the **Insert Picture** dialog box where you can select an image to insert in the control.

6   Make sure that the Office XP SBS\Access\Chap11\Controls folder is
selected and that **Graphics Interchange Format** is the **Files of type** setting.
Then double-click **tgc_logo2**.

The Garden Company logo appears inside the image control.

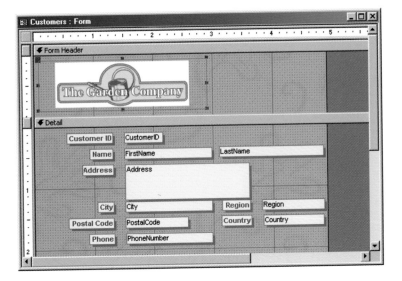

Tip

If the control isn't large enough, the image is cropped. You can enlarge the control to display the entire image. (You might also have to enlarge the **Form Header** section.)

Label

7 To add a caption to the header, click the **Label** control in the toolbox, and then drag another rectangle in the header section.

Access inserts a label control containing the insertion point, ready for you to enter a caption.

8 Type the caption **Customers**, and press Enter.

The Customers label takes on the formatting of the other labels.

9 With the **Customers** label selected, press the F4 key to display the **Properties** dialog box.

10 Change **Font Size** to **18**, and change **Text Align** to **Center**. Then close the **Properties** dialog box.

11 On the **Format** menu, point to **Size**, and then click **To Fit**.

12 Play with the size and position of the two controls you added until they look something like what you see on the next page.

249

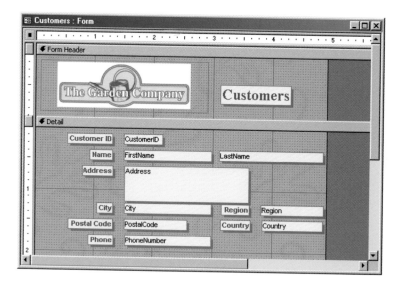

Control Wizards

13 If the **Control Wizards** button is active in the toolbox (has a border around it), click it to deselect it.

Combo Box

14 Insert a combo box in the **Details** section by clicking the **Combo Box** control in the toolbox, and then dragging a rectangle just below the current **Country** text box.

When you release the mouse, Access displays a combo box control, which is **unbound** (not attached to a field in the Customers table).

Format Painter

15 Copy the formatting of the **Country** text box to the new combo box control by clicking the **Country** text box, clicking the **Format Painter** button on the tool-bar, and then clicking the combo box control.

Both the combo box control and its label take on the new formatting.

16 Select the combo box again, and then display the **Properties** dialog box.

17 Click the **Data** tab, set **Control Source** to **Country**, and then type the following in the **Row Source** box:

SELECT DISTINCT Customers.Country FROM Customers;

(Note that there is no space between *Customers* and *Country*; there is only a period.)

This line is a query that extracts one example of every country in the **Country** field of the Customers table and displays the results as a list when you click the box's arrow.

The **Properties** dialog box now looks like this (you'll have to widen it to display the whole query):

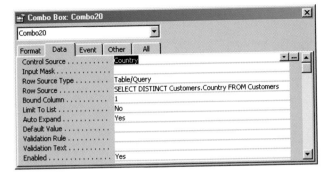

Tip

If you need to add a new customer from a country that is not on the list, you can type the new country in the combo box. After the record is added to the database, that country shows up when the combo box list is displayed.

18 If necessary, set the **Row Source Type** to **Table/Query**.

19 Click the label to the left of the combo box, click the dialog box's **Format** tab, change the caption to Country, and close the dialog box.

20 Delete the **Country** text box and its label, and move the new combo box and label into their place, resizing them as needed.

View

21 Click the **View** button to see your form, which looks similar to this:

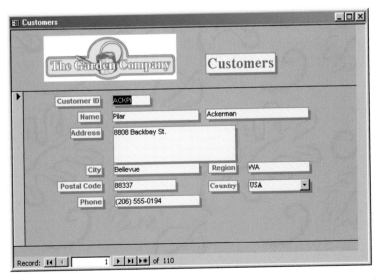

22 Scroll through a couple of records, and drop down the combo box's list to see how you can select a country.

23 You don't need the **record selector**—the gray bar along the left edge of the form—so return to Design view, display the form's **Properties** dialog box, and on the **Format** tab, change **Record Selectors** to **No**. While you're at it, change **Scroll Bars** to **Neither**. Then close the dialog box.

24 Save the form's new design, and switch to Form view for a final look.

25 Close the form and the database.

Using VBA to Enter Data in a Form

As you may have suspected by now, almost everything in Access, including the Access program itself, is an object. One of the characteristics of objects is that they can recognize and respond to **events**, which are essentially actions. Different objects recognize different events. The basic events, recognized by almost all objects, are Click, Double Click, Mouse Down, Mouse Move, and Mouse Up. Most objects recognize quite a few other events. A text control, for example, recognizes about 17 different events; a form recognizes more than 50.

Tip

You can see the list of events recognized by an object by looking at the **Event** tab on the object's **Properties** dialog box.

While you use a form, objects are signaling events, or **firing events**, almost constantly. However, unless you attach a macro or VBA procedure to an event, the object is really just firing blanks. By default, Access doesn't do anything obvious when it recognizes most events. So without interfering with the program's normal behavior, you can use an event to specify what action should happen. You can even use an event to trigger the running of a **macro** or a **Visual Basic for Applications (VBA) procedure** that performs a set of actions.

Sound complicated? Well, it's true that events are not things most casual Access users tend to worry about. But because knowing how to handle events can greatly increase the efficiency of objects like forms, you should take a glimpse of what they're all about while you have a form open.

For example, while looking at customer records in the GardenCo database, you might have noticed that the CustomerID is composed of the first three letters of the customer's last name and the first two letters of his or her first name, all in capital letters. This technique will usually generate a unique ID for a new customer. If you try to enter an ID that is already in use, Access won't accept the new entry, and you have to add a number or change the ID in some other way to make it unique. Performing trivial tasks, such as combining parts of two words and then converting the results to capital letters, is something a computer excels at. So rather than typing the ID for each new customer record that is added to The Garden Company's database, you can let VBA do it instead.

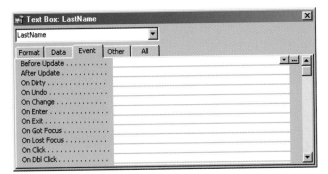

GardenCo
AftUpdate

In this exercise, you will write a few lines of VBA code and attach the code to the After Update event in the **LastName** text box on the Customers form. When you change the content of the text box and attempt to move out of it, the Before Update event is fired. In response to that event, Access updates the record in the source table, and then the After Update event is fired. This is the event you are going to work with. This is by no means an in-depth treatment of VBA, but this exercise will give you a taste of VBA's power. The working folder for this exercise is Office XP SBS\Access\Chap11\Events. Follow these steps:

1 Open the **GardenCo** database located in the working folder.

2 With **Forms** selected on the **Objects** bar, click **Customers** in the list of forms, and click the **Design** button.

3 Click the **LastName** text box to select it, and if necessary, press ⌧ to open the **Properties** dialog box.

4 Click the **Event** tab to see these options:

This tab lists all the events that the **LastName** text box control can respond to.

5 You want to attach VBA code to the After Update event, so click **After Update** in the list, and then click the **...** button.

The **Choose Builder** dialog box appears, offering you the options of building an expression, a macro, or VBA code.

6 Click **Code Builder**, and then click **OK** to open the VBA Editor.

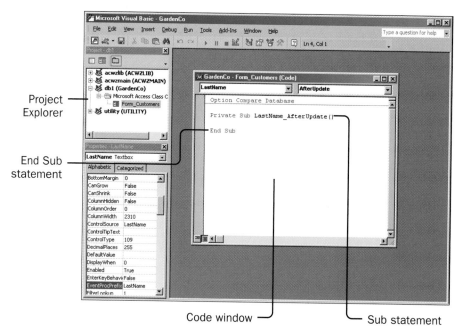

Project Explorer

End Sub statement

Code window —

Sub statement

In the **Project Explorer** pane, the editor lists any objects you have created to which you can attach code; in this case, only the Customers form (**Form_Customers**) is listed. As you create more forms and reports, they will appear here.

The Code window displays a placeholder for the procedure that Access will use to handle the After Update event for the LastName text control. This procedure is named *LastName_AfterUpdate()*, and at the moment it contains only the Sub and End Sub statements that mark the beginning and end of any procedure.

7 Type the following lines between the Sub and End Sub statements, or open the file named *AftUpdate.txt* in the Office XP SBS\Access\Chap11\Events folder, and copy and paste the lines:

```
'Create variables to hold first and last names
' and customer ID.
Dim fName As String
Dim lName As String
Dim cID As String

'Assign the text in the LastName text box to
' the lName variable.
lName = Forms!customers!LastName.Text

'You must set the focus to a text box before
' you can read its contents.
```

```
Forms!customers!FirstName.SetFocus
fName = Forms!customers!FirstName.Text

'Combine portions of the last and first names
' to create the customer ID.
cID = UCase(Left(lName, 3) & Left(fName, 2))

'Don't store the ID unless it is 5 characters long,
' (which indicates both names have been filled in).
If Len(cID) = 5 Then
    Forms!customers!CustomerID.SetFocus

    'Don't change the ID if it has already been
    ' entered; perhaps it was changed manually.
    If Forms!customers!CustomerID.Text = "" Then
        Forms!customers!CustomerID = cID
    End If
End If

'Set the focus where it would have gone naturally.
Forms!customers!Address.SetFocus
```

Important

When a line of text is preceded by an apostrophe, the text is a comment that explains the purpose of the next line of code. In the VBA Editor, comments are displayed in green.

Save

8 Click the **Save** button on the VBA Editor's toolbar.

View Microsoft Access

9 Click the **View Microsoft Access** button to return to the Access window, and close the **Properties** dialog box.

10 Click the **View** button on the toolbar to switch to Form view.

New Record

11 Size the window as necessary. Then on the **Navigation** bar, click the **New Record** button to create a new record.

12 Press the ⍤ key to move the insertion point to the **FirstName** text box, type John, press ⍤ to move to the **LastName** text box, type Coake, and then press ⍤ again.

If you entered the VBA code correctly, *COAJO* appears in the **CustomerID** text box.

13 Change the first and last name to something else and notice that the **CustomerID** text box doesn't change even if the names from which it was derived do change.

14 Press the Esc key to remove your entry, and then try entering the last name first, followed by the first name.

Access does not create a Customer ID. The code does what it was written to do (but not necessarily what you want it to do), which is create an ID regardless of the order in which the names are entered. There are several ways to fix this problem. You could write a similar procedure to handle the After Update event in the **FirstName** text box, or you could write one procedure to handle both events and then jump to it when either event occurs. You won't do either in these exercises, but if you are interested, you can look at the code in the database file for the next exercise to see the second solution.

15 Press Esc to clear your entries, and then close the **Customers** form and the database.

16 Press Alt+Tab to switch to the VBA Editor, which is still open, and close the editor.

Creating a Form Using AutoForm

Although a form doesn't have to include all the fields from a table, when it is used as the primary method of creating new records, it usually does include all of them. The quickest way to create a form that includes all the fields from one table is to use an **AutoForm**. And as with the forms created by a wizard, you can easily customize these forms.

GardenCo

In this exercise, you will create an AutoForm that displays information about each of the products carried by The Garden Company. The working folder for this exercise is Office XP SBS\Access\Chap11\AutoForm. Follow these steps:

1 Open the **GardenCo** database located in the working folder.

2 On the **Objects** bar, click **Forms**.

New

3 On the database window's toolbar, click the **New** button to display the **New Form** dialog box, which lists all the ways you can create a form.

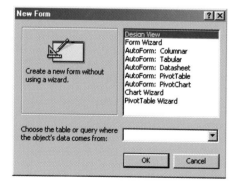

4 Click **AutoForm: Columnar** in the list of choices, select the **Categories** table from the drop-down list at the bottom of the dialog box, and then click **OK**.

The dialog box closes, and after a moment a new Categories form is displayed in Form view.

5 Click the **Save** button, accept the default name of **Categories** in the **Save As** dialog box, and click **OK** to view your form, which looks like this:

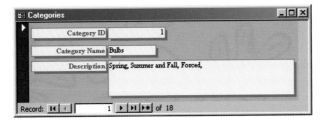

Tip

When AutoForm creates a form, Access applies the background style you selected the last time you used the **Form Wizard** (or the default style, if you haven't used the wizard). If your form doesn't look like this one, switch to Design view, and on the **Format** menu, click **AutoFormat**. You can then select **The Garden Company** style from the list displayed.

6 This form looks pretty good as it is, but switch to Design view so that you can make a few minor changes.

7 Delete the word *Category* from the **Category Name** label.

8 The **CategoryID** value is provided by Access and should never be changed, so disable that control by clicking it and, if necessary, pressing [F4] to display the control's **Properties** dialog box.

9 On the **Data** tab, change **Enabled** to **No**, and close the dialog box.

10 Switch to Form view, and scroll through a few categories. Try to edit entries in the **Category ID** field, to confirm that you can't.

11 You don't need the record selector for the form, so return to Design view, display the form's **Properties** dialog box, and on the **Format** tab, change **Scroll Bars** to **Neither** and **Record Selectors** to **No**.

12 Save and close the **Categories** form.

13 Close the database.

Adding a Subform to a Form

A form can display information (fields) from one or more tables or queries. If you want to display fields from several tables or queries on one form, you have to give some thought to the **relationships** that must exist between those objects.

In Access, a relationship is an association between common fields in two tables, and it allows you to relate the information in one table to the information in another table. For example, in the GardenCo database a relationship can be established between the Categories table and the Products table because both tables have a CategoryID field. Each product is in one category, and each category can contain many products, so this type of relationship—the most common—is known as a **one-to-many relationship**.

As you create forms and queries, Access might recognize some relationships between the fields in the underlying tables. However, it probably won't recognize all of them without a little help from you.

Other Types of Relationships

In addition to one-to-many relationships, you can create **one-to-one relationships** and **many-to-many relationships**, but they are not as common.

In a one-to-one relationship each record in one table can have one and only one related record in the other table. This type of relationship isn't commonly used because it is easier to put all the fields in one table. However, you might use two related tables instead of one to break up a table with many fields, or to track information that applies to only some of the records in the first table.

A many-to-many relationship is really two one-to-many relationships tied together through a third table. For example, the GardenCo database contains Products, Orders, and Order Details tables. The Products table has one record for each product sold by The Garden Company, and each product has a unique ProductID. The Orders table has one record for each order placed with The Garden Company, and each record in it has a unique OrderID. However, the Orders table doesn't specify which products were included in each order; that information is in the Order Details table, which is the table in the middle that ties the other two tables together. Products and Orders each have a one-to-many relationship with Order Details. Products and Orders therefore have a many-to-many relationship with each other. In plain language, this means that every product can appear in many orders, and every order can include many products.

GardenCo

In this exercise, you will first define the relationship between the Categories and Products tables in the GardenCo database. You will then add a **subform** to a form. For each category displayed on the main form, this subform will display all the products in that category. The working folder for this exercise is Office XP SBS\Access\Chap11\Subform. Follow these steps:

1 Open the **GardenCo** database located in the working folder.

Relationships

2 On the Access toolbar, click the **Relationships** button to open the Relationships window.

Show Table

3 If the **Show Table** dialog box isn't displayed, click the **Show Table** button on the toolbar, and then double-click **Categories** and **Products** in the list displayed. Close the **Show Table** dialog box to view the Relationships window, which looks like this:

4 Point to **CategoryID** in one table, and drag it on top of **CategoryID** in the other table.

Access displays the **Edit Relationships** dialog box, which lists the fields you have chosen to relate and offers several options, as shown here:

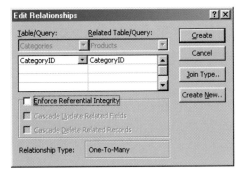

5 Click the **Enforce Preferential Integrity** check box, click the other two check boxes, and then click **Create**.

Tip

Access uses a system of rules called **referential integrity** to ensure that relationships between records in related tables are valid, and that you don't accidentally delete or change related data. When the Cascade Update Related Fields check box is selected, changing a primary key value in the primary table automatically updates the matching value in all related records. When the Cascade Delete Related Records check box is selected, deleting a record in the primary table deletes any related records in the related table.

Access draws a line representing the one-to-many relationship between the **CategoryID** fields in each of the tables, as shown here:

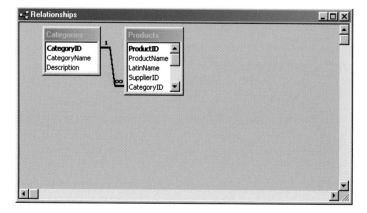

Tip

You can edit or delete a relationship by right-clicking the line and clicking the appropriate command on the shortcut menu.

6 Close the Relationships window, clicking **Yes** when prompted to save its layout.

7 Open the **Categories** form in Design view.

8 Enlarge the Form window, and drag the **Form Footer** section selector down about 1 inch to give yourself some room to work.

9 If the toolbox isn't displayed, click the **Toolbox** button.

10 Make sure the **Control Wizards** button in the toolbox is active (has a border around it).

Subform/
Subreport

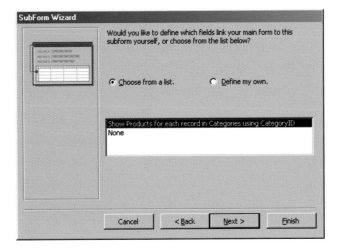

11 Click the **Subform/Subreport** button, and drag a rectangle in the lower portion of the **Details** section.

A white object appears on the form, and the first page of the **Subform Wizard** opens.

12 Leave **Use existing Tables and Queries** selected, and click **Next**.

13 In the **Tables/Queries** list, click **Table: Products**.

14 Add the **ProductName**, **CategoryID**, **QuantityPerUnit**, **UnitPrice**, and **UnitsInStock** fields to the **Selected Fields** list by clicking each one and then clicking the **>** button. Then click **Next** to display this third page of the wizard:

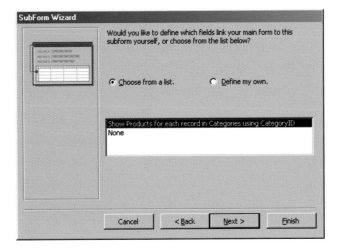

Because a field in the subform is related to a field in the main form (**CategoryID**), the wizard selects **Show Products for each record in Categories using CategoryID** as the **Choose from a list** option.

Tip

If the wizard can't figure out which fields are related, it selects the **Define my own** option and displays list boxes in which you can specify the fields to be related.

15 Click **Next** to accept the default selection, and then click **Finish** to accept the default name for the subform and complete the process.

Access displays the Categories form in Design view, with an embedded Products subform. The size and location of the subform is determined by the original rectangle you dragged on the form.

16 Adjust the size and location of the objects on your form so that it resembles the one on the next page.

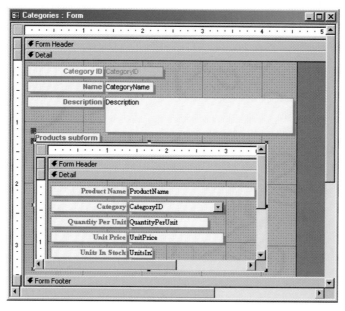

17 Notice the layout of the subform, and then click **View** to switch to Form view, where the form looks like this:

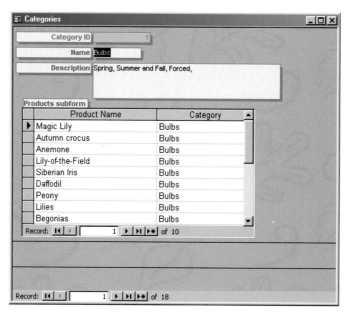

The format of the subform has totally changed. In Design view, it looks like a simple form, but in Form view, it looks like a datasheet.

18 Switch back to Design view, make any necessary size adjustments, and if necessary, open the **Properties** dialog box.

Form Selector

19 Click the **Form** selector in the upper left corner of the subform twice.

The first click selects the Products subform control, and the second click selects the form. A small black square appears in the button.

20 On the **Format** tab of the Properties dialog box, change both **Record Selectors** and **Navigation Buttons** to **No**.

While on this tab, notice the **Default View** property, which is set to **Datasheet**. You might want to return to this property and try the other options after finishing this exercise.

21 Switch back to Form view, and drag the dividers between column headers until you can see all the fields. Here are the results:

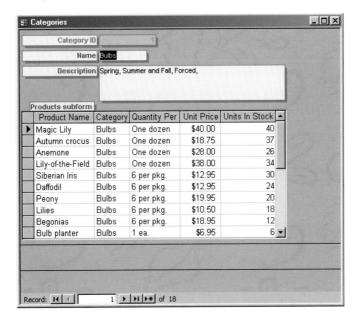

Tip

You can quickly adjust the width of columns to fit their data by double-clicking the double arrow between column headings.

First Record

22 Click the navigation buttons to scroll through several categories. When you are through, click the **First Record** button to return to the first category (**Bulbs**).

As each category is displayed at the top of the form, the products in that category are listed in the datasheet in the subform.

23 Click the category name to the right of the first product.

The arrow at the right end of the box indicates that this is a combo box.

24 Click the arrow to display the list of categories, and change the category to **Cacti**.

Next Record

25 Click the **Next Record** navigation button to move to the next category (Cacti).

You can see that the first product is now included in this category.

26 Display the list of categories, and restore the first product to the **Bulbs** category.

27 You don't want people to be able to change a product's category, so return to Design view. Then in the subform, click the **CategoryID** combo box control, and press ⌫.

Important

You included the **CategoryID** field when the wizard created this subform because it is the field that relates the Categories and Products tables. The underlying Products table uses a combo box to display the name of the category instead of its ID number, so that combo box also appears on the subform.

28 Save the form, then switch back to Form view, and adjust the width of the subform columns and the size of the Form window until your form looks like this:

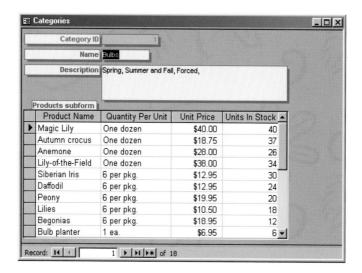

29 Close the **Categories** form, saving your changes to both the form and the subform.

30 Close the database.

Creating a Form and Subform with a Wizard

If you know when you create a form that you are going to add a subform, you can do the whole job with the **Form Wizard**, like this:

1 On the **Objects** bar, click **Forms**, and then click the **New** button on the database window's toolbar.

2 Click **Form Wizard**, select the form's base table from the list at the bottom of the page, and then click **OK**.

3 Verify that the table you selected is shown in the **Table/Queries** list, and then click the **>>** button to include all the fields in the new form.

4 Drop down the **Tables/Queries** list, and select the subform's base table.

5 Double-click the desired fields to add them to the list of selected fields, and then click **Next**.

6 Accept the default options, and click **Next**.

7 Accept the default **Datasheet** option, and click **Next**.

8 Click **Finish** to create the form and subform.

You can then clean up the form to suit your needs, just as you did in this exercise.

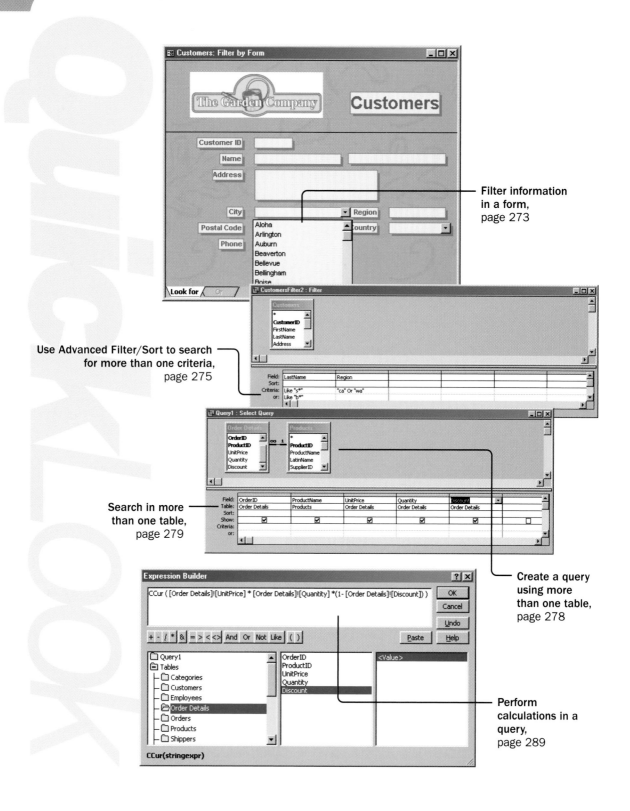

Filter information
in a form,
page 273

Use Advanced Filter/Sort to search
for more than one criteria,
page 275

Search in more
than one table,
page 279

Create a query
using more
than one table,
page 278

Perform
calculations in a
query,
page 289

Chapter 12
Locating Specific Information

After completing this chapter, you will be able to:

✔ Sort information on one or more fields.

✔ Filter information in various ways.

✔ Create queries that find information in one or more tables.

✔ Create a query to calculate totals.

A database is a repository for information. It may hold a few records in one table or thousands of records in many related tables. No matter how much information is stored in a database, it is useful only if you can locate the information you need when you need it. In a small database you can find information simply by scrolling through a table until you spot what you are looking for. But as a database grows in size and complexity, locating specific information becomes more difficult.

Microsoft Access provides a variety of tools you can use to organize the display of information in a database and to locate specific items of information. Using these tools, you can focus on just part of the information by quickly sorting a table based on any field (or combination of fields), or you can filter the table so that information containing some combination of characters is displayed (or excluded from the display). With a little more effort, you can create queries to display specific fields from specific records from one or more tables. You can even save these queries so that you can use them over and over again.

A query can do more than simply return a list of records from a table. You can use functions in a query that perform calculations on the information in the table to produce the sum, average, count, and other mathematical values.

In this chapter you will learn how to pinpoint precisely the information you need in a database through the use of sort and filter tools, and queries. You will be working with the GardenCo database files that are stored in the following subfolders of the Office XP SBS\Access\Chap12 folder: Sort, FilterDS, FilterForm, AdvFilter, QueryDes, QueryWiz and Aggregate.

Sorting Information

Information stored in a table can be sorted in either ascending or descending order, based on the values in one or more fields in the table. You could, for example, sort a customer table alphabetically based first on the last name of each customer and then on the first name. Such a sort would result in this type of list, which resembles those found in telephone books:

Smith	Denise
Smith	James
Smith	Jeff
Smith	Neil
Smith	Samantha

Occasionally you may need to sort a table to group all entries of one type together—for example, to get a discount on postage, The Garden Company might want to sort customer records on the Postal Code field to group the codes before printing mailing labels.

GardenCo

In this exercise, you will learn several ways to sort the information in a datasheet or a form. The working folder for this exercise is Office XP SBS\Access\Chap12\Sort. Follow these steps:

1 Open the **GardenCo** database located in the working folder.

2 Open the **Customers** table in Datasheet view.

Sort Ascending

3 To sort by Region, click anywhere in the **Region** column, and then click the **Sort Ascending** button.

Tip

You can also use the **Sort Ascending** or **Sort Descending** commands on the **Records** menu; or you can right-click the column in the datasheet and click either command on the shortcut menu.

The records are rearranged in order of region.

Sort Descending

4 To reverse the sort order, while still in the **Region** column, click the **Sort Descending** button.

The records for Washington State (WA) are now at the top of your list. In both sorts, the region was sorted alphabetically, but the **City** field was left in a seemingly random order, when what you really want to see is the records arranged by city within each region.

How Access Sorts

The concept of sorting seems pretty intuitive, but sometimes the computer's approach to such a concept is not so intuitive. Sorting "numbers" is a case in point. In Access, numbers can be treated as text or as numerals. Because of the spaces, hyphens, and punctuation typically used in street addresses, Postal Codes, and telephone numbers, the numbers in these fields are usually treated as text, and sorting them follows the logic applied to sorting all text. Numbers in a price or quantity field, on the other hand, are typically treated as numerals. When Access sorts text, it sorts first on the first character in the selected field in every record, then on the next character, then on the next, and so on—until it runs out of characters. When Access sorts numbers, it treats the contents of each field as a single value, and sorts the records based on that value. This tactic can result in seemingly strange sort orders. For example, sorting the list in the first column of the following table as text produces the list in the second column. Sorting the same list as numerals produces the list in the third column.

Original	Sort as Text	Sort as Number
1	1	1
1234	11	2
23	12	3
3	1234	4
11	2	5
22	22	11
12	23	12
4	3	22
2	4	23
5	5	1234

If a field with the Text data type contains numbers, you can sort the field numerically by padding the numbers with leading zeros so that all entries are the same length. For example, 001, 011, and 101 sort correctly even if the numbers are defined as text.

Tip

Access can sort on more than one field, but it sorts consecutively from left to right. So the fields you want to sort must be adjacent, and they must be arranged in the order in which you want to sort them.

5 To move the **Region** field to the left of the **City** field, click its header to select the column, and then drag the column to the left until a dark line appears between **Address** and **City**.

6 Because **Region** is already selected, hold down the ⎡shift⎤ key and click the **City** header to extend the selection so that both the **Region** and **City** columns are selected.

7 Click the **Sort Ascending** button to arrange the records with the regions in ascending order and the city names also in ascending order within each region (or in this case, each state).

Tip

You sort records while viewing them in a form. Simply click the box of the field on which you want to base the sort, and then click one of the **Sort** buttons. However, you can't sort on multiple fields in Form view.

8 The order of the columns in the Customer table doesn't really matter, but go ahead and move the **Region** column back to where it was.

9 Save and close the **Customers** table.

10 Close the database.

Filtering Information in a Table

Sorting the information in a table organizes it in a logical manner, but you still have the entire table to deal with. If your goal is to locate all records containing information in one or more fields that match a particular pattern, one of the available **Filter** commands will satisfy your needs. For example, you could quickly create a filter to locate every customer of The Garden Company who lives in Seattle. Or you could find everyone who placed an order on January 13. Or you could locate all customers who live outside of the United States.

You can apply simple filters while viewing information in a table or a form. These filters are applied to the contents of a selected field; but you can also apply another filter to the results of the first one, to further refine your search.

Tip

The **Filter** commands you will use in this exercise are available by pointing to **Filter** on the **Records** menu; by clicking buttons on the toolbar; and on the shortcut menu. However, not all **Filter** commands are available in each of these places.

GardenCo

In this exercise, you will practice several methods of filtering information in a table. The working folder for this exercise is Office XP SBS\Access\Chap12\FilterDS. Follow these steps:

1 Open the **GardenCo** database located in the working folder.

2 Open the **Customers** table in Datasheet view.

Filter By Selection

3 Click any instance of **Sidney** in the **City** field, and then click the **Filter By Selection** button.

The number of customers displayed in the table changes from 110 to 2, both of whom live in Sidney.

Important

When you filter a table, the records that don't match the filter aren't removed from the table; they are simply not displayed.

Remove Filter

4 Click the **Remove Filter** button to redisplay the rest of the customers.

5 What if you want a list of all customers who live anywhere that has a Postal Code starting with *V3F*? Find one example, select the characters **V3F**, and then click the **Filter By Selection** button again.

Only the 2 records with Postal Codes starting with *V3F* are now visible.

6 Click **Remove Filter**.

7 What if this table is enormous and you aren't sure if it contains even one *V3F*? Right-click any Postal Code, click **Filter For** on the shortcut menu, type **V3F*** in the cell, and press [Enter] to see the same results.

The asterisk (*) is a wildcard character that tells Access to search for any entry in the Postal Code field that starts with *V3F*.

8 To find out how many customers live outside the United States, remove the current filter, right-click the **Country** field in any USA record, and click **Filter Excluding Selection** on the shortcut menu.

You see all customers from other countries (in this case, only Canada).

9 To experiment with one more filtering technique, remove the filter, save and close the **Customers** table, and open the **Orders** table in Datasheet view.

Wildcard Characters

When you don't know or aren't sure of a character or set of characters, you can use **wildcard characters** as placeholders for those unknown characters in your search criteria. The most common wildcard characters are:

Character	Description	Example
*	Match any number of characters.	Lname = Co* returns Colman and Conroy.
?	Match any single alphabetic character.	Fname = eri? returns Eric and Erik.
#	Match any single numeric character.	ID = 1## returns any ID from 100 through 199.

10 To find all orders taken by Michael Emanuel on January 23, right-click **Emanuel, Michael** in the **Employee** field, and click **Filter By Selection** on the shortcut menu.

11 Right-click **23-Jan-2001** in the **OrderDate** field, and again click **Filter By Selection** on the shortcut menu.

You now have a list of Michael's orders on the 23rd. You could continue to refine this list by filtering on another field, or you could sort the results by clicking in a field and then clicking one of the **Sort** buttons.

Tip

After you have located just the information you want and have organized it appropriately, you can display the results in a form or report. Simply click the **New Object** button on the toolbar, and follow the directions.

12 Remove the filters by clicking the **Remove Filter** button.

13 Save and close the **Orders** table.

14 Close the database.

Tip

You can use the **Filter** commands to filter the information in a table when you are viewing it in a form. The **Filter For** command is often useful with forms because you don't have to be able to see the desired selection.

Filtering By Form

The **Filter By Form** command provides a quick and easy way to filter a table based on the information in several fields. If you open a table and then click the **Filter By Form** button, what you see looks like a simple datasheet. However, each of the blank cells is a combo box with a scrollable drop–down list of all the entries in that field, like this:

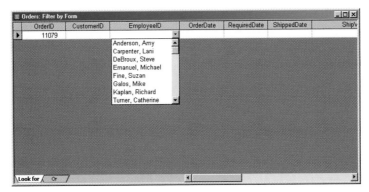

You can make a selection from the list and click the **ApplyFilter** button to display only the records containing your selection.

Using **Filter By Form** on a table that has only a few fields, such as this one, is easy. But using it on a table that has a few dozen fields gets a bit cumbersome. Then it's easier to use **Filter By Form** in the form version of the table. If you open a form and then click **Filter By Form**, you see an empty form. Clicking in any box and then clicking its arrow displays a list of all the entries in the field, like this:

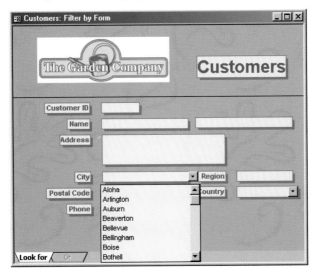

273

If you make a selection and click the **ApplyFilter** button, clicking the **Next Record** navigation button displays the first record that meets your selection criteria, then the next, and so on.

Tip

Filter By Form offers the same features and techniques whether you are using it in a form or a table. Because defining the filter is sometimes easier in a form and viewing the results is sometimes easier in a table, you might consider using **AutoForm** to quickly create a form for a table. You can then use the form with **Filter By Form** rather than the table, and then switch to Datasheet view to look at the results.

GardenCo

In this exercise, you will try to track down a customer whose last name you have forgotten. You are pretty sure the name starts with *S* and the customer is from California or Washington, so you are going to use **Filter By Form** to try and locate the customer's record. The working folder for this exercise is Office XP SBS\Access\Chap12\Filter-Form. Follow these steps:

1 Open the **GardenCo** database located in the working folder.

2 Open the **Customers** form in Form view.

Filter By Form

3 Click the **Filter By Form** button on the toolbar.

The Customers form, which displays the information from one record, is replaced by its Filter By Form version, which has a blank box for each field and the **Look for** and **Or** tabs at the bottom.

4 Click the **LastName** box, type **s***, and press [Enter] to tell Access to display all last names starting with s.

Access converts your entry to the proper format, or **syntax**, for this type of expression: *Like "s*"*

5 Click the **Region** box, and select **CA** from the drop-down list.

Apply Filter

6 Click the **Apply Filter** button on the Standard toolbar to see only the customers living in California whose last names begin with s.

Access replaces the filter window with the regular Customers form, and the navigation bar at the bottom of the form indicates that three filtered records are available.

7 Click the **Filter By Form** button to switch back to the filter.

Your filter criteria are still displayed. When you enter filter criteria using any method, they are saved as a form property and are available until replaced by other criteria.

8 To add the customers from another state, click the **Or** tab.

This tab has the same blank cells as the **Look for** tab. You can switch back and forth between the two tabs to confirm that your criteria haven't been cleared.

Tip

When you display the **Or** tab, a second **Or** tab appears so that you can include a third state if you want.

9 Type **s*** in the **LastName** box, type or select **WA** in the **Region** box, and then click the **Apply Filter** button.

You can scroll through the filtered Customers form to view the six matched records.

10 Close the **Customers** form, and then close the database.

Locating Information with the Advanced Filter/Sort Command

Filter By Selection, **Filter For Input,** and **Filter By Form** are quick and easy ways to home in on the information you need, as long as your filter criteria are fairly simple. But suppose The Garden Company needs to locate all the orders shipped to Midwest states between specific dates by either of two shippers. When you need to search a single table for records that meet multiple criteria, or that require complex expressions as criteria, you can use the **Advanced Filter/Sort** command.

You work with the **Advanced Filter/Sort** command in the design grid shown here:

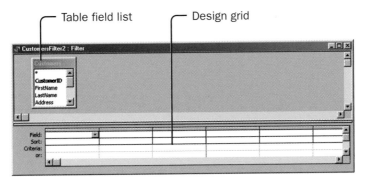

This **design grid** is similar to the query design grid, except that you cannot use it to work with multiple tables. If you create a complex filter that you want to have available for future use, you can save it as a query.

Tip

If you create a simple query in the filter window that you think you might like to use again, you can save it as a query. Click **Save As Query** on the **File** menu; click the **Save As Query** button on the toolbar; or right-click in the filter window, and click **Save As Query** on the shortcut menu.

GardenCo

In this exercise, you will create a filter to locate customers in two states by using the **Advanced Filter/Sort** command. After locating the customers, you will experiment a bit with the design grid to get a better understanding of the possibilities. The working folder for this exercise is Office XP SBS\Access\Chap12\AdvFilter. Follow these steps:

1 Open the **GardenCo** database located in the working folder.

2 Open the **Customers** table in Datasheet view.

3 On the **Records** menu, point to **Filter**, and then click **Advanced Filter/Sort**.

   Access opens the filter window with the **Customers** field list in the top area.

4 If the design grid is not blank, click **Clear Grid** on the **Edit** menu.

5 Double-click **LastName** to copy it to the **Field** cell in the first column of the design grid.

6 Click in the **Criteria** cell under **LastName**, type s*, and press ⏎Enter⏎.

   Access changes the criterion to *"Like "s*"*.

7 Scroll to the bottom of the **Customer** field list, and double-click **Region** to copy it to the next available column of the design grid.

8 Click in the **Criteria** cell under **Region**, type ca or wa, and press ⏎Enter⏎.

   The design grid looks like this:

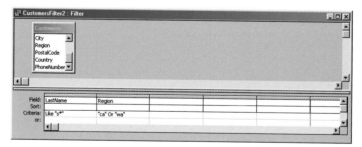

   Your entry has changed to *"ca" Or "wa"*. The filter will now match customers with a last name beginning with s who live in California or Washington.

9 On the **Filter** menu, click **Apply Filter/Sort** to view these records that match the criteria:

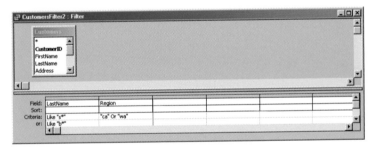

Tip

You can keep an eye on both the filter window and the table window if you reduce both in size so that you can see them at the same time.

10 Return to the filter window by clicking **Filter** and then **Advanced Filter/Sort** on the **Records** menu.

11 Click in the **or** cell in the **LastName** column, type **b***, and press Enter. The design grid now looks like this:

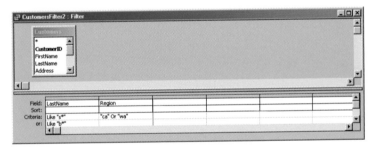

12 Click **Apply Filter/Sort** on the **Filter** menu.

The result includes records for all customers with a last name that begins with *s* or *b*, but some of the *b* names live in Montana and Oregon. If you look again at the design grid, you can see that the filter is formed by combining the fields in the **Criteria** row with the *And* operator, combining the fields in the **or** row with the *And* operator, and then using the *Or* operator to combine the two rows. So the filter is searching for customers with names beginning with *s* who live in California or Washington, or customers with names beginning with *b*, regardless of where they live.

13 Close the **Customers** table, without saving your changes.

14 Close the database.

Expressions

The word **expressions**, as used in Access, is synonymous with *formulas*. An expression is a combination of **operators**, **constants**, **functions**, and **control properties** that evaluates to a single value. Access builds formulas using the format *a=b+c*, where *a* is the result and *=b+c* is the expression. An expression can be used to assign properties to tables or forms, to determine values in fields or reports, as part of a query, and in many other places in Access.

The expressions you use in Access combine multiple **criteria** to define a set of conditions that a record must meet before Access will select it as the result of a filter or query. Multiple criteria are combined using logical, comparison, and arithmetic operators. Different types of expressions use different operators.

The most common **logical operators** are *And*, *Or*, and *Not*. When criteria are combined with the *And* operator, a record is selected only if it meets them all. When criteria are combined with the *Or* operator, a record is selected if it meets any one of them. The *Not* operator selects all records that don't match its criterion.

Common **comparison operators** include < (less than), > (greater than), and = (equal). These basic operators can be combined to form <= (less than or equal to), >= (greater than or equal to), and <> (not equal to). The *Like* operator is sometimes grouped with the comparison operators and is used to test whether or not text matches a pattern.

The common **arithmetic operators** are + (add), - (subtract), * (multiply), and / (divide), which are used with numerals. A related operator, & (a text form of addition), is used to concatenate two text strings.

Creating a Query in Design View

Sorting and filtering information is quick, easy, and useful. When you want to work with more than one table, however, you need to move beyond filters and into the realm of queries. The most common type of query selects records that meet specific conditions, but there are several other types, as follows:

■ A **select query** retrieves data from one or more tables and displays the results in a datasheet. You can also use a select query to group records and calculate sums, counts, averages, and other types of totals. You can work with the results of a select query in Datasheet view to update records in one or more related tables at the same time.

■ A **parameter query** prompts you for information to be used in the query—for example, a range of dates. This type of query is particularly useful if the query is the basis for a report that is run periodically.

- A **crosstab query** calculates and restructures data for easier analysis. It can calculate a sum, average, count, or other type of total for data that is grouped by two types of information—one down the left side of the datasheet and one across the top. The cell at the junction of each row and column displays the results of the query's calculation.

- An **action query** updates or makes changes to multiple records in one operation. It is essentially a select query that performs an action on the results of the selection process. Four types of actions are available: **delete queries**, which delete a group of records from one or more tables; **update queries**, which make changes to records in one or more tables; **append queries**, which add records from one or more tables to the end of one or more other tables; and **make-table queries**, which create a new table from all or part of the data in one or more tables.

Tip

Access also includes SQL queries, but you won't work with this type of query in this book.

Filters and Sorts vs. Queries

The major differences between using a filter or sort and using a query are:

- The **Filter** and **Sort** commands are usually faster to implement than queries.

- The **Filter** and **Sort** commands are not saved, or are saved only temporarily. A query can be saved permanently and run again at any time.

- The **Filter** and **Sort** commands are applied only to the table or form that is currently open. A query can be based on multiple tables and other queries, which don't have to be open.

You can create a query by hand or by using a wizard. Regardless of how you create the query, what you create is a statement that describes the conditions that must be met for records to be matched in one or more tables. When you run the query, the matching records appear in a datasheet in Datasheet view.

GardenCo

In this exercise, you will create an order entry form that salespeople can fill in as they take orders over the phone. The form will be based on a select query that combines information from the Order Details table and the Products table. The query will create a datasheet listing all products ordered with the unit price, quantity ordered, discount, and extended price. Because the extended price isn't stored in the database, you will calculate this amount directly in the query. The working folder for this exercise is Office XP SBS\Access\Chap12\QueryDes. Follow these steps:

1   Open the **GardenCo** database located in the working folder.

2   On the **Objects** bar, click **Queries**.

3   Double-click **Create query in Design view**.

Access opens the query window in Design view, and then opens the **Show Table** dialog box, like this:

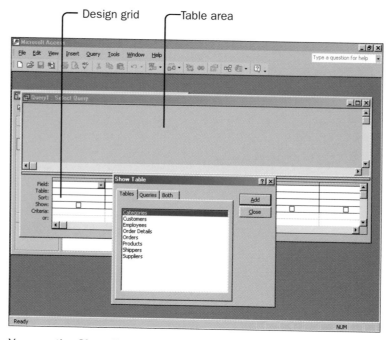

Design grid   Table area

You use the **Show Table** dialog box to specify which tables and saved queries to include in the current query.

4   With the **Tables** tab active, double-click **Order Details** and **Products** to add both tables to the query window. Then close the dialog box.

Each table you added is represented in the top portion of the window by a small field list window with the name of the table in its title bar, as shown here:

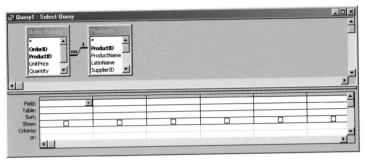

At the top of each list is an asterisk, which represents all the fields in the list. Primary key fields in each list are bold. The line from **ProductID** in the **Order Details** table to **ProductID** in the **Products** table indicates that these two fields are related.

Tip

To add more tables to a query, re-open the **Show Table** dialog box by right-clicking the top portion of the query window and clicking **Show Table** on the shortcut menu; or by clicking the **Show Tables** button on the toolbar.

The bottom area of the query window is taken up by a design grid where you will build the query's criteria.

5   To include fields in the query, you drag them from the lists at the top of the window to consecutive columns in the design grid. Drag the following fields from the two lists:

Field	From Table
OrderID	Order Details
ProductName	Products
UnitPrice	Order Details
Quantity	Order Details
Discount	Order Details

Tip

You can quickly copy a field to the next open column in the design grid by double-clicking the field. To copy all fields to the grid, double-click the title bar above the field list to select the entire list, and then drag the selection over the grid. When you release the mouse button, Access adds the fields to the columns in order. You can drag the asterisk to a column in the grid to include all the fields in the query, but you have to also drag individual fields to the grid if you want to sort on those fields or add conditions to them.

The query window now looks like this:

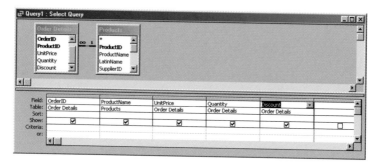

Run

6 Click the **Run** button to run the query and display the results in Datasheet view, like this:

OrderID	Product Name	UnitPrice	Quantity	Discount
11091	Autumn crocus	$18.75	4	0
11079	Compost Bin	$58.00	1	0
11083	Compost Bin	$58.00	1	0
11138	Compost Bin	$58.00	1	0
11152	Compost Bin	$58.00	1	0
11085	Cactus Sand Potting Mix	$4.50	2	0
11093	Cactus Sand Potting Mix	$4.50	2	0
11121	Cactus Sand Potting Mix	$4.50	1	0
11132	Cactus Sand Potting Mix	$4.50	1	0
11148	Cactus Sand Potting Mix	$4.50	1	0
11114	Weeping Forsythia	$18.00	3	0
11147	Weeping Forsythia	$18.00	1	0
11082	Bat Box	$14.75	3	0

Record: 1 of 215

The results show that the query is working so far. There are two things left to do: sort the results on the **OrderID** field and add a field for calculating the extended price, which is the unit price times the quantity sold minus any discount.

View

7 Click the **View** button to return to Design view.

The third row in the design grid is labeled *Sort*. If you click in the **Sort** cell in any column, you can specify whether to sort in ascending order, descending order, or not at all.

8 Click in the **Sort** cell in the **OrderID** column, click the arrow, and click **Ascending**.

Neither of the tables includes an extended price field. There is no point in entering this information in a table, because you can use the Expression Builder to insert an expression in the design grid that computes this price from existing information.

Expression Builder

When an expression is a valid filter or query option, you can usually either type the expression or use the Expression Builder to create it. You open the Expression Builder by either clicking **Build** on a shortcut menu or clicking the **...** button (sometimes referred to as the **Build** button) at the right end of a box that can accept an expression.

The Expression Builder isn't a wizard; it doesn't lead you through the process of building an expression. But it does provide a hierarchical list of most of the elements that you can include in an expression. After looking at the list, you can either type your expression in the expression box, or you can select functions, operators, and other elements to copy them to the expression box, and then click **OK** to transfer them to the filter or query.

9 Right-click the **Field** row of the first blank column in the design grid (the sixth column), and click **Build** on the shortcut menu.

The **Expression Builder** dialog box opens, as shown here:

Operator buttons — Expression box —

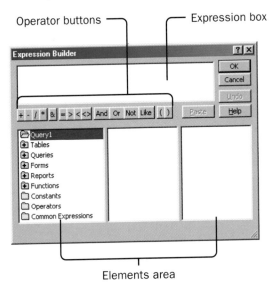

Elements area

Here is the expression you will build:

CCur([Order Details].[UnitPrice]*[Quantity]*(1-[Discount])/100)*100

Look at it, think about it, and see if it makes sense. The only part you probably can't figure out is the CCur function, which converts the results of the math inside its parentheses to currency format.

10 Double-click the **Functions** folder in the first column of the elements area, and then click **Built-In Functions**.

The categories of built-in functions are displayed in the second column.

11 Click **Conversion** in the second column to limit the functions in the third column to those in that category. Then double-click **CCur** in the third column.

The Expression Builder now looks like this:

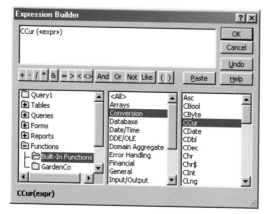

You have inserted the currency conversion function in the expression box. The **<<expr>>** inside the parentheses represents the other expressions that will eventually result in the number Access should convert to currency format.

12 Click **<<expr>>** to select it so that the next thing you enter will replace it.

13 The next element you want in the expression is the **UnitPrice** field from the Order Details table. Double-click **Tables**, click **Order Details**, and then double-click **UnitPrice**.

The Expression Builder now looks like this:

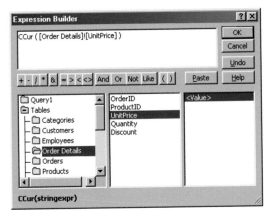

Your last action left the insertion point after UnitPrice, which is exactly where you want it.

14 You want to multiply the amount in the **UnitPrice** field by the amount in the **Quantity** field. Click the * (asterisk) button in the row of operator buttons below the expression box.

Access inserts the multiplication sign and another **<<expr>>** placeholder.

15 Click **<<Expr>>** to select it, and then insert the **Quantity** field by double-clicking it in the second column.

What you have entered so far would multiply the price by the number ordered, which would result in the total cost for this item. However, The Garden Company offers discounts on certain items at different times of the year. The amount of the discount is entered by the sales clerk and stored in the Order Details table. In the table, the discount is expressed as the percentage to deduct—usually 10 to 20 percent. But it is easier to compute the percentage the customer will pay—usually 80 to 90 percent of the regular price—than it is to compute the discount and then subtract it from the total cost.

16 Type *(1-, then double-click **Discount**, and type).

The Expression Builder now looks as shown on the next page (you will have to widen the window to see the whole expression).

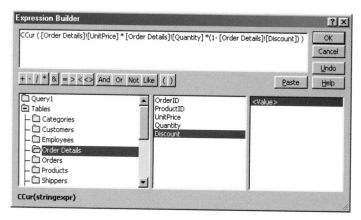

Remember that the discount is formatted in the datasheet as a percentage, but it is stored as a decimal number between 0 and 1. When you look at it you may see 10%, but what is actually stored in the database is 0.1. So if the discount is 10 percent, the result of *(1-Discount) is *.9. In other words, the formula multiplies the unit price by the quantity, and then multiplies that result by 0.9.

17 Click **OK**.

Access closes the Expression Builder and copies the expression to the design grid.

18 Press Enter to move the insertion point out of the field, which completes the entry of the expression.

Tip

You can quickly make a column in the design grid as wide as its contents by double-clicking the line in the gray selection bar that separates the column from the column to its right.

19 Access has given the expression the name **Expr1**. This name isn't particularly meaningful, so rename it by double-clicking **Expr1** and then typing **ExtendedPrice**.

20 Click the **View** button to see these results in Datasheet view:

OrderID	Product Name	UnitPrice	Quantity	Discount	ExtendedPrice
11079	Crushed Rock	$62.50	1	0	$62.50
11079	Compost Bin	$58.00	1	0	$58.00
11080	Douglas Fir	$18.75	1	0	$18.75
11080	Fortune Rhododendron	$24.00	2	0.1	$43.20
11081	Golden Larch	$27.00	1	0	$27.00
11081	Lawn cart	$85.00	1	0.1	$76.50
11082	Bat Box	$14.75	3	0	$44.25
11083	Compost Bin	$58.00	1	0	$58.00
11083	GrowGood Potting Soil	$6.35	1	0	$6.35
11083	QwikRoot	$18.00	1	0	$18.00
11083	Grass Rake	$11.95	1	0	$11.95
11084	Gooseberries	$7.50	3	0	$22.50
11084	Ambrosia	$6.25	1	0	$6.25

Record: 1 of 215

The orders are now sorted on the **OrderID** field, and the extended price is calculated in the last field.

21 Scroll down to see a few records with discounts.

If you check the math, you will see that the query calculates the extended price correctly.

22 Close the query window, and when prompted to save the query, click **Yes**. Type **Order Details Extended** to name the query, and then click **OK** to close it.

23 Close the database.

Creating a Query with a Wizard

The process used to create a simple select query with the **Query Wizard** is almost identical to that for creating a form with the **Form Wizard.** With the **Query Wizard**, you can add one or more fields from existing tables or queries to the new query.

For Access to work effectively with multiple tables, it must understand the relationships between the fields in those tables. You have to create these relationships before using the **Query Wizard**, by clicking the **Relationships** button and then dragging a field in one table over the identical field in another table.

GardenCo

In this exercise, you will use the **Query Wizard** to create a new query that combines information from the Customers and Orders tables to provide information about each order. These tables are related through their common **CustomerID** fields. (This relationship is already established in the GardenCo database files used in this chapter.) The working folder for this exercise is Office XP SBS\Access\Chap12\QueryWiz. Follow these steps:

1 Open the **GardenCo** database located in the working folder.

2 On the **Objects** bar, click **Queries**, and then double-click **Create query by using wizard**.

The first pane of the **Simple Query Wizard** opens.

Tip

You can also start the **Query Wizard** by clicking **Query** on the **Insert** menu or clicking the **New Object** button, and then double-clicking **Simple Query Wizard**.

3   Select **Table: Orders** from the **Tables/Queries** list.

4   Click the **>>** button to move all the available fields to the **Selected Fields** list.

5   Select **Table: Customers** from the **Tables/Queries** list.

6   Double-click the **Address**, **City**, **Region**, **PostalCode**, and **Country** fields to move them to the **Selected Fields** list, and then click **Next**.

Tip

If the relationship between two tables hasn't already been established, you will be prompted to define it and then start the wizard again.

7   Click **Next** again to accept the default option of showing details in the query result.

8   Change the query title to Orders Qry, leave the **Open the query to view information** option selected, and then click **Finish**.

Access runs the query and displays the results in Datasheet view. You can scroll through the results and see that information is displayed for all the orders.

9   Click the **View** button to view the query in Design view.

Notice that the **Show** box is, by default, checked for each of the fields used in the query. If you want to use a field in a query—for example, to sort on, to set criteria for, or in a calculation—but don't want to see the field in the results datasheet, you can clear its **Show** check box.

10   Clear the **Show** check box for **OrderID**, **CustomerID**, and **EmployeeID**, and then click the **View** button to switch back to Datasheet view.

The three fields have been removed from the results datasheet.

11   Click the **View** button to return to Design view.

This query returns all records in the Orders table. To have this query match the records for a range of dates, you can convert it to a parameter query, which asks for the date range each time you run it.

12   In the **OrderDate** column, click in the **Criteria** cell, and type the following:

Between [Type the beginning date:] And [Type the ending date:]

13   Click the **Run** button to run the query.

Access displays this dialog box:

14 Type **1/1/01**, and press ⌈Enter⌉.

15 In the second **Enter Parameter Value** dialog box, type **1/31/01**, and press ⌈Enter⌉ again.

The datasheet is displayed again, this time listing only orders between the parameter dates.

16 Close the datasheet, clicking **Yes** to save the query.

17 Close the database.

Performing Calculations in a Query

You typically use a query to locate all the records that meet some criteria. But sometimes you are not as interested in the details of all the records as you are in summarizing them in some way. For example, you might want to know how many orders have been placed this year, or the total dollar value of all orders placed. The easiest way to get this information is to create a query that groups the necessary fields and does the math for you. To do this, you use **aggregate functions** in the query.

Access queries support the following aggregate functions:

Function	Calculates
Sum	Total of the values in a field
Avg	Average of the values in a field
Count	Number of values in a field, not counting Null (blank) values
Min	Lowest value in a field
Max	Highest value in a field
StDev	Standard deviation of the values in a field
Var	Variance of the values in a field

GardenCo

In this exercise, you will create a query that calculates the number of products in The Garden Company's inventory, the average price of all the products, and the total value of the inventory. The working folder for this exercise is Office XP SBS\Access\Chap12\Aggregate. Follow these steps:

1 Open the **GardenCo** database in the working folder.

2 On the **Objects** bar, click **Queries**, and then double-click **Create query in Design view**.

Access first opens the query window in Design view and then displays the **Show Table** dialog box.

3 In the **Show Table** dialog box, double-click **Products**, and click **Close**.

Access adds the Products table to the query window and closes the **Show Table** dialog box.

4 In the list of fields in the Products table, double-click **ProductID** and then **UnitPrice**.

Access moves both fields to the design grid.

Totals

Σ

5 Click the **Totals** button on the toolbar.

A row named *Total* is added to the design grid, which should now look like this:

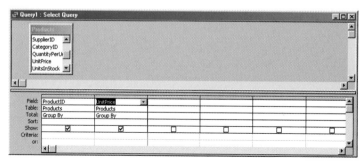

6 Click the **Total** cell of the **ProductID** column, click the arrow, and select **Count** from the drop-down list.

Access enters the word *Count* in the **Total** cell. When you run the query, this function will return a count of the number of records containing a value in the **ProductID** field.

7 In the **UnitPrice** column, set the **Total** cell to **Avg**.

When you run the query, this function will return the average of all the **Unit-Price** values.

Run

!

8 Click the **Run** button.

The result of the query is a single record containing the count and the average price, as shown here:

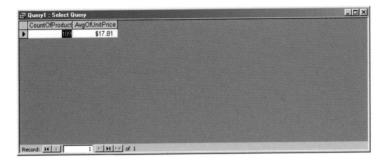

View

9   Click the **View** button to return to Design view.

10   In the **Field** cell of the third column, type **=UnitPrice*UnitsInStock** and press [Enter].

The text you typed is changed to *Expr1: [UnitPrice]*[UnitsInStock]*. This expression will multiply the price of each product by the number of units in stock.

11   Select **Expr1:**, and type **Value of Inventory:**.

12   Set the **Total** cell to **Sum** to return the sum of all the values calculated by the expression.

13   Run the query again.

The results are shown here:

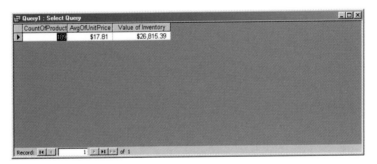

14   Close the query window, clicking **No** when asked if you want to save the query.

15   Close the database.

16   Quit Access.

IV

Microsoft PowerPoint

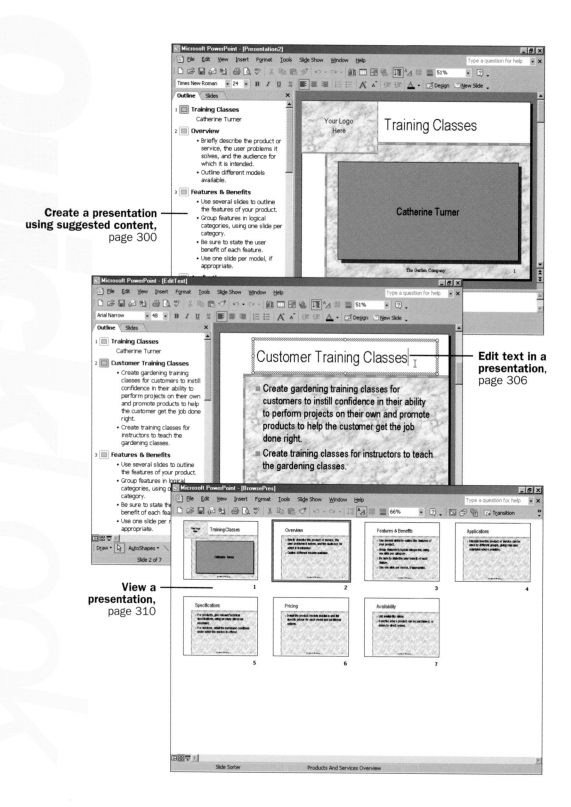

Create a presentation using suggested content, page 300

Edit text in a presentation, page 306

View a presentation, page 310

Chapter 13
Creating a Presentation

After completing this chapter, you will be able to:

✔ **Get started with PowerPoint.**

✔ **Choose the best method to start a presentation.**

✔ **Create a presentation using suggested content.**

✔ **Browse through a presentation.**

✔ **Edit text in a presentation.**

✔ **View a presentation.**

✔ **Get help using PowerPoint.**

Microsoft PowerPoint is a presentation program that allows you to create overhead slides, speaker notes, audience handouts, and outlines—all in a single presentation file. For example, you can create presentations for training, brainstorming, business planning, progress reports, project management, and marketing. PowerPoint offers powerful tools to help you create and organize a presentation step by step.

Catherine Turner is the owner of The Garden Company, a fictional business used in the Step by Step series. She wants to increase the name recognition of the company and promote its products in the marketplace. As part of her promotional efforts, she wants to provide gardening classes to increase product awareness and customer skills.

In this chapter, you'll create a presentation that promotes upcoming gardening classes provided by The Garden Company. During the process, you'll create the presentation using suggested content from PowerPoint, browse through the presentation slides, edit the suggested text, look at content in different views, and get help if you have a question.

This chapter uses the practice files BrowsePres, EditText, and ViewPres that are stored in the Office XP SBS\PowerPoint\Chap13 subfolder that you installed from this book's CD-ROM. For details about installing the practice files, see "Using the Book's CD-ROM" at the beginning of this book.

Important

If you haven't done so yet, you should install the book's practice files so that you can work through the exercises in this chapter. You can find instructions for installing the practice files in the "Using the CD-ROM" section at the beginning of the book.

Getting Started with PowerPoint

The most common way to start PowerPoint is to use the **Start** button on the Windows taskbar. When you start PowerPoint, the program window displays a blank presentation and a Task pane on the right side of the screen. The **program window** is an area of the screen that is used to display the PowerPoint program and the presentation window. The **presentation window** is the electronic canvas on which you type text, draw shapes, create graphs, add color, and insert objects. The program window contains many components common to every Microsoft Office XP program—such as the title bar, menu bar, Standard and Formatting toolbars, Ask a Question box, and status bar—and other components unique to PowerPoint—such as the view buttons, Slide pane, Notes pane, and several other Task panes. As with any Windows program, you can adjust the size of the PowerPoint window with the **Minimize** and **Restore/ Maximize** buttons, and you can close PowerPoint with the **Close** button on the title bar or close the presentation with the **Close Window** button on the menu bar.

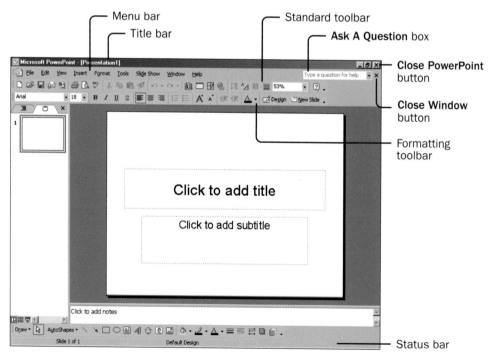

Tip

PowerPoint uses personalized menus and toolbars to reduce the number of menu commands and toolbar buttons that you see on the screen and to display the ones that you use most often. When you click a menu name, a short menu appears, containing the commands that you use most. To make the complete long menu appear, you can leave the pointer over the menu name for several seconds, you can double-click the menu name, or you can click the menu name and then click the small double arrow at the bottom of the short menu. When the long menu is displayed, the commands that did not appear on the short menu are light gray.

Important

When the Standard and Formatting toolbars share one row, which is the default setting, you can't see all the available buttons, but you can access other buttons by clicking the **Toolbar Options** down arrow at the end of the toolbar. If a button mentioned in this book doesn't appear on a toolbar, click the **Toolbar Options** down arrow on that toolbar to display the rest of the buttons available on that toolbar. To make it easier for you to find buttons, the Standard and Formatting toolbars in this book appear on two rows. To change your settings to match the screens in this book, click **Customize** on the **Tools** menu, select the **Show Standard and Formatting toolbars on two rows** check box on the **Options** tab, and then click **Close**.

Outline/Slides pane

At the bottom of the presentation window are view buttons that allow you to look at a presentation in different ways. **Normal view** is the main editing view, which you use to write and design your presentation. The view is made up of three panes: Outline/Slides, Slide, and Notes. The Outline/Slides pane shows tabs that let you alternate between seeing an outline of your slide text (**Outline** tab) and seeing the slides displayed as thumbnails (**Slides** tab). The Slide pane shows slides as they will appear in the presentation. The Notes pane is where you enter speaker notes. You can resize any of the panes by dragging the gray bar that separates them.

Task pane
new for
OfficeXP

On the right side of the PowerPoint window is a **Task pane**, which displays commonly used commands that you'll need as you work on your presentation. A Task pane allows you to quickly access commands related to a specific task without having to use menus and toolbars. PowerPoint displays a Task pane when you need it. For example, when you start PowerPoint, you'll see the New Presentation Task pane with commands that you can use to create a presentation. When you add a new slide to your presentation, you'll see the Slide Layout Task pane with common slide designs from which you can choose. If you want to use a Task pane and the one that you want does not appear, you can manually show the Task pane and then select the specific Task pane that you want from the **Other Task Panes** menu on the Task pane. If you no longer need the Task pane, you can hide it to free up valuable screen space in the program window. On the **View** menu, click **Task Pane**; clicking the command hides the Task pane if it is currently displayed or shows it if it is currently hidden.

Outline/Slides pane

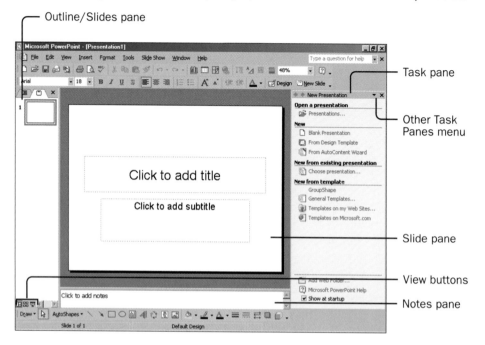

Task pane

Other Task
Panes menu

Slide pane

View buttons

Notes pane

In this exercise, you start PowerPoint and close and open a Task pane.

1   On the taskbar, click **Start**, point to **Programs**, and then click **Microsoft PowerPoint**.

The PowerPoint program window opens.

Tip

You can also start PowerPoint by creating a shortcut icon on the Windows desktop. Simply double-click a shortcut icon to start its associated program. To create a shortcut, click the **Start** button, point to **Programs**, right-click **Microsoft PowerPoint**, point to **Send To**, and then click **Desktop (create shortcut)**.

2   In the title bar of the New Presentation Task pane, click the **Other Task Panes** down arrow.

The **Other Task Panes** menu appears.

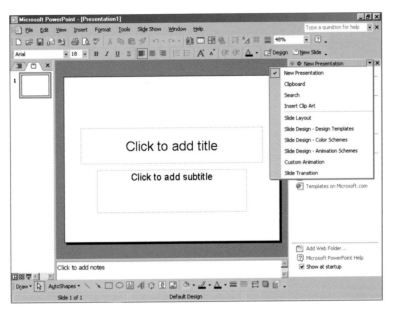

3   Press the [Esc] key, or click an empty place in the slide.

PowerPoint deselects the **Other Task Panes** menu and doesn't perform any commands on the menu.

Close

4   On the title bar of the New Presentation Task pane, click the **Close** button to close the New Presentation Task pane.

5   On the **View** menu, click **Task Pane**.

The New Presentation Task pane appears.

Choosing the Best Method to Start a Presentation

To begin working with PowerPoint, you can create a new presentation or you can open one that you've already worked on. You can use the New Presentation Task pane as your starting point. The option that you choose on the Task pane depends on how you want to start a presentation. If you need help with content and a presentation look, choose the **From AutoContent Wizard** option. If you have content ready but need help with a presentation look, choose the **From Design Template** option. If you have content ready and have a design in mind, choose the **Blank Presentation** option. The following table describes the methods available to you when you start or open a presentation from the New Presentation Task pane.

Click	To
From AutoContent Wizard under **New**	Create a new presentation using the **AutoContent Wizard**, which prompts you for a presentation title and information about the presentation. After you choose a presentation style and type, PowerPoint provides a basic outline to help you organize the content into a professional presentation.
From Design Template under **New**	Create a new presentation based on a design template, which is a presentation with predefined slide colors and text styles. After you click this option, the Slide Design Task pane appears, in which you can choose a template.
Blank Presentation under **New**	Create a new, blank presentation. After you click this option, the Slide Layout Task pane appears with 27 predesigned slide layouts from which you can choose to create a new slide.
Presentations or **More presentations** under **Open a presentation**	Open an existing PowerPoint presentation. A list of recently opened files appears above the option. If the file that you want is not in the list, click **Presentations** or **More presentations**. The **Open** dialog box appears, from which you can browse to find the presentation that you want to open.

Creating a Presentation Using Suggested Content

The **AutoContent Wizard** can save you time by helping you organize and write the text for a new presentation. The wizard takes you through a step-by-step process, prompting you for presentation information, starting with the type of presentation that you want to give and output that you will use, and ending with the **title slide**, which is the first slide in the presentation. When you finish, the wizard provides you with suggested content on your slides, which you can modify to meet your specific needs.

When you create a presentation, the work that you complete is stored only in your computer's temporary memory until you save it. To save your work for further use, you must give the presentation a name and store it on your computer's hard disk. The first time that you save a new presentation, the **Save As** dialog box opens, where you name the presentation and choose where to save it. After you've saved the presentation once using the **Save As** dialog box, you can save new changes that you make by clicking the **Save** button on the Standard toolbar. In other words, the newer version overwrites the original version. If you want to keep both the original file and the version with your recent changes, you click the **Save As** command on the **File** menu to save the new version with a new name.

In this exercise, you use the **AutoContent Wizard** to create a presentation promoting The Garden Company's upcoming gardening classes, and then you save the results.

1   In the **New Presentation** Task pane, click **From AutoContent Wizard** under **New**.

The **New Presentation** Task pane closes, and the **AutoContent Wizard** appears, displaying the **Start** page. On the left side of the wizard is a list of the pages in the wizard.

Troubleshooting

If the Office Assistant appears, click **No, don't provide help now** in the help screen.

2   Read the introduction, and then click **Next**.

The second page in the **AutoContent Wizard** appears, and the square next to *Presentation type* on the left side of the wizard turns green to indicate that this is the current page. The wizard prompts you to select a presentation type. To help you identify presentation types quickly, the wizard organizes presentations by category.

3   Click the **Sales/Marketing** button.

Presentations in the sales and marketing category appear in the list on the right side of the page.

4   In the list, click **Product/Services Overview**.

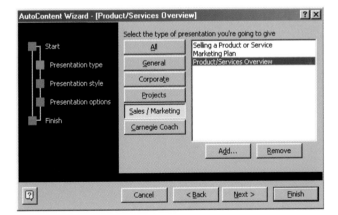

5   Click **Next**.

The wizard prompts you to select a media type for the presentation.

6   Click the **On-screen presentation** option, if necessary, to select that presentation type, and then click **Next**.

The wizard prompts you to enter information for the title slide and for footer information to be included on each slide.

7 Click in the **Presentation title** box, type Training Classes, and then press the Tab key to move the insertion point to the **Footer** box.

8 In the **Footer** box, type The Garden Company.

9 Clear the **Date last updated** check box to not include the date on each slide.

10 Verify that the **Slide number** check box is selected to include the slide number on each slide.

11 Click **Next**, and then click **Finish**.

The PowerPoint presentation window appears with content provided by the wizard in outline form on the left and the title slide on the right. The name on the title slide is the name of the registered PowerPoint user.

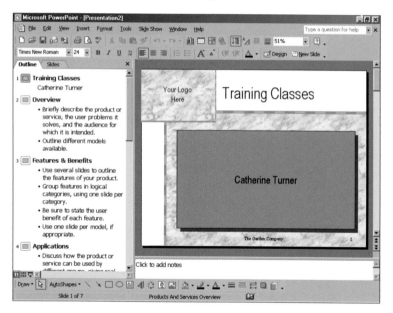

Save

12 On the Standard toolbar, click the **Save** button.

PowerPoint displays the **Save As** dialog box. The text in the **File name** box is selected.

13 In the **File name** box, type AutoContent.

14 Click the **Save in** down arrow, and then click your hard disk, typically drive C.

15 In the list of file and folder names, double-click the **Office XP SBS** folder, double-click the **PowerPoint** folder, and then double-click the **Chap13** folder.

The files and folders in the Chap13 folder appear.

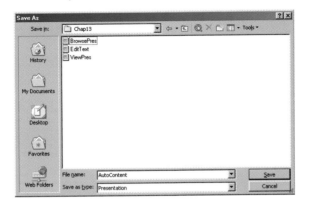

Tip

Depending on your Windows setup, file names might appear with an extension, a dot followed by a three-letter program identifier. For PowerPoint, the extension is .ppt.

16 Click **Save,** or press the [Enter] key to save the presentation.

The title bar name changes from *Presentation2* to *AutoContent.*

Tip

PowerPoint saves presentations for recovery in case the program stops responding or you lose power. PowerPoint saves the changes in a recovery file based on the amount of time indicated in the AutoRecover option. To turn on the AutoRecover option and specify a time interval in which to save, on the **Tools** menu, click **Options**, click the **Save** tab, select the **Save AutoRecover info** check box, specify the period of time, and then click **OK**.

Close Window

☒

17 Click the **Close Window** button in the presentation window.

The AutoContent presentation closes.

Browsing Through a Presentation

You might want to browse through a completed presentation to view the contents and design of each slide and to evaluate the types of changes that you want to make. In PowerPoint, you can browse through the slides in a presentation in several ways. You can click the scroll arrows to scroll line by line, click either side of the scroll box to scroll window by window, or drag the scroll box to move immediately to a specific slide. In the Slide pane, you can click the **Next Slide** and **Previous Slide** buttons, which are located at the bottom of the vertical scroll bar, to switch between slides in the presentation. You can also press the [Page Up] or [Page Down] key to scroll window by window. If you use these keys, the slides in the Slide pane will change also.

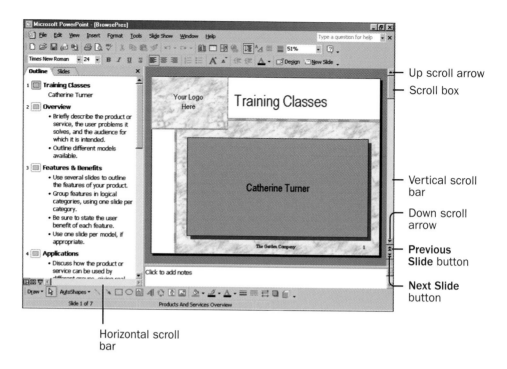

In this exercise, you use scroll bars and the **Next Slide** and **Previous Slide** buttons to move around in the Outline/Slides pane and to move from slide to slide in the Slide pane to browse through the presentation.

BrowsePres

Open

1 On the Standard toolbar, click the **Open** button.

The **Open** dialog box appears.

2 Navigate to the Office XP SBS folder on your hard disk, double-click the **PowerPoint** folder, double-click the **Chap13** folder, and then double-click the **BrowsePres** file.

The BrowsePres presentation opens, displaying Slide 1 in Normal view.

3 In the Outline/Slides pane, click the scroll arrow a few times to see the text below the current window.

4 In the Outline/Slides pane, click below the scroll box in the scroll bar.

The next window of information in the outline appears.

5 In the Outline/Slides pane, drag the scroll box to the bottom of the scroll bar.

The end of the outline appears.

6 In the Slide pane, click below the scroll box in the vertical scroll bar.

Slide 2 appears in the Slide pane. Notice that the **Outline** tab in the Outline/Slides pane jumps to Slide 2 as well, and the slide icon next to Slide 2 on the **Outline** tab is gray to indicate that this is the current slide.

Previous Slide

7 In the Slide pane, click the **Previous Slide** button.

Slide 1 appears in the Slide pane.

Next Slide

8 In the Slide pane, click the **Next Slide** button repeatedly until you reach the end of the presentation.

9 In the Slide pane, drag the scroll box in the vertical scroll bar until you see *Slide 3 of 7* in the slide indicator box, but don't release the mouse button.

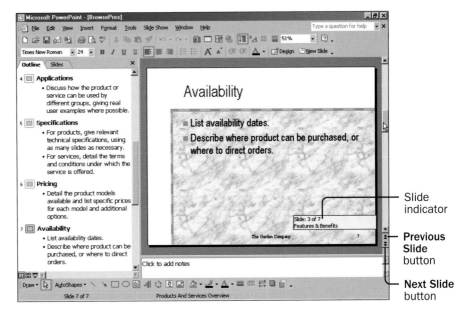

A slide indicator box appears, telling you the slide number and title of the slide to which the scroll box is pointing. In the scroll bar, the scroll box indicates the relative position of the slide in the presentation.

10 Release the mouse button.

The status bar changes from *Slide: 7 of 7* to *Slide: 3 of 7*.

Tip

You can click the slide icon next to a slide in the **Outline** tab to select the slide in the **Outline** tab and display the slide in the Slide pane.

Save

11 On the Standard toolbar, click the **Save** button to save the presentation.

12 Click the **Close Window** button in the presentation window.

Close Window

The BrowsePres presentation closes.

Editing Text in a Presentation

As you create a presentation, you'll often need to delete, modify, and add text to fine-tune your message. You can edit text in the Slide pane or the **Outline** tab of the Outline/Slides pane. In the Slide pane, you edit text one slide at a time, while on the **Outline** tab, you can edit text in all of the slides. A typical slide contains a title, called **title text**, and the major points below the title, called a **paragraph** or **bullet text**. In the Slide pane, slide text appears in boxes called **text objects**, while on the **Outline** tab, slide text appears in bulleted outline form.

I-beam

As you move the pointer over text in PowerPoint, it changes to the I-beam. When you click text in the **Outline** tab or in a text object on the slide, a blinking line, called an insertion point, appears. The **insertion point** indicates where text will be entered or edited as you type. To delete text, you first select the text or place the insertion point next to the text that you want to delete and then press the ⟦Del⟧ key or the ⟦Backspace⟧ key. To modify text in a presentation, you select the text that you want to change and type the revised text. To add an additional bullet point, you place the insertion point at the end of a line of text, press ⟦Enter⟧, and then add another line of text. When you place the insertion point in a text object, the text is surrounded by a rectangle of gray slanted lines, called a **selection box**, with the blinking insertion point placed in the text. The selection box identifies what object you want to change on the slide.

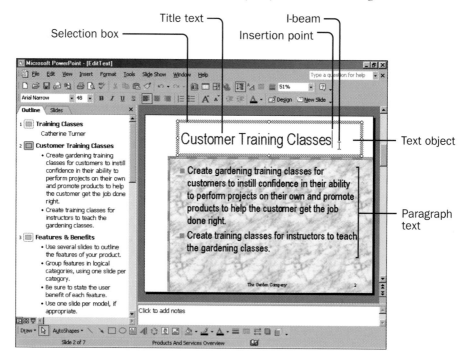

Whenever you perform an action that is not what you intended, you can reverse the action by clicking the **Undo** button. The **Undo** command can reverse up to the last 20 actions, one at a time, unless you change the maximum number of undos in the **Options** dialog box. For example, if you deleted some text by mistake, you can click the **Undo** button to restore the text that you just deleted. If you decide that the undo action is not what you wanted, you can click the **Redo** button to restore the undone action. You must undo or redo actions in the order in which you performed them. That is, you cannot undo your fourth previous action without first reversing the three actions that precede it. To undo a number of actions at the same time, you can click the down arrow next to the **Undo** button and then choose from among the actions that you can undo on the menu.

EditText

In this exercise, you change text in the **Outline** tab of the Outline/Slides pane, undo and redo actions that you recently performed, and change and add text in the Slide pane.

Open

1   On the Standard toolbar, click the **Open** button.

The **Open** dialog box appears.

2   Navigate to the Office XP SBS folder on your hard disk, double-click the **PowerPoint** folder, double-click the **Chap13** folder, and then double-click the **EditText** file.

The EditText presentation opens, displaying Slide 1 in Normal view.

I-beam pointer

I

3   In the **Outline** tab on the Outline/Slides pane, position the pointer (which changes to an I-beam) to the right of the text *Overview* in Slide 2, and then double-click the blank area to select the title text.

The text is selected, and the subsequent text that you type—regardless of its length—will replace the selection.

4   Type **Customer Training Classes**.

If you make a typing mistake, press Backspace to delete it. Note that the text changes in the Slide pane also.

Tip

You might notice red wavy lines under some of your text. These lines indicate possible spelling errors. You can right-click a word with a red wavy line to display a menu with a list of possible spellings, and then click the correct spelling.

Four-headed
arrow pointer

5   Position the I-beam pointer (which changes to the four-headed arrow) over the bullet next to the text *Briefly describe the product ...* in Slide 2 in the **Outline** tab, and then click once to select the bulleted text.

6 Type **Create gardening classes for customers to instill confidence in their ability to perform projects on their own and promote products to help the customer get the job done right.**

7 In Slide 2, click the bullet next to the text *Outline different models available* to select the text.

8 Type **Create training classes for instructors to teach the gardening classes.**

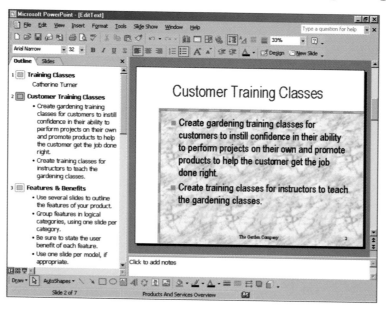

Undo

9 On the Standard toolbar, click the **Undo** button to reverse your last action, the text typing.

10 On the Standard toolbar, click the down arrow next to the **Undo** button.

The **Undo** button menu appears, displaying the first two items in the list as *Typing*.

11 Click the second item in the list, **Typing**.

The first bullet and title in Slide 2 reverts to the AutoContent Wizard's text.

Tip

You can change the number of actions that the **Undo** command will undo by adjusting the number of actions that appear on the **Undo** list. To do this, click **Options** on the **Tools** menu, click the **Edit** tab, and then change the maximum number of undos at the bottom of the dialog box.

Redo

12 On the Standard toolbar, click the **Redo** button to restore the title text in Slide 2.

13 On the Standard toolbar, click the **Redo** button down arrow, and then click the second item in the list, *Typing*, to restore both bulleted text items that you just undid.

Next Slide

14 Click the **Next Slide** button in the Slide pane to display Slide 3.

I-beam pointer

15 In the Slide pane, position the pointer (which changes to the I-beam) over the title text object before the text *Features*, and then click the title text.

A selection box surrounds the text with the blinking insertion point placed in the text.

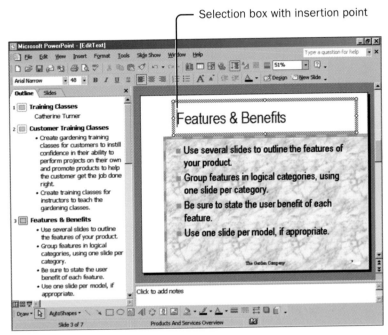

Selection box with insertion point

16 Type **Class**, and then press the [Space] key.

As you change text in the Slide pane, the text in the **Outline** tab changes, too.

17 In the Slide pane, position the pointer (which changes to the I-beam) over any of the bulleted text in Slide 3, and then click the bulleted text to select the text object and place the insertion point.

Four-headed
arrow pointer

18 Position the I-beam pointer (which changes to the four-headed arrow) over the bullet next to the text in the first bullet *Use several slides to outline ...*, click the bullet, and then type **Hands-on training**.

19 Position the pointer (which changes to the four-headed arrow) over the bullet next to the text *Group features in logical ...* in Slide 3, and then click the bullet.

20 Type **Step-by-step instruction**, and then press [Enter].

A new bullet appears in the slide. The new bullet appears gray until you add text.

21 Type **Full color handouts**.

22 Click the bulleted text *Be sure to state the user ...* in Slide 3, and then press
[Del] to delete the bullet.

23 Click the bulleted text *Use one slide per model ...* in Slide 3, and then press
[Del] to delete the bullet.

24 Click outside of the selection box to deselect the text object.

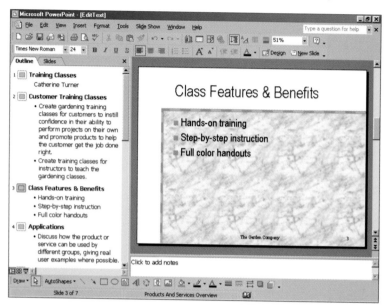

25 In the **Outline** tab on the Outline/Slides pane, click the slide icon in Slide 4,
and then press [Del] to delete the slide entitled *Applications*.

26 On the **Edit** menu, click **Delete Slide** to delete the slide entitled *Specifications*.

Save

27 On the Standard toolbar, click the **Save** button to save the presentation.

28 Click the **Close Window** button in the presentation window.

Close Window

The EditText presentation closes.

Viewing a Presentation

PowerPoint has four views to help you create, organize, and display presentations:
Normal, Slide Sorter, Notes Page, and Slide Show. You can click the view buttons at
the bottom of the presentation window to switch among the different views. You can
also access all of these view commands on the **View** menu. There is no view button
to switch to Notes Page view; instead, you must click the **Notes Page** command on
the **View** menu.

In **Normal view**, you can work with your presentation in three different ways: as an outline or slide miniature in the Outline/Slides pane, as a slide in the Slide pane, and as speaker notes in the Notes pane.

In **Slide Sorter view**, you can preview an entire presentation as slide miniatures—as if you were looking at photographic slides on a light board—and easily reorder the slides in a presentation. If you want to return to the view that you were in before you switched to Slide Sorter view, you can simply double-click a slide miniature to display that slide in the previous view. When PowerPoint displays slides formatted in Slide Sorter view, titles might be hard to read. You can hide the slide formatting to read the slide titles.

Notes Page view differs slightly from the Notes *pane*. While you can add speaker notes in the Notes pane, you must be in Notes Page view if you want to add graphics as notes.

Slide Show view displays slides as an electronic presentation, with the slides filling the entire screen. At any time during the development of a presentation, you can quickly and easily review the slides for accuracy and flow in Slide Show view. Slide Show view also displays the slides in order by slide number, using the entire screen on your computer.

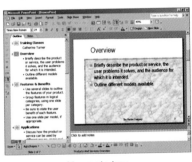

Normal view

Slide Sorter view

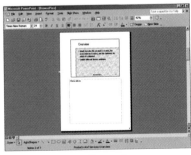

Notes Page view

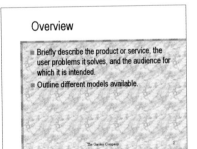

Slide Show view

ViewPres

In this exercise, you switch to different PowerPoint views and then display slides in a slide show.

Open

1 On the Standard toolbar, click the **Open** button.

The **Open** dialog box appears.

2 Navigate to the Office XP SBS folder on your hard disk, double-click the **PowerPoint** folder, double-click the **Chap13** folder, and then double-click the **ViewPres** file.

The ViewPres presentation opens, displaying Slide 1 in Normal view.

3 In the Outline/Slides pane, click the **Slides** tab.

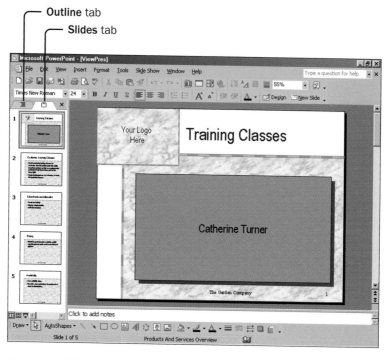

Slide Sorter View

4 Click the **Slide Sorter View** button.

All the slides now appear in miniature on the screen. Slide 1 is surrounded by a dark box, indicating that the slide is selected.

5 Hold down the Alt key, and then click an individual slide.

The formatting for the slide disappears, and the title appears clearly. When you release the mouse button, the display format reappears.

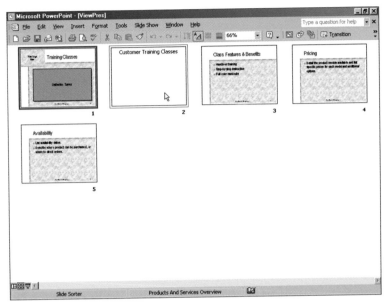

6 Double-click **Slide 1** to switch to Normal view.

The presentation view changes back to Normal view, showing Slide 1.

Slide Show

7 Click the **Slide Show** button.

PowerPoint displays the first slide in the presentation.

8 Click the screen to advance to the next slide.

Tip

To end a slide show before you reach the last slide, press [Esc].

9 Click one slide at a time to advance through the presentation.

After the last slide in the presentation, PowerPoint displays a black screen.

Troubleshooting

The black screen appears by default when you run a slide show unless you clear the **End with black screen** check box in the **Options** dialog box. To check the setting, on the **Tools** menu, click **Options**, and then click the **View** tab.

10 Click the black screen to return to the current view.

Normal view appears.

Save

11 On the Standard toolbar, click the **Save** button to save the presentation.

12 Click the **Close Window** button in the presentation window.

Close Window

The ViewPres presentation closes.

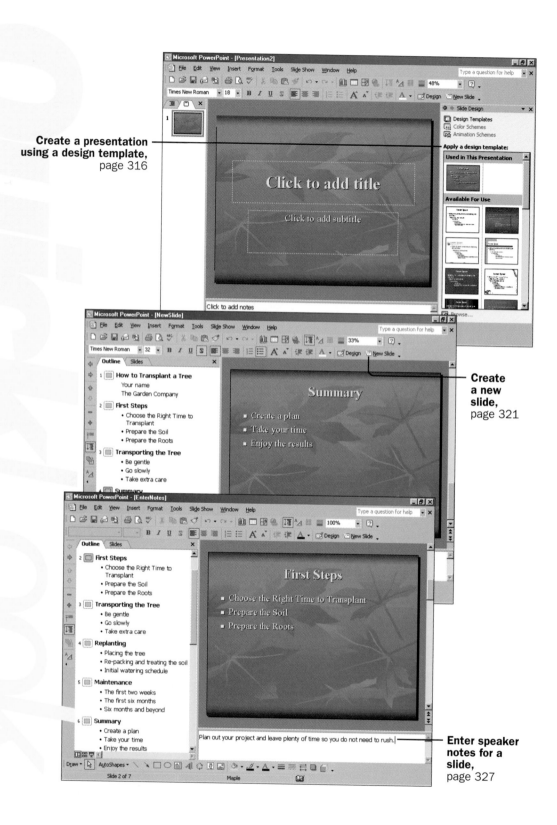

Create a presentation using a design template, page 316

Create a new slide, page 321

Enter speaker notes for a slide, page 327

Chapter 14
Working with a Presentation

After completing this chapter, you will be able to:

✔ Create a presentation using a design template.

✔ Enter text in a slide.

✔ Create a new slide.

✔ Insert slides from other presentations.

✔ Rearrange slides in a presentation.

✔ Enter speaker notes.

✔ Create a folder to store a presentation.

To work efficiently with Microsoft PowerPoint, you need to become familiar with the important capabilities of the product, such as creating a presentation using a design template, creating a new slide and entering text, inserting slides from other presentations and rearranging them in the presentation, and adding speaker notes.

The owner of The Garden Company has decided to use PowerPoint to develop the presentation content for a gardening class to offer customers. The first step is to start a new presentation and develop the content for the first gardening class, "How to Transplant a Tree." The assistant manager has developed several slides to include in the presentation.

In this chapter, you'll start a new presentation using a design template for the first gardening class, enter slide text, create new slides, insert slides from other presentations, rearrange slides, enter speaker notes, and create a folder in which to store a presentation.

 This chapter uses the practice files EnterText, NewSlide, InsertSlide, SlideInsert, OrderSlides, EnterNotes, and StorePres that are stored in the Office XP SBS\Power-Point\Chap14 subfolder that you installed from this book's CD-ROM. For details about installing the practice files, see "Using the Book's CD-ROM" at the beginning of this book.

Creating a Presentation Using a Design Template

Instead of starting a presentation with suggested text from the **AutoContent Wizard**, you can start a new presentation without any sample text. You can choose a design template or a blank presentation. A **design template** is a presentation with a professionally designed format and color scheme to which you need only add text. You can use one of the design templates that come with PowerPoint, or you can create your own. After you select a design template, you can choose a different layout for each slide to create a specific design look, such as a slide with a graph. You select a layout by clicking it in the Slide Layout Task pane in the right margin of your screen. The layout title for the selected slide layout appears as you roll the mouse over each choice.

In this exercise, you start a new presentation for the gardening class with a design template.

1   On the taskbar, click **Start**, point to **Programs**, and then click **Microsoft PowerPoint**.

The PowerPoint program window opens.

2   On the **View** menu, click **Task Pane**, if necessary, to display the New Presentation Task pane.

3   In the New Presentation Task pane, click **From Design Template**.

The Slide Design Task pane appears with a variety of design templates in alphabetical order.

Tip

To create a blank presentation or a presentation using the **AutoContent Wizard**, open the New Presentation Task pane, and then click **Blank Presentation** or **AutoContent Wizard**. The templates listed in the Slide Design Task pane are the same ones that the AutoContent Wizard uses.

4   In the Slide Design Task pane, point to a design template.

The name of the design template appears as a ScreenTip, and a down arrow appears on the right side of the design.

5   In the Slide Design Task pane, click the down arrow on the right side of the design template.

A menu appears with commands that let you apply the design template to the entire presentation or to selected slides or change the size of the preview design templates in the Slide Design Task pane.

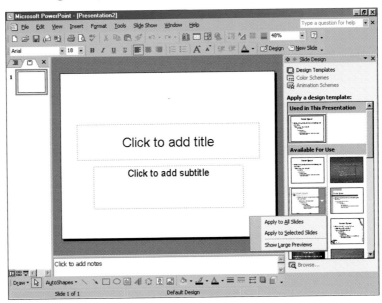

6   On the menu, click **Show Large Previews**.

The size of the preview design templates increases to make it easier to find the design that you want to use.

7   In the Slide Design Task pane, drag the scroll box down until the Maple slide design appears in the Task pane, and then click the **Maple** slide design.

A title slide with the Maple design appears in the slide pane.

8   Click the down arrow on the right side of the design template, click **Show Large Previews** to display the design templates in a smaller size, and then drag the scroll box to the top of the Slide Design Task pane.

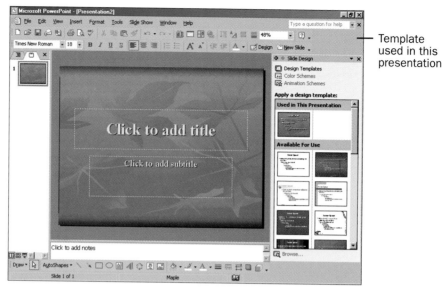

Template
used in this
presentation

9   In the Slide Design Task pane, click the **Other Tasks Panes** down arrow to
display a list of the Task panes, and then click **Slide Layout**.

The Slide Layout Task pane appears with slide layouts that you can apply to
selected slides. The default Title Slide is currently applied to the selected
slide in the Slide pane.

Other Task
Panes

10 In the Slide Layout Task pane, click the **Title Only** slide layout under **Text Layouts**.

PowerPoint applies the Title Only slide layout to the selected slide.

11 In the Slide Layout Task pane, point to several slide layout choices to read the description of each one.

Close

12 In the Slide Layout Task pane, click the **Close** button.

Save

13 On the Standard toolbar, click the **Save** button.

The **Save As** dialog box appears.

14 In the **File name** box, type **DesignTemp**.

15 Navigate to the Office XP SBS folder on your hard disk, double-click the **PowerPoint** folder, and then double-click the **Chap14** folder.

16 Click **Save**.

PowerPoint saves the DesignTemp presentation.

Close Window

17 Click the **Close Window** button in the presentation window.

The DesignTemp presentation closes.

Entering Text in a Slide

To add text to a presentation, including titles and subtitles, you can enter text into either the Slide pane or the Outline tab in Normal view. The Slide pane allows you to enter text on a slide using a visual method, while the Outline tab allows you to enter text using a content method. The Slide pane displaying the Title Slide slide layout includes two text boxes called **text placeholders**. The upper box is a placeholder for the slide's title text. The lower box is a placeholder for the slide's subtitle text. After you enter text into a placeholder, the placeholder becomes a text object, a box that contains text in a slide.

EnterText

In this exercise, you enter text in the first slide of the gardening presentation.

Open

1 On the Standard toolbar, click the **Open** button.

The **Open** dialog box appears.

2 Navigate to the Office XP SBS folder on your hard disk, double-click the **PowerPoint** folder, double-click the **Chap14** folder, and then double-click the **EnterText** file.

The EnterText presentation opens, displaying Slide 1 in Normal view.

3 In the Slide pane, click the text placeholder **Click to add title**.

A selection box surrounds the placeholder, indicating that the placeholder is ready for you to enter or edit text. The placeholder text disappears, and a blinking insertion point appears.

4 Type **How to Transplant a Tree**.

Notice that the text appears in the Outline pane at the same time. If the Thumbnail view is showing instead of the Outline view, click the **Outline** tab.

Tip

If you make a typing error, press Backspace to delete the mistake, and then type the correct text.

5 Click the text placeholder **Click to add subtitle**.

The title object is deselected, and the subtitle object is selected.

6 Type **Catherine Turner**, and then press the Enter key.

7 Type **The Garden Company**.

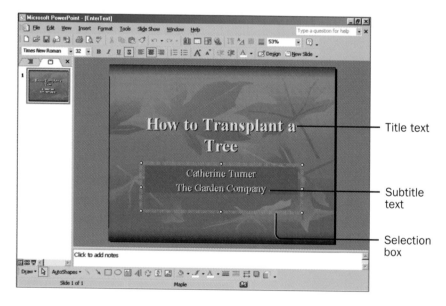

Title text

Subtitle text

Selection box

Save

8 On the Standard toolbar, click the **Save** button to save the presentation.

Close Window

9 Click the **Close Window** button in the presentation window.

The EnterText presentation closes.

Creating a New Slide

You can quickly and easily add more slides to a presentation in two ways: by clicking the **New Slide** button on the Formatting toolbar directly above the Task pane, or by clicking the **New Slide** command on the **Insert** menu. When you use either of these methods, PowerPoint inserts the new slide into the presentation immediately after the current slide, and the Slide Layout Task pane appears with 27 predesigned slide layouts, one of which you can apply to your new slide. You select a layout by clicking it in the Slide Layout Task pane. The layout title for the selected slide layout appears as you roll your mouse across each scheme. To apply a slide layout to your new slide, simply click on one of the 27 choices.

Once you have created a new slide, you can enter and organize slide title and paragraph text in the Slide or Outline pane. In the Outline pane, the slide title text appears to the right of each slide icon, and the paragraph text underneath each title appears, indented one level. To enter text in the Outline pane, you click where you want the text to start, and then you begin typing. In the Outline pane, you can also create a new slide and add title and paragraph text by using the **New Slide** command or by pressing the [Enter] key.

NewSlide

In this exercise, you create a new slide and then enter text in the Slide pane. You then switch to the Outline pane, enter paragraph text in the existing slide, create a new slide, and add text to that slide in the Outline pane.

Open

1   On the Standard toolbar, click the **Open** button.

The **Open** dialog box appears.

2   Navigate to the Office XP SBS folder on your hard disk, double-click the **PowerPoint** folder, double-click the **Chap14** folder, and then double-click the **NewSlide** file.

The NewSlide presentation opens, displaying Slide 1 in Normal view.

New Slide

3   On the Formatting toolbar, click the **New Slide** button.

If it was not already showing, the Slide Layout Task pane appears, and PowerPoint adds a new, empty slide after the current slide in the Slide pane and creates a new slide icon in the Outline pane. PowerPoint applies the default Title and Text slide layout (a title and bulleted list) to the new slide. The status bar displays *Slide 2 of 2*.

4   Type First Steps.

Notice that the new slide and the new title appear in the Outline pane when you create them in the Slide pane. PowerPoint lets you work directly in the Slide and Outline panes and in Slide and Outline views.

Tip

If you start typing on an empty slide without first having selected a placeholder, PowerPoint enters the text into the title object.

Close

5 In the Slide Layout Task pane, click the **Close** button, and then click the **Outline** tab in the Outline/Slides pane, if necessary.

6 Position the pointer (which changes to the I-beam pointer) to the right of the title in Slide 2 in the **Outline** tab, and then click the blank area to place the insertion point.

A blinking insertion point appears.

7 Press Enter.

PowerPoint adds a new slide in the Slide pane and a new slide icon in the **Outline** tab, with the blinking insertion point next to it.

8 Press the Tab key.

Press Tab to indent the text to the right one level. The slide icon changes to a small gray bullet on Slide 2 in the **Outline** tab.

9 Type **Choose the Right Time to Transplant**, and then press Enter.

PowerPoint adds a new bullet at the same indent level. Notice that once you press Enter after typing bulleted text, the bullet becomes black. Also note that the text wraps to the next line in the **Outline** tab without your having to press Enter.

10 Type **Prepare the Soil**, and then press Enter to insert a new bullet.

11 Type **Prepare the Roots**, and then press Enter to insert a new bullet.

Promote

12 On the Outlining toolbar, click the **Promote** button.

Important

If the Outline toolbar is not visible on your screen, click the **View** menu, point to **Toolbars**, and then click **Outlining**.

PowerPoint creates a new slide with the insertion point to the right of the slide icon.

Outline toolbar

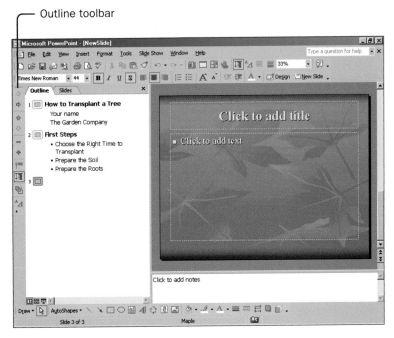

13 Type **Transporting the Tree**, and then press `Enter` to insert a new bullet.

14 Press `Tab`.

PowerPoint creates a new indent level for Slide 3.

15 Type **Be gentle**, and then press `Enter`.

A new bullet appears.

16 Type **Go slowly**, press `Enter`, and then type **Take extra care**.

17 Hold down the `Ctrl` key, and then press `Enter`.

A new slide appears.

18 Type **Summary**, press `Enter`, and then press `Tab`.

PowerPoint creates a new indent level for Slide 4.

19 Type **Create a plan**, and then press `Enter` to insert a new bullet.

20 Type **Take your time**, and then press `Enter` to insert a new bullet.

21 Type **Enjoy the results**.

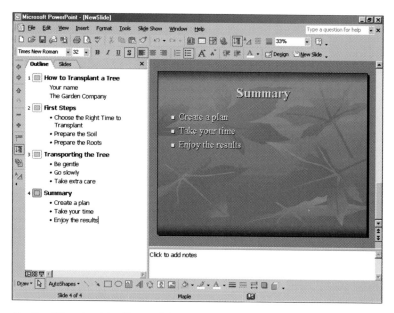

22 On the Standard toolbar, click the **Save** button to save the presentation.

23 Click the **Close Window** button in the presentation window.

The NewSlide presentation closes.

Inserting Slides from Other Presentations

You can save time while creating a presentation by using slides that you or someone else has already made. When you insert slides from one presentation into another, the slides conform to the color and design of the current presentation so you don't have to make many changes.

InsertSlide
SlideInsert

In this exercise, you insert slides from one presentation into another.

Open

1 On the Standard toolbar, click the **Open** button.

The **Open** dialog box appears.

2 Navigate to the Office XP SBS folder on your hard disk, double-click the **PowerPoint** folder, double-click the **Chap14** folder, and then double-click the **InsertSlide** file.

The InsertSlide presentation opens, displaying Slide 1 in Normal view.

3 Position the pointer (which changes to the I-beam pointer) to the right of the last bullet in Slide 4 in the **Outline** tab, and then click the blank area to place the insertion point.

4   On the **Insert** menu, click **Slides from Files**.

The **Slide Finder** dialog box appears.

5   Click the **Find Presentation** tab, if necessary, and then click **Browse**.

The **Browse** dialog box appears.

6   Navigate to the Office XP SBS folder on your hard disk, double-click the **PowerPoint** folder, and then double-click the **Chap14** folder.

7   In the list of file names, click the **SlideInsert** file, and then click **Open**.

The **Slide Finder** dialog box reappears.

8   Click **Display**, if necessary to display the slides in the preview boxes.

9   Click Slide 2, click Slide 3, click the right scroll arrow, and then click Slide 4 to select the slides that you want to insert.

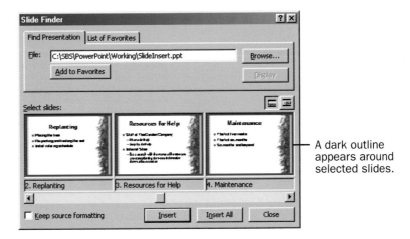

A dark outline appears around selected slides.

Tip

If you use one or more slides in several presentations, you can click **Add to Favorites** to save the selected slides in the **List of Favorites** tab in the **Slide Finder** dialog box.

10   Click **Insert**.

PowerPoint inserts the slides into the new presentation after the current slide.

11   Click **Close**.

The inserted slide text appears in the **Outline** tab and the last slide appears in the Slide pane.

12   On the Standard toolbar, click the **Save** button to save the presentation.

Close Window

13   Click the **Close Window** button in the presentation window.

The InsertSlide presentation closes.

Rearranging Slides in a Presentation

After you insert slides from another presentation into the current one, you may need to rearrange the slides into the order that most effectively communicates your message. This is best done in Slide Sorter view, where you can drag one or more slides from one location to another.

OrderSlides

In this exercise, you rearrange slides in Slide Sorter view.

Open

1 On the Standard toolbar, click the **Open** button.

The **Open** dialog box appears.

2 Navigate to the Office XP SBS folder on your hard disk, double-click the **PowerPoint** folder, double-click the **Chap14** folder, and then double-click the **OrderSlides** file.

The OrderSlides presentation opens, displaying Slide 1 in Normal view.

Slide Sorter View

3 Click the **Slide Sorter View** button.

Notice that the Slide Sorter toolbar appears above the presentation window.

4 Drag Slide 4 ("Summary") to the empty space after Slide 7 ("Maintenance").

Drag pointer

Notice that the pointer changes to the drag pointer when you begin to drag. When you release the mouse button, Slide 4 moves to its new position, and PowerPoint repositions and renumbers the other slides in the presentation.

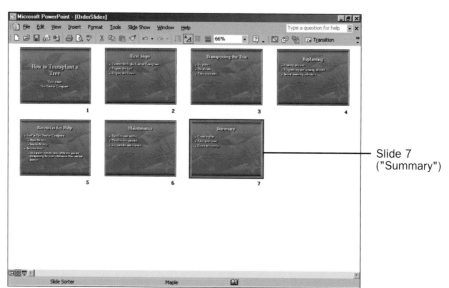

Slide 7 ("Summary")

Tip

In Slide Sorter view, you can also move slides between two or more open presentations. Open each presentation, switch to Slide Sorter view, and then click **Arrange All** on the **Window** menu. Drag the slides from one presentation window to another.

5 Drag Slide 5 ("Resources for Help") between Slides 6 and 7.

6 Double-click Slide 2 to return to the previous view, Normal view.

7 On the Standard toolbar, click the **Save** button to save the presentation.

Close Window

8 Click the **Close Window** button in the presentation window.

The OrderSlides presentation closes.

Entering Speaker Notes

As you create each slide in a presentation, you can also enter speaker notes that relate to the content on the slide and that you can use while you give the presentation. In the Notes pane, you can create speaker notes that appear on separate notes pages. Each slide in a presentation has a corresponding notes page. To enter speaker notes in the Notes pane, you click the **Notes** pane, and then you begin typing. Entering text and changing text in the Notes pane work the same way they do in the Slide and Outline panes. You can also enter speaker notes in Notes Page view by clicking **Notes Page** on the **View** menu. If you want to read all of the speaker notes, it might be easier if you switch to Notes Page view, in which you can move from notes page to notes page the same way as in Slide view.

EnterNotes

In this exercise, you enter text in the Notes pane, switch to Notes Page view, and move from notes page to notes page in Notes Page view.

Open

1 On the Standard toolbar, click the **Open** button.

The **Open** dialog box appears.

2 Navigate to the Office XP SBS folder on your hard disk, double-click the **PowerPoint** folder, double-click the **Chap14** folder, and then double-click the **EnterNotes** file.

The EnterNotes presentation opens, displaying Slide 1 in Normal view.

3 In the Slide pane, click the **Next Slide** button, and then click the text place-holder **Click to add notes** in the **Notes pane** in Slide 2.

The notes placeholder text disappears, and a blinking insertion point appears.

4 Type **Plan out your project and leave plenty of time so you do not need to rush.**

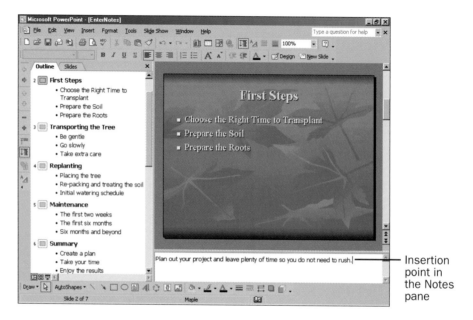

Insertion point in the Notes pane

Tip

If you make a mistake, press ⌫Backspace to delete the mistake, and then type the correct text.

5 On the **View** menu, click **Notes Page**.

Notes Page view appears at approximately 40% view on most screens to display the entire page. Your view percentage might be different.

Reduced slide image

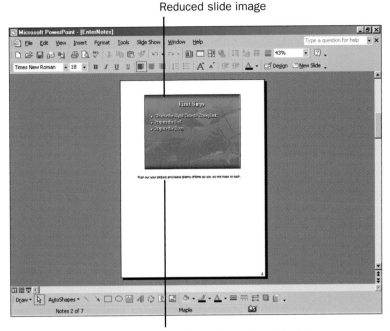

Speaker notes entered in the
Notes pane in Normal view

Tip

Your view scale might differ from the example shown here, depending on the size of
your monitor.

Zoom

`100%` ▾

6 On the Standard toolbar, click the **Zoom** down arrow, and then click **75%**. If
necessary, click the **Toolbar Options** down arrow on the Standard toolbar to
display the option.

The view scale increases to 75%.

Next Slide

7 Click the **Next Slide** button.

The status bar displays *Notes 3 of 7.*

8 Click the text placeholder **Click to add text** in the **Notes** placeholder in Slide 3.

The selection box surrounds the area that contains the Notes text.

9 Type **It is important to have a large enough vehicle to transport the tree,
dirt, and supplies that you will need.**

10 On the Standard toolbar, click the **Zoom** down arrow, and then click **Fit**.

The entire notes pages appears in the window.

Normal View

11 Click the **Normal View** button.

The notes that you entered in Notes Page view appear in Notes pane in Normal view.

12 On the Standard toolbar, click the **Save** button to save the presentation.

Close Window

13 Click the **Close Window** button in the presentation window.

The EnterNotes presentation closes.

Creating a Folder to Store a Presentation

To keep your presentations organized and easily accessible, you can store them in separate folders that you create and name. For example, the marketing department at The Garden Company might create a folder named New Catalog in which to store all presentations relating to the catalog. If, after a time, there are too many files in the New Catalog folder, the marketing department can create a **subfolder** within the New Catalog folder and name it *Products*. In the Products folder, they can store files that describe each product included in the catalog.

Create New
Folder

My Documents is the default folder displayed in the **Save As** dialog box. If you want to create another folder, you can click the **Create New Folder** button provided in the **Save As** dialog box.

Up One Level

Before clicking the **Create New Folder** button, you might need to click the **Save in** down arrow to locate the drive on which you want to store the new folder. You can also click the **Up One Level** button provided in the dialog box to move up a level in the hierarchy of folders, or use the Places Bar to move to another location in your computer. The **Places Bar** on the left side of the Save As and Open dialog boxes provides quick access to commonly used locations in which to store and open files.

You might sometimes need to save a presentation with another name, thus creating a copy of the original. For example, if you update a presentation for a gardening class, you can save the most recent version with a new name. You can then make changes to the copy saved with another name and then compare the differences between it and the original.

You can save the presentation with the new name in the same folder as the original or in a new folder. You can never store two presentations in the same folder if the presentations have the same name.

StorePres

In this exercise you create a folder and save an existing presentation with a new name.

Open

1 On the Standard toolbar, click the **Open** button.

The **Open** dialog box appears.

2 Navigate to the Office XP SBS folder on your hard disk, double-click the **PowerPoint** folder, double-click the **Chap14** folder, and then double-click the **StorePres** file.

The StorePres presentation opens, displaying Slide 1 in Normal view.

3 On the **File** menu, click **Save As**.

The **Save As** dialog box appears and displays the Chap14 folder as the current folder.

Troubleshooting

If the **Chap14** folder is not displayed in the **Save in** box, click the **Save in** down arrow to locate the folder.

Create New
Folder

4 Click the **Create New Folder** button.

The **New Folder** dialog box appears. Note that the folder that you are creating is a subfolder.

Important

Without the **Create New Folder** button provided in the **Open** and **Save As** dialog boxes, you would have to open Windows Explorer or My Computer to create a new folder.

5 Type **NewFolder**, and then click **OK**.

NewFolder becomes the current folder.

6 In the **File name** box, type **StoreFolder** to rename the file.

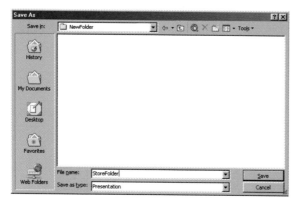

7   Click **Save**.

The file name in the title bar changes to *StoreFolder*. The original StorePres presentation on which this new presentation is based is stored in the **Chap14** folder, and the StoreFolder presentation is stored in the **NewFolder** subfolder.

Close Window

8   Click the **Close Window** button in the presentation window.

The StorePres presentation closes.

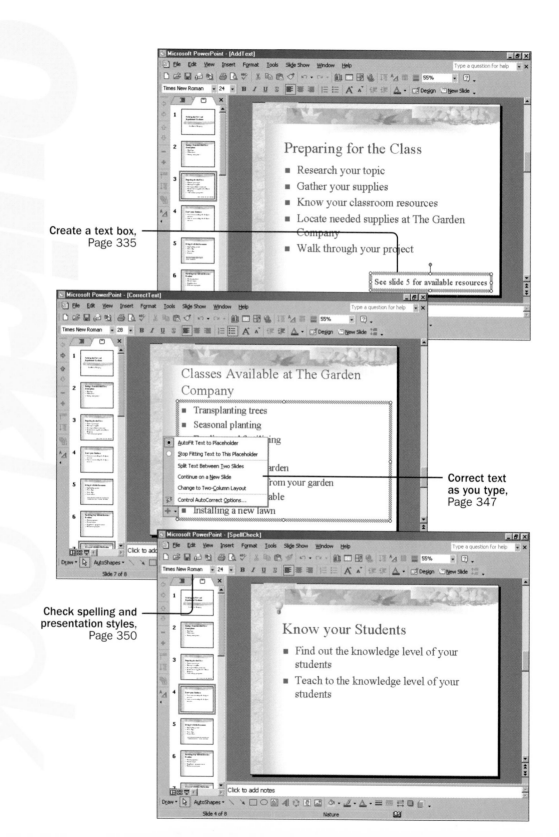

Create a text box,
Page 335

Correct text as you type,
Page 347

Check spelling and presentation styles,
Page 350

Chapter 15
Adding and Modifying Slide Text

After completing this chapter, you will be able to:

✔ **Add and move text on slides.**

✔ **Change text alignment and spacing.**

✔ **Find and replace text and fonts.**

✔ **Correct text while typing.**

✔ **Check spelling and presentation styles.**

In Microsoft PowerPoint, you can add text to your presentation and then modify it to fine-tune your message. You also have complete control over the placement and position of text. PowerPoint offers several alternatives for placing text on your slides: text placeholders for entering slide titles and subtitles, text labels for short notes and phrases, and text boxes for longer text. You can also place text inside objects, such as circles, rectangles, or stars.

The owner of The Garden Company has been working on a training presentation for new gardening class teachers and wants to add and modify supplementary text to fine-tune her message.

In this chapter, you'll create several kinds of text objects, edit text, change the appearance of text, find and replace text, replace fonts, let PowerPoint correct text while you type, check spelling, and check presentation style.

 This chapter uses the practice files AddText, AlignText, ReplaceText, CorrectText, and SpellCheck that are stored in the Office XP SBS\PowerPoint\Chap15 subfolder that you installed from this book's CD-ROM. For details about installing the practice files, see "Using the Book's CD-ROM" at the beginning of this book.

Adding and Moving Text on Slides

In addition to title and bulleted text, you can also add supplemental text to your slides. While the title and bulleted text appear in the outline and on the slide, the supplemental text appears only on the slide. Before you can add and move supplemental text on slides, you need to know how PowerPoint represents text on slides. An **object** is anything that you can manipulate, including text. For example, the title object on a slide is all of the text in the title, which is treated as a unit. To make formatting changes to all of the text in a text object, you need to first select the object. To select an object, you click a part of the object by using the pointer. To deselect an object, you move the pointer to a blank area of the slide and then click the blank area.

In PowerPoint, you can select a text object in two ways. The first way is to click the text in the text object, which displays a **slanted-line selection box**, consisting of gray slanted lines, around the text object. You can edit any content within the text object; for example, you can type or delete text. The second way is to click the edge of a slanted-line selection box, which selects the entire object. When you select the entire object, a fuzzy outline, called a **dotted selection box**, appears around the text object and is ready for you to edit as an object; that is, you can manipulate it as a whole. The white circles at each corner of either type of selection box are **resize handles**, which you can use to adjust and resize the object. A sample of each selection box is shown in the following illustrations:

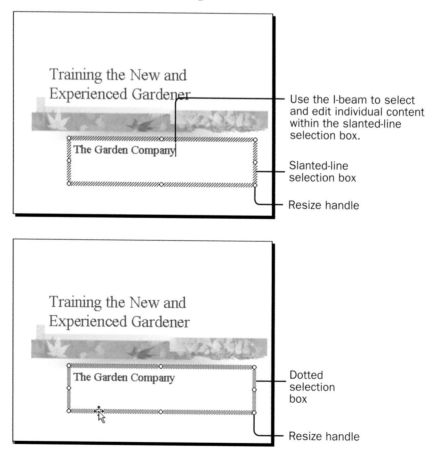

Once you have selected a text object with the dotted selection box, you can move or copy the text object to any place on a slide to change the appearance of a presentation. Dragging a text object is the most efficient way to move or copy it on a slide. The mouse is used to drag a text object from one location to another on a slide. While you drag an object, you can hold down the [Ctrl] key to make a copy of it.

Slides usually contain text boxes for title and bulleted text into which you enter your main ideas. You can also place other text objects on a slide by using the Text Box button on the Drawing toolbar. Text boxes are used when you need to include annotations or minor points that do not belong in a list.

You can create two types of text objects: a **text label**, which is text that does not **word wrap** within a defined box; and a **word processing box**, which is text that word wraps inside the boundaries of an object. Text labels are usually used to enter short notes or phrases: you use a word processing box for longer text or sentences. You can create a text label on a slide by using the Text Box tool to select a place on the slide where you will begin typing your text. You can create a word processing box by using the Text Box tool to drag the pointer to create a text box of the appropriate width.

Once you have created a word processing box or a text label, you can change one object into the other by changing the word-wrap option and the fit text option in the **Format Text Box** dialog box. You can also reduce the size of a text label to create a word processing box by dragging one of the corner resize handles. The text rewraps to adjust to the new size.

AddText

In this exercise, you select and deselect a text object, move a text object by dragging the edge of the text object's selection box, add text in a text object, and then create a text label and a word processing box.

1   Start PowerPoint, if necessary.

Open

2   On the Standard toolbar, click the **Open** button.

The **Open** dialog box appears.

3   Navigate to the Office XP SBS folder on your hard disk, double-click the **PowerPoint** folder, double-click the **Chap15** folder, and then double-click **AddText**.

The AddText presentation opens, displaying Slide 1 in Normal view.

4   On Slide 1, click the subtitle object.

The text box is selected with the slanted-line selection box.

5 Position the pointer directly on top of an edge of the slanted-line selection box.

Selection
Pointer

The pointer changes to the selection pointer, shown in the margin.

6 Click the edge of the slanted-line selection box.

The selection box changes to a dotted selection box.

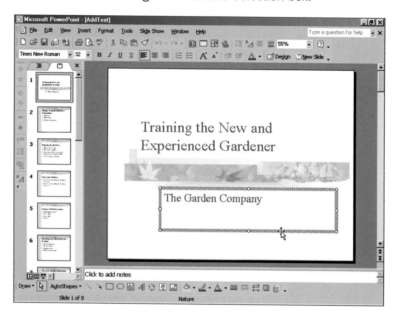

Tip

You can select an object with just one click. Position the pointer above or below the object until it changes to the selection pointer, and then click the slide. The dotted selection box appears.

7 Click outside the selection box in a blank area of the slide.

The text box is deselected.

Tip

To copy a text object, hold down the [Ctrl] key, and then drag the selection box of a text object to a new location on the slide.

8 In the Slide pane, drag the scroll box to Slide 3.

9 Double-click the text *TGC* in the bulleted list to select the text.

10 Type **The Garden Company**.

The paragraph wraps in the text object.

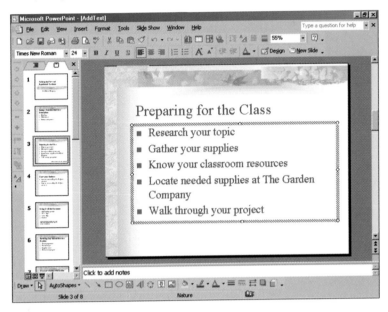

Text Box

abl

11 Click outside of the selection box in a blank area of the slide.

The text box is deselected.

12 On the Drawing toolbar, click the **Text Box** button.

Upside-down T-pointer

↓

The pointer changes to the upside-down T-pointer.

13 Position the pointer at the bottom left of the slide.

14 Click the slide to create a text label.

A small, empty selection box composed of gray slanted lines appears with the blinking insertion point in it.

15 Type **See slide 5 for available resources**.

16 Click any edge of the slanted-line selection box, and then drag the box to the right. Your slide will look similar to the one shown on the next page.

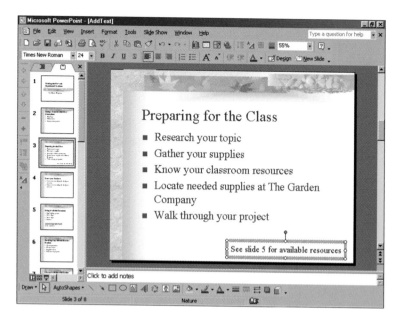

Tip

The text that you create on a slide using the Text Box tool does not appear in Outline view. Only text entered in a title placeholder or a main text placeholder appears in Outline view.

17 Click a blank area of the slide.

The text label is deselected.

18 In the Slide pane, drag the scroll box to Slide 5.

Text Box

19 On the Drawing toolbar, click the **Text Box** button.

The pointer changes to the upside-down T-pointer.

20 Position the upside-down T-pointer below the last bullet, and then drag the pointer to create a box that extends approximately three-fourths of the way across the slide.

When you release the mouse button, a slanted-line selection box appears with the blinking insertion point in it.

21 Type **The Garden Company staff can create PowerPoint presentations for you prior to your class session.**

The width of the box does not change, but the words wrap, and the box height increases to accommodate the complete entry.

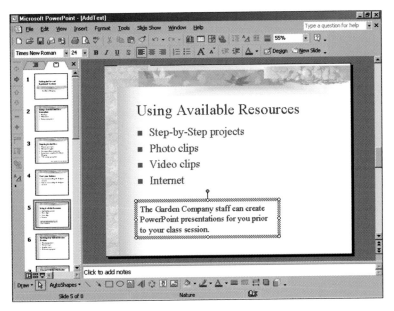

22 Click a blank area of the slide to deselect the text object.

Save

23 On the Standard toolbar, click the **Save** button to save the presentation.

Close Window

24 Click the **Close Window** button in the presentation window.

The AddText presentation closes.

Changing Text Alignment and Spacing

PowerPoint enables you to control the way text lines up on the slide. You can align text to the left or right or to the center in a text object. You can adjust the alignment of text in an object by selecting the object and clicking an alignment button (Align Left, Center, or Align Right) on the Formatting toolbar. The **Align Left** button aligns text evenly along the left edge of the text box and is useful for paragraph text. The **Align Right** button aligns text evenly along the right edge of the text box and is useful for text labels. The **Center** button aligns text in the middle of the text box and is useful for titles and headings. You can also adjust the vertical space between selected lines and the space before and after paragraphs by selecting the object and clicking a line spacing button (**Increase Paragraph Spacing** or **Decrease Paragraph Spacing**) on the Formatting toolbar or by using the **Line Spacing** command on the **Format** menu.

A text object can be any size. Sometimes the text within a text object doesn't fill the entire object. PowerPoint allows you to adjust the text object to fit the amount of text. If you draw a shape and add text to it, you can adjust the text to fit inside the object. You can adjust the position of text in a text object by selecting or clearing the

341

Resize AutoShape to fit text option on the **Text Box** tab in the **Format AutoShape** dialog box.

AlignText

In this exercise, you adjust a text object and a text placeholder, change the alignment of text in a text object, decrease paragraph spacing, and adjust line spacing.

Open

1   On the Standard toolbar, click the **Open** button.

The **Open** dialog box appears.

2   Navigate to the Office XP SBS folder on your hard disk, double-click the **PowerPoint** folder, double-click the **Chap15** folder, and then double-click **AlignText**.

The AlignText presentation opens, displaying Slide 1 in Normal view.

3   In the Slide pane, drag the scroll box to Slide 5.

4   Click the bottom text box on Slide 5, and then click the edge of the text box to select it with the dotted selection box.

Two-headed
arrow pointer
↔

5   Position the pointer (which changes to the two-headed arrow pointer) over the right middle resize handle of the text box.

6   Drag the resize handle to the right to extend the text box about an inch.

The text box enlarges, and the text wraps to the text object.

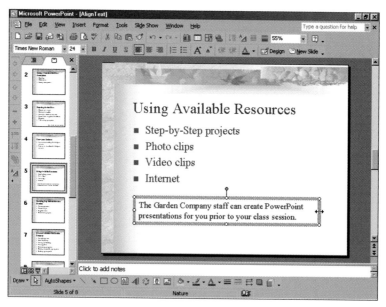

7   On the **Format** menu, click **Text Box**.

The **Format Text Box** dialog box appears.

8   Click the **Text Box** tab.

9   Clear the **Word wrap text in AutoShape** check box.

10 Click **OK**.

The word processing box changes to a text label and stretches across the slider beyond the slide boundary.

Tip

You can also convert a text label to a word processing box by dragging a resize handle to reduce the width of the text box. The text inside wraps to adjust to the new dimensions of the text box.

Undo

11 On the Standard toolbar, click the **Undo** button.

Selection
Pointer

12 Position the pointer near the bulleted text on Slide 5 until it changes to the selection pointer, and then click to select the paragraph text object.

Notice that the dotted selection box is larger than it needs to be.

13 On the **Format** menu, click **Placeholder**.

The **Format AutoShape** dialog box appears.

Tip

The command on the **Format** menu changes, depending on the type of object selected. If you resize a text box, the command on the **Format** menu is **Text Box**, and the dialog box that opens is titled **Format Text Box**.

14 Click the **Text Box** tab to display text spacing and alignment options.

15 Select the **Resize AutoShape to fit text** check box, and then click **OK**.

The object adjusts to fit the size of the text.

16 Click a blank area of the slide to deselect the text box.

17 In the Slide pane, drag the scroll box to Slide 8, and then select the text box at the bottom of the slide.

Center

18 On the Formatting toolbar, click the **Center** button.

The text in the text object aligns to the center of the text box.

Increase Para-
graph Spacing

19 On the Formatting toolbar, click the **Increase Paragraph Spacing** button.

The paragraph spacing in the text box increases by increments of 0.1 lines, from 1.0 to 1.1.

Important

If the **Increase Paragraph Spacing** button is not available on the Formatting toolbar, click the **Toolbar Options** down arrow, and then point to **Add or Remove Buttons** to display a list of additional Formatting buttons, click the button to place it on the toolbar, and then click a blank area of the slide to deselect the menu.

20 Click a blank area of the slide to deselect the text box.

Selection
Pointer

21 Click the edge of the bulleted paragraph text box on Slide 8 with the selection pointer.

The dotted selection box appears.

22 On the **Format** menu, click **Line Spacing**.

The **Line Spacing** dialog box appears.

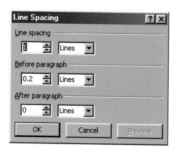

23 Click the **Before paragraph** down arrow until _0.1_ appears, and then click **OK**.

The paragraph spacing before each paragraph decreases by 0.1 lines.

24 Click a blank area of the slide to deselect the text box.

Tip

Everything that you can do to manipulate a text label or word processing box you can also do to any text object, including title and paragraph text objects.

Save

25 On the Standard toolbar, click the **Save** button to save the presentation.

Close Window

26 Click the **Close Window** button in the presentation window.

The AlignText presentation closes.

Finding and Replacing Text and Fonts

The **Find** and **Replace** commands on the **Edit** menu allow you to locate and change specific text in a presentation. **Find** helps you locate each occurrence of a specific word or set of characters, while **Replace** locates every occurrence of a specific word or set of characters and replaces it with a different one. You can change every occurrence of specific text all at once, or you can accept or reject each change individually. The **Find** and **Replace** commands also give you options for more detailed searches. If you want to search for whole words so that the search doesn't stop on a word that might contain only part of your search word, you select the **Find whole words only** check box. If you want to find a word or phrase that matches a certain capitalization exactly, you select the **Match case** check box. In addition to finding text, you can also find and replace a specific font in a presentation. The **Replace Fonts** command allows you to replace every instance of a font style that you have been using with another.

ReplaceText

In this exercise, you use the **Replace** command to find and replace a word and then replace a font.

Open

1 On the Standard toolbar, click the **Open** button.

The **Open** dialog box appears.

2 Navigate to the Office XP SBS folder on your hard disk, double-click the **PowerPoint** folder, double-click the **Chap15** folder, and then double-click **ReplaceText**.

The ReplaceText presentation opens, displaying Slide 1 in Normal view.

3 On the **Edit** menu, click **Replace**.

The **Replace** dialog box appears.

4 Click in the **Find what** box, if necessary, and then type Supplies.

5 Press the [Tab] key, or click in the **Replace with** box.

6 Type Supplies and equipment.

345

7 Select the **Match case** check box to find the text in the **Find what** box exactly as you typed it.

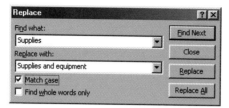

8 Click **Find Next**.

PowerPoint finds and selects the word *Supplies* on Slide 6.

Tip

If the dialog box covers up the selected text, move the **Replace** dialog box out of the way by dragging its title bar.

9 Click **Replace**.

PowerPoint replaces the selected text *Supplies* with the text *Supplies and equipment*. An alert box appears, telling you that PowerPoint has finished searching the presentation.

10 Click **OK**, and then click **Close** to close the **Replace** dialog box.

11 Click a blank area of the slide to deselect any text boxes.

12 On the **Format** menu, click **Replace Fonts**.

The **Replace Font** dialog box appears.

13 Click the **Replace** down arrow, and then click **Arial**.

14 Click the **With** down arrow, scroll down, and then click **Impact**.

15 Click **Replace**.

Throughout the presentation, the text formatted with the Arial font changes to the Impact font.

16 Click **Close** in the **Replace Font** dialog box.

17 In the Slide pane, drag the scroll box to Slide 8.

The Arial font in the bottom text box is now Impact.

Save

18 On the Standard toolbar, click the **Save** button to save the presentation.

Close Window

19 Click the **Close Window** button in the presentation window.

The ReplaceText presentation closes.

Correcting Text While Typing

As you type text in a presentation, you might be aware of making typographical errors, but when you look at the text, some of the mistakes have been corrected. With AutoCorrect, PowerPoint corrects common capitalization and spelling errors as you type. For example, if you frequently type *tehm* instead of *them*, you can create an AutoCorrect entry named *tehm*. Then, whenever you type *tehm* followed by a space or a punctuation mark, PowerPoint replaces the misspelling with *them*. You can customize AutoCorrect to recognize or ignore misspellings that you routinely make or to ignore specific text that you do not want AutoCorrect to change. You can also use AutoCorrect to recognize abbreviations or codes that you create to automate typing certain text. For example, you could customize AutoCorrect to type your full name when you type in only your initials.

AutoCorrect
Options
new for
OfficeXP

When you point to a word that AutoCorrect changed, a small blue box appears under the first letter. When you point to the small blue box, the **AutoCorrect Options** button appears. The **AutoCorrect Options** button gives you control over whether you want the text to be corrected. You can change text back to its original spelling, or you can stop AutoCorrect from automatically correcting text. You can also display the **AutoCorrect** dialog box and change AutoCorrect settings.

AutoFit Options
new for
OfficeXP

As you type text in a placeholder, PowerPoint uses AutoFit to resize the text, if necessary, to fit into the placeholder. The **AutoFit Options** button, which appears near your text the first time that it is resized, gives you control over whether you want the text to be resized. The **AutoFit Options** button displays a menu with options for controlling how the option works. For example, you can stop resizing text for the current placeholder while still maintaining your global AutoFit settings. You can also display the **AutoCorrect** dialog box and change the AutoFit settings so that text doesn't resize automatically.

CorrectText

In this exercise, you add an AutoCorrect entry, use AutoCorrect to fix a misspelled word, and then use AutoFit to resize a text box.

Open

1 On the Standard toolbar, click the **Open** button.

The **Open** dialog box appears.

2 Navigate to the Office XP SBS folder on your hard disk, double-click the **PowerPoint** folder, double-click the **Chap15** folder, and then double-click **CorrectText**.

The CorrectText presentation opens, displaying Slide 1 in Normal view.

3 On the **Tools** menu, click **AutoCorrect Options**, and then click the **AutoCorrect** tab, if necessary.

The **AutoCorrect** dialog box appears.

4 Click in the **Replace** box, if necessary, and then type **likns**.

The word *links* can be easily mistyped as *likns*.

5 Press [Tab], type **links**, and then click **Add**.

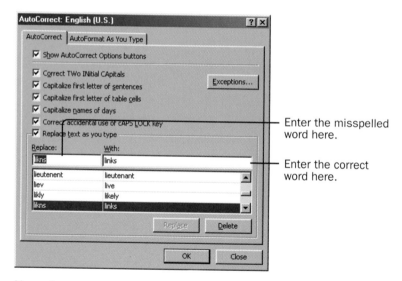

Enter the misspelled word here.

Enter the correct word here.

Now whenever you type *likns* in any presentation, PowerPoint replaces it with *links*.

6 Click **OK**.

7 In the Slide pane, drag the scroll box to Slide 5.

8 Click the blank area immediately after the word *Internet*, press the [Space] key, and then type **likns**.

9 Press the [Space] key.

PowerPoint corrects the word to *links*.

AutoCorrect
Options

10 Point to the small blue box under the word *links* to display the **AutoCorrect Options** button, and then click the **AutoCorrect Options** down arrow.

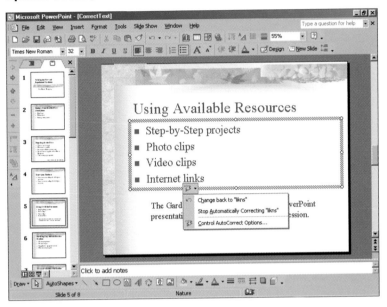

11 Click a blank area of the slide to deselect the **AutoCorrect Options** menu.

12 In the Slide pane, drag the scroll box to Slide 7.

13 Click to the right of the word *table* in the last line of the text box, and then press the [Enter] key.

14 Type **Installing a new lawn**.

The text box automatically resizes to fit the text in the box. The **AutoFit Options** button appears to the left of the text box.

AutoFit Options

15 Point to the **AutoFit Options** button, and then click the **AutoFit Options** down arrow, as shown on the next page.

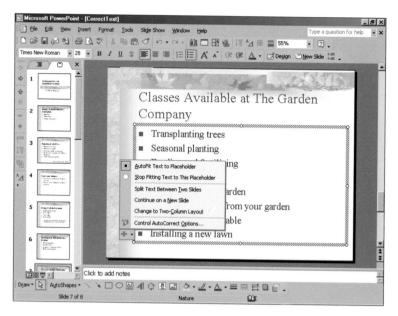

16 Click **Change to Two-Column Layout**.

Another bulleted list appears on the slide.

17 Type **Installing a sprinkler system** in the bulleted list on the right.

18 Click a blank area of the slide to deselect the text box.

Save

19 On the Standard toolbar, click the **Save** button to save the presentation.

Close Window

20 Click the **Close Window** button in the presentation window.

The CorrectText presentation closes.

Checking Spelling and Presentation Styles

PowerPoint's spelling checker checks the spelling of the entire presentation, including all slides, outlines, notes pages, and handout pages. To help you identify misspelled words or words that PowerPoint's built-in dictionary does not recognize, PowerPoint underlines them with a wavy red line. To turn this feature off, you can clear the **Check spelling as you type** check box on the **Spelling and Style** tab of the **Options** dialog box (available on the **Tools** menu). PowerPoint includes several built-in dictionaries so you can check presentations that use languages other than English. You can also create custom dictionaries in PowerPoint to check the spelling of unique words, or you can use custom dictionaries from other Microsoft programs. If a word is in a foreign language, you can mark it as such, and PowerPoint won't flag it as a misspelling anymore.

You can correct misspelled words in your presentation in two different ways. You can use the **Spelling** button on the Standard toolbar to check the entire presentation, or when you encounter a wavy red line under a word, you can right-click the word and choose the correct spelling from the list on the shortcut menu.

PowerPoint's style checker works with the Office Assistant to help you correct common presentation style errors so that your audience focuses on content, not visual mistakes. When the Office Assistant is visible, the style checker reviews the presentation for typical mistakes, such as incorrect font size, too many fonts, too many words, inconsistent punctuation, and other readability problems. The style checker then suggests ways to improve the presentation.

SpellCheck

In this exercise, you mark a word as a foreign language word, select and correct a misspelled word, check spelling in the entire presentation, and then set the style options and check the presentation style.

Open

1   On the Standard toolbar, click the **Open** button.

The **Open** dialog box appears.

2   Navigate to the Office XP SBS folder on your hard disk, double-click the **PowerPoint** folder, double-click the **Chap15** folder, and then double-click **SpellCheck**.

The SpellCheck presentation opens, displaying Slide 1 in Normal view.

3   In the Slide pane, drag the scroll box to Slide 8.

The words *Je*, *ne*, *sais*, and *quois* appear with a wavy red underline, indicating that they are misspelled or not recognized by the dictionary.

4   Select the French phrase *Je ne sais quois* in the text box.

5   On the **Tools** menu, click **Language**.

The **Language** dialog box appears.

6   Scroll down the list, click **French** (**France**), click **OK**, and then click in the text box to deselect the French words.

PowerPoint marks the selected words as French words for the spelling checker.

The red lines under the words no longer appear, indicating that the dictionary now recognizes the words.

7   Right-click the word *quois*, and then click **quoi** on the shortcut menu.

PowerPoint corrects the misspelled word.

Spelling

8   On the Standard toolbar, click the **Spelling** button.

PowerPoint begins checking the spelling in the presentation. The spelling checker stops and selects the proper name *Galos*.

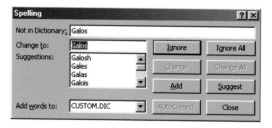

Galos does not appear in your dictionary, but you know it is a proper name that is spelled correctly.

Tip

The custom dictionary allows you to add words that the standard dictionary doesn't recognize. *Galos* is a proper name that you can add to your custom dictionary.

9   Click **Add**.

The word *Galos* is added to the custom dictionary and the spelling checker continues to check the presentation.

Tip

If you do not want to add a name or word to the spelling checker, you can click **Ignore** or **Ignore All**. The spelling checker will ignore the word or all appearances of the word in the current presentation.

10   The spelling checker stops and selects the misspelled word *Saeting*. A list appears in the **Suggestions** box, showing possible correct spellings of the misspelled word. The correct word spelling, *Seating*, appears in the list.

Tip

Click **AutoCorrect** in the **Spelling** dialog box to add the misspelling and the correct spelling of a word to the AutoCorrect table of entries.

11   Click the suggested spelling *Seating*, if necessary, and then click **Change** to correct the spelling.

The spelling checker continues to check the presentation for misspelled words or words not found in the dictionary. A dialog box appears when PowerPoint completes checking the entire presentation.

12   Click **OK** to continue, and then drag the scroll box up to Slide 1.

13   On the **Tools** menu, click **Options**.

The **Options** dialog box appears.

14   Click the **Spelling and Style** tab to display a list of options.

15 Select the **Check style** check box, and then click **Style Options**.

The **Style Options** dialog box appears. If PowerPoint prompts you to enable the Office Assistant, click **Enable Assistant**.

16 Select the **Body punctuation** check box to check for consistent body punctuation in the presentation.

17 Click the **Body punctuation** down arrow, and then click **Paragraphs have consistent punctuation**.

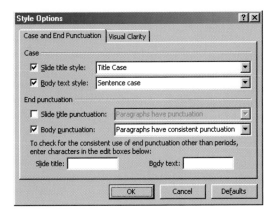

18 Click **OK** to close the **Style Options** dialog box, and then click **OK** again to close the **Options** dialog box.

19 In the Slide pane, drag the scroll box to Slide 4.

A light bulb appears on Slide 4.

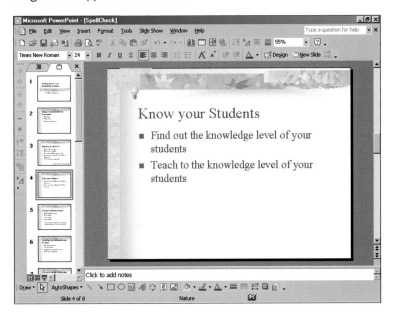

20   Click the **light bulb**.

A dialog balloon containing several options appears over the Office Assistant. The Office Assistant noticed that the text in the placeholder should be capitalized. The default style for title text is to capitalize all words in the title.

Tip

If you make a decision based on an Office Assistant tip and then change your mind, you may need to display the tip again. To do this, you need to reset your tips so that the Office Assistant will display all of them again. To reset your tips, right-click the Office Assistant, click **Options**, click **Reset my tips**, and then click **OK**.

21   Click the **Change the text to title case** option.

PowerPoint capitalizes the word *Your* in the title. The dialog balloon disappears.

Save

22   On the Standard toolbar, click the **Save** button to save the presentation.

Close Window

23   Click the **Close Window** button in the presentation window.

The SpellCheck presentation closes.

Changing Capitalization

As part of the style checking process, PowerPoint checks the capitalization, or case, of sentences and titles in the presentation, but you can independently change text case for selected text with a command on the **Format** menu. The **Change Case** command allows you to change text to sentence case, title case, uppercase, lowercase, or toggle case, which is a mixture of cases.

To change the text case:

1   Select the text that you want to change.

2   On the **Format** menu, click **Change Case**.

The **Change Case** dialog box appears with the **Sentence case** option button set as the default.

3   Click the change case option that you want to apply to the selected text.

4   Click **OK** to apply the change option to the presentation.

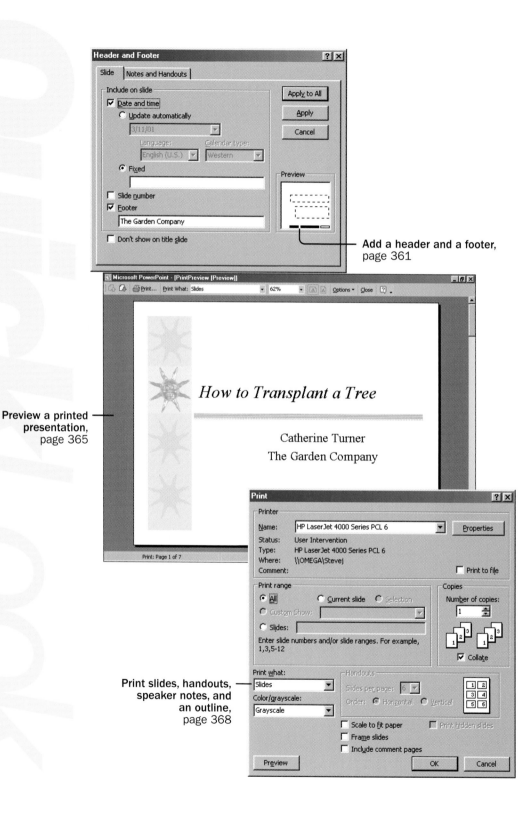

Add a header and a footer, page 361

Preview a printed presentation, page 365

Print slides, handouts, speaker notes, and an outline, page 368

Chapter 16
Printing a Presentation

After completing this chapter, you will be able to:

✔ **Work with an existing presentation.**

✔ **Add a header and a footer.**

✔ **Choose the right print settings.**

✔ **Preview a presentation.**

✔ **Print a presentation.**

Microsoft PowerPoint gives you flexibility when you are preparing to print slides, handouts, and speaker notes. Before you print your presentation, you can add a header and a footer to display the date and time, page number, or other important information. You can easily customize your printouts by selecting the paper size, page orientation, print range, and printer type that meet your needs. When you are ready to print, you can preview your presentation on the screen to make sure it appears the way you want. If you are working on a color presentation, you can preview your presentation in black and white to see how color slides will look after they are printed on a grayscale printer.

The owner of The Garden Company has completed the initial content development on a presentation for a gardening class. The next step is to preview and print the presentation to see how it looks.

In this chapter, you'll open an existing presentation, preview slides, add a header and a footer, choose the right printer settings, and print slides, audience handouts, outlines, and accompanying speaker notes.

 This chapter uses the practice files FilePrint, HeaderFooter, PrintSetting, PrintPreview, and PrintFile that are stored in the Office XP SBS\PowerPoint\Chap16 subfolder that you installed from this book's CD-ROM. For details about installing the practice files, see "Using the Book's CD-ROM" at the beginning of this book.

Working with an Existing Presentation

You can open an existing presentation—for example, one that you or a coworker has already created—and work on it in the same way that you would a new presentation. To open an existing presentation, you must first identify the presentation and its location.

FilePrint

In this exercise, you open an existing presentation.

Open

1 Start PowerPoint, if necessary.

2 On the **View** menu, click **Task Pane**, if necessary, to display the New Presentation Task pane.

3 In the New Presentation Task pane, under **Open a presentation**, click **Presentations**, or on the Standard toolbar, click the **Open** button to display the **Open** dialog box.

PowerPoint displays the **Open** dialog box, which is where you specify the name and location of the presentation that you want to open.

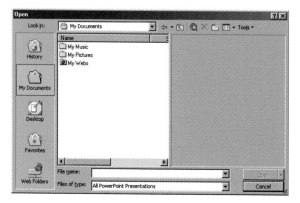

4 Click the **Look in** down arrow, and then click your hard disk, typically drive C.

5 In the list of file and folder names, double-click the **Office XP SBS** folder, double-click the **PowerPoint** folder, and then double-click the **Chap16** folder.

6 In the list of file and folder names, click the **FilePrint** file, and then click **Open**.

PowerPoint displays the **FilePrint** presentation in Normal view.

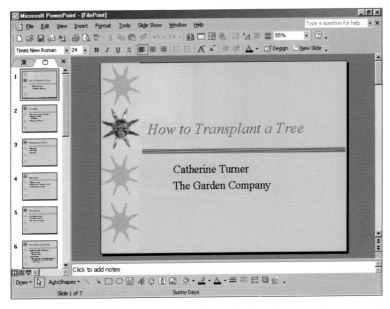

7   On the Standard toolbar, click the **Save** button to save the presentation.

Close Window

8   Click the **Close Window** button in the presentation window.

The FilePrint presentation closes.

Searching for a Presentation

If you can't remember the exact name or location of a presentation file, but you know part of the name or some of its contents, you can search for a presentation that contains part of the file name or specific words in the file by using the Basic Search Task pane. For more advanced searches, you can use properties, conditions, and values in the Advanced Search Task pane to make the search criteria more specific. The Advanced Search pane contains a set of properties—such as file name, text, creation date, last modified, and number of slides—and associated conditions—such as equal to, on or before, more than, and yes/no—to help you find a specific file or set of files. For example, you can type the search criteria *file name includes garden*, where *file name* is the property, *includes* is the condition, and *garden* is the value, to find all files that contain the word *garden*. If the fast searching option is installed on your computer, PowerPoint can search through files and organize information for faster retrieval. If fast searching is not installed, you can click **Install** in the Basic Search Task pane to install it.

At any time, you can enter presentation property values in the **Presentation Properties** dialog box. These presentation property values can assist you or others later when using the Search functions.

(continued)

To enter presentation property values and search for a file:

1 On the **File** menu, click **Properties**.

The **Presentation Properties** dialog box appears.

2 Click the **Summary** tab.

3 In the **Summary** tab, type presentation information into the specified boxes.

4 Click **OK** to add the presentation properties to the presentation.

5 On the Standard toolbar, click the **Search** button.

The Basic Search Task pane appears. If the Advanced Search Task pane appears, click **Basic Search** at the bottom of the Task pane.

6 In the **Search text** box, type the text to search for the files that you want to find.

7 Click the **Search in** down arrow, and then select the check box locations to look for presentation files. Or, select the **Everywhere** check box to search all files on your computer.

8 Click the **Results should be** down arrow, and then select the check box for the types of items to find, or select the **Anything** check box to find all types of files.

9 Click **Advanced Search** at the bottom of the Basic Search Task pane to display the Advanced Search Task pane.

10 Click the **Property** down arrow.

The **Property** box displays the properties available in the currently open presentation.

11 Choose a property from the list, or type the property name that you are searching for.

12 In the **Condition** box, choose a condition from the list, or type in a condition.

13 In the **Value** box, type the value to associate with the condition.

14 If previous search criteria exist, click **And** to add criteria that must be true in addition to previous criteria, or click **Or** to add a criteria that is sufficient regardless of previous criteria.

15 Click **Add** to add the search criteria.

16 Click **Search**.

PowerPoint searches through the selected files in the indicated folders. When the search is complete, PowerPoint displays the files that meet the search criteria in the **Search Results** Task pane. You can double-click files in the **Search Results** Task pane to open them.

Adding a Header and a Footer

Before you print your presentation, you can add a header and a footer, which will appear on every slide, handout, or notes page. Headers and footers contain useful information about the presentation, such as the author or company name, the date and time, and the page number. Because PowerPoint lets you add more than one header and footer to a presentation, you can have different headers and footers for slides and for notes and handouts. You can quickly and easily add a header and a footer to your slides, audience handouts, outlines, and speaker notes with the **Header and Footer** command on the **View** menu. Header and footer information appear only on the master slide.

HeaderFooter

In this exercise, you add a header and a footer to a presentation.

Open

1 On the Standard toolbar, click the **Open** button.

The **Open** dialog box appears.

2 Navigate to the Office XP SBS folder on your hard disk, double-click the **PowerPoint** folder, double-click the **Chap16** folder, and then double-click the **HeaderFooter** file.

The HeaderFooter presentation opens, displaying Slide 1 in Normal view.

3 On the **View** menu, click **Header and Footer**.

The **Header and Footer** dialog box appears, displaying the **Slide** tab.

4 Select the **Footer** check box, and then type The Garden Company.

In the **Preview** box, a black rectangle highlights the placement of the footer on the slides. Your dialog box should look like the following illustration:

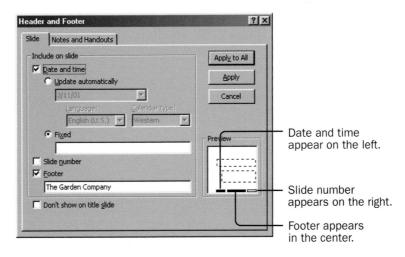

Date and time appear on the left.

Slide number appears on the right.

Footer appears in the center.

5 Select the **Don't show on title slide** check box, if necessary, so that the footer won't appear on the title slide.

6 Click the **Notes and Handouts** tab.

The header and footer settings for the notes and handout pages appear. All four check boxes are selected.

7 Click in the **Header** box, and then type **Transplanting a Tree**.

8 Click in the **Footer** box, and then type **The Garden Company**.

9 Clear the **Date and time** check box so that the date and time won't appear on each slide.

PowerPoint includes the header, footer, and page number on each notes or handout page that you print.

10 Click **Apply to All**.

PowerPoint applies the header and footer information to the slides, notes pages, outlines, and handouts pages.

11 On the Standard toolbar, click the **Save** button to save the presentation.

Close Window
☒

12 Click the **Close Window** button in the presentation window.

The HeaderFooter presentation closes.

Choosing the Right Print Settings

Additional paper sizes new for **Office**XP

Before you print a presentation, you should review the settings in the **Page Setup** dialog box and the **Print** dialog box. You can use the **Page Setup** dialog box to set the proportions and orientation of your slides, notes pages, handouts, and outlines on the printed page. For a new presentation, PowerPoint opens with default slide page settings: on-screen slide show, **landscape** orientation (10 x 7.5 inches), and slides starting at number 1. Notes, handouts, and outlines are printed in **portrait** orientation (7.5 x 10 inches). You can change these options at any time.

There are eleven slide sizes that you can select from in the **Page Setup** dialog box:

■ **On-screen Show** Use this setting when you are designing an on-screen slide show. The slide size for the screen is smaller than the Letter Paper size.

■ **Letter Paper (8.5 x 11 in)** Use this setting when you are printing a presentation on U.S. letter paper.

■ **Ledger Paper (11 x 17 in)** Use this setting when you are printing a presentation on legal size paper.

■ **A3 Paper (297 X 420 mm), A4 Paper (210 x 297 mm), B4 (ISO) Paper (250 X 353 mm), B5 (ISO) Paper (176 X 250 mm)** Use one of these settings when you are printing on international paper.

- ■ **35mm Slides** Use this setting when you are designing a presentation for 35mm slides.
- ■ **Overhead** Use this setting when you are printing transparencies for an overhead projector (8.5 x 11 in).
- ■ **Banner** Use this setting when you are designing a banner (8 x 1 in) for a Web page.
- ■ **Custom** Use this setting to design slides with a special size.

Tip

PowerPoint prints presentations on your default Windows printer unless you select a different printer. Your default printer is set up in the Windows print settings in the Control Panel. To change the default printer, click **Start** on the taskbar, point to **Settings**, click **Printers**, right-click the printer that you want to set as default, and then click **Set as Default**. You can select another printer in PowerPoint's **Print** dialog box.

PrintSetting

In this exercise, you change the slide size setting from **On-screen Show** to **Letter Paper** and select a printer for a presentation.

Open

1   On the Standard toolbar, click the **Open** button.

The **Open** dialog box appears.

2   Navigate to the Office XP SBS folder on your hard disk, double-click the **PowerPoint** folder, double-click the **Chap16** folder, and then double-click the **PrintSetting** file.

The PrintSetting presentation opens, displaying Slide 1 in Normal view.

3   On the **File** menu, click **Page Setup**.

The **Page Setup** dialog box appears.

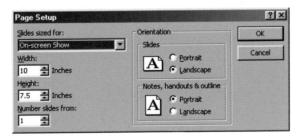

4   Click the **Slides sized for** down arrow, and then click **Letter Paper (8.5 x 11 in)**.

5   Click **OK**.

The slide size changes to Letter Paper.

Troubleshooting

> Before you print, it is important to verify that your printer is turned on, connected to your computer, and loaded with paper.

6 On the **File** menu, click **Print**.

The **Print** dialog box appears.

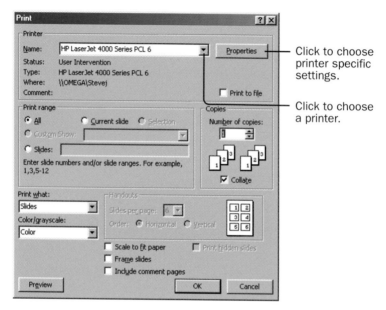

Click to choose printer specific settings.

Click to choose a printer.

7 In the **Printer** area, click the **Name** down arrow.

A drop-down list appears with the installed printers on your computer.

8 Click one of the printers in the list.

After choosing a printer, you can customize your printer settings.

9 Click **Properties**.

The **Properties** dialog box appears, showing the current printer settings. The **Properties** dialog settings differ, depending on the specific printer that you selected.

10 In the **Properties** dialog box, click **OK**.

The **Properties** dialog box closes to display the **Print** dialog box. The print setup is complete.

Close Window

11 In the **Print** dialog box, click **OK** to print the presentation with the selected print settings.

12 On the Standard toolbar, click the **Save** button to save the presentation.

13 Click the **Close Window** button in the presentation window.

The PrintSetting presentation closes.

Previewing a Presentation

Print Preview allows you to see how your presentation will look before you print it. While in print preview, you have the option of switching between various views, such as notes, slides, outlines, and handouts, or even landscape and portrait. If you are using a black and white printer to print a color presentation, you need to verify that the printed presentation will be legible. For example, red text against a shaded background shows up well in color, but when seen in black and white or shades of gray, the text tends to be indistinguishable from the background. To prevent this problem, you can preview your color slides in pure black and white or *grayscale* in Print Preview to see how they will look when you print them. Pure black and white displays colors in black and white, while grayscale displays colors in shades of gray. If you want to make changes to your slides while viewing them in black and white, you can change the color setting to black and white in Normal view.

PrintPreview

In this exercise, you preview your presentation handouts, switch to Pure Black and White view, and then change the way the slide looks in black and white.

Open

1 On the Standard toolbar, click the **Open** button.

The **Open** dialog box appears.

2 Navigate to the Office XP SBS folder on your hard disk, double-click the **PowerPoint** folder, double-click the **Chap16** folder, and then double-click the **PrintPreview** file.

The PrintPreview presentation opens, displaying Slide 1 in Normal view.

Print Preview

3 On the Standard toolbar, click the **Print Preview** button.

The screen switches to Print Preview and shows your presentation in the currently selected settings, as shown on the next page.

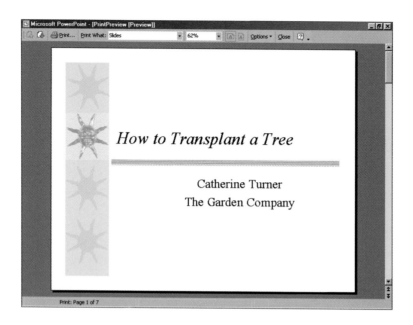

If you are printing to a grayscale printer, your slides are shown in grayscale in print preview.

4 On the Print Preview toolbar, click the **Print What** down arrow, and then click **Handouts (2 slides per page)**.

The preview screen displays your presentation in handout format with two slides per page.

5 On the Print Preview toolbar, click the **Options** down arrow, point to **Color/ Grayscale**, and then click **Color (On Black and White Printer)**.

The preview screen displays your presentation in a shaded grayscale color.

Important

If you are printing to a color printer, your options will be different; click **Color** on the **Color/Grayscale** menu.

6 On the Print Preview toolbar, click the **Next Page** button.

The preview screen displays the next handout page.

Magnifying
glass (+)

7 Position the pointer (which changes to a magnifying glass with a plus sign) in the preview area, and then click the center of the top slide.

The view in the preview screen increases to display a magnified view of the slide.

Magnifying
glass (-)

8 Position the pointer (which changes to a magnifying glass with a minus sign) in the preview area, and then click the center of the slide.

The preview screen is reduced to display the original view of the slide.

9 On the Print Preview toolbar, click the **Previous Page** button.

The preview screen displays the previous handout page.

Close Preview

Close

10 On the Print Preview toolbar, click the **Close Preview** button.

The preview screen closes, and your PowerPoint presentation returns to the previous view.

11 Click the **Normal View** button, if necessary, and then click the **Slides** tab, if necessary, to display slide miniatures in the Outline/Slides pane.

Color/Gray-
scale

12 On the Standard toolbar, click the **Color/Grayscale** button, and then click **Grayscale**.

The slide switches from color to grayscale and the Grayscale View toolbar opens. You can still view the slide miniatures in color on the **Slides** tab, making it easier to compare the color slides with the black and white slides.

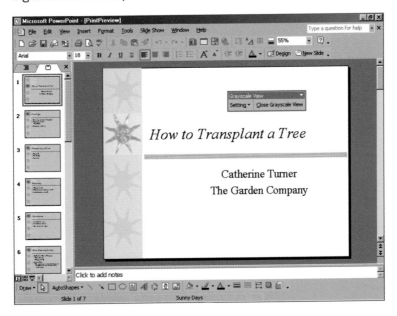

Next Slide

13 Click the **Next Slide** button.

The next slide appears, also in black and white with the slide miniature in color.

Slide Sorter
View

🔲

14 Click the **Slide Sorter View** button.

All of the slides in the Slide Sorter view appear in black and white.

15 Double-click **Slide 1** to display Slide 1 in Normal view.

16 On the Grayscale View toolbar, click the **Setting** button, and then click **Black with Grayscale Fill**.

The slide background changes from white to gray.

17 On the Grayscale View toolbar, click the **Setting** button, and then click **White**.

The slide background is white again.

18 On the Grayscale View toolbar, click the **Close Grayscale View** button.

The slide switches back to color.

19 On the Standard toolbar, click the **Save** button to save the presentation.

Close Window

❌

20 Click the **Close Window** button in the presentation window.

The PrintPreview presentation closes.

Printing a Presentation

You can print your PowerPoint presentation in several ways: as slides, speaker notes, audience handouts, or an outline. PowerPoint makes it easy to print your presentation; it detects the type of printer that you chose—either color or black and white—and prints the appropriate version of the presentation. For example, if you select a black and white printer, your presentation will be set to print in shades of gray (grayscale).

PowerPoint prints slides and supplements based on settings in the **Print** dialog box. In the **Print** dialog box, you can select a printer and set the print range, which defines which slides to print. You can also choose to print multiple copies of a presentation, and if you do print more than one copy of each slide, you can choose to collate the presentation as you print. When you collate the presentation, PowerPoint prints a complete copy before printing the next copy. The **Print** dialog box also contains a **Preview** button that takes you to the **Print Preview** window, allowing you to preview any changes that you may have made.

Tip

If you are working with a professional printer to print your slides, you will need to print your slides to a file instead of to a printer. To print your slides to a file, select the **Print to file** check box in the **Print** dialog box.

By clicking the **Print what** down arrow in the **Print** dialog box, you can choose to print a presentation as one of four output types:

- ■ **Slides** Prints slides as they appear on the screen, one per page. You can print a slide as an overhead transparency in the same way that you print any other slide, except you put transparency film in the printer instead of paper.
- ■ **Handouts** Prints one, two, three, four, six, or nine slides per page.
- ■ **Notes Pages** Prints each slide with the speaker notes under it. The notes pages appear with a reduced image of the slide at the top of the page.
- ■ **Outline View** Prints an outline with formatting according to the current view setting. What you see in the Outline pane is what you get on the printout.

An example of each printing type is shown in the following illustrations:

Slide (landscape)

Notes Page

Handout

Outline View

By clicking the **Color/grayscale** down arrow in the **Print** dialog box, you can choose to print a presentation as one of three color options:

■ **Color** Use this option to print a presentation in color on a color printer. If you select a black and white printer with this option, the presentation prints in grayscale.

■ **Grayscale** Use this option to print a presentation in grayscale on a color or black and white printer.

■ **Pure Black and White** Use this option to print a presentation in only black and white with no gray on a color or black and white printer.

Finally, at the bottom of the **Print** dialog box, you can select from the following print options to enhance a printout:

■ **Scale to fit paper** Use this option to scale slides to fit the paper size in the printer if the paper in the printer does not correspond to the slide size and orientation settings.

■ **Frame slides** Use this option to add a frame around the presentation slides when you print.

■ **Include comment pages** Use this option to print any comments that you have inserted throughout the presentation.

■ **Print hidden slides** Use this option to print all hidden slides.

Print

If you are satisfied with the current **Print** dialog box settings, you can click the **Print** button on the Standard toolbar to print directly without first viewing the settings. Otherwise, click the **Print** command on the **File** menu to print with new settings.

PrintFile

In this exercise, you review print output types and options. You then print presentation slides, audience handouts, and speaker notes.

Open

1 On the Standard toolbar, click the **Open** button.

The **Open** dialog box appears.

2 Navigate to the Office XP SBS folder on your hard disk, double-click the **PowerPoint** folder, double-click the **Chap16** folder, and then double-click the **PrintFile** file.

The PrintFile presentation opens, displaying Slide 1 in Normal view.

3 On the **File** menu, click **Print**.

The **Print** dialog box appears.

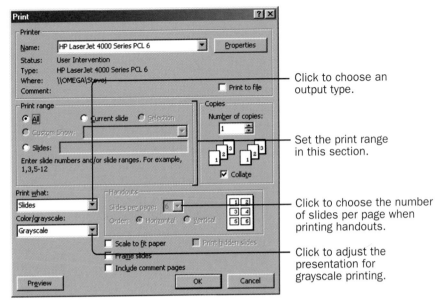

Click to choose an output type.

Set the print range in this section.

Click to choose the number of slides per page when printing handouts.

Click to adjust the presentation for grayscale printing.

4   In the **Print range** area, click the **Current slide** option.

5   Click the **Print what** down arrow, and then click **Slides** in the list that appears.

6   Click the **Color/grayscale** down arrow, click **Grayscale** in the list that appears, and then click **OK**.

PowerPoint prints the current slide in the presentation. A small print icon appears on the status bar located at the bottom of your screen, showing the printing status.

Tip

Every printer prints text and graphics slightly differently. PowerPoint sizes presentation slides to the printer that you choose. Using scalable fonts, such as TrueType fonts, PowerPoint allows you to print a presentation on different printers with the same results. When you print a presentation with scalable fonts, PowerPoint reduces or enlarges the size of the text in the presentation for each printer to get consistent results.

7   On the **File** menu, click **Print**.

The **Print** dialog box appears.

Tip

You can print audience handouts in six formats: one, two, three, four, six, or nine slides per page.

8 Click the **Print what** down arrow, and then click **Handouts**.

9 Click the **Slides per page** down arrow, and then click **2**.

PowerPoint selects the **Frame slides** check box when you select handouts.

10 Click **OK**.

PowerPoint prints the presentation slides as handout pages.

11 On the **File** menu, click **Print**.

The **Print** dialog box appears.

12 Click the **Print what** down arrow, and then click **Notes Pages**.

13 In the **Print range** area, click the **Slides** option.

The insertion point appears in the box next to the **Slides** option.

14 Type **1-2,4**.

Tip

You can print slides or notes pages in any order by entering slide numbers and ranges separated by commas. For example, if you enter 1,3,5-12 in the **Slides** box in the **Print** dialog box, PowerPoint prints slides 1, 3, and 5 through 12.

15 Click **OK**.

PowerPoint prints notes pages 1, 2, and 4.

Tip

When you send a document to a printer with background printing turned on, Windows can work in the background to print the job and let you continue to work. Background printing uses additional system memory. If printing is slow, you can turn off background printing to speed up the process. On the **Tools** menu, click **Options**, click the **Print** tab, and then clear the **Background printing** check box.

16 On the Standard toolbar, click the **Save** button to save the presentation.

Close Window
☒

17 Click the **Close Window** button in the presentation window.

The PrintFile presentation closes.

Printing a Presentation to a Printer on the Web

If your organization uses Microsoft Windows 2000 and the Active Directory directory service, you can search for and use printers across your network, intranet, or Web. **Active Directory** is a network service that stores information about resources, such as computers and printers.

To search for printers on your network, you use the **Find Printer** button in the **Print** dialog box. If Active Directory is not used at your site or if your operating system does not support it, the **Find Printer** button will not be available.

To find a printer on the Web and print a presentation using the **Print** dialog box:

1 On the **File** menu, click Print.

The **Print** dialog box appears.

2 Click **Find Printer**.

The **Find Printer** dialog box appears.

3 Click **Find Now** to find all printers on your network, intranet, or Web site.

4 In the **Find Printer** dialog box, select the printer that you want.

5 Click **OK**.

The **Printer** dialog box appears, and the selected printer appears in the **Name** box.

6 Specify the print settings that you want, and then click **OK** to print the presentation.

373

Microsoft FrontPage

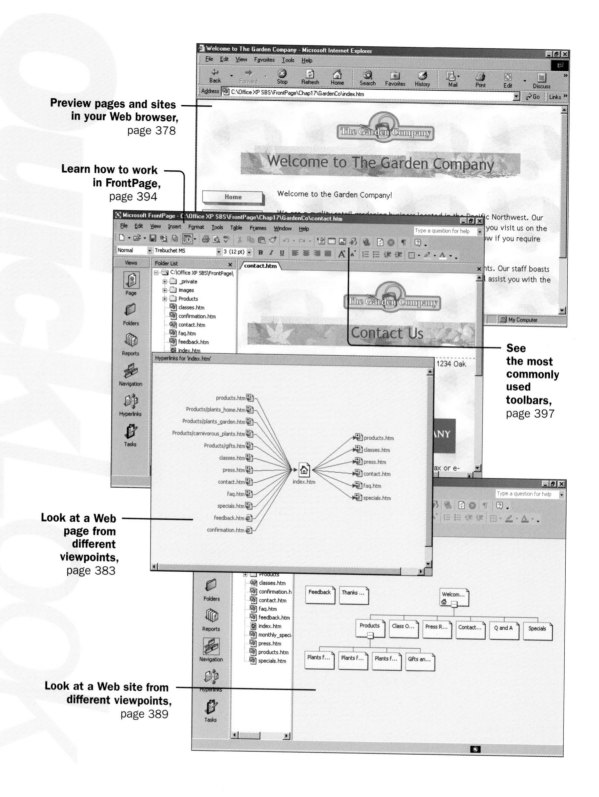

Preview pages and sites in your Web browser, page 378

Learn how to work in FrontPage, page 394

See the most commonly used toolbars, page 397

Look at a Web page from different viewpoints, page 383

Look at a Web site from different viewpoints, page 389

Chapter 17
Understanding How FrontPage Works

After completing this chapter, you will be able to:

✔ **Open and preview a FrontPage-based Web site.**

✔ **Open and preview an individual Web page.**

✔ **Look at a Web site from a variety of viewpoints.**

✔ **Look "behind the scenes" at the HTML code that does all the work.**

Microsoft FrontPage 2002 is a comprehensive application that you can use to develop Web sites. This sophisticated program provides everything you need to create Web sites ranging from a simple Web-based résumé to a complex Web-based retail store.

In spite of its sophistication, FrontPage is easy to use. As a member of the **Microsoft Office XP** suite of applications, it works pretty much the same way the other Office applications do. If you've avoided trying to create Web sites because you didn't want to learn how to program in **Hypertext Markup Language (HTML)**, FrontPage might well be the answer you've been waiting for. With FrontPage, you can easily create good-looking, interesting Web sites that incorporate complex elements, without typing a single line of programming code. But if you have some HTML programming experience or want to feel more in control, FrontPage gives you easy access to the code that it creates behind the scenes. You can view and edit the underlying HTML code at any time, but the great thing is that you don't have to. No programming experience is necessary to become a successful FrontPage developer.

This chapter introduces FrontPage and explains the concept of a FrontPage-based Web site. You will learn how to open an existing Web site, how to navigate between Web pages, and how to view the pages in different ways. You will then look at various ways of working in FrontPage and learn how to locate and control the FrontPage features you are likely to want to use in your own Web sites. In addition, you will learn how to view the underlying HTML code that makes all Web sites work. You will also get an overview of the different types of Web sites you can create with FrontPage and of the decision-making tools and resources that are necessary to create, manage, and maintain a personal or commercial Web site.

The exercises in this chapter and throughout the book are built around a Web site created for a fictitious garden and plant store called *The Garden Company*. This Web site, which is named *GardenCo*, contains realistic examples of content and structure that serve to demonstrate the concepts covered in each chapter. In this particular chapter, you will be working with the sample Web site that is stored in the Office XP SBS\FrontPage\Chap17 folder.

Tip

To follow along with the exercises in this book, you need to install the practice files from the companion CD-ROM. (You cannot just copy the files.) You'll find instructions for installing the files in the "Using the Book's CD-ROM" section at the beginning of the book.

Exploring an Existing Web Site

When you work with other Office XP applications, you create self-contained documents that can be individually opened from within Windows Explorer. When you work with FrontPage, you create a group of interconnected files that collectively make up each FrontPage-based Web site. As a result, Web sites must be opened from within FrontPage; clicking a single file name in Windows Explorer might open that file, but it won't open the Web site that the file belongs to.

In this exercise, you will start FrontPage and open a sample FrontPage-based Web site. You will then preview the Web site.

GardenCo

The working folder for this exercise is Office XP SBS\FrontPage\Chap17.

Follow these steps:

1 At the left end of the taskbar at the bottom of your screen, click the **Start** button. Then on the **Start** menu, point to **Programs**, and click **Microsoft FrontPage**.

Tip

Depending on your system resources, you might see a message box notifying you of additional system requirements for using certain Office XP features, such as Speech Recognition. If you see this message box, click **OK** to continue.

When FrontPage opens for the first time, you see a new page file called *new_page_1.htm* in the Page view editing window, as shown here:

The Standard toolbar   The New Page or Web Task pane

The Formatting toolbar

The Views bar

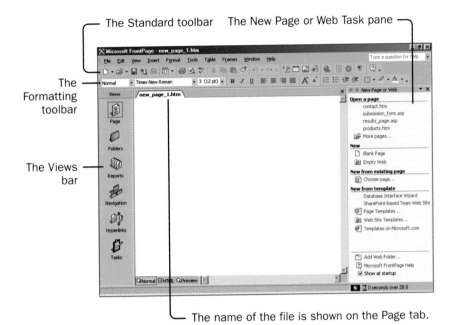

The name of the file is shown on the Page tab.

Office task panes

new for **Office**XP

The New Page or Web Task pane opens when FrontPage starts with no Web site open. If you don't want the Task pane to be shown by default, clear the **Show at startup** check box on the bottom of the Task pane.

2   On the **File** menu, click **Open Web** to open this dialog box:

The icons in the Views bar represent frequently used folders.

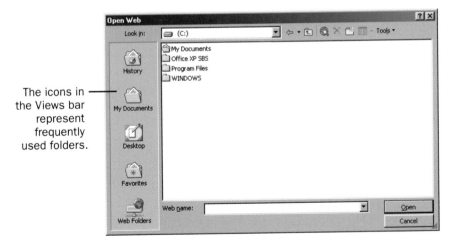

3   In the **Open Web** dialog box, browse to the Office XP
SBS\FrontPage\Chap17 folder.

Web site icon

A FrontPage-based Web site called *GardenCo* is located here, as indicated by
the **Web site** icon preceding the name.

4   Click **GardenCo** to select the Web site, and then click **Open**.

The New Page or Web Task pane closes, the new_page_1.htm file closes,
and the **Folder List** opens with the folders and files that make up the
GardenCo Web site displayed, like this:

The **Folder
List** displays
the visible
structure of
the Web site.

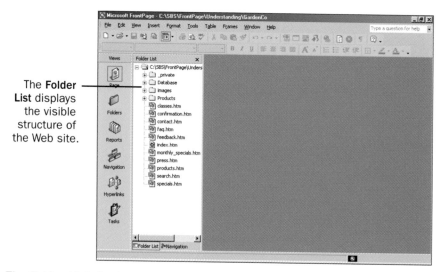

The **Folder List** displays the visible folders and files that you can access in
the Web site. You can open files of all types from the **Folder List** by double-
clicking them.

Important

A FrontPage-based Web site includes hidden folders and files generated by FrontPage
for behind-the-scenes operations. Deleting or changing these files and folders might
"break" the site by damaging the navigation structure, rendering links invalid, or
worse, so FrontPage designates them as hidden. Provided your computer is not set
to show hidden files and folders (this setting is on the **View** tab of the Microsoft
Windows **Folder Options** dialog box), you will not see these files, and there will be no
danger than you might accidentally delete or alter them.

5   Click the plus sign preceding each of the folders to view the folder contents.

Web page icon

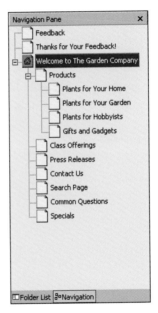

Different icons designate the various types of files that make up this site. For example, the **Web page** icon precedes the **file name** of each page of the FrontPage-based Web site, and the **home page** icon indicates the **home page** of the site.

Toggle Pane

The **Toggle Pane** button on the Standard toolbar is selected by default, indicating that you can click it to toggle the current pane between open and closed.

6   Click the **Toggle Pane** button to close the **Folder List**, and click it again to open the list.

7   At the bottom of the **Folder List**, click the **Navigation** button to switch to the Navigation Pane.

8   Drag the right border of the Navigation Pane to the right until all the **page titles** are visible, like this:

The Navigation Pane displays the page titles of all of the files that have been added to the **navigational structure** of the Web site. This view of the navigational structure is essentially a hierarchical map of how pages are connected within the site and what routes you can take to get from one page to another. As with the **Folder List**, you can open each of these files by double-clicking the page icon or title in the Navigation Pane.

9   Click the **Toggle Pane** button to close the Navigation Pane, and click it again to open the pane.

10 Click the **Toggle Pane** button's arrow, and select **Folder List** from the drop-down list to switch back to the **Folder List**.

11 In the **Folder List**, click **index.htm** to select the file.

12 To see how the site looks in your **Web browser**, click **Preview in Browser**, on the **File** menu.

The **Preview in Browser** dialog box opens:

Installed Internet browsers are shown in the Browser list.

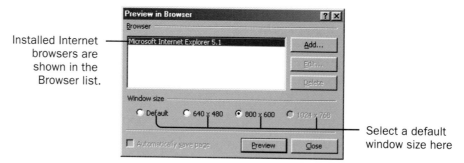

Select a default window size here

13 Select your preferred browser and window size (a minimum of 800 x 600 is recommended), and click **Preview**.

The GardenCo Web site opens in your selected browser, like this:

Page title   Company logo

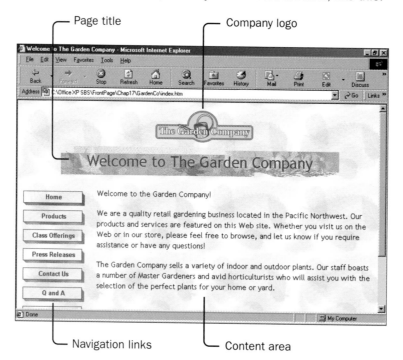

Navigation links   Content area

14 Click each of the navigation links to move between pages.

Close

15 When you're done previewing the Web site, click the **Close** button to close the browser and return to FrontPage.

16 On the **File** menu, click **Close Web** to close the Web site.

Optimizing Your Screen Display Properties

The width and height of your **screen area** is measured in pixels. When personal computers first became popular, most computer monitors were capable of displaying a screen area of only 640 pixels wide by 480 pixels high (more commonly known as 640 x 480). Now most computer monitors can also display at 800 by 600 pixels and 1024 by 768 pixels. Some monitors can even display a screen area of 1152 by 864 pixels, or larger.

Most computer users have the choice of at least two different screen area sizes. Some people prefer to work in the 640 by 480 area because everything on screen appears larger. Others prefer being able to fit more information on their screen with a 1024 by 768 display.

When designing a Web page that consists of more than free-flowing text, it is important to consider the likely screen area of your Web visitors. It is currently common practice to design Web sites to look their best when the visitor's screen area is set to 800 by 600 pixels. This means that visitors who view your site with a 640 by 480 area will have to scroll to display the entire page.

To determine your current screen area settings on a Windows 98 computer:

1 Click **Start**, point to **Settings**, and then click **Control Panel**.

2 In the Control Panel window, double-click **Display** to open the **Display Properties** dialog box.

3 On the **Settings** tab, look at the **Screen area** slider. The current screen area appears beneath the slider.

4 Click **Less** or **More** to move the slider to change the screen area.

Exploring an Existing Web Page

Web pages are the building blocks of every Web site. When you view a Web site in a browser, you are usually viewing Web pages. When you are developing a Web site, you are also working with pages. When you want to edit a Web page that is part of a FrontPage-based Web site, you first open the site in FrontPage and then open the individual page. Opening the page in FrontPage rather than as an individual file in another program avoids the possibility that you might damage the site. It also ensures that changes made on an individual page are reflected across the entire site as appropriate.

Important

If FrontPage is your default HTML editor, you can open individual Web pages from outside FrontPage by double-clicking the page file in Windows Explorer. However, if FrontPage is not your default editor, accessing and changing files individually from outside FrontPage could result in damage to the Web site.

In this exercise, you will open an individual Web page, view the HTML code generated by FrontPage, and preview a Web page both in FrontPage and in a browser.

GardenCo

The working folder for this exercise is Office XP SBS\FrontPage\Chap17.

Follow these steps:

1   On the **File** menu, click **Open Web**.

2   Browse to the Office XP SBS\FrontPage\Chap17 folder in the **Open Web** dialog box, select **GardenCo**, and click **Open** to open the Web site located in the working folder.

The Web site opens in FrontPage with the **Folder List** displayed, like this:

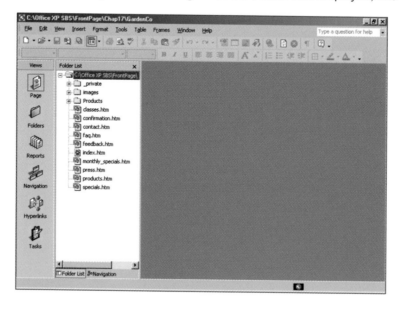

Tip

If the **Folder List** is not displayed, click **Folder List** on the **View** menu to open it.

3 In the **Folder List**, right-click the **contact.htm** file, and click **Open** on the shortcut menu.

Open Web
page icon

The file icon changes to an **open Web page** icon, and the file opens in the **Page view editing window**, like this:

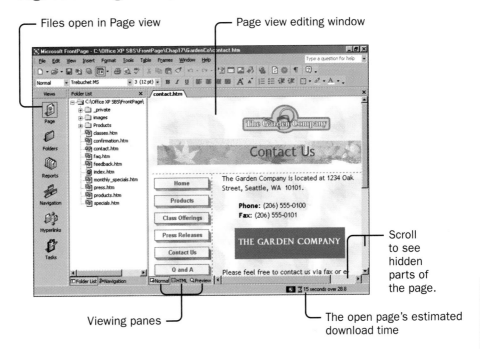

Files open in Page view

Page view editing window

Scroll
to see
hidden
parts of
the page.

Viewing panes

The open page's estimated
download time

4 Use the scroll bars to look at the entire page.

This page has **shared borders** at the top and left side of the page, delineated by the dotted lines, as shown in the example on the next page.

Top shared border

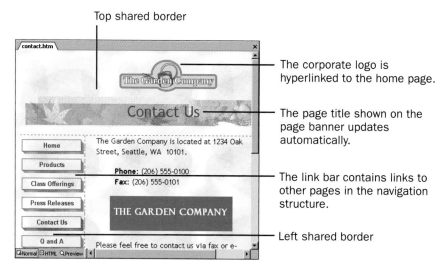

The corporate logo is hyperlinked to the home page.

The page title shown on the page banner updates automatically.

The link bar contains links to other pages in the navigation structure.

Left shared border

The shared borders appear on every page of the Web site and contain the same information, giving the site a consistent look. The top shared border contains a corporate logo and a title, or **page banner**. The left shared border contains a **Link bar** displaying **hyperlinks** that you can click to jump to other pages in the site.

The content area in the center of the page contains text, a graphic, a table, and two **e-mail links**, as shown here:

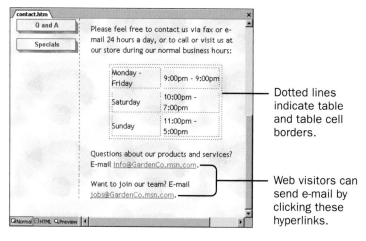

Dotted lines indicate table and table cell borders.

Web visitors can send e-mail by clicking these hyperlinks.

5   Now that you've seen the outside, let's look at the inside. Click the **HTML** button at the bottom of the Page view editing window to switch to the **HTML pane**.

The HTML code making up this page looks like this:

```html
<html>

<head>
<meta http-equiv="Content-Language" content="en-us">
<meta name="GENERATOR" content="Microsoft FrontPage 5.0">
<meta name="ProgId" content="FrontPage.Editor.Document">
<meta http-equiv="Content-Type" content="text/html; charset=windows-
1252">
<title>Contact Us</title>
<meta name="Microsoft Theme" content="modified-nature-theme 011,
default">
<meta name="Microsoft Border" content="tl, default">
</head>

<body>

<p>The Garden Company is located at 1234 Oak Street, Seattle, WA 
10101.</p>
<blockquote>

<p><b>Phone:</b> (206) 555-0100<br>
<b>Fax:</b> (206) 555-0101</p>
</blockquote>

<p align="center">
<applet code="fprotate.class" codebase="images/" width="264"
height="72">
  <param name="image1" valuetype="ref" value="images/banner1.gif">
  <param name="image2" valuetype="ref" value="images/banner2.gif">
  <param name="image3" valuetype="ref" value="images/banner3.gif">
  <param name="rotatoreffect" value="blindsHorizontal">
  <param name="time" value="2">
</applet></p>

<p>Please feel free to contact us via fax or e-mail 24 hours a day, or
to call or visit us at our store during our normal business hours:</p>
<div align="left">
  <blockquote>
  <table border="0" cellpadding="0" cellspacing="6" style="border-col-
lapse: collapse" id="AutoNumber1" height="57">
    <tr>
      <td height="19">Monday - Friday</td>
      <td height="19">9:00pm - 9:00pm</td>
    </tr>
    <tr>
      <td height="19">Saturday</td>
```

(continued)

```
      <td height="19">10:00pm - 7:00pm</td>
    </tr>
    <tr>
      <td height="19">Sunday</td>
      <td height="19">11:00pm - 5:00pm</td>
    </tr>
  </table>
  </blockquote>
</div>

<p>Questions about our products and services? E-mail
<a href="mailto:info@GardenCo.msn.com">info@GardenCo.msn.com</a>.</p>
<p>Want to join our team? E-mail
<a href="mailto:jobs@GardenCo.msn.com">jobs@GardenCo.msn.com</a>.</p>

</body>

</html>
```

6 Find each section of text within the page code and study the surrounding HTML code. Try to identify the code that creates each page element.

7 Click the **Normal** button at the bottom of the Page view editing window to switch back to the **Normal pane**.

8 Now see how the page will look to **Web visitors**. Click the **Preview** button at the bottom of the Page view editing window to switch to the **Preview pane**, where FrontPage displays the page like this:

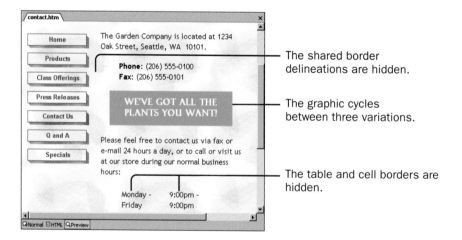

The shared border delineations are hidden.

The graphic cycles between three variations.

The table and cell borders are hidden.

Preview in
Browser

9 Next, preview the page in your default Web browser. On the Standard toolbar, click the **Preview in Browser** button.

Although you've chosen to preview only this page, you can still open the other pages of the site by clicking the hyperlinked buttons on the link bar.

10 When you're done previewing the Web site, click the **Close** button to close the browser and return to FrontPage.

11 Use the buttons at the bottom of the Page view editing window to switch between the Normal, HTML, and Preview panes as much as you like. When you're done looking at the page, click the **Close** button in the upper right corner of the Page view editing window to close the file.

12 On the **File** menu, click **Close Web** to close the Web site.

Looking at a Web Site in Various Ways

FrontPage 2002 provides six different **views** of a Web site:

Page tabs
new for
OfficeXP

- **Page view** displays the open page or pages in the Page view editing window. A tab at the top of each page shows the file name. If multiple pages are open, you can switch to another page by clicking its tab or by clicking its file name on the **Window** menu.

- **Folders view** displays the visible files and folders that are part of the open Web site. For each file, this view shows the file name, page title, file size, file type, the date the file was last modified and by whom, and any comments that have been added to the file information.

- **Reports view** displays any of 27 reports about the open Web site. Reports view defaults to the last opened report. If no other report has been open during the current FrontPage session, the default is a Site Summary report that collates the results of the other 26 reports. The various reports can be chosen from the **View** menu or from the Reporting toolbar.

- **Navigation view** graphically displays a hierarchical view of all the files that have been added to the navigation structure of the open Web site. To add a file to the navigation structure, you simply drag the file into the Navigation view window and drop it in the appropriate location. To fit the site content into the window, you can switch between Portrait mode (vertical layout) and Landscape mode (horizontal layout) or zoom in or out using the buttons on the Navigation toolbar.

- **Hyperlinks view** displays the hyperlinks to and from any selected page in the open Web site. Internal hyperlinks are shown as well as external hyperlinks and e-mail hyperlinks. You select a file in the **Folder List** to see the hyperlinks to and from that file, and then click the plus sign next to any file name to further expand the view.

- **Tasks view** displays a list of tasks to be completed in the open Web site. FrontPage creates these **tasks** when you use a wizard to create a Web site, or you can create your own tasks. For each task, you see the status, name, and description. You are also told to whom the task is assigned; whether the task has been categorized as High, Medium, or Low priority; and when the task was last modified. Tasks are a useful way of tracking the readiness status of a site.

You can switch between views by clicking the desired view on the **View** menu or on the **Views** bar.

In this exercise, you will look at Web pages in each of the FrontPage views, to get an idea of what information is available to you in each view.

GardenCo

The working folder for this exercise is Office XP SBS\FrontPage\Chap17.

Follow these steps:

Open

1   On the Standard toolbar, click the **Open** button's arrow, and then click **Open Web** on the drop-down list.

2   In the **Open Web** dialog box, browse to the Office XP SBS\FrontPage\ Chap17 folder, select **GardenCo**, and click **Open** to open the Web site located in the working folder.

3   In the **Folder List**, double-click **classes.htm** to open the file in the Page view editing window.

    On the **Views** bar, the Page view icon is selected to indicate that you are working in Page view.

Folders

4   On the **Views** bar, click the **Folders** icon.

    FrontPage displays the contents of the Web site in Folders view, like this:

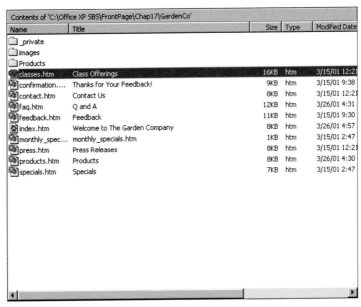

5 Use the scroll bars to view the entire screen.

Reports

6 On the **Views** bar, click the **Reports** icon.

FrontPage turns on the Reporting toolbar and displays the Site Summary report for the open Web site, like this:

Name	Count	Size	Description
All files	27	449KB	All files in the current Web
Pictures	10	333KB	Picture files in the current Web (GIF, JPG, BMP, etc.)
Unlinked files	5	247KB	Files in the current Web that cannot be reached by starting from your home page
Linked files	22	201KB	Files in the current Web that can be reached by starting from your home page
Slow pages	0	0KB	Pages in the current Web exceeding an estimated download time of 30 seconds at 28.8
Older files	0	0KB	Files in the current Web that have not been modified in over 72 days
Recently added fi...	21	292KB	Files in the current Web that have been created in the last 30 days
Hyperlinks	109		All hyperlinks in the current Web
Unverified hyperli...	2		Hyperlinks pointing to unconfirmed target files
Broken hyperlinks	0		Hyperlinks pointing to unavailable target files
External hyperlinks	2		Hyperlinks pointing to files outside of the current Web
Internal hyperlinks	107		Hyperlinks pointing to other files within the current Web
Component errors	1		Files in the current Web with components reporting an error
Uncompleted tasks	0		Tasks in the current Web that are not yet marked completed
Unused themes	1		Themes in the current Web that are not applied to any file

To see the individual reports that are collated into the Site Summary report, you can click the hyperlinked report names in the Site Summary or select the desired report from the **Reports** drop-down list on the Reporting toolbar.

Navigation

7 On the **Views** bar, click the **Navigation** icon.

FrontPage displays the Navigation toolbar and the navigational structure of the open Web site.

8 Select a percentage display size from the **Zoom** drop-down list on the Navigation toolbar so that the entire site fits in the window. (For example, for an 800 by 600 display, you might want to select **75**.)

Your screen now looks like this:

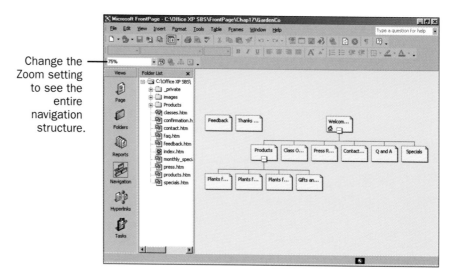

Change the Zoom setting to see the entire navigation structure.

Portrait/ Landscape

The **home page** icon indicates the home page of the site. Each page displays its page title rather than its file name.

9 On the Navigation toolbar, click the **Portrait/Landscape** button to change the orientation of the navigation structure.

View Subtree Only

10 Click the **Products** page to select it. On the Navigation toolbar, click the **View Subtree Only** button.

If you are working with a particularly large Web site you can use this technique to single out one section of the navigation structure.

11 Click the **View Subtree Only** button again to see the entire **site map**.

Hyperlinks

12 On the **Views** bar, click the **Hyperlinks** icon.

Because no specific page is selected, the screen reads *Select a page from the Folder List to view hyperlinks to and from that page.*

13 In the **Folder List**, click **index.htm**, the home page.

All the hyperlinks to and from the home page are displayed, like this:

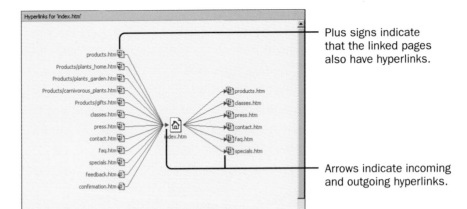

Plus signs indicate that the linked pages also have hyperlinks.

Arrows indicate incoming and outgoing hyperlinks.

14   Right-click **contact.htm**, and click **Move to Center** on the shortcut menu to move that file to the center point of the hyperlink structure.

Notice that different icons represent different types of links.

15   Click the plus sign next to any file icon to see the other hyperlinks from that file's page.

16   Click the minus sign to collapse the hyperlink view.

Tasks

17   On the **Views** bar, click the **Tasks** icon.

Tasks view shows you a reminder list of the things that need to be done in the open Web site. Tasks are automatically created when you use a FrontPage wizard to create a Web site. Tasks can also be created manually by anyone working on the Web site. The tasks that have been assigned to this Web site are shown here:

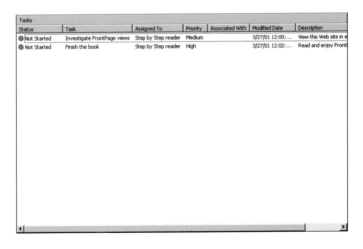

18 Use the scroll bars to view the entire list.

19 Double-click the task titled *Investigate FrontPage views* to open it. Read the description and study the task details, and then click **OK** to close the task.

20 Right-click the task titled *Investigate FrontPage views*, and click **Mark Complete** on the shortcut menu.

The task's **Status** setting changes from *Not Started* to *Completed*.

21 Double-click the task titled *Finish the book* to open it. Read the description and study the task details, and then click **OK** to close the task.

22 On the **File** menu, click **Close Web** to close the Web site.

Looking Around in FrontPage 2002

For those of you who are learning FrontPage without having much experience with the other applications in the Office XP suite, here is a summary of some of the basic techniques you will use to work with FrontPage.

FrontPage 2002 commands are available from 10 separate **menus**. Office XP applications feature the same expanding, dynamic menus that were first made available in Office 2000. The menu commands you use most often move to the top of each menu, making them easier to access. The menu commands you don't use are tucked out of sight, but can be easily accessed by clicking a double chevron at the bottom of the menu. Menu commands that are followed by an arrowhead have submenus. Menu commands that are followed by an ellipsis open dialog boxes where you provide the information necessary to carry out the command.

Most of the menu commands are also represented graphically on 12 **toolbars**, all of which are customizable. The graphic on the toolbar buttons corresponds to the graphic next to the same command on the menu. Each of the buttons has a **Screen-Tip** to tell you the name of the command.

Menu and toolbar options are unavailable when the option can't be applied either to the environment you're working in or to the specific object that is selected. Available menu commands are displayed in black; unavailable commands are **dimmed**, or displayed in a gray font.

The FrontPage 2002 Help file contains information that will assist you when you have questions about FrontPage. The opening screen of the Help file features the latest topics, such as *What's New* and *Get Started*, as well as a link to the Microsoft Office

Web site and other resources. The tabs across the top of the Help file give you three different ways to access information:

- The **Contents** tab displays the Help file topics in a traditional table of contents view.

More convenient
access to Help
new for
OfficeXP

- The **Answer Wizard** tab accepts questions in plain language and then matches your question up with topics that contain possible answers. The Answer Wizard is also accessible through the Ask A Question box at the right end of the FrontPage menu bar.

- The **Index** tab lists topic keywords for the entire Help file. You can either scroll through the list or type the word or words that you're looking for into the **Type keywords** box to search for them.

In this exercise, you will look at the commands that are available on the FrontPage 2002 menus and toolbars. You will also look at the Help file to learn about the types of information that are available to you when you need additional help.

There is no working folder for this exercise. Follow these steps:

Create a new
normal page

1   On the Standard toolbar, click the **Create a new normal page** button.

A new page called *new_page_1.htm* opens in the Page view editing window.

2   Click the **File** menu to open it, and then click the double chevron at the bottom of the menu to expand the complete menu.

3   Study the commands available on the menu, and think about how you might use each one.

The **Close Web**, **Publish Web**, and **Export** commands are dimmed because they are unavailable at this time—in this case, because they apply to Web sites rather than Web pages, and no Web site is open at the moment.

4   Arrowheads follow the **New**, **Recent Files**, and **Recent Webs** commands to indicate that each has a submenu. Point to the **New** command to see its submenu, as shown on the following page.

5 Repeat steps 2 through 4 for each of the remaining menus: **Edit**, **View**, **Insert**, **Format**, **Tools**, **Table**, **Frames**, **Window**, and **Help**. Study the available and unavailable options, and expand the submenus.

6 Click any command that is followed by an ellipsis to open the command's dialog box, and then click **Cancel** to close it.

7 When you get to the **Help** menu, click **Microsoft FrontPage Help**.

The Help window opens.

8 Click each of the three tabs to see the types of information that are available and the different ways that information can be accessed.

9 Click the **Close** button to close the Help window.

10 Right-click anywhere in the menu and toolbar area at the top of the window to open the toolbar shortcut menu, which looks like this:

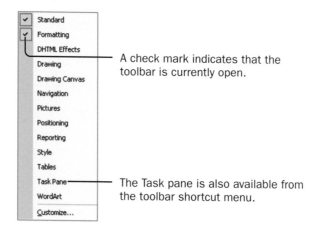

A check mark indicates that the toolbar is currently open.

The Task pane is also available from the toolbar shortcut menu.

Check marks indicate that the Standard and Formatting toolbars are currently turned on. This is the Standard toolbar:

And this is the Formatting toolbar:

FrontPage automatically turns on these two toolbars because they include buttons for the most commonly used page and file commands.

11 Point to each of the buttons on the Standard and Formatting toolbars to read their command names.

Each available button is highlighted as you point to it.

12 Click the top, left, bottom, or right border of the Formatting toolbar, and when the pointer turns into a four-headed arrow, drag the toolbar to the center of the screen, like this:

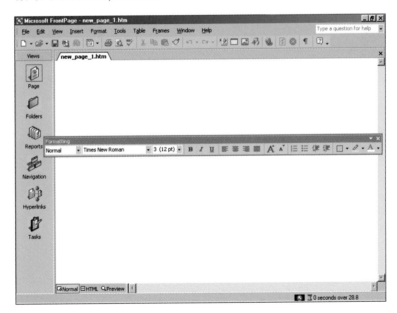

13 Now drag the Formatting toolbar by its title bar to the left edge of the screen so that it changes from horizontal to vertical orientation, as shown on the next page.

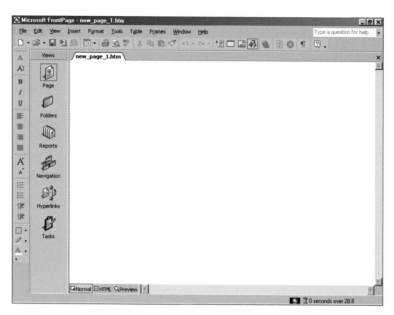

Moving a toolbar to one edge of the window is called **docking** the toolbar. You can dock the FrontPage toolbars at the top, left, bottom, or right edge of the window. The toolbar's orientation changes as it is moved. Toolbars docked on the left or right are vertically oriented; toolbars docked on the top or bottom and undocked toolbars are horizontally oriented.

14 On the toolbar shortcut menu, click **Drawing**.

The Drawing toolbar opens in its default location at the bottom of the screen, like this:

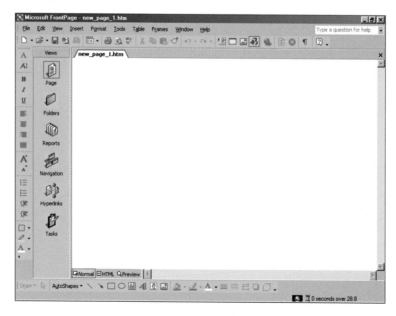

15 Click the arrow at the right end of the Drawing toolbar to display the **Add or Remove Buttons** command. Point to **Add or Remove Buttons**, and then click **Drawing** to open this list of the commands that are available from the Drawing toolbar:

A similar list is available for each of the toolbars.

16 In turn, click **AutoShapes**, **Line**, and **Arrow** buttons to remove them from the Drawing toolbar.

17 Click **Reset Toolbar** to return the toolbar to its original state, and then close the list.

18 Click the **Close** button to close FrontPage.

19 Reopen FrontPage by clicking **Start**, pointing to **Programs**, and then clicking **Microsoft FrontPage**.

When FrontPage reopens, notice that the changes you made are still in effect; the Formatting toolbar is still docked at the left side of the window.

20 Move the Formatting toolbar back to its original location below the Standard toolbar at the top of the window.

21 Right-click in the toolbar area, and click **Drawing toolbar** to turn it off.

22 On the **File** menu, click **Close Web** to close the Web site.

Understanding FrontPage Concepts

This section discusses the types of sites that can be developed with FrontPage and the system requirements that are necessary to take full advantage of the FrontPage 2002 development environment.

There are two kinds of Web sites: **disk-based Web sites** and **server-based Web sites**. A disk-based Web site can be run on any kind of computer, or even from a floppy disk or CD-ROM. Disk-based Web sites support only basic HTML functionality. Many of the more interesting **Web components** that FrontPage supplies won't work on a disk-based site.

Server-based Web sites run on a Web server—a computer that is specifically configured to **host** Web sites. On a small scale, a Web server might be a local computer such as your own, or it might be an intranet server within your company. On a larger scale, Web servers that host corporate Internet sites are usually located at professional **server farms** run by an **Internet service provider (ISP)** or **Web hosting company**.

Most Web sites are initially developed as disk-based sites; that is, you develop them on your local computer. You then publish them to a Web server, either within your organization or at your hosted Web location.

FrontPage 2002 makes it easy to develop both disk-based and server-based Web sites. However, a variety of factors, such as what capabilities you can add to your site, and whether those capabilities can be previewed in FrontPage or in the browser, depend on the type of site you are working with. For instance:

- Some FrontPage **Web components**—ready-made elements that provide capabilities such as link bars and tables of contents—work only when they are placed on a page that is part of a FrontPage-based Web site.

- Some components require that the Web page or site be located on a Web server running SharePoint Team Services from Microsoft.

- Other common Web components work only in a server-based Web site located on a Web server running the FrontPage Server Extensions.

- Some components pull their content directly from Web sites, so they require an Internet connection to be visible.

- Server administration features are available only for server-based Web sites stored on Web servers running SharePoint Team Services or the FrontPage Server Extensions 2002.

- To display database information, your site must be hosted on a Web server that supports Active Server Pages (ASP) and ActiveX Data Objects (ADO).

FrontPage-based Web sites can run on any kind of Web server, but the full functionality of your Web site might not be available unless your site is hosted on a Web server with the FrontPage Server Extensions 2002 installed. If you maintain your own Web server, installing the server extensions is a simple exercise; they are available on the Office XP installation CD-ROM. If you are looking for a company to host your Web site, or if you already have an ISP but you have never asked them to host a FrontPage–based Web site before, be sure to ask whether their servers have the FrontPage Server Extensions 2002 installed.

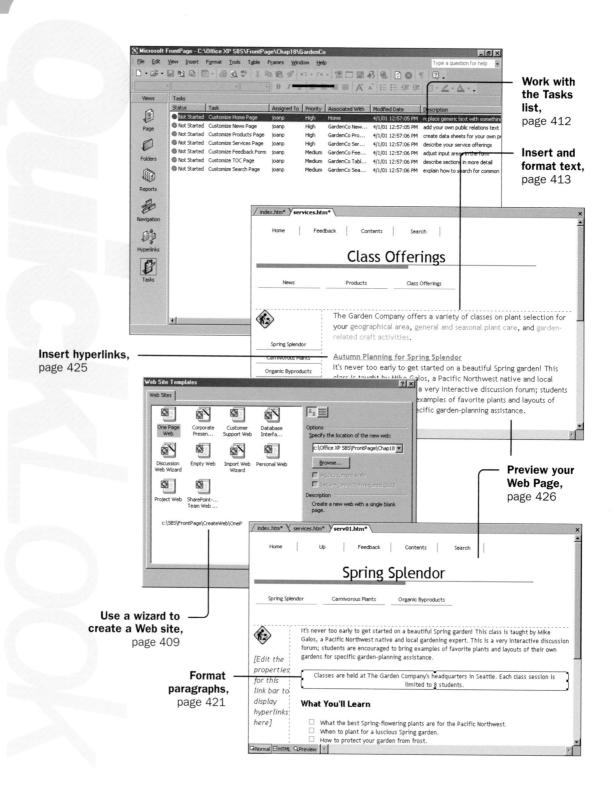

Work with the Tasks list, page 412

Insert and format text, page 413

Insert hyperlinks, page 425

Preview your Web Page, page 426

Use a wizard to create a Web site, page 409

Format paragraphs, page 421

Chapter 18
Creating a Web Site to Promote Yourself or Your Company

After completing this chapter, you will be able to:

✔ Create a Web site using a template or a wizard.
✔ Keep track of the tasks necessary to complete a Web site.
✔ Insert, edit, and format content from a variety of sources.
✔ Insert hyperlinks.
✔ Preview a Web site in FrontPage and in a browser.
✔ Delete a Web site.

All Microsoft Office XP applications provide tools for jump-starting the creation of common types of files. In the case of Microsoft FrontPage, you can use templates and wizards to set up the structure for basic types of Web pages and even entire Web sites. When you use one of these tools, FrontPage does most of the structural work for you, leaving you free to concentrate on the site's content.

You can use the FrontPage templates and wizards to create everything from a bare-bones Web page to a complex, multi-page, interactive site. These are great tools to use if you are new to Web design and want to explore the possibilities, or if you are looking for a quick way to get started on the creation of a real Web site.

In this chapter, you walk through the steps for creating a couple of Web sites, including a corporate site that we will work with throughout most of the book. You learn how to enter and format text, how to preview a Web site, and how to delete a site you no longer need.

You will be working with the following practice files, which are stored in the Office XP SBS\FrontPage\Chap18 folder: TasksList, InsertText, InsertExist, FormatText, InsertHype, and PreviewPage. For details about installing the practice files, see "Using the Book's CD-ROM" at the beginning of this book.

Creating a New Web Site Using a Template

The easiest way to create a new Web site is by using one of FrontPage's **templates**. Templates create the layout for a specific type of Web page or Web site, designating with placeholders the type of content you should put in each location. All you have to do is replace the placeholders with your own content, and you have a finished page or site to show off.

To create a Web site using a template, you simply select the template and specify the location where the site should be created. FrontPage then creates the new Web site and applies the template's structure to it, leaving it up to you to fill in the content and customize the look of the site to suit your needs.

In this exercise, you will create two different types of Web sites using templates: a simple one-page site and a personal Web site.

There is no working folder for this exercise.

Follow these steps:

1 If FrontPage is not already open, start it now.

2 If the New Page or Web Task pane is not open, point to **New** on the **File** menu, and then click **Page or Web**.

Your screen now looks like this:

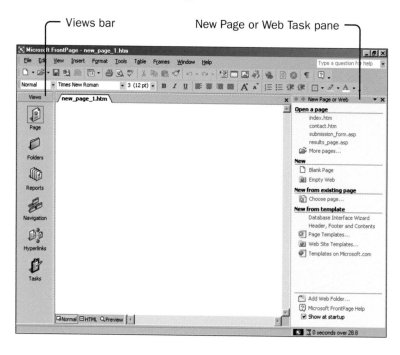

Views bar   New Page or Web Task pane

New Page or Web Task Pane

The New Page or Web Task pane contains convenient links to the Web sites and individual pages that you have created or worked with in FrontPage. It also contains links to templates and wizards you can use to create new pages or Web sites. If this Task pane is not already open, you can open it using the following three methods:

■ On the **File** menu, point to **New**, and then click **Page or Web**,

■ On the **View** menu, click **Task Pane**. Then if a different Task pane is displayed, click the arrow at the right end of the Task pane's title bar, and click **New Page or Web** in the drop-down list.

■ Right-click in the toolbar area, and click **Task Pane** on the toolbar shortcut menu. Then if a different Task pane is displayed, click **New Page or Web** in the Task pane's drop-down list.

To open the Task pane every time you start FrontPage:

■ On the **Tools** menu click **Options**, and then select the **Startup Task Pane** check box.

3   In the **New from template** area of the New Page or Web Task pane, click **Web Site Templates**.

This **Web Site Templates** dialog box opens:

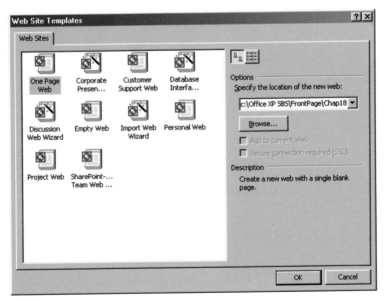

4 In the **Web Site Templates** dialog box, click the **One Page Web** icon.

5 Under **Options**, specify what you want to call your Web site and where you want to store it. In this case, type **C:\Office XP SBS\FrontPage\Chap18\ OnePage** in the **Specify the location of the new web** box to create a disk-based Web site in the working folder for this exercise.

Tip

If you installed the practice files to a drive other than your C: drive, substitute that drive letter in the above path. If your computer is set up as a server, you can store your Web site on your computer as a **server-based Web site**; otherwise you have to store it as a **disk-based Web site**.

6 Click **OK**.

In about three seconds, you have created a new, one-page Web site.

7 If the **Folder List** is not open, click **Folder List** on the **View** menu to open it.

8 In the **Folder List**, double-click **index.htm** to open it.

Your screen now looks like this:

Newly created one-page Web site files

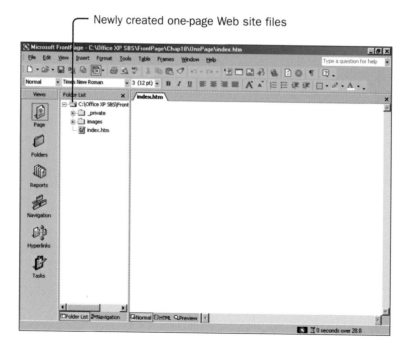

Tip

FrontPage opens your new Web site in whatever view was active last. If your screen doesn't look like our graphic, check the **Views** bar, and make any adjustments necessary to make your view the same as ours.

In FrontPage, it appears that your one-page Web site consists of a single file called *index.htm* and two empty folders called *_private* and *images*. However, as you can see from this view of the site in Windows Explorer, many files and folders (some of them hidden) support this single page:

Hidden file ———————————   ┌— Hidden folders

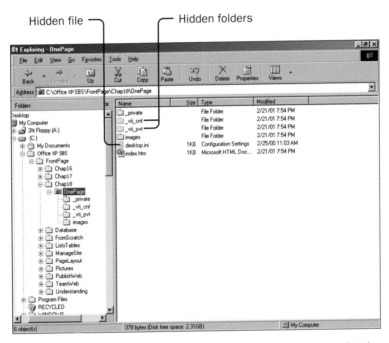

When index.htm is displayed in Page view, the page is completely empty—a blank canvas upon which you can create a veritable work of art! But how? Let FrontPage give you the starting framework. Now you'll test another template by creating a personal site to showcase your new skills.

Create a new normal page

9   Click the arrow to the right of the **Create a new normal page** button, and then click **Web**.

The **Web Site Templates** dialog box opens.

10   In the **Web Site Templates** dialog box, click the **Personal Web** icon, specify the location as **C:\Office XP SBS\FrontPage\Chap18\Personal**, and click **OK**.

Tip

FrontPage suggests a location for your new Web site based on the location of the last Web site you created.

A second FrontPage window opens, and FrontPage creates the personal Web site in the second window. You now have two instances of the program running on your computer at the same time.

11 Double-click the **index.htm** file in the **Folder List** to open the personal Web site in Page view.

The home page of the site is shown here:

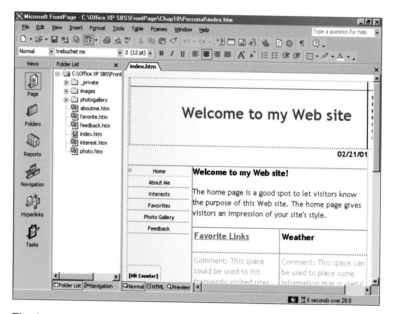

The home page provides links to pages about you, your interests, and your favorite Web sites. You can display photos of yourself, your family, your friends, your dog, and your vacations (real or imagined) in the photo gallery, and Web visitors can contact you by using the feedback page.

Placeholders currently represent all the information in this Web site. By replacing the placeholders with your own information, you can have an attractive site ready to publish in no time at all.

12 On the **File** menu, click **Close Web** to close the personal Web site.

Close

❌

13 Click the **Close** button to close the second instance of FrontPage and return to the first instance.

14 On the **File** menu, click **Close Web** to close the one-page Web site.

Creating a New Web Site Using a Wizard

Now let's create something a little more complex using one of FrontPage's **wizards**. Wizards are similar to templates, but even better. A wizard not only creates the layout of a page or site for you, but it also leads you through the process of personalizing the content and the appearance of the final product.

In this exercise, you will create a corporate Web site for a fictitious plant and garden store, The Garden Company. To provide some context for the sample site, imagine that The Garden Company has a small store located in Seattle, Washington. The owner of the company is Catherine Turner, who would like to communicate with her existing customers and expand her customer base by having a corporate presence on the Internet. If maintaining a Web site meets these modest goals, she may later choose to expand the site's capabilities to permit online retailing. You will use the **Corporate Presence Wizard** to create the basic corporate Web site.

Online Retailing

On the surface, expanding your business by selling goods or services via the Internet seems like a good idea. However, this decision should not be made without a good deal of analysis and planning. First, what you have to offer has to be so compelling that people will want to buy it, and second, you have to offer it under terms and conditions that will make people want to buy it from you, rather than from someone else. Unless you have an exclusive right to sell your particular product, you are going to be competing on many fronts, including price, cost and speed of delivery, and customer service. You must also consider how you will provide a secure environment for the handling of other people's money. All these topics are beyond the scope of this book, but if you are interested in learning more about online retailing, you might want to check out *Small Business Solutions for E-Commerce*, by Brenda Kienan (Microsoft Press, 2000).

There is no working folder for this exercise.

Follow these steps:

1   Click the arrow to the right of the **New** button, and then click **Web**.

The **Web Site Templates** dialog box opens.

2   In the **Web Site Templates** dialog box, click the **Corporate Presence Wizard** icon, specify the location and name of your Web site as C:\Office XP SBS\FrontPage\Chap18\GardenCo, and click **OK**.

The first of a series of **Corporate Presence Wizard** dialog boxes, called *pages*, opens. The wizard uses these pages to prompt you to make choices and enter basic corporate information.

409

3 Read the information on the first page, and then click **Next** to move to the second page.

4 Continue reading the information and clicking **Next** to accept all the default selections in each of the **Corporate Presence Wizard** pages, until you come to the one that requests the name and address of the company.

5 Type the information shown here (or your own personalized information), and click **Next**.

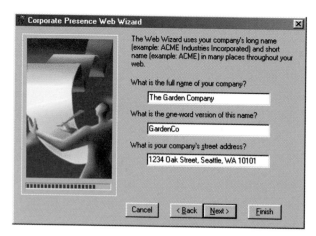

6 Enter the corporate contact information shown here (or your personalized information), and click **Next**.

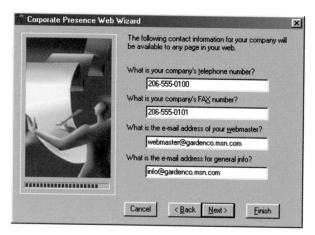

Creating a Web Site to Promote Yourself or Your Company

Generic E-Mail Addresses

It's wise to use generic e-mail addresses in your contact information instead of specific peoples' addresses, so that the address can stay the same no matter who is actually assigned to respond to the inquiry. For example, if The Garden Company listed its information contact address as that of Catherine Turner and then Catherine was away for an extended period of time, messages might build up in her mailbox with no one to answer them. Using a generic address and then forwarding all e-mail sent to that address to one or more individuals ensures that customers' questions are always answered promptly.

7 Most sites created by wizards come with a default graphic theme that gives all the Web pages in the site a consistent look. At this point in the process you could choose to change the default theme. We won't do so at this time, so click **Next**, and then click **Finish.**

FrontPage creates your site using the information you have provided and then displays this list of the tasks that need to be completed to finish the site:

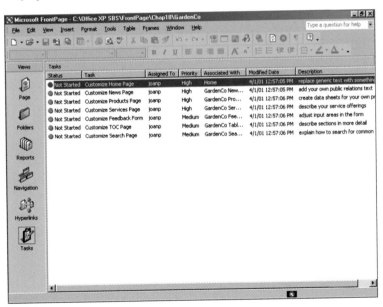

Tip

If you have previously created sites in FrontPage, the program knows who you are because of information saved in your user profile, and FrontPage will assign the tasks to you. If this is the first time you have created a site, FrontPage will assign the tasks to "nobody."

8 On the **File** menu, click **Close Web** to close the current Web site.

Working with the Tasks List

All of the tasks listed for the corporate presence site have something to do with customizing the content. The tasks are listed in order of priority. The first high-priority task is to customize the home page by replacing its generic text with something more specific to your company, so let's tackle that task now.

GardenCo

The working folder for this exercise is Office XP SBS\FrontPage\Chap18\TasksList.

Follow these steps:

1 On the **File** menu, click **Open Web**.

2 Browse to the GardenCo Web site that is located in the working folder, and click **Open** to open the Web site.

Tasks

3 If you are not already in Tasks view, click the **Tasks** icon on the Views bar.

4 Double-click **Customize Home Page**, the first high-priority task, to open a **Task Details** dialog box like this:

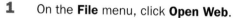
Your personal information appears here.

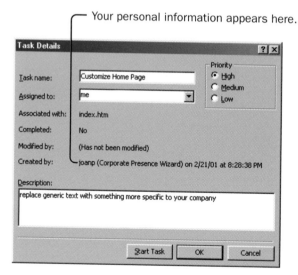

5 In the **Assigned to** box, double-click or drag to select the current entry. Assign the task to yourself by typing your name, username, or initials, and then click the **Start Task** button.

The home page (index.htm) opens in Page view, ready for you to replace the comments that have been inserted by the **Corporate Presence Wizard** with your own content.

6 You won't actually edit this page now, so click **Close Web** on the **File** menu to close the current Web site.

Inserting and Editing Comments

You can use comments to make notes to yourself, or to communicate with other people working on a Web site. Comments don't show up in the published version of a Web page.

To insert a comment, click **Comment** on the **Insert** menu. Then type your notes in the text box, and click **OK**.

To edit a comment, double-click anywhere in the comment's text block to open an editing window. Make your changes, and click **OK**. To delete a comment, click it once to select it, and then press the [Del] key.

Inserting and Editing Text

You can enter new text in a Web page by typing it directly in each page. When you use a FrontPage wizard to create a new Web site, the wizard uses **comments** as placeholders for the text that you need to personalize. The comments inserted by the wizard suggest the type of information you should enter in each area.

In this exercise, you will replace each of the three main blocks of placeholder text on the home page of a Web site created by the **Corporate Presence Wizard**.

GardenCo

The working folder for this exercise is Office XP SBS\FrontPage\Chap18\InsertText.

Follow these steps:

1   On the Standard toolbar, click the **Open** button's arrow, and then click **Open Web** on the drop-down list.

2   In the **Open Web** dialog box, browse to the **GardenCo** Web site that is located in the working folder, and click **Open** to open the Web site in FrontPage.

3   In the **Folder List**, double-click **index.htm** to open the home page in the Page view editing window, then click the **Close** button to close the **Folder List** and enlarge your work area.

4   In the body of the home page, click the introductory comment, and press the [End] key to position the insertion point at the end of the paragraph.

Tip

Although you can delete the comments before typing new text, you don't have to. The comments will not be visible to your Web site visitors.

5 Type the following text:

Welcome to The Garden Company. We are a quality retail gardening business located in the Pacific Northwest. Our products and services are featured on this Web site. Whether you visit us on the Web or in our store, please feel free to browse, and let us know if you require assistance or have any questions!

6 Position the insertion point at the end of the comment under the Our Mission heading, and then enter the following text:

At The Garden Company, we take pride in offering only the highest-quality plants and garden-related products to our customers.

7 After the comment under the Contact Information heading, enter the following text:

Please feel free to contact us via fax or e-mail 24 hours a day, or to call or visit us at our store during our normal business hours: Monday - Friday 9:00am - 9:00pm, Saturday and Sunday 10:00am - 5:00pm.

Your screen looks something like this:

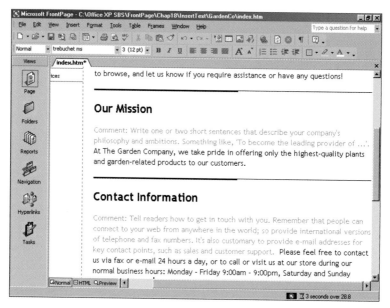

You can change the text that you've entered or add more text at any time.

8 Position the insertion point at the end of the paragraph under the Our Mission heading.

9 Press [Enter] to create a new paragraph, and then type the following text:

We also offer a variety of classes on plant selection for rainy regions, general and seasonal plant care, and garden-related craft activities.

10 Now you'll place an e-mail icon next to the Electronic mail heading in the **Contact Information** area of the page. Position the insertion point to the left of the *E* in *Electronic mail.*

11 On the **Insert** menu, click **Symbol** to display the **Symbol** dialog box.

12 In the **Font** drop-down list, select **Webdings**.

13 Scroll down until you see the three mail icons, and click the first mail icon to select it, like this:

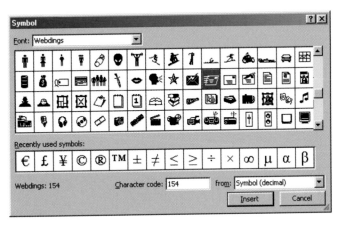

14 Click **Insert**, and then click **Close**.

In the Normal pane, your contact information now appears as shown here:

The symbol does not look correct in the Normal pane.

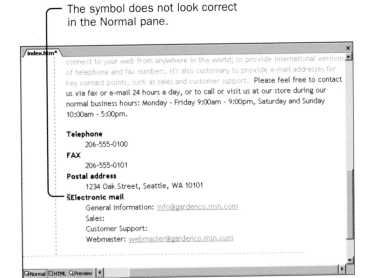

That sure doesn't look like the mail icon you just inserted!

15 Switch to the Preview pane by clicking the **Preview** button at the bottom of the Page view editing window.

Now you can see the symbol as your Web visitors will see it:

The symbol looks correct in the Preview pane.

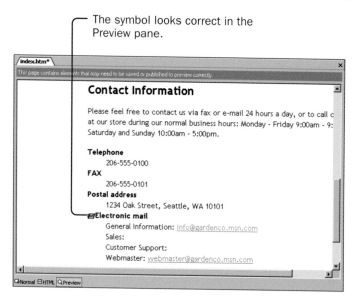

Save

16 On the Standard toolbar, click the **Save** button to save your Web page.

17 On the Views bar, click the **Tasks** icon to open Tasks view.

18 Right-click the first task, and select **Mark Complete** from the shortcut menu to mark the task as completed.

19 On the **File** menu, click **Close Web** to close the current Web site.

Inserting Existing Text

If you have already created material for another purpose, such as a press release or company brochure, you probably don't want to have to create it all over again in your Web site. And you don't have to. FrontPage makes it quite simple to copy and paste text into a template-based Web site in order to personalize it to your own taste. You can even insert entire files.

Office Clipboard task pane new for **Office**XP

You can copy or cut multiple pieces of content from Microsoft Office programs and then paste the content into your Web pages. The Office Clipboard Task pane stores text, tables, graphics, and other file elements in a convenient and accessible location and can archive up to 24 different elements across all the Office applications.

Paste the way
you want

new for
OfficeXP

Each time you paste content from the Clipboard into FrontPage, the floating **Paste Options** button appears, allowing you to choose to apply the destination styles, keep the source formatting, or keep only the text for your pasted selection. The default option is to keep the source formatting. You can ignore the **Paste Options** button if you do not want to select something other than source formatting.

Tip

To stop the **Paste Options** button from appearing, click **Options** on the **Tools** menu, and clear the **Show Paste Options button** check box.

In this exercise, you will insert text from external files into two existing Web pages of the GardenCo Web site: News and Services. In this site, the second high-priority task is to add public relations text to the News page. The text on this page currently consists of a Web Changes heading and a discussion of site updates. Because you have decided that site updates won't be of interest to patrons of The Garden Company, you will change this page to one that contains press releases. You will also modify the Services pages, using text contained in a Microsoft Word document. You will then update the page title of each page to reflect its new content.

GardenCo
PR2.doc
Classes.doc

The working folder for this exercise is Office XP SBS\FrontPage\Chap18\InsertExist.

Follow these steps:

1   Open the GardenCo Web site located in the working folder.

2   Switch to Tasks view.

Important

You can display previously completed tasks by right-clicking on the background of the Tasks list, and then clicking **Show History** on the shortcut menu.

3   Edit the Customize News Page task, assign it to yourself, and then click **Start Task** to open news.htm.

4   Click to the left of the **Web Changes** heading to select it, and type **Press Releases**.

The text of the heading is replaced, but its formatting is retained.

5   Replace the default opening paragraph text with the following:

Keep up with the news! Recent press releases and links to archived press releases are available here.

6   Select the comment below the paragraph you just typed.

7   On the **Insert** menu, click **File** to open the **Insert File** dialog box.

8   Browse to the Office XP SBS\FrontPage\Chap18\InsertExist folder.

9   In the **Files of type** drop-down list, select **Word 97-2002 (*.doc)**.

10   Select **PR2.doc** from the list of available files, and then click **Open** to insert the full text of the document in your Web page.

The text of the document is converted to rich text format and then to HTML and inserted into the News page, just as if you had created it there originally. The original formatting is retained.

Tip

Don't spend time making a document perfect before you import it. You can always make adjustments to the text of the document after it is imported into your Web page.

The contact information at the top of the imported text is contained in a table. The table and cells are indicated by dotted lines.

11   Click the insertion point inside the table. On the **Table** menu, point to **Select**, and then click **Table**.

The table and its contents are selected.

12   Right-click the selection, and click **Delete Cells** on the shortcut menu to delete the table.

13   Triple-click the Press Release heading to select the entire paragraph, and press the [Del] key to remove it from the Web page.

14   Click the **Save** button to save your Web page.

FrontPage prompts you to update your Tasks list.

15   Click **Yes**, and then click the **Close** button in the top right corner of the work area to close the page file.

16   On the Views bar, click the **Tasks** icon to open Tasks view.

The Customize Home Page and Customize News Page tasks are now shown as Completed.

17   Next you will add text to the Services page. Assign the Customize Services Page task to yourself and start the task.

The Services page opens.

18   Now you'll customize the **page banner**. Right-click the **Services** page banner, and select **Page Banner Properties** from the shortcut menu, as shown here:

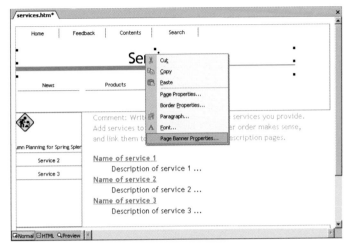

The **Page Banner Properties** dialog box opens.

19 In the **Page banner** box, select and delete the current text, and then type **Class Offerings** in the Page banner box, like this:

20 Click **OK** to close the dialog box and change the page title.

This change affects the page title shown both on the page banner and in Navigation view.

21 In Windows Explorer, browse to the Office XP SBS\FrontPage\Chap18\ InsertExist folder, and double-click **classes.doc** to open it in Word.

22 Triple-click anywhere in the introductory paragraph to select it, and press Ctrl+C to copy the text to the Office Clipboard.

23 On the services.htm page, click the comment text to select it, and then press Ctrl+V to copy the overview text of the Class Offerings document from the Office Clipboard.

The copied text replaces the comment.

24 Select and delete the extra (empty) paragraph inserted with the text.

25 From the **Folder List**, open **serv01.htm**, **serv02.htm**, and **serv03.htm** (the three individual service files) for editing.

26 In each file, repeat steps 17 and 18 to change the page title to the following short versions of the class names described in the Class Offerings document:

Change *Service 1* to **Spring Splendor**.

Change *Service 2* to **Carnivorous Plants**.

Change *Service 3* to **Organic Byproducts**.

As you update each page banner, note that the navigational links under the page banners and the Navigation view page titles update simultaneously.

27 Return to the **services.htm** file, and note that the vertical navigation links along the left have also been updated to reflect the new page titles.

28 For each of the three *Name of service* links, double-click the link to select it, and type the full name of the corresponding course from the Class Offerings document, as follows:

Replace *Name of service 1* with **Autumn Planning for Spring Splendor**.

Replace *Name of service 2* with **Carnivorous Plants: Vicious or Delicious?**

Replace *Name of service 3* with **Organic Byproducts: Use Them or Lose Them!**

Because these are hyperlinks, it is preferable to retype the link than to copy and paste it, to ensure that the link remains active.

29 Now copy and paste the first descriptive paragraph for each class from the Class Offerings document into services.htm, replacing the corresponding service description.

When you're done, your page looks something like this:

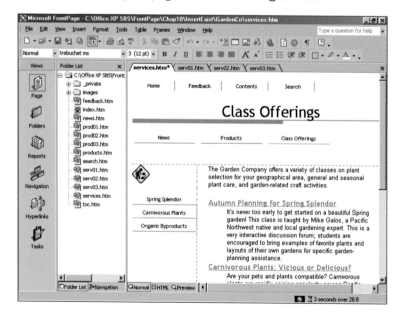

30 On each of the three individual class description pages (serv01.htm, serv02.htm, and serv03.htm), click anywhere in the body of the page, press ⌘+Ａ to select all the content, and then press the Ｄｅｌ key.

31 In the Class Offerings document, select and copy the descriptive text, learning objectives, and class schedule for each class to the Office Clipboard, and then paste the Clipboard contents into the appropriate service page.

32 On the **File** menu, select **Save All** to save your changes, and mark the task as completed when prompted to do so.

33 On the **File** menu, click **Close Web** to close the Web site.

Formatting Text

Web sites and Web pages created by FrontPage wizards are already formatted to look terrific without you having to do anything. However, there are times when you will want to give a word or two a special look or to make a paragraph stand out in some way. Most of the techniques you use in FrontPage to format text are the same as those you use in the other Office applications, so in this section, you will quickly review the types of formatting you are most likely to want to apply to your text, without much explanation.

In this exercise, you will format text and paragraphs using common Office formatting techniques.

GardenCo

The working folder for this exercise is Office XP SBS\FrontPage\Chap18\FormatText.

Follow these steps:

1 Open the GardenCo Web site that is located in the working folder.

2 Open index.htm (the home page) in the Page view editing window.

3 Select and delete the three comment blocks to make the page easier to read.

4 In the first paragraph, select the company name.

Increase Font Size

5 On the Formatting toolbar, click the **Increase Font Size** button.

Note that the font size shown in the **Font Size** drop-down list box changes from *3 (12 pt)* to *4 (14 pt)* as the text size increases.

Italic

6 Select the last sentence in the first paragraph (beginning with *Whether you visit us*), and click the **Italic** button to italicize the text.

7 Click the **Preview** button at the bottom of the Page view editing window to switch to the Preview pane, and locate the mail icon in the Contact Information section.

Notice that at its current size, the icon is not very legible.

8 Switch back to the Normal pane, and select the mail icon.

Font Size
12 ▾

9 On the Formatting toolbar, click the arrow to the right of the **Font Size** box, and click **6 (24 pt)** in the drop-down list to increase the size of the mail icon.

Tip

Font sizes are expressed in FrontPage in two ways: in **points** (as you are used to seeing in other applications, such as Word and Microsoft Excel) and in **sizes** of 1 through 7. Eight options are given in the **Font Size** drop-down list: **Normal, 1 (8 pt), 2 (10 pt), 3 (12 pt), 4 (14 pt), 5 (18 pt), 6 (24 pt)**, and **7 (36 pt)**.

10 Insert a space between the icon and the adjacent text for tidiness, and then switch to the Preview pane to see the effects of the change.

Your page looks something like this:

11 Open services.htm (the Class Offerings page) in Page view.

Notice that the text on this page is a different font than the default font on the home page.

12 Select the first paragraph.

Font
Times New Roman ▾

13 Click the arrow to the right of the **Font** box, and click **Trebuchet MS** in the drop-down list.

Notice that the font size is still different from that on the home page.

14 With the first paragraph still selected, press Ctrl + Space to restore the original page formatting. Repeat this step with each of the three class description paragraphs.

15 For each paragraph, position the insertion point at the end of the paragraph, and press [Enter] to insert a line break.

In the introductory paragraph, select the words *geographical area*.

Font Color

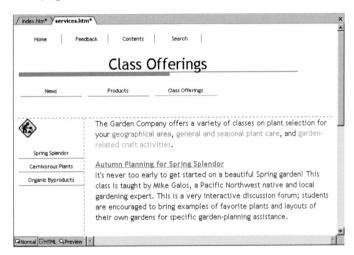

16 On the Formatting toolbar, click the **Font Color** button's arrow, and change the font color to **Blue**. Repeat this procedure to change the words *general and seasonal plant care* to **Green** and *garden-related craft activities* to **Red**.

Your page looks like this:

17 Open **serv01.htm** (the Spring Splendor page) in the Page view editing window.

Notice that the font on this page does not match the default site font on the home page.

18 Press [Ctrl]+[A] to select all the page content. In the **Font** box's drop-down list, click **(default font)**.

The font of each of the page elements changes to the default font, Trebuchet MS.

19 Select the paragraph that gives details about the class location and size.

Borders

20 On the Formatting toolbar, click the **Borders** button's arrow to display the **Borders** toolbar.

This toolbar can be detached and docked elsewhere, or it can float independently.

21 Click the **Outside Borders** option to apply a border to the paragraph.

22 With the paragraph still selected, click **Paragraph** on the **Format** menu.

23 In the **Paragraph** dialog box, do the following:

- In the **Alignment** drop-down list, click **Center**.

- In the **Indentation** section, set **Before text** and **After text** to **15**.
- In the **Spacing** section, set **Before** and **After** to **0**.

The dialog box now looks like this:

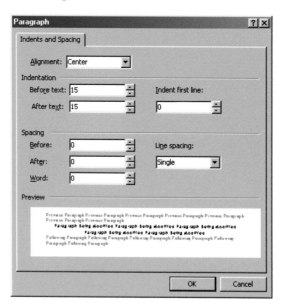

24 Click **OK** to apply the paragraph formatting.

Your page looks as shown here:

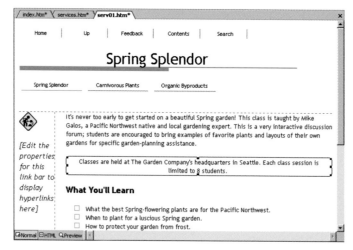

25 Repeat steps 17 through 25 to reformat serv02.htm (the Carnivorous Plants page) and serv03.htm (the Organic Byproducts page).

26 On the **File** menu, click **Save All** to save all the open files.

27 On the **File** menu, click **Close Web** to close the Web site.

Cascading Style Sheets

Cascading style sheets (CSS) are documents defining formats and styles for different page elements (headings, paragraphs, tables, lists, and so forth) in a central location, either as an **embedded cascading style sheet** within a Web page or as an **external cascading style sheet**. External style sheets can be referenced by multiple documents to provide a consistent look across pages and sites.

Cascading style sheets also allow a Web author to stipulate how page elements are to be displayed by different browsers. Many Web sites utilize a **browser sniffer** that detects the Web browser and version used by each Web visitor and attaches the appropriate cascading style sheet to the site at that time.

To create an embedded cascading style sheet in FrontPage, click **Style** on the **Format** menu, and then define your own styles. The definitions are saved in the HTML code of the page.

To create an external cascading style sheet in FrontPage, select the CSS type from the options available on the **Style Sheets** tab of the **Page Templates** dialog box, click **OK** to create a CSS file, and then define your styles within the file.

To attach a style sheet in FrontPage, click **Style Sheet Links** on the **Format** menu, and browse to the CSS file on your computer or (if you have an Internet connection) anywhere on the Web.

Alternatively, you can select the **Apply using CSS** option in the **Themes** dialog box when applying a theme to your page or site.

The World Wide Web Consortium (W3C) originally developed cascading style sheets. For more information about current and future CSS specifications and how various browsers support CSS, visit *www.w3c.org*.

Inserting Hyperlinks

When you use a wizard to generate a Web site, the wizard creates hyperlinks between the pages of the Web site. However, you will often want to add hyperlinks of your own. These hyperlinks might be to specific items of information on the same page or on a different page, to other Web sites, or to documents that are not part of any Web site.

In this exercise, you will create hyperlinks from the News page of the GardenCo Web site to important press releases that are stored in an external Word document.

GardenCo

The working folder for this exercise is Office XP SBS\FrontPage\Chap18\InsertHype.

Follow these steps:

1 Open the GardenCo Web site that is located in the working folder.

2 Open news.htm in Page view, and press `Ctrl`+`End` to move the insertion point to the end of the document.

3 Press `Enter` to move to a new line. Type **Archived Press Releases**, and press `Enter`.

4 On the **Insert** menu, click **Hyperlink**.

Browse for File

5 Click the **Browse for File** button, browse to the Office XP SBS\FrontPage\ Chap18\InsertHype folder, select **PR1.doc**, and then click **OK**.

A hyperlink to the press release is inserted at the insertion point, like this:

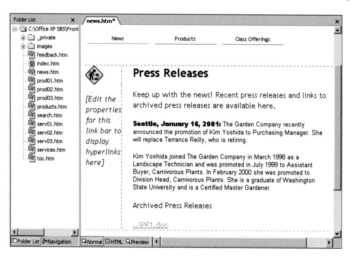

6 To view the contents of the linked file from within FrontPage, press the `Ctrl` key and click the link.

A press release dated September 23, 1998 opens in Word.

7 Close the press release to return to your Web site.

8 Save and close the open file.

9 On the **File** menu, click **Close Web** to close the current Web site.

Seeing Your Web Pages as Visitors Will

We've made a pretty good start at personalizing The Garden Company's Web site, and you are probably anxious to see the results of your work. There are two ways to view a Web site created with FrontPage before it is published: in FrontPage or in a browser.

Previewing your Web site in FrontPage is a good way to look at the basic layout and evaluate the overall presentation of the site, but it doesn't always represent the site as a visitor will experience it. Apart from the fact that you probably can't see as much of the page as you intend your visitors to see, none of the advanced controls that you might choose to add later will work in this view. To see an accurate preview of your Web site before it is published, you will need to preview it in a browser.

Viewing the Web site in a browser is a great opportunity to test its usability and functionality before exposing it to the scrutiny of the real world. Always be sure to take the time to test your site before publishing it.

In this exercise, you will look at the GardenCo Web site in the Preview pane, and then you will preview it in a Web browser.

GardenCo

The working folder for this exercise is Office XP SBS\FrontPage\Chap18\PreviewPage.

Follow these steps:

1 Open the GardenCo Web site located in the working folder.

2 Open the home page in Page view.

Preview

Q Preview

3 Click the **Preview** button at the bottom of the screen to switch to the Preview pane.

The Web page is displayed in FrontPage as shown here:

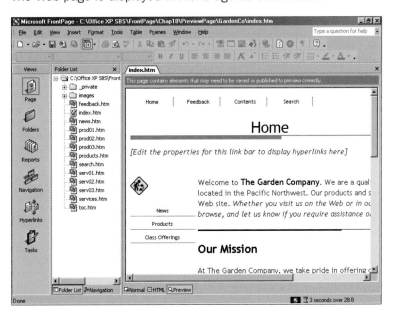

4 Click the navigation links on the left to jump to the News page.

5 Click **Home** at the top of the page to move back to the home page.

At the top of the screen, a message tells you that the page contains elements that might need to be saved or published to preview correctly.

Preview in
Browser

6 Click the **Preview in Browser** button.

7 The **Preview in Browser** dialog box opens. Select a browser and a window size, and click **Preview**.

Your screen now looks something like this one, which shows the home page of the GardenCo site displayed in Microsoft Internet Explorer 5.1:

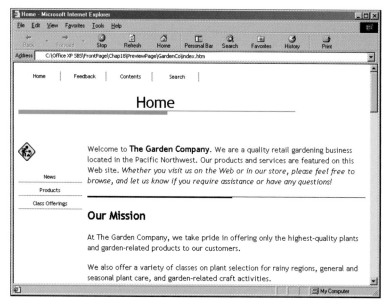

8 Browse through the site just as a visitor would, clicking various links to ensure that they work.

9 Close the browser and return to FrontPage.

Troubleshooting

You cannot edit a file in FrontPage while you are previewing it in a browser. Attempting to do so causes an error called an **access violation**. Always close the browser, and then make any necessary changes to your site in FrontPage.

10 On the **File** menu, click **Close Web** to close the current Web site.

Deleting a Web Site

When you first start creating Web sites with FrontPage, you will probably want to experiment. As a result, you will more than likely end up with Web sites on your hard disk drive that you no longer need. What's more, if you make a mess when creating a real Web site and decide to start over, because you already have a Web site with your chosen name stored on your hard disk drive, FrontPage will not allow you to over-write the existing site with a new one. It will insist that you create a whole new set of files by appending a number to the name you want to use.

To solve these problems, you might be tempted to simply delete existing sites in Windows Explorer, but if you do, you risk leaving behind extraneous hidden files. Instead you must delete the sites from FrontPage. In this section, we show you how to delete the two Web sites you created with templates at the beginning of the chapter.

Important

If you did not create the Web sites in the first two exercises of this chapter, you will obviously not be able to delete them in this exercise.

There is no working folder for this exercise.

Follow these steps:

1 On the **File** menu, click **Open Web**.

2 In the **Open Web** dialog box, browse to C:\Office XP SBS\FrontPage\ Chap18\OnePage, and click **Open** to open the Web site.

3 Open the **Folder List** if it is not already open.

4 In the **Folder List**, right-click the top-level folder of the site, and click **Delete** on the shortcut menu to open this **Confirm Delete** dialog box:

5 Select the **Delete this Web entirely** option, and click **OK** to delete the Web site.

The Web site is deleted and the **Folder List** closes, because the displayed content no longer exists.

6 Repeat steps 1 through 4 to delete the Personal Web site created at the beginning of this chapter.

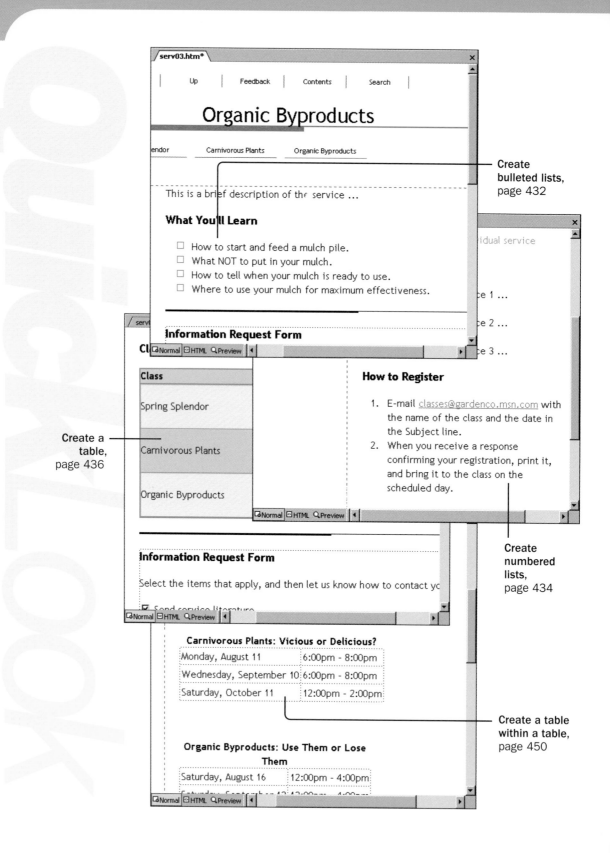

serv03.htm*   ✕

| Up | Feedback | Contents | Search |

Organic Byproducts

endor   Carnivorous Plants   Organic Byproducts

Create
bulleted lists,
page 432

This is a brief description of the service ...

What You'll Learn

☐ How to start and feed a mulch pile.
☐ What NOT to put in your mulch.
☐ How to tell when your mulch is ready to use.
☐ Where to use your mulch for maximum effectiveness.

Information Request Form

Cl ⬚Normal ⊞HTML ⚲Preview ◀

idual service

e 1 ...

e 2 ...

e 3 ...

Class

Spring Splendor

Carnivorous Plants

Organic Byproducts

Create a
table,
page 436

How to Register

1. E-mail classes@gardenco.msn.com with the name of the class and the date in the Subject line.
2. When you receive a response confirming your registration, print it, and bring it to the class on the scheduled day.

⬚Normal ⊞HTML ⚲Preview ◀

Create
numbered
lists,
page 434

Information Request Form

Select the items that apply, and then let us know how to contact yo

☑ Send service literature

⬚Normal ⊞HTML ⚲Preview ◀

Carnivorous Plants: Vicious or Delicious?

Monday, August 11	6:00pm - 8:00pm
Wednesday, September 10	6:00pm - 8:00pm
Saturday, October 11	12:00pm - 2:00pm

Create a table
within a table,
page 450

Organic Byproducts: Use Them or Lose Them

| Saturday, August 16 | 12:00pm - 4:00pm |

⬚Normal ⊞HTML ⚲Preview ◀

Chapter 19
Presenting Information in Lists and Tables

After completing this chapter, you will be able to:

✔ **Create bulleted and numbered lists.**

✔ **Create a table in various ways.**

✔ **Enter, edit, and format information in a table.**

✔ **Edit a table's structure.**

✔ **Create a table within a table.**

You are probably familiar with the kinds of lists and tables you can create in applications such as Microsoft Word and Microsoft PowerPoint. In Microsoft FrontPage, you use similar techniques to create lists and most kinds of tables.

Both lists and tables are traditionally used to present information in structured, easy-to-grasp formats. In Web pages, you use lists and tables for their traditional purposes, but you can also use tables to structure entire Web page layouts. (Using tables to establish the look of an entire Web page minimizes browser display variations and gives you more control than if you depend on a non-structured presentation.)

In this chapter, we'll first add a few lists to some of the pages of The Garden Company's Web site. Then we'll create tables using three simple methods:

■ By using the **Insert Table** button.

■ By using the **Insert Table** command.

■ By drawing lines to create the table's rows and columns.

You will be working with practice files that are stored in the following subfolders of the Office XP SBS\FrontPage\Chap19 folder: CreateList, CreateTable, TableText, TableStruct, FormatTable, and TableInTable. For details about installing the practice files, see "Using the Book's CD-ROM" at the beginning of this book.

Creating a List

You use **lists** to break out items of information that might otherwise be buried in a text paragraph. If the items don't have to appear in a particular order, they usually appear in **bulleted lists**; for example, a list of plants that are drought tolerant would be presented in a bulleted list. If the items do have to appear in a particular order, they usually appear in **numbered lists**; for example, instructions for repotting a particular houseplant would be presented in a numbered list.

In this exercise, you will personalize the content in a version of The Garden Company's Web site that was created using the **Corporate Presence Wizard** by adding some lists. To create bulleted and numbered lists in FrontPage, you use the same techniques you would use in Microsoft Word, so you'll move quickly through the exercise without going into a lot of detail.

GardenCo

The working folder for this chapter is Office XP SBS\FrontPage\Chap19\CreateList.

Follow these steps:

1 If FrontPage is not already open, start it now.

Open

2 Click the **Open** button's arrow, and click **Open Web** on the drop-down list to display this **Open Web** dialog box:

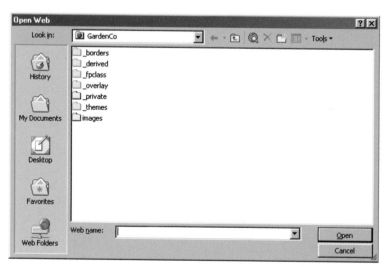

3 Browse to the working folder, select **GardenCo**, and click **Open**.

The Garden Company's Web site opens in the view that was active when you last quit FrontPage. If you are in Page view, your work area is blank because none of the Web site's pages is open.

4   If the **Folder List** is not already open, click **Folder List** on the **View** menu. Then double-click **serv01.htm** to open the Spring Splendor page.

5   Select the Key Benefits heading, and type **What You'll Learn** to replace the heading text.

6   Select and replace the three bulleted items with these:

- **Which spring-flowering plants are best for the Pacific Northwest.**
- **When to plant for a luscious spring garden.**
- **How to protect your garden from frost.**

Close

⊠

7   Click the serv01.htm file's **Close** button to close the Spring Splendor page, saving your changes when prompted.

8   In the **Folder List**, double-click **serv02.htm** to open the Carnivorous Plants page in the Page view editing window.

9   Repeat steps 5 and 6 on the Carnivorous Plants page, replacing the bulleted items with these:

- **What types of carnivorous plants thrive in the Pacific Northwest.**
- **Which plants are appropriate for indoor and outdoor locations.**
- **What risks pets and livestock face during periods of extreme growth.**

10   Click the serv02.htm file's **Close** button to close the Carnivorous Plants page, saving your changes when prompted.

11   In the **Folder List**, double-click **serv03.htm** to open the Organic Byproducts page in the Page view editing window.

12   Repeat steps 5 and 6 on the Organic Byproducts page, replacing the bulleted items with these:

- **How to start and feed a mulch pile.**
- **What NOT to put in your mulch.**
- **How to tell when your mulch is ready to use.**

13   To add a new bulleted item to the Organic Byproducts list, position the insertion point at the end of the third item, and press Enter .

A new, blank bulleted list line is created.

14   Type **Where to use your mulch for maximum effectiveness** as the fourth bullet.

The bulleted list looks like the example shown on the next page.

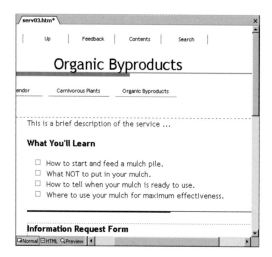

Changing Paragraphs to Lists

As in Word, to convert a series of regular paragraphs to a bulleted list, select the paragraphs and click the **Bullets** button on the Formatting toolbar. To convert the bulleted items back to regular paragraphs, select the items and click the **Bullets** button to toggle it off. Similarly, to convert regular paragraphs to a numbered list, select the paragraphs and click the **Numbering** button on the Formatting toolbar.

15 Click the serv03.htm file's **Close** button to close the Organic Byproducts page, saving your changes when prompted.

16 In the **Folder List**, double-click **services.htm** to open the Class Offerings page in the Page view editing window.

17 Press ⌃+⟶ to move the insertion point to the bottom of the page.

18 Type **How to Register**, then hold down the ⇧ key and press ⟵ to select the text.

19 On the **Style** drop-down list, click **Heading 3** to format the text as a third-level heading.

20 Press ⟶ to move the insertion point to the end of the heading, and then press ⏎ to start a new line.

21 Type **E-mail classes@gardenCo.msn.com with the name of the class and the date in the Subject line.**

As you type, the e-mail address will automatically be formatted as a hyperlink.

Numbering

22 Click the **Numbering** button on the Formatting toolbar to turn the paragraph into a numbered item, and then press [Enter] to create a new line.

FrontPage assumes that the next paragraph will also be a numbered item.

23 Type **When you receive a response confirming your registration, print it, and bring it to the class on the scheduled day.**

24 Press [Enter] to create a new line, and then click the **Numbering** button to turn off numbering and convert the new numbered item to a regular paragraph.

The numbered list looks like this:

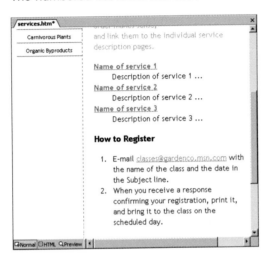

Tip

If you're interested, you might want to click the **HTML** button to display the underlying source code for the numbered list in the HTML pane. As you will see, FrontPage designates the entire list as an **ordered list** by enclosing it in <ol> and </ol> tags. Each list item is enclosed in <li> and </li> tags. A bulleted list has a similar structure, except that the entire list is designated as an **unordered list** by enclosing it in <ul> and </ul> tags.

25 Click the services.htm file's **Close** button to close the Class Offerings page, saving your changes when prompted.

26 On the **File** menu, click **Close Web** to close the current Web site.

No Tabular List?

Sometimes text or numbers would stand out better for your Web visitors if they were presented in columns and rows, but they don't need the structure of a full-blown table. In Word, you would use a tabular list—a set of pseudo columns and rows in which you use tabs to line everything up—instead of setting up a full-blown table structure. But FrontPage doesn't accommodate this type of list. When you want to put information in columns and rows, you need to create a real table.

Creating a Table

A **table** consists of vertical **columns** and horizontal **rows**. A table might have an over-all **table title** that appears either as a separate paragraph above the body of the table or in the table's top row. It usually has a **header row**, which contains a title for each column, and it might have a **header column**, which contains a title for each row.

In this exercise, you'll learn one way of creating a table as you set up the structure for a Class Schedules table to organize information about the gardening classes offered by The Garden Company.

GardenCo

The working folder for this chapter is Office XP SBS\FrontPage\Chap19\CreateTable.

Follow these steps:

1   On the **File** menu, click **Open Web**.

2   In the **Open Web** dialog box, browse to the GardenCo Web site located in the working folder, and then click **Open**.

3   In the **Folder List**, double-click the **serv01.htm** file to open the Spring Splendor page in the Page view editing window.

4   Click the black horizontal rule about halfway down the page, and then press `Home` to position the insertion point at the beginning of the line.

5   Type **Class Schedule**, and then hold down the `Shift` key and press `Home` to select the text.

6   On the **Style** drop-down list, click **Heading 3** to format the text as a third-level heading.

7   Press `End` to move the insertion point to the end of the heading, and then press `Enter` to start a new line.

Insert Table

8   On the Standard toolbar, click the **Insert Table** button.

FrontPage displays this grid of five columns and four rows:

Cancel

9   Point to the first **cell**—the intersection of the first row and the first column—
and hold down the left mouse button. Then, without releasing the button,
drag the pointer until an area three cells wide by ten cells high is highlighted
(the grid will expand as you drag the mouse to the edge), and then release
the mouse button.

FrontPage inserts a table with the number of rows and columns you highlighted, like this:

Converting Existing Text to a Table

If you have an existing block of text with items separated by commas, tabs, or paragraph marks, you can convert the text to a table. Select the text you want to convert,
and then on the **Table** menu, point to **Convert** and click **Text To Table**. The **Convert
Text To Table** dialog box opens so that you can tell FrontPage how the elements of
the selected text are separated. Make your selection, and click **OK**. FrontPage converts the text to a table, and because the table is selected, the Tables toolbar opens
so that you can make any necessary adjustments.

You can also convert a table to text. Select the table, and on the **Table** menu, point
to **Convert** and click **Table To Text**. Then in the **Convert Table To Text** dialog box,
select the character you want to use to separate items, and click **OK**.

10 Click the serv01.htm file's **Close** button to close the Spring Splendor page, saving your changes when prompted.

11 In the **Folder List**, double-click **serv02.htm** to open the Carnivorous Plants page in the Page view editing window.

12 Repeat steps 4 through 7 to create the Class Schedule heading and blank line.

13 On the **Table** menu, point to **Insert**, and then click **Table** to display this dialog box:

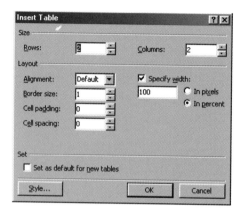

Unlike most corresponding menu commands and toolbar buttons in Microsoft Office XP, the **Insert Table** command and the **Insert Table** button work differently. The command displays a dialog box, whereas the button displays a grid.

14 In the **Size** section, specify **9** rows and **4** columns for your table.

15 In the **Layout** section, set **Border size** to **0** and **Cell padding** to **3**.

Tip

Cell padding is space between the borders of the cells and the text inside them. This padding is similar to the margins of a page.

16 Check that the width is set to **100** percent, and click **OK** to create this table:

17   Click the serv02.htm file's **Close** button to close the Carnivorous Plants page, saving your changes when prompted.

18   In the **Folder List**, double-click **serv03.htm** to open the Organic Byproducts page in the Page view editing window.

19   Repeat steps 4 through 7 to create the Class Schedule heading and blank line.

20   On the **Table** menu, click **Draw Table**.

The Tables toolbar opens, and the mouse pointer changes to a pencil.

Toolbars, Toolbars Everywhere

In FrontPage, whenever you select a type of object that has a toolbar associated with it, the toolbar pops up on the screen. FrontPage assumes that you have selected the object in order to work with it in some way and that the buttons on the toolbar probably provide the quickest way of accomplishing the task at hand. Selecting something else automatically closes the toolbar, but if you want to close the toolbar while you are working with the object to reduce screen clutter, you can either click the **Close** button at the right end of the title bar of a floating toolbar, or right-click the toolbar and click its name on the shortcut menu. If you close a toolbar in this way, it might not pop up the next time you select the associated type of object. To display a hidden toolbar, right-click any visible toolbar and then click the name of the toolbar you want on the shortcut menu.

21 Click where you want to position the top-left corner of the table, and drag the pencil pointer to where you want to position the bottom-right corner.

FrontPage creates a single-cell table.

22 Using the pencil pointer, draw lines to create the table's rows and columns, ending up with a table three columns wide by ten columns high, something like this one:

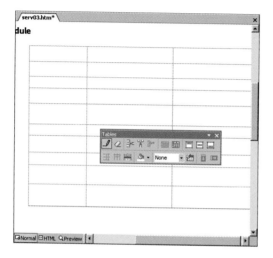

Tip

Experiment with the locations of the lines separating columns and rows; you will find that the table expands to meet your needs.

23 Press the [Esc] key to change the pointer back to its original shape.

24 Click the serv03.htm file's **Close** button to close the Organic Byproducts page, saving your changes when prompted.

25 On the **File** menu, click **Close Web** to close the Web site.

Entering and Editing Information in a Table

The Garden Company's Web site has the structures for three tables on three separate pages, but you need to fill the tables with information to make them useful. You enter information in FrontPage tables the same way you would enter it in Word tables.

In this exercise, you will fill three existing tables with information. For The Garden Company's Web site, you'll place the same information in each table, but you would probably fill your own tables with different types of information.

GardenCo
ClassList.doc

The working folder for this chapter is Office XP SBS\FrontPage\Chap19\TableText.

Follow these steps:

1 On the **File** menu, click **Open Web**.

2 In the **Open Web** dialog box, browse to the **GardenCo** Web site located in the working folder, and then click **Open**.

3 In the **Folder List**, click the **serv01.htm** file to select it, and then hold down the ⌨Ctrl key and click **serv02.htm** and **serv03.htm** so that all three files are selected.

4 Press ⌨Enter to open the three files in the Page view editing window.

5 On the Spring Splendor page, enter the column titles Class, Date, and Time in the cells of the first row of the table, thereby creating a header row.

6 Now enter the following information in the three columns of the table, under the respective headings:

Class	Date	Time
Spring Splendor	Tuesday, August 5	6:00pm – 9:00pm
Spring Splendor	Thursday, September 4	6:00pm – 9:00pm
Spring Splendor	Saturday, October 4	11:00am – 2:00pm
Carnivorous Plants	Monday, August 11	6:00pm – 8:00pm
Carnivorous Plants	Wednesday, September 10	6:00pm – 8:00pm
Carnivorous Plants	Saturday, October 11	12:00pm – 2:00pm
Organic Byproducts	Saturday, August 16	12:00pm – 4:00pm
Organic Byproducts	Saturday, September 13	12:00pm – 4:00pm
Organic Byproducts	Saturday, October 18	12:00pm – 4:00pm

Tip

If you don't feel like typing, you can copy and paste this information from the Class-List.doc file stored in the Office XP SBS\FrontPage\Chap19\TableText folder.

7 Click the **serv03.htm** page tab to switch to that file.

8 On the Organic Byproducts page, fill the hand-drawn table with the same header row and the same three columns of information.

9 Click the **serv02.htm** page tab to switch to that file.

10 For the table on the Carnivorous Plants page, ignore the header row, fill in the first two columns with the class and date information, and then fill in the fourth column with the time information.

11 On the **File** menu, click **Save All** to save the open files.

12 On the **File** menu, click **Close Web** to close the Web site.

Editing the Structure of a Table

Unless you are very skilled at creating tables, you will rarely create one that you don't have to later adjust in one way or another. Most likely, you will have to add or delete rows or columns and move information around until it is in the right place. Almost certainly, you will also have to adjust the size of rows and columns that are too big, too small, or unevenly spaced. Luckily, with FrontPage it is simple to fix all these structural problems.

Tip

When columns are much wider than the information they contain, your Web visitors might have to scroll from side to side to see all of the information in a table. When columns are too narrow, your Web visitors might have to scroll up and down. Whenever possible, you want to avoid making them scroll by resizing one or more of the rows or columns in a table.

In this exercise, you will change the structure of an existing table in order to rearrange the information it contains. On the Carnivorous Plants page of our sample Web site, the class schedule is currently presented in nine rows and four columns, one of which is blank. You will move the time information from the fourth to the third column, and add a header row to this table.

GardenCo

The working folder for this exercise is Office XP SBS\FrontPage\Chap19\TableStruct.

Follow these steps:

1 Open the **GardenCo** Web site located in the working folder.

2 In the **Folder List**, double-click **serv02.htm** to open the Carnivorous Plants page in the Page view editing window.

3 On the Carnivorous Plants page, click anywhere in the fourth column of the table.

4 On the **Table** menu, point to **Select**, and then click **Column**.

5 Point to the selection, and drag the time information from the fourth column to the third column.

6 Click anywhere in the top row of the table.

7 On the **Table** menu, point to **Insert**, and then click **Rows or Columns** to display this dialog box:

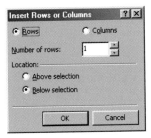

8 Specify that you want to insert one row above the current selection, and click **OK**.

FrontPage inserts a new row at the top of the table.

9 Now click anywhere in the fourth column of the table.

10 On the **Table** menu, point to **Select**, and then click **Column**.

11 Right-click the selection, and click **Delete Cells** on the shortcut menu to delete the blank column from the right side of the table.

12 In the new header row, enter the same column headings as those in the other two tables: **Class**, **Date**, and **Time**.

The table on the Carnivorous Plants page now looks like those on the Spring Splendor and Organic Byproducts pages.

13 Click the serv02.htm file's **Close** button to close the Carnivorous Plants page, saving your changes when prompted.

14 In the **Folder List**, double-click **serv03.htm** to open the Organic Byproducts page in the Page view editing window.

15 To adjust the size of the columns in the table on this page, start by pointing to the right border of the table's Date column.

The pointer changes to a double-headed arrow.

16 Double-click the border.

FrontPage resizes the column so that it can hold all its entries on one line.

17 Now click anywhere in the table, and on the **Table** menu, click **AutoFit to Contents**.

All the columns adjust to the exact width of their contents, as shown on the next page.

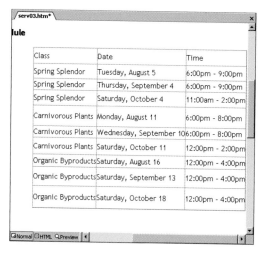

18 Right-click anywhere in the table, and click **Table Properties** on the shortcut menu to display this **Table Properties** dialog box:

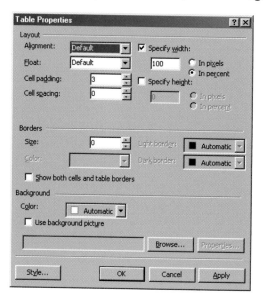

19 In the **Table Properties** dialog box, do the following:

- In the **Alignment** drop-down list, click **Left**.
- Set **Cell padding** to **3**.
- In the **Specify width** box, type **100**, and then click **In percent**.
- In the **Borders** area, set **Size** to **0**.

20   Click **OK** to close the dialog box and apply your changes.

21   Next move the pointer to the top of the first column so that it changes to a down arrow. Hold the left mouse button down to select the column, and drag to the right until all three columns are selected.

22   On the **Table** menu, click **Distribute Columns Evenly** to make all the columns the same width.

23   Click the serv03.htm file's **Close** button to close the Organic Byproducts page, saving your changes when prompted.

24   On the **File** menu, click **Close Web** to close the Web site.

Formatting a Table

In FrontPage as in Word, you have several options for formatting tables. You can choose from a large variety of preformatted table styles or create your own look. You can even merge two or more cells into one cell so that a table entry spans several columns or rows.

More table formatting options

new for **Office**XP

FrontPage 2002 now supports more of the standard Office table-formatting options:

■   **Fill right** and **fill down** allow you to quickly copy content from one table cell to several others.

■   **Auto Format** provides a fast and easy way to create professional-looking tables by simply selecting a preformatted option from a list.

■   The **border drop-down tool** button enables you to format table and cell borders as easily as you can in Word and Excel, by clicking your selection.

In this exercise, you'll format the tables in The Garden Company's Web site, first by doing things "the hard way"—and seeing just how easy that can be—and then by checking out a few of FrontPage's ready-made formats.

GardenCo

The working folder for this chapter is Office XP SBS\FrontPage\Chap19\FormatTable.

Follow these steps:

1   Open the **GardenCo** Web site located in the working folder.

2   In the **Folder List**, double-click **serv02.htm** to open the Carnivorous Plants page in the Page view editing window.

3   Scroll down to the table, and select the three cells of the header row.

4   Right-click the selection, and click **Cell Properties** on the shortcut menu to display the dialog box shown on the next page.

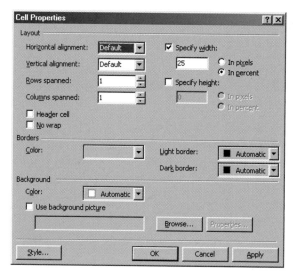

5 In the **Cell Properties** dialog box, select the **Header cell** check box.

6 In the **Background** area, click the **Color** box's arrow to display this color palette:

The default color selections include the 16 standard colors of the "Web-safe" palette, as well as the colors that are currently used in the open document.

Tip

When a theme is attached to a Web page, the default colors include those used in the theme. It is generally best to select colors from the theme to maintain a consistent look and feel throughout your Web site.

If you click **More Colors**, FrontPage opens this dialog box:

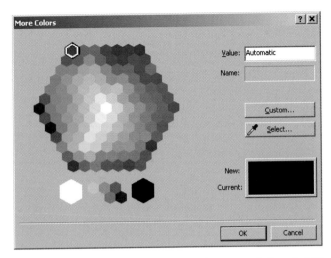

In this dialog box, you can select from a palette of 127 colors or specify a custom color using the hexadecimal or RGB value. Your options are practically limitless!

7   Select your favorite color from the default set, and then click **OK** to close the **Cell Properties** dialog box and apply your changes.

The background color is applied, as shown here:

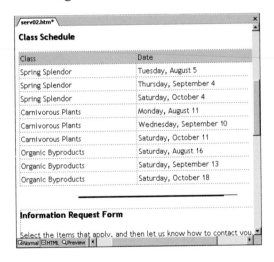

8 In the **Folder List**, double-click **serv01.htm** to open the Spring Splendor page in the Page view editing window.

9 Click the insertion point anywhere in the table on that page.

10 On the **Table** menu, click **Table AutoFormat**.

11 In the **Table AutoFormat** dialog box, scroll through the **Formats** list on the left, clicking each format in turn.

When you select a format, a sample table with that format applied is displayed in the Preview window, like this:

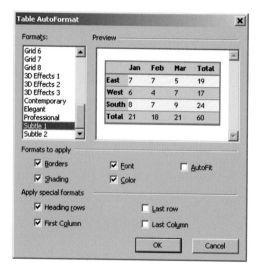

12 Select the **Subtle 1** format.

13 Because this table does not have a special first column, clear the **First Column** check box in the **Apply special formats** section.

14 Click **OK** to apply the selected format to the table.

15 Click the **Preview** button at the bottom of the Page view editing window to switch to the Preview pane.

When Web visitors view the table, it will look something like this:

This table looks good, but it would look tidier if each class name appeared only once and spanned three rows.

16 Click the **Normal** button at the bottom of the Page view editing window to switch to the Normal pane.

17 In the first column, select the three cells containing the words *Spring Splendor*, and on the **Table** menu, click **Merge Cells**.

FrontPage merges the three cells into one cell that still contains three instances of *Spring Splendor*.

18 Select and delete two instances of the class name, leaving just one.

19 Repeat steps 16 and 17 for the Carnivorous Plants and Organic Byproducts classes. The table now looks like this:

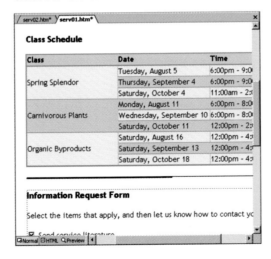

Tip

To split one cell into multiple cells, right-click the cell and click **Split Cells** on the shortcut menu. In the **Split Cells** dialog box, specify the number of rows or columns you want to split the merged cell into, and click **OK**.

20   On the **File** menu, click **Save All** to save the open pages.

21   On the **File** menu, click **Close Web** to close the Web site.

Creating a Table Within a Table

In the same way that you can split and merge individual cells, you can split and merge entire tables. You can also nest one table within another. These options might seem pretty complex for presenting straightforward information, but they offer wonderful possibilities, particularly when you want to organize an entire Web page with one table.

In this exercise you will split the Class Schedule table into three separate tables, one for each class, with each class name as the table title.

GardenCo

The working folder for this chapter is Office XP SBS\FrontPage\Chap19\TableInTable.

Follow these steps:

1   Open the **GardenCo** Web site located in the working folder.

2   In the **Folder List**, double-click **serv02.htm** to open the Carnivorous Plants page in the Page view editing window.

3   Scroll down to the table, and click in the first row containing the words *Carnivorous Plants*.

4   On the **Table** menu, click **Split Table**.

FrontPage splits the table into two tables.

5   Click in the first row containing the words *Organic Byproducts*, and split the table again.

You now have three distinct tables.

6   Click in the row containing the words *Class*, *Date*, and *Time*.

7   On the **Table** menu, point to **Select**, and then click **Row**.

8   Right-click the selection, and click **Delete Cells** on the shortcut menu.

9   Click anywhere in the Spring Splendor table, point to **Insert** on the **Table** menu, and then click **Caption**.

A centered caption row is inserted at the top of the table.

10 Type **Autumn Planning for Spring Splendor** as the table caption.

11 Select the caption, and make it bold.

12 Select the first column. Right-click the selection, and click **Delete Cells** on the shortcut menu to delete the column.

13 Click the insertion point anywhere in the table, and click **AutoFit to Contents** on the **Table** menu.

14 Repeat steps 9 through 13 for the Carnivorous Plants and Organic Byproducts tables, using the following class titles as the table captions:

- **Carnivorous Plants: Vicious or Delicious?**

- **Organic Byproducts: Use Them or Lose Them!**

The results look something like this:

15 Click the serv02.htm file's **Close** button to close the Carnivorous Plants page, saving your changes when prompted.

16 On the **File** menu, click **Close Web** to close the Web site.

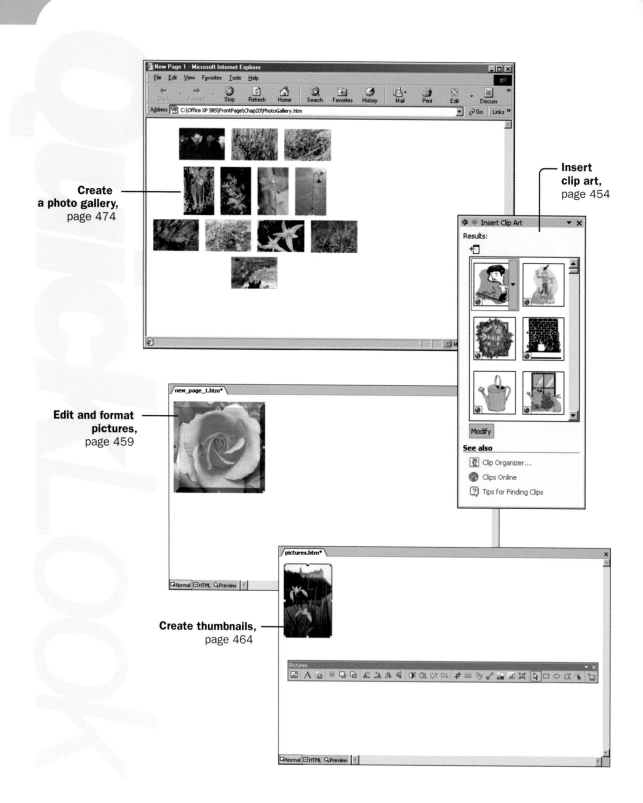

**Create
a photo gallery,**
page 474

**Insert
clip art,**
page 454

**Edit and format
pictures,**
page 459

Create thumbnails,
page 464

Chapter 20
Enhancing Your Web Site with Graphics

After completing this chapter, you will be able to:

✔   Add clip art, pictures, and other graphic elements to a Web page.

✔   Change the size and look of pictures.

✔   Create picture thumbnails.

✔   Create a photo gallery.

You can do a lot to get your message across and increase the appeal of your Web pages by using well-crafted language and formatting words and paragraphs in various ways. However, there are times when no matter how you format your text, it's not enough to grab the attention of your visitors and make your Web site stand out from all the others they might browse.

At times like these, you need the pizzazz that pictures and other graphic images can give your pages. With Microsoft FrontPage, you can insert a variety of graphic elements, including clip art, picture files, scanned images, drawings, shapes, WordArt objects, and videos.

It is safe to assume that a large part of the appeal of The Garden Company's Web site, which is used as the example for most of the exercises in this book, would be pictures of plants, "idea" shots of gardens to provide inspiration, garden bed designs, and other visually enticing elements. No amount of text will do the trick for a Web site that is about things you have to see to appreciate, just as no amount of text can possibly substitute for a music clip on a site dedicated to a particular band or genre of music.

To make The Garden Company's Web site visually appealing, you would need to use graphics judiciously, carefully selecting an appropriate style and exercising some restraint in order to avoid a confusing effect. Because you will be learning how to add a wide variety of graphic elements in this chapter, you will use the GardenCo Web site only when it's appropriate, practicing otherwise in a new page that you can discard later.

In this chapter, you will be working with practice files that are stored in the following subfolders of the Office XP SBS\FrontPage\Chap20 folder: AddPicture, Thumbnail, and PhotoGallery. For details about installing the practice files, see "Using the Book's CD-ROM" at the beginning of this book.

Adding Clip Art

FrontPage makes it easy to insert all kinds of **media** including graphics, pictures, videos, and even sound effects, into a Web page. When you're looking for a quick and simple graphic representation that won't cost you a licensing fee, an easy solution is to use **clip art**. A large library of clip art is supplied with Microsoft Office XP, and a seemingly endless selection is available on the Microsoft Design Gallery Live Web site at *dgl.microsoft.com*. If neither of these sources has what you need, you can find hundreds of small clip art galleries on the Web. You can also purchase clip art CD-ROMs, many of which focus on particular themes or on particular styles of clip art.

Office XP stores different clip art elements in different folders with the applications they are most often used with, and all of them are available to you in FrontPage. The first time you access the clip art feature, you will be prompted to create a catalog of all the clip art items on your computer. You have to run through this simple process only once.

Updated Clip
Organizer
new for
OfficeXP

The new and improved Clip Organizer (formerly known as the Clip Gallery) enables you to access and organize media files through an easy-to-use Task pane interface. The Clip Organizer contains hundreds of new pieces of clip art and makes it easy to find additional digital art on the World Wide Web.

You can find, access, and insert a variety of media files from the Insert Clip Art Task pane. In addition to traditional clip art, which usually consists of cartoon-like drawings, you can choose from photographs, movies, and sounds. This great resource area is a lot of fun to explore.

In this exercise, you will run through the initial configuration of the media files (if you haven't already done so), and then you'll insert a piece of clip art on a practice page.

There is no working folder for this exercise.

Follow these steps:

1   If FrontPage is not already open, start it now.

Create a new
normal page

2   If a new page is not already open, click the **Create a new normal page** button on the Standard toolbar to open a new blank page to use as a canvas for your artwork.

3   On the **Insert** menu, point to **Picture**, and then click **Clip Art**.

4   If this is the first time you've opened the Insert Clip Art Task pane, this **Add Clips to Organizer** dialog box appears:

In this dialog box, you can do the following:

5   Click **Options** to access this listing of folders from which clip art will be imported:

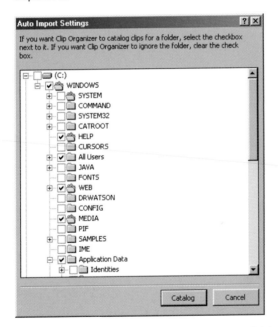

6   Click **Cancel** to accept the default import folders and close the **Auto Import Settings** and **Add Clips to Organizer** dialog boxes.

7   On the **Insert** menu, point to **Picture**, and click **Clip Art** again.

8   Click **Now** to catalog all the media files available on your computer.

The Insert Clip Art Task pane changes to look like the example on the next page.

9   Make sure that **All media file types** is displayed in the **Results should be**
    box, and then search for a piece of garden-related clip art by typing garden in
    the **Search text** box and clicking **Search**.

    The results of your search are displayed in this **Results** box:

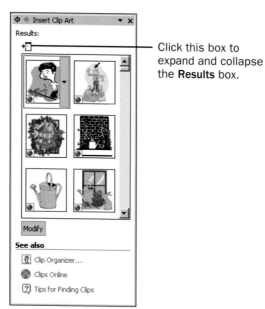

Click this box to
expand and collapse
the **Results** box.

Results

You can expand and collapse the **Results** box by clicking the button above the window.

10 Hover the mouse pointer over the graphics to display their descriptions, sizes, file sizes, and formats.

11 Scroll through the search results until you find a graphic you like.

12 Right-click the graphic, and click **Insert** on the shortcut menu.

FrontPage inserts the selected graphic in your page at the insertion point, like this:

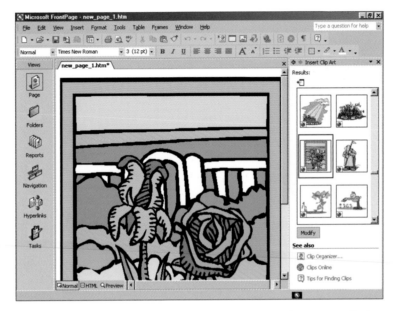

As you can see, the clip art is huge. Later in the chapter, we'll show you how to resize graphics.

13 Click the file's **Close** button to close the current file; click **No** when prompted to save your work.

Adding a Picture

Where Web pages are concerned, it's worth keeping in mind the well-worn saying "A picture is worth a thousand words." You will often find it beneficial to add photographs to your Web pages to illustrate or enhance the text or to demonstrate a difficult concept. You can obtain Web-ready pictures in a variety of ways: by taking photographs with a digital camera, by scanning existing photographs to create digital files, or by buying art files or downloading public-domain files from the Internet.

FrontPage 2002 can access picture files that are on your computer, on another computer on your network, or if you have an Internet connection, even on a Web site.

For the highest display quality, you should use pictures that have been saved as **Graphics Interchange Format (GIF)** or **Joint Photographic Experts Group (JPG)** files. Both display well over the Web. The GIF file format supports up to 256 colors. The JPG file format was specifically developed for photographs and is the best format to use for photos and other graphics with more than 256 colors. JPG files are usually smaller and therefore take less time to download over the Web.

Tip

You can easily convert graphics of other file types to GIF or JPG format in FrontPage. In Page view, right-click the graphic, and then click **Picture Properties** on the shortcut menu. In the **Type** area of the **General** tab, click **GIF** or **JPG**.

In this exercise, you will insert a picture file on a practice page.

Garden4.gif

The working folder for this exercise is Office XP SBS\FrontPage\Chap20\AddPicture.

Follow these steps:

1 On the Standard toolbar, click the **Create a new normal page** button to create a new page.

The new page opens in the Page view editing window with the insertion point positioned at the top of the page.

2 On the **Insert** menu, point to **Picture**, and then click **From File** to open the **Picture** dialog box.

3 In the **Picture** dialog box, browse to the working folder.

The Garden4.gif file is selected because it is the only file in the directory.

Views

4 If you don't see a preview of the graphic in the dialog box, click the **Views** button's arrow on the **Picture** dialog box's toolbar, and then click **Preview** in the drop-down menu.

The dialog box displays a preview of the selected graphic, as shown here:

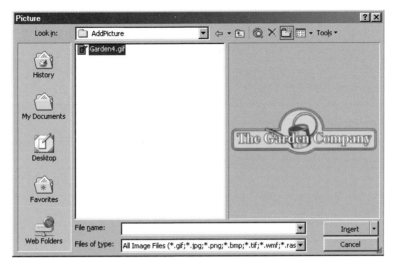

5   Click **Insert** to insert the graphic in the Web page at the insertion point.

6   Click the file's **Close** button to close the current file; click **No** when prompted to save your work.

Editing and Formatting Pictures

Sometimes the picture you add to a Web page won't produce exactly the result you are looking for—perhaps it's too large or too small, or perhaps it includes a variety of elements that distract from the thing you're trying to draw the visitor's attention to. For really drastic changes, you will need to manipulate the picture in a graphics-editing program before adding it to the Web page. But for small modifications and for such enhancements as sizing, **cropping**, and adding a frame, you can do the job within FrontPage.

The commands used to edit and format pictures are contained on the Pictures toolbar, shown here:

■   Click **Insert Picture From File** to open the **Picture** dialog box, where you can search for and insert another picture.

■   Use the **Text** button to create a text box in the picture area into which you can insert your own text.

459

- Click **Auto Thumbnail** to create a small preview version of your picture that is hyperlinked to the original. Viewers can click the thumbnail to view the full-size version.

- Use the **Position Absolutely**, **Bring Forward**, and **Send Backward** buttons to control the position of the picture on the page in relation to other elements, whether it is in front of or behind other objects, and whether it moves with the surrounding text.

- Click the **Rotate Left**, **Rotate Right**, **Flip Horizontal**, and **Flip Vertical** buttons to reverse and rotate your picture.

- Click the **More Contrast**, **Less Contrast**, **More Brightness**, and **Less Brightness** buttons to increase and decrease the brightness and contrast of the selected picture.

- Use the **Crop** button to cut the picture down to a smaller size; this will not shrink the picture, but will instead trim the picture as you indicate.

- Click the **Line Style** button to open the **Line Style** dialog box, in which you can change the width, length, color, and pattern of lines.

- Click the **Format Picture** button to open the **Format Picture** dialog box.

- Use the **Set Transparent Color** button to indicate that a particular color will be transparent when the graphic is viewed on a Web page. This is ideal when you want to display an irregularly shaped object (one without straight borders).

- Click the **Color** button to recolor your picture as a black and white, grayscale (black, white, and shades of gray), or washed out version of the original.

- Click **Bevel** to create a beveled self-framing effect.

- Use the **Resample** button to refine the focus of a picture that has been enlarged or shrunken.

- Click **Select** to change the insertion point to a pointer so that you can select a picture for editing. This button is selected by default when the Pictures toolbar is opened.

- Use the **Rectangular Hotspot**, **Circular Hotspot**, **Polygonal Hotspot**, and **Highlight Hotspots** buttons to select and view **hotspots**, or **image maps**, on your picture. These are areas that can be hyperlinked to jump to other graphics, other Web pages, or other Web sites. They can even generate e-mail messages!

- Click **Restore** to undo any changes that have been made to the picture since the Pictures toolbar was opened.

The Pictures toolbar opens automatically when you select a picture for editing, or you can open it at any time by clicking the toolbar area and then clicking **Pictures** on the shortcut menu.

In this exercise, you work with a photograph to practice using some of FrontPage's picture editing and formatting capabilities. First you size the picture and crop away the parts you don't want; then you convert the picture to black and white and give it a bevel frame.

There is no working folder for this exercise.

Follow these steps:

1   On the Standard toolbar, click the **Create a new normal page** button to create a new page.

2   If the Insert Clip Art Task pane is not already open, click **Task Pane** on the **View** menu and select **Insert Clip Art** from the drop-down title bar.

3   If the Insert Clip Art Task pane still shows the results of your previous search, click **Modify** to start a new search.

4   In the **Search text** box, type roses. In the **Results should be** drop-down list, clear the **Clip Art**, **Movies**, and **Sounds** check boxes, leaving only the **Photographs** check box selected. Then click away from the drop-down list to close it and click **Search** to look for pictures of roses.

5   Click the first photo to insert it on the page.

6   Close the Insert Clip Art Task pane to give you more room to work.

7   On the **View** menu, point to **Toolbars**, and then click **Pictures** to open the Pictures toolbar.

Your screen now looks like this:

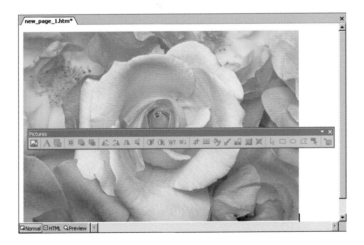

8 Drag the Pictures toolbar down until it docks at the bottom of the screen and is not covering the rose.

Crop

9 Click the picture to select it, and then click the **Crop** button on the Pictures toolbar.

A dashed box appears in the picture, defining the edges of the area to be cropped.

10 Drag the handles of the crop box until the box contains the central rose, like this:

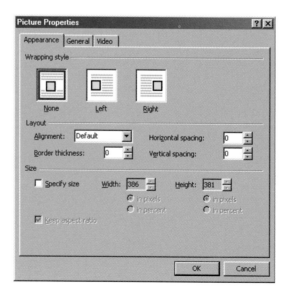

The crop box is indicated by this dotted line.

11 Click the **Crop** button again to crop the picture to the specified shape and size.

12 Double-click the picture to display a **Picture Properties** dialog box like this one:

13 Select the **Specify size** check box, and set the **Width** to **200** pixels.

14 To prevent distortion, ensure that the **Keep aspect ratio** check box is selected.

The height will automatically resize to match the new width.

15 Click **OK** to close the dialog box and apply your changes.

FrontPage resizes the graphic to your specified dimensions, as shown here:

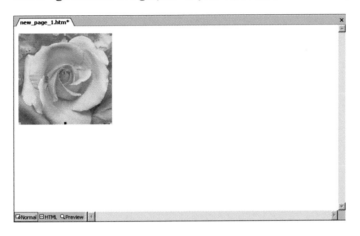

Color

16 On the Pictures toolbar, click the **Color** button.

17 On the **Color** drop-down menu, click **Grayscale**.

The picture is converted to shades of gray, but retains the original quality of detail.

Bevel

18 On the Pictures toolbar, click **Bevel**.

The colors at the edges of the picture change to make it appear that the center is raised, like this:

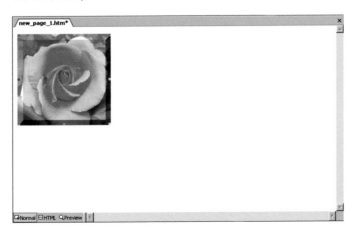

19 Click the file's **Close** button to close the current file; click **No** when prompted to save your work.

Creating and Displaying Thumbnails

Thumbnails are small versions of graphics that are hyperlinked to full-size versions. Thumbnails are often used on Web pages containing many graphics that Web visitors may or may not want to see (catalog items, for example). Because thumbnails are small, they download faster, so visitors are less likely to get impatient and move to another site.

In this exercise, you create a thumbnail of a picture and test it in FrontPage.

pictures.htm

The working folder for this exercise is Office XP SBS\FrontPage\Chap20\Thumbnail.

Follow these steps:

1 Open the **pictures.htm** file located in the working folder.

2 Click the picture on the page to select it, and open the Pictures toolbar.

Auto Thumbnail

3 On the Pictures toolbar, click the **Auto Thumbnail** button.

The picture shrinks to thumbnail size and is now surrounded by a blue border that indicates the presence of a hyperlink, as shown here:

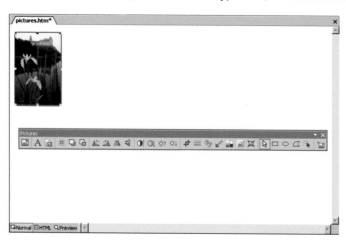

The hyperlink surrounding the graphic links the thumbnail version of the graphic to the original, which is no longer displayed on the page.

4 Click the **HTML** button at the bottom of the Page view editing window to display the HTML code that links the thumbnail to the original graphic.

The code looks similar to this:

```
<img border="2" src="../../../WINDOWS/TEMP/FrontPageTempDir/
PH01245J[1]_small.jpg" width="100" height="151" xthumbnail-orig-
image="PH01245J[1].jpg">
```

5   Click the **Normal** button at the bottom of the Page view editing window to return to the Normal pane.

6   Drag the handles surrounding the selected thumbnail to make it bigger.

The thumbnail becomes blurry and grainy, or *pixilated*, when you make it bigger, because the thumbnail version is not as detailed as the original picture.

Undo

7   After you have seen the effect of enlarging the thumbnail, click the **Undo** button on the Standard toolbar to return the thumbnail to its original size.

8   To test the thumbnail link, click the **Preview** button at the bottom of the Page view editing window to switch to the Preview pane, and then click the thumbnail to open the original picture in the Preview pane.

Troubleshooting

Certain types of files, including Windows Metafile (WMF) files, won't open in the Preview pane. To preview these images, hold down the [Ctrl] key in the Normal pane and click the thumbnail to open the original picture in a separate window.

9   To experience the thumbnail link as your Web visitors will, click **Preview in Browser** on the Standard toolbar. Save the page and embedded graphics if prompted to do so.

Your Web page opens in your browser, with the thumbnail and hyperlink displayed.

10   Click the thumbnail to display the full-size graphic, and then click the browser's **Back** button to return to the thumbnail.

11   Close the browser to return to FrontPage.

12   Close the page without saving your changes.

Adding a Line, Shape, or Drawing

When it comes to dressing up your pages with graphic elements, you are not limited to images such as clip art, pictures, and photographs. You can also create designs with lines, squares, circles, and other shapes, and if you are artistically inclined, you can even create entire drawings from within FrontPage. For professional-quality art, you should use a dedicated graphics program, but you can use FrontPage to turn out simple, Web-ready artwork.

Cross-browser
enhanced
drawing tools
new for
OfficeXP

FrontPage 2002 includes enhanced drawing tools that make it easy to incorporate specially formatted lines, a wide variety of preformed shapes, WordArt objects, text boxes, and shadowing using the same techniques that are available in Microsoft Word and Microsoft PowerPoint. These lines, shapes, and drawings are collectively known as **Office Drawings**. Office Drawings can be copied from other Office applications and pasted directly into your FrontPage-based Web site.

The commands used to work with most graphics are represented as buttons on the Drawing toolbar and the Drawing Canvas toolbar. Both of these toolbars can be opened at any time by right-clicking the toolbar area and clicking their names on the toolbar shortcut menu. The Drawing toolbar opens automatically when you select an Office Drawing for editing. It contains these buttons:

- Use the commands on the **Draw** menu to control the grouping, position, and movement of objects.

- Click the **AutoShapes** button to display a menu of over 130 shapes ranging from basic geometric shapes and arrows to fully formed weather indicators. Special flowchart, banner, and call-out symbols are included. You can drag the **AutoShapes** menu away from the Drawing toolbar so that it functions as its own free-floating toolbar.

- Use the **Line**, **Arrow**, **Rectangle**, and **Oval** buttons to draw these basic shapes in any size by clicking and dragging the shape onto the page.

- Click the **Text Box** button to insert text frames within graphics.

- Click the **Insert WordArt**, **Insert Clip Art**, and **Insert Picture From File** buttons to insert new graphic elements.

- Use the **Fill Color**, **Line Color**, and **Font Color** buttons to control the colors of their respective elements. The buttons display the currently selected colors. To apply the current selection, simply select an element and click the button. To change the current color selection, click the button's arrow and select a color the same way you would in any other Office application.

- Use the **Line Style**, **Dash Style**, and **Arrow Style** buttons to format the thickness, color, solidity, and end caps of line elements.

- Apply shadows to graphic elements and modify the properties of shadows using the **Shadow Style** button.

- Give graphic elements a three-dimensional look using the **3-D Style** button.

You can **group** several drawing elements together so that you can treat them as one. In this way, you can create a drawing out of several shapes and then copy and paste the entire drawing, or shrink or enlarge it. If you want to treat the drawing as individual elements again, you can **ungroup** them at any time.

The "frame" in which Office Drawings are created in FrontPage is called the **drawing canvas**. You can have the drawing canvas act as an actual frame by formatting it with visible borders and background colors, but its main purpose is to contain all the elements of the drawing that you create so that the underlying HTML code for the drawing can be selected and treated as a single unit. The formatting of the drawing canvas also determines the way in which text wraps around the drawing and the position of the drawing in relation to other objects on the page.

The Drawing Canvas toolbar opens when you insert a new drawing. It includes these buttons:

- Click **Fit** to enlarge or shrink the drawing canvas to the same size as the drawing it contains.
- Click **Expand** to stretch the drawing to the current size of the canvas.
- Click **Scale Drawing** to enlarge the drawing to the current size of the canvas, but maintain its original height to width ratio.

In this exercise, you first draw a horizontal rule, then you create and insert a drawing that incorporates predefined shapes, and finally you insert a shape directly on the page.

There is no working folder for this exercise.

Follow these steps:

1 Create a new normal page.

2 On the **Insert** menu, click **Horizontal Line** to draw a rather boring line.

3 Right-click the line, and then click **Horizontal Line Properties** on the shortcut menu to display the dialog box shown on the next page.

In the **Horizontal Line Properties** dialog box, do the following:

4 Set the **Width** to **80** percent of the window.

5 Set the **Height** to **3** pixels.

6 In the **Color** drop-down box, click **Green**.

Tip

Move the mouse over the colors in the **Color** drop-down box to see each color's name displayed as a ScreenTip.

7 Click **OK** to close the dialog box and apply your settings.

The page now looks like this:

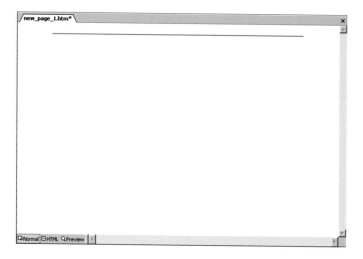

8 Now press ⌃Ctrl⌄+⌃End⌄ to move the insertion point to the end of the page.

9 On the **Insert** menu, point to **Picture**, and then click **New Drawing**.

FrontPage displays an empty drawing canvas, the Drawing Canvas toolbar, and the Drawing toolbar, like this:

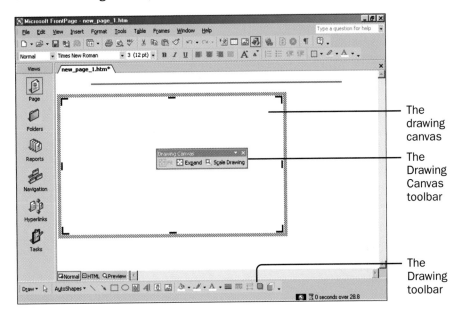

The drawing canvas

The Drawing Canvas toolbar

The Drawing toolbar

Tip

You can drag the toolbars out of the way while you're working.

10 On the Drawing toolbar, click **AutoShapes** to see the menu of available shapes.

Tip

When you see a drop-down menu with a "handle" on it (horizontal lines in a shaded stripe), you can drag the menu onto the work area, and it will float there until you click the toolbar's **Close** button. Alternatively, you can drag the menu onto the toolbar or dock it at the left, right, or bottom edge of the window.

11 Point to **Stars and Banners**, and then click the **Explosion 2** symbol, shown here:

Tip

Move the pointer over a symbol to see the symbol's name displayed as a ScreenTip.

12 Drag down from the top right corner of the drawing canvas to create a small "explosion" shape, like this:

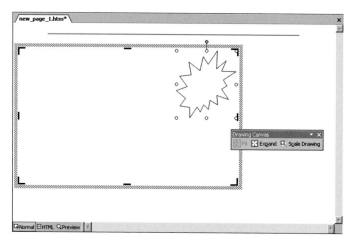

This explosion will become the head of a flower.

13 Use the Terminator and Decision shapes available on the **AutoShapes Flow-chart** menu to create a stem and leaves for your flower, as shown here:

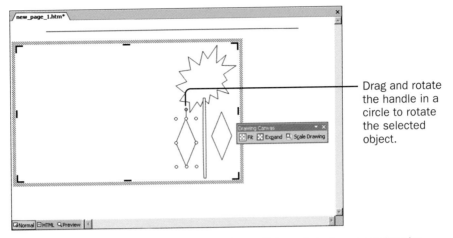

Drag and rotate the handle in a circle to rotate the selected object.

14 To rotate the leaves to appropriate angles, click each in turn and drag its rotate handle (the green dot) to move it into the position shown here:

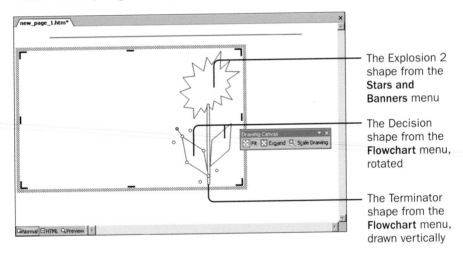

The Explosion 2 shape from the **Stars and Banners** menu

The Decision shape from the **Flowchart** menu, rotated

The Terminator shape from the **Flowchart** menu, drawn vertically

15 Right-click the explosion, and on the shortcut menu, point to **Order**, and then click **Bring to Front**.

The head of the flower now appears in front of the stem. Depending on how closely you overlapped your stem and flower head, this repositioning might be difficult to see.

16 Use the available shapes to create a garden scene like the one shown on the next page.

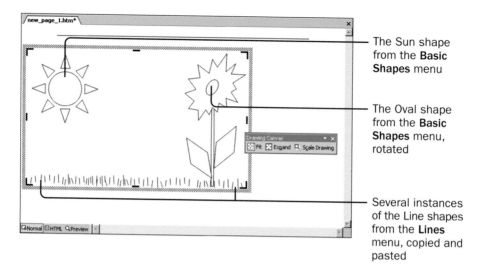

The Sun shape from the **Basic Shapes** menu

The Oval shape from the **Basic Shapes** menu, rotated

Several instances of the Line shapes from the **Lines** menu, copied and pasted

17 Click the head of the flower to select it, hold down the [Shift] key, and click each of the other flower elements so that they are all selected, like this:

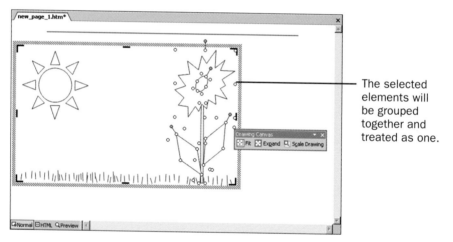

The selected elements will be grouped together and treated as one.

18 Right-click the selected elements, and on the shortcut menu, point to **Grouping**, and then click **Group**.

The elements of the flower are grouped into one element so that you can work with the flower as a whole.

Tip

To separate grouped elements, select the group and click **Ungroup** on the **Grouping** menu.

Copy

19 Using the **Copy** and **Paste** buttons on the Standard toolbar or the keyboard shortcuts `Ctrl`+`C` to copy and `Ctrl`+`V` to paste, paste multiple copies of the flower into your drawing to create an entire field.

Paste

20 Use the flowers' sizing handles to make them different sizes.

21 Right-click each flower, point to **Grouping** on the shortcut menu, and then click **Ungroup** to separate the elements so that they can be individually colored.

22 Right-click the sun in your picture, and click **Format AutoShape** on the shortcut menu to display this dialog box:

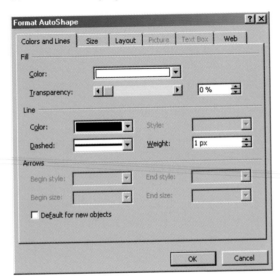

In the **Format AutoShape** dialog box, do the following:

23 On the **Colors and Lines** tab, set the **Fill Color** to **Yellow**.

24 On the **Layout** tab, set the **Wrapping style** to **None** and the **Positioning style** to **Absolute**.

25 Click **OK** to close the dialog box and apply your settings.

26 Color the flower elements in your favorite colors to create a cheerful garden scene like the one shown on the next page.

27 Close the Drawing toolbar when you're finished.

28 Click the page's **Close** button to close the current file; save your work when prompted if you want to.

Creating a Photo Gallery

Companies like The Garden Company often want to include photo galleries on their Web sites—sometimes of products, sometimes of offices or other company buildings, or sometimes of key people Web visitors will deal with. To create a photo gallery by hand, you can simply add your pictures to a page, format them as thumbnails, and arrange them the way you want them.

Photo Gallery
new for
OfficeXP

FrontPage offers an even easier method. You can use the Photo Gallery Web component to quickly and easily create an attractive display of personal or business photos or images. You can choose from four styles, arranging your pictures either horizontally, vertically, in a tableau-style montage, or in a slideshow. With the Photo Gallery Web component, you can add captions and descriptions to your images and update the layout and content in seconds.

About Web Components

FrontPage 2002 offers many exciting, ready-made **Web components** that can be dropped onto a Web page to give your site added zing with very little effort.

FrontPage Web components range from decorative to informative to downright useful, and they are one of the most appealing aspects of the program. Web components enable any FrontPage-savvy designer to create a well-programmed, fully functional site without ever having to go "behind the scenes" to actually do any programming.

In this exercise, you will create a photo gallery in a pre-existing Web site using the Photo Gallery Web component. The photos used in this exercise are from the Carnivorous Plant Database at *www2.labs.agilent.com/bot/cp_home/* and are used by permission of the database owner.

GardenCo

The working folder for this exercise is Office XP SBS\FrontPage\Chap20\PhotoGallery. In addition to the GardenCo Web site, you will link to the 12 plant photographs located in the working folder. Because the Photo Gallery Web component must be saved as part of a FrontPage-based Web site in order for it to work, you will complete this exercise within the structure of a sample Web site.

Follow these steps:

1 On the **File** menu, click **Open Web**. Browse to the working folder, click **GardenCo**, and then click **Open** to open the Web site.

2 On the Standard toolbar, click the **Create a new normal page** button to open a new page.

3 On the **Insert** menu, click **Web Component**, and then select **Photo Gallery** to see these options:

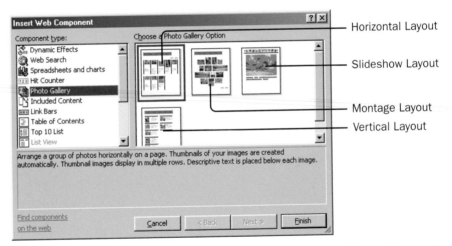

4 In the **Choose a Photo Gallery Option** box, click each of the four options and read the description that appears in the pane below.

5 Select the **Montage Layout** option, and click **Finish**.

The **Photo Gallery Properties** dialog box opens so that you can add photos to the photo gallery.

6 Click **Add**, and then click **Pictures from Files**.

7 Browse to the Office XP SBS\FrontPage\Chap20\PhotoGallery folder, where you'll find 12 photos of carnivorous plants.

8   Select all the files at once by clicking the first file, holding down the [Shift] key, and clicking the last file. Then click **Open**.

FrontPage imports the pictures into the photo gallery and displays them in the **Photo Gallery Properties** dialog box.

9   Select **plant1.jpg** on the file list.

10   In the **Caption** box, type Four Deadly Beauties.

11   In the **Description** box, type These delicate flowers are four of the wonders of the world of carnivorous plants!

12   Click **Override and use custom font formatting**.

13   Select the text in the **Caption** box.

14   In the **Font** drop-down list, click **Batang**.

15   In the **Font Size** drop-down list, click **2 (10 pt)**.

16   In the **Font Color** drop-down list, click **Purple**.

17   Click the **Bold** button.

18   Select the text in the **Description box**, and repeat steps 14 and 15 to change the font and font size.

The dialog box now looks something like this:

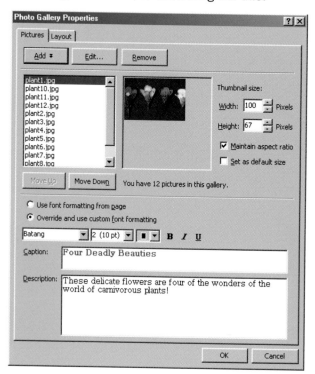

19 Click **OK** to close the **Photo Gallery Properties** dialog box and generate the photo gallery.

20 On the Standard toolbar, click the **Preview in browser** button to preview the file in your default browser and window size. When prompted to do so, save the page file with the name *Gallery.htm* and the embedded graphics with their default names.

Your photo gallery looks something like this:

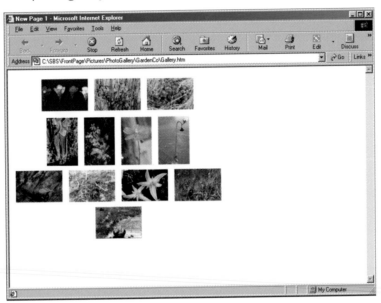

Pretty impressive for a few minutes' work!

21 Close the browser to return to FrontPage.

22 Click the page's **Close** button to close its file; save your work when prompted if you want to.

23 On the **File** menu, click **Close Web** to close the Web site.

Tip

If you later change your mind about the layout of your photo gallery, simply right-click the Photo Gallery Web component in Page view, and click **Photo Gallery Properties** on the shortcut menu to display the **Photo Gallery Properties** dialog box. On the **Layout** tab, select a different layout option, and click **OK** to reformat your photo gallery.

Adding Fancy Text

WordArt objects are text objects with special formatting applied. You can choose from 30 basic formatting options and then make further changes from the WordArt toolbar. This toolbar opens automatically when you insert a WordArt object and contains the following buttons:

- Click **Insert WordArt** to open the **WordArt Gallery** dialog box so that you can create a new WordArt object.

- Click **Edit Text** to open the **Edit WordArt Text** dialog box, where you can change the text, font, font size, and font formatting of your WordArt object.

- Select from 30 basic formatting styles in the **WordArt Gallery**.

- Change the colors and lines, size, layout, and alternate Web text of your WordArt object through the **Format WordArt** dialog box.

- Click **Edit Shape** to choose from 40 basic shapes, curves, and angles around which your WordArt is built.

- Click **WordArt Same Letter Heights** to make uppercase and lowercase letters the same height.

- Click **WordArt Vertical Text** to change the text from the default horizontal alignment to vertical alignment.

- Use the **WordArt Alignment** button to specify that the WordArt text be aligned to the left, center, or right within the available space, or that it be word-justified or stretched to fill the space.

- Use the **WordArt Character Spacing** button to control the **kerning** between letters.

If you have already used **WordArt** to create fancy headings in Word documents, you know how easy it is to work with this tool to create effects that would be very hard, if not impossible, to replicate with regular formatting. For those times when ordinary formatting simply will not do the trick, you can use WordArt in FrontPage to create headings for your Web pages.

In this exercise, you create an eye-catching WordArt page title in a sample page.

There is no working folder for this exercise.

Follow these steps:

1   On the Standard toolbar, click the **Create a new normal page** button to create a new page.

The new page opens in the Page view editing window with the insertion point
positioned at the top of the page.

2   On the **Insert** menu, point to **Picture**, and then click **WordArt**.

3   Select your favorite style in this **Word Art Gallery** dialog box:

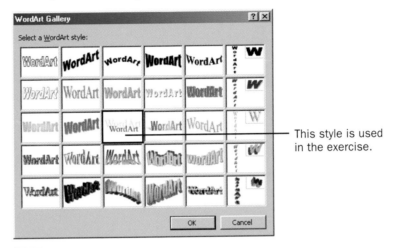

This style is used
in the exercise.

4   Click **OK** to display this **Edit WordArt Text** dialog box:

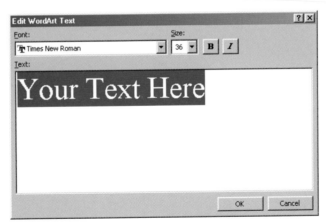

5   In the **Text** box, type **Carnivorous Plants**.

6   In the **Font** drop-down list, click **Verdana**.

7   In the **Size** drop-down list, click **24**.

8   Click the **Bold** button.

9 Click **OK** to close the dialog box and apply your settings.

FrontPage creates the page title according to your specifications, inserts it in the Web page at the insertion point, and displays the WordArt toolbar.

10 Click the WordArt toolbar's **Close** button to close the toolbar.

11 Right-click the WordArt object, and click **Paragraph** on the shortcut menu to display the **Paragraph** dialog box.

12 In the **Alignment** drop-down list, click **Center**, and then click **OK** to close the dialog box and display this result:

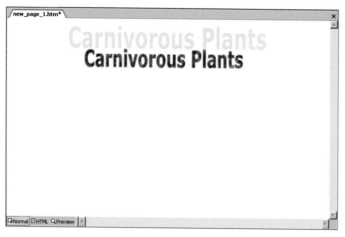

13 Close the page file without saving your changes.

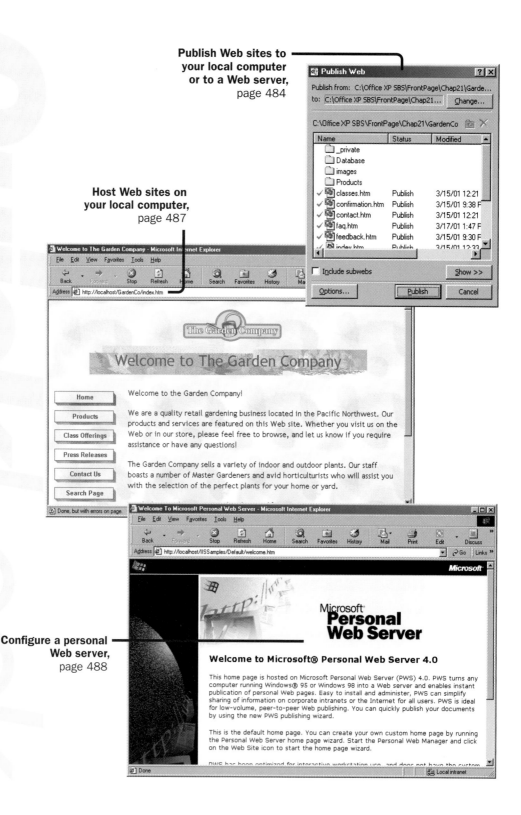

Publish Web sites to your local computer or to a Web server, page 484

Host Web sites on your local computer, page 487

Configure a personal Web server, page 488

Chapter 21
Publishing Your Web Site

After completing this chapter, you will be able to:

✔ **Configure a computer as a personal Web server.**

✔ **Find a Web hosting company or Internet service provider.**

✔ **Publish a Web site to a personal Web server.**

✔ **Publish a Web site to an intranet or Internet server.**

There is no point in going to all the trouble of building an attractive, informative, creative Web site if no one is going to look at it. The culmination of all your work is the moment when you make your Web site available to the outside world by publishing it either to an intranet or to the Internet.

In Web site terms, **publishing**, also known as **launching**, means copying all of your Web site files to a **Web server**. After the site is published, it is considered "live"; that is, the intended private group of people (in the case of an intranet) or the general public (in the case of the Internet) can view the site in their Web browsers.

You can publish a Web site in three ways:

■ You can use **Hypertext Transfer Protocol (HTTP)** to publish to a Web server that has the FrontPage Server Extensions or SharePoint Team Services from Microsoft installed.

■ You can use **File Transfer Protocol (FTP)** to publish to a Web server that does not have the FrontPage Server Extensions or SharePoint Team Services installed. To use FTP, you need to know the name of the FTP server that will receive your files and have a valid user name and password.

■ You can copy your Web site to a folder on your own computer. With a FrontPage-based Web site, it is advisable to publish the Web folder rather than simply copying the files, to ensure that the structure and integrity of the site is maintained.

This chapter discusses how and where you can publish your FrontPage-based Web site. For the first exercise, you don't need any sample files. For the remaining exercises, you will be working with a sample Web site that is stored in the Office XP SBS\FrontPage\Chap21 folder. For details about installing the practice files, see "Using the Book's CD-ROM" at the beginning of this book.

Important

The second exercise in this chapter shows you how to configure your computer as a personal Web server. In the fourth exercise, you publish a Web site to your personal Web server, so you will need to complete the second exercise before you can complete the fourth.

Finding a Suitable Host for Your Web Site

Web sites fall into two categories: **disk-based Web sites** and **server-based Web sites**. When you are developing a Web site, it's important to understand the difference.

Disk-based Web sites can be run on any kind of computer, or even from a floppy disk or CD-ROM. They support basic HTML functionality, and that's all. Most of the Web components provided with FrontPage won't work in disk-based sites.

Server-based Web sites are run on a Web server—a computer that is specifically configured to host Web sites. On a small scale, a local computer such as your own might be designated as a Web server, or the server that hosts your company's intranet might serve this function. Personal Web sites are often hosted on the servers of **Internet service providers (ISPs)**. On a larger scale, Web servers that host corporate Web sites are usually located at professional **Web hosting companies**.

A bewildering number of Web hosting companies are available to choose from, each offering different rate plans and different levels of support. As is the case when choosing any kind of a service provider—from cellular phones to hairdressers—it can be difficult to evaluate all the choices and determine which one will best fit your needs.

The Web hosting industry is large and worldwide. Several paper-based and online magazines are dedicated to reviewing and reporting on the field of Web hosting, such as *Web Hosting Magazine*, which you can buy at full-service newsstands and bookstores, and *The Web Host Industry Review*, which you can browse at *www.thewhir.com*. Both types of magazines are filled with news, information, and advertising.

The best way to start your search for a Web hosting company is to do a search on the World Wide Web for *Web hosting*. You will find a variety of Web sites representing individual Web hosting companies. You can also find sites that collate and categorize hosting companies. Good resources to check out include TopHosts at *www.tophosts.com*, HostSearch at *www.hostsearch.com*, and Web Host Directory at *www.webhostdir.com*. These sites help you sort through the choices based on different criteria.

Some Web hosting companies offer free or very inexpensive hosting services; be wary of these offers, though, because this is one of those times when you really do get what you pay for. Reliable high-speed servers and reliable high-speed technicians are neither free nor inexpensive! Changing Web hosting services can be difficult (although not impossible), so it is a good idea to make an informed decision from the beginning rather than learning from your mistakes.

Geographic location should not be a factor in your choice of Web hosting companies, but do choose a Web host located in your own country to avoid any potential problems if there is a disagreement over payment. You will never need to physically visit your hosting company's office, and almost all companies have toll-free numbers in the event that you need to telephone them.

One good way to make a decision, or at least to narrow the field to fewer choices, is to talk to people who have established businesses and ISP-hosted corporate Web sites and ask for their positive and negative impressions of any ISPs they have used. Most of the professional ISPs offer very good information on their own Web sites that should also help you to decide.

As the developer of a FrontPage-based Web site, your choices are already limited because if you use any of the special FrontPage functionality, your ISP must support FrontPage Server Extensions. Web hosting companies that support FrontPage Server Extensions will advertise this fact on their Web sites. Many of the resources listed above will enable you to search specifically for FrontPage-enabled hosting services.

Microsoft also maintains a list of registered Web Presence Providers—ISPs that have agreed to offer full support of FrontPage Server Extensions. A list of Web Presence Providers around the world is available at *www.microsoftwpp.com/wppsearch/*.

What Are FrontPage Server Extensions?

FrontPage Server Extensions are a set of **server-side applications**—programs that are run on the Web server rather than on the Web visitor's own computer—that enable you to do the following:

- Publish content directly to the Web server via the Internet.

- Include forms, discussion Webs, and hit counters on a Web site.

- Provide full-text site search capability.

Because the programs are run on the server, Web designers are spared the need to write the code and scripting that would be necessary to embed the functionality of these types of elements in the Web pages themselves. Instead, the code is "called" from the page and run on the Web server.

The FrontPage Server Extensions are not necessary to host FrontPage-based Web sites; however, they extend what the Web site is capable of doing. For a full list of the features that currently require FrontPage Server Extensions, visit *www.microsoft.com/frontpage/*.

Choosing and Registering a Domain Name

Before launching a commercial Web site on the Internet, you will need to choose and register a **domain name**. The domain name is the base of the alphanumeric address, called the **uniform resource locator (URL)**, where visitors locate your Web site on the World Wide Web. For example, Microsoft Corporation's URL is *www.microsoft.com*, and its domain name is *microsoft.com*. Your domain name may be your name, the name of your company, a word or phrase that represents what your company does, or any string of letters and numbers you desire.

When choosing a domain name, it is prudent to look for a name that will be easy for people to remember and easy for people to spell. Domain names that spell common words are good choices. Your domain name might be made up of more than one word, in which case you must decide either to run the words together as one string, or to separate them with other characters such as underscores. Remember, though, that you will need to spell the name out over the phone, so you should look for something short and simple!

Choose a name that means something to your company; if you have a registered trademark, consider using that. Domain names are not case-sensitive. You can use uppercase and lowercase letters in your written material to separate and differentiate between words, but visitors do not need to follow your capitalization to get to your site.

Part of your choice of a domain name is the extension. Depending on the type of Web site you are registering, you might choose an extension of .com, .org, .net, .edu, or one of the new extensions that have recently been made available in order to handle the increasing numbers of new Web site registrations. Each of these extensions has a meaning: .com is for companies, .org is for nonprofit organizations, .net is for networks, and .edu is for educational institutions.

Some examples of domain names tied to product lines include QuickCourse.com and eclecticClassroom.com. You can use humor or wit in your choice of a domain name, such as eFishinSea.com, which is owned by a witty boat enthusiast. (When you pronounce the name it sounds like "efficiency.")

Obviously, for URLs to work, each domain name must be unique. To avoid duplication, all domain names are registered. You can register a domain name through many Web hosting companies; some of them will even help you with your search for the right name. Network Solutions (*www.networksolutions.com*) is a good one-stop shop for researching and registering domain name/extension combinations. You can also go directly to *www.InterNIC.com*, the United States Department of Commerce's domain registry Web site for more information.

Configuring Your Own Computer to Host a Web Site

Most Web sites are initially developed as disk-based sites; that is, the site is developed and tested on a local computer. Only after a site is finished is it published to a Web server that is maintained either by the organization that owns the Web site or by a Web hosting company. And only at that point does it become a server-based site. The drawback to this strategy is that the server-specific components of the site won't work until the site is published to the server, at which time you might find out that they don't work at all.

If you're going to do a significant amount of Web site development, you might consider configuring your own computer as a server. For FrontPage 2002, Microsoft recommends the following configuration for a Web server:

- Windows 2000
- Internet Information Services 5
- FrontPage Server Extensions 2002 or SharePoint Team Services

If your computer does not meet these requirements, or if you do not want to run a full-blown Web server on your computer, you can set up your Windows 98 computer as a personal Web server, using the following configuration:

- Windows 98
- Microsoft Personal Web Server 4.0
- FrontPage 2000 Server Extensions

Troubleshooting

FrontPage Server Extensions 2002 does not support Windows 9x operating systems. As a workaround, Windows 98 users can install FrontPage 2000 Server Extensions from the Microsoft Web site at *http://office.microsoft.com/downloads/2000/winfpse.aspx*.

By using a personal Web server, you can develop and run server-based sites locally; that is, on your own computer. You will still need to publish the site to a server that is accessible by its intended audience, but the risk of showing your mistakes to the world will be significantly lower if you thoroughly test your site on your personal Web server first.

Important

The drawback to configuring your computer as a Web server is that, depending on the computer's configuration, you might find that its overall speed and performance is slightly reduced. You might not want to do this if you have other ways of testing the server-specific components of your Web site.

In this exercise, you will configure a Windows 98 computer as a personal Web server by installing **Personal Web Server (PWS)** and the FrontPage 2000 Server Extensions. (PWS is supplied on the Windows 98 installation CD-ROM; however, by default it is not fully installed with the operating system.) You will then test the installation, first by opening your default home page, and then by opening a Web site.

GardenCo

To work through this exercise, you will need to have available the Windows 98 CD-ROM and an Internet connection.

The working folder for this exercise is Office XP SBS\FrontPage\Chap21.

Follow these steps:

1   Close any programs that might be running on your computer.

2   At the left end of the taskbar at the bottom of the screen, click **Start**, point to **Settings**, and click **Control Panel**.

The Control Panel window opens.

3   Double-click **Add/Remove Programs** to open the **Add/Remove Programs Properties** dialog box.

4   Click the **Windows Setup** tab to display these options:

Selections vary based on your computer setup.

5   In the **Components** list, click the words **Internet Tools** (do not click the check box, because you might inadvertently tell Windows to uninstall currently installed components).

Internet Tools are the tools that come with Windows 98 to help you use the Internet.

The Windows Internet Tools

Personal Web Server is just one of the tools included in Windows 98 to help you work with the Internet. Two others are related to FrontPage, and the rest provide miscellaneous Internet-related capabilities, as follows:

■ Microsoft FrontPage Express is a simple HTML page editor.

■ Web Publishing Wizard provides services that enable you to easily upload Web sites to a Web server.

■ Microsoft Virtual Reality Modeling Language (VRML) 2.0 Viewer is a viewer for VRML objects, which are three-dimensional full-color objects with special texture, animation, and lighting effects.

■ Microsoft Wallet provides a secure place to store private information such as credit card details for use while shopping on the Internet.

■ Real Audio Player displays live and on-demand audio, video, and animation.

■ Web-Based Enterprise Management components provide remote problem tracking and system administration capabilities to system administrators and support technicians.

6 Click **Details** to see the available Internet Tools components.

7 In the **Components** list, select the **Personal Web Server** check box, and click **OK** to close the **Internet Tools** dialog box.

8 Click **OK** again to close the **Add/Remove Programs Properties** dialog box and install the Personal Web Server.

You are prompted to insert your Windows 98 CD-ROM.

9 Insert the Windows 98 CD-ROM in the drive, and click **OK**.

Windows searches for a file called *pws_main.htm*. If it does not find the file in the expected location, you will see a message like this one:

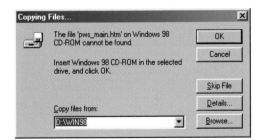

Troubleshooting

This message might be displayed because Windows is looking on the wrong drive, or because the wrong CD-ROM is in the disk drive. Often the best response to this message is to click the **Browse** button and manually search for the file. More often than not, it will be simple to find. In this case, Windows is looking for a file that can be found inside a Cabinet (CAB) file called *Precopy2.cab*. Browse to this file and then click **OK** to continue.

After locating the file, Windows copies the necessary information to your hard disk and returns you to the Control Panel.

10 Close the Control Panel window.

You now need to run the Personal Web Server setup program.

11 In Windows Explorer, browse to the *add-ons\pws* folder on the Windows 98 CD-ROM, and double-click **setup.exe**.

The first page of the **Microsoft Personal Web Server Setup Wizard** opens, as shown here:

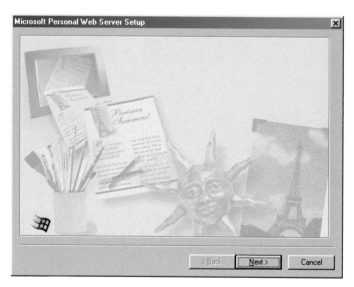

12 Click **Next**.

The next page of the wizard appears, offering **Minimum**, **Typical**, and **Custom** installation options:

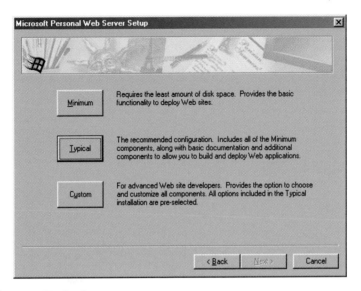

13 Click **Typical**.

The next page of the wizard appears, with the default Web publishing directory identified as *C:\Inetpub\wwwroot*:

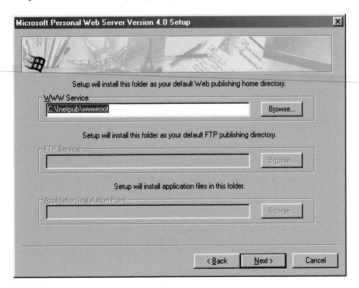

Unless you have a good reason, you should always accept the default installation locations. If you change the default publishing folder, it is important to enter an **absolute path** that includes a drive letter. The setup program might misinterpret a **relative path**.

14 Click **Next**.

The setup program displays a progress bar while it copies the necessary files to your computer and configures a variety of settings. When the setup is complete, this final page of the wizard is displayed:

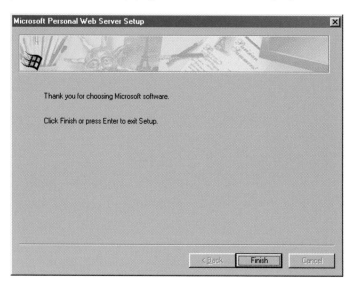

15 Click **Finish** to close the program.

You are prompted to restart your computer:

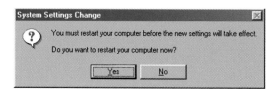

Prepare to restart your computer by doing the following:

16 Save and close all open applications.

17 Leave the Windows 98 CD-ROM in your CD-ROM drive; it will be accessed again after you restart.

18 If there is a floppy disk in the disk drive, eject it.

19 Click **Yes** in the message box to restart your computer.

When your computer restarts (and after you log on, if necessary), Windows 98 updates its systems settings, and your computer is now configured as a personal Web server.

20 Remove the Windows 98 CD-ROM from your hard drive, and return it to a safe storage location.

21 If necessary, start your Internet connection. Open your Web browser, and in the **Address** box, type http://www.microsoft.com/frontpage.

The Microsoft FrontPage Web site opens in your browser. (This page is updated frequently. Information given here is current as of April 1, 2001.)

22 In the Resources area, click **FrontPage Server Extensions**.

You are redirected to the FrontPage section of the MSDN Online Web site.

23 Click the **Download the FrontPage Server Extensions for Microsoft Windows-Based Servers** link.

The Downloads for Microsoft Windows-Based Servers page opens.

24 Scroll down and click the link to the download file for your operating system.

The **File Download** dialog box opens.

25 Click **Run this program from its current location**, and then click **OK**.

A progress bar estimating the time left appears while the file is downloaded.

26 Select the **Close this dialog box when download completes** check box, if it is not already selected.

When the download is complete, a **Security Warning** dialog box appears.

27 Click **Yes** to continue.

The FrontPage Server Extensions installation begins. A setup program walks you through a short registration process and then installs the server extensions on your computer. When the installation is complete, you are prompted to restart your computer.

28 Click **Yes** in the message box to restart your computer.

When your computer restarts (and after you log on, if necessary), Windows finishes the configuration of the FrontPage Server Extensions.

29 To test whether the installation was successful, start your browser.

30 In the **Address** box, type http://localhost and press Enter.

Tip

When you configure your computer as a personal Web server, a specific **Internet Protocol (IP)** address is assigned to the PWS root Web site. *Localhost* is a **friendly name** for this IP address, meaning that it is easier to remember than the address itself. Entering *http://localhost* in the browser **Address** box displays the root Web site of any configured Web server.

The default PWS home page opens, as shown here:

31 Open Windows Explorer, and browse to the C: drive.

Windows created a new folder called *Inetpub* on your C: drive. The Inetpub folder contains four subfolders: iissamples, scripts, webpub, and wwwroot.

32 Copy the **GardenCo** Web site from the Office XP SBS\FrontPage\Chap21 folder to the C:\Inetpub\wwwroot folder.

33 Start your browser, type **http://localhost/GardenCo/index.htm** in the **Address** box, and press Enter .

The home page of The Garden Company's Web site is displayed in your browser, like this:

34 Test the Web site by displaying various pages and clicking different links and components.

All of the components should be fully functional, including the hit counter and search page.

35 Close the browser.

Publishing a Web Site to a Local Folder

If you have developed a FrontPage-based Web site on your local machine and you want to move the Web site files to a different location or create a copy of the Web site, it is prudent to publish the site to the new location rather than simply moving or copying the files in Windows Explorer. This guarantees that the underlying structure of the site will be updated as necessary to maintain the integrity of the links.

In this exercise, you will publish a disk-based Web site to a local folder.

GardenCo

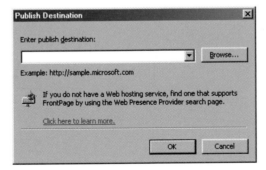

The working folder for this exercise is Office XP SBS\FrontPage\Chap21.

Follow these steps:

1 If FrontPage is not already open, start it now.

2 On the **File** menu, click **Open Web**.

3 In the **Open Web** dialog box, browse to the Office XP SBS\FrontPage\ Chap21 folder, select **GardenCo**, and then click **Open** to open the disk-based Web site.

4 On the **File** menu, click **Publish Web**.

The **Publish Destination** dialog box opens:

Publish Destination   ☒

Enter publish destination:

▼   Browse...

Example: http://sample.microsoft.com

If you do not have a Web hosting service, find one that supports FrontPage by using the Web Presence Provider search page.

Click here to learn more.

OK   Cancel

5 Click the **Browse** button to open the **New Publish Location** dialog box, and browse to Office XP SBS\FrontPage\Chap21.

Create New
Folder

6 Click the **Create New Folder** button on the dialog box's toolbar to open the **New Folder** dialog box.

7 In the **Name** box, type **PublishLocal**, and then click **OK** to return to the **New Publish Location** dialog box with your newly created folder selected.

8 Click **Open** to return to the **Publish Destination** dialog box.

FrontPage has entered the specified path in the **Enter publish destination** box.

9 Click **OK**.

This message appears:

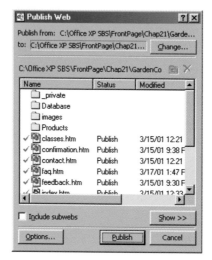

10 Click **OK** to create the new Web at the specified location.

The **Publish Web** dialog box opens, listing these files to be published:

11 Click the **Options** button.

12 Review the many settings that you can work with in the **Options** dialog box, and then click **Cancel** to maintain the default settings.

13 Click **Publish** to publish the Web site to your local drive.

You see this warning:

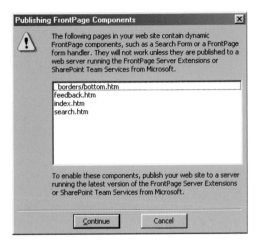

14 Click **Continue**.

FrontPage displays a progress bar while publishing the selected files, and when the publishing process is finished, this message is displayed:

15 Click the **Click here to view your publish log file** option.

Because the Publish Log is an HTML file, it opens in your browser. It contains the date and time of each transaction involved in the publishing process.

16 Scroll through the file and review the publishing process that just finished.

FrontPage first creates the required folder structure, copies each individual file, and then copies the navigation structure. The entire process takes about one minute. (The publishing time depends on the size and complexity of the individual Web site.)

Tip

You can filter this report to display only certain types of transactions: Publish Starts, Folder Creations, File Copies, File Renames, File Deletions, Confirmations, or Warnings. The default is to display all of the transactions.

17 Close the browser to return to FrontPage.

18 Now click the **Click here to view your published web site** option.

The Garden Company's Web site opens in your browser at the default window size.

19 Browse around the site, testing its functionality.

Notice that FrontPage Web components, such as the hit counter on the home page and the search engine on the search page, do not work properly.

20 Close the browser.

21 Click **Done** to close the message box.

Back in FrontPage, the original disk-based Web site is still open, as shown here in the **Folder List**:

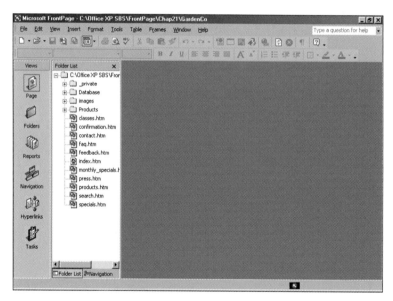

22 Close the Web site.

Publishing a Web Site to a Web Server

Developing a Web site is an iterative process. You work on a few pages, and you publish them to see whether they work as intended. Then you make corrections, work on a few more pages, and publish again. Gradually the pages evolve into a full-fledged Web site that you are ready to present to its intended audience.

While you are working on the site, you will want to publish it to a development server, not to one that is accessible to outsiders. Depending on your resources, this development server might be another computer, or it might be a personal Web server hosted on your own computer. When you are finally ready to launch the site, you will need to publish it again, this time to a Web server that is capable of supporting the many visitors you hope will come to take a look.

Single-page publishing

new for OfficeXP

FrontPage 2002 enables you to publish only the files that you want to rather than the entire Web site. You can even publish a single Web page by right-clicking the file name in the **Folder List** or in Folders view and clicking **Publish Selected Files** on the shortcut menu.

You can also mark specific files for exclusion from the publishing process by right-clicking the file name in the **Folder List** or in Folders view and clicking **Don't Publish** on the shortcut menu.

In this exercise, you will first publish a disk-based Web site to your personal Web server, and you will then publish the site from the personal Web server to a remote Web server.

Important

To complete this exercise, you must have Personal Web Server and FrontPage 2000 Server Extensions installed on your computer. You must also have access to a Web server on a different computer.

GardenCo

The working folder for this exercise is Office XP SBS\FrontPage\Chap21.

Follow these steps:

1 Open the **GardenCo** Web site located in the working folder.

2 On the **File** menu, click **Publish Web**.

The **Publish Web** dialog box opens with the previous publish destination shown in the **Publish to** box.

3 Click **Change**.

4 In the **Publish Destination** dialog box, type **http://localhost** in the **Enter publish destination** box, and then click **OK**.

The **Publish Web** dialog box now shows the location to which the Web site will be published.

5 Click **Publish**.

The **Publishing FrontPage Components** dialog box opens to let you know which components might not work without the current version of the FrontPage Server Extensions.

Troubleshooting

If you're working on a Windows 98 computer, most of the Web site pages are listed here because the program is searching for FrontPage Server Extensions 2002, and these are not supported by Windows 98. Instead, Windows 98 users need to install FrontPage 2000 Server Extensions. Most features usually work when published to a Windows 98 system, in spite of what this dialog box says.

6 Click **Continue**.

FrontPage displays a progress bar while copying folders and files to your personal Web server, and informs you when the procedure has been successfully completed.

7 Click the option to view the Web site in your browser.

All of the FrontPage Web components are fully functional.

8 Next take a look at the Publish Log, shown here:

Friday, March 23, 2001	11:05:06 AM	Copied "images/custrel3.gif".
Friday, March 23, 2001	11:05:06 AM	Copied "images/fprotate.class".
Friday, March 23, 2001	11:05:06 AM	Copied "images/fprotatx.class".
Friday, March 23, 2001	11:05:06 AM	Copied "images/isao74.jpg".
Friday, March 23, 2001	11:05:06 AM	Copied "images/jmhvulg.jpg".
Friday, March 23, 2001	11:05:09 AM	Copied "images/pxweser.jpg".
Friday, March 23, 2001	11:05:09 AM	Copied "images/September.gif".
Friday, March 23, 2001	11:05:09 AM	Copied "images/tgdogo_sm.gif".
Friday, March 23, 2001	11:05:10 AM	Copied "Products/carnivorous_plants.htm".
Friday, March 23, 2001	11:05:10 AM	Copied "Products/gifts.htm".
Friday, March 23, 2001	11:05:10 AM	Copied "Products/plants_garden.htm".
Friday, March 23, 2001	11:05:10 AM	Copied "Products/plants_home.htm".
Friday, March 23, 2001	11:05:11 AM	Copied home page from "index.htm" to "Default.htm".
Friday, March 23, 2001	11:05:11 AM	Renamed "index.htm" to "Default.htm".
Friday, March 23, 2001	11:05:12 AM	Copied navigation structure.
Friday, March 23, 2001	**11:05:30 AM**	**Finished publish from "C:\Office XP SBS\FrontPage\Chap21\GardenCo" to "http://localhost".**

Notice that the process of publishing the site to the personal Web server included an additional transaction. The index.htm home page file was renamed to *Default.htm* in order to support the expected server-based Web site structure.

9 Close the browser to return to FrontPage.

10 Click **Done** to close the message box.

The original Web site is open in FrontPage.

11 On the **File** menu, click **Open Web**.

12 Browse to *C:\Inetpub\wwwroot*, and click **Open** to open the site you just published to your personal Web server.

13 Now publish the personal Web server-based site to a remote Web server (a different computer). Start by clicking **Publish Web** on the **File** menu.

The **Publish Web** dialog box opens with the previous publish destination shown in the **Publish to** box.

14 Click **Change** to open the **Publish Destination** dialog box.

15 In the **Enter publish destination** box, type **http://<server>/PublishServer**, where <server> is the name of your Web server, and then click **OK**.

16 When you are prompted to create a new Web site at the specified location, click **OK**.

The **Publish Web** dialog box now displays the new publish location.

17 Click **Publish**.

FrontPage displays a progress bar while copying files and folders to the Web server, and displays the message box when the procedure has been successfully completed.

18 View the Web site in your browser, testing its functionality.

All of the FrontPage Web components are fully functional.

19 Look at the Publish Log to see what transactions were included in the publishing process.

20 Return to FrontPage, and click **Done** to close the message box.

21 Close the Web site.

22 Quit FrontPage.

Publishing a Web Site from a Remote Web Server to a Local Computer

FrontPage enables you to publish any Web site to which you have access to any location. The publishing process goes both ways. In addition to publishing from a local computer to a remote server, you can do the opposite: publish a Web site from the Internet to your computer. In order to publish from the Web to your computer:

- The remote server must have FrontPage Server Extensions installed.

- You must have a valid user name and password for the remote server.

- You must have a working Internet connection.

To publish a FrontPage Web site from a remote server to a local folder or to your personal Web server, follow these steps:

1 If necessary, start your Internet connection.

2 On the **File** menu, click **Open Web**.

3 In the **Web name** box, type the **URL** or **IP** address of the remote Web site preceded by *http://* to indicate that it is a server-based site (for example, http://www.microsoft.com/frontpage/ or http://207.46.131.13/frontpage/), and then click **Open**.

4 If the remote server requires a user name and password, it will prompt you for them. Supply a valid user name and password, and click **OK**.

The remote Web site opens in FrontPage.

5 On the **File** menu, click **Publish Web**.

6 In the **Publish Destination** box, type the disk or server location where you want to publish the Web site, and then click **OK**.

7 In the **Publish Web** dialog box, click **Publish**.

VI

Microsoft
Publisher

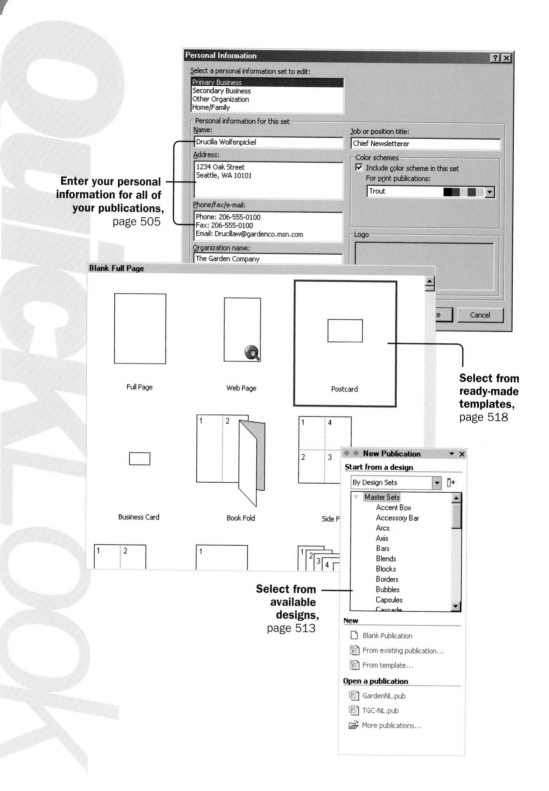

Personal Information

Select a personal information set to edit:

Primary Business
Secondary Business
Other Organization
Home/Family

Personal information for this set

Name:

Drucilla Wolfenpickel

Address:

1234 Oak Street
Seattle, WA 10101

Phone/fax/e-mail:

Phone: 206-555-0100
Fax: 206-555-0100
Email: Drucillaw@gardenco.msn.com

Organization name:

The Garden Company

Job or position title:

Chief Newsletterer

Color schemes

☑ Include color scheme in this set
For print publications:

Trout

Logo

Enter your personal information for all of your publications, page 505

_e_   Cancel

Blank Full Page

Full Page

Web Page

Postcard

Business Card

Book Fold

Side F

1   2

1

Select from ready-made templates, page 518

New Publication

Start from a design

By Design Sets

Master Sets
 Accent Box
 Accessory Bar
 Arcs
 Axis
 Bars
 Blends
 Blocks
 Borders
 Bubbles
 Capsules
 Cascade

New

 Blank Publication
 From existing publication...
 From template...

Open a publication

 GardenNL.pub
 TGC-NL.pub
 More publications...

Select from available designs, page 513

Chapter 22
Creating a Document

After completing this chapter, you will be able to:

✔ Create a publication using the Publication Wizard.

✔ Create a publication using the Publication Design Set.

✔ Save a publication as a template.

✔ Create a publication using a template.

✔ Create a publication from scratch.

Publisher 2002 makes it fun to create a variety of publications from newsletters and flyers to complex brochures and catalogs. Because Publisher 2002 offers a broad variety of formats and printing options, you can use it both at work (to produce marketing, sales, management, or other professional documents) or at home (to produce invitations, flyers, holiday letters, scrapbook pages, or just about anything you could think of).

This chapter uses the BusinessCard practice file. For details about installing the practice files, see "Using the Book's CD-ROM" at the beginning of this book.

Creating a Publication for the First Time

The first time you create a publication using the Publication Wizard, Publisher 2002 gathers information from you for its Personal Information Set. There are four different sets available: Primary Business, Secondary Business, Other Organization, and Home/Family. Once you provide the information for these sets, Publisher 2002 automatically plugs it into your documents so you don't have to keep typing it in.

In this exercise, you will complete the Personal Information Set for the Primary Business, The Garden Company, while beginning the company's newsletter.

1 Click the **Start** button.

The **Start** menu opens.

2 Click **Programs**.

The **Programs** submenu opens.

3   Click **Microsoft Publisher 2002**.

Publisher 2002 opens.

New
Publication
Task pane
new for
OfficeXP

4   In the New Publication Task pane, click the down arrow of the **Start from a design** box to see the options.

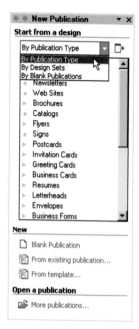

5   Click **By Publication Type**.

The box immediately beneath the **By Publication Type** box lists the various publication types available. If *Quick Publications* is highlighted, the preview window to the right of the list will show the Quick Publications samples.

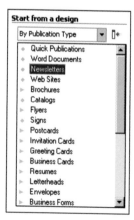

6   Click **Newsletters**.

The preview window shows the newsletter samples.

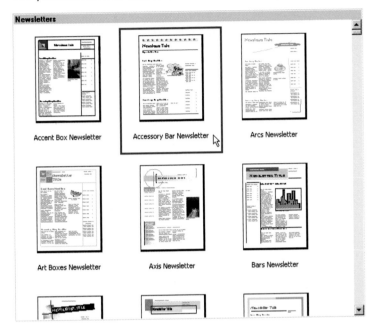

7   Position the cursor over the **Accessory Bar Newsletter** option.

A frame appears around the Accessory Bar Newsletter option.

8   Click inside the frame to select the **Accessory Bar Newsletter** format.

Three things happen when you make your selection. First, the Task pane shows the Newsletter Options. Second, the Accessory Bar Newsletter's first page appears, ready for you to reformat it. And third, a dialog box appears informing you that the wizard will automatically fill in information about your company and inviting you to click **OK** to verify that information.

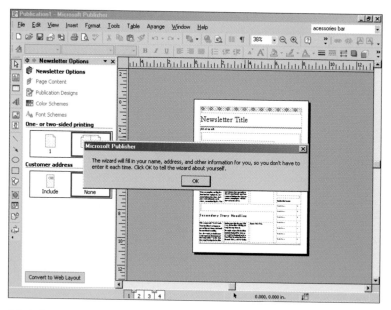

9 Click **OK**.

The **Personal Information** dialog box appears.

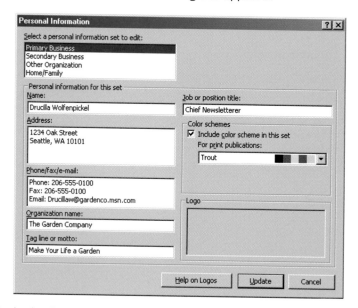

10 In the **Select a personal information set to edit** box, click **Primary Business**.

11 In the **Personal information for this set** box, type Drucilla Wolfenpickel.

12 Press ⊞ to move to the next field.

13 In the **Address** field, type 1234 Oak Street, Seattle, WA 10101.

14 Press Tab to move to the next field.

15 In the **Phone/fax/e-mail** box, type Phone: 206-555-01. Press Enter. On the next line, type Fax: 206-555-01. Press Enter. On the next line, type Drucillaw@gardenco.msn.com.

16 Press Tab to move to the next field.

17 In the **Organization name** box, type The Garden Company.

18 Press Tab to move to the next field.

19 In the **Tag Line Or Motto** box, type Make Your Life a Garden.

20 In the **Job or position title** box, type Chief Newsletterer.

21 In the **Color schemes** area, select the **Include color scheme in this set** check box.

22 Click the down arrow of the **For print publications** box.

The default color scheme is Trout. When you click the down arrow, you see lots of color scheme options.

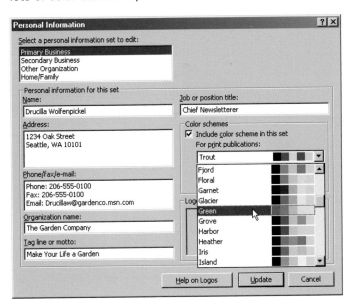

23 Select **Green**.

24 Click the **Update** button.

The information you just typed in will be retained and inserted into this newsletter and any other document you create. You will not have to enter the information again; however, you can change it at any time.

Save

25 Click the **Save** button.

The **Save As** dialog box appears.

26 Navigate to the Office XP SBS\Publisher\Chap22 folder, type **TGC-NL** in the **File name** box, and then click **Save**.

Close

27 Click the **Close** button.

TGC-NL.pub closes.

Creating a Publication Using the Publication Wizard

Publisher 2002 provides a Publication Wizard that makes it easy for you to create just about any kind of document you'll ever need, including a variety of Quick Publications (flyers, brochures, and so on), newsletters, Web sites, catalogs, signs, postcards, greeting cards, business cards, resumes, letterhead, envelopes, business forms, banners, calendars, ads, award certificates, gift certificates, labels, menus, programs, and even paper airplanes and origami designs.

In this exercise, you will create Spouts 'n Sprouts, The Garden Company's newsletter, with the help of the Publication Wizard.

New

1 On the Standard toolbar, click the **New** button.

If the New Publication Task pane is not open, choose **Task Pane** from the view menu.

2 In the New Publication Task pane, click the down arrow of the **Start from a design** box.

3 Click **By Publication Type**.

4 In the box immediately beneath the **Start from a design** box, click **Newsletters**.

The preview window to the right will show newsletter samples.

5 Position the cursor over the **Accessory Bar Newsletter** option.

A frame appears around the Accessory Bar Newsletter option.

6 Click to select the **Accessory Bar Newsletter** format.

If you haven't provided any personal information to Publisher 2002, you will see the **Personal Information** dialog box. In this box you can specify your name, company address, and other pertinent information. If you have already provided this information, it will automatically be inserted into the business card template. Of course, you can change anything on the template.

Tip

It may take several seconds for your computer to bring up the selected newsletter template.

7 Select the words *Newsletter Title* and replace them with **Spouts 'n Sprouts**.

Tip

Press `F9` to zoom in on the selected area if it is too small to read. When you're through, you can press `F9` again to zoom back to whole-page display.

8 Press `Tab` eight times and type **Spring 2001**.

9 Select the words *Lead Story Headline* and replace them with **Best Sprouts For Spring**.

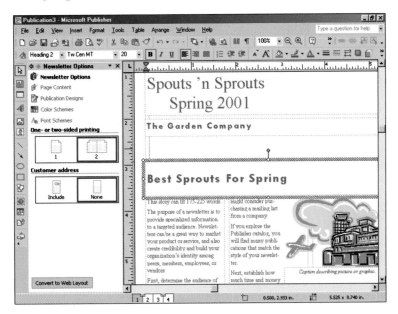

The text box contains important information about writing a newsletter that you should read before replacing it with your own text. This box is where you would write the actual article about the best spring sprouts.

Page
Navigation

```
1  2  3  4
```

10 Click the **2** on the **Page Navigation** button at the bottom of the screen.

The view switches to a 2-page spread of the inside pages (pages 2 and 3).

11 Select the middle **Inside Story Headline** on page 3 and replace it with **Flower Power**.

This article would tell readers how different plants can make a room more healthful.

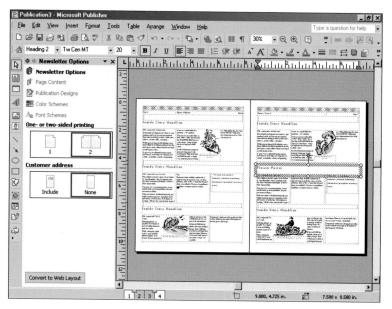

12 Click the **4** on the **Page Navigation** button at the bottom of the screen.

Page 4 appears on the screen all by itself.

13 Click the bottom text box part of the default logo in the top left corner of the page.

14 Press and hold the ⎡Shift⎤ key while clicking to select the top pyramid part of the default logo.

This allows you to select both components of the default logo.

15 Press the **Delete** key.

The default logo disappears.

16 Click the **Insert** menu, click **Picture**, and then click **From File**.

The **Insert Picture** dialog box opens.

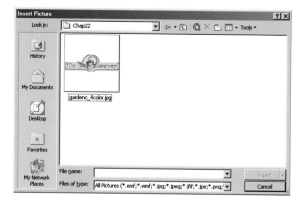

17 Navigate to the Office XP SBS\Publisher\Chap22 folder.

18 Select **gardenc_4color.jpg**, and then click **Insert**.

The file contains the company logo, which will probably appear oversized. If this happens, right-click the logo, click **Format Picture**, and then click the **Size** tab. Change the height to *35%*. If you use the down arrow to do this, the width automatically matches the height. If you typed *35%*, press ⟨Tab⟩ to change the width to match the height.

19 Position the properly sized logo as shown in the figure.

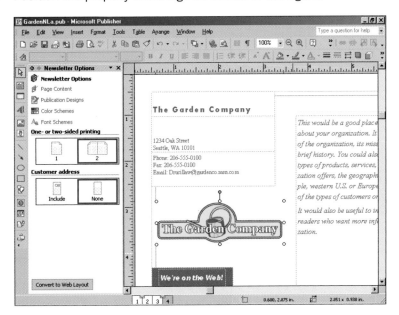

Save

20 On the Standard toolbar, click the **Save** button.

The **Save As** dialog box opens.

21 In the **File name** field, type GardenNL.

22 Click the **Save** button.

Publisher 2002 saves the changes to GardenNL.pub.

Close

23 Click the **Close** button.

24 GardenNL.pub closes.

Creating a Business Card
Using the Publication Design Set

To help you create many different kinds of documents without having to labor over their design, Publisher 2002 includes several preformatted types of documents. These design sets include preformatted stationery (business cards, letterhead, envelopes, thank-you notes, "with compliments" cards, and postcards), business forms (expense reports, fax cover sheets, inventory lists, invoices, purchase orders, job quotes, refund forms, billing statements, and weekly records), calendars, catalogs, gift certificates, brochures, flyers, newsletters, party invitations, shipping labels (for Avery 5164 labels), Web sites, and Microsoft Word documents.

In this exercise, you will create a business card for Catherine Turner, owner of The Garden Company.

New

1   On the Standard toolbar, click the **New** button.

If the New Publication Task pane is not open, choose **Task Pane** from the **View** menu.

2   Click the down arrow of the **Start from a design** box.

The **Start from a design** box opens to reveal three options.

3   Click **By Design Sets**.

The box immediately beneath the **Start from a design** box changes to display the various design sets available.

4   Click **Accessory Bar**.

Tip

It's a good idea to keep your publications consistent in format. The newsletter reflects a design that will be common to the business card you create here as well as any other documents that you might create, from letterhead to shipping labels and everything in between.

All design sets using the Accessory Bar format are presented in the preview window.

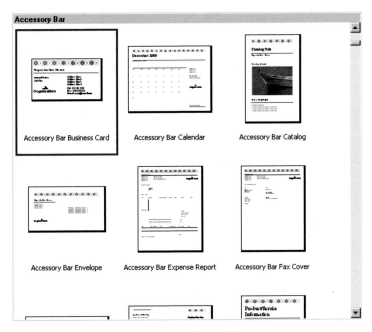

5 Double-click **Accessory Bar Business Card**.

If you haven't provided any personal information to Publisher 2002, you will see the **Personal Information** dialog box. In this box you can specify your name, company address, and other pertinent information. If you have already provided this information, it will automatically be inserted into the business card template. Of course, you can change anything on the template.

6 Click the text box portion of the default logo.

7 Hold the [Shift] key down and click the pyramid portion of the default logo.

This allows you to select all parts of the default logo at the same time.

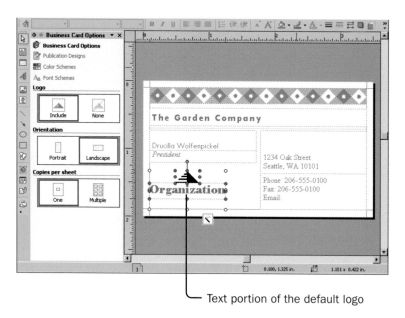

Text portion of the default logo

8   Press the ⌜Del⌝ key.

A dialog box appears asking if you want to change the design to one that does not use a logo.

9   Click **No**.

The default logo disappears, leaving a blank spot so that you can insert The Garden Company's logo.

10   On the Standard toolbar, click **Insert**, click **Picture**, and then click **From File**.

The **Insert Picture** dialog box appears.

11   Navigate to where you installed the practice files and select the **garden_4color.jpg** file.

12   Click **Insert**.

The Garden Company's logo appears, but you may have to drag it into position.

Tip

The Garden Company logo might appear too large. In fact, it might completely cover the business card you're designing. If this happens, right-click on the logo and click **Format Picture**. Click the **Size** tab and, in the **Scale** area, change the height to a smaller percentage, such as 20%. If you use the down arrow to do this, the width will automatically change to match 20%. If you simply select the default 100% and type 20% over it, you will have to press ⌨Tab to get the width to match the height. After changing the height and width to 20%, click **OK**.

Save

13 On the Standard toolbar, click the **Save** button.

The **Save As** dialog box appears.

14 In the **File name** field, type **MyBusinessCard**.

15 Click the **Save** button.

Publisher 2002 saves the changes to a file named MyBusinessCard. When you save this document for the first time, you might be asked if you want to add the new logo to the Primary Business personal information set. Click **Yes**. Now your logo will also be automatically inserted into any document you create.

Close

16 Click the **Close** button.

MyBusinessCard.pub closes.

Saving a Publication as a Template

Once you've created a document that you plan to use over and over again, like a business card or a newsletter, you can save it as a template. Then, when it's time to create the next one, you can just replace existing text or images with the new ones.

In this exercise, you will save the BusinessCard file as a business card template.

Open

1   On the Standard toolbar, click the **Open** button.

The **Open Publication** dialog box appears.

2   Navigate to Office XP SBS\Publisher\Chap22 and double-click the **BusinessCard** file.

BusinessCard.pub opens.

3   On the Standard toolbar, click **File**, and then click **Save As**.

The **Save As** dialog box appears.

4   In the **File name** box, type **B-Card Template**.

5   Click the down arrow of the **Save as type** box, and click **Publisher Template**.

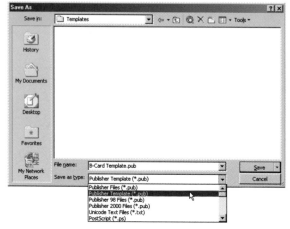

6   Click **Save**.

Publisher 2002 saves your changes to B-Card Template.

Close

7   Click the **Close button**.

B-Card Template.pub closes.

Creating a Publication from a Template

Templates make life so much simpler. When you labor over a document and then save it as a template, the next time you need to make a similar document, you need only open the template, make your changes, save them, and zip zap, you're done.

In this exercise, you will use the B-Card Template to create a business card for a new employee of The Garden Company.

1   On the Standard tool bar, click **File**, and then click **New**.

If the New Publication Task pane is not open, choose **Task Pane** from the **View** menu.

2   In the **New** area of the New Publication Task pane, click **From template...**.

The **Open Template** dialog box appears.

3   Navigate to the B-Card Template and click it.

4   Click **Create New**.

The B-Card Template opens.

5   Click the default name, and then type **Mike Galos**.

6   Click the default title, and then type **Head Dirt Bagger**.

7   Click the name portion of the e-mail address (the part to the left of the @ symbol), and then type **Mikeg**.

8 On the Standard toolbar, click **File**, and then click **Save As**.

The **Save As** dialog box opens.

9 In the **File name** box, type **B-Card Mikeg**.

10 Click **Save**.

Publisher 2002 saves your changes to B-Card Mikeg.

Close

11 Click the **Close** button.

12 B-Card Mikeg.pub closes.

Creating a Publication from a Blank Page

Even though Publisher 2002 provides several easy-to-use publication types and design sets, sometimes it's easier to start from scratch. For example, you may have an idea of how you want the document to look, and none of the templates or predesigned forms suit you. Or, you might just be one of those people who thinks better facing a blank sheet rather than when facing one that illustrates someone else's ideas.

In this exercise you will create a postcard advertising a Valentine's Day special on dirt.

1 On the Standard toolbar, click **File**, and then click **New**.

If the New Publication Task pane is not open, choose **Task Pane** from the **View** menu.

2 In the **Start from a design** box, select **By Blank Publications**.

3 In the preview window, click **Postcard**.

After a few seconds, a new, blank postcard opens.

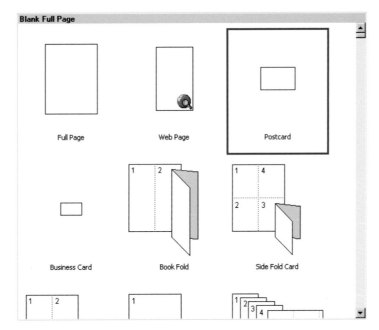

4 In the **Apply a design** section of the Task pane, scroll down until you see *Jungle* and click it.

Publisher applies the Jungle design to the postcard.

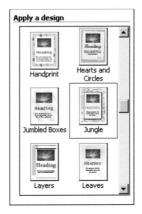

5 Click inside the postcard and type Worship the dirt she walks on?

6 Press Enter, and then type Show her you love her with a big bag of Valentine dirt.

7   On the Standard toolbar, click **Insert**, click **Picture**, and then click **From File**.

The **Insert Picture** dialog box appears.

8   Navigate to Office XP SBS\Publisher\Chap22, and then double-click the **garden_4color.jpg** file.

9   Click **OK**.

The Garden Company logo appears on the postcard.

Tip

The Garden Company logo might appear too large. In fact, it might completely cover the postcard you're designing. If this happens, right-click on the logo and click **Format Picture**. Click the **Size** tab and, in the **Scale** area, change the height to a smaller percentage, such as 20%. If you use the down arrow to do this, the width will automatically change to match 20%. If you simply highlight the default 100% and type 20% over it, you will have to press [Tab] to get the width to match the height. After changing the height and width to 20%, click **OK**.

10   With the logo still selected, position the cursor over the little green handle and drag it to the right to reposition the logo at a 90-degree angle.

11   Position the logo so that it is directly beneath the text.

Click anywhere in the postcard to deselect the logo, and then position the cursor at the end of the last sentence you typed.

12   Press ⌤ᴱⁿᵗᵉʳ three times to move the cursor to a position a little below the logo.

13   Click the down arrow of the **font size** box on the Standard toolbar and click **12**.

Center

14   On the Formatting toolbar, click the **Center** button.

The cursor moves to the center of the postcard.

15   Type **1234 Oak Street**, and then press ⌤ᴱⁿᵗᵉʳ.

16   Type **Seattle, WA 10101**, and then press ⌤ᴱⁿᵗᵉʳ.

17   Type **206-555-0100**.

18 On the Standard toolbar, click **File**, and then click **Save As**.

The **Save As** dialog box appears.

19 In the **File name** box, type **DirtPostcardSale**.

Save

20 Click **Save**.

Publisher 2002 saves your changes to DirtPostcardSale.

Close

21 Click the **Close** button.

DirtPostcardSale.pub closes.

22 On the Standard toolbar, click **File**, and then click **Exit**.

Publisher 2002 closes.

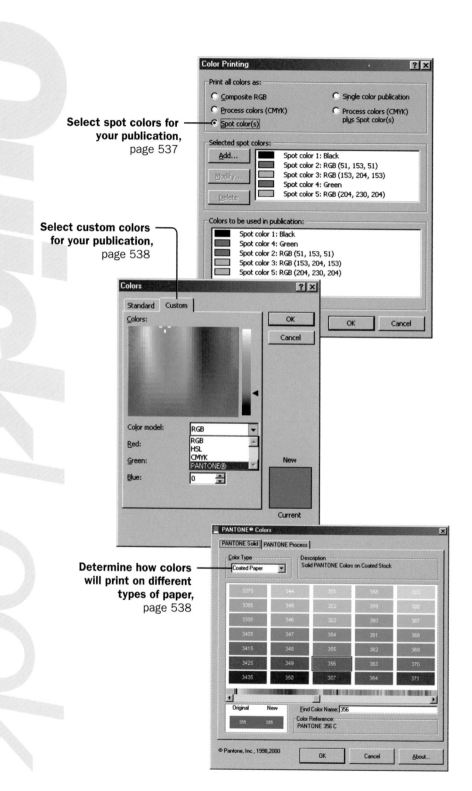

Select spot colors for your publication, page 537

Select custom colors for your publication, page 538

Determine how colors will print on different types of paper, page 538

Chapter 23
Printing Your Documents

After completing this chapter, you will be able to:

✔ Determine the nonprinting region for your printer.

✔ Prepare and send documents to a standard printer.

✔ Prepare and send documents to a commercial printer.

After you finish creating a document, you'll probably want to print it. Publisher 2002 makes it easy for you to format your document for printing, whether at a standard printer in your home or office or at a commercial printer. When you are creating a document for internal use or limited distribution, you will probably choose to print it at your standard printer; however, if you are creating a document for wide distribution, you will find it more economical to use an outside printing service (in other words, a **commercial printer**).

Regardless of your choice, you must consider two things. First, you should have your potential printing option in mind, as it dictates how you create the document. Second, be assured that no matter which printing option you design into the document, you can always change your mind and switch to the other printing method.

This chapter uses the practice files PrintDoc1, PrintDoc2, SpotColor, SpotColor2, and ProcessColor that you installed from this book's CD-ROM. For details about installing the practice files, see "Using the Book's CD-ROM" at the beginning of this book.

Determining Your Printer's Nonprintable Region

Most desktop printers, whether laser or inkjet, have an area on the page that they simply won't print. When you design your document onscreen, it will appear perfect, but when you print it, the edges may be cut off. When this happens, you must reformat your entire document, resizing illustrations and possibly even rearranging text. This can be extremely frustrating and time consuming.

In this exercise, you will determine your printer's nonprintable area.

1   Click **Start**.

The **Start** menu opens.

2 Click **Settings**, and then click **Printers**.

The Printers folder opens, revealing all the printers that are connected to your computer and available for use.

3 Right-click the printer you expect to use, and then click **Properties**.

The **Printer Properties** dialog box opens.

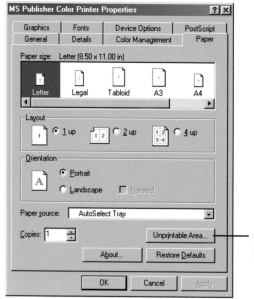

Determine your document's unprintable range.

4   In the **Printer Properties** dialog box, click the **Paper** tab.

Tip

Your **Properties** dialog box may not have a paper tab. If it does not, click the other tabs until you find one that contains information on the nonprintable area. If you do not find any information, consult your printer manual or contact your printer manufacturer.

5   Click the **Unprintable Area** button.

The **Unprintable Area** dialog box opens. The numbers in the Top, Left, Right, and Bottom boxes represent the distance in from the paper's edge that is unprintable. The default measurement is in inches. You can change it to millimeters by clicking **Millimeters** in the **Units** area.

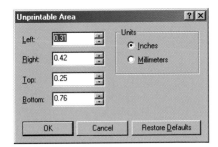

6   Click **OK** to close the **Unprintable Area** dialog box.

7   Click **OK** again to close the **Print Properties** dialog box.

Printing a Document to a Standard Printer

Most of the time, you'll choose to print your document on your standard printer. There are several ways to print a file. Publisher 2002 makes all of them easy—one method is so easy it takes only one click of the mouse (assuming the file is already open). You can also choose the target standard printer, and you can preview a file before printing it. This way you can "eyeball" it to see if there are any gross errors that you can correct before actually printing it.

PrintDoc1

In this exercise, you'll print the PrintDoc1 practice file three times. First you'll open it and print it with one click.

Open

1   On the Standard toolbar, click the **Open** button.

The **Open Publication** dialog box appears.

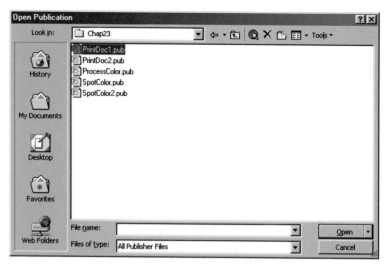

2 Navigate to Office XP SBS\Publisher\Chap23, and double-click the
PrintDoc1.pub file.

PrintDoc1.pub opens.

Print

3 Position the cursor over the **Print** button on the Formatting toolbar.

After a couple of seconds, a tooltip will appear identifying the printer to
which this file will be printed.

4 Verify that the selected printer is correct.

5 Click the **Print** icon to print your document.

The document will print on the designated printer.

Close

6 Click the **Close** button.

The file PrintDoc1.pub closes.

Even though it took a lot of steps to describe this process, once the file was
open, you printed it with just one click!

PrintDoc1

Now you're ready to select the target printer for the second printing. You'll use
PrintDoc1 to select the target printer.

Open

1 On the Standard toolbar, click the **Open** button.

The **Open Publication** dialog box appears.

2 Navigate to the Office XP SBS\Publisher\Chap23 folder, and double-click the **PrintDoc1.pub** file.

PrintDoc1.pub opens.

3 On the Standard toolbar, click **File**, and then click **Print**.

The **Print** dialog box opens.

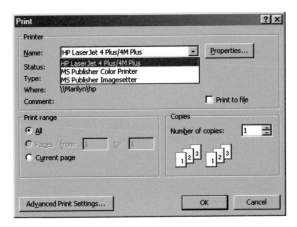

4 Click the down arrow of the **Name** box.

If you have more than one printer connected to your computer, you will see a list of the connected printers. If you have only one printer, you will see just one printer listed.

5 Click the printer to which you want to print this file.

6 In the **Print Range** area, verify that the **All** check box is selected.

7 In the **Copies** area, verify that *1* is listed in the **Number of copies** box.

8 Click **OK**.

The file will print on the designated printer.

Close

9 Click the **Close** button.

PrintDoc1.pub closes.

PrintDoc1

Finally you're ready to preview the document before printing it. This is always a good step to take so that you can catch errors before wasting paper, toner, or ink (or your valuable time). It's also a good idea to preview a file before printing it so that you can avoid costly errors, especially if you are printing on a color inkjet printer whose color cartridges are expensive. In this exercise, you'll preview PrintDoc1 before printing it.

Open

1 On the Standard toolbar, click the **Open** button.

The **Open Publication** dialog box appears.

2 Navigate to the Office XP SBS\Publisher\Chap23 folder, and double-click the **PrintDoc1.pub** file.

PrintDoc1.pub opens.

Print Preview
new for
OfficeXP

3 On the Standard toolbar, select **File**, and then click **Print Preview**.

Magnifying
Glass (+)

The file will appear in the Preview window. The cursor turns into a little magnifying glass with a plus sign in it. You can click it anywhere to zoom in and see the targeted area enlarged.

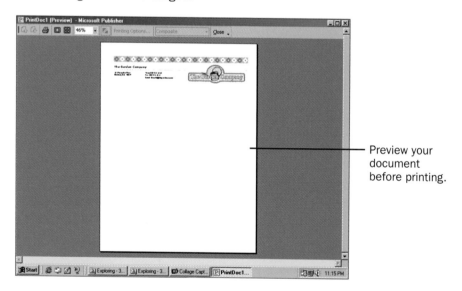

Preview your
document
before printing.

Print

4 On the Print Preview toolbar, click the **Print** button.

PrintDoc1.pub prints on the designated printer.

Tip

Instead of printing the file, you could click the **Close** button on the toolbar to return to the file to fix any errors you saw in the preview.

5 Click **Close** to return to the file.

The Print Preview window closes.

Close

6 Click the **Close** button.

PrintDoc1.pub closes.

Printing a Range of Pages to a Standard Printer

Sometimes you may want to print just a portion of your file because, for whatever reason, you don't need all the pages. For example, The Garden Company might want to print just the inside of the newsletter to see if it has the proper "eye appeal." Publisher 2002 makes it possible for you to specify the exact page or range of pages you want to print.

PrintDoc2

In this exercise, you will print pages 2 and 3 of PrintDoc2.

Open

1 On the Standard toolbar, click the **Open** button.

The **Open Publication** dialog box appears.

2 Navigate to Office XP SBS\Publisher\Chap23 folder, and double-click the **PrintDoc2.pub** file.

PrintDoc2.pub opens.

3 On the Standard toolbar, select **File**, and then click **Print**.

The **Print** dialog box opens.

4 In the **Print range** area, click **Pages from**.

5 In the **Pages from** box, type the number 2.

6 In the **Pages to** box, type the number 3.

7 Click **OK**.

Only pages 2 and 3 will print to the designated printer.

Close

8   Click the **Close** button.

PrintDoc2.pub closes.

Printing a Single Page to a Standard Printer

Sometimes you want to print just a single page in a document. This is especially handy if you want to use a page as a sample or show it to a colleague.

PrintDoc2

In this exercise, you will print page 4 of PrintDoc2.

Open

1   On the Standard toolbar, click the **Open** button.

The **Open Publication** dialog box appears.

2   Navigate to the Office XP SBS\Publisher\Chap23 folder, and then double-click the **PrintDoc2.pub** file.

PrintDoc2 opens

3   Click on the *4* on the **Page Navigation** button at the bottom of the screen.

PrintDoc2.pub opens to the last page.

4   On the Standard toolbar, click **File**, and then click **Print**.

The **Print** dialog box opens.

5   In the **Print range** area, select the **Current page** option.

6   Click **OK** to close the **Print** dialog box.

Page 4 of PrintDoc2.pub will print on the designated printer.

Close

7   Click the **Close** button.

PrintDoc2.pub closes.

Canceling a Print Job on a Standard Printer

Oops. You just clicked **Print** and then realized that you forgot to fix something. No problem. If your print job is not too short and you're quick enough on the draw, you can cancel it.

PrintDoc2

In this exercise, you will send PrintDoc2 to the standard printer and then immediately cancel the print job.

Open

1   On the Standard toolbar, click the **Open** button.

The **Open Publication** dialog box appears.

2 Navigate to the Office XP SBS\Publisher\Chap23 folder, and then double-click the **PrintDoc2.pub** file.

PrintDoc2 opens.

Print

3 On the Standard toolbar, click the **Print** button.

This will send the entire file to your standard printer without your having to make any print layout decisions. A little printer icon appears in the notification area of the Taskbar, which is usually at the bottom right of your screen.

4 Double-click the **Printer** icon in the notification area of your screen.

The printer status window opens, listing all jobs in the print queue.

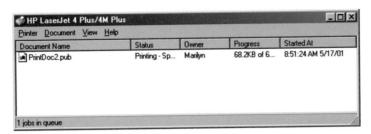

5 Click your print job in the list.

6 Click the **Printer** menu, and then click **Purge Print Documents**.

The printer will probably not stop immediately, because it will continue to print any data it already received, but it will stop as soon as it has printed that data.

Close

7 Click the **Close** button.

The printer status window closes.

8 Click the **Close** button in the Publisher window.

PrintDoc2.pub closes.

Preparing a Document for a Commercial Printer

A commercial printer is a printing service that produces your project using **printing plates**. Some large companies have an in-house printing service, but most businesses use outside companies. A commercial printer is a good choice for publishing your document if you are going to print a large quantity for wide distribution or if you have a lot of photographs or complex graphics. Standard computer printers are typically slow, printing only a few pages per minute, and expensive, especially if you're using a color inkjet.

Commercial printers also offer you a greater choice of **paper stocks**. Not all papers will work in laser or inkjet printers, so as you design your project you should keep in mind the paper on which you plan to print it. Heavy paper like cardstock is especially wearing on a standard printer. If you envision your document being printed on a heavier-than-normal (normal is referred to as 20-28 pound) paper stock, you should seriously consider setting it up for a commercial printer.

Process-Color or Spot-Color Processing?

If you're planning to send your document to a commercial printer, you need to make a few decisions even before you begin designing it. You should consult with the commercial printer to determine which printing process is best for your document: **process color** (also called CMYK, which stands for cyan-magenta-yellow-black), **spot color**, or a combination of the two processes. Once you've made that decision, you can begin to design your document with the color printing process in mind.

- Process-color (CMYK) printing can reproduce all the colors on a printed page. It is especially appropriate for printing documents that include full-color photographs, detailed and/or multi-colored graphics or any illustrations that require exceptionally high-quality resolution. These types of documents might include catalogs, product flyers, or other marketing pieces where the depiction of your product must be as accurate or high-quality as possible.

- Spot-color processing uses shadings of black and one or more other colors. It's especially effective when you're printing a document with headings, borders, or logos that require emphasis, or line drawings or other graphics that require color matching. It's also the best choice when your document will use special inks or **varnish**. These types of documents might be newsletters or booklets (where the cover would be varnished).

Another consideration is cost. Because every color in a process-color job requires a separate color plate, it is a more expensive choice. This is especially significant if the document you are printing is going to have a small print run. Spot-color processing is not only less expensive, it's also more flexible in its pricing. Screen tints allow the commercial printer to create various shades without having to use separate plates. Of course, there are other elements that dictate cost, too, like paper choice, graphics, number of graphics, and final printed quantities.

Setting Up a Publication for Spot-Color Printing

Publisher 2002 includes a **Commercial Printing** option that allows you to prepare any document for printing by an outside service. Spot-color printing uses semi-transparent, pre-mixed inks that usually come from standard color-matching guides. Your commercial printer should have a library of colors for you to look at. Be aware that the colors you see on your computer screen may not match the final outcome. You should discuss this with your commercial printer to ensure your satisfaction with the final product.

SpotColor

In this exercise, you will prepare the practice file SpotColor for spot-color printing by a commercial printer. The Garden Company might choose this method of printing for a flyer that uses more line art than photo art as it is less expensive and the color resolution is not as important.

Open

1 On the Standard toolbar, click the **Open** button.

The **Open Publication** dialog box appears.

2 Navigate to the Office XP SBS\Publisher\Chap23 folder, and double-click the **SpotColor.pub** file.

SpotColor.pub opens.

3 Click the **Tools** menu, click **Commercial Printing Tools**, and then click **Color Printing**.

The **Color Printing** dialog box appears.

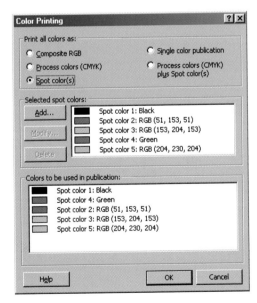

4 In the **Print all colors as** area, click the **Spot color(s)** option.

Tip

When you select **Spot color(s)**, Publisher 2002 automatically includes black as one of the colors in your document. The default number of colors is two but you may add up to five additional spot colors. When you choose black and one spot color, Publisher automatically converts all nonblack colors in your document to tints of the selected spot color. If you choose two spot colors in addition to black, Publisher changes all colors that match spot color #2 to 100% of that color and all other colors (except black) to tints of spot color #1.

5 Click **OK** to close the **Color Printing** dialog box.

The changes will be reflected in the document.

Close

6 Click the **Close** button.

SpotColor.pub closes.

Changing Colors in a Spot-Color Document

When you prepare a document for spot-color printing, you may want to include more than the default colors or you may even want to add a color that Publisher 2002 didn't include. Using the **Add** and **Modify** buttons, this becomes an easy task.

In this exercise, you will change a green spot color to mauve in the SpotColor2 practice file.

Open

1 On the Standard toolbar, click the **Open** button.

The **Open Publication** dialog box appears.

2 Navigate to the Office XP SBS\Publisher\Chap23 folder, and then double-click the **SpotColor2.pub** file.

SpotColor2.pub opens.

3 Click the **Tools** menu, click **Commercial Printing Tools**, and then click **Color Printing**.

The **Color Printing** dialog box opens.

4 In the **Print all colors as** area, select the **Spot color(s)** option.

The selected colors appear in the **Selected spot colors** box and the **Add** button becomes active. The selected colors also appear in the **Colors to be used in publication** box.

5 In the **Selected spot colors** area, select **Spot color 4: Green**.

The **Modify** and **Delete** buttons become active.

6 Click **Modify**.

The **Colors** dialog box opens.

Standard tab

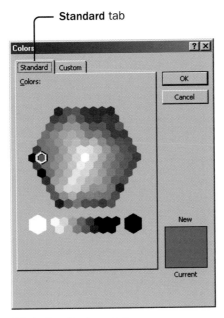

7 Click the **Custom** tab.

The **Color model** drop-down list offers these four options: RGB, CMYK, HSL, or PANTONE® .

Tip

A **color model** is a method of specifying color. When you choose an option, keep in mind that RGB (red-green-blue) and HSL (hue-saturation-luminance) are models for devices that transmit light, like your video monitor, while CMYK (cyan-magenta-yellow-black) and PANTONE are for actual printed documents.

Custom tab

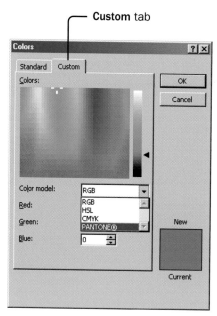

8   Click the down arrow of the **Color model** box, and select **PANTONE®** .
    The **PANTONE® Colors** dialog box opens.

Choose paper type.

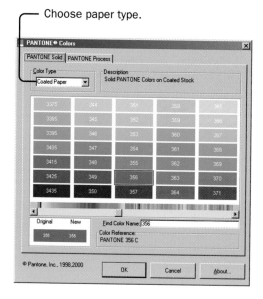

Tip

The first time you choose **PANTONE®**, you will see a copyright notice. Read it, then click **OK** to close the box. It will not appear again.

9 If the **PANTONE® Colors** dialog box did not open to the **PANTONE® Solid** tab, click it.

Tip

When the **PANTONE® Colors** dialog box opens, it will open to the tab most recently accessed, so if you or someone else used Publisher 2002 previously and used the **PANTONE® Process** tab, that will be the one to come up.

The **PANTONE® Solid** tab offers a number of paper type and color choices.

10 In the **Color Type** area, click the down arrow to reveal the color type options.

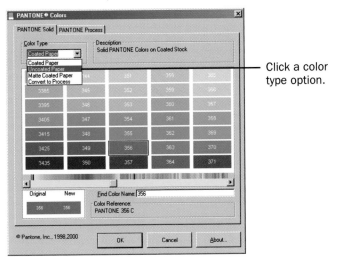

Click a color type option.

11 Select the **Uncoated Paper** option.

12 In the **Find Color Name** box, type 530.

13 Press [Enter].

The color designated as PANTONE 530 C (a mauve) is selected.

14 Click **OK** to return to the **Colors** dialog box.

15 Click **OK** to return to the **Color Printing** dialog box.

Notice that Spot Color #4, which was originally green, is now the mauve represented by PANTONE 530 C.

16 Click **OK** to return to the file.

Save

17 On the Standard toolbar, click the **Save** button.

Publisher saves your changes.

Close

18 Click the **Close** button.

SpotColor2.pub closes.

Setting Up a Publication for Process-Color Printing

When your document includes full-color photographs, detailed multi-colored graphics, or simply requires high resolution or high-quality images, your best printing choice is to use a commercial or outside printing service and process-color printing. Because process-color printing can reproduce all colors on a printed page, it is especially effective for documents like brochures where products are illustrated with detailed artwork or photographs. In anticipation of Mother's Day, The Garden Company has prepared a flyer offering orchids, and process-color printing is the best option for producing it.

ProcessColor

In this exercise, you will prepare the ProcessColor practice file for process-color printing by an outside, commercial printer.

Open

1 On the Standard toolbar, click the **Open** button.

The **Open Publication** dialog box appears.

2 Navigate to the Office XP SBS\Publisher\Chap23 folder, and then double-click the **ProcessColor.pub** file.

ProcessColor.pub opens.

3 Click the **Tools** menu, click **Commercial Printing Tools**, and then click **Color Printing**.

The **Color Printing** dialog box opens.

4 In the **Print all colors as** area, click the **Process color (CMYK)** option.

Publisher 2002 automatically identifies the colors to be used in the document and lists them in the **Colors to be used in publication** box.

5 Click **OK** to close the **Color Printing** dialog box and return to the file.

Save

6 On the Standard toolbar, click the **Save** button.

Publisher saves your changes.

Close

7 Click the **Close** button.

ProcessColor.pub closes.

VII

Microsoft
Outlook

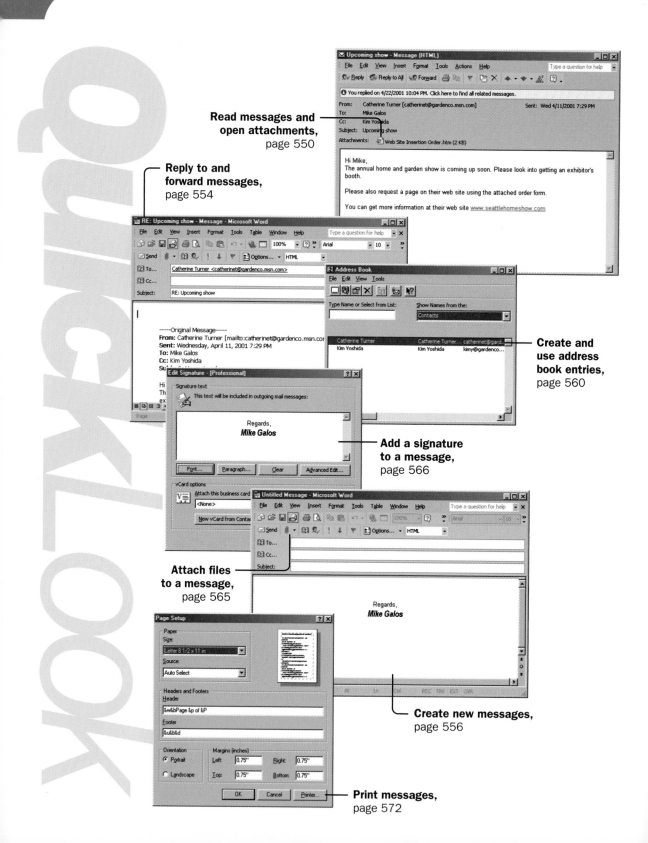

Read messages and open attachments, page 550

Reply to and forward messages, page 554

Create and use address book entries, page 560

Add a signature to a message, page 566

Attach files to a message, page 565

Create new messages, page 556

Print messages, page 572

Chapter 24
Working with E-Mail

After completing this chapter, you will be able to:

✔ **Read messages and open attachments.**

✔ **Reply to and forward messages.**

✔ **Create new messages and attach files and signatures.**

✔ **Create and use address book entries.**

✔ **Print messages.**

Microsoft Outlook 2002 is a desktop communications program that helps you manage your time and information more effectively and enables you to share information and collaborate with others more easily.

Electronic mail, or **e-mail**, is an essential form of communication in today's workplace. Outlook gives you all the tools you need to use e-mail effectively and to manage your electronic messages. With Outlook, you can

■ Send and receive e-mail messages

■ Attach files to your messages

■ Create and manage an address book

■ Organize and archive your messages

■ Personalize your messages

This chapter uses the practice files NewSupplier, NextShow, and Attachment that you installed from this book's CD-ROM onto your hard disk and copied into Outlook. For details about installing and copying the practice files, see "Using the Book's CD-ROM" at the beginning of this book.

This chapter first discusses the various ways Outlook can be set up and what to expect when you first start the program. Then you'll learn how to read and write messages, send and receive messages, attach files to messages, and create and use an address book.

Important

The exercises in this chapter assume that you are using Word as your default e-mail editor.

Starting Outlook for the First Time

Outlook 2002 supports e-mail accounts that work with a computer running Microsoft Exchange Server or a computer set up as an Internet mail server. This section discusses these two types of accounts and explains what you might expect to see the first time you start Outlook.

If you are connected to a **local area network (LAN)** that includes a computer running **Microsoft Exchange Server**, you send and receive e-mail both internally (within your organization) and externally (over the Internet) using that server. Your network or system administrator will supply the information you need to set up an Exchange e-mail account.

If you are working on a stand-alone computer or on a network that does not have its own mail server, using Internet mail requires that you have an e-mail account with an **Internet service provider (ISP)**. You connect to the ISP using a modem and a phone line, DSL line, or cable; or through a LAN.

- If you are using a modem, you can manually establish a connection when you need it, or you can set up dial-up networking to automatically connect whenever you start Outlook. Your ISP can provide the phone number, modem settings, and any other special information you need for both types of connection.

- If you are connected to a LAN, it must be configured to provide access to your ISP from your computer. Your network or system administrator can provide you with the appropriate information to gain access to Internet mail via the LAN.

- Regardless of how you connect to your ISP, in order to send and receive Internet mail, you will need to know the names of your incoming and outgoing e-mail servers, your account name, and your password.

Different Types of Internet Mail Accounts

Microsoft Outlook 2002 supports more types of Internet e-mail accounts than ever—POP3, IMAP, and HTTP (including Hotmail).

- **Post Office Protocol 3 (POP3)** is a very common type of e-mail account provided by ISPs. With a POP3 account, you connect to an e-mail server and download your messages to your local computer.

- **Internet Message Access Protocol (IMAP)** is similar to POP3 except that your messages are stored on the e-mail server. You connect to the server to read message headers and select which messages you want to download to your local computer.

Hotmail
Support
new for
OfficeXP

- **Hypertext Transfer Protocol (HTTP)** is used whenever you access Web pages from the Internet. When HTTP is used as an e-mail protocol, messages are stored, retrieved, and displayed as individual Web pages. Hotmail is an example of an HTTP e-mail account.

When you start Outlook for the first time, what you see depends on whether you have upgraded Outlook or are using it on this computer for the first time.

Upgrading to Outlook 2002

If you have used a previous version of Outlook on your computer, you already have an Outlook **profile**. This profile is a collection of all the data necessary to access one or more e-mail accounts and address books. In this case, Outlook 2002 picks up your existing profile settings, and you don't have to enter them again to start using the new version of Outlook.

Using Outlook for the First Time

If this is the first time you have ever used Outlook on this computer, you will be asked to create a profile. To complete this step, you will need specific information about your e-mail account, including your account name, your password, and the names of the incoming and outgoing e-mail servers that handle your account. Your system administrator or ISP can provide you with this information.

Here are the general steps for setting up Outlook:

Microsoft
Outlook

1   On the desktop, double-click the **Microsoft Outlook** icon.

When Outlook starts, you see the **New Profile** dialog box.

2   Type a name for your profile (typically your full name), and click **OK**.

The **E-mail Accounts** dialog box appears.

3   Click **Add a new e-mail account**, and then click **Next**.

The **Server Type** dialog box appears.

4   Select the type of your e-mail account, and click **Next**.

An **account settings** dialog box appears. The content of this dialog box is determined by the type of e-mail account you selected in the **Server Type** dialog box.

5   From here on, you will need to enter the information and follow the instructions provided by your system administrator or ISP.

When you complete the process, the Outlook window appears.

Important

If you upgraded to Outlook 2002 from an earlier version, any custom settings you made for your old version of the program carry over to the new version. As a result, as you work your way through the exercises in this book, some of the instructions might not work quite the same way for you, and your screen might not look the same as the book's graphics. The instructions and graphics are based on a default installation of Outlook on a networked computer with an Exchange e-mail account. If you are not working on a network or you have changed the default settings, don't worry. You will still be able to follow along with the exercises, but you might occasionally have to reverse a setting or skip a step. (For example, if AutoPreview is already active on your screen, you would skip the step to turn on AutoPreview.)

Reading Messages and Opening Attachments

When you start Outlook, any new messages are moved from your e-mail server, or **downloaded**, to your Inbox. With Outlook, you can view and read your messages in several ways:

■   You can scan for your most important messages by using AutoPreview, which displays the first few lines of messages in your Inbox.

■   You can quickly read a message without opening it by looking at the **Preview** pane.

■ You can open the message in its own window for easier reading.

E-mail messages can contain many types of files as attachments. For example, a colleague might send a Microsoft Word document to you by attaching it to an e-mail message. You can open these files from the **Preview** pane or from an open message.

NextShow

For the exercises in this chapter, you'll act as Mike Galos, the administrative assistant for The Garden Company, a plant and garden accessories store. The practice files used in this book will reflect this assumed identity. In this exercise, you will preview a message, open a message, and open an attachment.

Inbox

1 If your Outlook window shows a summary of the appointments, tasks, and messages you need to attend to today, click the **Inbox** icon on the Outlook Bar on the left side of the window. Then if necessary, maximize the window.

You now see the **Inbox**, which is where you store and manage your e-mail messages.

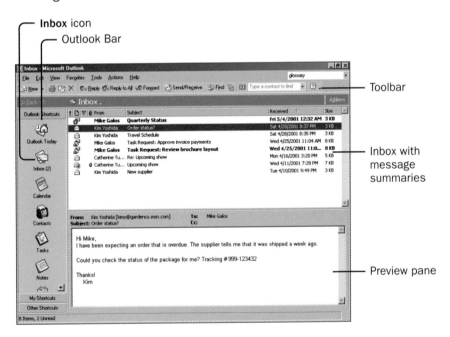

— **Inbox** icon
— Outlook Bar
— Toolbar
— Inbox with message summaries
— Preview pane

2 Turn on AutoPreview by clicking **AutoPreview** on the **View** menu.

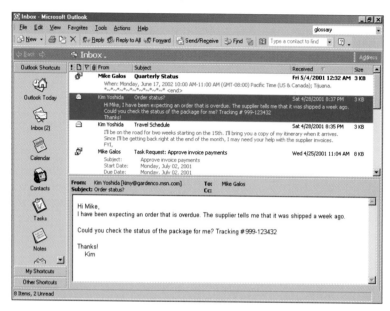

You can now see up to three lines of each of the messages in your Inbox.

3 If necessary, scroll up or down in your Inbox to locate the **Upcoming show** message from Catherine Turner, the owner of The Garden Company. Then click the message to display it in the Preview pane.

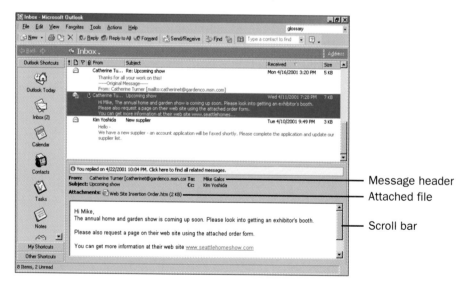

Message header

Attached file

Scroll bar

Enhanced
Preview Pane
new for
OfficeXP

Using the scroll bar in the Preview pane, you can see the full content of the message. Note that the Preview pane shows the full **message header** (the information that appears at the top of the e-mail message, including the sender, recipient, and date) and the names of any attached files.

4 To open the attachment double-click **Web Site Insertion Order.htm**.

5 If you see a message warning you about opening attachments, click the **Open it** option, and then click **OK**.

The Web Site Insertion Order form appears in your Web browser.

6 Return to the Inbox by clicking its name on the Windows taskbar.

7 Close the Preview pane by clicking **Preview Pane** on the **View** menu.

If your Inbox contains many messages, you can now see more of them at a glance.

8 Open the **Upcoming show** message by double-clicking it in the Inbox.

The message appears in its own **Message** window.

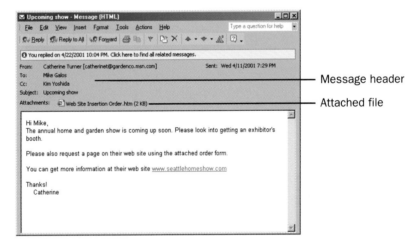

Message header

Attached file

Note the message header and the names of any attached files at the top.

Tip

Don't worry if your window is not the same size as this one. As with other windows, you can size Outlook windows to suit the way you work by using the **Maximize** and **Restore** buttons or by dragging the window's frame.

Close

9 Click the **Close** button to close the **Message** window.

Responding to Messages

You can respond to messages in several ways. You can reply to only the person who sent the message, or you can reply to the person who sent the message and all the people whose addresses were on the original To and Cc lines. Whether you reply to only the sender or to everyone, your reply will not include any files that were attached to the original message.

You can forward a message you have received to anyone, not just the person who originally sent the message or any of the other recipients. A forwarded message will include any files that were attached to the original message.

NextShow

As Mike Galos, the administrative assistant for The Garden Company, your first task of the day is to read and respond to your e-mail messages. In this exercise, you will reply to and forward messages.

1 With your Inbox displayed, double-click the **Upcoming show** message from Catherine Turner.

The message appears in the **Message** window.

Note that this message was sent to you, Mike Galos, and was copied to Kim Yoshida, the head buyer for The Garden Company. The message also includes an attachment.

Reply

2 On the toolbar, click the **Reply** button.

The Reply form is displayed on your screen.

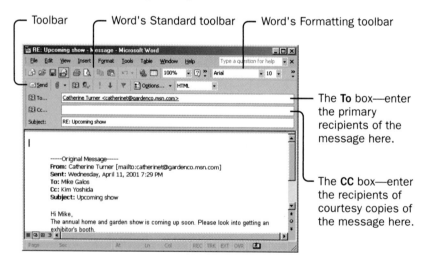

Note that the reply will be sent only to Catherine Turner and that the attachment is not included. Note also that a prefix, *RE:*, has been added to the subject line. This prefix indicates that this is a response to an earlier message.

Tip

If Microsoft Word is your default e-mail editor, the Reply form displays Word's Standard and Formatting toolbars in addition to the regular toolbar. If you don't use the buttons on Word's toolbars, you can turn the toolbars off to save space. On the form's **View** menu, point to **Toolbars**, and then click **Standard** or **Formatting**.

3 The insertion point is already in the message box, so type **What size booth would you like?**

4 Click the **Send** button.

Important

The e-mail addresses in these exercises are fictitious—any messages you send to these addresses will be returned to your Inbox because the messages are undeliverable. Simply delete any returned message by clicking it and then clicking the **Delete** button.

5 If sending the message closes the **Message** window, double-click the message to open the window again.

6 On the toolbar, click the **Reply to All** button.

The Reply form appears. You can see from the message header that this reply will be sent to both Catherine Turner and Kim Yoshida. Again, the attachment is not included.

Important

Because this practice message was copied into your Inbox rather than sent to you, your address (*mikeg@gardenco.msn.com*) also appears in the **To** box. When you reply to a message that someone else sent to you, your address will not appear in the **To** box, and your reply will not be sent back to you.

7 Type **I have faxed the form to the show organizers**, and then click the **Send** button.

The Reply form closes.

8 If necessary, reopen the **Message** window, and then on the toolbar, click the **Forward** button.

The Forward Message form appears.

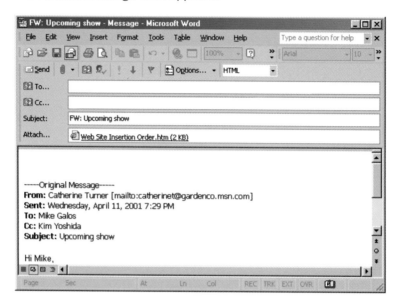

Note that the address lines are blank and that the attachment is included. Note also that a prefix, *FW:*, has been added to the subject line. This prefix indicates that this is a forwarded message.

9 In the **To** box, type your own e-mail address (not that of Mike Galos).

10 Press the ⎚ key until you get to the message body, type **Thought you might be interested in this**, and click the **Send** button.

The message closes, and it will now be forwarded back to you. If the message arrives quickly, look at it in your Inbox, and then open it and examine the message header. Note how the subject line and attachment appear. If your message doesn't arrive quickly, you can examine it later.

Close

11 If necessary, close the open **Message** window by clicking its **Close** button.

Creating New Messages

With Outlook, communicating by e-mail is quick and easy. You can send messages to people in your office and at other locations. And, in addition to using Outlook's many formatting options, you can embed hyperlinks and attach files to your messages.

Word as default editor
new for OfficeXP

If you installed Word 2002 when you installed Outlook, Outlook 2002 will use Word as its default e-mail editor. Many of Word's powerful text editing capabilities, including styles, tables, and themes, are available to you as you create messages in Outlook. Also, Word will check your spelling as you type, correcting many errors automatically. You can also tell Word to check the spelling of your message when you send it.

Tip

If Word is not your default e-mail editor and you would like it to be, click **Options** on the **Tools** menu. Click the **Mail Format** tab, and click the **Use Microsoft Word to edit e-mail messages** check box. To turn off Word as your default e-mail editor, make sure the check box is cleared.

Important

The exercises in this chapter assume that you are using Word as your default e-mail editor.

In this exercise, you will compose a new e-mail message. You don't need any practice files for this exercise.

New Mail Message

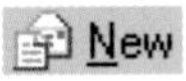

1 On the toolbar, click the **New Mail Message** button.

A new, blank message appears in the Message form.

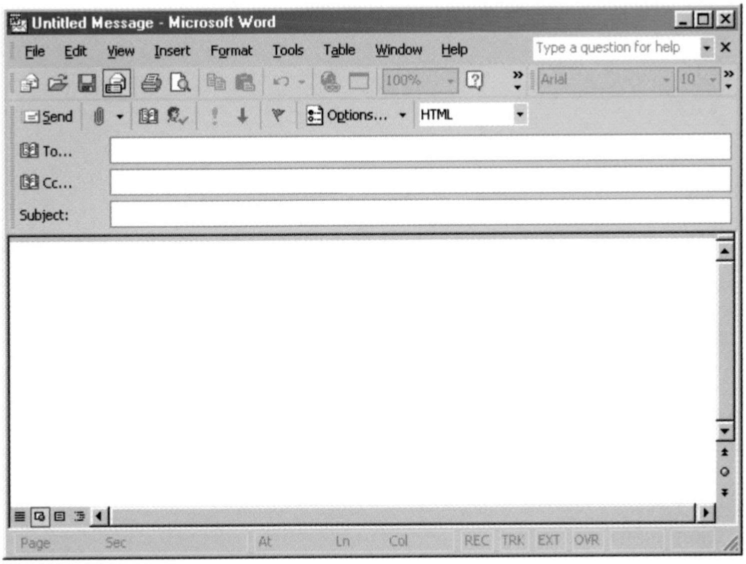

Take a few minutes to investigate the menus and menu options. If you are familiar with Word, you will recognize many of them.

Tip

By clicking the down arrow to the right of the **New Mail Message** button, you can create something other than a new e-mail message. You can create new appointments, contacts, tasks, and Office documents as well.

2 In the **To** box, type catherinet@gardenco.msn.com. Then type ; (a semi-colon) and a space, and type kimy@gardenco.msn.com.

Note that you use semicolons to separate multiple addresses.

Tip

If you are working on a network that uses Exchange Server, when you send messages to other people on your network, you can type just the part of the address that is to the left of the @ sign. The remaining part of the address identifies the server that handles the e-mail account, and within an organization, the server name is not needed.

Automatically completes addresses

new for **Office**XP

When your recipient's address is in your **address book** or you've typed it in a message header before, Outlook automatically completes the address for you, and pressing the [Tab] key inserts the entry. If there are multiple matches, Outlook presents a list of items that match what you've typed so far. Use the arrow keys to select the item you want, and press [Enter].

3 Press the [Tab] key, and in the **Cc** box, type your own e-mail address.

Tip

If you want to send a copy of a message to a person without the other recipients' being aware of it, you can send a "blind" copy. Display the **Bcc** box by clicking the arrow to the right of the **Options** button, and then clicking **Bcc**. Then type the person's e-mail address in the **Bcc** box.

4 Press the [Tab] key to move to the **Subject** box, and type Today's schedule.

5 Press the [Tab] key again, and type Here are the people who will be working today. Then press the [Enter] key twice.

Important

After your message has been open for a period of time, Outlook saves a **draft** of it in the Drafts folder so that any work you have done is saved if you are somehow disconnected from Outlook before you send the message. If you close a message without sending it, Outlook asks you if you want to save the message in the Drafts folder. To find these messages later, click the Drafts folder in the **Folder List**. If the **Folder List** is not visible, click **Folder List** on the **View** menu to display it.

6 On the **Table** menu, point to **Insert**, and then click **Table**.

Word's **Insert Table** dialog box appears.

7 Change the number of columns to **4**, and click **OK**.

A table appears in your message.

8 Fill in the cells of the table as shown here, pressing ⓣⓐⓑ to move from cell to cell:

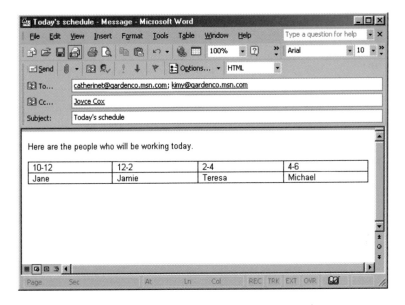

9 Click the **Send** button.

The Message form closes, and the message is sent on its way.

Using an Address Book

You can store cumbersome e-mail addresses in an address book so that you can avoid having to type them each time you send a message. With an address book, you can click the **To** button in the Message form, and then select recipients by name.

Tip

With or without an address book, you can address messages by typing the full address into the **To**, **Cc**, or **Bcc** boxes in the Message form.

If you are using Outlook with Exchange Server, an Exchange address book, which is called a **Global Address List** and contains the e-mail addresses of all the people on your network, might already be available to you. If a Global Address List is available to you, Outlook will use this as your default address book. Because the Global Address List is maintained by your system administrator, you cannot add to it; you must use another address book to create any entries not included in that list. By default, entries you created are stored in your Contacts folder, which is a type of address book.

Address book entries can be for an individual contact or for a **distribution list**—a group of individual addresses stored under a single name. For example, to facilitate communication with a team, you might create a distribution list including the addresses for all the people working on a particular project.

As Mike Galos, the administrative assistant of The Garden Company, you want to add a couple of addresses to your address book. You also want to create a **distribution list** so that you can quickly send mail to both addresses at once. In this exercise, you will add, update, and delete address book entries, create a distribution list, and address a message using your address book. You don't need any practice files for this exercise.

1　On the **Tools** menu, click **Address Book**.

　　The **Address Book** window appears. If you are working on a network, the **Show Names from the** setting is **Global Address List**. Otherwise, it is **Contacts**.

2　If necessary, click the down arrow to the right of the **Show Names from the** box, and click **Contacts** in the drop-down list.

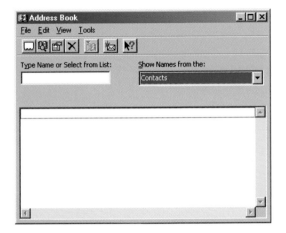

New Entry

3   On the toolbar, click the **New Entry** button.

The **New Entry** dialog box appears.

4   In the **Select the entry type** box, click **New Contact**, and then click **OK**.

The Contact form appears.

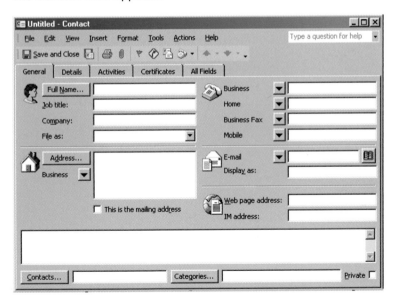

5 In the **Full Name** box, type your boss's name, Catherine Turner.

6 In the **E-mail** box, type your boss's e-mail address, catherinet@gardenco.msn.com.

7 Click the **Save and Close** button.

The Contact form closes, and the contact appears in the **Address Book** window.

8 Now you'll add another entry. On the toolbar, click the **New Entry** button.

The **New Entry** dialog box appears.

9 In the **Select the entry type** box, click **New Contact**, and then click **OK**.

The Contact form appears.

10 In the **Full Name** box, type the name of The Garden Company's head buyer, Kim Yoshida.

11 In the **E-mail** box, type the head buyer's e-mail address, kimy@gardenco.msn.com.

Friendly names instead of e-mail addresses
new for
OfficeXP

12 Press the Tab key, and in the **Display as** box, delete the e-mail address and parentheses so that the box contains only the name *Kim Yoshida*.

13 Click the **Save and Close** button.

The Contact form closes, and the contact appears in the **Address Book** window. Your address book should look like this:

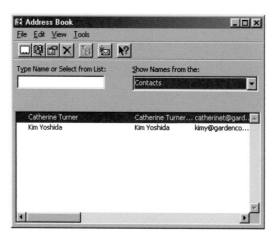

14 Now you'll create a distribution list. On the toolbar, click the **New Entry** button.

The **New Entry** dialog box appears.

15 In the **Select the entry type** box, click **New Distribution List**, and then click **OK**.

The Distribution List form appears.

Tip

If a form window is too small to work with easily, you can click the **Maximize** button or resize it by dragging its frame.

16 In the **Name** box, type **Garden Co**, and then click the **Select Members** button.

The **Select Members** dialog box appears.

17 If necessary, click the down arrow to the right of the **Show Names from the** box, and click **Contacts** in the drop-down list.

18 In the **Name** list, click **Kim Yoshida**, and click the **Members** button.

Kim Yoshida is added to the distribution list.

19 In the **Name** list, click **Catherine Turner**, and click the **Members** button.

Catherine Turner is added to the distribution list.

Tip

To add multiple names to the distribution list simultaneously, click a name in the **Name** list, hold down the Ctrl key, click any additional names you want to add, and then click the **Members** button.

20 Click **OK** to close the **Select Members** dialog box.

You return to the Distribution List form.

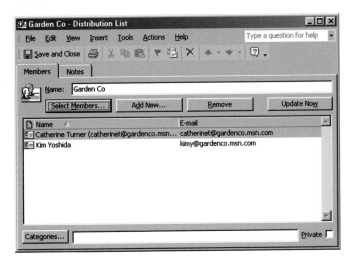

21 Click the **Save and Close** button.

The Distribution List form closes, and the **Address Book** window appears.

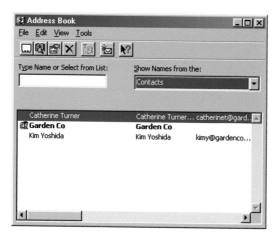

Close

22 Click the **Close** button.

The **Address Book** window closes.

New Mail
Message

New

23 On the toolbar, click the **New Mail Message** button.

A new, blank message opens in the Message form.

To...

24 Click the **To** button to the left of the **To** box.

The **Select Names** dialog box appears.

25 If necessary, change the **Show Names from the** setting to **Contacts**.

26 In the **Name** list, click **Kim Yoshida**, and then click the **To** button.

Kim's name is added to the list of recipients in the **To** box.

27 In the **Name** list, click **Garden Co**, and then click the **Cc** button.

The distribution list's name is added to the list of recipients in the **Cc** box.

28 Click **OK**.

The **Select Names** dialog box closes, and the recipient names are added to the **To** and **Cc** boxes on the Message form.

Tip

You can type distribution list names in the **To** and **Cc** boxes just like any other e-mail address. Outlook will then match what you type with the name in your address book and will display the name as bold and underlined, which indicates that the name represents a distribution list rather than an individual address.

29 Click in the **Subject** box, and type Test.

30 Close the message without sending it. When prompted to save it, click **No**.

Attaching Files to Messages

Sending files such as documents or spreadsheets via e-mail is a convenient way to share your files with others. Outlook makes it easy to attach files to your messages.

Important

> You can attach any type of file to an e-mail message, but when sending attachments, be sure that your recipients have the software required to open your file. For example, if you are attaching a Word document, your recipients must have Word installed on their computers to open your attachment.

Attachment

As the assistant for The Garden Company, you have been asked to craft a standard form for a company letter. You want to send your first draft to the company's owner for review. In this exercise, you will attach a Word document to an e-mail message. The document you will use is located in the Office XP SBS\Outlook\Chap24 folder on your hard disk.

New Mail
Message

1 On the toolbar, click the **New Mail Message** button.

A new, blank message appears in the Message form.

2 In the **To** box, type catherinet@gardenco.msn.com; and then type your own address.

3 Click in the **Subject** box, and type The First Draft.

4 Press the ⌨Tab key, type Here it is – let me know what you think in the message body, and press ⌨Enter.

Insert File

5 On the form's toolbar, click the **Insert File** button.

The **Insert File** dialog box appears.

6 Browse to the Office XP SBS\Outlook\Chap24 folder (which is probably located on drive C), and double-click the folder name.

The contents of the folder are displayed.

7 Click the **Attachment** document, and then click the **Insert** button.

The document appears in the **Attach** box in the message header. Your message now looks similar to this one:

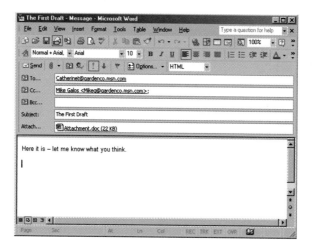

Tip

You can embed a hyperlink to a Web site in an e-mail message simply by including the site's **uniform resource locator (URL)**. To embed a hyperlink, simply type the URL (for example, *www.microsoft.com*) followed by a space. Outlook formats the URL to appear as a link. Your recipients can simply click the link in the message to open the Web page.

8   Close the message without sending it. If prompted to save it, click **No**.

Adding Signatures to Messages

By using a **signature**, you can personalize your messages and save time. A signature is a predefined block of text that can be inserted, manually or automatically, at the end of your messages. Your signature can include any text you like but typically includes your name, title, and company name. Signatures can also be formatted in the same ways that message text can be formatted. You can define several different signatures to choose from, perhaps one for professional use and one for personal use.

In this exercise, you will create a signature and then set Outlook to insert it in all new messages. You don't need any practice files for this exercise.

1   On the **Tools** menu, click **Options**.

The **Options** dialog box appears.

2   Click the **Mail Format** tab.

These options are shown:

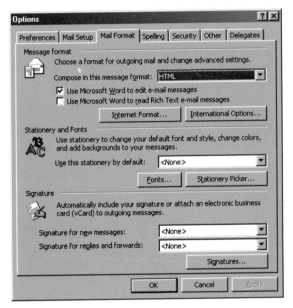

3   Click the **Signatures** button, and then click the **New** button.

The **Create New Signature** dialog box appears.

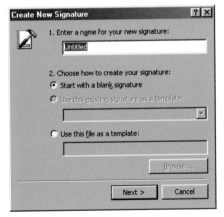

4   Type Professional as the name of your signature, and click the **Next** button.

The **Edit Signature** dialog box appears.

5   In the **Signature text** box, type Regards and a comma, press Enter, and then type Mike Galos.

6   Select **Mike Galos**, and then click the **Font** button.

The **Font** dialog box appears.

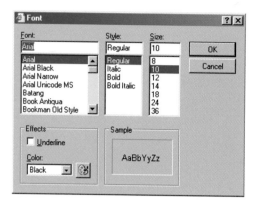

7 Change the font to **Arial Narrow**, the style to **Bold Italic**, and the size to **14**. Then click **OK**.

The name changes to reflect the new font, style, and size.

8 Select both lines of the signature, and click the **Paragraph** button.

The **Paragraph** dialog box appears.

9 Click **Center**, and click **OK**.

Your professional signature looks like this:

10 When you are satisfied with your signature, click **Finish**.

The **Create Signature** dialog box appears.

11 Click **OK**.

The **Options** dialog box appears. Note that the signature you just created is selected in the **Signature for new messages** list. Outlook will automatically insert your signature into all new e-mail messages when you click **New Mail Message**.

12 Click **OK**.

The **Options** dialog box closes.

New Mail
Message

📝 New

13 On the toolbar, click the **New Mail Message** button.

A new message, containing your new signature, appears in the Message form.

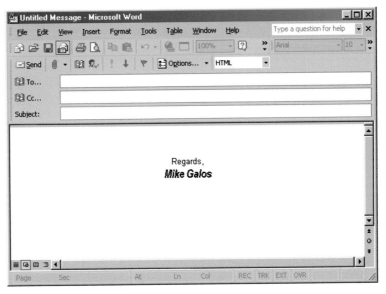

14 Close the message.

Tip

To have your signature automatically inserted into replies or forwarded messages, too, click **Options** on the **Tools** menu, and click the **Mail Format** tab. Click the signature you want in the **Signature for replies or forwards** list, and click **OK**.

15 On the **Tools** menu, click **Options**.

The **Options** dialog box appears.

16 Click the **Mail Format** tab.

17 In the **Signature for new messages** list, click **<none>**.

New messages will appear without a signature.

18 In the **Options** dialog box, click **OK**.

The **Options** dialog box closes.

Sending and Receiving Messages

Depending on your e-mail account and network configuration, messages you send could go out instantaneously or be kept in your Outbox until you choose to send them. If you are connected to a LAN, your messages will usually go out instantaneously. If you are not connected to a LAN (for example, if you connect to an ISP via phone line, DSL line, or cable), your messages will typically be kept in your Outbox.

How you receive messages also depends on your type of e-mail account and your Outlook configuration. Outlook might check for new messages periodically and download them automatically. Or, you might need to check for new messages.

Copies of messages you send are kept in the Sent Items folder by default. To see these messages, click **Sent Items** in the **Folder** list. If you do not want to keep copies of your sent messages, click **Options** on the **Tools** menu, click the **E-mail Options** button, clear the **Save copies of messages in Sent Items folder** check box, and click **OK**.

In this exercise, you will send a message and check for new messages. You don't need any practice files for this exercise.

New Mail
Message

🖼 **New**

1 On the toolbar, click the **New Mail Message** button.

A new message appears in the Message form.

2 In the **To** box, type your own e-mail address.

3 Click in the **Subject** box, and type the subject of the message: Sending and Receiving Test.

Send

✉ **Send**

4 Press the ⎀ key, and in the message body, type This is a test. Then click the **Send** button.

The message closes.

5 On the **View** menu, click **Folder List**.

The **Outlook** window now looks like this:

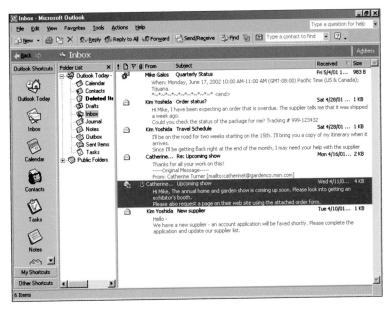

6 In the **Folder** list, click **Outbox**.

The contents of the Outbox are displayed. If the message you sent appears in the Outbox, you must send the message manually. If the Outbox is empty, your message was sent automatically.

When a message is waiting to be sent, your Outbox looks similar to this one:

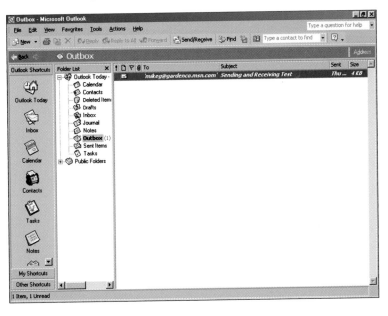

7 To send any messages in your Outbox and download any new messages from your e-mail server, on the toolbar, click the **Send/Receive** button.

Outlook connects to your e-mail server to send and receive messages. Depending on your setup, it might access your modem and connection line. When your message is sent, it disappears from the Outbox. When it is received, the message appears in your Inbox, along with any other new messages.

8 In the **Folder** list, click **Inbox** to see your new message(s).

The contents of the Inbox are displayed.

Multiple E-mail Accounts

Accounts
button
new for
OfficeXP

With Outlook, you can get all your e-mail in one place by configuring more than one account in your profile. To add an e-mail account to your profile:

1 On the **Tools** menu, click **E-mail Accounts** to start the **E-mail Accounts Wizard**.

2 Click the **Add a new e-mail account** option, and click **Next**.

3 Click the option for the appropriate server type, and click **Next**.

4 Enter the required server and account settings, and click **Next**.

5 Click **Finish** to close the **E-mail Accounts Wizard**.

If you have more than one e-mail account in your profile, you can send your mail from any of your accounts. In the Message form, on the toolbar, click the down arrow to the right of the **Accounts** button, and click the account you want in the drop-down list.

Printing Messages

Occasionally, you might need a hard copy, or printout, of an e-mail message. For example, you might need to print the directions to an afternoon appointment or distribute copies of a message at a meeting. With Outlook, you can print your e-mail messages in much the same way you would any other document.

Depending on the format (HTML, Rich Text, or Plain Text) of the message you want to print, you can set a number of page setup options, including paper size, margins, and orientation. You can also use Print Preview to see how a message will appear when printed. (Print Preview is not available for messages in HTML format.)

NextShow

In this exercise, you will change the page setup for a message and then print it.

1 In the Inbox, double-click the **Upcoming show** message from Catherine Turner to open it.

The message appears in the **Message** window.

2 On the **File** menu, point to **Page Setup**, and click **Memo Style**.

The **Page Setup** dialog box appears.

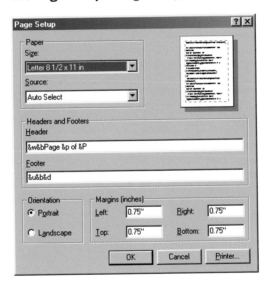

Tip

To display the **Page Setup** dialog box, you must have at least one printer installed. If you are working on a network, your administrator can provide the information you need to install a printer. If you are working on a stand-alone computer, click the **Start** button, point to **Settings**, and click **Printers**. Then click the **Add Printer** icon, and follow the wizard's instructions.

3 In the **Left** box, type **1.0** to set the left margin to 1 inch, and click **OK**.

The **Page Setup** dialog box closes, and your new settings are now in effect for this message.

Print

4 On the toolbar, click the **Print** button.

The message is printed with the default print options.

Tip

You can change print options, including which pages and how many copies should be printed, in the **Print** dialog box. Other print options may be available, depending on your printer. On the **File** menu, click **Print** to display the **Print** dialog box.

5   Click **AutoPreview** on the **View** menu to turn off AutoPreview.

AutoPreview is turned off.

6   Click **Preview Pane** on the **View** menu to turn the Preview Pane on.

The Preview Pane appears.

Close

7   On the **Folder** list, click the **Close** button.

The **Folder** list is no longer displayed.

8   If you are not continuing on with the next chapter, on the **File** menu, click **Exit** to quit Outlook.

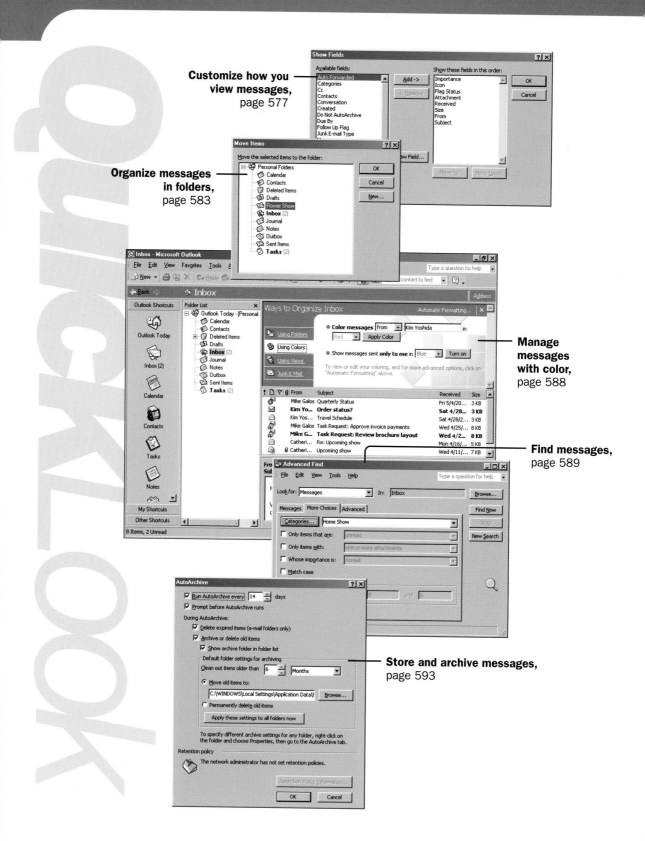

Customize how you view messages, page 577

Organize messages in folders, page 583

Manage messages with color, page 588

Find messages, page 589

Store and archive messages, page 593

Chapter 25
Managing E-Mail Messages

After completing this chapter, you will be able to:

✔ Customize how you view messages.

✔ Organize messages.

✔ Find messages.

✔ Store and archive messages.

In today's business world, e-mail is an essential method of communication. But when you use your e-mail regularly and receive a large volume of messages, it can be difficult to manage them all. Microsoft Outlook 2002 has many features to help you read, organize, find, and store e-mail messages quickly.

You can choose to view your messages in a way that makes it easier for you to scan, read, and respond to them. You can organize your messages in folders, search for messages by category and other criteria, and archive your messages in Outlook and on your hard disk.

 In this chapter, you will work specifically with the OrderStatus, NextShow, ReNext-Show, and Schedule practice files that came on this book's CD-ROM. If you have not already installed these files on your hard disk and copied them into Outlook, see "Using the Book's CD-ROM" at the beginning of the book.

Customizing How You View Messages

As your Inbox gathers messages, it can be challenging to prioritize them. You can use Outlook to customize how you view, group, and sort messages. You can then quickly determine which are the most important, decide which can be deleted, and locate that message from your boss that you haven't responded to yet.

Regardless of the **view** you choose, you can sort your messages by any column simply by clicking the column heading. By default, messages in your Inbox are sorted by the received date in descending order—the most recent messages appear at the top of the list. But you can sort columns in either ascending or descending order. You can also group your messages by the contents of any column—by the sender of the message, for instance, or by the subject.

In this exercise, you will sort and group messages, select a defined message view, and customize your message view.

1   If it is not already open, start Outlook. Then if necessary, maximize the **Outlook** window.

2   In the Inbox, click the heading of the **From** column.

Outlook sorts the messages by the name in the **From** column, in ascending order.

3   Click the heading of the **From** column again.

Outlook sorts the messages in descending order.

4   Click the heading of the **Received** column.

Outlook sorts the messages by the date received in descending order.

5   Right-click the heading of the **Subject** column, and click **Group By This Field** on the shortcut menu.

Outlook groups your messages by subject and sorts the subjects in ascending order.

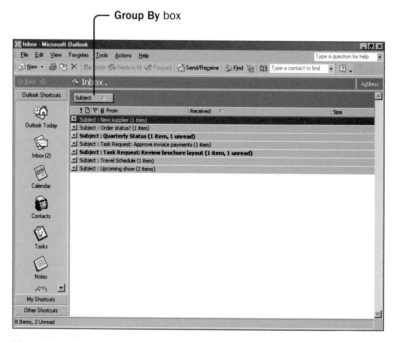

Note that the total number of items and the number of unread items in each group is indicated in parentheses following the subject line.

Tip

Unread items are distinguished from read ones by their bold type and closed-envelope icons. If you do not have any unread messages in your Inbox, for purposes of this exercise, right-click a message, and click **Mark as Unread** on the shortcut menu. The message header in the Inbox will then change to bold, and its message icon will change from an open to a closed envelope.

6   Click the plus sign (+) to the left of the **Subject: Upcoming show** line.

The messages in that subject group are displayed.

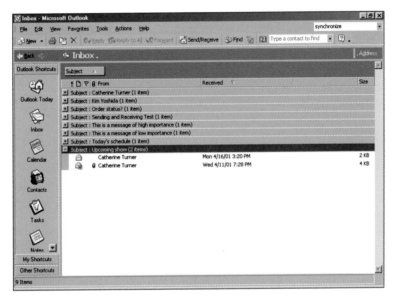

7   In the **Group By** box, click the **Subject** button.

The subjects are sorted in descending order.

8   In the **Group By** box, right-click the **Subject** button, and click **Don't Group By This Field** on the shortcut menu.

Messages are no longer grouped by subject.

9   Right-click any column heading, and click **Group By Box** on the shortcut menu.

The **Group By** box disappears.

10   If none of the messages in your Inbox appears in bold type, which indicates that you have not yet read them, right-click the **Order Status** message from Kim Yoshida, and click **Mark as Unread** on the shortcut menu.

11   On the **View** menu, point to **Current View**, and click **Unread Messages**.

Outlook filters the messages to show only unread messages.

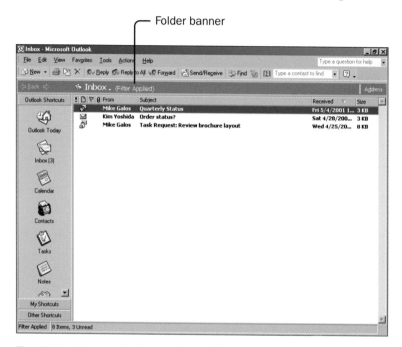

Folder banner

The **Folder banner** indicates that a **filter** has been applied. (If you have no unread messages in your Inbox, it will appear to be empty.)

12   On the **View** menu, point to **Current View**, and click **Messages**.

The messages are no longer filtered.

Tip

The Ways to Organize Inbox pane provides an alternative method for selecting a view for your messages. On the **Tools** menu, click **Organize** to open the pane. Then click **Using Views**, and click a view in the list.

13 On the **View** menu, point to **Current View**, and click **Customize Current View**.

The **View Summary** dialog box appears.

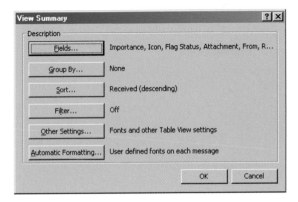

14 Click the **Fields** button.

The **Show Fields** dialog box appears.

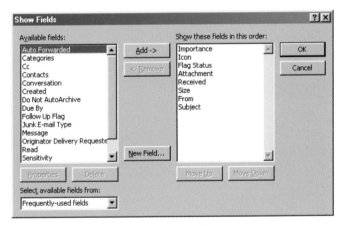

15 In the **Available fields** list, click **Sensitivity**, and click the **Add** button.

The **Sensitivity** field is added to the list of columns to be shown in this view.

16 In the **Show these fields in this order** list, drag **Sensitivity** to appear just after **Importance**, and click **OK**.

The **Show Fields** dialog box closes, and you return to the **View Summary** dialog box.

Tip

To change the order of columns in any view, simply drag the column headings to the locations you prefer. While you are dragging a column heading, red arrows indicate where the column will appear if you release the mouse button.

17 Click the **Other Settings** button.

The **Other Settings** dialog box appears.

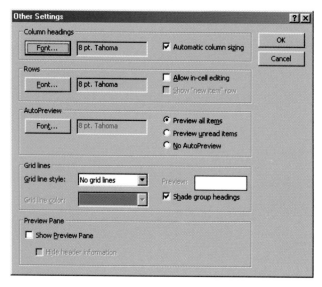

18 Click the down arrow to the right of the **Grid line style** box, click **Small dots**, and click **OK**.

The **Other Settings** dialog box closes, and you return to the **View Summary** dialog box.

19 In the **View Summary** dialog box, click **OK**.

The **View Summary** dialog box closes, and the Inbox is displayed with the new view settings.

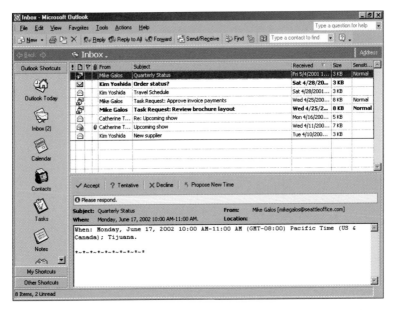

20 Drag the **Sensitivity** column heading downward, and release the mouse button when a large black X appears over the heading.

The Sensitivity column is removed from the view.

21 To return to the default settings, on the **View** menu, click **Current View**, and then click **Define Views**.

The **Define Views** dialog box appears.

22 Click the **Reset** button, and then click **Close**.

The Inbox is displayed with the default view settings.

Organizing Messages in Folders

After you've read and responded to messages, you might want to keep some for future reference. With Outlook, you can organize your messages in a variety of ways.

Creating folders to organize your messages helps you avoid an accumulation of unrelated messages in your Inbox. For example, you can create a folder for each project you're working on and store all messages regarding a particular project in its own folder. Or, you can create a folder to store all messages from your boss. You can move messages to the folders manually or have Outlook move them for you.

Tip

If you are using a Microsoft Exchange Server account, the **Out of Office Assistant** can help you manage messages while you are away from the office. When you have more experience with Outlook, you might want to explore this handy helper. On the **Tools** menu, click **Out of Office Assistant** to see what options are available.

NextShow
NewSupplier

In this exercise, you will create a new folder, move messages to that folder, move and rename the folder, and then delete a message and delete the folder.

1   On the **Tools** menu, click **Organize**.

The Ways to Organize Inbox pane appears.

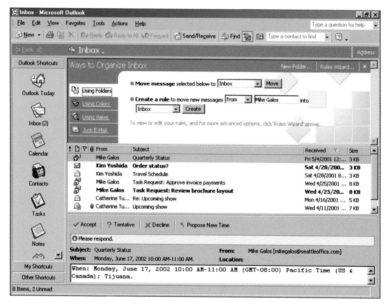

2   At the top of the Ways to Organize Inbox pane, click the **New Folder** button.

The **Create New Folder** dialog box appears.

Tip

If you are working on a stand-alone computer, the first item in the **Select where to place the folder** box is **Personal Folders** because your Outlook information is stored on your hard disk, not on a server.

3 In the **Name** box, type Home Show as the name of your new folder, and click **OK**.

The **Create New Folder** dialog box closes.

4 If Outlook asks whether you want to put a shortcut for this folder on the Outlook Bar, click **No**.

The new Home Show folder appears in the **Folder** list as a subfolder of the Inbox folder. (You can scroll the **Folder** list to see the folder.)

5 To display the **Folder** list, click **Folder List** on the **View** menu.

The **Folder** list is displayed.

New folder

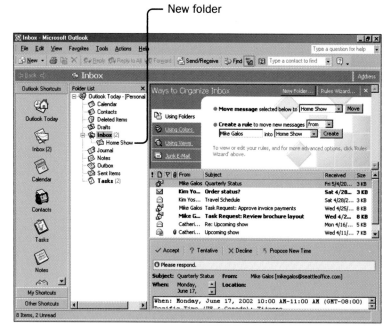

6 In the Inbox, click the **Upcoming show** message from Catherine Turner, and in the Ways to Organize Inbox pane, click the **Move** button.

The message is moved to the new folder.

7 Repeat step 6 to move the **New Supplier** message to the new folder.

Tip

You can move messages to another folder automatically by creating a rule. To create a simple rule, such as moving all messages received from your boss to a separate folder, use the **Using Folders** tab of the Ways to Organize Inbox pane. For more complex rules, click the **Rules Wizard** button in the top right corner of the Ways to Organize Inbox pane.

8 In the **Folder** list, click the Home Show folder.

The contents of the new folder are displayed.

9 In the **Folder** list, drag the Home Show folder to **Outlook Today**.

The new folder is now listed at the same level in the **Folder** list as the Inbox and in alphabetical order with the other items at this level.

10 In the **Folder** list, right-click the Home Show folder, and click **Rename "Home Show"** on the shortcut menu.

The name of the folder appears in the **Folder** list in an editable text box.

11 Type **Flower Show**, and press the Enter key.

The folder name is changed.

12 In the **Folder** list, click the **Flower Show** folder to display its contents.

Move to Folder

13 Click the **Upcoming show** message. Then click the **Move to Folder** button, and click **Move to Folder**.

The **Move Items** dialog box is displayed.

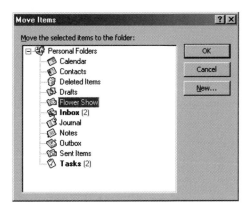

14 Click **Inbox**, and click **OK**.

The message is moved to the Inbox.

Delete

15 Now click the **New Supplier** message, and click the **Delete** button.

The message is deleted, and the folder is now empty.

16 In the **Folder** list, click the Flower Show folder, and click the **Delete** button.

17 When asked if you are sure you want to delete the folder, click **Yes**.

The folder is deleted. When you delete a folder, any messages contained within that folder are also deleted. (In this case, the folder is empty.)

18 Close the **Folder** list by clicking its **Close** button.

The **Folder** list closes.

Important

When you delete any item in Outlook, it is moved to the Deleted Items folder. You can view your deleted items by clicking that folder in the **Folder** list. You can tell Outlook to empty the Deleted Items folder every time you close the program by setting an option in the **Options** dialog box. On the **Tools** menu, click **Options**, click the **Other** tab, and then click the **Empty the Deleted Items folder upon exiting** check box, clicking **OK** when you are finished. You can empty the Deleted Items folder at any time by right-clicking the folder in the **Folder** list and clicking **Empty "Deleted Items" Folder** on the shortcut menu.

Managing Messages with Color

Color-coding messages can help you easily distinguish messages sent to or received from certain people. You can also choose to have messages that were sent directly to you displayed in a different color to distinguish them from messages sent to a distribution list. For example, you might show all messages from your boss in red, and all messages from the Finance department in green.

In this exercise, you will color-code messages.

NextShow

Inbox

1   Display the **Folder** list by clicking **Folder List** on the **View** menu.

The **Folder** list appears.

2   In the **Folder** list, click **Inbox**, and on the **Tools** menu, click **Organize**.

The Ways to Organize Inbox pane appears.

3   In the Ways to Organize Inbox pane, click **Using Colors**.

The **Using Colors** tab is displayed.

4   Click the **Upcoming show** message from Catherine Turner.

5   In the **Color Messages** section, make sure **From** is selected in the first box and Catherine Turner appears in the second box.

6   In the third box, select **Fuschia** from the drop-down list, and click the **Apply Color** button.

The specified messages are displayed in the selected color.

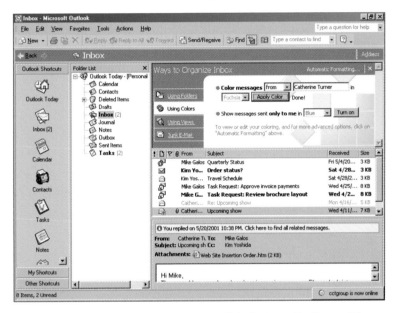

7   In the Ways to Organize Inbox pane, click **Automatic Formatting**.

The **Automatic Formatting** dialog box appears.

8   In the **Rules for this view** list, click **Mail received from Catherine Turner**, and then click the **Delete** button.

The Mail received from Catherine Turner rule is deleted.

9   In the **Automatic Formatting** dialog box, click OK.

The dialog box closes.

10   Close the Ways to Organize Inbox pane by clicking its **Close** button.

11   Close the **Folder** list by clicking its **Close** button.

The **Folder** list closes.

Finding Messages

Find
new for
OfficeXP

If you can't locate a message in your Inbox or other message folders, you can find it using Outlook's **Find** and **Advanced Find** features. You can look for messages in one folder, the folders you select, or all folders. You can search the text of the whole message or only the Subject field.

To make finding messages easier, you can create categories and assign messages to them. With categories, you group messages by a common characteristic. Outlook includes a set of predefined categories, and you can create your own. For example, you might assign all messages about invoices and payments to the Finance category, or you might create a Payroll category for all messages related to timesheets and paychecks.

NextShow
ReNextShow

In this exercise, you will find a message using the Find feature, create a category, assign messages to it, and find messages using the Advanced Find feature.

Find

1   On the toolbar, click the **Find** button.

The Find pane appears above the Inbox.

2   In the **Look for** box in the Find pane, type **show**, which you know is contained within a message in your Inbox. Then click the **Find Now** button.

Outlook searches your messages and displays only those that contain the word you typed.

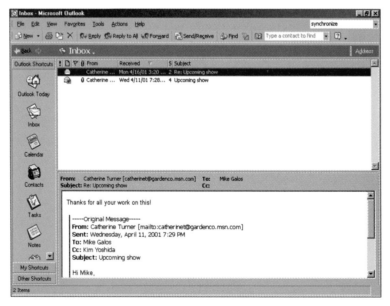

3   To show all messages again, click the **Clear** button.

All your messages are displayed.

4   In the Inbox, click the **Upcoming show** message from Catherine Turner, and on the **Edit** menu, click **Categories**.

The **Categories** dialog box appears.

5 In the **Item(s) belong to these categories** box, after **Practice Files**, type ; (a semicolon) and then **Home Show** as the name of a new category, and click the **Add to List** button.

The category is added to the list and automatically selected for the message.

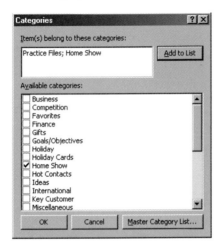

6 In the **Categories** dialog box, click **OK**.

The message is assigned to the new category.

7 In the **Find** pane, click the **Options** button, and then click **Advanced Find** in the **Options** drop-down list.

The **Advanced Find** window appears.

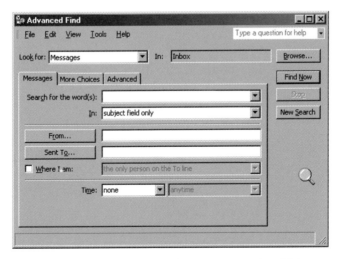

Take a moment to look over the many ways in which you can search for messages.

8 In the **Advanced Find** window, click the **More Choices** tab.

The **More Choices** tab is displayed.

9 Click the **Categories** button.

The **Categories** dialog box appears.

10 In the **Available categories** list, select the **Home Show** check box, and click **OK**.

The **Categories** dialog box closes, and you return to the **Advanced Find** window. Your category appears in the **Categories** box.

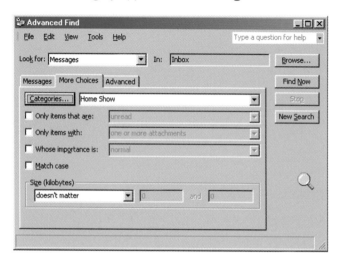

11 Click the **Find Now** button.

Outlook searches your messages and displays the matching items in a list at the bottom of the **Advanced Find** window.

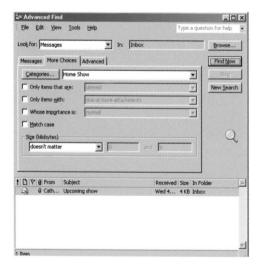

Close

☒

12 Close the **Advanced Find** window by clicking its **Close** button.

Storing and Archiving Messages

As messages accumulate in your Inbox and other message folders, you might need to consider other ways to store them. For example, you might want to **archive** all messages sent or received before a certain date, or save all messages related to a project as files on your hard disk. With Outlook, you can store your messages as text or HTML files on your hard disk, or archive your messages to an Outlook message file. Archiving messages in a separate Outlook message file helps you manage clutter and the size of your primary message file, while allowing easy access to archived messages from within Outlook.

Global AutoArchive Settings
new for **Office**XP

You can archive messages manually or automatically. When archived messages are moved to a separate message file, the messages are removed from their original folder. By default, Outlook automatically archives messages in all folders at regular intervals to a location determined by your operating system. You can change the default global settings for **AutoArchive** and choose settings for specific folders. Archive settings selected for a specific folder override the global settings for that folder. If you don't specify AutoArchive settings for a folder, Outlook uses the global settings.

OrderStatus Schedule

In this exercise, you will save a message as a text file, save a message as an HTML file, archive messages manually, and set automatic archive options.

1 In the Inbox, click the **Order Status** message from Kim Yoshida, and on the **File** menu, click **Save As**.

The **Save As** dialog box appears.

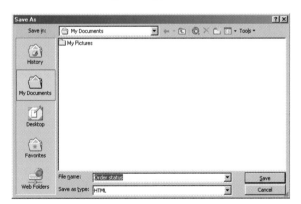

By default, messages are saved as HTML files in the My Documents folder.

Tip

Your **Save As** dialog box will reflect the contents of your My Documents folder. If you have file extensions turned on, the name in the **File Name** box will be *Order Status.htm*.

2   In the **Save As** dialog box, click **Save**.

The message is saved in the My Documents folder.

3   In the Inbox, click the **Travel Schedule** message from Kim Yoshida, and on the **File** menu, click **Save As**.

The **Save As** dialog box appears.

4   Click the down arrow to the right of the **Save as type** box, click **Text Only** in the drop-down list, and click **Save**.

The message is saved in the My Documents folder.

5   On the **Start** menu, point to **Documents**, and then click **My Documents**.

The My Documents folder opens, containing the messages you saved.

Web page icon   **6**   Double-click the HTML file you saved, which is indicated by a **Web page** icon.

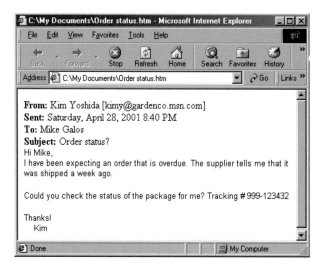

The message opens in your Web browser.

If the message contained any formatting, the HTML format would preserve it.

7   Close the browser window

Text page icon   **8**   In the My Documents folder, double-click the text file you saved, which is indicated by a **text page** icon.

The message opens in Notepad.

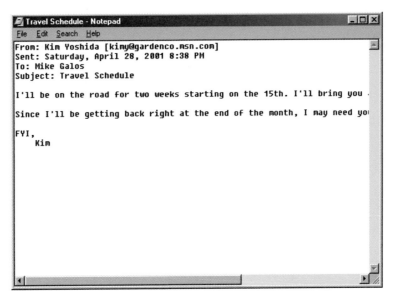

9   Close Notepad.

10   Close the My Documents folder.

11   Now you'll try archiving messages. In Outlook, on the **Tools** menu, click **Options**.

The **Options** dialog box appears.

12   Click the **Other** tab, and then click the **AutoArchive** button.

The **AutoArchive** dialog box appears.

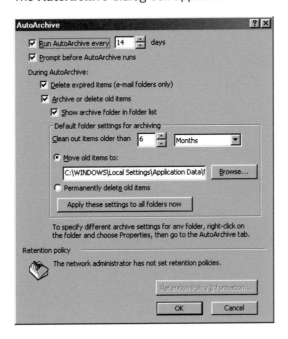

13   Review your AutoArchive default settings—particularly note the interval at which the archive will happen, the age at which items will be archived, and the location in the **Move old items to** box—and click **Cancel**.

The **AutoArchive** dialog box closes.

Tip

With **Mailbox Cleanup**, you can see the size of your mailbox, find and delete old items or items that are larger than a certain size, start AutoArchive, or view the size of and empty your Deleted Items folder. On the **Tools** menu, click **Mailbox Cleanup**.

14   In the **Options** dialog box, click **Cancel**.

The **Options** dialog box closes.

15   Open the **Folder** list by clicking **Folder List** on the **View** menu.

The **Folder** list appears.

16   In the **Folder** list, click **Sent Items**.

17   On the **File** menu, point to **Folder**, and click **Properties for "Sent Items"**.

The **Sent Items Properties** dialog box appears.

18   Click the **AutoArchive** tab.

The AutoArchive options are displayed.

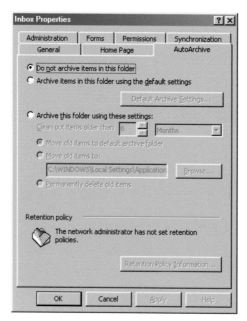

19   Click the **Archive this folder using these settings** option.

20 In the **Clean out items older than** box, click **4** and **Months**.

21 Be sure the option to **Move old items to default archive folder** is selected, and click **OK**.

The **Sent Items Properties** dialog box closes. Items in the Sent Items folder will be archived according to the new settings, whereas items in all other folders will be archived according to the default settings.

22 Now you'll set Outlook to archive your messages according to your settings. On the **File** menu, click **Archive**.

The **Archive** dialog box appears.

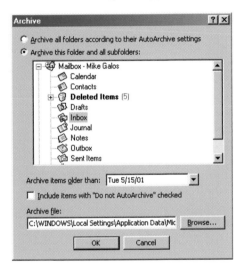

23 Be sure the **Archive this folder and all subfolders** option is selected and that the Sent Items folder is selected in the list.

24 In the **Archive items older than** list, select a date that you know is later than the date of some messages in your Sent Items folder, and click **OK**.

Outlook archives the messages in your Sent Items folder according to your settings.

25 In the **Folder** list, double-click **Archive Folders** to expand it, and click the **Sent Items** folder that appears within that folder.

The contents of the archived Sent Items folder are displayed. (Items that are copied to Outlook folders are archived based on the date they were copied rather than the date of the item itself.)

26 On the **Edit** menu, click **Select All**.

Outlook selects all the messages in the archived Sent Items folder.

Move to Folder

27 On the toolbar, click the **Move to Folder** button, and click **Sent Items** in the drop-down list.

The messages are returned to the Sent Items folder.

28 On the Outlook Bar, click the **Inbox** icon.

The contents of the Inbox are displayed.

29 In the **Folder** list, click **Sent Items**.

30 On the **File** menu, point to **Folder**, and click **Properties for "Sent Items"**.

The **Sent Items Properties** dialog box appears.

31 Click the **AutoArchive** tab.

The AutoArchive options are displayed.

32 Click the **Do not archive items in this folder** option, and then click **OK**.

The **Sent Items Properties** dialog box closes.

33 Close the **Folder** list, and then close the Find pane. Then on the **File** menu, click **Exit** to quit Outlook.

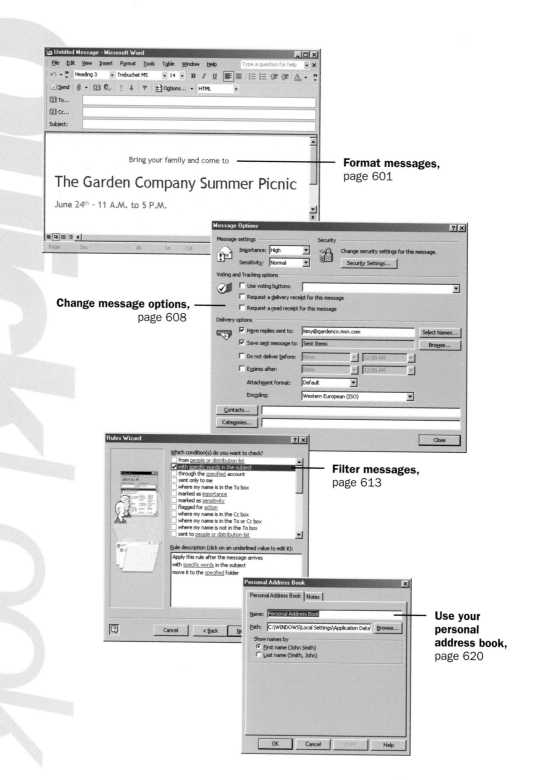

Format messages,
page 601

Change message options,
page 608

Filter messages,
page 613

**Use your
personal
address book,**
page 620

Chapter 26
Customizing and Organizing E-Mail Messages

After completing this chapter, you will be able to:

✔ **Format messages.**

✔ **Change message options.**

✔ **Filter messages.**

✔ **Use personal folders and address books.**

As you learn the fundamentals of sending, receiving, and managing your e-mail, you will see how using e-mail can help you work more efficiently. Because you can customize the format of your messages, select from a number of message and delivery options, filter messages, and set up personal folders and address books, you can configure Microsoft Outlook to be as convenient and useful as possible. For example, you might ask your project team to use a particular phrase in the subject line of messages related to the project. Then, when you need to focus on the project, you can filter messages to display only those items related to it.

This chapter uses OrderStatus, NextShow, ReNextShow, and Schedule (which are all messages) and GardenCo (which is a personal address book) that you installed from this book's CD-ROM onto your hard disk and copied into Outlook. For details about installing and copying the practice files, see "Using the Book's CD-ROM" at the beginning of this book.

Formatting Messages

E-mail messages are sent in one of three formats: HTML, Plain Text, or Outlook Rich Text Format (RTF). Outlook supports all three formats. Other e-mail programs might be able to work with only some of them.

- **HTML** is the default message format in Outlook. HTML supports text formatting, numbering, bullets, pictures and backgrounds in the message body, styles, and stationery. Most popular e-mail programs support HTML messages.

- **Outlook Rich Text Format** supports a host of formatting options including text formatting, bullets, numbering, background colors, borders, and shading. Rich Text Format is supported by some Microsoft e-mail clients, including Outlook 97 and Outlook 2000. Microsoft Outlook Express, which is distributed with several versions of Microsoft Windows, supports only HTML and Plain Text.

- **Plain Text** is supported by all e-mail programs, but as the name implies, messages in plain text do not include any formatting.

For the most part, HTML format will meet your needs. In fact, Microsoft recommends using the HTML format, whether you are sending messages over the Internet or using Microsoft Exchange Server. When you send an HTML message to someone whose e-mail program doesn't support HTML format, the message is displayed as plain text in the recipient's e-mail program. Outlook automatically converts RTF messages you send over the Internet into HTML format. When you reply to or forward a message, by default Outlook uses the format of the original message. However, you can choose the format for any message you send.

When sending messages in HTML format, you can enhance the appearance of your messages using **stationery** and **themes**. When you use stationery, you can specify the set of fonts, bullets, background color, horizontal lines, images, and other elements you want to use in outgoing e-mail messages. You can choose from a collection of predefined stationery, customize one of the patterns, create new stationery, or download new patterns from the Web. If you use Microsoft Word as your e-mail editor, you can choose from additional patterns available as Word themes.

Important

This chapter assumes that Microsoft Word is your default e-mail editor. If it's not, you can make it the default by clicking **Options** on the **Tools** menu, clicking the **Mail Format** tab, clicking the **Use Microsoft Word to edit e-mail messages** check box, and clicking **OK**.

In this exercise, you will format messages in HTML, Rich Text, and plain text formats. You will also compose messages using stationery and themes. You don't need any practice files for this exercise.

1 If Outlook is not already open, start it now. Then if necessary, maximize the window.

Inbox

2 On the Outlook Bar, click the **Inbox** icon.

The contents of the Inbox are displayed.

New Mail
Message

3 On the Standard toolbar, click the **New Mail Message** button.

A blank Message form appears.

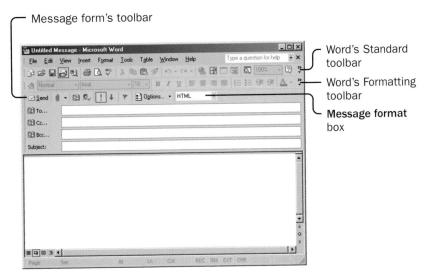

4 Click in the body of the message, and type Wow! Have you seen the new roses?

By default, the text is formatted in 10-point Arial (the Normal style).

5 Drag the gray bar at the left end of the Formatting toolbar to the right as far as it will go so that you can see more of its buttons.

Font Size

12

6 Select the word *Wow!*, and change its size by clicking the down arrow to the right of the **Font Size** box and clicking **16**.

Font Color

A

7 Click the down arrow to the right of the **Font Color** button, and click the red square.

8 On the Message form's toolbar, click the down arrow to the right of the **Message format** box, and click **Plain Text**.

A message box appears indicating that **Plain Text** format does not support some of the formatting in the message.

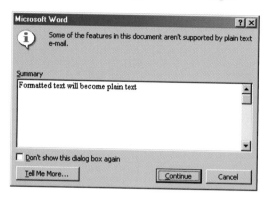

Tip

You can choose to bypass this message in the future. Before clicking **Continue**, click the **Don't show this dialog box again** check box.

9 Click the **Continue** button.

The text is formatted in 10-point Courier New (the Plain Text style), and the Formatting toolbar is unavailable.

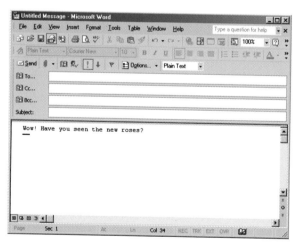

10   On the Message form's toolbar, click the down arrow to the right of the **Message format** box, and click **Rich Text**.

The message format is changed to **Rich Text** format, but the text remains in the Plain Text style. You can now use the Formatting toolbar to change the style or other text formatting.

Close

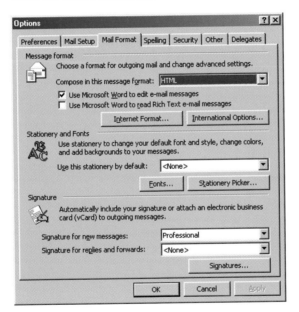

11   Click the Message form's **Close** button, and when asked if you want to keep a draft of the message, click **No**.

The Message form closes.

12   On the **Tools** menu, click **Options**.

The **Options** dialog box appears.

13   Click the **Mail Format** tab.

14   In the **Message format** area, click the down arrow to the right of the **Compose in this message format** box, click **Plain Text**, and then click **OK**.

The **Options** dialog box closes. The default message format for new messages is set to **Plain Text** format.

15   On the Standard toolbar, click the **New Mail Message** button.

The Message form appears, with the **Plain Text** format selected.

16   Click the **Close** button.

The Message form closes.

17 On the **Tools** menu, click **Options**.

The **Options** dialog box appears.

18 Click the **Mail Format** tab.

19 In the **Message format** area, click the down arrow to the right of the **Compose in this message format** box, and then click **HTML**.

20 In the **Stationery and Fonts** area, click the down arrow to the right of the **Use this stationery by default** box, click **Clear Day**, and click **OK**.

The **Options** dialog box closes. New messages will be formatted in **HTML** format using the Clear Day stationery.

21 On the Standard toolbar, click the **New Mail Message** button.

The Message form appears, using the Clear Sky stationery.

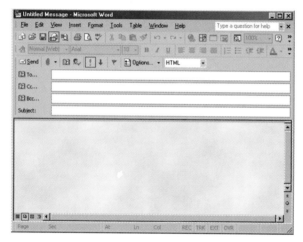

22 Click in the body of the message, and type **Bring your family and come to**.

By default, the text is formatted in 10-point Arial (the Normal style for this stationery).

Tip

You can customize message stationery. On the **Mail Format** tab of the **Options** dialog box, click the **Stationery Picker** button. To edit existing stationery, click the stationery design you want, click the **Edit** button, apply the font, background, and color formatting you want, and then click **OK**. To create new stationery, click the **New** button in the **Stationery Picker** dialog box, and follow the directions in the wizard that appears.

23 On the **Format** menu, click **Theme**.

The **Theme** dialog box appears.

24 In the **Choose a Theme** list, click **Artsy**.

A preview of the Artsy theme appears in the **Theme** dialog box.

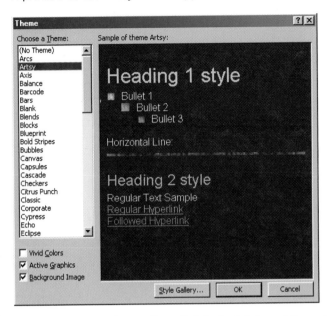

25 In the **Choose a Theme** list, click **Industrial**, and then click **OK**.

The **Theme** dialog box closes, and the Industrial theme is applied to the message, replacing the Clear Day stationery.

26 In the body of the message, press [Enter], type **The Garden Company Summer Picnic**, press [Enter], type **June 24th – 11 A.M. to 5 P.M.**, and press [Enter] again.

Center

27 Click in the first line of text, and on the Formatting toolbar, click the **Center** button.

The line is now centered in the body of the message.

28 Click in the second line of text, and on the Formatting toolbar, click the down arrow to the right of the **Style** box, and then click **Heading 1**.

Tip

If you can't see the **Style** box, click the **Toolbar Options** button to display a drop-down menu of additional buttons, and set the style for the paragraph there. The **Style** box will then join the other buttons on the visible part of the Formatting toolbar.

The line is now formatted with the Heading 1 style.

29 Click the third line of text, and on the Formatting toolbar, click the down arrow to the right of the **Style** box, and then click **Heading 3**.

The line is now formatted with the Heading 3 style. The message looks like this:

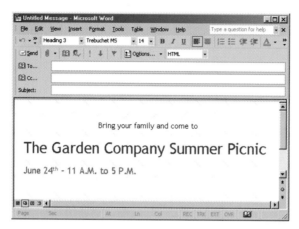

30 Click the **Close** button on the Message form, and when asked if you want to keep a draft of the message, click **No**.

The Message form closes, discarding the draft.

31 On the **Tools** menu, click **Options**, and then click the **Mail Format** tab.

32 In the **Stationery and Fonts** area, click the down arrow to the right of the **Use this stationery by default** box, click **<None>** at the top of the drop-down list, and then click **OK**.

The **Options** dialog box closes. New messages will now be formatted in HTML with no stationery applied.

Changing Message Settings and Delivery Options

To help you manage your e-mail and convey the meaning of your messages more effectively, you can set the importance, sensitivity, and a number of delivery options for e-mail messages.

You can set a message to High, Normal, or Low **importance**. Messages sent with High importance are marked with a red exclamation point. Messages sent with Normal importance have no special marker. Messages sent with Low importance are marked with a blue arrow pointing downward. These markers show up in the Importance column in the Inbox.

You can also set message **sensitivity** to Normal, Personal, Private, or Confidential. Messages marked as Private cannot be modified after they are sent.

To help you manage messages you receive, you can choose to have people's replies to your messages sent to another e-mail address. For example, you may have replies sent to a new e-mail address as you transition from one to another. To help you manage messages you send, you can choose whether to save copies of your sent messages and in which folder they should be saved. You can also specify when a message will be delivered and make a message unavailable after a certain date.

In this exercise, you will set the importance and sensitivity of a message. You will also modify the delivery options for a message. You don't need any practice files for this exercise.

New Mail
Message

1 With your Inbox displayed in the **Outlook** window, on the Standard toolbar, click the **New Mail Message** button.

A blank Message form appears.

Options

Options...

2 On the Message form's toolbar, click the **Options** button.

The **Message Options** dialog box appears.

3 In the **Message settings** area, click the down arrow to the right of the **Importance** box, and click **High** in the drop-down list.

4 In the **Delivery options** area, click the **Have replies sent to** check box, and click in the text box. Delete text in the box, and type the e-mail address **kimy@gardenco.msn.com**.

The dialog box looks like this:

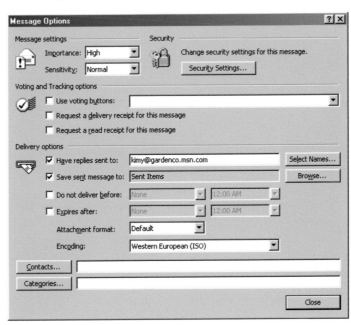

5 Click the **Close** button.

The **Message Options** dialog box closes, and you return to the Message form.

6 In the **To** box, type your own e-mail address.

Send

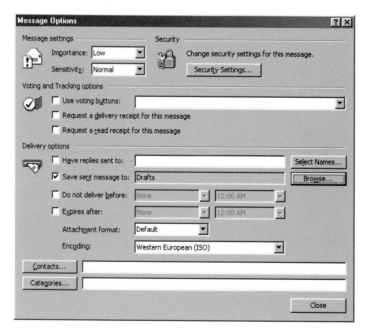

7 Click in the **Subject** box, type **This is a message of high importance**, and on the Message form's toolbar, click the **Send** button.

The Message form closes, and the message is sent.

8 On the Standard toolbar, click the **New Mail Message** button.

A blank Message form appears.

9 On the Message form's toolbar, click the **Options** button.

The **Message Options** dialog box appears.

10 In the **Message settings** area, click the down arrow to the right of the **Importance** box, and click **Low** in the drop-down list.

11 In the **Delivery options** area, click the **Browse** button.

The **Select Folder** dialog box appears.

12 In the **Folders** list, click the **Drafts** folder, and click **OK**.

The sent message will be saved in the Drafts folder.

13 Click the **Close** button.

The **Message Options** dialog box closes, and you return to the Message form.

14 In the **To** box, type your own e-mail address.

15 Click in the **Subject** box, type **This is a message of low importance**, and on the Message form's toolbar, click the **Send** button.

The Message form closes, and the message is sent.

16 If the messages have not yet arrived in your Inbox, click the **Send/Receive** button.

Outlook downloads any new messages. The message sent with High importance is marked with a red exclamation point. The message sent with Low importance is marked with a blue arrow pointing downward.

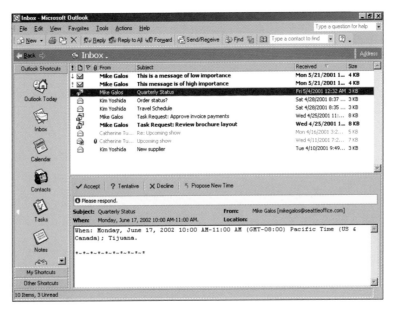

17 Double-click the message sent with High importance.

The **Message** window appears. The message header indicates that this message was sent with High importance.

Reply

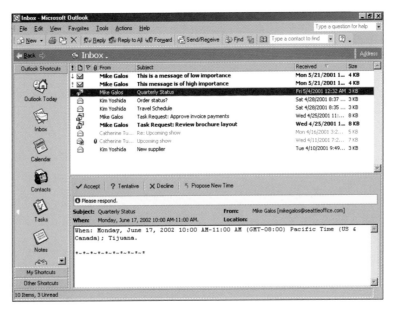

18 On the Standard toolbar, click the **Reply** button.

The Reply form appears. The **To** box contains the e-mail address you entered earlier, *kimy@gardenco.msn.com*.

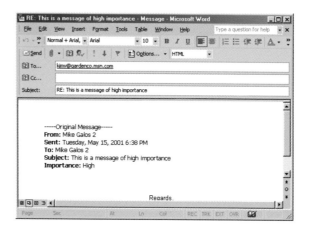

Close

❌

19 Click the **Close** button.

The Reply form closes.

20 Click the **Close** button in the **Message** window.

The **Message** window closes.

21 On the Folder banner, click the down arrow to the right of *Inbox*, and then click **Drafts** in the drop-down list.

The contents of the Drafts folder are displayed, including the copy of the message you sent with Low importance.

22 On the Outlook Bar, click **Inbox**.

The contents of the Inbox are displayed.

Recalling Messages

If you are connected to a network that uses Microsoft Exchange Server, you can recall messages you've sent. For example, if you discover errors in a message you've sent, you can recall the message so that you can correct the error and resend the message.

To recall a message:

1 If the **Folder** list is not open, click **Folder List** on the **View** menu.

2 In the **Folder** list, click **Sent Items**.

3 Double-click the message you want to recall to open it in a **Message** window.

4 On the **Actions** menu, click **Recall This Message**.

5 Select whether you want to delete unread copies of the message or delete unread copies and replace them with a new message, and then click **OK**.

You can recall or replace a message only if its recipient is logged on, is using Microsoft Outlook, and has not yet read the message or moved it from the Inbox.

Filtering Messages

As messages accumulate in your Inbox, it can be a challenge to find a message you need when you need it. To help meet this challenge, you can **filter** your messages by customizing views. When you filter messages, you display only those messages that meet common criteria, helping you identify a specific collection of messages. You can also create rules to move your messages to selected folders as you receive them, and you can filter out junk e-mail or e-mail with adult content.

Schedule
NextShow
ReNextShow

In this exercise, you will create a view to filter messages and create a rule that will move messages out of the Inbox.

1   With your Inbox displayed in Outlook, on the **View** menu, point to **Current View**, and click **Define Views**.

The **Define Views for "Inbox"** dialog box appears.

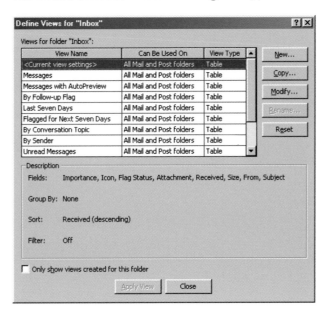

2   Click the **Copy** button.

The **Copy View** dialog box appears.

3   In the **Name of new view** box, type Filtered for Show, and click **OK**.

The **Copy View** dialog box closes, and the **View Summary** dialog box appears, showing the settings from the view you copied.

4   Click the **Filter** button.

The **Filter** dialog box appears.

5   In the **Search for the word(s)** box, type show, and click **OK**.

The **Filter** dialog box closes, and the **View Summary** dialog box appears, showing the new filter settings.

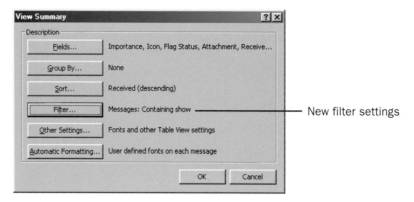

New filter settings

6 In the **View Summary** dialog box, click **OK**.

The **View Summary** dialog box closes, and you are returned to the **Define Views for "Inbox"** dialog box, which shows the new view in the **View Name** list.

7 Make sure **Filtered for Show** is highlighted in the **View Name** list, and click the **Apply View** button.

The **Define Views for "Inbox"** dialog box closes, and the Inbox is displayed, containing only the messages with the word *show* in the subject. The Folder banner indicates that a filter is applied.

Folder banner

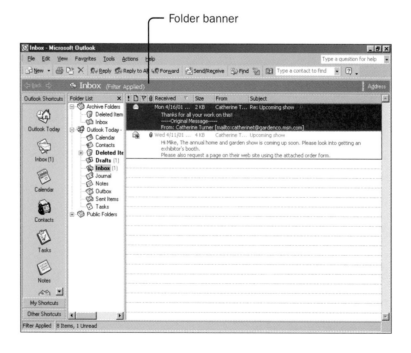

8   On the **View** menu, point to **Current View**.

The list of available views appears, including the new Filtered for Show view.

9   Click **Messages** on the **Current View** submenu.

The filter is removed, and all your messages appear in the Inbox.

10   Now you'll create a rule to manage messages that meet specific criteria. On the **Tools** menu, click **Rules Wizard**.

The first page of the **Rules Wizard** appears.

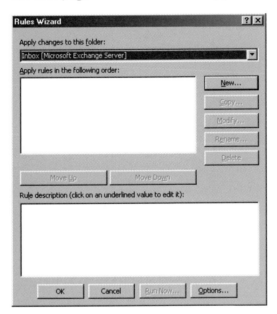

11   Click the **New** button.

The next page of the **Rules Wizard** appears. The **Start creating a rule from a template** option is selected. Take a moment to look over the types of rules you can create from a template. (If the Office Assistant offers to help you, click **No, don't provide help now**.)

12   Be sure that **Move new messages from someone** is selected, and click the **Next** button.

The next page of the **Rules Wizard** appears.

13   In the **Which condition(s) do you want to check?** list, clear the **from people or distribution list** check box, and select the **with specific words in the subject** check box.

The description in the **Rule description** box is updated to reflect the change. The underlined words in the description are values that you must specify to complete the rule.

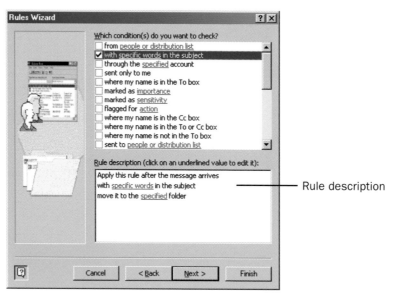

Rule description

14 In the **Rule description** box, click the underlined words **specific words**.

The **Search Text** dialog box appears.

15 In the **Specify words or phrases to search for in the subject** box, type
Travel, click the **Add** button, and then click **OK**.

The **Rule description** box is updated to reflect the change.

16 Click the **Next** button.

The next page of the **Rules Wizard** is displayed.

17 In the **What do you want to do with the message?** box, be sure the **move it
to the specified folder** check box is selected, and in the **Rule description**
box, click the underlined word **specified**.

The **Rules Wizard** dialog box appears, showing a list of folders for you to
choose from.

18 Click the **New** button.

The **Create New Folder** dialog box appears.

19 In the **Name** box, type Travel, and in the **Select where to place the folder**
list, click **Inbox**.

The dialog box now looks like this:

20 Click **OK**.

21 If prompted to add a shortcut to the **Outlook Bar**, click **No**, and then in the **Rules Wizard** dialog box, click **OK**.

The dialog box closes, and the **Rule description** box is updated to reflect your folder selection.

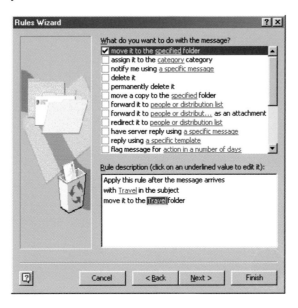

22 Click the **Next** button.

The next page of the **Rules Wizard** is displayed.

23 In the **Add any exceptions (if necessary)** list, click the **except if it is flagged for action** check box, and in the **Rule description** box, click the underlined word **action**.

The **Flagged Message** dialog box appears.

24 Click the down arrow to the right of the **Flag** box to see the available options, click **Any**, and click **OK**.

The **Rule description** box is updated to reflect your selection.

25 Click the **Next** button.

The final page of the **Rules Wizard** is displayed, summarizing the parameters you have set for the Travel rule.

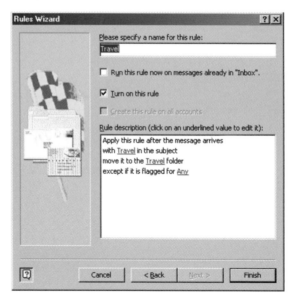

26 Select the **Run this rule now on messages already in "Inbox"** check box, and click the **Finish** button.

The rule is saved and is now listed in the **Rules Wizard** dialog box.

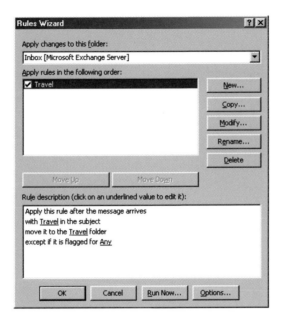

27 Click **OK**.

The rule is now active, and Outlook applies it to the messages in the Inbox.

28 In the **Folder** list, click the plus sign (+) to the left of the Inbox folder, and then click the **Travel** folder.

The contents of the Travel folder are displayed, including the Travel Schedule message from Kim Yoshida.

29 In the **Folder** list, click **Inbox**.

The contents of the Inbox are displayed.

Tip

If you are using Microsoft Exchange Server, you can filter messages even when you are away from the office by using the Out of Office Assistant. When you have more experience with Outlook, you might want to explore this feature by clicking **Out of Office Assistant** on the **Tools** menu.

Filtering Junk E-Mail Messages

Outlook offers several options for managing junk e-mail messages—the unsolicited advertisements and solicitation letters that can swamp your Inbox if your e-mail address finds its way into the hands of unscrupulous mailing list vendors. You can color-code junk messages for easy identification, or you can move them to another folder to reduce clutter in your Inbox. You can manage messages with adult content in the same way.

To filter junk e-mail or adult-content messages:

Organize

1   On the Standard toolbar, click the **Organize** button.

   The Ways to Organize Inbox pane appears.

2   In the Ways to Organize Inbox pane, click **Junk E-Mail**.

3   To color-code junk messages, in the first line, click **color** in the first box, and in the second box, click a color in the drop-down list.

   You can also set the first box to **move** and select a destination folder in the second box.

4   Click the **Turn On** button to turn on the rule for filtering junk messages.

5   To filter adult-content messages, in the second line, click either **color** or **move**, and then select a specific color or destination.

6   Click the **Turn On** button to turn on the rule for filtering messages with adult content.

7   Close the Ways to Organize Inbox pane.

The filtering rules remain in effect behind the scenes until you turn them off.

Using Personal Folders and Address Books

The items you create and receive in Outlook—messages, appointments, tasks, notes, and journal entries—are kept in a data file either on a server on your network or on the hard disk in your own computer.

■   If your information is kept on a server, which is the case when you are working on a network that uses Microsoft Exchange Server, it is part of a file called a **private store**. You can access this store only when you are connected to your server.

■   If your information is kept on your own computer, it is stored in a **Personal Folders file** that has a .pst file extension. The default Personal Folders file is Outlook.pst. You can access this file whether or not you are connected to your ISP.

Whether you are working on a networked or a stand-alone computer, you can create Personal Folders files to store Outlook items on the hard disk of your own computer. If you are working on a network, you might want to do this so that certain items are available whether or not you are connected to the server—if you work on a laptop that you use both in the office and at home, for example. If you are not working on a network, you might want to do this so that you can keep items related to a particular project in a separate Personal Folders file. Then you can back up that file separately from your other Outlook items, or you can copy that file to another computer.

For the same reason, you might want to create a **Personal Address Book** to store e-mail addresses and distribution lists separately from your Contacts folder. Personal Address Book files have a .pab file extension and can also be stored on your local computer.

GardenCo
Travel

In this exercise, you will create a Personal Folders file, move messages and folders to the new file, add a Personal Address Book, and create a personal distribution list. The Personal Address Book you will use is located in the Office XP SBS\Outlook\Chap26 folder on your hard disk.

Important

If you did not work through the previous exercise in this chapter, you need to complete steps 1 through 7 of this exercise. If you did work through the previous exercise, you can skip these steps.

1   On the **File** menu, click **Import and Export**.

The **Import and Export Wizard** appears.

2   In the **Choose an action to perform** list, click **Import from another program or file**, and click **Next**.

The next page of the **Import and Export Wizard** appears.

3   In the **Select file type to import from** list, click **Personal Folder File (.pst)**, and click **Next**.

The next page of the **Import and Export Wizard** appears.

4   Click the **Browse** button.

The **Open Personal Folders** dialog box appears.

5   Click the down arrow at the right end of the **Look in** box, browse to the Office XP SBS\Outlook\Chap26 folder, click **Travel**, and click the **Open** button.

The **Open Personal Folders** dialog box closes, and the path to the folder you selected appears in the **File to import** box.

6   In the **Import and Export Wizard**, make sure the **Replace duplicates with items imported** option is selected, and click **Next**.

The next page of the **Import and Export Wizard** appears.

7 In the **Select the folder to import from** list, click the **Travel** folder, and click **Finish**.

The Travel folder is added to your **Folder** list. (If the **Folder** list is not visible, display it by clicking **Folder List** on the **View** menu.)

8 On the **Tools** menu, click **Options**, and then click the **Mail Setup** tab.

The **Options** dialog box appears, with the **Mail Setup** options displayed.

9 Click the **Data Files** button.

The **Outlook Data Files** dialog box appears.

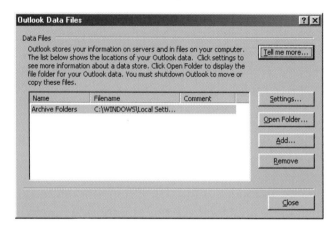

10 Click the **Add** button, and in the **New Outlook Data File** dialog box, click **OK** to create a new Personal Folders file.

The **Create or Open Outlook Data File** dialog box appears.

11 In the **File name** box, type **personal.pst**, and click **OK**.

The **Create Microsoft Personal Folders** dialog box appears.

12 In the **Name** box, type MikeG as a distinct name for this file, and click **OK**.

The **Outlook Data Files** dialog box is displayed, showing the new Personal Folders file.

13 Click the **Close** button, and in the **Options** dialog box, click **OK**.

The **Options** dialog box closes.

14 In the **Folder** list, double-click **MikeG**.

The contents of the Personal Folders file are displayed in the Inbox (currently the file is empty), and the folder is expanded in the **Folder** list. By default, the Personal Folders file contains its own Deleted Items folder.

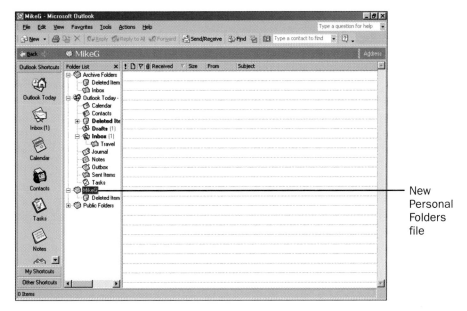

New Personal Folders file

15 In the **Folder** list, click **Inbox**.

The contents of the Inbox are displayed.

16 Click the **Upcoming show** message from Catherine Turner, and then hold down the ⌃ctrl⌄ key and click the **RE: Upcoming show** message.

The messages are selected.

Move to Folder

17 On the Standard toolbar, click the **Move to Folder** button, and then click **Move to Folder** on the drop-down menu.

The **Move Items** dialog box appears.

18 In the **Move the selected items to the folder** list, click **MikeG**, and then click **OK**.

The **Move Items** dialog box closes, and the messages are moved to the new Personal Folders file.

19 In the **Folder** list, click **MikeG**.

The contents of the new Personal Folders file, including the two messages you just moved, are displayed.

20 In the **Folder** list, drag the **Travel** folder to the **MikeG** folder.

The folder and its contents are moved to the new Personal Folders file.

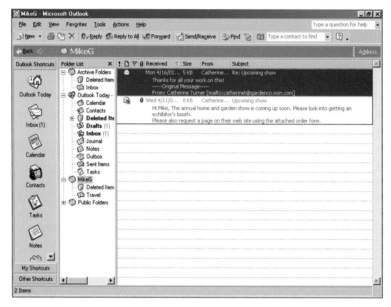

21 Now you will add a Personal Address Book to Outlook. On the **Tools** menu, click **E-mail Accounts**.

The **E-mail Accounts** dialog box appears.

22 Click the **Add a new directory or address book** option, and click **Next**.

The **Directory or Address Book Type** page appears.

23 Click the **Additional Address Books** option, and click **Next**.

The **Other Address Book Types** page appears.

24 In the **Additional Address Book Types** list, click **Personal Address Book**, and click **Next**.

The **Personal Address Book** dialog box appears.

25 Click the **Browse** button.

The **Use Personal Address Book** dialog box appears.

26 Click the down arrow to the right of the **Look in** box, browse to the Office XP SBS\Outlook\Chap26 folder, click **GardenCo**, and then click the **Open** button.

In the **Personal Address Book** dialog box, the path to the GardenCo file appears in the **Path** box.

27 Click **OK**, and in the **Add E-mail Account** message box, click **OK** again.

The address book is added, but you must restart Outlook before you can use it.

28 On the **File** menu, click **Exit** to exit Outlook.

Microsoft
Outlook

29 On your desktop, double-click the **Microsoft Outlook** icon to start Outlook again.

30 On the **Tools** menu, click **Address Book**. Then click the down arrow to the right of the **Show Names from the** box, and click **Personal Address Book**.

The contents of the Personal Address Book are displayed, including entries for Catherine Turner and Kim Yoshida.

New Entry

31 On the Standard toolbar, click the **New Entry** button.

The **New Entry dialog** box appears.

32 In the **Put this entry** area, click the down arrow to the right of the **In the** box, and then click **Personal Address Book** in the drop-down list.

33 In the **Select the entry type** list, click **Personal Distribution List**, and then click **OK**.

The **New Personal Distribution List Properties** dialog box appears.

34 In the **Name** box, type Team, and click the **Add/Remove Members** button.

The **Edit Members of Team** dialog box appears.

35 In the **Show Names from the** list, click **Personal Address Book**.

The names in the Personal Address Book appear in the **Name** list.

Tip

You can also add contacts to your personal distribution lists. In the **Edit Members** dialog box, click **Contacts** in the **Show Names from the** list to show names from the Contacts folder, and then click the names you want.

36 In the **Name** list, click **Catherine Turner**, hold down the shift key and click **Kim Yoshida**, and then click the **Members** button.

The names are added to the **Personal Distribution List** box.

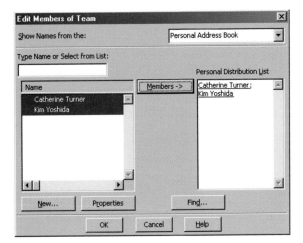

37   Click **OK**, and in the **New Personal Distribution List Properties** dialog box, click **OK**.

The Address Book shows the new distribution list. Distribution lists appear in bold and are marked with an icon.

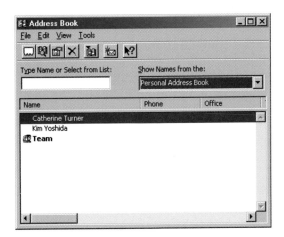

Close

38   Click the **Close** button.

The **Address Book** window closes.

New Mail
Message

39   On the Standard toolbar, click the **New Mail Message** button.

A new, blank Message form appears.

To

40 Click the **To** button, click the down arrow to the right of the **Show Names from the** box, and click **Personal Address Book** in the drop-down list.

The contents of the Personal Address Book are displayed in the **Name** list.

41 In the **Name** list, click the **Team** distribution list, click the **To** button, and click **OK**.

The **Team** distribution list appears in the **To** box.

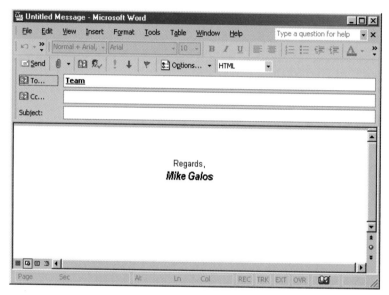

42 Click the **Close** button, and click **No** when prompted to save the message draft.

The Message form closes, discarding the draft.

43 Close the **Folder** list by clicking its **Close** button. If you are not continuing on to the next chapter, close any open messages, and on the **File** menu, click **Exit** to exit Outlook.

Checking Addresses

By default, Outlook will check any e-mail address you type against the entries in the Outlook Address Book. If the address book does not contain an entry for a name that you type in the **To**, **Cc**, or **Bcc** boxes of a new message, when you send the message, Outlook will prompt you to select an address book entry or provide a full address.

To have Outlook check entries from your Personal Address Book:

1   On the **Tools** menu, click **Address Book**.

2   On the **Address Book** window's **Tools** menu, click **Options**.

3   In the **Addressing** dialog box, click the **Add** button.

4   In the **Add Address List** dialog box, click **Personal Address Book**, and click the **Add** button.

5   Click the **Close** button.

6   In the **Addressing** dialog box, click **OK**.

7   In the **Address Book** window, click the **Close** button.

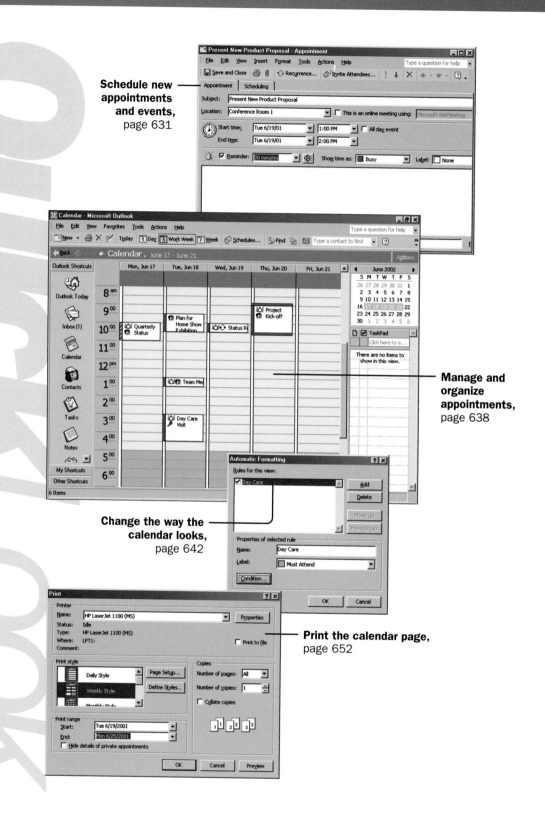

Schedule new appointments and events, page 631

Manage and organize appointments, page 638

Change the way the calendar looks, page 642

Print the calendar page, page 652

Chapter 27
Managing Your Calendar

After completing this chapter, you will be able to:

✔ **Schedule appointments and events.**

✔ **Manage and organize appointments.**

✔ **Change the way the Calendar looks.**

✔ **Print your Calendar.**

Managing time effectively is a constant challenge for most people today. Microsoft Outlook's **Calendar** makes it easy for you to manage your schedule, including both appointments and events, as well as view and print your schedule for a day, a week, or a month.

This chapter uses the practice files DayCareVisit and TeamMeeting (which are appointments) that you installed from this book's CD-ROM onto your hard disk and copied into Outlook. For details about installing and copying the practice files, see "Using the Book's CD-ROM" at the beginning of this book.

Scheduling Appointments and Events

Adding your time commitments to a calendar can help you manage your daily schedule. You can use Outlook's Calendar to schedule **appointments** (which typically last just part of a day) or **events** (which typically last all day long). For example, you might create an appointment in your Outlook Calendar for the time you will spend seeing your doctor, and you might schedule an event for an all-day seminar you plan to attend. Both appointments and events can be **recurring**, meaning they occur repeatedly at regular intervals—for example, daily, weekly, or monthly. You can specify a subject and location for each Calendar item as well as the date and time. You can indicate your availability as available, tentative, busy, or out of office during the scheduled time, and you can choose to receive a reminder of an appointment or event. Reminders appear in a small dialog box that appears as the time of the appointment or event approaches. Outlook must be open for you to receive reminders.

You can also mark an appointment as **private**. Private appointments appear on your Calendar, but the details are hidden from others.

By default, your Calendar looks like this:

Appointment area

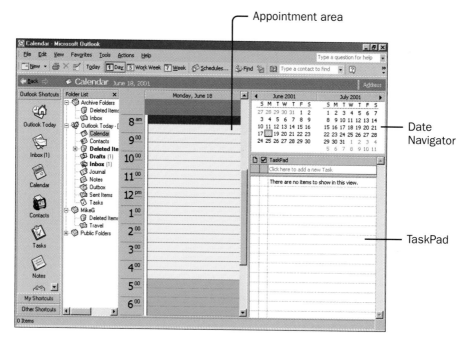

Date Navigator

TaskPad

In Outlook's Calendar, the day is broken into half-hour increments, with the hours between 8 A.M. and 5 P.M. on weekdays highlighted as the default **work week**. You can change the Calendar's work week to reflect your own working hours, and you can schedule appointments for any time of any day.

The **Date Navigator** serves as a handy month calendar and an easy way to view your schedule for specific dates. To view your schedule for a particular date, simply click that date in the Date Navigator.

In this exercise, you will view and move around your Calendar, schedule an appointment, make a recurring appointment, and schedule an event. You don't need any practice files for this exercise.

1   If it is not already open, start Outlook, and then maximize its window.

Calendar

2   In the Outlook Bar, click the **Calendar** icon.

Your Calendar is displayed, showing today's schedule.

3 If necessary, close the **Folder** list by clicking **Folder List** on the **View** menu. Then in the Date Navigator, click tomorrow's date.

Tomorrow's schedule is displayed.

4 Double-click the **1 PM** time slot.

The Appointment form appears.

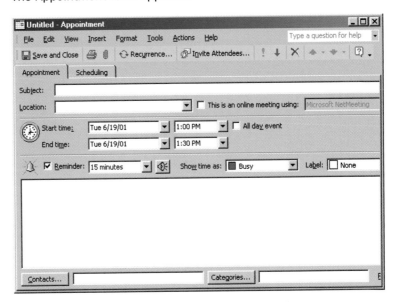

5 In the **Subject** box, type **Present New Product Proposal**.

6 Press the ⌨Tab key, and in the **Location** box, type **Conference Room 1**, which is the location for your appointment.

7 Click the down arrow to the right of the second **End time** box, and click **2:00 PM** in the drop-down list to extend the meeting duration to an hour.

8 Click the down arrow to the right of the **Reminder** box, and click **30 minutes** in the drop-down list to be reminded far enough in advance to set up for your presentation.

The Appointment form now looks like the example shown on the next page.

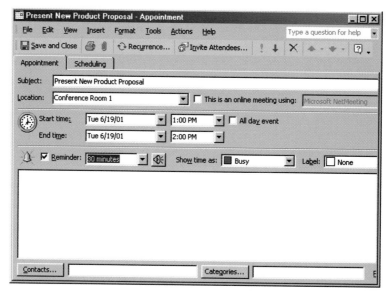

9 Click the **Save and Close** button.

The appointment is saved in your Calendar, where it looks like this:

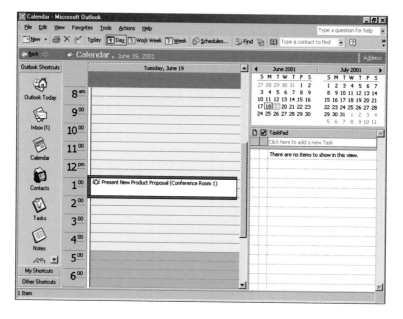

Tip

You can quickly create an appointment using the default reminder setting and without specifying a location. Simply click the time slot on the Calendar, type the subject, and press the [Enter] key.

10 In the Date Navigator, click the Wednesday of the third week of next month.

The schedule for the selected day of the month is displayed.

11 Double-click the **10 AM** time slot.

The Appointment form appears.

12 In the **Subject** box, type Status Report.

13 Press the [Tab] key, and in the **Location** box, type Boss's Office.

14 Click the **Recurrence** button.

The **Appointment Recurrence** dialog box appears.

15 In the **Recurrence pattern** area, click the **Monthly** option, and then click **The third Wednesday of every 1 month(s)** option.

The dialog box now looks like this:

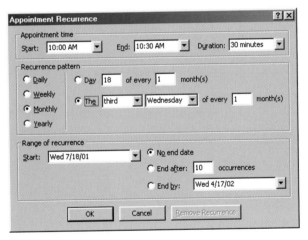

16 Click **OK**.

The recurrence settings are added to the Appointment form.

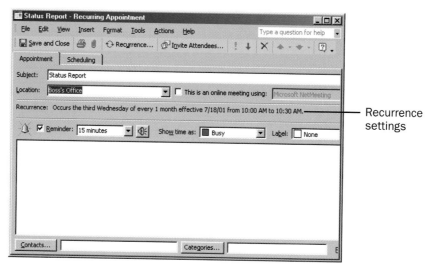

Recurrence settings

17 Click the **Save and Close** button.

The recurring appointment is added to your Calendar.

18 In the Date Navigator, click the right arrow.

The Date Navigator shows the next month, with the third Wednesday appearing in bold, indicating that an appointment is scheduled for that day.

19 On the **View** menu, point to **Go To**, and click **Go To Date**.

The **Go To Date** dialog box appears.

20 In the **Date** box, type 12/23/02, and click **OK**.

The schedule for December 23rd, 2002, is displayed.

21 Right-click the **9 AM** time slot, and click **New All Day Event** on the shortcut menu.

The Event form appears.

22 In the **Subject** box, type Out for the Holidays.

23 Clear the **Reminder** check box.

24 Click the down arrow to the right of the **Show time as** box, and click **Out of Office** in the drop-down list.

25 In the bottom right corner of the Event form, click the **Private** check box.

The form now looks like this:

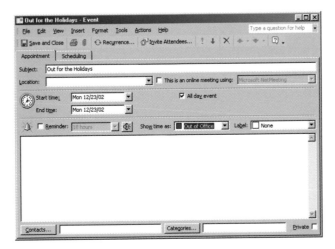

Tip

You can easily mark an existing appointment as private. Simply right-click the appointment in the Calendar, and click **Private** on the shortcut menu.

26 Click the **Save and Close** button.

The new event is added to your Calendar, with a **key** icon indicating that the appointment is marked as private.

Tip

By default, Outlook adds the typical holidays for your country as events on your Calendar, but you can add the holidays of other countries. On the **Tools** menu, click **Options**. On the **Preferences** tab, click **Calendar Options**, and click the **Add Holidays** button. Select the countries whose holidays you want to add, and then click **OK**. Click **OK** again to close the confirmation message that appears, and then click **OK** twice to close the remaining dialog boxes.

27 Navigate to the location of the Status Report event and right-click the event.

28 In the shortcut menu, click **Delete**. In the **Confirm Delete** dialog box that appears, click the **Delete All Occurrences** option.

The event is deleted.

29 Navigate to the location of the Present New Product Proposal event, and right-click the event.

30 On the shortcut menu, click **Delete**.

The event is deleted.

Today

31 On the toolbar, click the **Today** button.

Today's schedule is displayed.

Managing and Organizing Appointments

You can use the Outlook Calendar to manage and organize your appointments in a variety of ways. You can enter details about an appointment to help you remember important information, such as the agenda for a meeting or directions to a client's office. And as with e-mail messages, you can assign categories to help you sort your appointments. For example, you might assign a dentist appointment to the Personal category. Outlook includes a selection of useful categories, including Business, Personal, and more, but you can create additional categories to meet your needs. When your schedule changes, you can also move, copy, and delete appointments.

In this exercise, you will add details to an appointment, assign a category to an appointment, and move, copy, and delete an appointment. You don't need any practice files for this exercise.

1 With your Calendar displayed in Outlook, click tomorrow's date in the Date Navigator.

Tomorrow's schedule is displayed.

2 Click the **9 AM** time slot, type Budget Meeting, and press the Enter key.

The appointment is added to the Calendar.

3 Double-click the appointment to edit it.

The Appointment form appears.

4 Click in the **Location** box, and type Conference Room 1.

Tip

Outlook remembers the locations you type in the **Location** box. Instead of typing the location again, you can click the down arrow to the right of the **Location** box, and then click the location you want.

5   Click the down arrow to the right of the second **Start time** box, and click **9:30 AM** in the drop-down list.

6   Click the down arrow to the right of the second **End time** box, and click **10:30 AM** in the drop-down list.

7   Be sure the **Reminder** check box is selected, and in the **Reminder** list, click **1 hour**.

8   Click the **comments** area below the reminder, and type a rough agenda for the meeting like the one shown here:

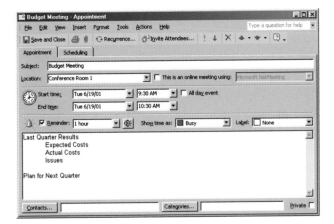

9   At the bottom of the Appointment form, click the **Categories** button.

The **Categories** dialog box appears.

10   Click in the **Item(s) belong to these categories** box, type Finance, and click the **Add to List** button.

The **Finance** category is added to the list and is selected.

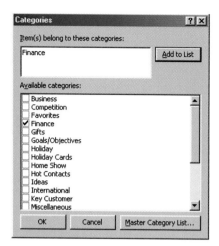

11 In the **Available categories** list, click the **Business** check box, and click **OK**.

The selected categories are added to the **Categories** box in the Appointment form.

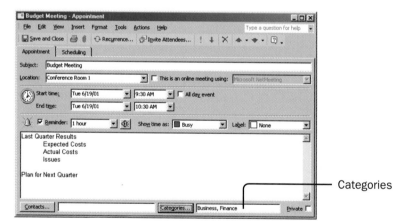

Categories

12 Click the **Save and Close** button.

The updated appointment is added to the Calendar.

13 Click the **12 PM** time slot, and type Lunch with Susan.

14 Point to the bottom border of the appointment, and when the pointer changes to a vertical double-headed arrow, drag the bottom of the appointment to 1 PM, and then press the [Enter] key.

The appointment is added to the Calendar.

Today

15 On the toolbar, click the **Today** button.

The schedule for today is displayed. In the Date Navigator, tomorrow's date appears in bold, indicating that appointments are scheduled for that day.

16 In the Date Navigator, click tomorrow's date.

Tomorrow's schedule is displayed.

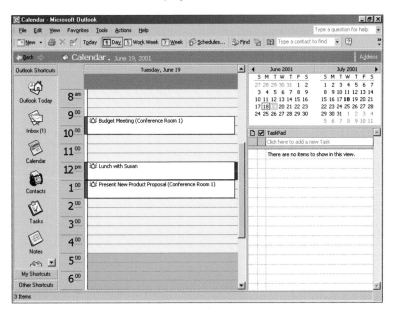

17 Point to the left border of the **Lunch with Susan** appointment.

The pointer becomes a four-headed arrow.

18 Drag the appointment to the 11:30 AM time slot.

The lunch appointment is rescheduled for 11:30 AM

19 Point to the left border of the **Budget Meeting** appointment.

The pointer becomes a four-headed arrow.

20 Using the right mouse button, drag the appointment to the same day of the following week in the Date Navigator.

A shortcut menu appears.

21 On the shortcut menu, click **Copy**.

The schedule for the same day next week is displayed, showing the Budget Meeting appointment.

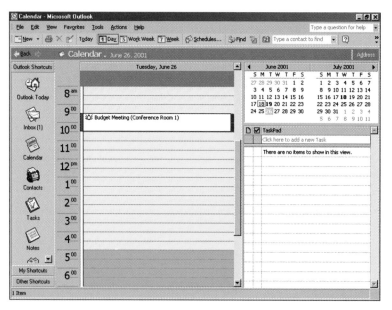

22 In the Date Navigator, click tomorrow's date.

Tomorrow's schedule is displayed, showing the original Budget Meeting appointment.

Delete

23 Click the **Lunch with Susan** appointment, and on the toolbar, click the **Delete** button.

The appointment is removed from your Calendar.

Changing the Way the Calendar Looks

To help you stay on top of your schedule, Outlook provides a variety of ways to view your Calendar. For daily use, you can look at one day at a time. For short-term planning, you can see a five-day work week or a seven-day week. For long-term planning, you can view an entire month. You can set your default work schedule as well as choose how appointments are displayed using a set of customizable views and filters, similar to those available for e-mail messages.

Calendar
Coloring
new for
OfficeXP

To make important appointments stand out in your Calendar, you can color-code them using labels. Labels allow you to color-code appointments so you know the type of an appointment at a glance. The available labels include Important, Business, Personal, and more. Labels can help you get ready for your appointments. You can apply the Travel Required label to remind you that an appointment takes place away from your office or apply the Needs Preparation label to an appointment for which you must prepare a presentation.

About Calendar Views

Outlook offers a number of ways to view your Calendar. To select the view, on the **View** menu, point to **Current View**, and then click the view you want.

Click This View	To See
Day/Week/Month	A calendar-like view of appointments, events, and meetings for the period of time you specify. This is the default view, and it includes the TaskPad.
Day/Week/Month With AutoPreview	The Day/Week/Month view with the addition of the first line of comment text for each Calendar item
Active Appointments	A list of appointments and meetings scheduled for today and in the future, showing details in columns
Events	A list of events, showing details in columns
Annual Events	A list of annual events, showing details in columns
Recurring Appointments	A list of recurring appointments, showing details in columns
By Category	A list of all items, grouped by category, showing details in columns

HomeShow
Kickoff
DayCareVisit
TeamMeeting

In this exercise, you will view items during a specified period of time, change your Calendar view, add colors to appointments manually and by using a rule, and change your default work week schedule.

1   With your Calendar displayed in Outlook, drag the right frame of the Calendar to the right until only one month is visible in the Date Navigator.

2   Navigate to June 2002 in the Date Navigator, click **18**, and then click the **Work Week** button on the toolbar.

The Calendar shows the schedule for Monday through Friday of the week containing the date you selected.

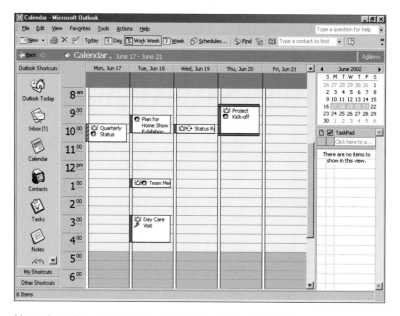

Note that the week is shaded in the Date Navigator.

   3   On the toolbar, click the **Week** button.

The Calendar now shows the schedule for the seven-day week containing the date that was selected when you clicked the **Week** button. The week is shaded in the Date Navigator.

4   In the Date Navigator, click to the left of Sunday of the next week.

The Calendar now shows the schedule for next week.

   5   On the toolbar, click the **Month** button. (If necessary, click the **Toolbar Options** button at the right end of the toolbar, and click the **Month** button on the drop-down menu.)

The Calendar shows the schedule for the current month.

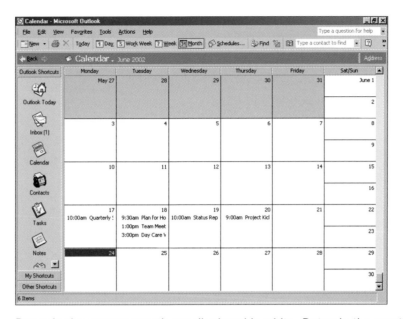

Dates in the current month are displayed in white. Dates in the months immediately preceding or following are displayed in gray. Gray and white alternate for each month thereafter.

6   On the toolbar, click the **Day** button.

You see the familiar display for a single day—in this case, showing any appointments scheduled for the date you selected in step 2.

7   Click the **Today** button.

The Calendar displays today's schedule.

8   On the **View** menu, point to **Current View**, and click **Day/Week/Month View With AutoPreview**.

9   Click tomorrow's date in the Date Navigator.

Calendar items are displayed with the first line of comment text. If you have no appointments on the date shown, click any Tuesday after July 2001 in the Date Navigator to see the Team Meeting appointment, which contains comment text.

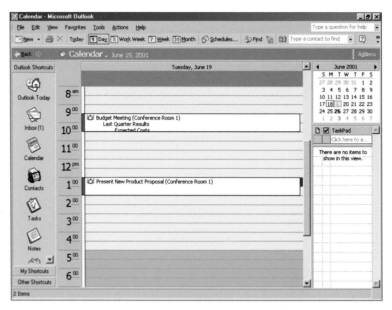

10 On the **View** menu, point to **Current View**, and click **By Category**.

Calendar items are displayed in a columnar list, grouped by category.

11 Click the plus sign (+) to the left of the Personal category.

The item in the Personal category is displayed.

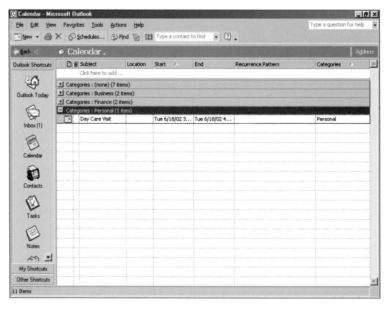

12 On the **View** menu, point to **Current View**, and click **Day/Week/Month**.

The Calendar displays today's schedule.

13 Navigate to June 18, 2002, add an appointment at 11:00 A.M. called **Budget Meeting**, and then double-click the **Budget Meeting** appointment.

The Appointment form appears.

14 Click the down arrow to the right of the **Label** box, click **Business**, and then click the **Save and Close** button.

The updated appointment is saved in your Calendar, appearing in blue to indicate it is business related.

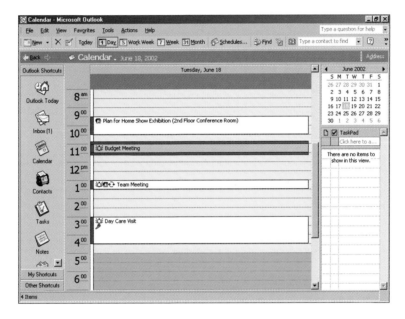

Calendar
Coloring

15 On the toolbar, click the **Calendar Coloring** button, and then click **Automatic Formatting**.

The **Automatic Formatting** dialog box appears so that you can create a new formatting rule.

16 Click the **Add** button, and in the **Name** box, type **Day Care**.

The rule is added to the **Rules for this view** area.

17 In the **Label** list, click **Must Attend**, and click the **Condition** button.

The **Filter** dialog box is displayed.

18 In the **Search for the word(s)** box, type **Day Care**, and click **OK**.

The condition specifying that the formatting should be applied to items that include the words *Day Care* is saved, and you return to the **Automatic Formatting** dialog box, which looks like the example shown on the next page.

19 Click **OK**.

Outlook applies the automatic formatting rule to your Calendar and displays the Day Care Visit appointment in orange, indicating that you must attend.

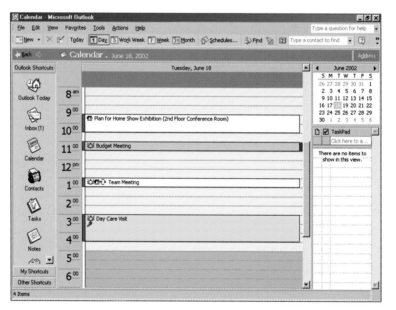

20 Now you'll change your work week. On the **Tools** menu, click **Options**.

The **Options** dialog box appears.

21 On the **Preferences** tab, click the **Calendar Options** button.

The **Calendar Options** dialog box appears.

22 In the **Calendar work week** area, click the **Sun** check box and clear the **Fri** check box.

23 Make sure that the **Start time** setting is 8:00 AM. Then click the down arrow to the right of the **End time** box, and click **4:30 PM**.

The dialog box now looks like this:

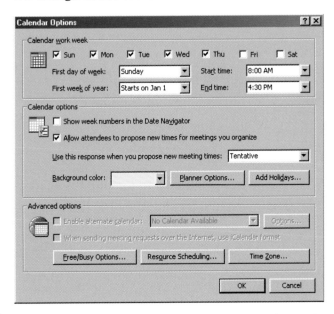

24 Click **OK**, and in the **Options** dialog box, click **OK** again.

The Calendar is displayed with your new default work hours—only the hours between 8 AM and 4:30 PM are highlighted.

25 On the toolbar, click the **Work Week** button.

The Work Week view displays Sunday through Thursday, according to your default work week settings.

26 On the toolbar, click the **Calendar Coloring** button, and then click **Automatic Formatting**.

The **Automatic Formatting** dialog box appears.

27 Click the **Day Care** rule, and click the **Delete** button.

The rule is deleted.

28 Click **OK**.

The **Automatic Formatting** dialog box closes.

29 On the **Tools** menu, click **Options**.

The **Options** dialog box appears.

30 On the **Preferences** tab, click the **Calendar Options** button.

The **Calendar Options** dialog box appears.

31 In the **Calendar work week** area, clear the **Sun** check box and click the **Fri** check box.

32 Click **OK**, and in the **Options** dialog box, click **OK** again.

Both dialog boxes close.

33 Drag the right frame of the Calendar to the left until two months are visible in the Date Navigator again.

34 On the toolbar, click the **Day** button.

The schedule for the date selected in the Date Navigator is displayed.

Time Zones in Your Calendar

If you frequently work with people from other countries or regularly travel internationally, you might want to change the time zone or view a second time zone in your Calendar. Note that changing your time zone in Outlook is equivalent to changing your time zone in Control Panel. It affects the time displayed on the Windows taskbar and in any other Windows programs.

To change your current time zone:

1 On the **Tools** menu, click **Options**.

2 On the **Preferences** tab, click the **Calendar Options** button.

3 In the **Calendar Options** dialog box, click the **Time Zone** button.

4 Click the down arrow to the right of the **Time zone** box, click a time zone other than your own, and then click **OK** three times to close all the dialog boxes.

To show a second time zone in your Calendar:

1 On the **Tools** menu, click **Options**.

2 On the **Preferences** tab, click the **Calendar Options** button.

3 In the **Calendar Options** dialog box, click the **Time Zone** button.

4 Select the **Show an additional time zone** check box.

5 Click in the **Label** box, and type the label you want for this time zone. (For example, if you are adding the Eastern Time Zone, you would type *EST*.)

6 Click the down arrow to the right of the **Time zone** box, click the time zone you want, and click **OK** three times to close all the dialog boxes. Your calendar will look something like this:

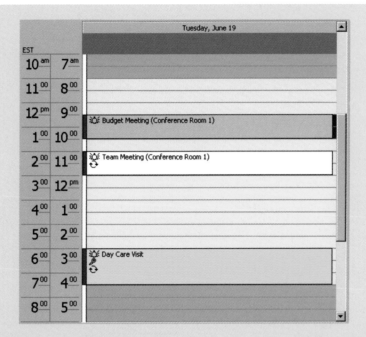

You can use the **Swap Time Zones** button in the **Time Zone** dialog box to replace the current time zone with the second one. Swapping time zones changes all time-related fields, such as when messages are received or the time of appointments, to the new time zone.

To reset the time zone display to its original settings:

1   On the **Tools** menu, click **Options**.

2   On the **Preferences** tab, click the **Calendar Options** button.

3   In the **Calendar Options** dialog box, click the **Time Zone** button.

4   Click the **Show an additional time zone** check box.

5   Clear the **Show an additional time zone** check box.

6   Click the down arrow to the right of the **Time zone** box, click your own time zone, and then click **OK** three times to close all the dialog boxes.

Printing Your Calendar

When your schedule is full and you find yourself running from one appointment to the next, you might not always be able to check your Outlook Calendar. By printing your Calendar, you can take your schedule with you. With Outlook, you can print your Calendar in a variety of formats, called **print styles**. You can select from a list of predefined print styles, including Daily, Weekly, and Monthly, or create your own. You can also select the range of dates to be printed.

In this exercise, you will print your Calendar in the daily, weekly, and monthly styles, and then create a new print style for your Calendar. You don't need any practice files for this exercise.

Important

To complete this exercise, you must have a printer installed. If you are working on a network, your administrator can provide the information you need to install a printer. If you are working on a stand-alone computer, click the **Start** button, point to **Settings**, and click **Printers**. Then click the **Add Printer** icon, and follow the wizard's instructions.

1 With your Calendar displayed in Outlook, click tomorrow's date in the Date Navigator.

The Calendar displays your schedule for tomorrow.

Print

2 On the toolbar, click the **Print** button. (If the toolbar button is not visible, click the **Toolbar Options** button to display it.)

The **Print** dialog box appears, with the **Daily Style** format and tomorrow's date as the default options.

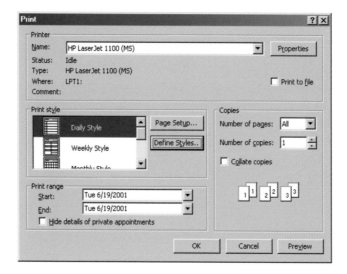

652

3   Click **OK**.

Outlook prints today's schedule in the Daily Style format, which approximates the Day view.

4   On the toolbar, click the **Print** button again.

The **Print** dialog box appears, with Daily Style and tomorrow's date as the default options.

5   In the **Print style** list, click **Weekly Style**.

6   In the **Print range** area, click the down arrow to the right of the **End** box, and click the date seven days from today.

The **Print** dialog box now looks like this:

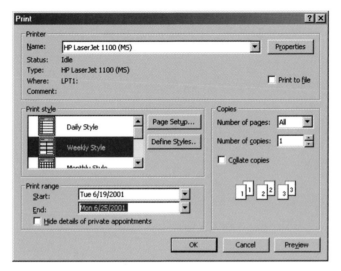

7   Click the **Hide details of private appointments** check box, and click **OK**.

Outlook prints the schedule for the selected dates in the Weekly Style format, which approximates the Week view.

8   On the toolbar, click the **Print** button again.

Note that Outlook doesn't retain your settings from one print session to the next.

9   In the **Print style** list, click **Monthly Style**, and then click the **Page Setup** button.

The **Page Setup** dialog box appears, showing the options for the Monthly Style format.

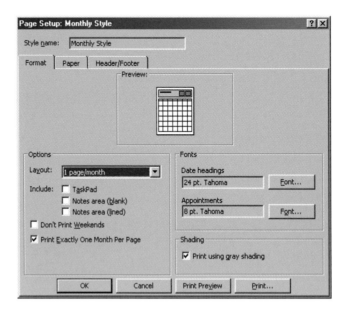

Tip

Each print style has a unique set of page setup options. When selecting a print style, be sure to click the **Page Setup** button to investigate these options.

10 On the **Format** tab, click the **Don't Print Weekends** check box, and click **OK**.

The **Page Setup** dialog box closes.

11 In the **Print** dialog box, click **OK**.

Outlook prints the Calendar for the current month.

12 Now you'll copy a built-in style and customize it to create your own print style. On the toolbar, click the **Print** button.

13 Click the **Define Styles** button.

The **Define Print Styles** dialog box appears.

14 In the **Print styles** list, make sure *Daily Style* is selected, and click the **Copy** button.

The **Page Setup** dialog box appears, showing the options for your copy of the Daily Style format.

15 Click in the **Style name** box at the top of the dialog box, delete the text in the box, and type **2 Per Day**.

16 Click the down arrow to the right of the **Layout** box, and click **2 pages/day**.

17 Clear the **Notes area (blank)** check box, and click the **Notes area (lined)** check box.

The dialog box now looks like this:

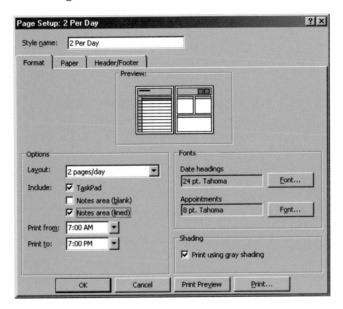

18 Click the **Paper** tab.

The options on the **Paper** tab are displayed.

19 In the **Orientation** area in the bottom right corner, click the **Landscape** option, and then click the **Print Preview** button.

The Print Preview window opens, showing your print style applied to today's schedule.

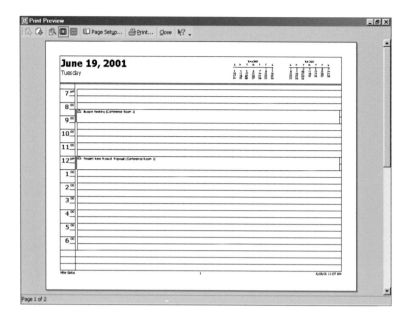

Close Preview

Close

20 On the Print Preview toolbar, click the **Close Preview** button.

The Print Preview window closes.

21 On the toolbar, click the **Print** button.

The **Print** dialog box appears.

22 In the **Print style** list, make sure *2 Per Day* is selected, and click **OK**.

Outlook prints the selected day's schedule in the 2 Per Day format.

23 If you are not continuing on to the next chapter, on the **File** menu, click **Exit** to exit Outlook.

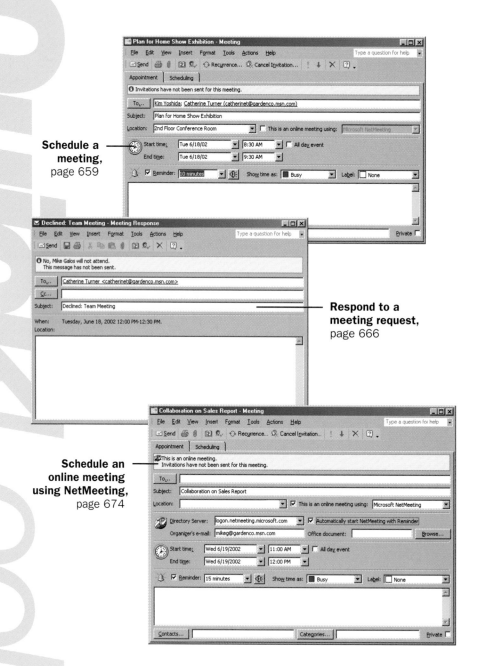

Schedule a meeting, page 659

Respond to a meeting request, page 666

Schedule an online meeting using NetMeeting, page 674

Chapter 28
Scheduling and Managing Meetings

After completing this chapter, you will be able to:

✔ Schedule a meeting.

✔ Respond to meeting requests.

✔ Update and cancel meetings.

✔ Schedule online meetings with NetMeeting.

Microsoft Outlook can help you with the often onerous task of organizing meetings. You can check the availability of attendees, find a location, distribute the meeting invitations, and track attendee responses. And as schedules change, you can update or cancel scheduled meetings. You can also respond to meeting invitations manually or automatically and view other users' calendars to check their availability.

This chapter uses the practice files HomeShow (which is a Calendar item); Kickoff, TeamMeet, and Status (which are meeting requests); and CatherineT and KimY (which are contact items) that you installed from this book's CD-ROM and copied into Outlook. For details about installing and copying the practice files, see "Using the Book's CD-ROM" at the beginning of this book.

Scheduling Meetings

With Outlook, you can schedule meetings, invite attendees—both those who work for your organization and those who don't—and reserve resources such as conference rooms or equipment. To choose a date and time for your meeting, you can check the availability of attendees and resources by viewing their free/busy information. Attendees who don't work for your organization must make this information available over the Internet.

You can also have Outlook select the meeting time for you. You can indicate whether the attendance of each invitee is required or optional. Outlook uses this information to find the best meeting times for required attendees and to optimize the availability of optional attendees.

Once you have selected a time, you send a **meeting request**—a type of e-mail message—to each invited attendee and requested resource. Responses from attendees and those responsible for scheduling the resources you requested are automatically tracked as you receive them.

CatherineT
KimY

In this exercise, you will plan a meeting, invite attendees, and set and then remove a meeting reminder.

Important

For this exercise, you will need contact information for Catherine Turner and Kim Yoshida in your Contacts list. Follow the instructions in "Using the Book's CD-ROM" to copy the CatherineT and KimY practice files from the Office XP SBS\ Outlook\Chap28\Journal folder to the **Contacts** icon on the Outlook Bar.

1   If it is not already open, start Outlook, and then maximize its window.

Calendar

2   On the Outlook Bar, click the **Calendar** icon.

The Calendar is displayed.

3   If Outlook displays reminders about appointments you entered in your Calendar in previous exercises, click **Dismiss All**, and then click **Yes** to close them.

4   In the Date Navigator, scroll to June 2002, and click **17** to display the Calendar for that day.

5   On the **Actions** menu, click **Plan a Meeting**.

The Plan a Meeting form appears, listing you as the only attendee in the **All Attendees** list.

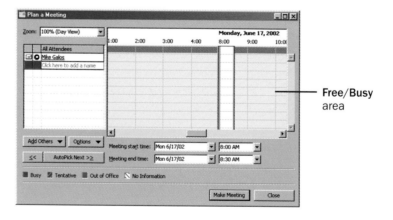

Free/Busy area

6 Click the **Add Others** button, and in the drop-down list, click **Add from Address Book**.

The **Select Attendees and Resources** dialog box appears.

7 If necessary, click the down arrow to the right of the **Show Names from the** box, and then click **Contacts**.

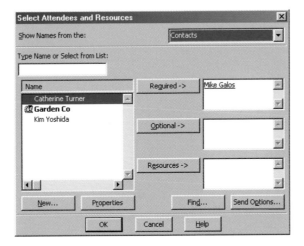

Important

In this exercise, you have been provided with contact information for fictitious employees of The Garden Company. If you want, you can use the names of your co-workers or other contacts to plan an actual meeting.

8 In the **Name** list, click **Kim Yoshida**, and click the **Required** button.

The name is added to the **Required Attendees** box.

9 In the **Name** list, click **Catherine Turner**, and click the **Optional** button.

The name is added to the **Optional Attendees** box.

10 Click **OK**. If prompted to join the Microsoft Office Internet Free/Busy Service, click **Cancel**.

The attendees are added to the **All Attendees** list, with icons that indicate whether their attendance is required or optional.

Required attendee icon

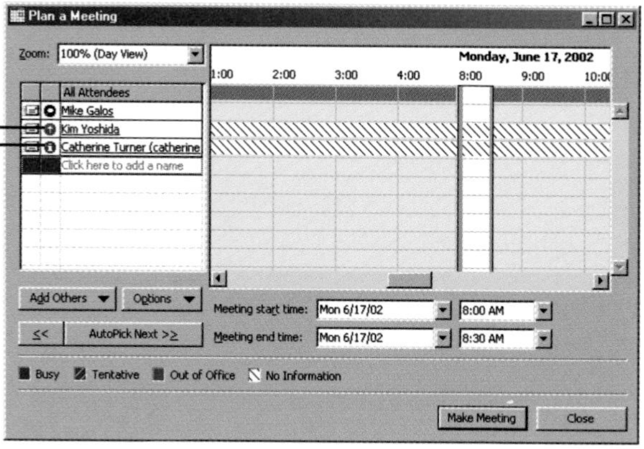

Optional attendee icon

11 Use the horizontal scroll bar in the **Free/Busy** area to view attendee availability for June 18, 2002.

This area shows whether attendees are free, tentatively scheduled, busy, or out of the office. Busy time appears in blue, tentative time in stripes, and time out of the office in purple. (If you are using fictitious names, free/busy information will not be available.)

12 Click the **8:30** time slot in the **Free/Busy** area to select that time.

The half-hour time slot you clicked appears as a vertical white bar. The **Meeting start time** and **Meeting end time** lists reflect the date and time you selected.

Tip

You can quickly find the next available free time for all attendees and resources. Click the **AutoPick Next** button in the **Plan a Meeting** dialog box or on the **Scheduling** tab of the Meeting form.

13 In the **Free/Busy** area, click the red bar on the right edge of the selected meeting time and drag it one half hour to the right.

The second **Meeting end time** setting reflects the change—the meeting is now scheduled to last for one hour.

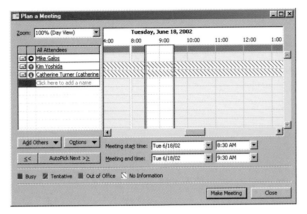

14 Click the **Make Meeting** button.

The Meeting form appears.

15 In the **Subject** box, type **Plan for Home Show Exhibition**, press the `Tab` key, and in the **Location** box, type **2nd Floor Conference Room**.

16 Be sure the **Reminder** check box is selected, click the down arrow to the right of the **Reminder** box, and then click **10 minutes**.

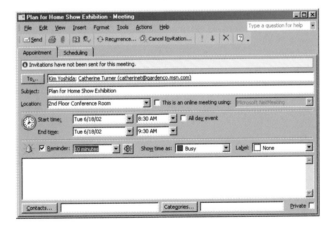

Send

≡ Send

17 On the toolbar, click the **Send** button.

The meeting request is sent.

Important

If the attendees you provided are fictitious, e-mail messages you send to them will be returned as undeliverable. You can delete the returned messages at any time.

18 Click the **Close** button.

The Plan a Meeting form closes.

19 In the Calendar, click June 18, 2002, in the Date Navigator.

The schedule for June 18 is displayed, with the meeting request in the 9:30-10:30 time slot.

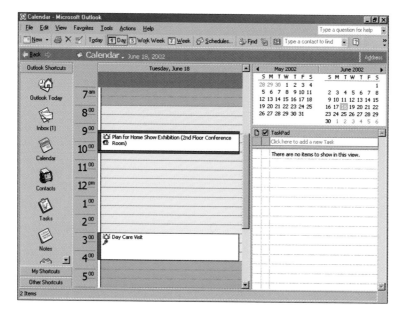

20 Double-click the **Plan for Home Show Exhibition** meeting.

The Meeting form opens.

21 Clear the **Reminder** check box, and on the toolbar, click **Save and Close**.

The updated meeting is saved. You will not receive a reminder for the meeting, but your meeting attendees will.

Scheduling Resources for a Meeting

If you are working on a network that uses Microsoft Exchange Server and your system administrator has added resources such as conference rooms or projection equipment to the organization's **Global Address List**, you can reserve those resources for your meeting. You reserve resources by inviting them to your meeting. Your invitation is sent to the person designated by your administrator to manage the schedule for the resource. That person responds to your meeting request based on the availability of the resource at the time you requested.

To schedule a resource for a new meeting:

1   On the Outlook Bar, click the **Calendar** icon.

2   On the **Actions** menu, click **Plan a Meeting**.

    The Plan a Meeting form appears.

3   Click the **Add Others** button, and then click **Add from Address Book**.

    The **Select Attendees and Resources** dialog box appears.

4   In the **Show Names from the** box, be sure that *Global Address List* is selected.

5   In the **Name** list, select the required and optional attendees as usual. Then click the resource you want, and click the **Resources** button.

6   Repeat step 5 for as many resources as you need, and then click **OK**.

7   In the Plan a Meeting form, click the **Make Meeting** button, and then click the **Close** button.

To schedule a resource for an existing meeting:

1   In the Calendar, double-click the meeting to open it, and then click the **Scheduling** tab.

2   Click the **Add Others** button, and then click **Add from Address Book**.

3   In the **Show Names from the** box, be sure that *Global Address List* is selected.

4   In the **Name** list, click the resource you want, and then click the **Resources** button.

5   Repeat step 4 for as many resources as you need, and then click **OK**.

6   Click the **Send Update** button.

Responding to Meeting Requests

Just as you can send meeting requests, you can receive meeting requests from others. When you do, you can respond in one of three ways. You can accept the request and inform the requester that you will attend. Meetings that you accept are automatically entered in your Calendar. You can tentatively accept a request, indicating that you might or might not be able to attend the meeting. Meetings that you accept tentatively are also entered in your Calendar, but your free/busy information will show you as only tentatively scheduled for that time. Finally, you can decline a meeting, in which case the request is deleted and no entry is made in your Calendar. When you decline a meeting, you can choose whether Outlook notifies the person who sent the request.

Kickoff Status
TeamMeet

In this exercise, you will accept a meeting request, decline a meeting request, and propose a new meeting time in response to a meeting request.

Inbox

1   On the Outlook Bar, click the **Inbox** icon.

The contents of the Inbox are displayed.

2   Double-click the **Quarterly Status** message.

The Meeting form appears.

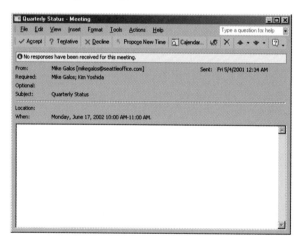

Calendar

3 To view the meeting in your Calendar before you respond, click the **Calendar** button on the toolbar.

Your Calendar appears in a new window, with the requested meeting shown on the desired date.

Close

4 In the Calendar window, click the **Close** button.

The Calendar window closes.

Accept

5 On the Meeting form, click the **Accept** button.

A message box appears, prompting you to choose how you want to respond.

6 With the **Send the response now** option selected, click **OK**.

Your response is sent to the person who requested the meeting, the Meeting form closes, the meeting is entered in your Calendar, and the next message in the Inbox opens.

Tip

When accepting or declining a meeting, you can choose to send a standard response, a response that you compose yourself, or no response.

7 Close the open message by clicking its **Close** button.

8 In the Inbox, double-click the **Team Meeting** message.

The Meeting form appears.

Decline

9 On the toolbar, click the **Decline** button.

A message box appears, prompting you to choose how you want to respond.

10 With the **Edit the response before sending** option selected, click **OK**.

The Meeting Response form appears. The **Subject** box indicates that you are declining the Team Meeting request.

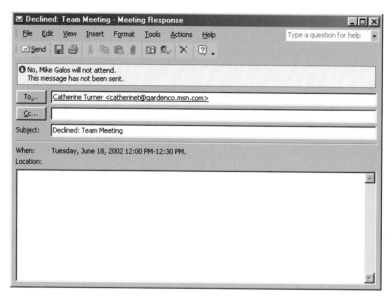

11 In the message body, type **I will be out of the office on this day**.

Send

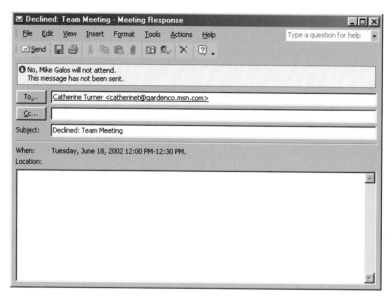

12 On the toolbar, click the **Send** button.

Your response is sent, and the Meeting form closes. The meeting is not added to your Calendar.

13 In the Inbox, double-click the **Project Kick-off** message.

The Meeting form appears.

Propose New
Time

new for
OfficeXP

14 On the toolbar, click the **Propose New Time** button. If prompted to join the Microsoft Office Internet Free/Busy Service, click **Cancel**.

The **Propose New Time** dialog box appears.

15 In the **Free/Busy** area, click the **11:00** column, and drag the right edge of the meeting time to 12:00.

The meeting start and end times are updated to reflect your changes.

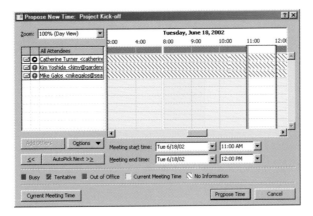

16 Click the **Propose Time** button.

The **Propose New Time** dialog box closes, and the Meeting Response form appears. The subject of the response indicates that you are proposing a new time for the meeting.

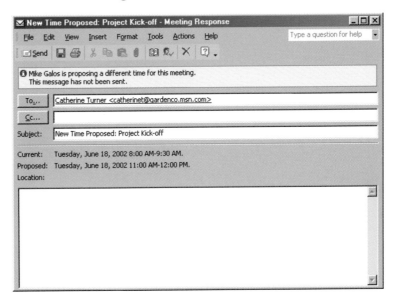

17 In the body of the message, type **I cannot attend meetings scheduled before 9am.**, and on the Standard toolbar, click the **Send** button.

Your response is sent, and the Meeting form closes. The meeting is added to your Calendar as tentatively scheduled for the original meeting time.

Responding to Meeting Requests Automatically

You can choose to respond to meeting requests automatically. Outlook will process meeting requests and cancellations as you receive them, responding to requests, adding new meetings to your calendar, and removing canceled meetings from your calendar. If you choose, Outlook will automatically decline meeting requests that conflict with existing items on your calendar. You can also choose to automatically decline any request for a recurring meeting.

1 On the **Tools** menu, click **Options**.

   The **Options** dialog box appears.

2 On the **Preferences** tab, click the **Calendar Options** button, and then click the **Resource Scheduling** button.

   The **Resource Scheduling** dialog box appears.

3 Click the **Automatically accept meeting requests and process cancellations** check box.

4 Click the **Automatically decline conflicting meeting requests** and the **Automatically decline recurring meeting requests** check boxes if desired, and click **OK**.

5 In the **Calendar Options** dialog box, click **OK**, and in the **Options** dialog box, click **OK**.

Updating and Canceling Meeting Requests

Project schedules can shift on a daily basis. As such, your meetings must be flexible. Outlook makes it easy to update or cancel meetings as your needs change. For example, you might learn that a required attendee is unavailable at the time you requested. In this case, you can change the date or time of the meeting or cancel the meeting altogether. You can also add people to or remove people from the list of attendees.

HomeShow

In this exercise, you will reschedule a meeting, revise a list of meeting attendees, and cancel a meeting.

Important

For this exercise, you will work with the Plan for Home Show Exhibition meeting. If you didn't create this meeting in an earlier exercise, follow the instructions in "Using the Book's CD-ROM" to copy the HomeShow practice file from the Office XP SBS\ Outlook\Chap28 folder to the **Calendar** icon on the Outlook Bar.

1 On the Outlook Bar, click the **Calendar** icon.

The Calendar is displayed.

2 Using the Date Navigator, click June 18, 2002—the date of the Plan for Home Show Exhibition meeting.

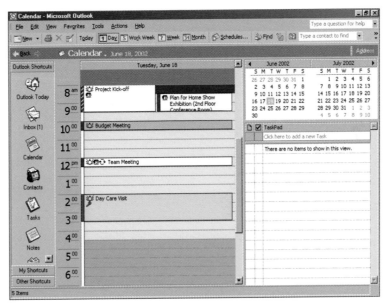

3 Double-click the **Plan for Home Show Exhibition** meeting.

The Meeting form appears.

4 Click the **Scheduling** tab, and in the **Free/Busy** area, scroll to the next business day.

5 Click the **11:00 AM** timeslot, and drag the right edge of the shaded area to 12:00 PM to schedule the meeting to last for one hour.

The start and end times reflect the changes you made to the date and time.

6 Click the **Add Others** button, and then click **Add from Address Book** in the drop-down list.

The **Select Attendees and Resources** dialog box appears.

7 In the **Optional** box, click **Catherine Turner**, and press the ⌨ Del key.

Catherine Turner is removed from the **Optional** box.

Tip

If you are working with an actual meeting and using the names of your co-workers, pick any one of the optional attendees to delete. You can add that person back to the meeting request at any time.

8 Click **OK**.

The **Select Attendees and Resources** dialog box closes. The Meeting form reflects your change in attendees.

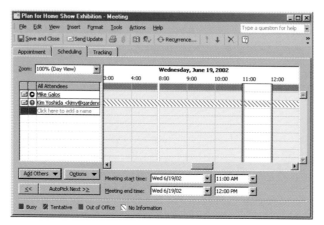

9 On the toolbar, click the **Send Update** button.

The updated Meeting form is sent.

10 In the Date Navigator, click the next business day.

The schedule for the next business day is displayed, including the rescheduled Plan for Home Show Exhibition meeting.

11 Double-click the **Plan for Home Show Exhibition** meeting.

The Meeting form appears.

12 Click the **Tracking** tab.

The **Tracking** tab is displayed, indicating the response received from each attendee. If you are using the practice files for this exercise, this tab will not reflect any responses to the meeting request because the attendees are fictitious people.

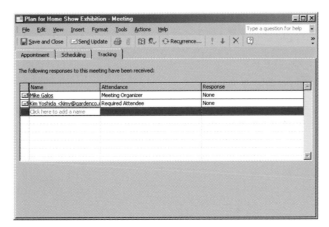

13 On the **Actions** menu, click **Cancel Meeting**.

A message box appears, asking you if you want to send a cancellation notice to the attendees.

14 With the **Send cancellation and delete meeting** option selected, click **OK**.

15 Click the **Appointment** tab.

The Meeting form is updated to indicate that the meeting has been canceled.

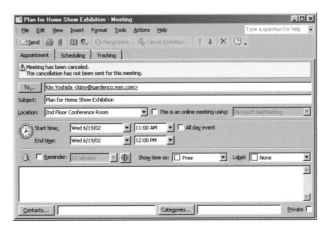

Send

☐ Send

16 On the toolbar, click the **Send** button.

The cancellation notice is sent to all remaining attendees (Kim Yoshida), the Meeting form closes, and the meeting is removed from your Calendar.

Tip

You can easily send a new e-mail message to all attendees of a particular meeting. Simply open the meeting, and on the **Actions** menu, click **New Message to Attendees**. (This method works only on meetings for which attendees have already been invited.)

Scheduling Online Meetings Using NetMeeting

With **NetMeeting**, a program that comes with Microsoft Internet Explorer, you can conduct online meetings via the Internet. NetMeeting allows you to conduct both audio and video conferences with one or more people. NetMeeting conference participants can share applications, collaborate on documents, draw on a shared electronic whiteboard, or transfer files.

Important

To take full advantage of NetMeeting's audio and video capabilities, you need an audio card, video card, speakers, microphone, and camera connected to your computer. Without a camera, you can view other people's video, but they cannot view yours.

CatherineT
KimY

In this exercise, you will schedule an online meeting using NetMeeting.

Important

For this exercise, you will need contact information for Catherine Turner and Kim Yoshida in your Contacts list. Follow the instructions in "Using the Book's CD-ROM" at the beginning of this book to copy the CatherineT and KimY practice files from the Office XP SBS\Outlook\Chap28\Journal folder to the **Contacts** icon on the Outlook Bar.

1   In the Calendar, display the schedule for June 19, 2002, and click the **11:00-12:00** time slot.

New
Appointment
⊞ **New** ▾

2   On the toolbar, click the down arrow to the right of the **New Appointment** button, and then click **Meeting Request**.

A blank Meeting form appears.

3   Click in the **Subject** box, and type **Collaboration on Sales Report**.

4   Click the **This is an online meeting using** check box, and be sure **Microsoft NetMeeting** is selected in the adjacent box. You might have to enlarge the window to see its entire contents.

5   Click in the **Directory Server** box, type **logon.netmeeting.microsoft.com** (the name of the Microsoft Internet Directory server), and then select the **Automatically start NetMeeting with Reminder** check box.

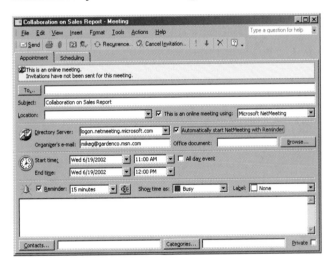

Important

Your organization might use another **directory server**. Contact your system administrator or your ISP for more information.

6   Click the **Scheduling** tab.

7   Click the **Add Others** button, and click **Add from Address Book** in the drop-down list.

The **Select Attendees and Resources** dialog box appears.

8   If necessary, click the down arrow to the right of the **Show names from the** list, and then click **Contacts**.

9   In the **Name** list, click **Kim Yoshida**, hold down the ⌃Ctrl key, and click **Catherine Turner**.

Both names are selected.

10   Click the **Required** button, and then click **OK**. If prompted to join the Microsoft Office Internet Free/Busy Service, click **Cancel**.

The names are added to the **All Attendees** list.

11   In the **Free/Busy** area, scroll to the next business day, click the **2:00 PM** time slot and drag the right edge of the selected time slot to 3:30 PM (halfway between 3:00 PM and 4:00 PM).

The meeting start and end times reflect the date and time you chose.

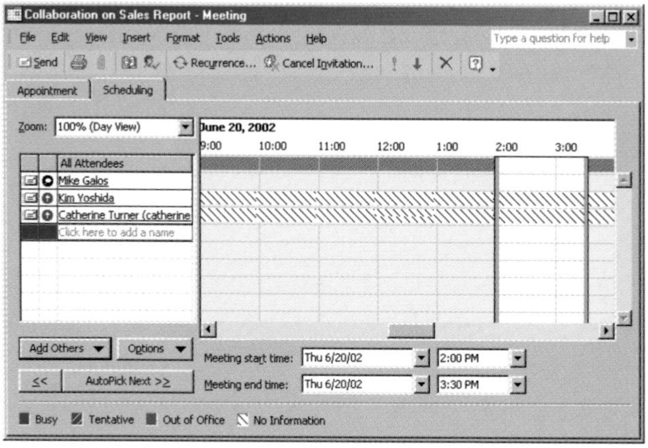

Send

🖃 Send

12 On the toolbar, click the **Send** button.

The meeting request is sent. When the meeting time arrives, NetMeeting will start automatically so that you and the other attendees can connect to the conference.

Tip

For more information on using NetMeeting, start NetMeeting, and on the **Help** menu, click **Help Topics**. To start NetMeeting, click the **Start** button, point to **Programs**, point to **Accessories**, point to **Communications**, and click **NetMeeting**.

Quick Reference

1 On the taskbar, click the **Start** button.

2 On the **Start** menu, point to **Programs**, and then click **Microsoft Word**.

1 On the right side of the menu bar, click in the **Ask A Question** box.

2 Type a question, press ⌷Enter⌷, and then click a topic.

● On the Standard toolbar, click the **New Blank Document** button.

1 Click in the document to place the insertion point where you want the text to begin.

2 Type the text.

1 On the Standard toolbar, click the **Save** button.

2 Click the **Save in** down arrow, and then select a location for the file.

3 In the **File name** box, type the file name.

4 Click **Save**.

1 On the **File** menu, click **Save As**.

2 In the **File name** box, type a new name for the document.

3 Click the **Save as type** down arrow, click the file format that you want to use, and then click **Save**.

1 On the Standard toolbar, click the **Open** button.

2 Navigate to the file you want to open, click the file, and then click **Open**.

19 **To edit text**

1 Select the text or click to place the insertion point where you want to edit.

2 Press ⌨Del⌨ or ⌨Backspace⌨ to delete text, and then retype the text.

21 **To close a document**

● On the **File** menu, click **Close**, or click the **Close Window** button in the document window.

23 **To find and replace text**

1 On the **Edit** menu, click **Replace** to open the **Find and Replace** dialog box.

2 In the **Find what** box, type the text you want to find.

3 Press ⌨Tab⌨ to move the insertion point to the **Replace with** box, type the text you want to use instead, and then click **Find Next**.

4 Click **Replace** or **Replace All** to replace text or **Find Next** to find text.

5 Click **OK**, and then click the **Close** button.

Chapter 2 **Changing the Look of Your Document**

Page 29 **To change the appearance of text**

1 Select the text you want to change.

2 On the Formatting toolbar, click a formatting button, or on the **Format** menu, click **Reveal Formatting** to open the Reveal Formatting task pane, and then use the links to open dialog boxes and make changes.

36 **To format a paragraph**

1 Click in the paragraph or select any part of it.

2 Apply the formats that you want from the toolbars, or on the **Format** menu, click **Paragraph** to open the **Paragraph** dialog box, and then make changes.

42 **To create a bulleted or numbered list**

1 Select the text.

2 On the Formatting toolbar, click the **Numbering** button or the **Bullets** button, or on the **Format** menu, click **Bullets and Numbering** to display the **Bullets and Numbering** dialog box, click a tab, and then click a bullet or numbering style.

48 **To change line and page break options**

1 On the **Format** menu, click **Paragraph** to display the **Paragraph** dialog box, and then click the **Line and Page Breaks** tab, if necessary.

2 Click the **Widow/Orphan control** check box, if desired, select the **Keep lines together** check box, if desired, and then click **OK**.

3 On the **Insert** menu, click **Break** to open the **Break** dialog box.

4 Select the option(s) you want, and then click **OK**.

49 **To add a header or footer to a document**

1 On the **View** menu, click **Header and Footer**.

2 Using the Header and Footer toolbar to move around and make selections, type header and/or footer text.

3 Use the Header and Footer toolbar to format and change the header and/or footer text.

4 On the Header and Footer toolbar, click the **Close** button.

53 **To open and use the Styles and Formatting task pane to change styles**

1 Select the text you want to change.

2 On the **Format** menu, click **Styles and Formatting** to open the Styles and Formatting task pane.

3 In the Styles and Formatting task pane, point to the preview box in the **Formatting of selected text** section to display information about the current style.

4 In the Styles and Formatting task pane, click an option from the **Pick formatting to apply** section, or click **New Style**, and then define a new style with the options in the **New Style** dialog box.

Chapter 3 Presenting Information in Tables and Columns

Page 62 **To create a new table**

1 Click in the document to place the insertion point where you want to create a table.

2 On the **Table** menu, point to **Insert**, and then click **Table**.

3 Type the number of columns and rows you want to use, and then click **OK**.

4 Click in a cell and type your text. Use the [Tab] key to navigate from cell to cell.

5 Use buttons on the Tables and Borders toolbar (such as **Merge Cells**, **Split Cells**, **Align**, or **Distribute**) to format and modify the table or individual cells.

64 **To convert existing plain text to a table**

1 Select the block of text that you want to convert to a table.

2 On the **Table** menu, point to **Convert**, and then click **Text to Table**.

3 Type the number of columns you want to use, and then click **OK**.

65   **To sort information in a table**

1   Click in the table to place the insertion point in the column where you want to sort the information.

2   On the **Table** menu, click **Sort**.

3   In the **Sort** dialog box, select the options you want to use, and then click **OK**.

67   **To format text in a table**

1   In Print Layout view, select the table text that you want to format.

2   Use the Formatting toolbar, the Tables and Borders toolbar, and the **Format** menu to make changes to the text and the table.

73   **To calculate data in a table**

1   Click in the table to place the insertion point.

2   On the **Table** menu, click **Formula** to display the **Formula** dialog box.

3   In the **Formula** dialog box, use the current formula or select another one, and then click **OK**.

73   **To embed an Excel worksheet in a Word document**

1   Click in the document to place the insertion point where you want to embed the Excel worksheet.

2   On the **Insert** menu, click **Object** to open the **Object** dialog box, and then click the **Create from File** tab.

3   Click **Browse**, navigate to the Excel worksheet you want to embed, click the file, and then click **OK**.

76   **To format text into columns**

1   On the **Format** menu, click **Columns**.

2   In the **Columns** dialog box, type the number of columns you want to use, and then click **OK**.

Chapter   **4**   **Proofreading and Printing a Document**
Page   **84**   **To check the spelling and grammar in a document**

1   On the Standard toolbar, click the **Spelling and Grammar** button.

2   Use the **Spelling and Grammar** dialog box to respond to text that is flagged.

3   Click **OK** to close the alert message that Word has finished checking the spelling and grammar in the document.

88   **To preview a document**

●   On the Standard toolbar, click the **Print Preview** button.

89 **To print a document**

1 On the **File** menu, click **Print**.

2 In the **Print** dialog box, select a printer, and then choose the print options you want to use.

3 Click **OK**.

90 **To print an envelope or label to accompany a letter document**

1 Select the inside address at the top of the document.

2 On the **Tools** menu, point to **Letters and Mailings**, and then click **Envelopes and Labels**.

3 In the **Envelopes and Labels** dialog box, click the **Envelopes** tab or the **Labels** tab, select the options you want to use, and then click **Print**.

Chapter 5 Getting to Know Excel

Page 98 **To open a workbook**

1 On the Standard toolbar, click the **Open** button.

2 Click the **Look in** down arrow, and select the hard disk where you stored the file.

3 Locate and double-click the target folder to display its contents.

4 Double-click the target file to open it.

99 **To save a workbook**

1 On the Standard toolbar, click the **Save** button.

2 Navigate to the folder where you want to save the workbook.

3 In the **File name** box, delete the existing file name, and type the name for your file.

4 Click **Save**.

100 **To save a workbook with a different file name and format**

1 On the **File** menu, click **Save As**.

2 Navigate to the folder where you want to save the workbook.

3 In the **File name** box, delete the existing file name, and type the name for your file.

4 Click the **Save as type** down arrow to expand the list, and click the desired type.

5 Click **Save**.

102 **To move to a worksheet**

● In the lower left corner of the Excel window, click the appropriate sheet tab.

103 **To select one or more cells**

● Click the first cell to be selected, and drag to the last cell to be selected.

105 **To select one or more columns or rows**

1 Click the column or row head for the column or row to be selected.

2 If necessary, drag to the row or column head at the edge of the group to be selected.

109 **To create a new workbook**

● On the Standard toolbar, click the **New** button.

109 **To enter data manually**

1 Click the cell in which you want to enter the data.

2 Type the data, and press Enter.

111 **To quickly enter a series of data**

1 Click the first cell in which you want to enter data.

2 Type a value, and press Enter.

3 In the new cell, type the second value in the series.

4 Grab the fill handle, and drag it to the last cell to be filled with data.

112 **To enter data in multiple cells**

1 Click a cell, and type the data to appear in multiple cells.

2 Select the cells in which you want the data in the active cell to appear.

3 Press Ctrl + Enter.

114 **To find specific data**

1 On the **Edit** menu, click **Find**.

2 In the **Find what** box, type the word or text you want to find, and then click **Find Next**.

3 Click **Find Next** again to find subsequent occurrences of the text.

115 **To replace specific data**

1 On the **Edit** menu, click **Replace**.

2 In the **Find what** box, type the word or text you want to replace.

3 In the **Replace with** box, type the word or text you want to substitute for the text in the **Find what** box.

4 Click **Find Next**.

5 Click **Replace** to replace the value in the highlighted cell.

115 **To replace cell data manually**

1 Click the cell with the data to be replaced.

2 Type the new data, and press Enter.

117 **To change an action**

1 Click the **Undo** button to remove the last change.

2 Click the **Redo** button to reinstate the last change you removed.

117 **To check spelling**

● On the Standard toolbar, click the **Spelling** button.

Chapter 6 Making Changes to Your Workbook
Page 122 **To name a worksheet**

1 In the lower left corner of the workbook window, right-click the desired sheet tab.

2 From the shortcut menu that appears, click **Rename**.

3 Type the new name for the worksheet, and press Enter.

123 **To reposition a worksheet**

● Click the sheet tab of the worksheet to move, and drag it to the new position on the tab bar.

123 **To adjust column width**

● Position the mouse pointer over an edge of the column head of the column to be resized, and drag the edge to the side.

124 **To adjust row height**

● Position the mouse pointer over an edge of the row head of the row to be resized, and drag the edge up or down.

124 **To merge cells**

1 Select the cells to be merged.

2 On the Formatting toolbar, click the **Merge and Center** toolbar button.

125 **To add a row or column**

1 Click any cell in the row below which you want the new row to appear, or click any cell in the column to the right of which you want the new column to appear.

2 On the **Insert** menu, click **Rows** or **Columns**.

125 **To hide a row or column**

1 Select any cell in the row or column to be hidden.

2 On the **Format** menu, point to **Row** or **Column**, and then click **Hide**.

126 **To unhide a row or column**

● On **Format** menu, point to **Row** or **Column**, and then click **Unhide**.

129 **To prevent text spillover**

1 Click the desired cell.

2 On the **Format** menu, click **Cells**.

3 If necessary, click the **Alignment** tab.

4 Click the **Wrap Text** check box, and click **OK**.

129 **To control how text appears in a cell**

1 Click the desired cell.

2 On the **Format** menu, click **Cells**.

3 Use the controls in the **Format Cells** dialog box to change the appearance of the cell text.

130 **To freeze column headings**

1 Select the rows you want to freeze.

2 On the **Window** menu, click **Freeze Panes**.

130 **To unfreeze column headings**

● On the **Window** menu, click **Unfreeze Panes**.

133 **To change cell formatting**

1 Click the cell you want to change.

2 On the Formatting toolbar, click the button corresponding to the formatting you want to apply.

134 **To add cell borders**

1 On the Formatting toolbar, click the **Borders** button's down arrow and then, from the list that appears, click **Draw Borders**.

2 Click the cell edge on which you want to draw a border.

3 Drag the mouse pointer to draw a border around a group of cells.

134 **To add cell shading**

1 Click the cell to be shaded.

2 On the Formatting toolbar, click the **Fill Color** button.

3 In the **Fill Color** color palette, click the desired square, and then click **OK**.

136 **To create a style**

1 On the **Format** menu, click **Style**.

2 In the **Style name** box, delete the existing value and then type a name for the new style.

3 Click **Modify**, and define the style with the controls of the **Format Cells** dialog box.

4 Click **OK** in the **Format Cells** dialog box and the **Styles** dialog box.

138 **To copy a format**

1 Click the cell with the format to be copied.

2 On the Standard toolbar, click the **Format Painter** button.

3 Click the cell or cells to which the styles will be copied.

141 **To format a number**

1 Click the cell with the number to be formatted.

2 On the **Format** menu, click **Cells**.

3 If necessary, click the **Number** tab.

4 In the **Category** list, click the general category for the formatting.

5 In the **Type** list, click the specific format, and then click **OK**.

141 **To format a number as a dollar amount**

1 Click the cell with the number to be formatted.

2 On the Formatting toolbar, click the **Currency Style** button.

142 **To create a custom format**

1 On the **Format** menu, click **Cells**.

2 In the **Category** list, click **Custom**.

3 In the **Type** list, click the item to serve as the base for the custom style.

4 In the **Type** box, modify the item, and then click **OK**.

146 **To create a conditional format**

1 Click the cell to be formatted.

2 On the **Format** menu, click **Conditional Formatting**.

3 In the second list box, click the down arrow and then click the operator to use in the test.

4 Type the arguments to use in the condition.

5 Click the **Format** button, and use the controls in the **Format Cells** dialog box to create a format for this condition.

6 Click **OK**.

Chapter 7 Performing Calculations on Data

Page 153 **To name a range of cells**

1 Select the cells to be included in the range.

2 Click in the **Name** box.

3 Type the name of the range, and press Enter.

153 **To name a range of cells using adjacent cell labels**

1 Ensure that the desired name for the cell range is in the topmost or leftmost cell of the range.

2 Select the cells to be part of the range.

3 On the **Insert** menu, point to **Name**, and then click **Create**.

4 Click the check box indicating the location of the cell with the name for the range, and then click **OK**.

160 **To write a formula**

1 Click the cell into which the formula will be written.

2 Type an equal sign, and then type the remainder of the formula.

160 **To copy a formula to another cell**

1 Click the cell containing the formula.

2 On the Standard toolbar, click the **Copy** button.

3 Click the cell into which the formula will be pasted.

4 On the Standard toolbar, click the **Paste** button.

171 **To create a custom filter**

   1   Click the top cell in the column to filter.

   2   On the **Data** menu, point to **Filter**, and then click **AutoFilter**.

   3   Click the down arrow, and then click **(Custom...)** in the list.

   4   In the upper left box of the **Custom AutoFilter** dialog box, click the down arrow, and from the list that appears, click a comparison operator.

   5   Type the arguments for the comparison in the boxes at the upper right, and click **OK**.

171 **To remove a filter**

   ●   On the **Data** menu, point to **Filter**, and then click **AutoFilter**.

172 **To filter for a specific value**

   1   Click the top cell in the column to filter.

   2   On the **Data** menu, point to **Filter**, and then click **AutoFilter**.

   3   Click the down arrow, and then, from the list of unique column values that appears, click the value for which you want to filter.

172 **To select a random row from a list**

   1   In the cell next to the first cell with data in it, type **=RAND()<#%**, replacing # with a number representing the likelihood that the row should be selected.

   2   Press [Tab].

   3   Click the cell into which you entered the RAND() formula, grab the fill handle, and drag to the cell next to the last cell in the data column.

173 **To extract a list of unique values**

   1   Click the top cell in the column to filter.

   2   On the **Data** menu, point to **Filter**, and then click **Advanced Filter**.

   3   Click the **Unique records only** check box, and then click **OK**.

176 **To find a total**

   ●   Select the cells with the values to be summed. The total appears on the status bar, in the lower right corner of the **Excel** window.

179 **To set acceptable values for a cell**

   1   Click the cell to be modified.

   2   On the **Data** menu, click **Validation**.

3 In the **Allow** box, click the down arrow, and from the list that appears, click the type of data to be allowed.

4 In the **Data** box, click the down arrow, and from the list that appears, click the comparison operator to be used.

5 Type values in the boxes to complete the validation statement.

6 Click the **Input Message** tab.

7 In the **Title** box, type the title for the message box that appears when the cell becomes active.

8 In the **Input Message** box, type the message the user will see in the message box.

9 Click the **Error Alert** tab.

10 In the **Style** box, click the down arrow, and from the list that appears, choose the type of box you want to appear.

11 In the **Title** box, type the title for the message box that appears when a user enters invalid data. Then click **OK**.

182 **To allow only numeric values in a cell**

1 Click the cell to be modified.

2 On the **Data** menu, click **Validation**.

3 In the **Allow** box, click the down arrow, and from the list that appears, click **Whole number**.

4 Click **OK**.

Chapter 9 Getting to Know Access
Page 190 **To open an existing database**

1 On the taskbar, click the **Start** button, point to **Programs**, and then click **Microsoft Access**.

2 Click the **Open** button on the toolbar, browse to the folder that stores the database you want to open, and double-click the file name.

3 If necessary, click the **Don't show this screen again** check box, and then click **OK**.

193 **To view details about objects listed in the database window**

● Click the **Details** button on the toolbar at the top of the database window.

194 **To hide command shortcuts in the database window**

1 On the **Tools** menu, click **Options**.

2 On the **View** tab, clear the **New object shortcuts** check box, and click **OK**.

198 **To open a table, query, form, or report**

1 With the database open, click **Tables**, **Queries**, **Forms**, or **Reports** on the Objects bar.

2 Make your selection from the options available, and then click the **Open** button at the top of the database window.

Chapter 10 **Creating a New Database**

Page 213 **To change the default storage location**

1 When a database file is open, click **Options** on the **Tools** menu.

2 On the **General** tab, enter a new path in the **Default database folder** box, and then click **OK**.

220 **To create an empty database structure**

1 Click the **New** button on the toolbar to display the New File task pane.

2 In the **New** section of the task pane, click **Blank Database**.

3 Navigate to the storage location you want for the file, type a name for the new database, and click **Create**.

224 **To switch views of a database object**

1 Click the **View** button on the toolbar.

2 Click the **View** button's down arrow, and click an option in the drop-down list.

225 **To set the primary key field**

1 Display the table in Design view.

2 Select the field that you want to be the primary key field in the top portion of the window.

3 On the **Edit** menu, click **Primary Key**.

225 **To set a field's data type**

1 Display the table in Design view.

2 Click in the **Data Type** cell for the field you want to change, and then click the down arrow to display a list of all possible data types.

3 Click the type you want.

226 **To assign a caption (a column header that is different from the field name)**

1 Display the table in Design view.

2 Click the field to which you want to assign a caption.

3 Click the **Caption** box, and type the caption text.

690

226 **To set a text field's size**

1 Display the table in Design view.

2 Click the field whose size you want to change.

3 Click the **Field Size** box, and type the number of characters you want to allow in the field.

Chapter 11 **Simplifying Data Entry with Forms**

Page 239 **To edit form properties**

1 Display the form in Design view.

2 Use the buttons and boxes on the Formatting toolbar to change the formatting of labels and controls.

3 To change the properties of a control, right-click the control, and click **Properties** on the shortcut menu.

4 Make your changes in the **Properties** dialog box.

240 **To rearrange form controls**

1 Display the form in Design view.

2 Select the control you want to move.

3 Drag the open-hand pointer in the direction you want to move the control and its label, or drag the pointing-finger pointer to move just the selected control.

246 **To fine-tune the size or position of a form control**

1 Display the form in Design view.

2 Select the control you want to change.

3 Move the pointer until it becomes the shape for the change you want, and then press the appropriate arrow key—↑, ↓, ←, or →—to move the control in small increments in a specific direction.

246 **To create a style based on a form**

1 Display the form in Design view.

2 On the **Format** menu, click **AutoFormat**.

3 Click **Customize**.

4 Click **Create a new AutoFormat based on the Form <form name>**, and then click **OK**.

5 Type a name for the new style, and then click **OK**.

6 Click **OK** to close the **AutoFormat** dialog box.

248 **To add a graphic to a form**

1 Display the form in Design view.

2 If necessary, click the **Toolbox** button to open the toolbox.

3 Click the **Image** control in the toolbox, and then drag a rectangle the height and width that you want in the desired location on the form.

4 In the **Insert Picture** dialog box, navigate to the storage location of the file you want to use, and double-click it.

248 **To add a control to a form**

1 Display the form in Design view.

2 If necessary, click the **Toolbox** button to open the toolbox.

3 Click the appropriate control button in the toolbox, and then drag a rectangle in the desired location on the form.

4 If necessary, display the control's **Properties** dialog box, and make changes.

250 **To copy the formatting of one form control to another**

1 Display the form in Design view.

2 Click the control that contains the formatting you want to copy.

3 Click the **Format Painter** button on the toolbar, and then click the control to which you want to copy the formatting.

256 **To create a form using an AutoForm**

1 On the Objects bar, click **Forms**.

2 On the database window's toolbar, click the **New** button.

3 Click the option you want in the list, select the table on which you want to base the form, and then click **OK**.

4 Click the **Save** button, enter the name you want for the form in the **Save As** dialog box, and click **OK**.

259 **To define a relationship between tables**

1 With the database open, click the **Relationships** button on the toolbar to open the **Relationships** window.

2 If the **Show Table** dialog box isn't displayed, click the **Show Table** button on the toolbar. Double-click the tables you want to work with in the list, and then close the **Show Table** dialog box.

3 Drag a field from one table so that it is on top of the corresponding field in the other table.

4 Select the options you want in the **Edit Relationships** dialog box, and then click **Create**.

5 Close the Relationships window, clicking **Yes** when prompted to save its layout.

260 To edit or delete a table relationship

1 With the database open, click the **Relationships** button on the toolbar to open the **Relationships** window.

2 Right-click the line representing the relationship you want to edit or delete, and click the appropriate command on the shortcut menu.

260 To add a subform to a form

1 Open the form in Design view.

2 If the toolbox isn't displayed, click the **Toolbox** button.

3 Make sure the **Control Wizards** button in the toolbox is active (has a border around it).

4 Click the **Subform/Subreport** button, and drag a rectangle in the desired location of the form.

5 Follow the instructions of the **Subform Wizard**, and click **Finish** on the wizard's last page to complete the process.

6 Adjust the size and location of the objects on your form as necessary.

263 To adjust a subform's properties

1 Display the form that contains the subform in Design view.

2 If necessary, open the **Properties** dialog box.

3 Click the **Form Selector** button in the upper left corner of the subform twice.

4 Make the changes you want in the **Properties** dialog box.

Chapter 12 Locating Specific Information
Page 268 To sort information in a table

1 With the table open in Datasheet view, click anywhere in the column of the field on which you want to base the sort, and then click the **Sort Ascending** button or the **Sort Descending** button. (To sort on more than one column of information, arrange them so they are side-by-side in the order you want to sort them, select the columns, and then use the **Sort** buttons.)

2 To reverse the sort order, click the opposite **Sort** button.

271 To filter a table based on a selection

1 Open the table in Datasheet view.

2 Select the information you want to use as the filter criteria.

3   Click the **Filter By Selection** button.

4   If necessary, repeat steps 2 and 3 to filter the information further.

5   Click the **Remove Filter** button to redisplay all of the table's records.

271   **To filter a table based on text you type**

1   Open the table in Datasheet view.

2   Right-click any field in the appropriate column, and click **Filter For** on the shortcut menu.

3   Type the criteria you want to use as the filter, and press Enter. (You can use wildcard characters and simple expressions as the filter criteria.)

271   **To filter a table excluding a selection**

1   Open the table in Datasheet view.

2   Right-click the appropriate field in any record, and click **Filter Excluding Selection** on the shortcut menu.

274   **To filter by form to locate information**

1   Open the table or form you want to work with in either Datasheet or Form view.

2   Click the **Filter By Form** button on the toolbar.

3   Click the field box in which you want to create the filter, type the filter criteria you want, and press Enter; or select the criteria from the list of options. (Repeat this step for any other fields you want to filter.)

4   To add additional filter criteria for a particular field, click the **Or** tab and enter the criteria as necessary.

5   Click the **Apply Filter** button.

276   **To save a query created in the Advanced Filter/Sort window**

1   Click **Save As Query** on the **File** menu.

2   Name the query, and click **OK**.

280   **To create a select query**

1   On the Objects bar, click **Queries**.

2   Double-click **Create query in Design view**.

3   In the **Show Table** dialog box, double-click the tables you want to use in the query, and then close the dialog box.

4   To include fields in the query, drag them from the lists at the top of the window to a column in the design grid. To copy all fields to the grid, double-click the title bar above the field list to select the entire list, and then drag the selection over the grid.

5 Click the **Run** button to run the query and display the results in Data-sheet view.

283 **To add an expression to a query**

1 With the query window displayed, right-click the appropriate cell in the design grid, and click **Build** on the shortcut menu.

2 Double-click the **Functions** folder in the first column of the elements area, and then click **Built-In Functions**.

3 Click the function type you want in the second column. Then double-click the function you want in the third column.

4 Build the expression, and then click **OK**.

5 Press [Enter] to move the insertion point out of the field, which completes the entry of the expression.

6 To rename the expression, double-click **Expr1**, and then type the name you want.

288 **To turn off the display of a field in a query**

1 Display the query in Design view.

2 Clear the **Show** check box for any fields you don't want displayed.

3 Switch to Datasheet view to see the results.

Chapter 13 **Creating a Presentation**
Page 298 **To start Microsoft PowerPoint**

● On the taskbar, click **Start**, point to **Programs**, and then click **Microsoft PowerPoint**.

301 **To create a presentation using suggested content**

1 In the New Presentation task pane, click **From AutoContent Wizard**.

2 Click **Next**, click **All**, select a presentation, and then click **Next**.

3 Click a presentation style, and then click **Next**.

4 Click the **Presentation title** box, type a presentation title, press [Tab], and then type footer text.

5 Click **Next**, and then click **Finish**.

304 **To move from slide to slide in the Slide pane**

1 In Slide pane, click the **Previous Slide** button or the **Next Slide** button.

2 In Slide pane, drag the scroll box up or down the vertical scroll bar.

338 **To move a text object**

1 Click the text object.

2 Drag the edge of the selection box to place the text object where you want it.

339 **To create a text label**

1 On the Drawing toolbar, click the **Text Box** button.

2 Click where you want the text label to appear, and then type the text.

340 **To create a word processing box**

1 On the Drawing toolbar, click the **Text Box** button.

2 Position the pointer on the slide, drag the pointer to create a box the length you want, and then type the text.

341 **To change text alignment**

1 Click the text box.

2 On the Formatting toolbar, click an alignment button (**Align Left**, **Center**, or **Align Right**).

344 **To adjust line spacing**

1 Click the text object with the dotted selection box.

2 On the **Format** menu, click **Line Spacing**.

3 Click the **Before paragraph** or **After paragraph** arrow to select a setting, and then click **OK**.

345 **To replace text**

1 On the **Edit** menu, click **Replace**.

2 Click the **Find what** box, and then type the text you want to replace.

3 Click in the **Replace with** box, and then type the replacement text.

4 Click **Find Next**, and then click **Replace**.

5 Click **OK**, and then click **Close** to close the **Replace** dialog box.

348 **To add an AutoCorrect entry**

1 On the **Tools** menu, click **AutoCorrect Options**, and then click the **AutoCorrect** tab, if necessary.

2 Click in the **Replace** box, and then type a misspelled word.

3 Press [Tab], and then type the correctly spelled word.

4 Click **Add**, and then click **OK**.

361 **To add a header and a footer to a presentation**

    1   On the **View** menu, click **Header and Footer**.

    2   Click the **Slides** or **Notes and Handouts** tab.

    3   Select date and time, slide number, and footer options.

    4   Click **Apply to All**.

365 **To preview your presentation**

    1   On the Standard toolbar, click the **Print Preview** button.

    2   On the Print Preview toolbar, click the **Print what** down arrow, and then click an option in the list.

366 **To preview slides in pure black and white or grayscale**

    1   On the Standard toolbar, click the **Color/Grayscale** button or if in Print Preview, click the **Options** down arrow, and point to **Color/Grayscale**.

    2   On the menu, click **Pure Black and White** or **Grayscale**.

370 **To print presentation slides, audience handouts, or speaker notes**

    1   On the **File** menu, click **Print**.

    2   Click the **Print what** down arrow, and then click **Slides**, **Handouts Pages**, or **Notes Pages**.

    3   Type a range to choose the slides to print, and then click **OK**.

Chapter 17 **Understanding How FrontPage Works**

Page   **379** **To stop the FrontPage task pane from appearing automatically**

    ●   With the task pane open, clear the **Show at startup** check box on the bottom of the task pane.

381 **To close or open a FrontPage pane**

    ●   Click the **Toggle Pane** button; or click the **Toggle Pane** button's down arrow, and select the appropriate pane.

382 **To preview a Web site in a Web browser**

    1   Open the file in the Page view editing window, or click the file name in the **Folder** list to select the file.

    2   On the **File** menu, click **Preview in Browser**.

    3   Select your preferred browser and window size, and then click **Preview**.

386 **To view the HTML code for a Web page**

- With the page open in FrontPage, click the **HTML** button at the bottom of the Page view editing window to switch to the HTML pane.

390 **To switch views of a Web page**

- With the page open, click the desired view on the **View** menu or on the Views bar.

392 **To change the display size of a window**

- Select a percentage display size from the **Zoom** drop-down list on the toolbar.

394 **To mark a task as complete**

- With the Web site displayed in Tasks view, right-click the appropriate task, and then click **Mark Complete** on the shortcut menu.

Chapter 18 **Creating a Web Site to Promote Yourself or Your Company**
Page 405 **To create a Web site using a template**

1 Click **Web Site Templates** in the **New from template** area of the New Page or Web task pane.
2 In the **Web Site Templates** dialog box, select the appropriate icon for the type of Web site you want to create.
3 Under **Options**, specify what you want to call your Web site and where you want to store it, and then click **OK**.

405 **To open the task pane every time you start FrontPage**

- On the **Tools** menu, click **Options**, click the **Startup Task Pane** check box, and then click **OK**.

409 **To create a Web site using a wizard**

1 Click the **New** button's down arrow, and then click **Web**.
2 In the **Web Site Templates** dialog box, click the appropriate icon for the type of Web site you want to create, specify the location and name of your Web site, and then click **OK**.

412 **To use the tasks list**

1 With the Web site displayed in Tasks view, double-click the task you want to work on to open a **Task Details** dialog box.
2 Change any settings as necessary, and then click the **Start Task** button to open the page in Page view.

413 **To insert a comment**

● On the **Insert** menu, click **Comment**.

413 **To edit a comment**

1 Double-click anywhere in the comment's text block to open an editing window.

2 Make your changes, and then click **OK**.

415 **To insert a symbol**

1 On the **Insert** menu, click **Symbol** to display the **Symbol** dialog box.

2 In the **Font** drop-down list, select the font that contains the symbol you want to use, and then click the symbol to select it.

3 Click **Insert**, and then click **Close**.

418 **To insert an existing file**

1 Click where you want the text to appear, or select the text to be replaced.

2 On the **Insert** menu, click **File** to open the **Insert File** dialog box.

3 Browse to the folder where the text you want to insert is stored.

4 In the **Files of type** drop-down list, select the appropriate option.

5 Select the file you want from the list of available files, and then click **Open** to insert the full text of the document in your Web page.

418 **To delete a table**

● Select the table, right-click the selection, and then click ⌦ on the shortcut menu.

419 **To customize a page banner**

1 Right-click the page banner, and select **Page Banner Properties** from the shortcut menu.

2 Change the options you want, and then click **OK**.

421 **To increase the font size by one size**

● Select the text you want to change, and on the Formatting toolbar, click the **Increase Font Size** button.

423 **To add a border to a paragraph**

1 Select the paragraph you want to change.

2 On the Formatting toolbar, click the **Borders** button's down arrow to display the Borders toolbar, and then click the desired option.

2   Click the **Numbering** button or the **Bullets** button on the Formatting toolbar to turn the paragraph into a numbered or bulleted item, and then press `Enter` to create a new line.

436   **To create a table**

1   Click where you want the table to appear, and on the Standard toolbar, click the **Insert Table** button.

2   Point to the first cell and hold down the left mouse button. Then, without releasing the button, drag the pointer until the number of rows and columns you want is highlighted (the grid will expand as you drag the mouse to the edge), and then release the mouse button.

437   **To convert existing text to a table**

1   Select the existing text, and on the **Table** menu, point to **Convert** and click **Text to Table**.

2   Select the options you want and click **OK**.

437   **To convert a table to text**

1   Select the table, and on the **Table** menu, point to **Convert** and click **Table to Text**.

2   In the **Convert Table to Text** dialog box, select the character you want to use to separate items, and then click **OK**.

438   **To insert a table with specific formatting settings**

1   Click where you want the table to appear.

2   On the **Table** menu, point to **Insert**, and then click **Table**.

3   Specify the options that you want in the **Size** and **Layout** sections, and click **OK**.

439   **To draw a table**

1   On the **Table** menu, click **Draw Table**.

2   Click where you want to position the top-left corner of the table, and drag the pencil pointer to where you want to position the bottom-right corner.

3   Using the pencil pointer, draw lines to create the table's rows and columns.

443   **To insert a row in a table**

1   Click anywhere in the row that sits above or below where you want the new row to appear.

2   On the **Table** menu, point to **Insert**, and then click **Rows or Columns**.

3 Specify how many rows you want to insert and whether the row(s) should appear above or below the current selection, and then click OK.

443 **To delete a column in a table**

1 Click anywhere in the column you want to delete.

2 On the **Table** menu, point to **Select**, and then click **Column**.

3 Right-click the selection, and then click **Delete Cells** on the shortcut menu.

443 **To adjust the size of table columns so that all entries fit on one line**

1 Point to the right border of the column you want to adjust.

2 When the pointer changes to a double-headed arrow, double-click the border to resize the column so that it can hold all its entries on one line.

443 **To adjust the size of table columns to the exact width of their contents**

● Click anywhere in the table, and on the **Table** menu, click **AutoFit to Contents**.

444 **To change a table's properties**

1 Right-click anywhere in the table, and then click **Table Properties** on the shortcut menu.

2 In the **Table Properties** dialog box, change the options you want, and then click **OK**.

445 **To make all columns in a table the same width**

● Select the columns, and on the **Table** menu, click **Distribute Columns Evenly**.

446 **To change a cell's background color in a table**

1 Select the cells you want to format, right-click the selection, and then click **Cell Properties** on the shortcut menu.

2 In the **Background** area, click the **Color** box's down arrow.

3 Select the color you want from the palette that is displayed or click **More Colors** to select a custom color, and then click **OK**.

448 **To apply an AutoFormat to a table**

1 Click anywhere in the table.

2 On the **Table** menu, click **Table AutoFormat**.

3 Scroll through the **Formats** list and select the format you want, select any options you want in the **Apply special formats** section, and then click **OK**.

449 **To merge cells in a table**

● Select the cells you want to merge, and on the **Table** menu, click **Merge Cells**.

450 **To split one cell into multiple cells in a table**

1 Right-click the cell and click **Split Cells** on the shortcut menu.

2 In the **Split Cells** dialog box, specify the number of rows or columns you want to split the merged cell into, and then click **OK**.

450 **To split a table into multiple tables**

● Click in the row where you want the first table to end, and on the **Table** menu, click **Split Table**.

450 **To add a caption to a table**

1 Click anywhere in the table.

2 On the **Table** menu, point to **Insert** and then click **Caption**.

3 Type the text you want for the table caption.

Chapter 20 **Enhancing Your Web Site with Graphics**
Page 454 **To insert clip art in a page**

1 Click where you want the clip art to appear.

2 On the **Insert** menu, point to **Picture**, and then click **Clip Art**.

3 Make sure that **All media types** is displayed in the **Results should be** box, and then search for the type of clip art you want by typing a keyword in the **Search text** box and clicking **Search**.

4 Right-click the graphic you want to use, and then click **Insert** on the shortcut menu.

458 **To convert a graphic to GIF or JPG format**

1 In Page view, right-click the graphic, and then click **Picture Properties** on the shortcut menu.

2 In the **Type** area of the **General** tab, click **GIF** or **JPG**, and then click **OK**.

458 **To insert a picture file on a page**

1 Click where you want the picture to appear.

2 On the **Insert** menu, point to **Picture**, and then click **From File** to open the **Picture** dialog box.

3 In the **Picture** dialog box, browse to the folder that contains the file you want to use, and then click **Insert** to insert the graphic in the Web page at the insertion point.

462 **To crop a graphic**

1 Click the picture, and then click the **Crop** button on the Pictures toolbar.

2 Drag the handles of the crop box until the box contains the section of the graphic you want to keep.

3 Click the **Crop** button again to crop the picture to the specified shape and size.

462 **To size a graphic**

1 Double-click the picture to display a **Picture Properties** dialog box.

2 Select the **Specify size** check box, and set the **Width** to the setting you want. Make sure that the **Keep aspect ratio** check box is selected, and then click **OK**.

463 **To convert a graphic to black and white**

● Click the graphic you want to recolor, click **Color** on the Pictures toolbar, and then click **Grayscale** on the **Color** drop-down menu.

464 **To create a thumbnail**

1 With the picture selected, click the **Auto Thumbnail** button on the Pictures toolbar.

2 Drag the handles surrounding the selected thumbnail to resize it.

3 To test the thumbnail link, click the **Preview** button at the bottom of the Page view editing window to switch to the Preview pane, and then click the thumbnail to open the original picture in the Preview pane.

467 **To draw a horizontal rule**

1 Click where you want the line to appear.

2 On the **Insert** menu, click **Horizontal Line**.

3 Right-click the line, click **Horizontal Line Properties** on the shortcut menu, and then click **OK**.

469 **To insert a drawing with predefined shapes**

1 On the **Insert** menu, point to **Picture**, and then click **New Drawing**.

2 On the Drawing toolbar, click **AutoShapes** to see the menu of available shapes.

3 Click the shape you want, and then click the area where you want the shape to appear.

To group shapes together

1   Select a shape, hold down the [shift] key, and then click any other shapes you want to be included in the group.

2   Right-click the selected elements, and on the shortcut menu, point to **Grouping**, and then click **Group**.

To create a photo gallery

1   Click where you want the photo gallery to appear.

2   On the **Insert** menu, click **Web Component**, and then click **Photo Gallery**.

3   In the **Choose a Photo Gallery Option** box, click the option you want, and then click **Finish**.

To change a photo gallery's layout

1   Right-click the **Photo Gallery** Web component in Page view, and then click **Photo Gallery Properties** on the shortcut menu to display the **Photo Gallery Properties** dialog box.

2   On the **Layout** tab, select a different layout option, and then click **OK** to reformat your photo gallery.

To add fancy text with WordArt

1   Click where you want to add the fancy text, point to **Picture** on the **Insert** menu, and then click **WordArt**.

2   Select the style you want in the **Word Art Gallery** dialog box, and then click **OK** to display the **Edit WordArt Text** dialog box.

3   Enter the text, format it as necessary, and then click **OK** to close the dialog box and apply your settings.

Chapter 21   **Publishing Your Web Site**
Page   488   **To install the Personal Web Server**

1   At the left end of the taskbar at the bottom of the screen, click **Start**, point to **Settings**, and then click **Control Panel**.

2   Double-click **Add/Remove Programs** to open the **Add/Remove Programs Properties** dialog box, and then click the **Windows Setup** tab.

3   In the **Components** list, click the words **Internet Tools** (not the check box), and then click **Details** to see the available Internet Tools components.

4   In the **Components** list, click the **Personal Web Server** check box, and then click **OK** to close the **Internet Tools** dialog box.

5   Click **OK** again to close the **Add/Remove Programs Properties** dialog box and install the Personal Web Server.

6 Insert the Windows 98 CD-ROM in the drive, and then click **OK**.

7 If necessary, browse to the file called *pws_main.htm*, click **OK**, and then close the Control Panel window.

8 In Windows Explorer, browse to the *add-ons\pws* folder on the Windows 98 CD-ROM, and double-click **setup.exe**.

9 Follow the instructions in the **Microsoft Personal Web Server Setup Wizard**, and then click **Finish** on the wizard's last page to close the program.

10 Click **Yes** to restart your computer.

493 **To install the FrontPage Server Extensions**

1 If necessary, start your Internet connection. Open your Web browser, and in the **Address** box, type **http://www.microsoft.com/frontpage**.

2 In the **Resources** area of the Web page, click **FrontPage Server Extensions**, and then click the **Download the FrontPage Server Extensions for Microsoft Windows-based Servers** link.

3 Click the link to the download file for your operating system, click **Run this program from its current location**, and then click **OK**.

4 Click the **Close this dialog box when download completes** check box, if it is not already selected, and then click **Yes** to continue.

5 Work through the dialog boxes of the setup program, and when the installation is complete, click **Yes** in the message box to restart your computer.

495 **To publish a disk-based Web site to a local folder**

1 On the **File** menu, click **Open Web**, select the Web site you want to publish, and then click **Open**.

2 On the **File** menu, click **Publish Web**, and then click the **Browse** button to open the **New Publish Location** dialog box, and browse to the appropriate folder.

3 Click the **Create New Folder** button on the dialog box's toolbar to open the **New Folder** dialog box.

4 In the **Name** box, type the name you want for the folder, and then click **OK** to return to the **New Publish Location** dialog box with your newly created folder selected.

5 Click **Open** to return to the **Publish Destination** dialog box, and then click **OK**.

6 Click **OK** to create the new Web site, and then click the **Options** button to change any options as necessary.

7 Click **Publish** to publish the Web site to your local drive.

499   **To publish a single page of a Web site**

●   With the Web site open in FrontPage, right-click the file name in the **Folder** list or in Folders view, and click **Publish Selected Files** on the shortcut menu.

499   **To publish a disk-based Web site to your personal Web server**

1   With the Web site open, click **Publish Web** on the **File** menu.

2   To change the publish destination shown in the **Publish to** box, click **Change**.

3   In the **Publish Destination** dialog box, click in the **Enter publish destination** box, type **http://localhost**, and then click **OK**.

4   Click **Publish**, click **Continue**, and then click the view option you want.

500   **To publish a Web site from a personal Web server to a remote Web server**

1   With the Web site open in your personal Web server, click **Publish Web** on the **File** menu.

2   To change the publish destination shown in the **Publish to** box, click **Change**.

3   In the **Enter publish destination box**, type **http://<server>/PublishServer**, where *<server>* is the name of your Web server, and then click **OK**.

4   Click **OK** to create a new Web site at the specified location, and then click **Publish**.

501   **To publish a FrontPage Web site from a remote server to a local folder or to your personal Web server**

1   On the **File** menu, click **Open Web**.

2   In the **Web name** box, type the URL or IP address of the remote Web site preceded by *http://* to indicate that it is a server-based site (for example, **http://www.microsoft.com/frontpage/** or **http://207.46.131.13/frontpage/**), and then click **Open**.

3   Supply a valid user name and password if prompted, and then click **OK**.

4   On the **File** menu, click **Publish Web**.

5   In the **Publish Destination** box, type the disk or server location where you want to publish the Web site, and then click **OK**.

6   In the **Publish Web** dialog box, click **Publish**.

Chapter 22   Creating a Document
Page   505   **To start Microsoft Publisher**

1   On the taskbar, click the **Start** button.

2   On the **Start** menu, point to **Programs**, and then click **Microsoft Publisher**.

506 **Creating a newsletter for the first time**

1 In the New Publication Task pane, click the down arrow of the **Start from a design** box to see the options.

2 Click **By Publication Type**.

3 Click **Newsletters**.

4 Select one of the available newsletter formats.

508 **To complete the Personal Information Set for your business**

1 After you have used the **Publication Wizard** to select a predesigned publication, a dialog box appears to inform you that a wizard will automatically fill in all your company's information. Click **OK**.

2 In the **Select a personal information set to edit** box of the **Personal Information** dialog box, click **Primary Business**.

3 In the **Personal information for this set** box, type your name.

4 Press ⎵Tab⎵ to move to the remaining fields and enter your information.

5 Click **Update**.

510 **To create a newsletter using the Publication Wizard**

1 On the Standard toolbar, click the **New** button.

2 In the New Publication Task pane, click the down arrow of the **Start from a design** box.

3 Click **By Publication Type**.

4 In the box immediately beneath the **Start from a design** box, click **Newsletters**, and then select one of the formats.

5 Click the words *Newsletter Title* and replace them with the title of your newsletter. Click the other headline placeholders and replace them with your own headlines, and start typing your articles.

512 **To insert a picture**

1 From the **Insert** menu, click **Picture**, and then click **From File**.

2 Navigate to the folder that contains the image you want to use.

3 Select the image and then click **Insert**.

514 **To create a business card using the Publication Design Set**

1 On the Standard toolbar, click the **New** button.

2 Click the down arrow of the **Start from a design** box.

3 Click **By Design Sets**, and then click one of the design set options.

4 Double-click the business card in the design option you chose.

517 **To save a publication as a template**

1 On the Standard toolbar, click the **Open** button, and open your publication.

2 On the Standard toolbar, click **File**, and then click **Save As**.

3 In the **File name** box, type the new name of your document.

4 Click the down arrow in the **Save as type** box, and then click **Publisher Template**.

5 Click **Save**.

519 **To create a publication from a template**

1 On the Standard tool bar, click **File**, and then click **New**.

2 In the **New** area of the New Publication task pane, click **From template...**

3 Navigate to one of the templates and select it.

4 Click **Create New**.

5 Replace the default text with the new text.

6 On the Standard toolbar, click **File**, and then click **Save As**.

7 In the **File name** box, type the new name of the publication.

8 Click **Save**.

520 **To create a publication from a blank page**

1 On the Standard toolbar, click **File**, and then click **New**.

2 In the **Start from a design** box, click **By Blank Publications**.

3 In the preview window, click the publication you want to create.

4 When the document opens, select one of the predetermined designs in the **Apply a design** section of the task pane.

Chapter 23 **Printing Your Documents**
Page 527 **To determine your printer's nonprintable region**

1 From the **Start** menu, click **Settings**, and then click **Printers**.

2 Right-click the printer you expect to use, and then click **Properties**.

3 The **Printer Properties** dialog box opens.

4 In the **Printer Properties** dialog box, click the **Paper** tab.

5 Click the **Unprintable Area** button.

6 Change the defaults in the **Unprintable Area** dialog box, if desired.

7 Click **OK**.

530 **To print a document to a standard printer**

1 On the Standard toolbar, click the **Open** button, and open your publication.

2 Position the cursor over the **Print** button on the Formatting toolbar.

3 Click the **Print** icon to print your document.

531 **To select a target printer**

1 On the Standard toolbar, click the **Open** button, and open your publication.

2 On the Standard toolbar, click **File**, and then click **Print**.

3 Click the down arrow of the **Name** box.

4 Select the printer to which you want to print this file.

5 Click **OK**.

532 **To preview your document**

1 On the Standard toolbar, click the **Open** button, and open your publication.

2 On the Standard toolbar, click **File**, and then click **Print Preview**.

533 **To print a range of pages to a standard printer**

1 On the Standard toolbar, click the **Open** button, and open your publication. (Make sure the file has more than three pages.)

2 On the Standard toolbar, select **File**, and then click **Print**.

3 In the **Print range** area, click **Pages from**.

4 In the **Pages from** box, type the number **2**.

5 In the **Pages to** box, type the number **3**.

6 Click **OK**.

534 **To print a single page to a standard printer**

1 On the Standard toolbar, click the **Open** button, and open your publication. (Make sure the file has more than three pages.)

2 Click the page number of the single page you want to print on the **Page Navigation** button at the bottom of the screen.

3 On the Standard toolbar, click **File**, and then click **Print**.

4 In the **Print range** area, click the **Current page** option.

5 Click **OK**.

535 **To cancel a print job on a standard printer**

1 After you've already sent your document to the printer, double-click the **Printer** icon in the notification area of your screen.

2 Select your print job in the list.

3 Click the **Printer** menu, and then click **Purge Print Documents**.

4 Click **Close**.

1 On the Standard toolbar, click the **Open** button, and open your publication.

2 Click the **Tools** menu, click **Commercial Printing Tools**, and then click **Color Printing**.

3 In the **Print all colors as** area, click the **Spot color(s)** option.

1 On the Standard toolbar, click the **Open** button, and open your publication.

2 Click the **Tools** menu, click **Commercial Printing Tools**, and then click **Color Printing**.

3 In the **Print all colors as** area, click the **Spot color(s)** option.

4 In the **Selected spot colors** area, select one of the colors.

5 Click **Modify**.

6 Click the **Custom** tab.

7 Choose one of the selections in the **Color model** box.

8 Click **OK**.

1 On the Standard toolbar, click the **Open** button, and open your publication.

2 From the **Tools** menu, click **Commercial Printing Tools**, and then click **Color Printing**.

3 In the **Print all colors as** area, click the **Process color (CMYK)** option.

4 Click **OK** to close the **Color Printing** dialog box and return to the file.

1 On the desktop, double-click the **Microsoft Outlook** icon.

2 In the **New Profile** dialog box, type a name for your profile (typically your full name), and click **OK**.

3 In the **E-mail Accounts** dialog box, click **Add a new e-mail account**, and then click **Next**.

4 In the **Server Type** dialog box, select the type of your e-mail account, and click **Next**.

5 From here on, you will need to enter the information and follow the instructions provided by your system administrator or ISP. When you complete the process, the **Outlook** window appears.

552 **To preview a message**

1 Turn on AutoPreview by clicking **AutoPreview** on the **View** menu.

2 Select a message you want to preview, and then click the message to display it in the **Preview** pane.

553 **To open an attachment**

1 Double-click a message with an attachment.

2 Double-click the attached file.

3 If you see a message warning you about opening attachments, click the **Open it** option, and then click **OK**.

4 Return to the Inbox by clicking **Inbox** on the Windows taskbar.

554 **To reply to a message**

1 With your Inbox displayed, open a message to which you'd like to reply.

2 On the toolbar, click the **Reply** button if you want to respond to the sender or the **Reply to All** button if you want to respond to everyone in the **To** and **Cc** boxes of the original message.

3 The insertion point is already in the message box, so start typing your reply text.

4 Click the **Send** button.

556 **To forward a message**

1 With your Inbox displayed, open a message you'd like to forward to another recipient.

2 On the toolbar, click the **Forward** button.

3 In the **To** box, type the new recipient's e-mail address.

4 Press the Tab key until you get to the message body, type your message text, and then click the **Send** button.

557 **To create a new message**

1 On the toolbar, click the **New Mail Message** button.

2 In the **To** box, type your recipient's e-mail address. If you want to address the message to more than one person, remember to separate each e-mail address with a semicolon.

3 Press the Tab key, and in the **Cc** box, type the e-mail address of another recipient (or type your own address).

4 Press the Tab key to move to the **Subject** box, and type your message text.

5 Click the **Send** button.

560   **To add an entry to an address book**

1   On the **Tools** menu, click **Address Book**.

2   If necessary, click the down arrow to the right of the **Show Names from the** box, and click **Contacts** in the drop-down list.

3   On the toolbar, click the **New Entry** button.

4   In the **Select the entry type** box, click **New Contact**, and then click **OK**.

5   In the **Full Name** box, type your new contact's full name.

6   In the **E-mail** box, type your new contact's e-mail address.

7   Click the **Save and Close** button.

562   **To create a distribution list**

1   On the toolbar, click the **New Entry** button.

2   In the **Select the entry type** box, click **New Distribution List**, and then click **OK**.

3   In the **Name** box, type an easy-to-remember name for your distribution list, and then click the **Select Members** button.

4   If necessary, click the down arrow to the right of the **Show Names from the** box, and click **Contacts** in the drop-down list.

5   In the **Name** list, click the name of the person you want to add to the list, and click the **Members** button. Keep doing this until you've added all your distribution list members.

6   Click **OK** to close the **Select Members** dialog box.

7   Click the **Save and Close** button.

565   **To attach a file to a message**

1   On the toolbar, click the **New Mail Message** button.

2   In the **To** box, type your recipient's e-mail address.

3   Click in the **Subject** box, and type something to indicate what the attachment contains.

4   Press the ⌈Tab⌋ key, type your message text, and press ⌈Enter⌋.

5   On the form's toolbar, click the **Insert File** button.

6   Browse to the folder containing the file you want to attach, and double-click the folder name.

7   Click the **Attachment** document, and then click the **Insert** button.

8   Click the **Send** button.

566 **To add a signature to a message**

1 On the **Tools** menu, click **Options**.

2 Click the **Mail Format** tab.

3 Click the **Signatures** button, and then click the **New** button.

4 Type the name of your signature, and click the **Next** button.

5 In the **Signature text** box, type your signature text. Use the font and paragraph options to format your text.

6 When you are satisfied with your signature, click **Finish**.

7 Click **OK**.

573 **To print a message**

1 Open a message you want to print.

2 On the **File** menu, point to **Page Setup**, and click **Memo Style**.

3 In the **Left** box, type **1.0** to set the left margin to **1** inch, and click **OK**.

4 On the toolbar, click the **Print** button.

Chapter 25 **Managing E-Mail Messages**

Page 578 **To sort messages**

1 In the Inbox, click the heading of the **From** column, which sorts the messages by name in ascending order.

2 Click the heading of the **From** column again to sort the messages by name in descending order.

3 Right-click the heading of the **Subject** column, and click **Group By This Field** on the shortcut menu to group the messages by subject and sort the subjects in ascending order.

581 **To customize your current view**

1 On the **View** menu, point to **Current View**, and click **Customize Current View**.

2 Click the **Fields** button.

3 In the **Available fields** list, click a field you want to add to your view, and click the **Add** button.

4 In the **Show these fields in this order** list, drag each field up or down until they are in the order you want, and click **OK**.

5 In the **View Summary** dialog box, click **OK**.

6 To return to the default settings, on the **View** menu, click **Current View**, and then click **Define Views**.

7 Click the **Reset** button, and then click **Close**.

To create a new folder for messages

1 On the **Tools** menu, click **Organize**.

2 At the top of the Ways to Organize Inbox pane, click the **New Folder** button.

3 In the **Name** box, type the name of your new folder, and click **OK**.

To manage messages with color

1 Display the **Folder** list by clicking **Folder List** on the **View** menu.

2 In the **Folder** list, click **Inbox**, and on the **Tools** menu, click **Organize**.

3 In the Ways to Organize Inbox pane, click **Using Colors**.

4 Click a message or group of messages you want to color code.

5 In the **Color Messages** section, make sure **From** is selected in the first box and the name of the sender appears in the second box.

6 In the third box, select a color from the drop-down list, and click the **Apply Color** button.

To find a message

1 On the toolbar, click the **Find** button.

2 In the **Look for** box in the **Find** pane, type a word you know is contained within a message in your Inbox. Then click the **Find Now** button.

To add more parameters to your message search

1 In the Find pane, click the **Options** button, and then click **Advanced Find** in the **Options** drop-down list. Take a moment to look over the many ways in which you can search for messages.

2 In the **Advanced Find** window, click the **More Choices** tab.

3 Click the **Categories** button.

4 In the **Available categories** list, select a category to search on, and click **OK**.

5 Click the **Find Now** button.

To save a message as a text file

1 In the Inbox, click a message, and on the **File** menu, click **Save As**.

2 Click the down arrow to the right of the **Save as type** box, click **Text Only** in the drop-down list, and click **Save**.

1 On your Message form's toolbar, click the **Options** button.

2 In the Message settings area, click the down arrow to the right of the **Importance** box or **Sensitivity** box, and click on the setting that you want.

3 Click **Close**.

612 **To recall a message**

1 Click **Folder list** on the **View** menu.

2 In the **Folder** list, click **Sent Items**

3 Double-click the message you want to recall.

4 On the **Actions** menu, click **Recall This Message**.

5 Select whether you want to delete unread copies of the message or delete unread copies and replace them with a new message, and then click **OK**.

620 **To filter junk e-mail and adult-content messages**

1 On the Standard toolbar, click the **Organize** button.

2 In the Ways to Organize Inbox pane, click **Junk E-Mail**.

3 Click the **down arrows** to display lists of options for coloring or moving the unwanted messages, and select your preferences.

4 Click the **Turn On** button to turn on the rules you've selected.

5 Close the Ways to Organize Inbox pane.

629 **To allow Outlook to check an address using your Personal Address Book**

1 On the **Tools** menu, click **Address Book**.

2 On the **Address Book** window's **Tools** menu, click **Options**.

3 In the **Addressing** dialog box, click the **Add** button.

4 In the **Add Address List** dialog box, click **Personal Address Book**, and click the **Add** button.

5 Click the **Close** button.

6 In the **Addressing** dialog box, click **OK**.

7 In the **Address Book** window, click the **Close** button.

Chapter 27 **Managing Your Calendar**
Page 637 **To mark an appointment as private**

● In your Calendar, right-click the appointment, and then click **Private** on the shortcut menu.

643 **To change the view of your Calendar**

● On the **View** menu, point to **Current View**, and then click the view you want.

650 **To change the time zone in your Calendar**

1 On the **Tools** menu, click **Options**.

2 On the **Preferences** tab, click the **Calendar Options** button.

3 In the **Calendar Options** dialog box, click the **Time Zone** button.

4 Click the down arrow to the right of the **Time zone** box, click the time zone to which you want to change, and then click **OK** three times to close all the dialog boxes.

652 **To print your Calendar**

1 With your Calendar displayed in Outlook, click the **Print** button. (If the toolbar button isn't visible, click the **Toolbar Options** button to display it.)

2 In the **Print style** list, click the style you want (you can print one day per page or one week per page, for example).

3 Click the **Page Setup** button, choose a format, and then click **OK**.

4 In the **Print range** area, click the down arrows to the right of the **Start** box and to the right of the **End** box to choose the date range of the schedule that you want to print.

5 Click **OK**.

Chapter 28 **Scheduling and Managing Meetings**
Page 666 **To respond to a meeting request**

1 On the Outlook Bar, click the **Inbox** icon.

2 Double-click the **meeting request** message.

3 View the meeting in your Calendar by clicking the **Calendar** button on the toolbar.

4 In the Calendar window, click the **Close** button.

5 On the Meeting form, click the appropriate response button.

6 In the message box that appears, choose how you want to respond, and then click **OK**.

7 If you've chosen to edit your response before sending, a Meeting Response form appears. Type a message, and then on the toolbar, click the **Send** button.

670 **To respond to meeting requests automatically**

1 In the Calendar, on the **Tools** menu, click **Options**.

2 On the **Preferences** tab, click the **Calendar Options** button, and then click the **Resource Scheduling** button.

719

3   Click the **Automatically accept meeting requests and process cancellations** check box.

4   Click the **Automatically decline conflicting meeting requests** and the **Automatically decline recurring meeting requests** check boxes, if desired, and click **OK**.

5   In the **Calendar Options** dialog box, click **OK**, and in the **Options** dialog box, click **OK**.

673 **To cancel a meeting**

1   In the Calendar, use the Date Navigator to locate the meeting you want to cancel.

2   Double-click the meeting.

3   On the **Actions** menu, click **Cancel Meeting**.

4   If you want to send a cancellation notice to the attendees, select the **Send cancellation and delete meeting** option, and click **OK**.

5   Click the **Appointment** tab and type your message in the Meeting form.

6   On the toolbar, click the **Send** button.

Glossary

Active Directory A network service that stores information about resources, such as computers and printers.

absolute path A designation for the location of a file including the root directory and the descending series of subdirectories leading to the end file.

access violation An error caused by attempting to access a page or site that is not allowed.

action query A query that updates or makes changes to multiple records in one operation.

active cell The cell that is currently selected and open for editing.

address book A reference section listing individuals' e-mail addresses and names.

aggregate function A function that groups and performs calculations on multiple fields.

alignment The arrangement of objects in fixed or predetermined positions, rows, or columns.

appointment A predetermined meeting or event set on your Outlook Calendar.

argument Specific data that a function requires to calculate a value.

arithmetic operator A character that stands as a symbol for an arithmetic operation: + (addition), − (subtraction), * (multiplication), or / (division).

attribute A characteristic that determines the appearance of text. You can change the appearance of text by making it bold, italic, or colored.

auditing The process of examining a worksheet for errors.

AutoComplete The feature that allows you to complete data entry for a cell based on similar values in other cells in the same column.

AutoContent Wizard A wizard that takes you through a step-by-step process to create a presentation, prompting you for presentation information as you go.

AutoCorrect A feature that corrects commonly misspelled words as you type.

AutoFill A feature that extends a series of values based on the contents of a single cell.

AutoFilter An Excel tool you can use to create filters.

AutoForm A feature that efficiently creates forms using all the available fields and minimal formatting.

bound Linked, as when a form used to view information in a table is linked to that table. *See also* unbound.

browser sniffer A program that detects the Web browser and version used by each Web visitor.

bullet A small graphic, such as a large dot, that sets off an item in a list.

bullet text   A list of items in which each item is preceded by a symbol.

bulleted list   An unordered list of concepts, items, or options.

Calendar   A feature in Outlook used for highlighting dates and times, and for scheduling appointments, meetings, and events.

cell   The box at the intersection of a row and a column.

cell padding   The space between the borders of a cell and the text inside it.

cell range   A group of cells.

cell reference   The letter and number combination, such as C16, that identifies the row and column intersection of a cell.

character style   A style for selected words and lines of text within a paragraph.

clip art   Graphics that can be copied and incorporated into other documents.

color model   A method or convention for representing color in desktop publishing and graphic arts.

column   The vertical line of cells in a spreadsheet or table.

command button   A control shaped like a button to which you can attach code that runs when the button is clicked.

comment   In FrontPage, a note embedded in a Web page that is not visible in the published version of the Web page.
In Access, a note embedded in code that helps people reading the code understand its purpose.

commercial printer   A printing service that can supply large quantities of publications and can print publications on various kinds of paper stock and in any variety of colors.

comparison operator   An operator that compares values, such as < (less than), > (greater than), or = (equal to).

component   A part of a database that is used to store and organize information. Also known as a *database object*.

conditional format   A format that is applied only when cell contents meet certain criteria.

conditional formula   A formula that calculates a value using one of two different expressions, depending on whether a third expression is true or false.

constant   A named item that retains a constant value throughout the execution of a program, as opposed to a variable, whose value can change during execution.

control   An object such as a label, text box, option button, or check box in a form or report that allows you to view or manipulate information stored in tables or queries.

control property   A setting that determines the appearance of a control, what data it displays, and how that data looks. A control's properties can be viewed and changed in its Properties dialog box.

control source   The source of a control's data—the field, table or query whose data will be displayed in the control.

criteria   The specifications you give to Access so that it can find matching fields and records. Criteria can be simple, such as all the records with a ZIP code of 98052, or complex, such as the phone numbers of all customers who have placed orders for over $500 worth of live plants within the last two weeks and who live in ZIP codes 98052, 98053, and 98054.

cropping   Cutting off parts of a graphic to trim it to a smaller size.

crosstab query   A query that calculates and restructures data for easier analysis.

data access page   A dynamic Web page that allows users to directly manipulate data in a database via the Internet.

data list   A multi-element structure that has a linear organization but that allows data elements to be added or removed in any order.

data type   The type of data that can be entered in a field: text, memo, number, date/time, currency, AutoNumber, Boolean (Yes/No), OLE object, and hyperlink. You set the data type by displaying the table in Design view.

database application   A database that is refined and made simpler for the user by the sophisticated use of queries, forms, reports, a switchboard, and various other tools.

database program   A program that stores data. Programs range from those that can store one table per file (referred to as a flat database) to those that can store many related tables per file (referred to as a relational database).

database window   The window from which all database objects can be manipulated or accessed.

Datasheet view   The view in which the information in a table or query can be viewed and manipulated. *See also* view.

Date Navigator   The small calendar next to the appointment area in the Outlook Calendar.

dependents   The cells with formulas that use the value from a particular cell.

design grid   The name given to the structure used in Design view to manually construct and modify advanced filters and queries.

design template   A file that contains the styles in a document or presentation.

Design view   In Access, the view in which the structure of a table or query can be viewed and manipulated. Generally, a view of a form that allows you to modify the appearance of the form. *See also* view.

desktop publishing   A process that combines text and graphics in an appealing and easy-to-read format, such as a report, newsletter, or book.

destination file   The file into which you are inserting information.

dimmed   In reference to menu commands, unavailable and displayed in gray font.

directory server   A server on a network that returns mail addresses of other users or enables a user to locate hosts and services.

disk-based Web site   A Web site that is located on a floppy disk, a CD-ROM, or a computer that is not configured as a Web server.

distribution list   A list of recipients on an e-mail mailing list.

docking   Attaching a toolbar to one edge of a window.

domain name   The base of the alphanumeric address, called the uniform resource locator (URL), where Web visitors locate a Web site on the World Wide Web.

dotted selection box   The border of a selected object that indicates that you can manipulate the entire object.

download   To transfer a file from a remote computer to the requesting computer via a network.

drawing canvas   An area that contains drawing shapes and pictures.

e-mail   An electronic text message sent over local area networks or the Internet.

e-mail link   A hyperlink that initiates an e-mail message.

embedded cascading style sheet   A document embedded within a Web page that defines formats and styles for different page elements.

embedded object   An object that becomes part of the destination file and is no longer a part of the source file.

error code   A brief message that appears in a worksheet cell, describing a problem with a formula or a function.

event   An action performed by a user or by Access, to which a programmed response can be attached. Common user events include Click, Double Click, Mouse Down, Mouse Move, and Mouse Up. You can use macros or VBA modules to determine how Access responds when one of these events occurs.

expression   A combination of functions, field values, constants, and operators that yield a result. Expressions can be simple, such as *>100*, or complex, such as *((ProductPrice*Quantity)*.90)+(Shipping+Handling)*.

external cascading style sheet   A document outside of a Web page that defines formats and styles for different page elements. External style sheets can be referenced by multiple documents to provide a consistent look across pages and sites.

field   A column in a data list. An individual item of the information that is the same type across all records. Represented in Access as a column in a database table. *See also* record.

file   Information, such as a document, that a program saves with a unique name.

file format   The way a program stores a file so that the program can open it.

file name   The name of a file.

File Transfer Protocol (FTP)   A protocol that allows users to copy files between their local system and any system they can reach on the network.

fill handle   The square at the lower right corner of a cell that you drag to indicate other cells that should hold values in the series defined by the active cell.

FillSeries   The feature that extends a series of values based on the contents of two cells, where the first cell has the starting value for the series and the second cell shows the increment.

filter   To exclude records from a data list in a mail merge in Word. A rule that Excel uses to determine which worksheet rows to display.

flat database   A simple database consisting of one table. *See also* relational database.

Folder list   A FrontPage window in which the open Web site's visible folders and files are displayed.

Folders view   Displays the visible files and folders that are part of the open Web site.

font   *See* font typeface.

font effects   A way to emphasize text using formatting options, such as bold type, italics, all capital letters, or shadows.

font size   The size of text, usually expressed in points.

font typeface   A complete set of characters that uses the same design.

footer   The text that is printed at the bottom of each page of a document.

form   A database object used to enter, edit, and manipulate information in a database table. A form gives you a simple view of some or all of the fields of one record at a time.

Form view   The view in which you can enter and modify the information in a record. *See also* view.

formula   A mathematical expression that performs calculations, such as adding or averaging values.

freeze   To assign cells that will remain at the top of a worksheet regardless of how far down the worksheet a user scrolls.

friendly name   A simple name that translates into a more complex one; friendly names used to identify Web locations are translated by the computer to more complex Internet Protocol (IP) addresses.

FTP   *See* File Transfer Protocol (FTP).

function   A named procedure or routine in a program, often used for mathematical or financial calculations.

Graphics Interchange Format (GIF)   A file format for saving pictures that displays well over the Web.

group   One of four elements—the other three being object, permission, and user—on which the Access user-level security model is based.

header   The text that is printed at the top of each page of a document.

header column   The column in a table that contains the title of each row.

header row   The row in a table that contains the title of each column.

home page   The starting page for a set of Web pages in a Web site.

hosting   The process or service of storing a Web site on a configured Web server and serving it to the intended audience.

hotspot   A defined area on an image map that is hyperlinked to a bookmark, Web page, Web site, or e-mail address.

HTML   *See* Hypertext Markup Language (HTML).

HTML pane   The window in which the Hypertext Markup Language (HTML) code behind a FrontPage-based Web page is displayed.

HTTP   *See* Hypertext Transfer Protocol.

hyperlink   The text or graphic that users click to go to a file; a location in a file; an Internet or intranet site, page, or location; and so on. Hyperlinks can also lead to Gopher, telnet, newsgroup, and FTP sites. Hyperlinks usually appear underlined and in color, but sometimes the only indication is that the pointer changes to a hand.

Hyperlinks view   The FrontPage window that displays the hyperlinks to and from any selected page in the open Web site.

Hypertext Markup Language (HTML)   The language used for marking a document so that it can be published on the World Wide Web and viewed with a browser.

Hypertext Transfer Protocol (HTTP)   A protocol utilizing TCP/IP to transfer hypertext requests and information between servers and browsers.

image map   A graphic element containing hotspots.

Inbox   The default mailbox where Outlook stores incoming messages.

indent   Displacement of the left or right edge of a block of text in relation to the margin or to other blocks of text.

input mask   A field property that determines what data can be entered in a field, how the data looks, and the format in which it is stored.

insertion point   A blinking bar that indicates where text will be entered or edited as you type.

Internet Protocol (IP)   The number that uniquely identifies a specific computer on the Internet.

Internet Service Provider (ISP)   A business that provides Internet access to individuals and organizations.

Joint Photographic Experts Group (JPG)   A graphics format used for photos and other graphics with more than 256 colors.

kerning   The distance between letters in a word.

key combination   Two or more keys pressed at the same time that perform an action.

label control   An area on a form that contains text that appears on the form in Form view.

LAN   *See* Local Area Network (LAN).

landscape orientation   Horizontal orientation in which the page is wider than it is tall.

launching   *See* publishing.

Layout Preview   A view of a report that shows you how each element will look but without all the detail of Print Preview.

link bar   A hyperlinked list of Web pages within a Web site, providing access to the specified pages.

linked object   An object that maintains a direct link to the source file.

list   Items of information, either numbered or bulleted, set off from a paragraph.

Local Area Network (LAN)   A group of computers connected in such a way that any computer can interact with any other on a network.

localhost   The friendly name for the root Web site of a configured Web server.

logical operator   One of the Boolean operators: AND, OR, and NOT.

macro   A recorded series of commands (keystrokes and instructions) that are treated as a single command.

main form   One form that is linked to one or more tables. *See also* subform.

manual page break   A page break that you insert in a document. A manual page break appears as a dotted line across the page with the label *Page Break*.

many-to-many relationship   A relationship formed between two tables that each have a one-to-many relationship with a third table. *See also* one-to-many relationship; one-to-one relationship.

media   Graphics, videos, sound effects, or other material that can be inserted into a Web page.

meeting request   In Outlook, an invitation to a meeting received through e-mail, which is automatically added to your Calendar if you accept.

menu   A list of commands a user can select from in order to perform a desired action.

merge   The process of combining a data source document and a main document to create a single merged document.

message header   In Outlook, the portion at the top of an e-mail message that contains to To, Cc, and Subject information.

module   A Visual Basic for Applications (VBA) program.

named range   A group of related cells defined by a single name.

navigation button   One of the buttons found on a form or navigation bar that helps users display specific records.

Navigation view   A view of all the files that have been added to the navigational structure of the open Web site.

navigational structure   A hierarchical map of how Web pages are connected within a Web site and what routes the user can take to get from one page to another.

Normal pane   The window in which the standard FrontPage development environment is displayed.

Normal view   The default editing view, which you use to write and edit documents.

Notes Page view   View where you can add speaker notes and related graphics.

numbered list   An ordered list of concepts, items, or options.

object   One of the components of an Access database, such as a table, form, or report.

Object Linking and Embedding (OLE)   A feature that allows you to insert a file created in one program into a document that was created in another program.

Office Assistant   A help system that answers questions, offers tips, and provides help for Microsoft Office XP program features.

Office Clipboard   A storage area shared by all Office programs where multiple pieces of information from several different sources are stored.

Office Drawings   The specially formatted lines, preformed shapes, WordArt objects, text boxes, and shadowing that can be incorporated into Microsoft Office documents.

one-to-many relationship   A relationship formed between two tables in which each record in one table has more than one related record in the other table. *See also* many-to-many relationship; one-to-one relationship.

one-to-one relationship   A relationship formed between two tables in which each record in one table has only one related record in the other table. *See also* many-to-many relationship; one-to-many relationship.

operator   *See* arithmetic operator; comparison operator; logical operator.

option button   A control on a form that allows users to select preferred settings.

ordered list   The Hypertext Markup Language (HTML) term for a numbered list.

orphan   The first line of a paragraph printed by itself at the bottom of a page.

Outline view   A view that shows the structure of a document, which consists of headings and body text.

page   *See* data access page.

page banner   A textual or graphic image that displays the title of a Web page.

page orientation   The way in which a page is laid out in a printed document.

page title   The text that is displayed on the page banner of a Web page and in the title bar of a Web browser.

Page view editing window   The FrontPage window in which a Web page is edited.

paragraph   In a document, any block of text that ends when you press the Enter key.

paragraph styles   Styles for entire paragraphs, including their indents, alignment, and tabs.

parameter query   A query that prompts for the information to be used in the query, such as a range of dates.

Personal Web Server (PWS)   An application that transmits information in Hypertext Markup Language (HTML) pages by using the Hypertext Transport Protocol (HTTP). It provides the ability to publish Web pages on the Internet or over a local area network (LAN) on an intranet.

Pick From list   The feature that allows you to enter a value into a cell by choosing the value from the set of values already entered into cells in the same column.

Places bar   In PowerPoint, a bar on the left side of the Save As and Open dialog boxes that provides quick access to commonly used locations in which to store and open files.

point   A measurement for the size of text. A point is equal to about 1/72 of an inch.

populate   To fill a table or other object with data.

portrait orientation (or mode)   A display and printing mode whereby columns run parallel to the long edge of a sheet of paper.

precedents   The cells that are used in a formula.

presentation window   The electronic canvas on which you type text, draw shapes, create graphs, add color, and insert objects.

Preview pane   The FrontPage window in which Web pages can be viewed before they are published.

primary key   One or more fields that determine the uniqueness of each record in a database.

Print Layout view   A view that shows a document as it appears on the printed page.

Print Preview   A view of a report that allows users to see exactly how the report will look when printed.

profile   A record maintained about an authorized user of a multiuser computer system. The profile usually contains such information as the user's access restrictions, mailbox location, type of terminal, and so on.

property A setting that determines the content and appearance of the object to which it applies.

publishing Copying your Web site files to a Web server for the purpose of displaying the site to the intended audience.

query In Word, a set of selection criteria that indicate how to filter recipients in a mail merge. In Access, a database object that locates information so that the information can be viewed, changed, or analyzed in various ways. The results of a query can be used as the basis for forms, reports, and data access pages.

range A group of related cells.

record All the items of information (fields) that pertain to one particular entity, such as a customer, employee, or project. *See also* field.

record selector The gray bar along the left edge of a table or form.

record source The place from which information derives between two bound objects, such as a field that pulls information from a table. *See also* control source.

recurring In Outlook, an event or meeting that occurs every day, week, or month at the same time and for the same duration.

referential integrity The system of rules Access uses to ensure that relationships between tables are valid and that data cannot be changed in one table without also being changed in all related tables.

relational database A sophisticated type of database in which data is organized in multiple related tables. Data can be pulled from the tables just as if they were stored in a single table.

relationship An association between common fields in two tables.

relative path A designation of the location of a file in relation to the current working directory.

report In Excel, a special document with links to one or more worksheets from the same workbook. In Access, a database object used to display a table or tables in a formatted, easily accessible manner, either on the screen or on paper.

Reports view The FrontPage view that displays the available reports for the open Web site.

resize handle A white circle on each corner and side of an object that you can drag to change the object's size.

rows Cells that are on the same horizontal line in a worksheet.

running a query The process of telling Access to search the specified table or tables for records that match the criteria you have specified in the query and to display the designated fields from those records in a datasheet (table). *See also* criteria; query.

saving   The process of storing the current state of a database or database object for later retrieval. In Access, new records and changes to existing records are saved when you move to a different record; you don't have to do anything to save them. You do have to save new objects and changes to existing objects.

screen area   The width and height of your screen, measured in pixels.

ScreenTip   The small text box that appears when the cursor passes over a button, telling the user the name of the command.

section break   A portion of a document you can format with unique page settings, such as different margins. A section break appears as a double-dotted line across the page with the words *Section Break* and the type of section break in the middle of the line.

select query   A query that retrieves data matching specified criteria from one or more tables and displays the results in a datasheet.

selection area   A blank area to the left of a document's left margin that you can click to select parts of the document.

selection box   A gray slanted line or dotted outline around an object.

selector   A small box attached to an object that you click to select the object.

server farm   An area where multiple Web servers are located.

server-based Web site   A Web site that is located on a computer that is configured as a Web server.

server-side application   A program or protocol that is run on the Web server rather than on a Web visitor's own computer.

shared border   The areas at the top, bottom, left, or right of all or some of the pages in a Web site, in which common elements are displayed.

sheet tab   The indicator for a worksheet, located in the lower left corner of the workbook window.

signatures   Text or pictures that are automatically appended to outgoing e-mail messages.

site map   A graphical depiction of the locations of Web pages in a Web site.

slanted-line selection box   The border of a selected object that indicates that you can edit the object's content.

Slide Show view   The view where you can preview slides as an electronic presentation.

Slide Sorter view   The view where you can see all slides in a presentation in miniature.

soft page break   A page break that Word inserts in a document. A soft page break appears as a dotted line across the page.

sort   To reorder the contents of a worksheet based on a criterion.

source file   The original document created in the source program.

source program The program that created a document that is a linked object in Word.

Spelling and Grammar A feature that corrects errors and maintains professional writing standards.

splash screen An introductory screen containing useful or entertaining information. Often used to divert the user's attention while data is loading.

split bar A line that defines which cells have been frozen at the top of a worksheet.

style A collection of text and paragraph formatting choices that you can apply to text throughout a document.

Style area An area along the left side of a Word document that displays style names.

subdatasheet A datasheet that is embedded in another datasheet.

subfolder A folder within a folder.

subform A form inserted in a control that is embedded in another form.

switchboard A form used to navigate among the objects of a database application so that users don't have to be familiar with the actual database.

syntax The format that expressions must conform to in order for Access to be able to process them.

tab stop A location along the ruler that you use to align text.

table A structured presentation of information consisting of vertical columns and horizontal rows.

Table AutoFormat A set of 18 predesigned table formats that include a variety of borders, colors, and attributes that will give a table a professional look.

Table Wizard The Access tool that helps users construct tables.

task An individual item of work to be performed.

task pane A pane that allows you to access commands related to a specific task quickly without having to use menus and toolbars.

Tasks view The FrontPage window that displays a list of tasks to be completed in an open Web site.

template A special document that stores text, styles, formatting, macros, and page information for use in other documents.

text box control A control on a form or report where data from a table can be entered or edited.

text label A text object used primarily for short phrases or notes.

text object A box that contains text in a slide.

text placeholder A dotted-lined box that you can click to add text.

thesaurus   A feature that looks up alternative words or synonyms for a word.

thumbnail   A small version of a graphic that is hyperlinked to a full-size version.

title slide   The first slide in a presentation.

title text   Text that identifies the name or purpose of a slide.

toolbar   A graphical bar with buttons that perform some of the common commands in Office XP.

unbound   Not linked, as when a control is used to calculate values from two or more fields and is therefore not bound to any particular field. *See also* bound.

uniform resource locator (URL)   The alphanumeric address where Web visitors locate your Web site on the World Wide Web.

unordered list   The Hypertext Markup Language (HTML) term for a bulleted list.

URL   *See* uniform resource locator (URL).

validation rule   A field property that tests entries to ensure that only the correct types of information become part of a table.

view   The display of information from a specific perspective.

Web browser   A program used to view Web pages on the World Wide Web.

Web component   A ready-made programmatic element that provides capabilities such as link bars and tables of content.

Web hosting company   A business that provides Internet access to individuals and organizations.

Web Layout view   A view that shows a document as it appears as a Web page.

Web page   A special document in HTML designed to be viewed in a Web browser.

Web server   A storage location where you save a Web site or Web page for viewing on the World Wide Web or on a network.

Web site   A collection of Web pages with navigation tools and a designed theme.

Web visitor   An individual who views a Web site.

widow   The last line of a paragraph printed by itself at the top of a page.

wildcard character   A placeholder for an unknown character or characters in search criteria.

wizard   A program that creates the layout of a Web page or Web site and leads the user through the process of personalizing the content and the appearance of the final product.

word processing   A process by which you create, edit, and produce text documents.

word processing box   A text object used primarily for longer text.

word wrap   A feature that automatically moves the insertion point to the next line within an object as you type.

WordArt   A feature that allows you to change the shape and appearance of text in a document.

work week   In Outlook, the five days between Monday and Friday, inclusive. You can view the whole work week at once in the Calendar.

workbook   The basic Excel document, consisting of one or more worksheets.

worksheet   A page in an Excel workbook.

Index

Numbers and Symbols

3-D style, Microsoft FrontPage, 466
35mm slides, 363
+ (addition operator), 278
* (asterisk character), 272
#DIV/0! error code, 163
/ (division operator), 278
= (equal sign operator), 156
error code, 163
> (greater than operator), 278
>= (greater than or equal to operator), 278
< (less than operator), 278
<= (less than or equal to operator), 278
* (multiplication operator), 278
#NAME? error code, 163
<> (not equal to operator), 278
(pound sign character), 272
? (question mark character), 272
#REF! error code, 163
– (subtraction operator), 278
& (text addition operator), 278
#VALUE! error code, 163

A

abbreviations, Microsoft Word, 21–24
absolute path, Web server, 491
absolute references, Microsoft Excel, 159–60
accepting meeting requests, 667, 670
Access. *See* Microsoft Access
access violation, Microsoft FrontPage, 428
accounts, e-mail, 549, 572. *See also* e-mail
action queries, 197, 279
Active Appointments view, Calendar, 643
active cell, Microsoft Excel, 100
Active Server Pages (ASP), 400

ActiveX Data Objects (ADO), 400
addition operator (+), 278
address book, e-mail, 560–65, 621, 624–28, 629
addresses, e-mail, 411, 558, 560–65, 621, 624–28, 629
addresses, IP, Web server, 493
ADO, 400
ads, Microsoft Publisher, 510
adult-content e-mail, 620
Advanced Filter/Sort, Microsoft Access, 275–78
agendas, meeting, 638
aggregate functions, Microsoft Access, 289
alignment
    Microsoft Excel, 127, 129, 131
    Microsoft FrontPage, 423–24, 444, 479
    Microsoft PowerPoint, 341–45
    Microsoft Word, 33, 68, 75–78
And operator, Microsoft Access, 278
animation, 32, 489
Annual Events view, Calendar, 643
Answer Wizard
    Microsoft FrontPage, 395
    Microsoft Word, 6
appearance. *See* formatting
append query, Microsoft Access, 279
applications, server-side, 485
applying styles. *See* styles
appointments, Calendar
    about, 631–32
    categories, 638–40
    entering, 633–34
    managing, 638–42
    private, 631, 637
    recurring, 635, 638
    reminder, 635
archiving e-mail, 593–98
area, style, Microsoft Word, 52
arguments, Microsoft Excel, 157, 161
arithmetic
    Microsoft Access, 278
    Microsoft Excel, 151–65
    Microsoft Word, 70–75
arranging slides, 326–27

arrows, Microsoft FrontPage, 466
art. *See* clip art; graphics; photographs; pictures
ascending sort, Microsoft Access, 268–70
Ask A Question box
    Microsoft Excel, 97
    Microsoft FrontPage, 395
    Microsoft Word, 6
ASP, 400
attachments, e-mail, 550–53, 565–66
audio
    meetings, 674–76
    Real Audio Player, 489
auditing formulas, Microsoft Excel, 163–65
AutoArchive, 593, 596–98
AutoCalculate, Microsoft Excel, 174–77
AutoComplete, Microsoft Excel, 107
AutoContent Wizard, Microsoft PowerPoint, 299–302
AutoCorrect
    Microsoft PowerPoint, 347–54
    Microsoft Word, 21–24, 83
AutoDialer, Microsoft Access, 218
AutoFill, Microsoft Excel, 107–108
    Options, 108
AutoFilter, Microsoft Excel, 168, 169–73
AutoFit
    Microsoft FrontPage, 451
    Microsoft PowerPoint, 347
AutoForm, Microsoft Access, 256–57, 274
AutoFormat
    Microsoft FrontPage, 445, 448
    Microsoft Word, 66–67
AutoLookup queries, 197
AutoNumber, Microsoft Access, 225
AutoPreview, Microsoft Outlook, 550–53
AutoRecover, Microsoft PowerPoint, 303
AutoShapes
    Microsoft FrontPage, 466, 469, 473
    Microsoft PowerPoint, 342–45

735

E

Index

Kristen Crupi

Kristen Crupi has more than five years' experience as a technical writer and information architect. Kristen served as a technical resource on the *Windows 95 Resource Kit* team and contributed to the *Microsoft Excel 2000 Step by Step Courseware*, both from Microsoft Press. Her background includes extensive online help and training development, and most recently, information architecture for Web-based applications.

Curtis Frye

Curtis Frye is a freelance writer from Portland, Oregon. He is the author of *Master Access 2000 Visually* from IDG/Maran, Microsoft Press's *Microsoft Access 2000 Step by Step Courseware: Expert Skills Student Guide* for ActiveEducation, and ActiveEducation's *Introduction to ASP*, as well as three online courses for DigitalThink (*Excel 2000: Data Formatting and Customization, Excel 2000: Data Analysis and Dissemination*, and *Advanced Database Design*). He was also a major contributor to Eric and Deborah Ray's *Microsoft Access 2000 for Windows: Visual QuickStart*, from Peachpit Press, and writes "The Interoperability Corner," a monthly column for Jerry Olsen's *All About Microsoft Word* newsletter. When he's not writing, Curt is a professional improvisational comedian with ComedySportz.

Online Training Solutions, Inc. (OTSI)

OTSI is a traditional and electronic publishing company specializing in the creation, production, and delivery of computer software training. OTSI publishes the Quick Course and Practical Business Skills series of computer and business training products. Please visit the OTSI Web site at *www.otsiweb.com*.

Perspection, Inc.

Perspection, Inc., is a software training company that provides information and training to help people use software more effectively in order to communicate, make decisions, and solve problems. Perspection writes and produces software training books, and develops multimedia and Web-based training. Please visit the Perspection Web site at *www.perspection.com*.

MICROSOFT LICENSE AGREEMENT

Book Companion CD

user manual, in "online" documentation, and/or in other Microsoft-provided materials. Any supplemental software code provided to you as part of the Support Services shall be considered part of the SOFTWARE PRODUCT and subject to the terms and conditions of this EULA. With respect to technical information you provide to Microsoft as part of the Support Services, Microsoft may use such information for its business purposes, including for product support and development. Microsoft will not utilize such technical information in a form that personally identifies you.

- **Software Transfer.** You may permanently transfer all of your rights under this EULA, provided you retain no copies, you transfer all of the SOFTWARE PRODUCT (including all component parts, the media and printed materials, any upgrades, this EULA, and, if applicable, the Certificate of Authenticity), **and** the recipient agrees to the terms of this EULA.

- **Termination.** Without prejudice to any other rights, Microsoft may terminate this EULA if you fail to comply with the terms and conditions of this EULA. In such event, you must destroy all copies of the SOFTWARE PRODUCT and all of its component parts.

3. **COPYRIGHT.** All title and copyrights in and to the SOFTWARE PRODUCT (including but not limited to any images, photographs, animations, video, audio, music, text, SAMPLE CODE, REDISTRIBUTABLES, and "applets" incorporated into the SOFTWARE PRODUCT) and any copies of the SOFTWARE PRODUCT are owned by Microsoft or its suppliers. The SOFTWARE PRODUCT is protected by copyright laws and international treaty provisions. Therefore, you must treat the SOFTWARE PRODUCT like any other copyrighted material **except** that you may install the SOFTWARE PRODUCT on a single computer provided you keep the original solely for backup or archival purposes. You may not copy the printed materials accompanying the SOFTWARE PRODUCT.

4. **U.S. GOVERNMENT RESTRICTED RIGHTS.** The SOFTWARE PRODUCT and documentation are provided with RESTRICTED RIGHTS. Use, duplication, or disclosure by the Government is subject to restrictions as set forth in subparagraph (c)(1)(ii) of the Rights in Technical Data and Computer Software clause at DFARS 252.227-7013 or subparagraphs (c)(1) and (2) of the Commercial Computer Software—Restricted Rights at 48 CFR 52.227-19, as applicable. Manufacturer is Microsoft Corporation/One Microsoft Way/Redmond, WA 98052-6399.

5. **EXPORT RESTRICTIONS.** You agree that you will not export or re-export the SOFTWARE PRODUCT, any part thereof, or any process or service that is the direct product of the SOFTWARE PRODUCT (the foregoing collectively referred to as the "Restricted Components"), to any country, person, entity, or end user subject to U.S. export restrictions. You specifically agree not to export or re-export any of the Restricted Components (i) to any country to which the U.S. has embargoed or restricted the export of goods or services, which currently include, but are not necessarily limited to, Cuba, Iran, Iraq, Libya, North Korea, Sudan, and Syria, or to any national of any such country, wherever located, who intends to transmit or transport the Restricted Components back to such country; (ii) to any end user who you know or have reason to know will utilize the Restricted Components in the design, development, or production of nuclear, chemical, or biological weapons; or (iii) to any end user who has been prohibited from participating in U.S. export transactions by any federal agency of the U.S. government. You warrant and represent that neither the BXA nor any other U.S. federal agency has suspended, revoked, or denied your export privileges.

DISCLAIMER OF WARRANTY

NO WARRANTIES OR CONDITIONS. MICROSOFT EXPRESSLY DISCLAIMS ANY WARRANTY OR CONDITION FOR THE SOFTWARE PRODUCT. THE SOFTWARE PRODUCT AND ANY RELATED DOCUMENTATION ARE PROVIDED "AS IS" WITHOUT WARRANTY OR CONDITION OF ANY KIND, EITHER EXPRESS OR IMPLIED, INCLUDING, WITHOUT LIMITATION, THE IMPLIED WARRANTIES OF MERCHANTABILITY, FITNESS FOR A PARTICULAR PURPOSE, OR NONINFRINGEMENT. THE ENTIRE RISK ARISING OUT OF USE OR PERFORMANCE OF THE SOFTWARE PRODUCT REMAINS WITH YOU.

LIMITATION OF LIABILITY. TO THE MAXIMUM EXTENT PERMITTED BY APPLICABLE LAW, IN NO EVENT SHALL MICROSOFT OR ITS SUPPLIERS BE LIABLE FOR ANY SPECIAL, INCIDENTAL, INDIRECT, OR CONSEQUENTIAL DAMAGES WHATSOEVER (INCLUDING, WITHOUT LIMITATION, DAMAGES FOR LOSS OF BUSINESS PROFITS, BUSINESS INTERRUPTION, LOSS OF BUSINESS INFORMATION, OR ANY OTHER PECUNIARY LOSS) ARISING OUT OF THE USE OF OR INABILITY TO USE THE SOFTWARE PRODUCT OR THE PROVISION OF OR FAILURE TO PROVIDE SUPPORT SERVICES, EVEN IF MICROSOFT HAS BEEN ADVISED OF THE POSSIBILITY OF SUCH DAMAGES. IN ANY CASE, MICROSOFT'S ENTIRE LIABILITY UNDER ANY PROVISION OF THIS EULA SHALL BE LIMITED TO THE GREATER OF THE AMOUNT ACTUALLY PAID BY YOU FOR THE SOFTWARE PRODUCT OR US$5.00; PROVIDED, HOWEVER, IF YOU HAVE ENTERED INTO A MICROSOFT SUPPORT SERVICES AGREEMENT, MICROSOFT'S ENTIRE LIABILITY REGARDING SUPPORT SERVICES SHALL BE GOVERNED BY THE TERMS OF THAT AGREEMENT. BECAUSE SOME STATES AND JURISDICTIONS DO NOT ALLOW THE EXCLUSION OR LIMITATION OF LIABILITY, THE ABOVE LIMITATION MAY NOT APPLY TO YOU.

MISCELLANEOUS

This EULA is governed by the laws of the State of Washington USA, except and only to the extent that applicable law mandates governing law of a different jurisdiction.

Should you have any questions concerning this EULA, or if you desire to contact Microsoft for any reason, please contact the Microsoft subsidiary serving your country, or write: Microsoft Sales Information Center/One Microsoft Way/Redmond, WA 98052-6399.

PN 097-0002296